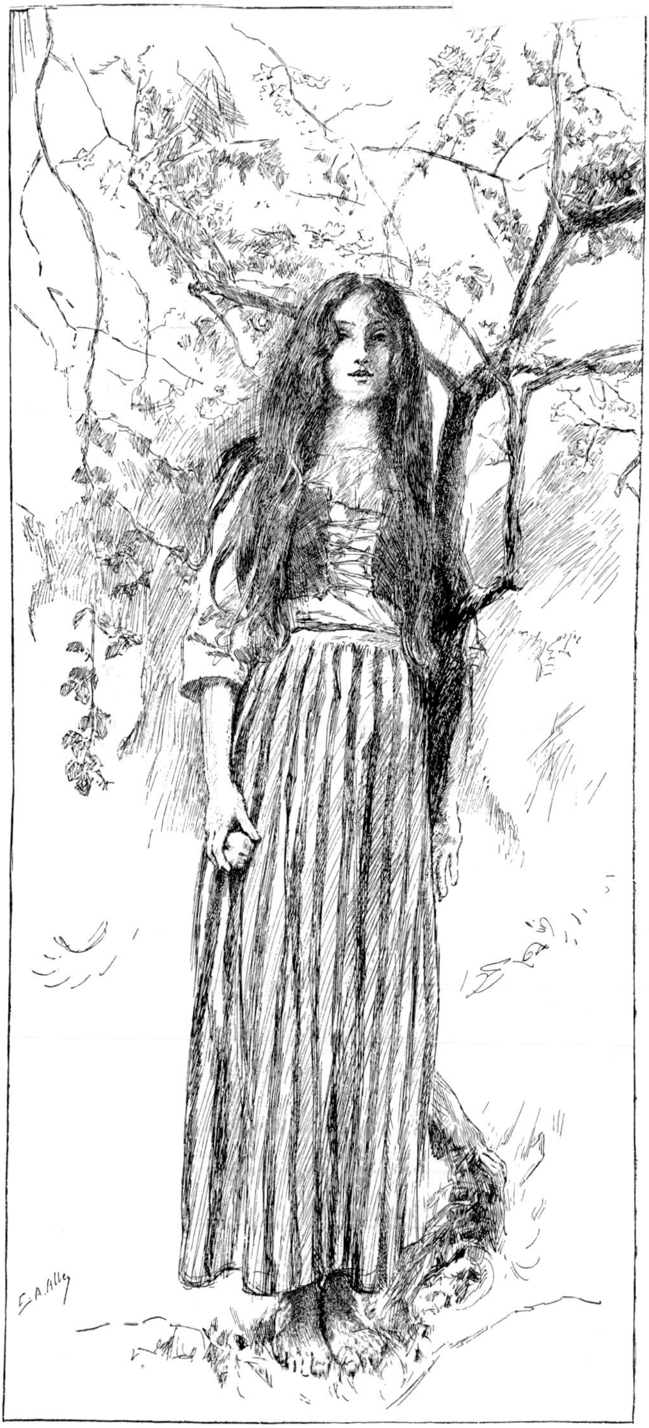

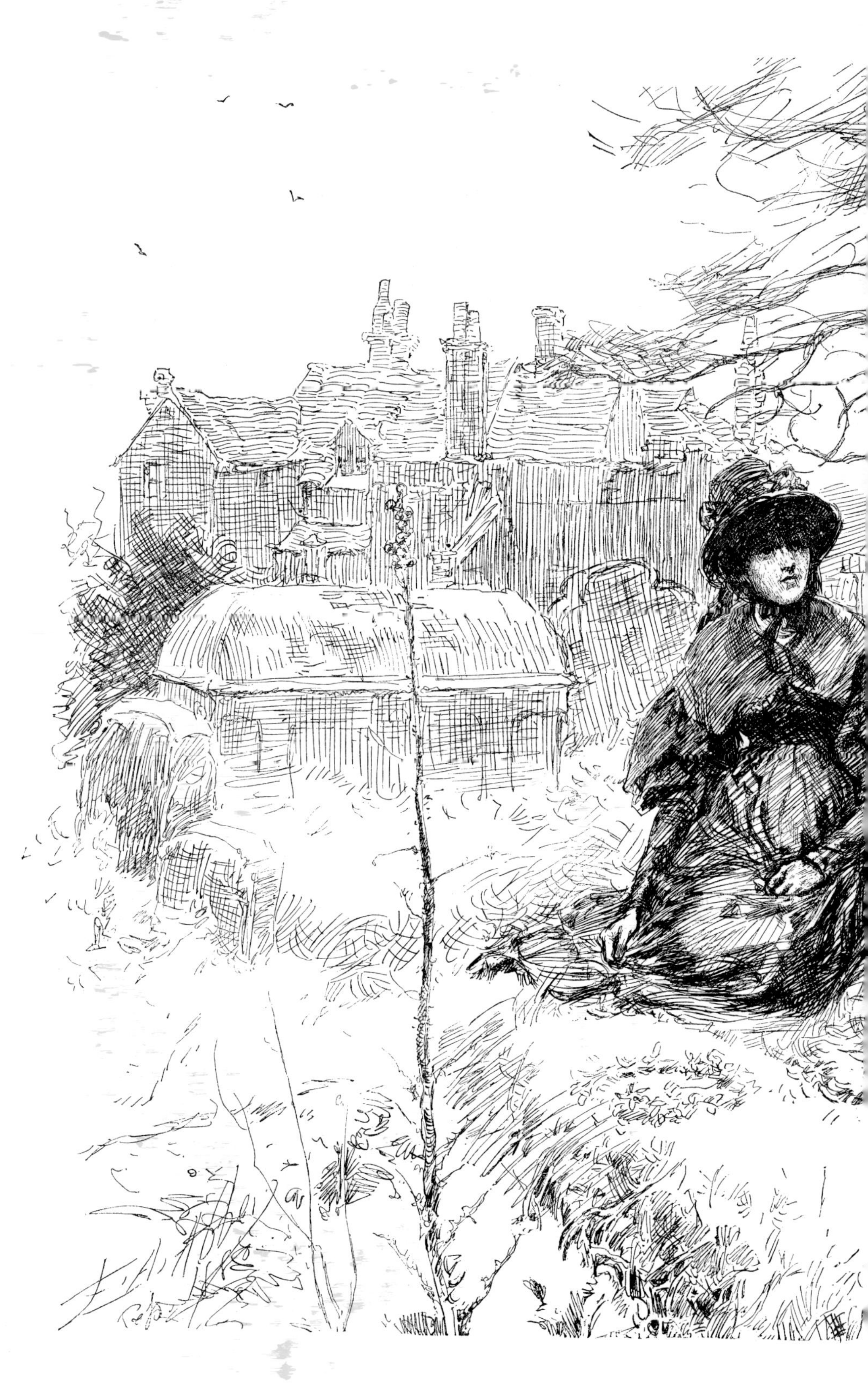

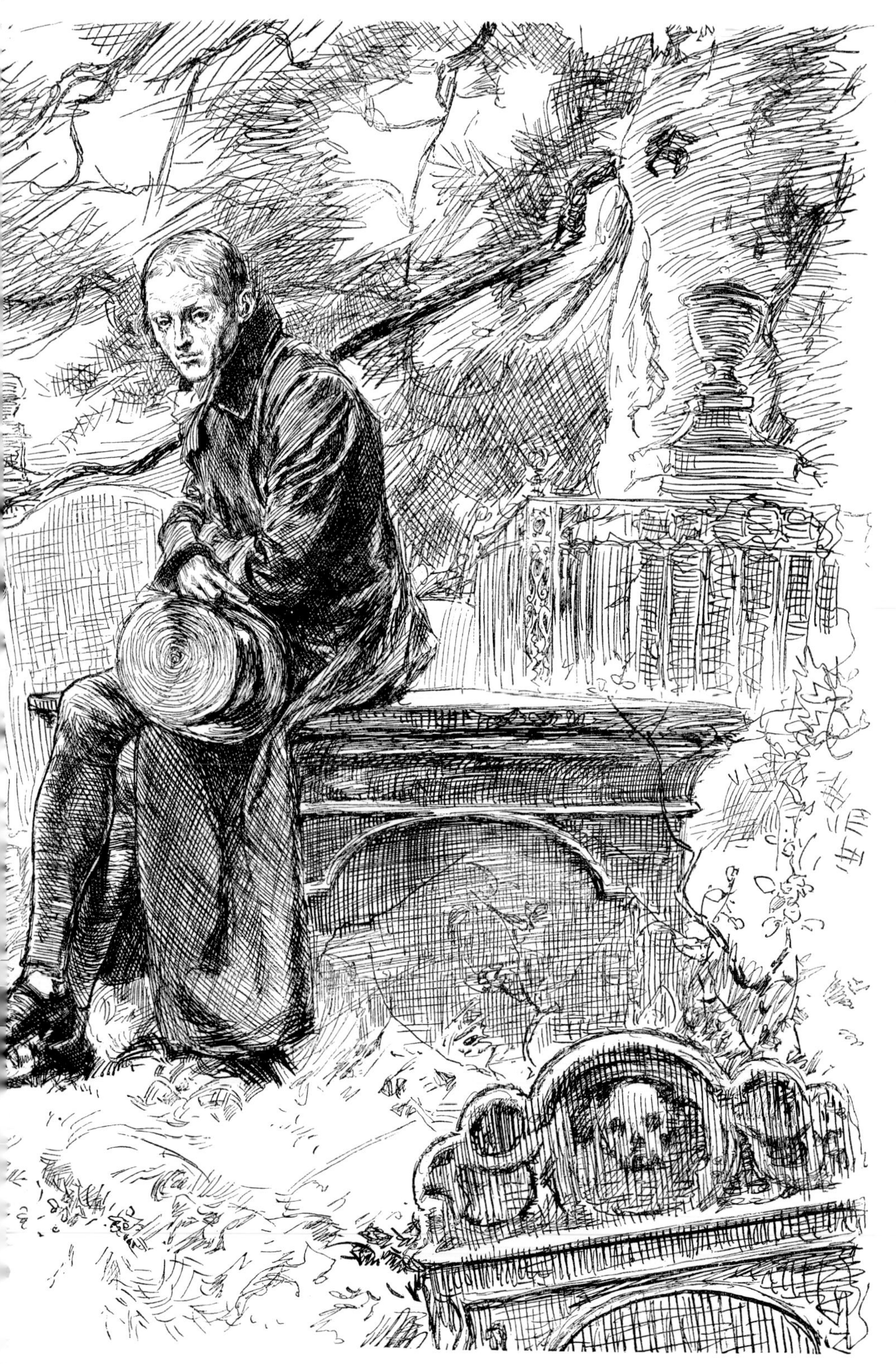

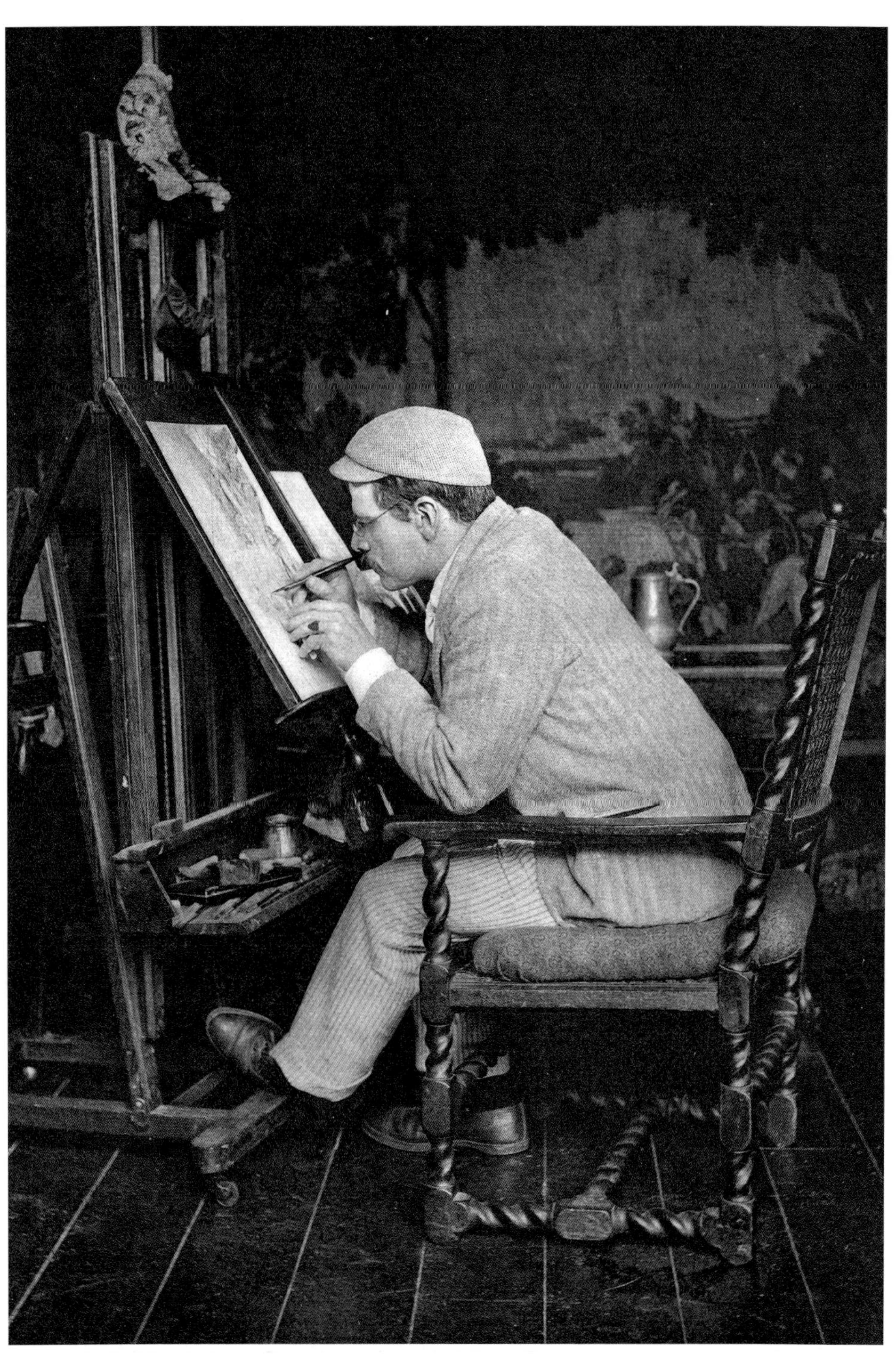

Edwin Austin Abbey, 1889

THE DRAWINGS OF
EDWIN AUSTIN ABBEY

by
Alice A. Carter
and
John Fleskes

FLESK

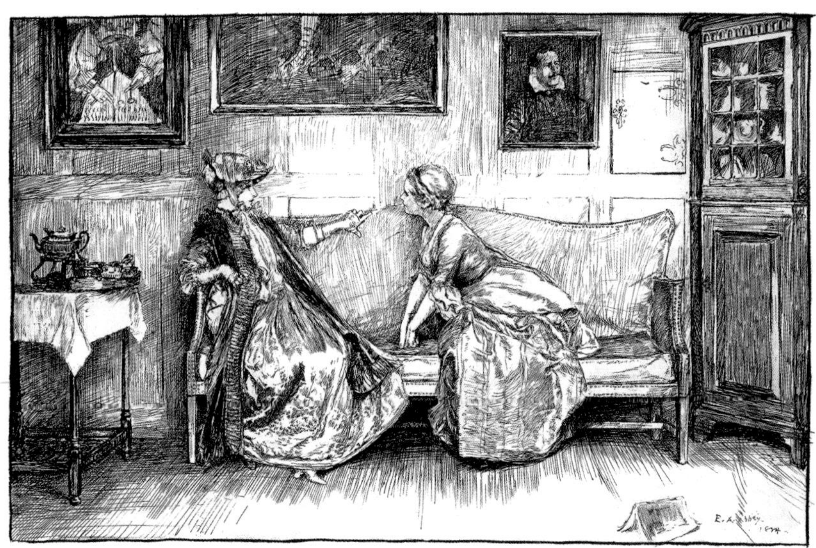

Edited and Designed by John Fleskes
Production, editing and design assistance by Katherine Chu
Production assistance by Keith Silva and James Walker II
Copyedited by Martin Timins

First printing
August 2021

Paperback edition ISBN: 978-1-64041-045-9
Hardbound edition ISBN: 978-1-64041-046-6
Library of Congress Control Number: 2020952121
Printed in China

Page 1: "Sweet as the primrose peeps beneath the thorn." The Deserted Village,
Harper & Brothers, October 1902
Originally published in Harper's New Monthly Magazine, July 1902
Pages 2-3: "November," *Harper's Bazar*, December 1880
Page 400: Imogen. "Ho! Who's here? If anything that's civil, speak." Harper's Monthly Magazine,
April 1909. "Cymbeline." Act III., Scene IV. — Country near Milford-Haven.

fleskpublications.com

CONTENTS

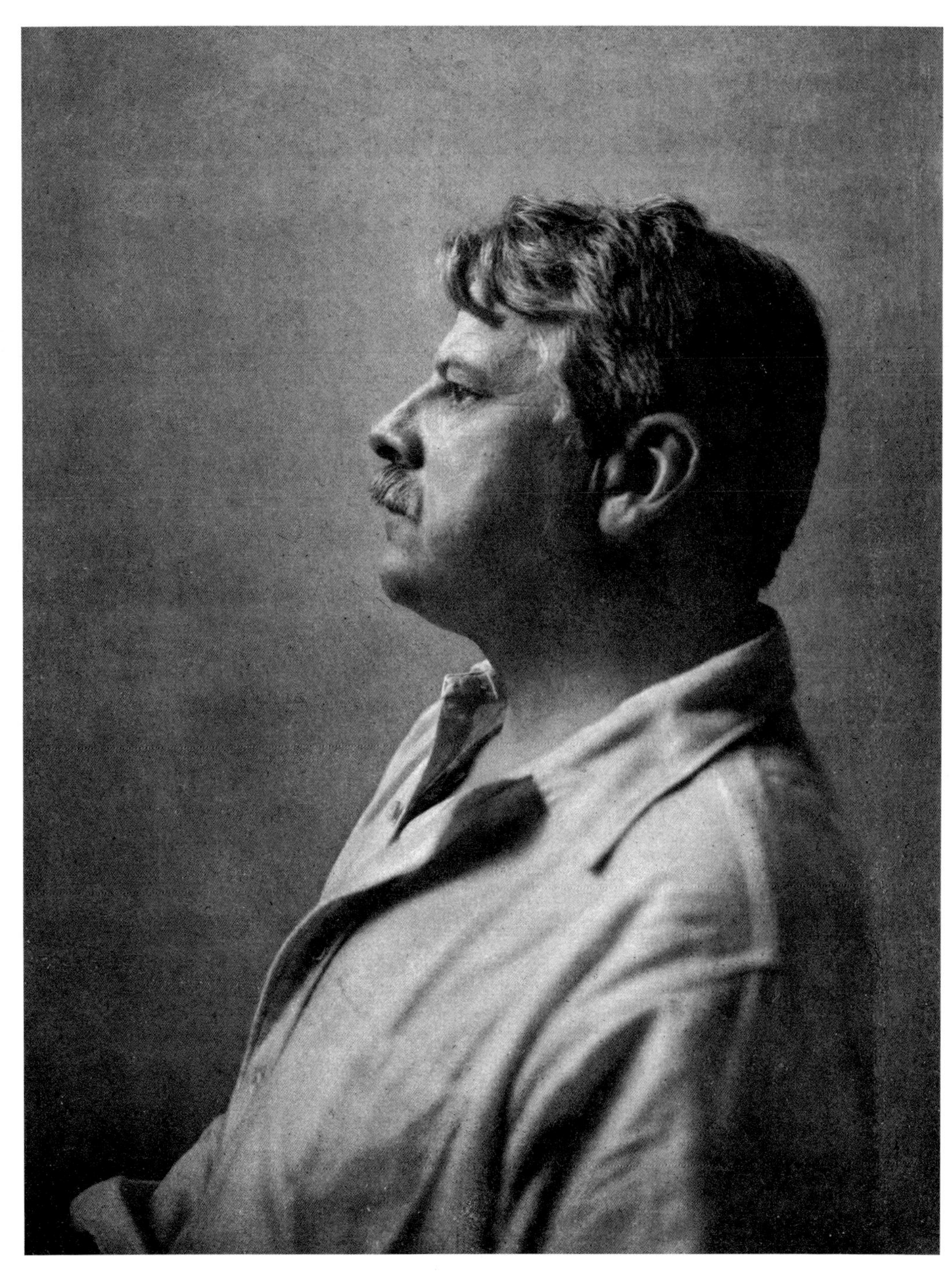

Undated photo from *The Life and Work of E.A. Abbey; Volume 2*

EDWIN AUSTIN ABBEY
and
THE HOUSE OF HARPER

by
Alice A. Carter

On April 1, 1883, Edwin Austin Abbey (1852-1911) celebrated his thirty-first birthday on the Dutch island of Walcheren. Seventy miles to the north, thirty-year-old Vincent van Gogh (1853-1890) was writing to his brother about a group of artists featured in a special Christmas issue of *Harper's Monthly Magazine*. "In my view," Van Gogh wrote, "Abbey is by far the cleverest... He has style—and that's a great thing. I write about it because I believe you'll agree with me that not all Americans are bad. That, on the contrary...besides a host of noisemakers and bunglers of the most insufferable and impossible sorts there are characters who have the effect of a lily or a snowdrop among thorns."[1]

Van Gogh was not alone in either his admiration for Abbey's illustrations or his opinion about the thorny state of American art. By 1883, the international distribution of Abbey's work in *Harper's Monthly Magazine, Harper's Weekly* and Harper & Brothers books had earned him a degree of fame that most of his contemporaries would struggle for years to attain—or, as in Van Gogh's case, never attain at all. And while the best-known American artists of the era were deeply influenced by European academic painting, the fluid spontaneity of Abbey's pen-and-ink drawings presented a startling departure from the rigid wood engravings that dominated American publications. Whether a lily or a snowdrop, Abbey did have style, and although not yet in full flower, he was poised at the beginning of a remarkable career that would jump-start a century of American dominance in mass-media entertainment.

The events that led Abbey to Walcheren Island began three decades earlier in antebellum Philadelphia, Pennsylvania. The night before his birth, the aurora borealis lit up the sky, and dawn yielded sun after days of rain. If these portents caused William and Margery Abbey to entertain high hopes for their firstborn, they would soon adjust their expectations. Edwin (called "Ned" all his life) was a high-spirited child with no patience for study. Even so, his parents made sure that like it or not, the boy got the best education possible. "My mother was a very well-read woman who, early in my life, as long as my memory goes back, did what she could to guide my tastes—primarily my literary tastes," Abbey recalled. "My father...although he was a poor man...sent my brother and myself to what he considered the best classical school in Philadelphia at the time (Henry D. Gregory's) hoping that we should enter the University of Pennsylvania and adopt a profession. This my brother did. I was a disappointment as a schoolboy."[2]

Abbey's poor academic performance was not for lack of persistence or ambition. He had an abundance of both and pursued his love of drawing from the time he was photographed clutching a pencil at age two until his sixteenth year, when his father, resigned to the inevitable, apprenticed him at the wood-engraving firm of Van Ingen and Snyder. There, Abbey's talents were quickly acknowledged. He was soon working as a draughtsman and an editor—making drawings on his own and selecting topics for other artists to illustrate. At night he attended classes at the Pennsylvania Academy of the Fine Arts, where his laissez-faire attitude toward formal education was again apparent. Although he admired his instructor, painter Christian Schussele (1824-1879), he balked at the traditional academic curriculum, which required drawing from ancient Greco-Roman sculpture. "I often wondered why the spirit of the class did not move him, for all he saw men and women making clever and bold studies from the antique," a classmate recalled.[3]

While his peers were working industriously, Abbey played truant, pursuing his interest in illustration at the Philadelphia library, where he spent hours looking at English periodicals—studying illustrations by Frederick Walker (1840-1875) in *The Cornhill* and cartoons by George du Maurier (1834-1896) in *Punch*. "I wonder what would have happened had my father known I was not at the Academy as he expected me to be, digging away at the antique?"[4] Abbey wrote years later. Fortunately, his father didn't suspect, and in 1870 with paternal pride he mailed his teenage son's drawings to Charles Parsons (1821-1910), art editor at

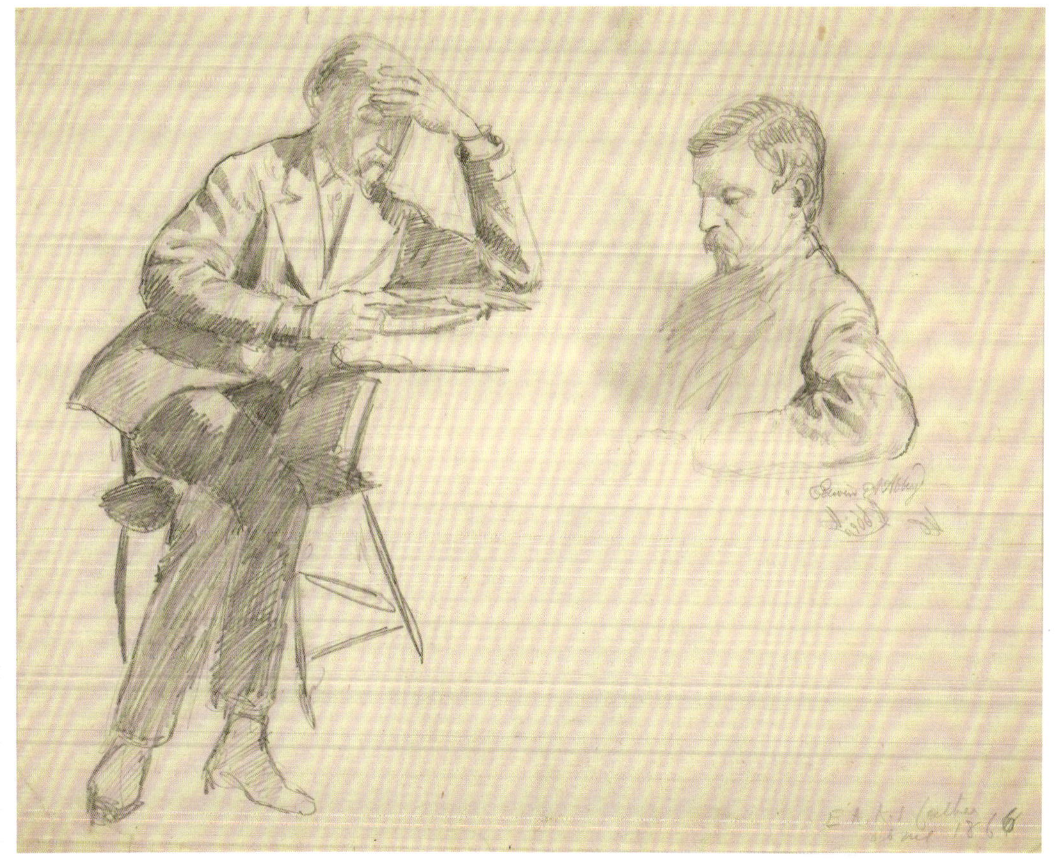

Edwin Austin Abbey (1852-1911), Portrait of the artist's father 2 views, 1866:
Edwin Austin Abbey Estate, 1937; Yale University Art Gallery, New Haven, Conn.

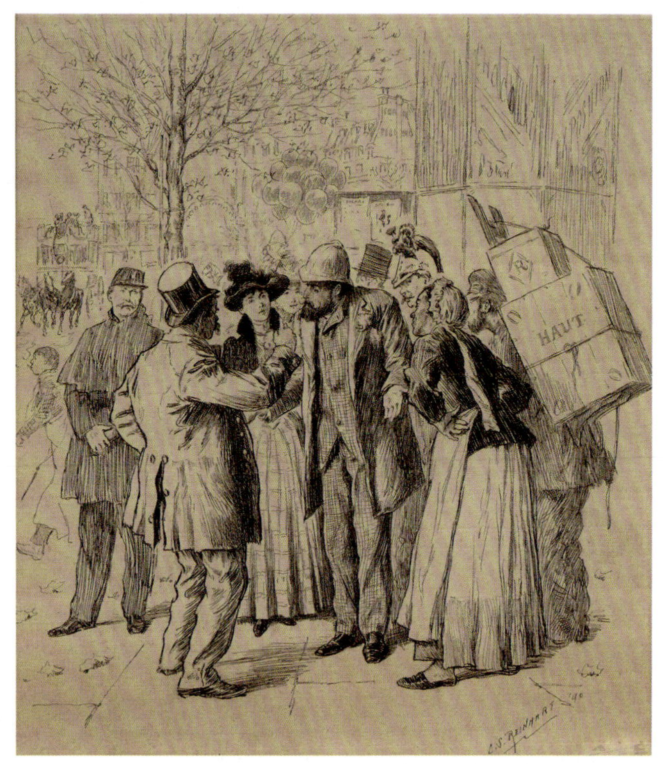

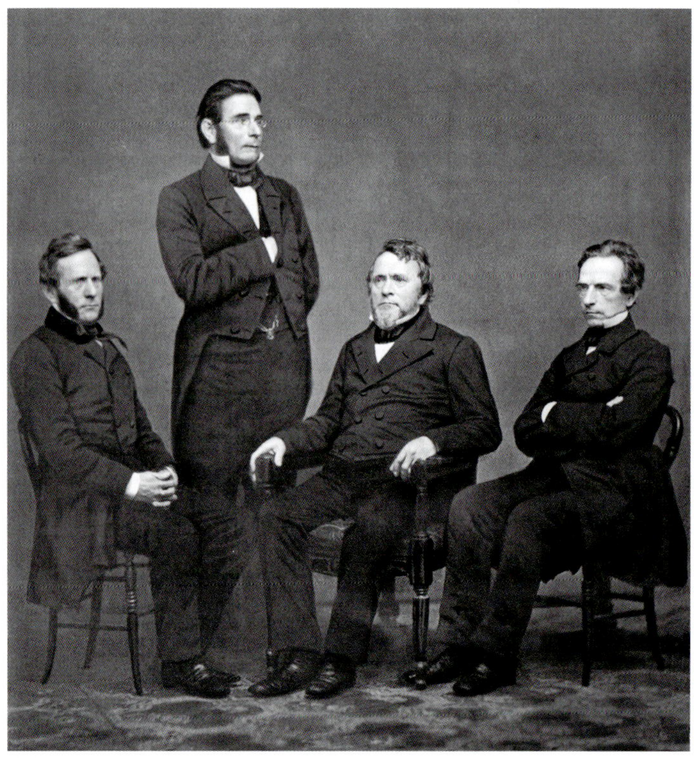

Top: Charles Stanley Reinhart (1844-1896), Eight Days in Paris, 1890; Carter/Granner Collection
Bottom: Mathew Brady (1822-1896), Group Portrait of the Four Harper Brothers c. 1860,
left to right: Fletcher, James, John, and Joseph

the publishing powerhouse of Harper & Brothers on Franklin Square in New York City.

Charles Parsons had prospered as a painter before discovering that his greater talent was spotting potential in others. By the time he received Abbey's drawings, he was eight years into his managerial position. Although he was famous for teasing young hopefuls by asking if they had anything else to live on, he took Abbey's work seriously.[5] Years later, Abbey praised Parsons in a letter to a friend: "I cannot forget the happy pride I felt when he wrote to my father nineteen years ago in answer to a letter enclosing some sketches of mine, 'What the young man needs is opportunity,' and he very shortly gave me an opportunity, and has given me other opportunities ever since."[6] Relying on intuition that rarely failed him, Parsons offered Ned Abbey his chance, publishing a drawing by the 18-year-old on December 3, 1870, and soon after offering him full-time employment.

In February 1871, Abbey hurried up the winding staircase at the heart of the House of Harper, crossed the iron bridge connecting the courtyard to the art department, shook hands with Charles Parsons and lead artist Charles Stanley Reinhart (1844-1896) and began a professional association that would last a lifetime.[7] Abbey's first assignments were for *Harper's Weekly: A Journal of Civilization*, a magazine launched in 1857 by Fletcher Harper (1806-1877), the youngest of the founding brothers. The highfalutin moniker (satirized in the *New York Tribune* as "*The Weakly Journal of Civilization*") belied the intent of the magazine.[8] The publication combined news, illustrations, serial fiction and advertising in a spirited amalgamation where the biting editorial cartoons of Thomas Nast (1840-1902) shared space with ads for novelties, sewing machines and yeast powder.

While the older, more-conservative *Harper's Monthly* avoided politics, the *Weekly* stepped into the fray. As Fletcher Harper liked to say, "When you fight, fight."[9] During the Civil War the *Weekly* embedded "special artists" with the troops honoring a promise to "give a well-drawn, well-engraved and well-printed illustration of every important event that occurs."[10] That promise was still at the heart of the magazine's mission in 1871. When news happened, the art staff went out on assignment. Scribbling down their impressions as best they could, they would hurry back to "The House," where their sketches were redrawn and handed over to the engravers.[11] At the time, illustration was a two-step collaboration between the artists who created the sketches and the engravers who cut away the negative areas leaving the line work in relief. The resulting woodblock could then be inked and printed along with the type.

The rush to get pictures into print "while news was still news" often yielded poor results, which Abbey was quick to note. Still, he was thrilled to be the youngest member in a congenial group of illustrators. One of his colleagues remembered that he worked "like a little demon shoveling coal."[12] During crises like the Orange riots and the Chicago fire, he often put in thirty-six hours at a stretch, recovering later with "cold coffee and a wet towel."[13] For his troubles he took home $15 a week, which even in 1871 was scanty compensation, especially since Harper's was willing to pay engravers up to $500 for carving out a full-page picture.[14]

The impetus for these extraordinary returns was a brand-new competitor, *Scribner's Monthly: An Illustrated Magazine for the People*.[15] It presented a direct threat to the primacy and profits of the Harper brothers' flagship periodical, *Harper's Monthly Magazine*. Editor Henry Mills Alden (1836-1919), who welcomed a fair fight, seized the gauntlet for *Harper's*, declaring exuberantly: "If you arc driving a mettlesome horse and another spirited steed comes alongside, your horse... naturally leaps forward, rejoicing in a good race."[16] When *Scribner's* revealed its plan to drive circulation with superior pictures, Charles Parsons rallied his troops and saw in young Ned Abbey the ability to take on the competition.

Abbey's first illustration for *Harper's Monthly* was an embarrassment he hoped would "never be dug out from its resting place."[17] His second attempt, a drawing of militia men lined up for inspection, showed the humor and attention to historical detail that would define his later illustrations. Abbey signed the piece—a rarity when much of the work done for *Harper's* involved recycling old engravings, replicating photographs or, in many cases, redrawing sketches submitted by other artists. On his first visit to the art department, the illustrator William Allen Rogers (1854-1931) was mortified to learn that Abbey and colleague Arthur Burdett Frost (1851-1928) had redrawn his submission to the *Weekly*. "We didn't know exactly what it meant," Abbey told Rogers with a chuckle, "but then Frost said that he didn't believe that you did either, so we went ahead."[18] Rogers, who soon joined the staff, never forget how quickly Abbey had put him at ease and embraced him in as a comrade.

Camaraderie was as much a part of Abbey's success as his improving skill. Everyone liked him. When pressure mounted, he entertained the staff by cartwheeling down the aisle. Although he was small, Abbey was athletic. One day he installed a trapeze on an overhead beam, hiked himself up and, while "skinning the cat," knocked the high silk hat off the head of Fletcher Harper Jr. (1828-1890). Fortunately, Fletcher admired the youngster's vitality and liked to watch him laugh so he could "see a fine set of teeth."[19] Abbey's exceptionally white teeth added to the consensus that he was well "set up" with broad shoulders, regular features and intense dark eyes that belied his carefree demeanor. "His friends could call him Ned and laugh at his merry pranks and his wit," Rogers

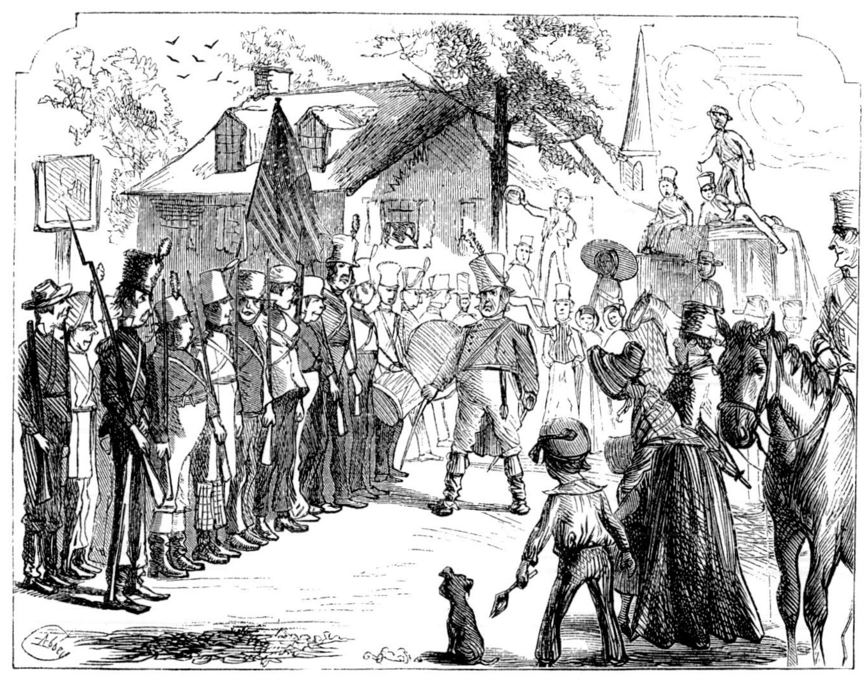

"And general muster-day."

Edwin Austin Abbey (1852-1911), *Harper's New Monthly Magazine*, July 1871
"When This Old Flag Was New."
Abbey recalled composing this charming scene in January of 1871.
It was his second drawing for Harper's.

later wrote, "but always, to me, what he did and what he said was the least of who he was."[20]

Rogers was right. Behind Abbey's office shenanigans lurked a focused drive for excellence. When he wasn't swinging from the ceiling, he studied the illustrated periodicals that accumulated in the art department, searching for a lodestar. Among the "good, bad, and indifferent," he found his mentors—the English illustrators George John Pinwell (1842-1875), William Small (1843-1929), Frederick Walker (1840-1875), John Everett Millais (1829-1896) and Charles Keene (1823-1891).[21] Inspired by their prowess, Abbey worked on weekends, holidays and after hours by candlelight, bundled up against the cold in his unheated room. His tenacity paid off in more-challenging assignments from Charles Parsons, whose practiced eye recognized the increasing competence in his protégé.

Management rewarded Abbey with a raise. By 1874 his pay had more than doubled to $35 a week. Still, he was always in debt—often drawing

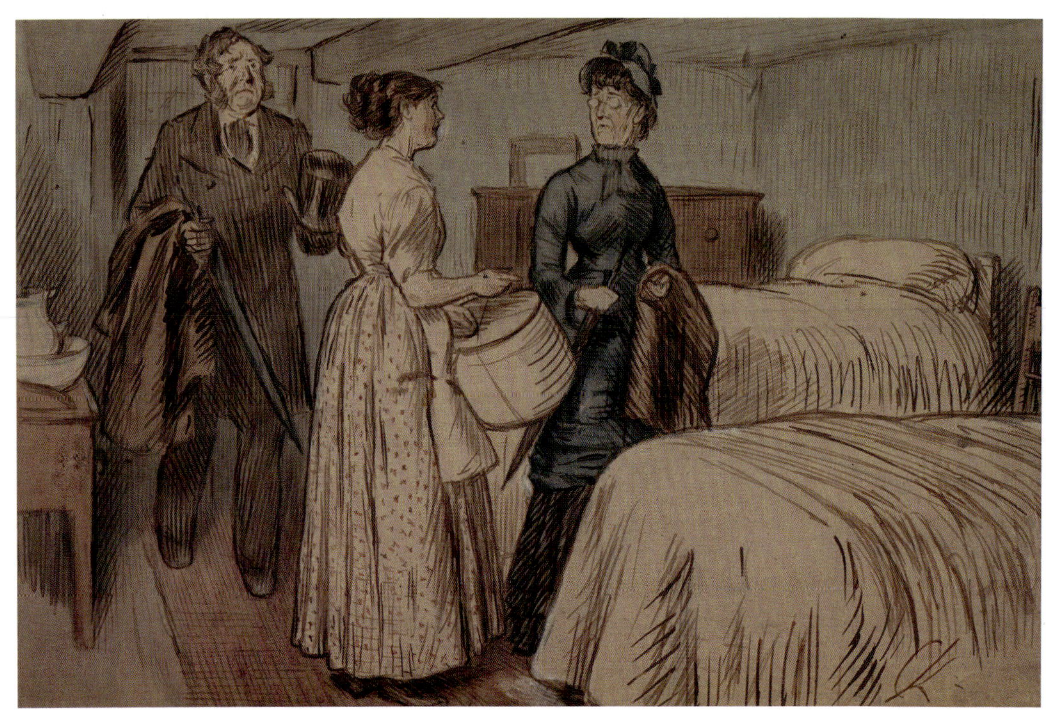

Charles Samuel Keene (1823-1891),
Checking in; Carter/Granner Collection

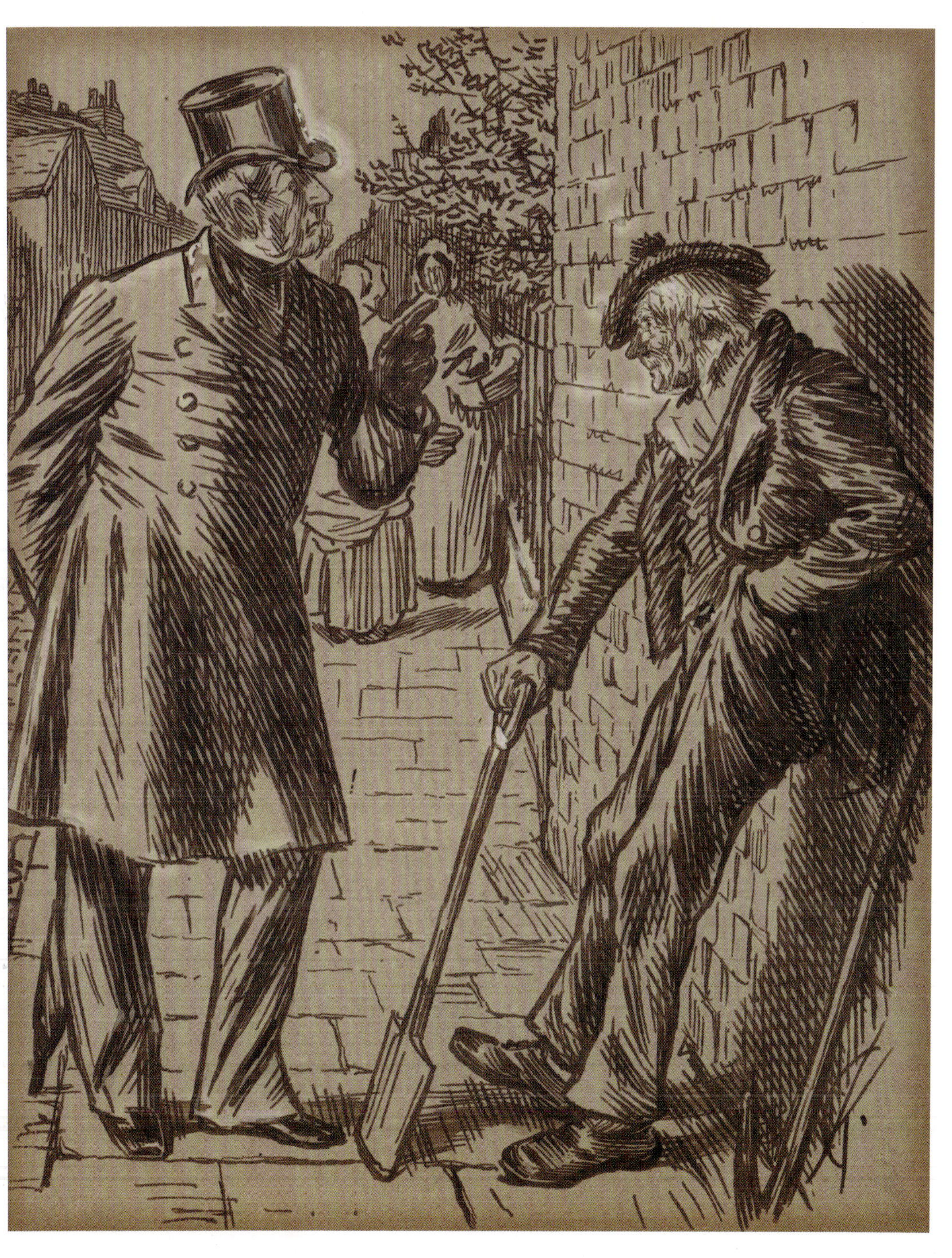

Charles Samuel Keene (1823-1891),
Live and Let Live; Carter/Granner Collection

on his account to send money to his family or to pay for costumes, props and books. Weary of the financial worry and embarrassed to be eating crackers in the office while his colleagues went out to lunch, Abbey requested $40 a week. When management refused, he decided to go out on his own. At twenty-two, it was a daring move for which he was unprepared. "That time I left Harpers and had to go to other publishers for work," he remembered, "I nearly died of sheer shyness."[22]

Abbey persevered. From his top-floor studio on Union Square, he worked with his customary good cheer on assignments for *Harper's*, *Scribner's* and other publications willing to hire him. On breaks, he entertained his nineteen-year-old assistant by belting out sentimental songs and ending the performance with a backflip. On Wednesday evenings, he unwound with fellow members of the Tile Club—an organization of artists who met weekly to eat cheese and crackers, drink beer and paint designs on eight-inch tiles in the idle hope of selling them. The Tilers adopted nicknames. Abbey was "The Chestnut" in honor of his facility for telling tall tales.[23]

When work was slow, Abbey visited local galleries. Once, on a whim, he dropped by an exhibition that included drawings by several of the British illustrators he admired. "These drawings were simply exquisite and were a revelation to me,"[24] Abbey remembered. Astounded by the difference between the original art and the engraved facsimiles he had been studying since boyhood, Abbey realized that he needed to change his working methods. Rather than making rough sketches and leaving the details to the engraver, he would create finished pen-and-ink drawings and insist that they be replicated exactly. This notion was revolutionary. Both in America and Europe, readers were accustomed to illustrations that mimicked fine-art prints. Line drawings were considered a preliminary step in creating artwork, not an end in themselves.

Sometime in 1876, Harper's offered Abbey $50 a week to return to the fold. Glad of a steady income, he agreed—although he kept his own studio. By May 10, he was back on the job and out on assignment. The nineteen-year-old future illustrator and writer Joseph Pennell (1857-1926) recalled spotting Abbey on opening day at the Centennial Exhibition in Philadelphia. "I saw Abbey and Reinhart and I do not know how many other illustrators, over a big doorway sketching President

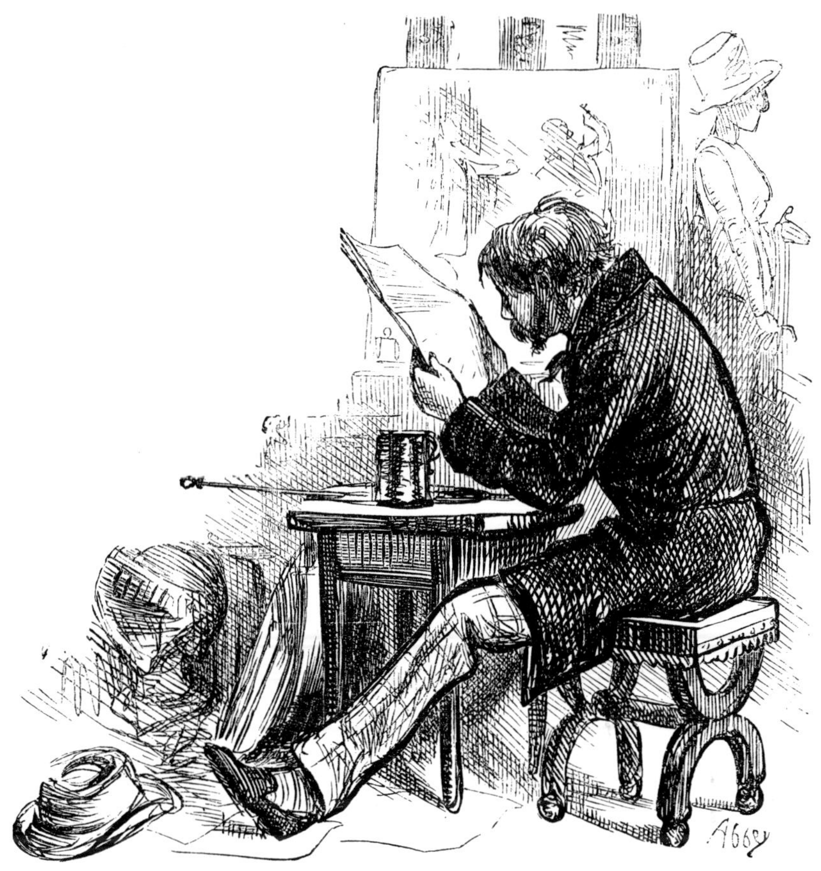

Brush "at work."

Edwin Austin Abbey (1852-1911), *Harper's New Monthly Magazine*, May 1873,
The Editor's Drawer, Our London Scrapbook: The Artist's Quarter.

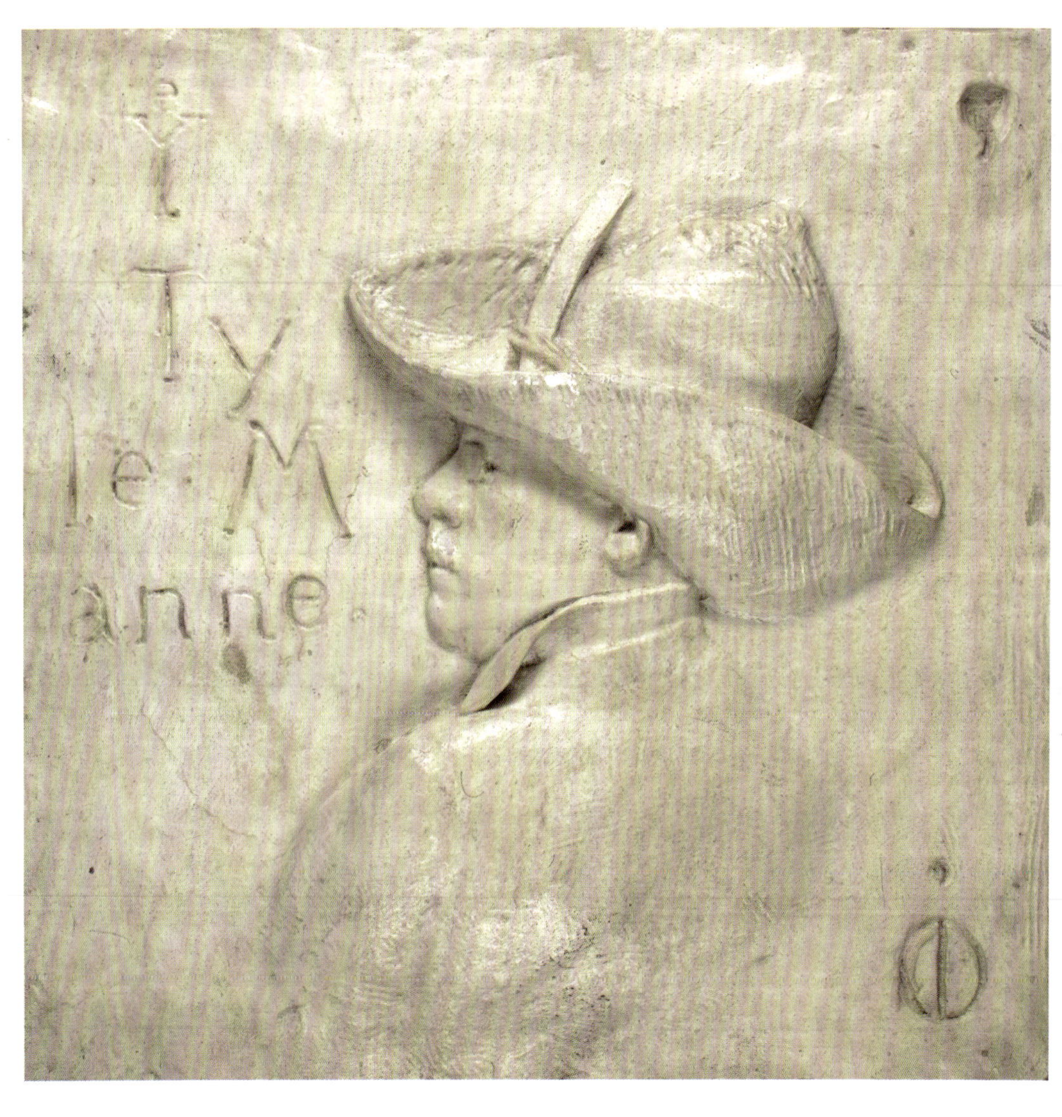

Ye Tyle Manne, Portrait tile of Edwin Austin Abbey (1852-1911) by William Rudolf O'Donovan, (1844-1920): Edwin Austin Abbey Estate, 1937; Yale University Art Gallery, New Haven, Conn.

Grant," Pennell wrote. "I turned my back on the President to watch the illustrators."[25] After completing his sketches, Abbey braved the crowds (estimated at 200,000 that day) and elbowed his way into the Centennial's art gallery.

The English paintings stopped him in his tracks. Thirty-two years later, the experience was still vivid. "I can close my eyes now and see nearly every picture," Abbey wrote. "These English things told me something of the things I had read about and reflected the ideas of the country that interested me so much. My heart lay with the English."[26] Abbey had been reading the works of British authors since childhood. With no international copyright law to prevent piracy, American periodicals regularly serialized novels by literary stars like Dickens and Thackery with impunity. What Abbey saw in the canvases of the British painters was the visual embodiment of the stories that had kindled his boyhood imagination. In that moment, he made a decision: As soon as possible, he would go to England.[27]

Abbey shared his enthusiasm at the office, urging his cohorts to embrace the principles of English Pre-Raphaelite painting and exchange visual clichés for acute observation. As William Allen Rogers admitted, "To Abbey, perhaps more than anyone else, was due the introduction of careful work from the model and all the details from nature itself."[28] The improvement was soon obvious, especially in Abbey's work. Inspired by the Centennial paintings, he incorporated authenticity into his pen-and-ink drawings. Signed or unsigned, his work stands out among the many of illustrations published in *Harper's Monthly* between 1876 and 1878.

Innovation is not always appreciated, however. Over time, the *Harper's* editor Henry Mills Alden received hundreds of letters protesting the "new style of drawing," which was "ruining the magazine."[29] Alarmed, Alden brought the letters to Charles Parsons, who knew exactly what to do: He locked them in his safe. Parsons had a paternal regard for the art staff, but his affection for Ned Abbey went beyond that. Despite the difference in their ages, they had become compatriots, and Parsons understood two things about his friend: Abbey was never going to compromise his work, and he was never going to be content until he set foot in England.

In November 1878, Parsons figured out a way to underwrite Abbey's dream. The adventure would be financed by a $600 advance from

Harper's for drawings of English subjects and a series of illustrations for an anthology of poems by the seventeenth-century British writer and cleric Robert Herrick (1591-1674).[30] If Herrick is remembered at all today, it is for a single line: "Gather ye rosebuds while ye may." In the Victorian era, however, the pastoral (and occasionally bawdy) works of the poet were enjoying a revival. Herrick's rhymes were featured in popular periodicals, and British publishers turned out twenty editions of his work between 1810 and 1900.[31]

Abbey refused Parson's offer. His financial judgement had not improved, and even though he was still under obligation to his family, he continued to splurge on reference material. "You know that I am attached to *Harper's Magazine* and would do more for them and at less prices than anyone else," Abbey explained to Parsons. "But you also know how I am situated and how necessary it is for me to put myself in a way to assist those dependent upon me...If the Harpers are willing to advance me 500 dollars now and 75 a page for the work...I think I would be willing to go."[32] Parsons negotiated an agreement. Tickets were purchased, and Abbey embarked on his journey with a sendoff befitting the publishers' favorite son.

On December 7, 1878, J. Henry Harper (1850-1938) hosted a farewell breakfast at Delmonico's with a guest list that read like a who's who of *fin de siècle* art and publishing. After the guests were seated, the host signaled the head waiter to begin serving. "He came over to me," Harper later recalled, "and whispered in what seemed to be stentorian tones, 'Hadn't you better wait until Mr. Abbey arrives?' I had forgotten our Hamlet."[33] The lead actor soon made his entrance to relief and applause. Following the meal, Abbey was transported regally to the docks in a coach and four—on time for the 2:30 p.m. departure of the *S.S. Germanic.* As the ship pulled away into the mist, Abbey looked back at the assembled throng and spotted a friend: The painter J. Alden Wier (1852-1919) had climbed a pole and was waving a handkerchief tied to a stick.

Ten days later, Abbey arrived in the land of his dreams. Staggering off the tender on sea legs, his great expectations dissolved. "Everything looks dirty; water is dirty, boats that we pass are beastly dirty, sails are almost black," he informed his family.[34] As he watched incredulously, a Dickensian cast of newsboys, porters and bootblacks with mud up to their armpits materialized out of the Liverpool fog. "I never believed that people could go about looking so desperately wretched," he recalled. "Our tramps are princes to them."[35] Abbey was reminded of Jo, the sweeper in *Bleak House*, and the misery that Luke Fildes (1843-1927) depicted in "Applicants for Admission to the Casual Ward," one Abbey's favorite paintings at the Centennial Exhibition.

A night's rest and a journey through the countryside changed everything. The next day, Abbey was snuggly housed at the Red Horse Inn in picturesque Stratford-upon-Avon—neat as a pin and festooned in holly and greens for Christmas. He was thrilled when the proprietor offered him the room that Washington Irving (1783-1859) had described in *The Sketch Book of Geoffrey Crayon*. As long as the traveler has "the wherewithal to pay his bill," Irving wrote, "he is, for the time being, the very monarch of all he surveys, the armchair is his throne, the poker his septre."[36] Irving's former room was configured for tourists, with a plaque affixed to the famous armchair, but Abbey was delighted. He stayed through New Year's making drawings for *Harper's Monthly* and attending the inn's holiday parties, where he won over the locals with his courtesy and humor.

Early in January, Abbey packed up for London. With his advance as collateral and his Stratford drawings in the mail to *Harper's*, it never occurred to him that he might lack "the wherewithal to pay his bill." At checkout, he was stunned to discover the cost of charm and hospitality. In London, Abbey rented an attic room suited to his reduced circumstances, nursed a bad cold and worried that he would be in real trouble if the *Harper's* drawings were rejected. Broke, sick and alone in the largest metropolis in the world, he considered his options and did what any intrepid man of twenty-six might do in the situation: Fortified with letters of introduction, Abbey shaved, put on a clean shirt and set out to find a friend.

Abbey's letters of introduction were a formality. The artists he wanted to meet already knew who he was. *Harper's* was widely distributed in Europe and, as predicted, the rivalry with *Scribner's* had indeed benefited both horses in the race. As *Scribner's* explained to its readers, "The success of American periodicals in a foreign market is generally attributed wholly to the superiority of American engraving and the prodigality of

illustration."[37] There is no doubt that Abbey's association with the House
of Harper helped him to put his foot in the door of London's artistic
community. But it was his warmth and humility that kept that door open.

Within a week, Abbey's new friends had extracted him from his attic
(deemed unsuitable) and moved him to better lodgings. In short order
he relocated again, this time close to the Anglo-American artist George
Henry Boughton (1833-1905). At the age of forty-five, Boughton was
established in West House, an impressive home where everything spoke of
"extremely fine taste, and—prosperity," as Abbey noted.[38] Boughton took
the young American under his wing and, like Henry Higgins, schooled
him in British manners. "English people are so plagued particular about
etiquette...but Boughton coached me up," Abbey assured his mother.[39]
Through Boughton, Abbey met the novelist William Black (1841-1898),
Dutch painter Lawrence Alma-Tadema (1836-1912), composer Johannes
Brahms (1833-1897), poet Robert Browning (1812-1889) and American
expatriate painter James Abbott McNeill Whistler (1834-1903).

During his first month in the city, Abbey attended social events that
were as different from the feet-on-the-table informality of the Tile Club
as Stratford was from London. "What a lucky fellow I am to drop into
the society I most enjoy and from which I can learn so much," he wrote
to his mother.[40] During a performance by the baritone George Henschel
(1850-1934), Abbey got "quivers way down in his boots."[41] His friend
Boughton, likewise moved, shed tears and pinched Abbey's arm with
such force that the marks were still there the next day. At the end of each
glittering evening, however, Abbey returned to his studio, hung up his
swallowtail jacket and faced a different reality: His Stratford drawings
were being held at the dead-letter office in Washington, D.C., for postage
due. Until they were ransomed and approved, he would not be paid.

Seeking to remedy his financial woes, Abbey accepted every assignment
Harper's was willing to commission—travel pieces, illustrations for Keats's
"The Eve of St. Agnes," designs for a ballad of Dick Whittington, as well
as drawings for the Herrick poems. Every illustration cost Abbey money
for models, props and research—often more than half of his commission.
He did his best to economize and, rather than taking the bus, walked
the ten-mile round trip from Campden Hill to Harper's London offices.
Eventually he was forced to borrow money from Boughton.

Under the pressure, Abbey's buoyant spirits flagged. In New York, his ability to work while simultaneously carrying on a conversation or slyly singing "Come into the garden, Maud...I am here at the gate alone" was legendary. Now he had to concentrate. Lacking the buttress of a formal art education to back up his intuitive talent, his work had become increasingly difficult. He told Charles Parsons that he felt like an impostor.

Eventually Abbey did get paid, although not as much as he expected. Printing technology had advanced, and artwork transferred to wood photographically could be reduced or enlarged. Since Abbey's pay was determined in inches (the art's size when published), he was horrified to see drawings that took weeks to create compressed into tiny spaces on the printed page. Unless he knew the final size of his illustrations in advance,

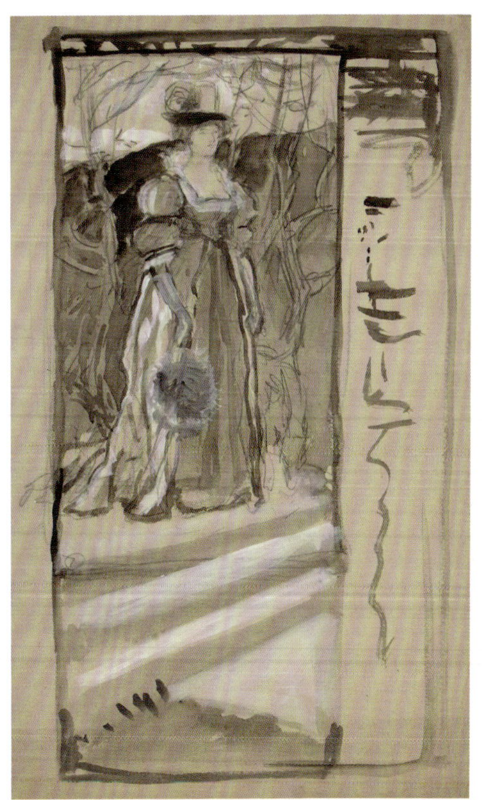
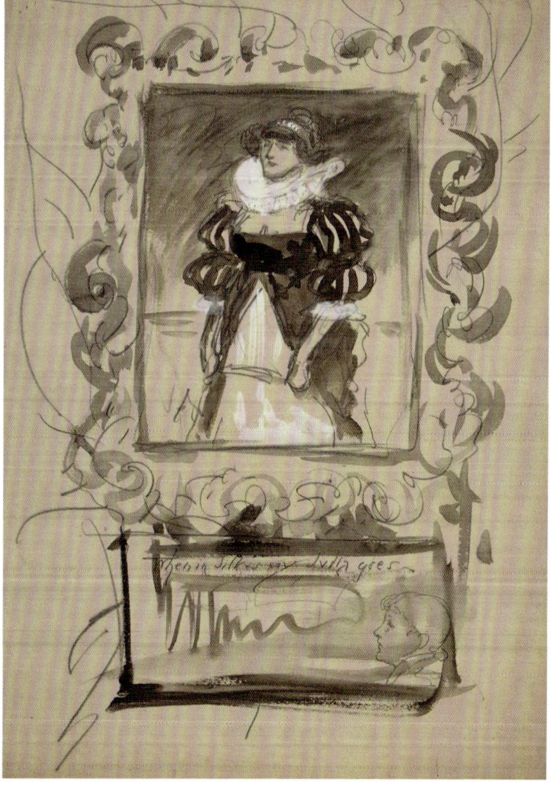

Edwin Austin Abbey, American (1852-1911),
Two studies for the final illustration for "Upon Julia's Clothes," p. 35 of Robert Herrick's Poems:
Studies from the Edwin Austin Abbey Estate, 1937; Yale University Art Gallery, New Haven, Conn.

it would be impossible to budget his time or to calculate his income. "It seems scarcely worthwhile to work a drawing up so highly as you have always impressed upon me you desired, and then make it so trifling in size that the detail is entirely lost," he complained to Charles Parsons.[42] Compounding Abbey's anxiety was his commitment to help his parents, who had no idea he was in financial trouble.

By the end of the year, Abbey was depressed and ill. Nevertheless, he decided to stay in England, and although he didn't suspect it at the time, his decision was final. In London he had access to the reference material he needed to make his illustrations "fairly smell" of their time."[43] Most of all, he was getting the education he had missed when he dove headfirst into the workforce as a teenager. He visited galleries and museums and even made a trip to the Salon in Paris, where Bastien Lepage's painting of Joan of Arc astonished him. "I have never had anything so stir me up in all

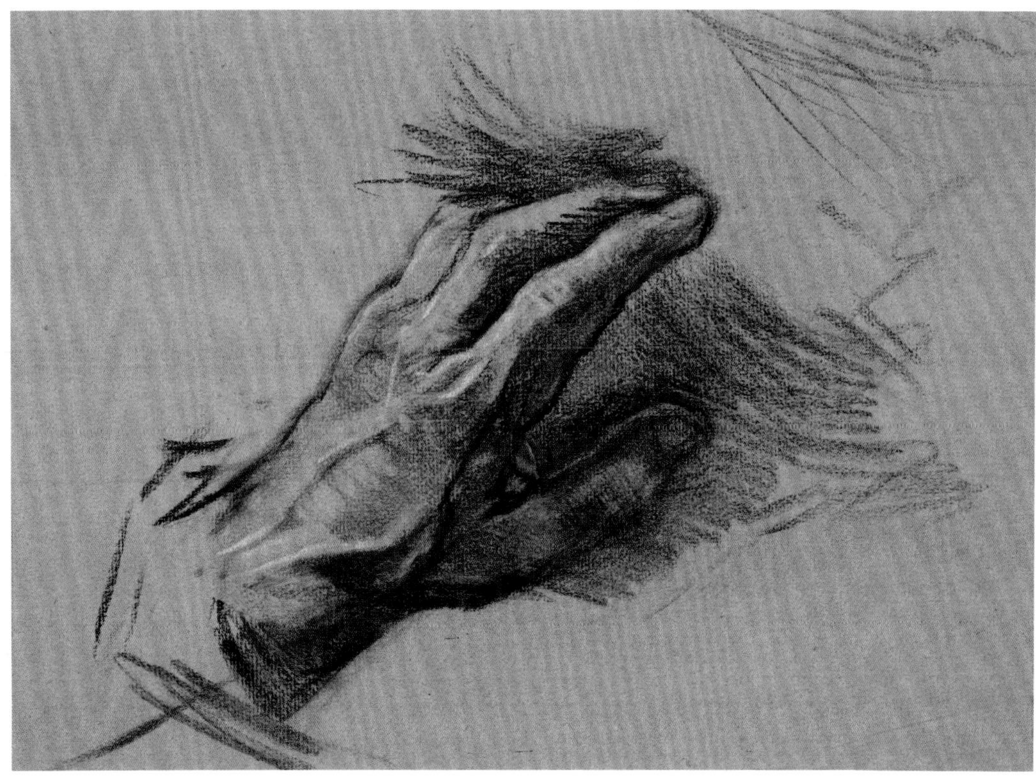

Edwin Austin Abbey (1852-1911), Sketch of a hand; Edwin Austin Abbey Estate, 1937;
Yale University Art Gallery, New Haven, Conn.

my life," he wrote to Parsons. "If I could express to you the wild longing within me to grab a brush and set my teeth and paint until I *dropped dead*, this pen would get *red hot*."[44] It would be years before Abbey could grab a brush with confidence. Meanwhile, Boughton helped him with his draughtsmanship. Frederic Leighton (1830-1896), whose work had impressed him at the Centennial, shared his "method," while Alma-Tadema was more direct. "You are too careless with your hands," he told Abbey. "Do as I do. If you have a small hand to draw, draw it large first—then draw it from nature again in your picture."[45]

Abbey's struggles were undetectable in pages of *Harper's Monthly*, where his work continued to outperform the competition. In the magazine's March 1879 issue, the author Samuel Benjamin (1837-1914) put a cap on the young artist's accomplishments in his article "Present Tendencies of American Art" with this assessment: "We think the artist

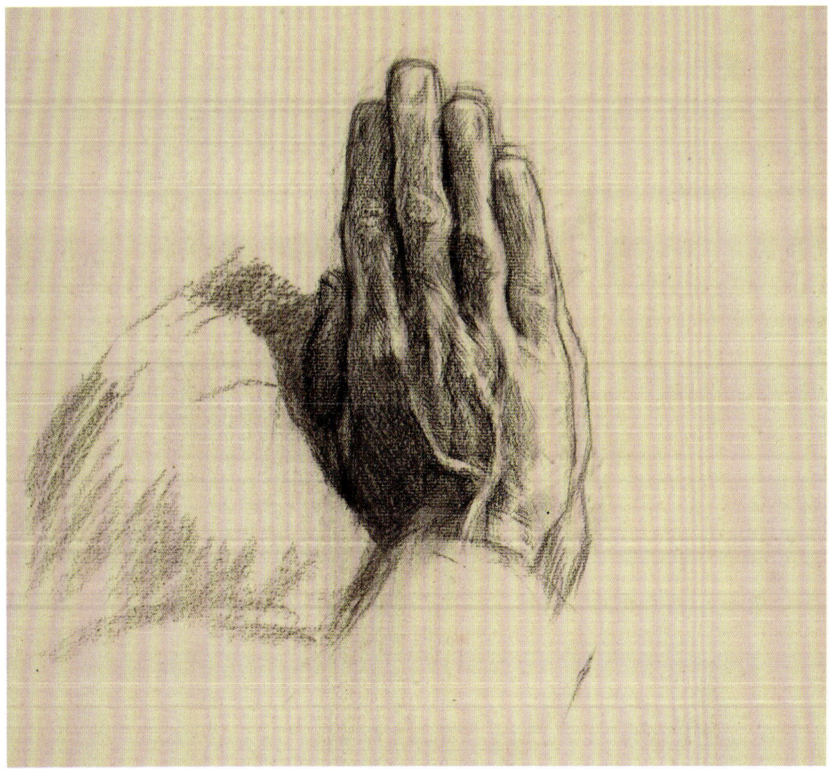

Edwin Austin Abbey (1852-1911), Sketch of two hands, clasped in prayer;
Edwin Austin Abbey Estate, 1937; Yale University Art Gallery, New Haven, Conn.

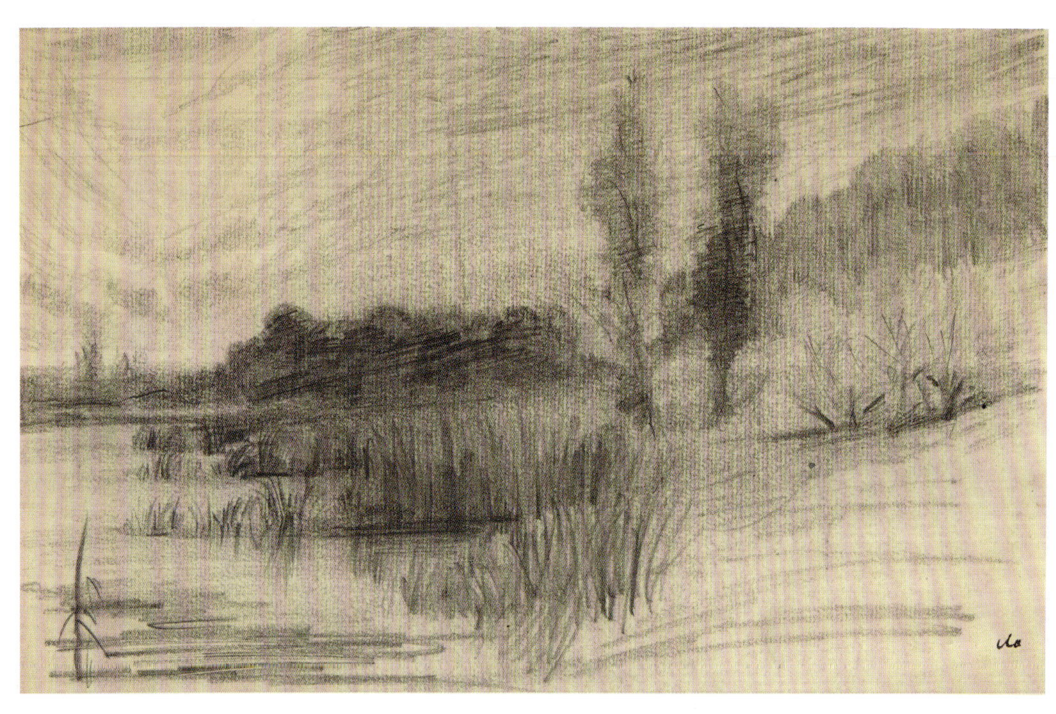

Edwin Austin Abbey (1852-1911), Landscape by water's edge,
Edwin Austin Abbey Estate, 1937; Yale University Art Gallery, New Haven, Conn.

who on the whole shows the most original inventive power, scarcely equaled by any other artist we have produced, is Mr. E. A. Abbey...We find represented in him genius of a high order."[46] Months later, Charles Reinhart—considered the lead artist at *Harper's*—appeared red-faced at Benjamin's door, ready to "knock him down" for giving Abbey's work precedence over his own. Abbey never heard about the incident, and Reinhart remained one of his dearest friends.[47]

Poor health dogged Abbey for most of 1880. When news reached him that his mother was gravely ill, he was too weak to travel. After she passed away, he was inconsolable. With what was left of his will and energy, Abbey applied himself to the Herrick drawings. His doctor forbade Abbey from working more than four hours a day, however, and progress was slow. With little money coming in, his debts mounted. In desperation, he pawned everything he could spare. In spring of 1881, Abbey gave up his apartment and moved into #54 Bedford Gardens, the home and studio of illustrator Alfred Parsons (1847-1920). Although only five years older than Abbey and no relation to Charles Parsons, he looked after his new roommate with similar protective kindness. Nevertheless, Abbey was mortified to have to depend on charity. He reluctantly began working for *The Graphic*, a London-based weekly that paid on receipt. In short order, a generous draft arrived from the House of Harper. Finally, after three years of struggle, life was good.

Alfred Parsons might have put the "e" in "Olde" England. He was as close to an Anglophile as possible for a British native and as enamored with English history as Abbey in his most sentimental moments. Parsons' paintings and illustrations were poems to a mythological countryside where trees and flowers swayed to gentle breezes and the "dark satanic mills" of William Blake (1757-1827) had yet to despoil the natural beauty.[48] Parsons was eager to introduce what was left of "Olde" England to his American friend. In the summer of 1881, the two men vacationed together in the village of Lechlade, perched in bucolic splendor on the banks of the Thames. Abbey wanted to reciprocate and show Parsons his own country, which, for all its flaws, churned with energy and potential.

In September 1881, Abbey and Alfred Parsons arrived in New York and rented a studio on West 10th Street. The first order of business was electing "The Englishman" to membership in the Tile Club. The return of

"The Chestnut" inspired the group to embark on a project. They would "get up a Christmassy thing."[49] The result was *Harper's Christmas*, the publication that impressed Van Gogh when it reached him in 1883.[50] Abbey and Parsons stayed in New York for eight months. During that time, Parsons created chapter headers for the Herrick book while Abbey finalized a contract to illustrate the *Monthly's* anticipated serialization of the theatrical comedy *She Stoops to Conquer*, by Oliver Goldsmith (1728-1774). At the end of May, Abbey and Parsons headed home to England.

Selections from the Poetry of Robert Herrick with Drawings by Edwin A. Abbey was published in late 1882, in time for Christmas. Abbey dedicated the book to Alfred Parsons, the friend who had visited him daily during his long illness, brought him grapes and jellies, read to him in the stifling heat of his sick room and housed him when he had nowhere else to go. The book was a landmark in Abbey's career, and the best of the Herrick drawings show his ability to create a genie's magic—a full-throttle, naturalistic recreation of times past conjured out of a bottle of ink. Still, some of the drawings reveal Abbey's struggles and anxiety in their rigid poses. "I like to feel in a man's work that it has hurt him a little, given him a wakeful night or two, and a little headache," Abbey wrote to Charles Parsons during the worst of his troubles.[51] The Herrick book hurt him more than a little, but it also vaulted Abbey to the forefront of his profession. *The New York Times* declared it "perfect in paper, type and binding, and all those thousand things which must be cared for in a book...for it is nothing else than an advance in American art."[52]

Fame washed over Ned Abbey like a summer shower, leaving him refreshed but unchanged. He remained generous, self-critical, self-effacing and, at the age of thirty, ready for a good time. The painter Luke Fildes described the young artist as "more consistently out for fun" than anyone he ever knew and marveled at Abbey's ability to carouse all night and still turn out a steady stream of exquisite illustrations.[53] In a letter to Charles Parsons, Abbey confessed that he often called on his bachelor friends at one or two in the morning and dragged them from their warm beds to walk with him along the Chelsea Embankment until the gas lights flicked out at sunrise. Armed with a cup of coffee and the energy of youth, Abbey would then go cheerfully back to his studio and get to work.

The main project at hand was *She Stoops to Conquer*, and during the

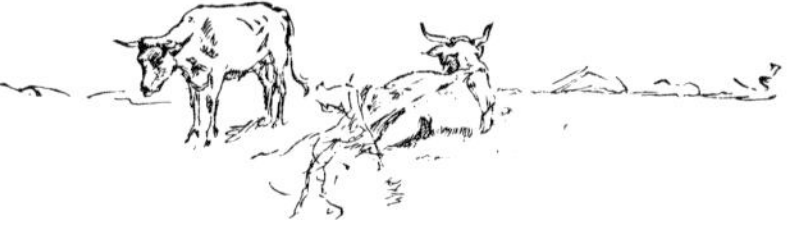

Edwin Austin Abbey (1852-1911),
Selections From The Hesperides & Noble Numbers of Robert Herrick
"A Beucolick, or Discourse of Neatherds," Harper & Brothers, 1882

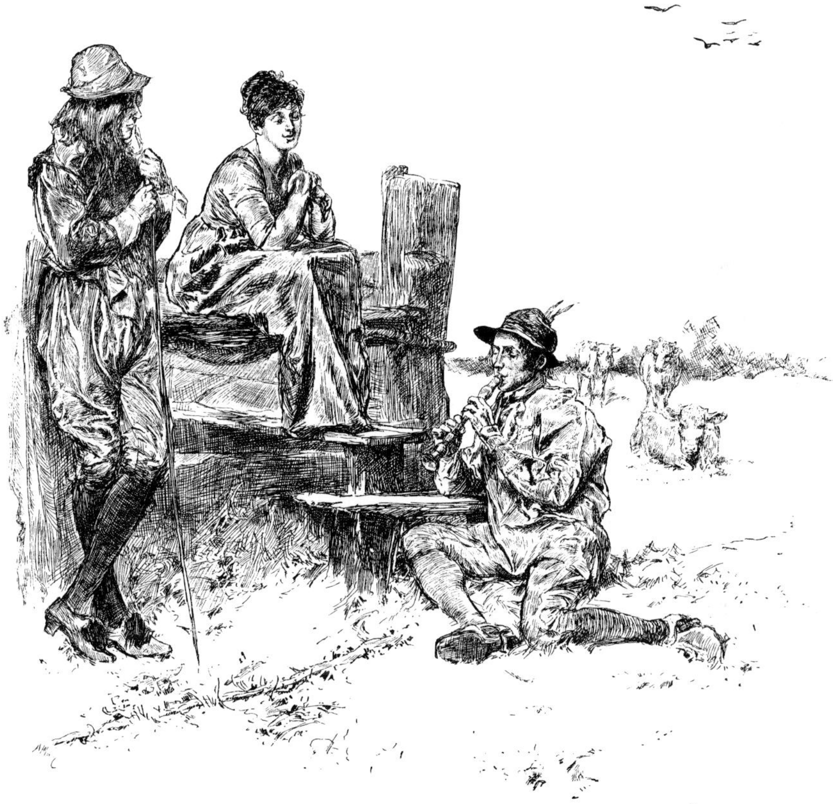

spring of 1883 Abbey was busy assembling the reference material he needed to translate Goldsmith's eighteenth-century script into pictures. By June, the project had paralyzed him. He was struggling with the faces and the complications of placing multiple characters in elaborate interiors. Everything had to be perfect. "My maxim in all my work is that if it is worth doing at all, it is worth doing as well as it is possible to do it—in every *minutest* respect," Abbey once wrote.[54] Not only did he feel the weight of his own expectations, he also felt a responsibility to *Harper's* and the thousands of subscribers who now eagerly anticipated his work.

The first installment of *She Stoops to Conquer* appeared in the December 1884 issue of *Harper's Monthly*. When Abbey saw it, he was furious. His layout had been ignored: Major illustrations were reduced, vignettes enlarged, and the resulting conglomeration jammed haphazardly together on a double-page spread. Abbey was no longer a supplicant at the door of the House of Harper, and he was going to be respected or would take his talents to the competition. "Money is not everything in this world," he told Charles Parsons. "I can make four or five

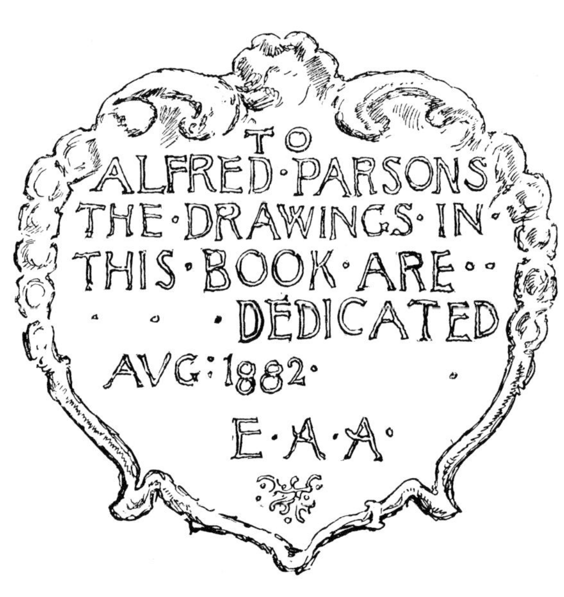

Edwin Austin Abbey (1852-1911), Dedication,
Selections From The Hesperides & Noble Numbers of Robert Herrick
Harper & Brothers, 1882

times the money elsewhere."[55] The next eleven installments were printed to Abbey's specifications.

In 1886, *She Stoops to Conquer* was released in book form. Joseph Pennell declared the volume "monumental."[56] *The New York Times* hailed it as magnificent, noting: "There is not a sketch or a head or tailpiece in the book which is not worth examination, while the page drawings are pictures remarkable for grace and character, charmingly drawn, beautifully printed. Mr. Abbey has undoubtedly accomplished his *chef*

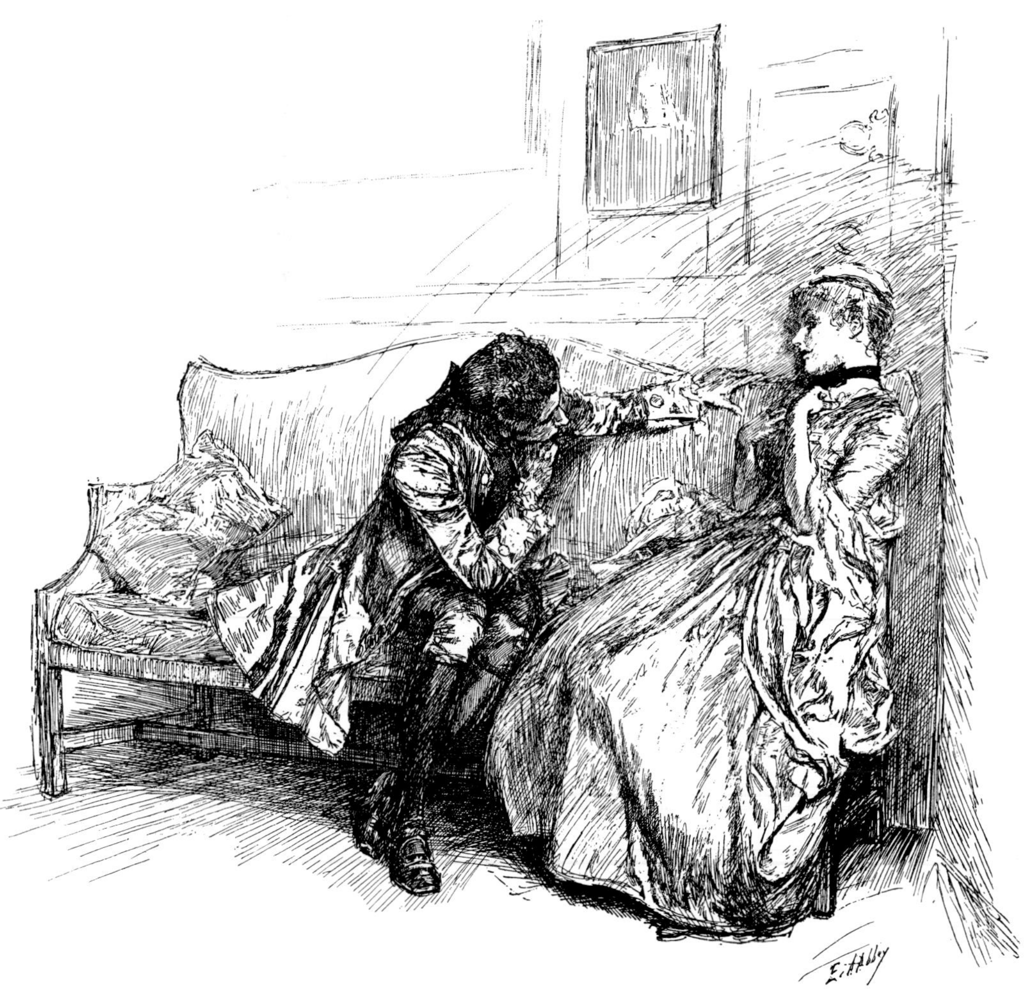

"Thou dear dissembler."

Edwin Austin Abbey (1852-1911), *Harper's New Monthly Magazine*, October 1885
"She Stoops to Conquer"

d'oeuvre in illustrating 'She Stoops to Conquer.'"[57] While the new book was superior to the Herrick edition, it would not be Abbey's masterpiece. Before he could fully represent the past in all its mysterious complexity, he would have to live it.

Starting in 1885, Abbey began spending time in the village of Broadway—ninety-five miles northwest of London and two hundred years back in time. The American painter Frank Millet (1848-1912) had "discovered" Broadway, and his various lodgings became the headquarters for an art colony that at over time included (besides Abbey and Alfred Parsons) the illustrator Fred Barnard (1846-1896), writers Edmund Gosse (1849-1928) and Henry James (1843-1916), poet Austin Dobson (1840-1921) and American émigré painter John Singer Sargent (1856-1925). Broadway's tumble-down, antiquated houses spoke of everyday life. An

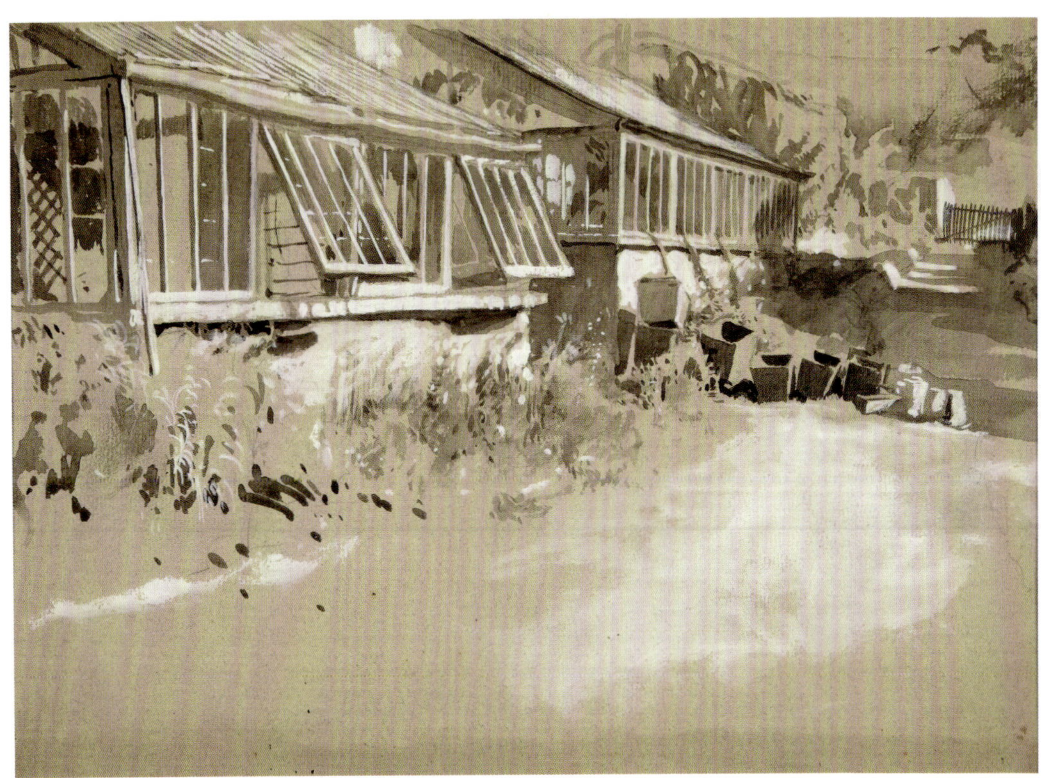

Edwin Austin Abbey (1852-1911), Shacks and shrubs,
Edwin Austin Abbey Estate, 1937; Yale University Art Gallery, New Haven, Conn.

old inn that had sheltered both Oliver Cromwell and Charles I lent historic significance, while an eighteenth-century tower commissioned by the Sixth Earl of Coventry provided aristocratic glamour.

Freed from their urban studios, Millet's guests swam, played tennis, danced and hiked. Dobson described the atmosphere as "jolly as a boys' school."[58] Even so, most days were dedicated to work. "We are all busy as bees at Broadway," Abbey wrote to Charles Parsons.[59] "Sargent has been painting a great big picture in the garden…Millet is painting two interiors; Barnard is doing various sketches."[60] Observing all the activity, Henry James quipped, "It is delicious to be at Broadway and not have to draw."[61] Abbey was glad to draw. Inspired by the old town, he painted watercolors, completed illustrations, filled sketchbooks and dreamed up two new

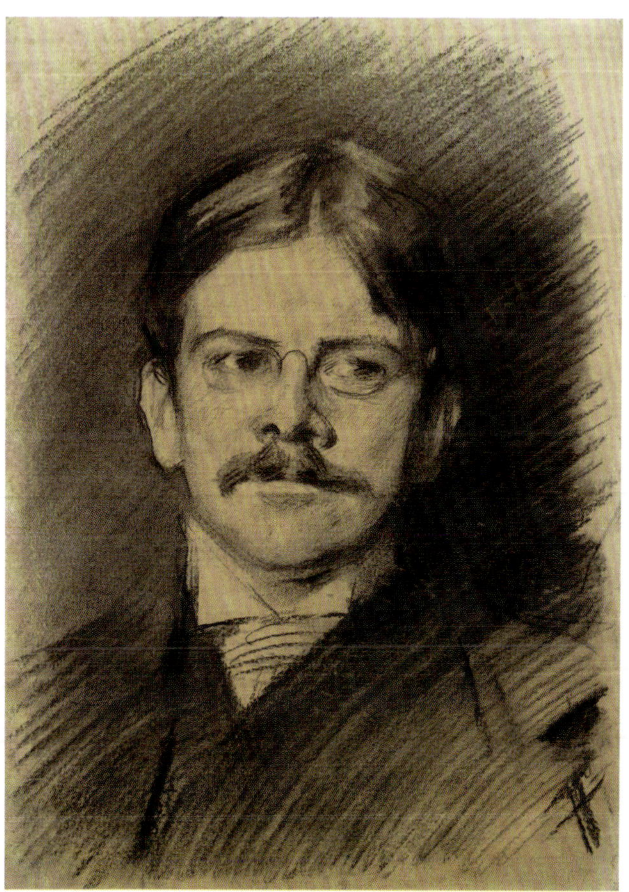

John Singer Sargent (1856-1925), Portrait of Edwin Austin Abbey ca. 1889; Edwin Austin Abbey Estate, 1937; Yale University Art Gallery, New Haven, Conn.

projects that he and Alfred Parsons could work on together: *Old Songs*, an illustrated volume of traditional English ballads; and *The Quiet Life*, a poetry anthology.

Harper's had a different idea. In February 1886, Abbey received a letter from the editor Henry Mills Alden, asking him to consider illustrating Shakespeare's comedies. "I would like to have your name go down to posterity associated with Shakespeare!" Alden wrote enthusiastically.[62] It is difficult to imagine the popular appeal of William Shakespeare in nineteenth-century America. Schoolchildren memorized long passages from the Bard's plays, and productions of his work were staged coast-to-coast in city theaters, town halls, parks and frontier saloons. There were Shakespeare calendars, Shakespeare trading cards, spoofs in minstrel shows and endless jokes of this sort: "When was Desdemona like a ship? When she was Moored."[63]

Abbey was hesitant to tackle a project so entrenched in popular imagination. Still, the proposal was intriguing enough to lure him to New York. In early spring he was back at Harper & Brothers, where his

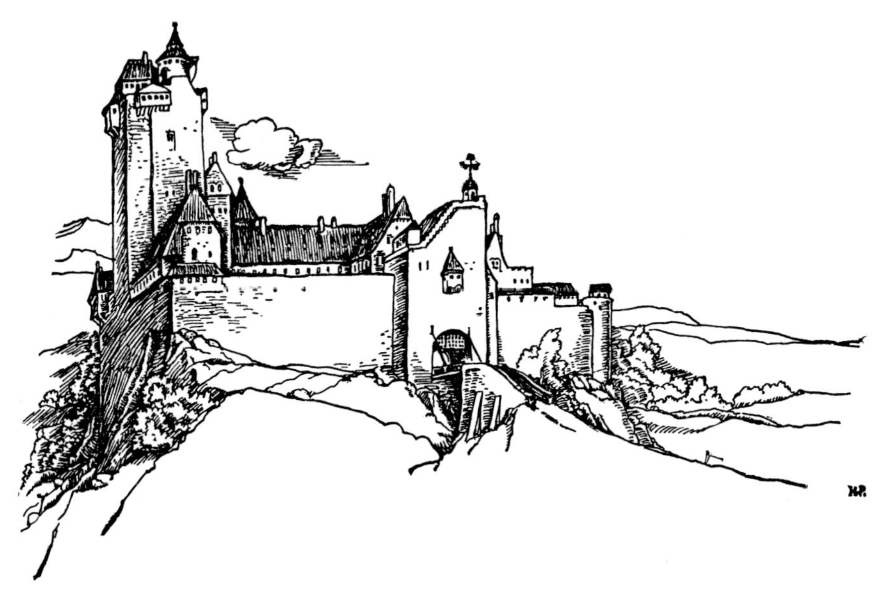

Howard Pyle (1853-1911), *Otto of the Silver Hand*,
"Castle Drachenhausen," Charles Scribner's and Sons, 1888

proposals for *Old Songs* and *The Quiet Life* were approved but Alden's Shakespeare scheme was reluctantly declined. During the short trip, Abbey reconnected with his friends from the Tile Club as well as Charles Parsons' expanding group of *Harper's* illustrators.

When he returned home, Abbey received a letter from the illustrator Howard Pyle (1853-1911), whose career with *Harper's* was just beginning. "I wonder whether two lives could be more different than yours and mine," Pyle wrote. "I doubt whether I shall ever cross the ocean to see those things which seem so beautiful and dreamlike in my imagination, and which if I saw, might break the bubble of my fancy and leave nothing behind but bitter soap suds."[64] Pyle meant no harm and genuinely liked Abbey, whom he described as a "chipper, jocund, little fellow, with a merry twinkle in his eyes and a laugh that means business."[65] Still, Abbey was angry at what he took as an affront to his entire career. "Don't waste any of your time imagining what has already been imagined," he wrote in response. "Your German and Dutch castles are much less picturesque than they really are…The first week I spent in England…made me wish back all the English drawings I had ever made. The country is as different from America as chalk is from cheese."[66] Abbey was not a man to burn bridges, however, and he never mailed the letter.

For much of 1887, Abbey and Alfred Parsons worked together on their collaborative projects. The selection of ballads for *Old Songs* required expert advice, so Abbey contacted the Rev. J.W. Ebsworth (1824-1908), proud president of England's Ballad Society. Ebsworth was a fan of Abbey's work and so thrilled about the project that he waxed poetic: "The world has gone sordid and shabby/ But there came from across the big main/ One to cheer the worn hearts, Edwin Abbey/ Who fills life with enjoyment again…" The tribute embarrassed Abbey, but it would not be the last time his work moved a tender Victorian heart to verse.

Although Abbey had enough on his plate, the Shakespeare proposal lingered in his mind. The plays were set in different eras, with locations as diverse as Italy, Yugoslavia and—in the case of *A Midsummer-Night's Dream*—Fairyland. Abbey was increasingly fastidious about his work and understood that illustrating Shakespeare to his own standards would be expensive. "I 'want to know, don't you know,' whether I could afford to do the book," he told Charles Parsons.[67] Harper's replied with a generous contract for 133 drawings at $325 for a full-page illustration, with the smaller ones pro-rated according to size.[68] Although he could not have foreseen it at the time, the project would eventually expand to include Shakespeare's tragedies and consume Abbey's attention for most of the next twenty years.

Abbey began 1888 with a research trip. He sketched Shakespearian backgrounds in Italy and traveled to Munich, where he visited museums and purchased an assortment of swords. Returning happily to London with armloads of "arms," he realized that the Parsons/Abbey abode could not accommodate the theatrical property for fourteen plays. When he discovered that the house next door was available, he converted it into a studio, hanging the walls with fabric, adding a glass conservatory, a room for his costume collection and a door connecting his new workspace and the home he and Alfred Parsons continued to share. He designed his studio for the long haul—a modern, well-equipped showplace suitable for an artist of thirty-five at the top of his game.

Outrageous fortune (as any young Hamlet knows) can change everything. In May 1888, Frank Millet invited Abbey for a weekend in Broadway. There he met Mary Gertrude Mead (1851-1931), born to American parents in Torquay, England, brought up in Greenwich, Connecticut, and destined to change Abbey's life. At thirty-seven, Miss Mead's own accomplishments were impressive. After graduating from Vassar, she had studied Romance languages in Europe, worked at the College of Mines in New York, taught at the Roxbury Latin School and maintained a more than passing interest in art. In 1884 she organized an exhibition by the British painter George Frederic Watts (1817-1904) at the Metropolitan Museum of Art in New York. When Abbey returned to Broadway in September, he saw Miss Mead (called Gertrude) every day until she went home to America in January. Was it love? Indeed, it was. The "selfish three-cornered bachelor," was smitten.[69] "I really feel the ambition I used to have long ago coming back to me," he wrote to Gertrude. "I owe that to you with many other things I cannot speak of."[70]

When Harper & Brothers published the book version of *Old Songs* in December 1888, a reviewer at *The Critic* declared it "the most beautiful book of the year.[71] Gertrude, perhaps less impressed, encouraged Abbey to turn his attention to painting. Although he had been exhibiting

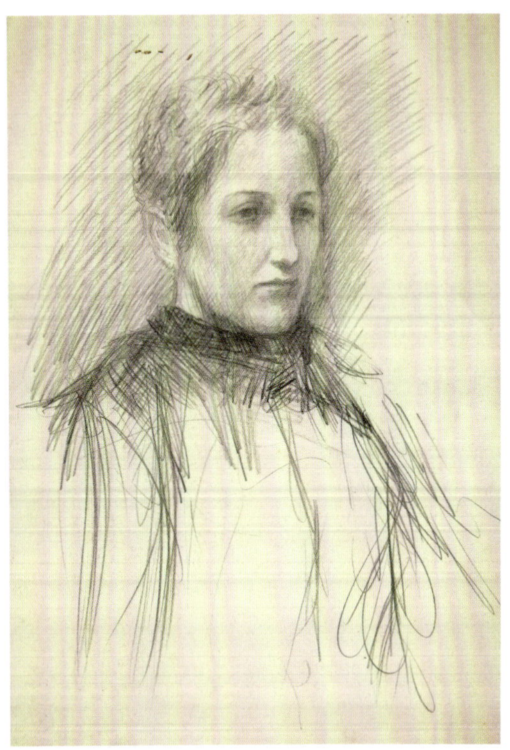 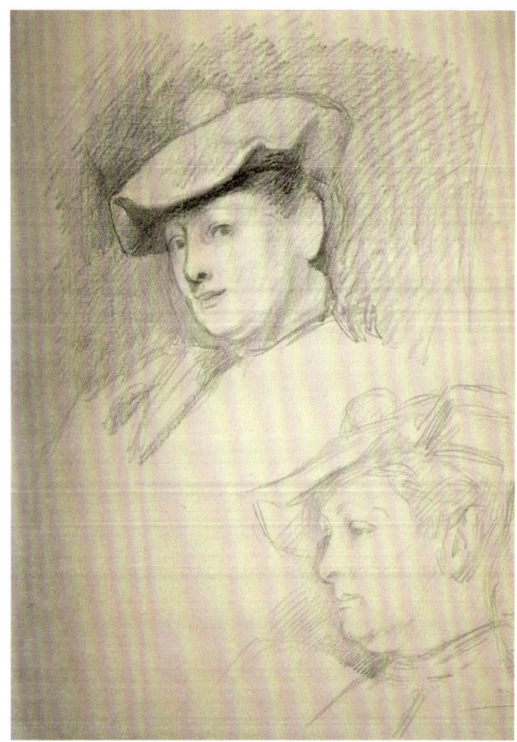

Left: Edwin Austin Abbey (1852-1911), Portrait of a young Mrs. Abbey (purported):
Edwin Austin Abbey Estate, 1937; Yale University Art Gallery, New Haven, Conn.
Right: Edwin Austin Abbey (1852-1911), Portrait of Mrs. Abbey: 2 views;
Yale University Art Gallery, New Haven, Conn.

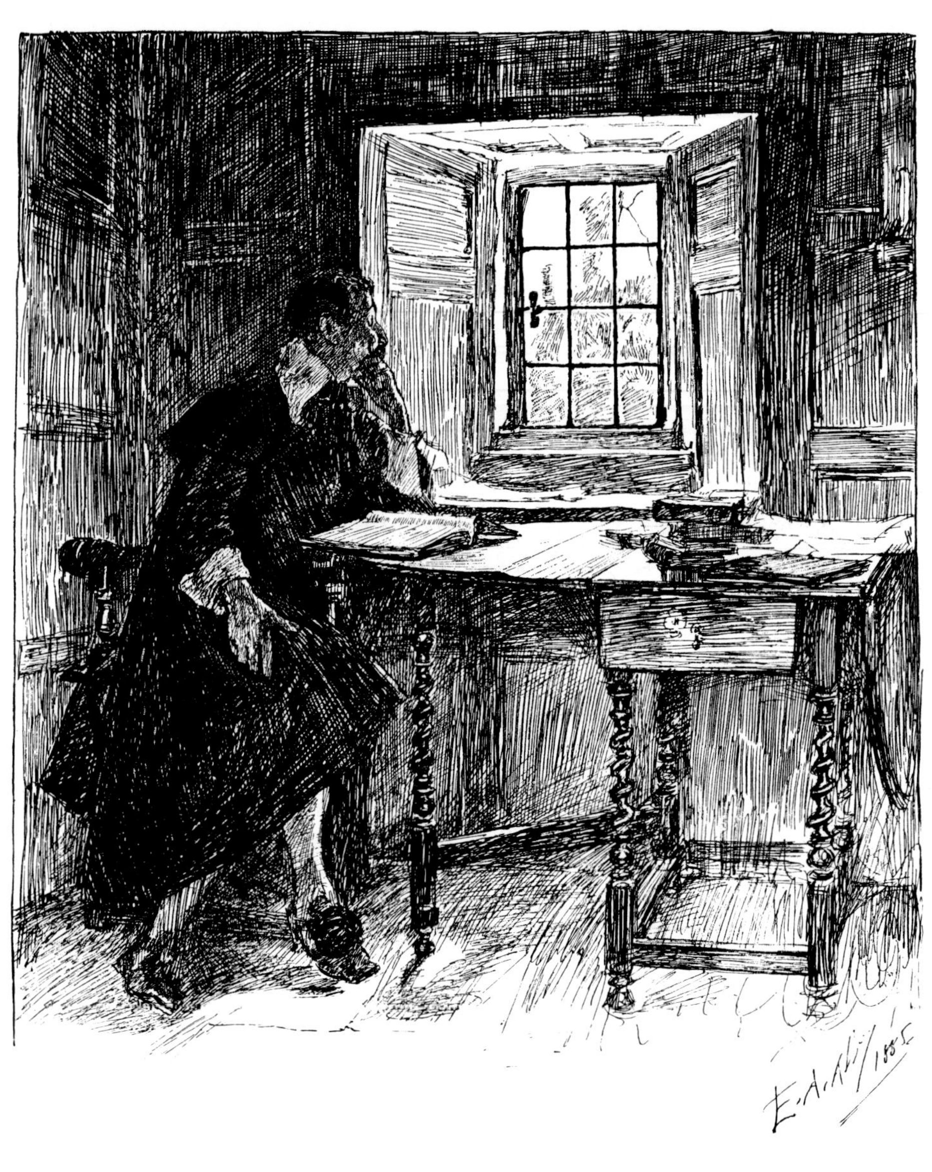

Edwin Austin Abbey (1852-1911), *The Quiet Life*
"The Wish," Harper & Brothers, 1889

his watercolors since 1874, Abbey had never considered himself a fine artist. "I cannot help having a guilty feeling whenever I am painting, as though I were wasting my time and energy that ought to be applied to my legitimate profession," he wrote to Gertrude.[72] Two weeks later, Abbey was referring to his illustration career in the past tense. "I really did try hard to do my best when I was only encouraged to do somebody else's best," he wrote. "And I may say without false modesty, or anything else, that I have raised the level of my particular art in my own country."[73] Abbey had an additional reason for reconsidering his illustration career that had nothing to do with Gertrude. He had just received word that Charles Parsons was retiring from Harper & Brothers, ending Abbey's professional relationship with the man who had wisely guided and quietly bankrolled his career for eighteen years.

Five days after his thirty-seventh birthday, Abbey was on his way to New York to supervise the design of *The Quite Life* and to see as much of Miss Mead as possible. When he returned to London, he went to work in his new studio but now found the space "beastly." He tried decorating and hanging pictures, but when the atmosphere failed to improve, he headed north to Broadway and the familiar dusty rooms filled with the floating particles he called "working impulse."[74] The magic took hold, and Abbey was soon engaged again in his work—although not on the drawings he had promised Harper's. Confessing as much to Charles Parsons, he wrote: "I may as well tell you, now that you are no longer in an official capacity, that I have been mostly *painting* since I returned."[75]

Harper & Brothers released *The Quiet Life* in December 1889. Austin Dobson wrote a prologue and epilogue, translating into verse the tranquility of bygone days in humble places like Broadway. "The peace which they celebrate is not always that which passeth understanding," a reviewer at *The Critic* informed readers. "It is more often that which may both be understood and experienced in walled gardens, deep English meadows, and old low-ceiling rooms."[76] Alfred Parson's landscape drawings and floral cartouches for *The Quiet Life* are among his best. Abbey's illustrations also are remarkable—intelligently conceived, elegantly composed and beautifully lit. Unlike his contemporaries, Abbey used broken or "fudged" edges that made his characters "of the scene rather than in it or on it."[77] One drawing is signed by both men: Abbey drew the figures, and Parsons supplied the background. Altogether, the book was their masterpiece—a tribute to friendship and a poignant eulogy to the village that had captured their hearts. Although Alfred Parsons would maintain a home there, Abbey's idyll was about to end.

Abbey's last summer at Broadway was productive. He completed illustrations for *A Comedy of Errors*, designed costumes for a London production of *La Tosca* and finished "May Day Morning," a large oil painting he exhibited at the Royal Academy in 1890. When Abbey wasn't in the studio, he rowed, played cricket and socialized with his friends. The activity and camaraderie energized him. "I am not a tender artistic plant," he wrote to Gertrude. "The more tired out I am the clearer my head seems to get and the more sensitive my hand. It's doing things that excites me, with active and appreciative minds."[78] In June, when he heard that he had won a first-class medal for his *Old Songs* illustrations at the Exposition Universelle in Paris, he opted to stay in England and keep busy.

Working simultaneously as an illustrator, a fine artist and costume designer eventually proved too much even for Ned Abbey. By late November, he was back at Bedford Gardens supervising dress rehearsals for *La Tosca* while recovering from shingles. After the opera opened, Abbey took a moment to explain himself to Gertrude before stepping into a future that would take him in a new direction: "I began so heedlessly and unconsciously my artistic career that I can only see *now* that the thing that has been of the greatest interest to me all these years is the personal, sympathetic quality of my little people. I know that unless, within five minutes after beginning a drawing, the little soul within doesn't begin to make itself manifest upon the paper, my interest flags and generally ceases altogether, until the little eyes begin to twinkle or the little lips to smile."[79]

Mary Gertrude Mead and Edwin Austin Abbey were married in New York on April 22, 1890. Alfred Parsons, who was recovering from an illness, was unable to attend, but John Sargent was there and served as an usher. At the end of May, the couple headed to Boston in a private railway car—not on a honeymoon but on a business trip. Although he had only completed two oil paintings in his life ("May Day Morning" and a wall decoration for a New York hotel), he was among three artists—including Sargent and Puvis de Chavannes (1824-1898)—selected to provide murals for Boston's new library, designed by the architects McKim, Mead and White and acclaimed as "A Palace for the People."

One of the firm's partners, William Rutherford Mead (1846-1928), was Gertrude's uncle. Her assurance that Abbey would accept the task, despite the small stipend, probably affected the decision to trust a novice with the commission.[80] In Boston, Abbey took in a baseball game, dined with the library's trustees and boarded the *S.S. Trave* for England with a new wife and a weighty assignment. The artist, whose greatest pleasure was seeing his little people come to life under his hand, had agreed to paint a spectacle—a frieze eight feet high and 180 feet long. For his troubles, Abbey was to receive $15,000, a sum he hoped would finally free him from debt.

Abbey was never prudent with money, however, and Gertrude failed to reform him. Upon returning to London, he began looking for a larger studio. He settled on Morgan Hall, a stately seventeenth-century house in the village of Fairford. A lease was negotiated, and renovations were under way by January 1891. The first order of business was construction of an enormous studio—the largest in England, at 64 feet by 40 feet, with 25 feet between the floor and the dark-timbered ceiling. Although it was common for successful nineteenth-century artists to work in sumptuous surroundings that doubled as sales galleries, Abbey designed a spartan workspace with room for a dozen large easels, stacks of canvases and huge tapestries, as well as all the paraphernalia he had amassed over the years— fabric samples, musical instruments, weapons, armor and books. A special room at one end of the building held hundreds of costumes.[81]

Morgan Hall was to be Abbey's home for the next twenty years. Sargent joined him in the studio as soon as it was finished, with Abbey occupying one end while his friend commandeered the other. Gertrude's mother came for a visit and stayed for more than three years, and Alfred Parsons was a frequent guest. Abbey, still an athlete, converted the lawn into a cricket pitch. The highlight of his year was "cricket week," when ten artist friends gathered to play matches, tell tales, listen to music and dine in the studio, flanked by huge canvases picturing Sir Galahad's search for the Holy Grail—Abbey's theme for the Boston Library. "Those big things take it out of me," he cheerfully told one of his guests. "I feel like a fly crawling around on them."[82]

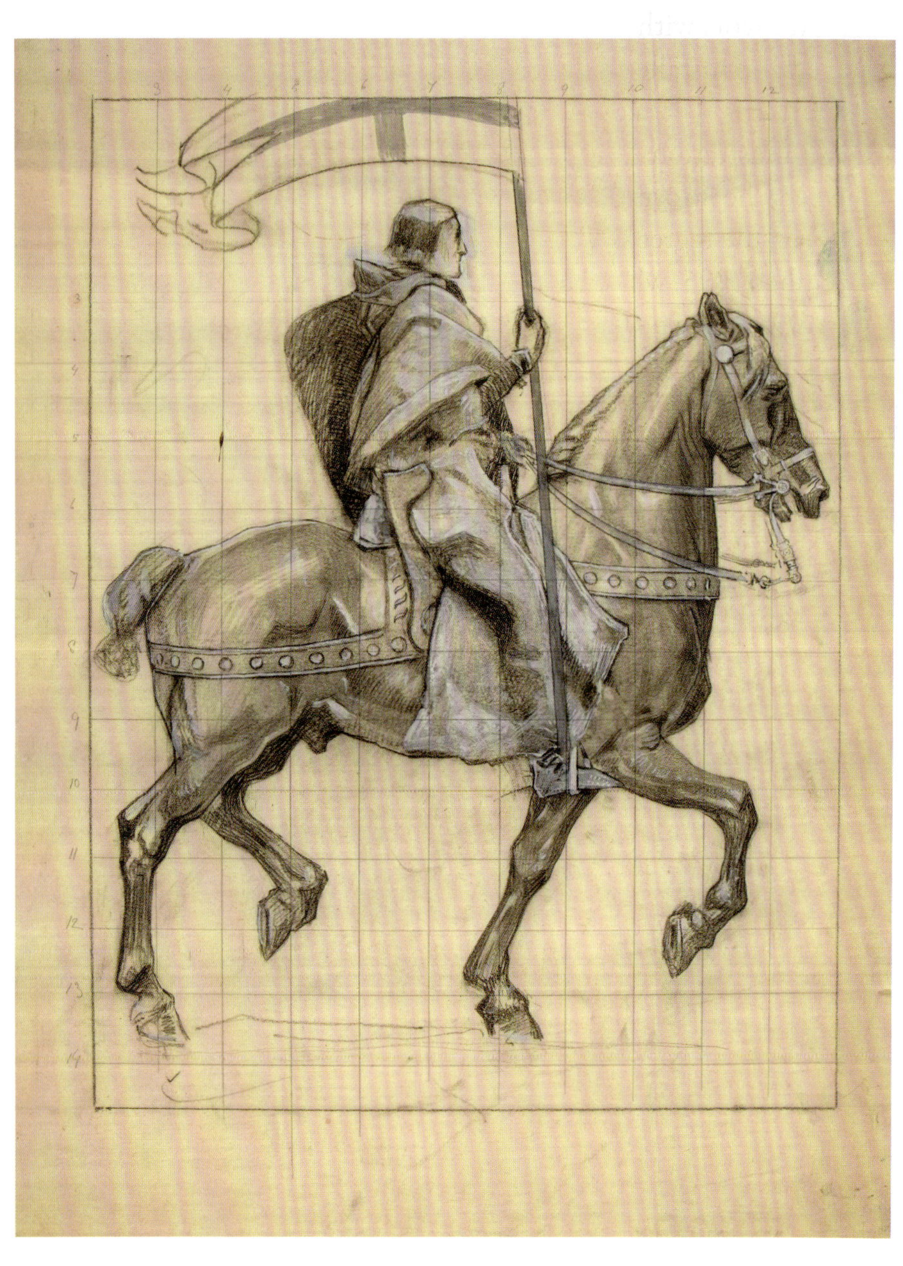

Edwin Austin Abbey, American (1852-1911),
Study for "Galahad Departs" in The Quest of the Holy Grail mural series at Boston Public Library

Although Sir Galahad dominated the real estate, Abbey tackled his diverse endeavors with equal enthusiasm. Between 1891 and 1895, he completed and installed five of the Boston Library paintings, exhibited watercolors, worked in pastel and dispatched "Enter Theseus," the last of his 133 illustrations for the Shakespearian comedies. "My Comedies are finished," he informed Charles Parsons. "And it is laughable as I think of it—the regret with which I hand over the *very last* drawing."[83] In November 1895, when Harper & Brothers released *The Comedies of William Shakespeare: With Many Drawings by Edwin A. Abbey*, as the collection was called, *The New York Times* proclaimed Abbey "head and shoulders above other illustrators of his time."[84]

Abbey's drawings for the comedies are among his best works. Marion Spielmann (1858-1948), editor of *The Magazine of Art*, wrote that "we cannot withhold applause from a man who, from a mere stage direction,

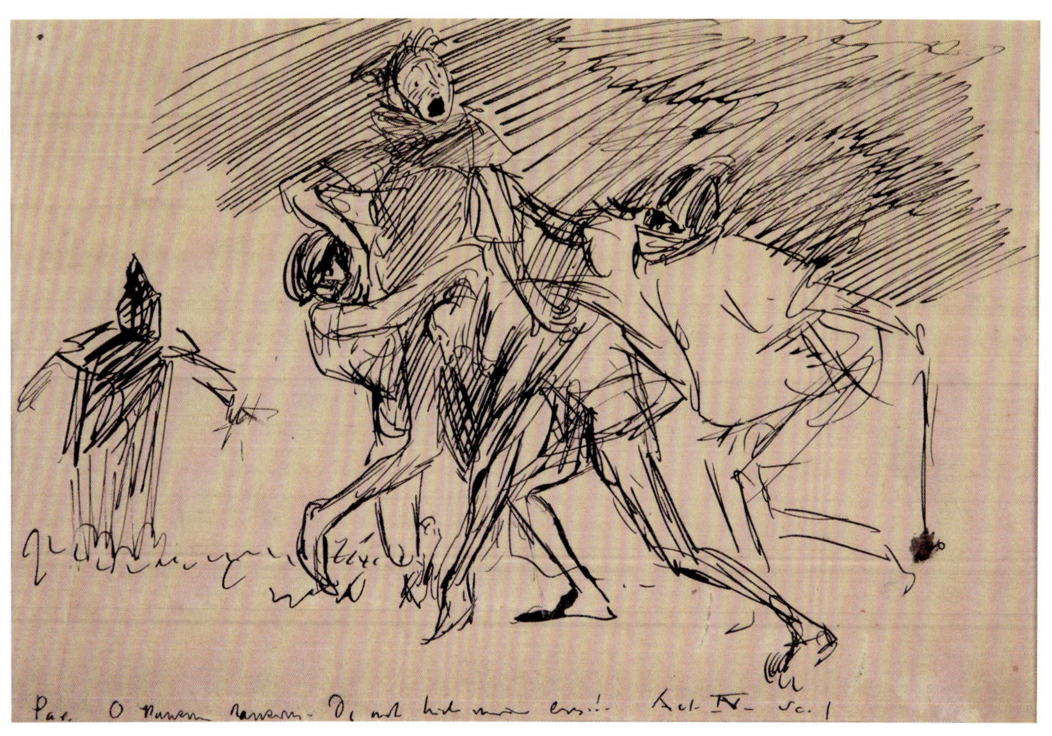

Edwin Austin Abbey (1852-1911), The Comedies of Shakespeare — "All's Well That Ends Well"
Act IV, Scene I. — "Oh, Ransome, Ransome, do no hide mine eyes" (preliminary sketch)
Edwin Austin Abbey Estate, 1937; Yale University Art Gallery, New Haven, Conn.

can evolve a fine composition full of suggestion while unswervingly loyal to the word and spirit of the text."[85] Abbey's increasing ability to create atmospheric pictures was partly attributable to advances in printing technology. By 1895, artwork could be photographed directly onto sensitized zinc plates or gelatin film ending the need to define edges as landmarks for the engravers. Abbey took full advantage this innovation, using lighting effects rather than outlines to delineate the elements in his pictures. The result was alchemy—pen-and-ink drawings with the life, drama and depth of the finest large-scale oil paintings.

With his *Harper's* commission completed, Abbey devoted himself to painting, continuing the Shakespearian theme in his canvases. In 1898 he was awarded a gold medal from his alma mater, the Pennsylvania Academy of the Fine Arts. The following year he was elected Royal

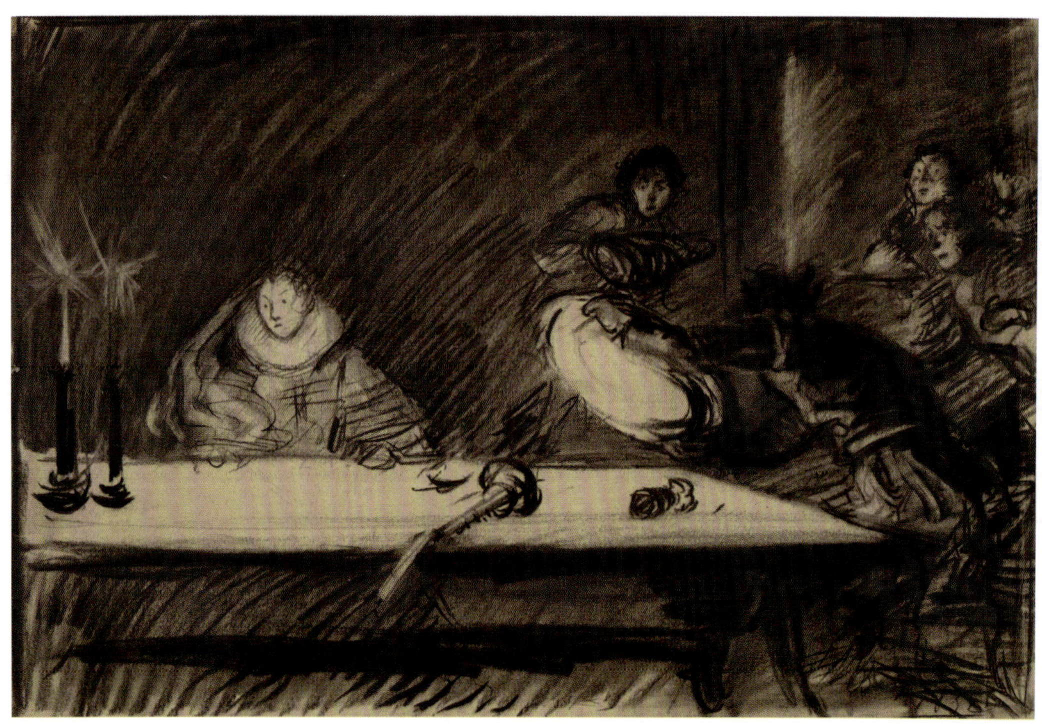

Edwin Austin Abbey (1852-1911), The Comedies of Shakespeare XIII. — "Taming of the Shrew"
Act IV., Scene I.— for Petruchio Overturns the Trencher (preliminary sketch)
Edwin Austin Abbey Estate, 1937; Yale University Art Gallery, New Haven, Conn.

Academician and leased a home and studio in London where he and
Gertrude stayed when Academy commitments called him to the city.
A gold medal at the 1900 Paris International Exposition added to
the honors awarded an artist who valued only work and friendship.
(When Abbey died, Gertrude lovingly saved every drawing, study and
sketchbook but had his medals melted down and the money donated
to the Red Cross.)

In July 1901, after a six-year hiatus, Harper's contacted Abbey about
illustrating Shakespeare's tragedies. The Holy Grail frieze was nearing
completion, so—although he was under contract to paint a 15-foot by
9-foot canvas to document the coronation of King Edward VII—Abbey
was eager to return to the work that "interested him the most." That year
he signed an agreement to complete seventy drawings for the tragedies

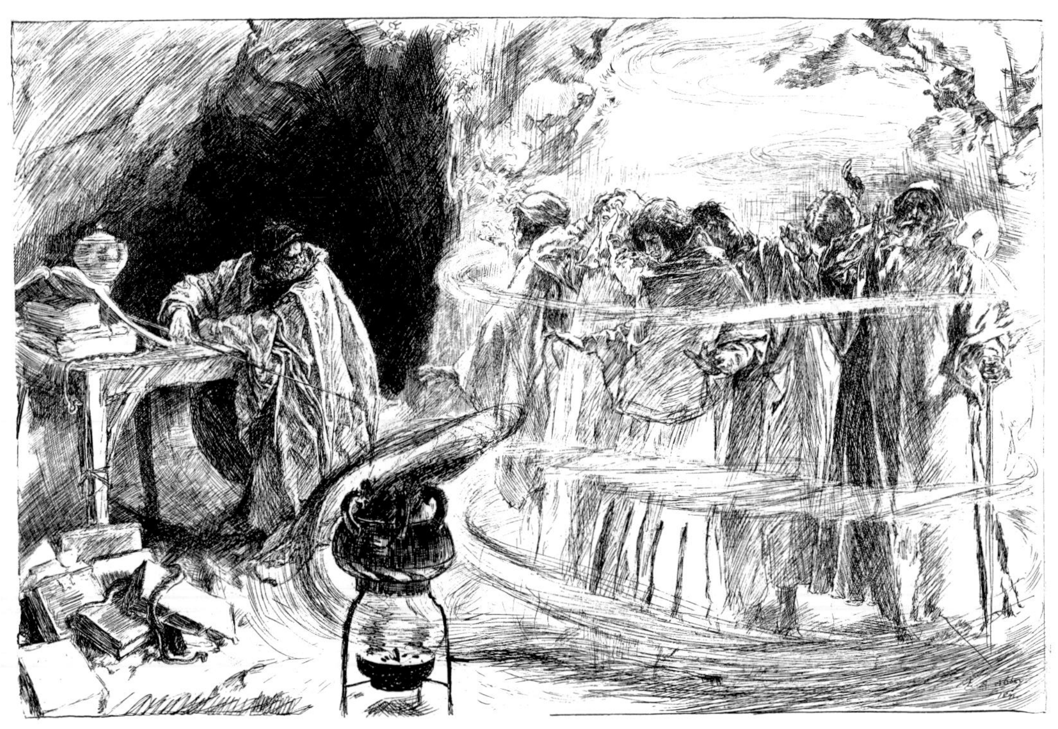

Prospero (in his magic robes). "There stand, for you are spell-stopp'd."

Harper's New Monthly Magazine, April 1892
The Comedies of Shakespeare — "The Tempest"
Act V., Scene I. — Alonzo and Gonzalo, Sebastian, Antonio, Adrian and Francisco.

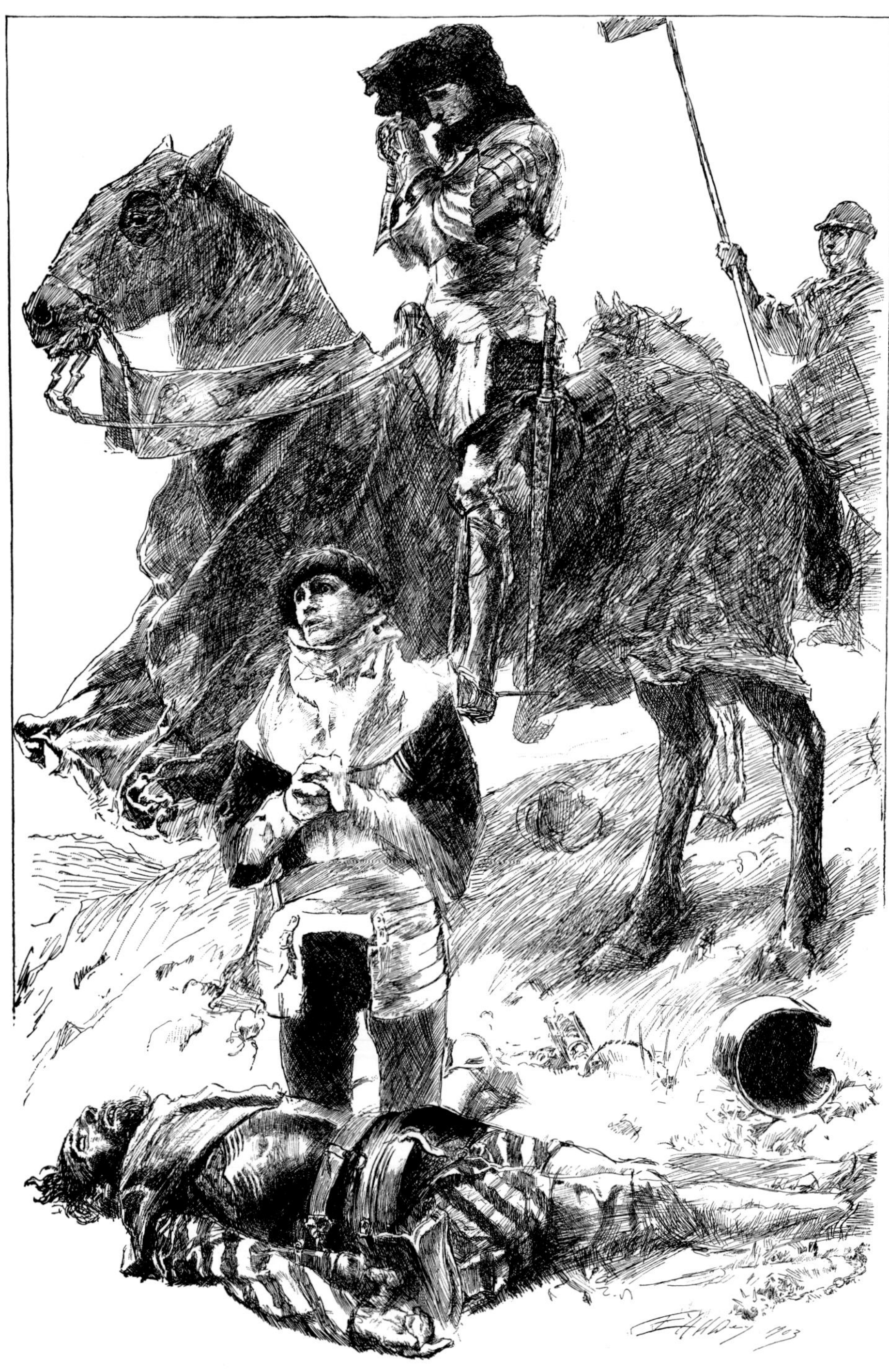

Lancastrian Soldier. "Who's this?—O God!
It is my father's face. Whom in this conflict I un'wares have kill'd."

Edwin Austin Abbey (1852-1911), *Harper's Monthly Magazine*, November 1905
Shakespeare's "King Henry VI."
Part III: Act II., Scene V. — Another part of the field.

and thirty for *The Deserted Village*, depicting Oliver Goldsmith's poem.
Harper's agreed to pay $50,000 for the Shakespeare illustrations and
$300 each for the Goldsmith drawings. Altogether, Abbey had more than
enough work to keep any artist busy and solvent. Still, in spring 1902, he
inexplicably agreed to create a series of enormous murals for the new State
Capitol Building in Harrisburg, Pennsylvania.

Abbey enlarged his already-vast studio to accommodate the Harrisburg
project and hired a series of student assistants to help him. All of them
later remembered the experience as a highlight in their careers. Although
the hours were long, Abbey's jovial disposition and complete lack of
pretention kept the atmosphere light. He wore a soft felt hat with a hole
in the middle and sang at his easel, blundering through Scottish ballads
with his American accent. "If a story came to his mind while he worked,"
one of his assistants recalled, "he appeared not to have the power to resist
coming to tell it to me at once...He was the kindest and most lovable man
I think I have ever met."[86]

Even with the extra help, the workload took a toll on Abbey's health,
and by 1903 he admitted to feeling the strain. "I have had a laborious year
of it," he wrote to his brother-in-law. "I am more and more convinced
that great physical strength is absolutely essential to any success in art...
Hard and incessant study, combined with a particularly nerve-trying sort
of labour—unless one is very strong one can't stand it."[87] Abbey stood it,
continuing work on the Harrisburg murals while completing his drawings
for the Shakespearian tragedies with his usual diligence. One of his
assistants recalled that Abbey's knowledge was "simply astonishing—
I saw him do many of the Shakespeare drawings for *Harper's*, and though
the actual drawings would only take him an hour or two, he would take
days and weeks to get up the material for each one."[88]

Six of the tragedies ran in *Harper's Monthly* between 1908 and 1909,
giving readers the opportunity to see more work by Edwin A. Abbey than
at any other time in his long association with the magazine. Remarkably,
he also finished his first eight murals for the Pennsylvania State Capitol—
four huge lunettes depicting "Science Revealing the Treasures of the
Earth," "The Spirit of Vulcan," "The Spirit of Religious Liberty" and "The
Spirit of Light," as well as four rondels decorated with nine-foot-tall
allegorical figures. A reporter from the *New York Sun* was on the scene

as the paintings were packed, and he was amused when Abbey—dressed formally in a silk hat—dipped a large brush into a jampot and, with a joyful flourish, wrote "To the Commonwealth of Pennsylvania" on the side of the massive crate.[89]

The Harrisburg murals occupied Abbey for the remaining two years of his life. By 1910, it was clear to his friends that his great energy was flagging. Yet he soldiered on, refusing to believe that anything was seriously wrong. When his doctors suspected cancer and suggested exploratory surgery, Abbey was incredulous. "I can't believe that!" he told them. "I have so much work to do, and I feel so capable of doing it."[90] Abbey was admitted to the hospital on June 25, 1911 and discharged to his home in London two weeks later. According to common practice, he was spared the knowledge that his condition was fatal. He remained

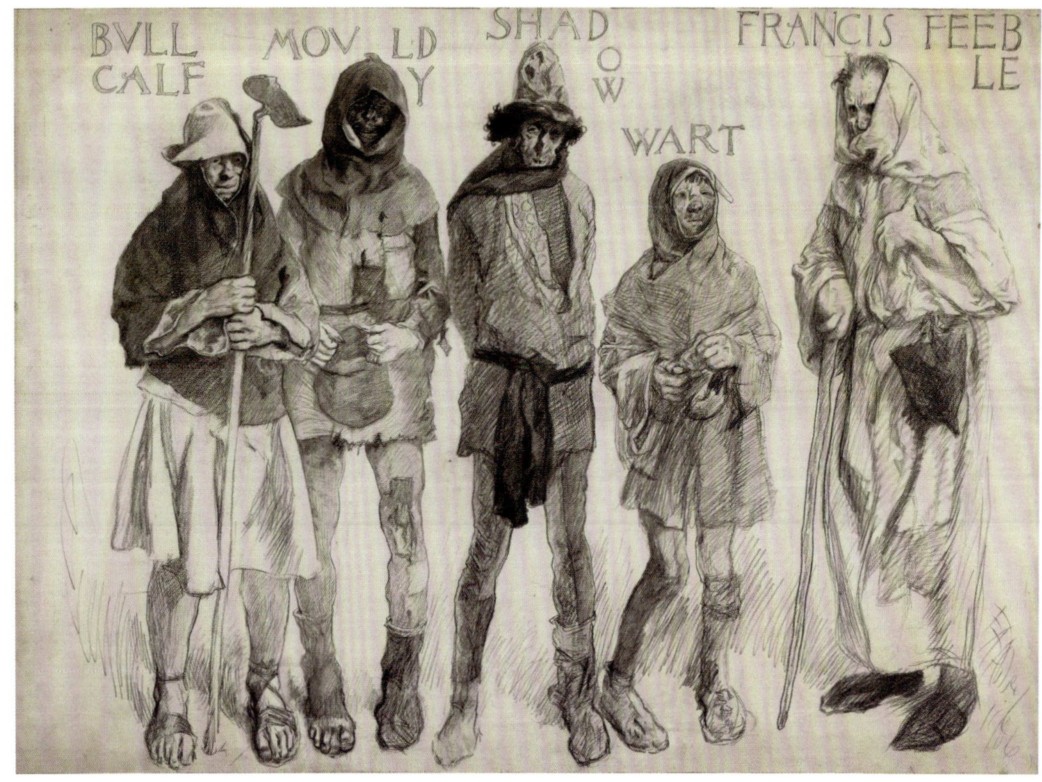

Edwin Austin Abbey (1852-1911), 1906
Shakespeare's "King Henry VI."
Part II: Act III., Scene II. — Before Justice Shallow's House in Gloucestershire:
Bull Calf, Mouldy, Shadow, Wart, Francis Feeble

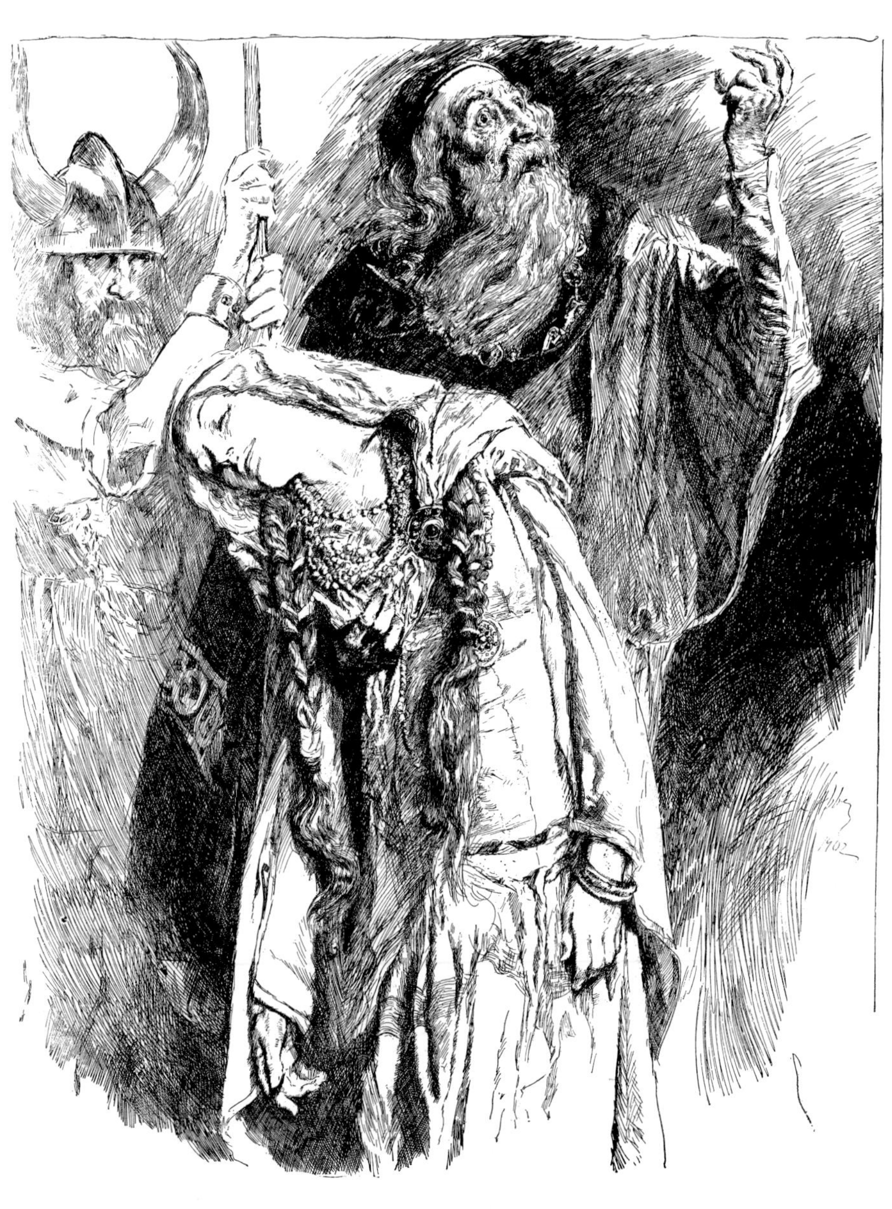

Edwin Austin Abbey (1852-1911), *Harper's Monthly Magazine*, December 1902
"King Lear"
Act V., Scene III. — Lear, with Cordelia dead in his arms.

confident of a full recovery and had his bed moved into the studio where he could assess the work that lay ahead. He ordered art supplies, dictated letters, received friends, and as his strength failed, closed his eyes and listened as Gertrude read aloud from his favorite novels.

Abbey died on August 1, 1911, at the age of fifty-nine. His unfinished canvases, detailed drawings, comprehensive designs and harmonious color schemes bore testimony to years of hard work on the grand project he would never complete. Still, as Henry James wrote, "He had *had* it, he hadn't missed it: he had sat at the full feast and had manfully, splendidly lived."[91] Edwin Austin Abbey never cared much for ceremonies or speeches or gigantic paintings in vaulted domes. He preferred the old songs, the quiet life and the intimacy of pictures you could hold in your hands.

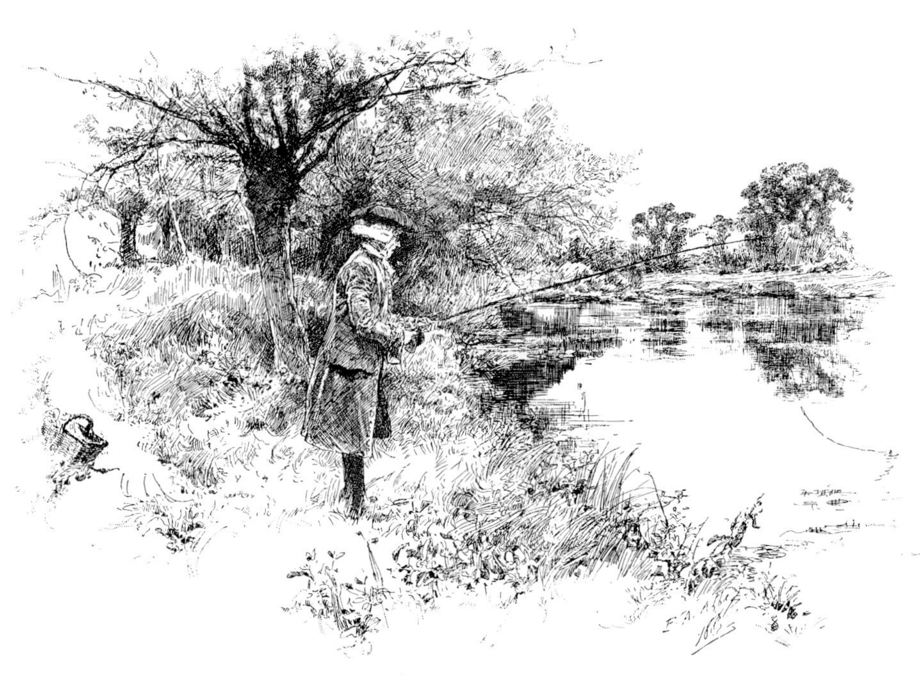

Edwin Austin Abbey (1852-1911), *The Quiet Life*
"Ode to Solitude," Harper & Brothers, 1889

THE DRAWINGS OF
EDWIN AUSTIN ABBEY

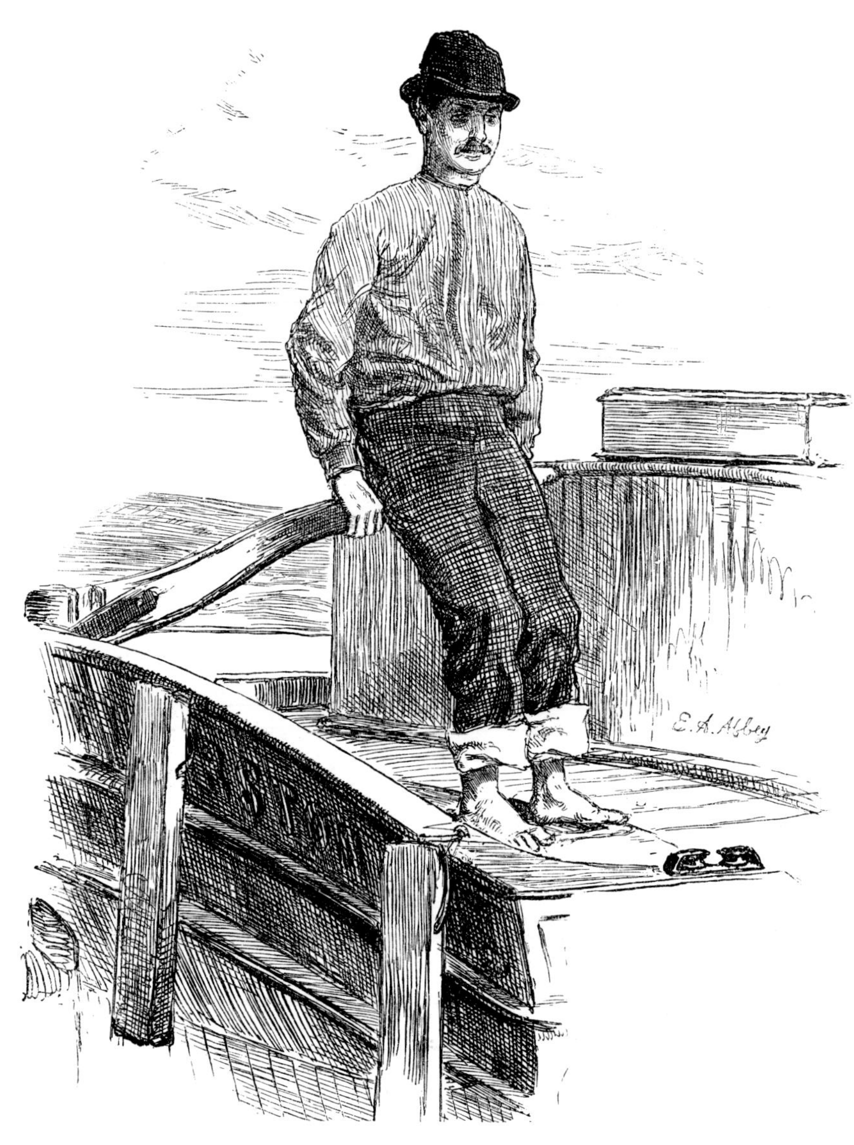

Buffalo Jack.

Harper's New Monthly Magazine, December 1873
"The Water Ways of New York"

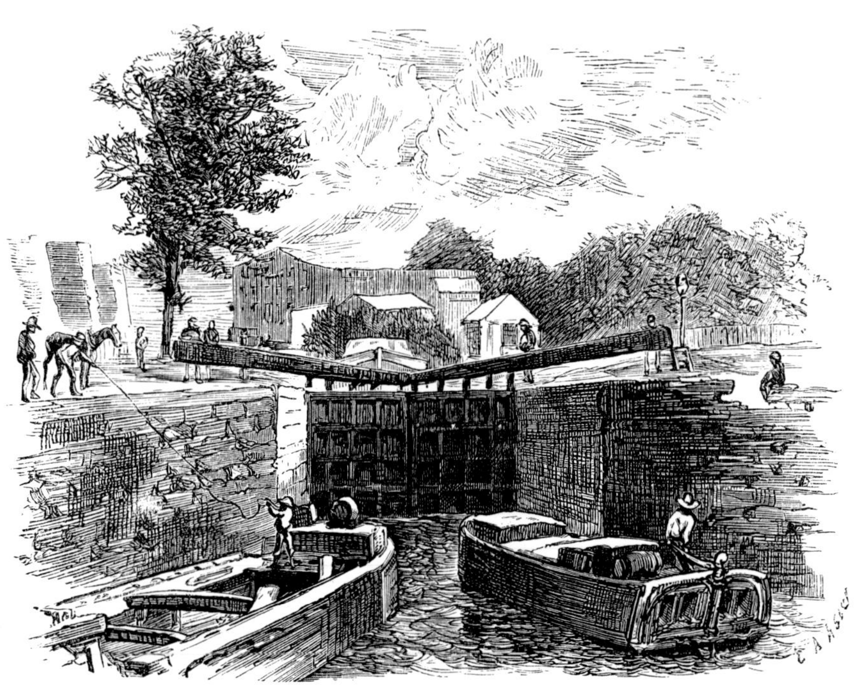

Enterance to the Erie Canal at Troy.

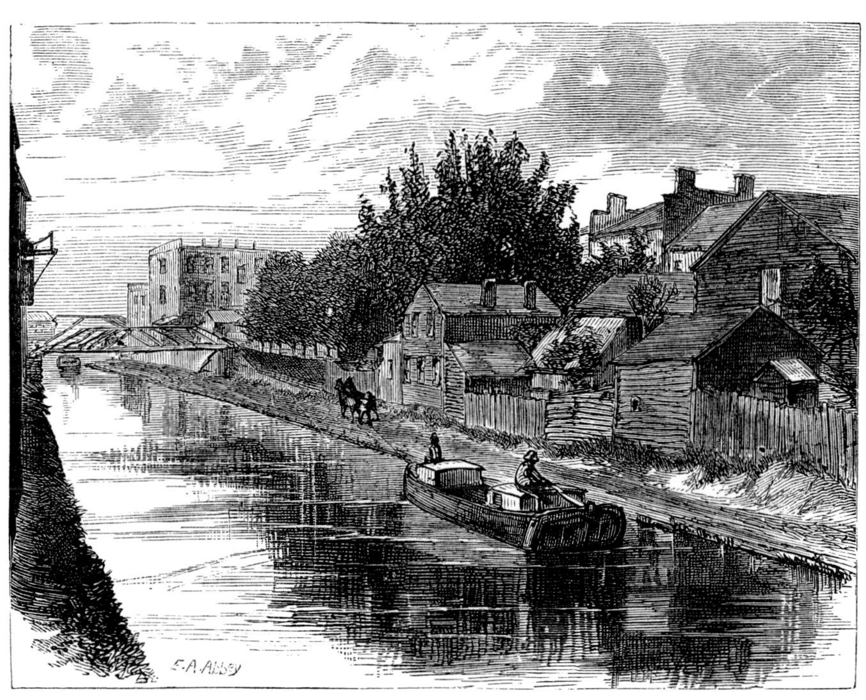

Soheneotady.

Harper's New Monthly Magazine, December 1873
"The Water Ways of New York"

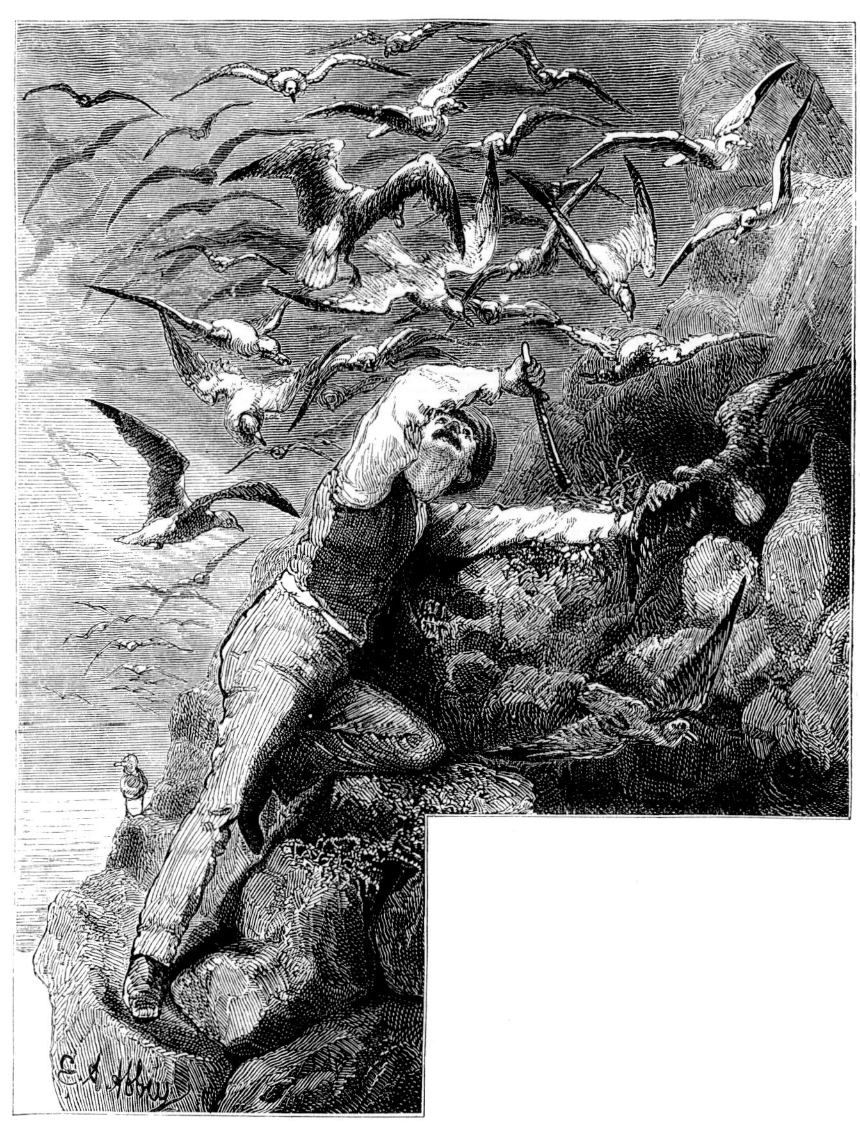

The contest for the eggs.

Harper's New Monthly Magazine, April 1874
"The Farallon Islands"

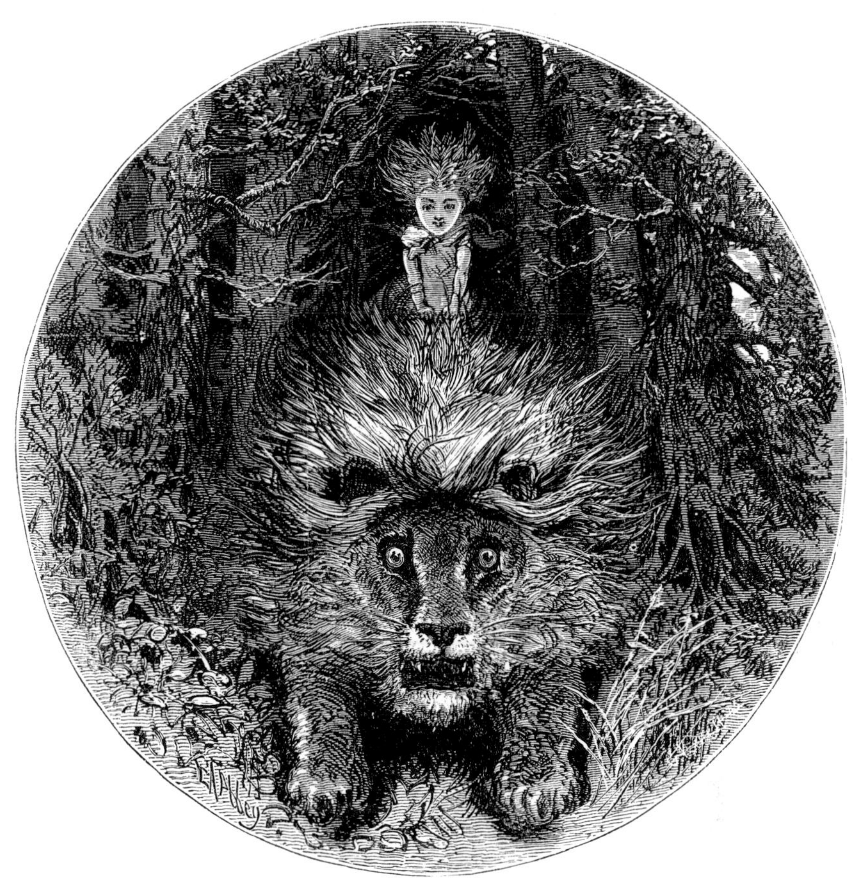

"And toward them rushing, with bristling mane,
came a hungry lion, lean and wild."

Harper's New Monthly Magazine, January 1875
"The Children's Night"

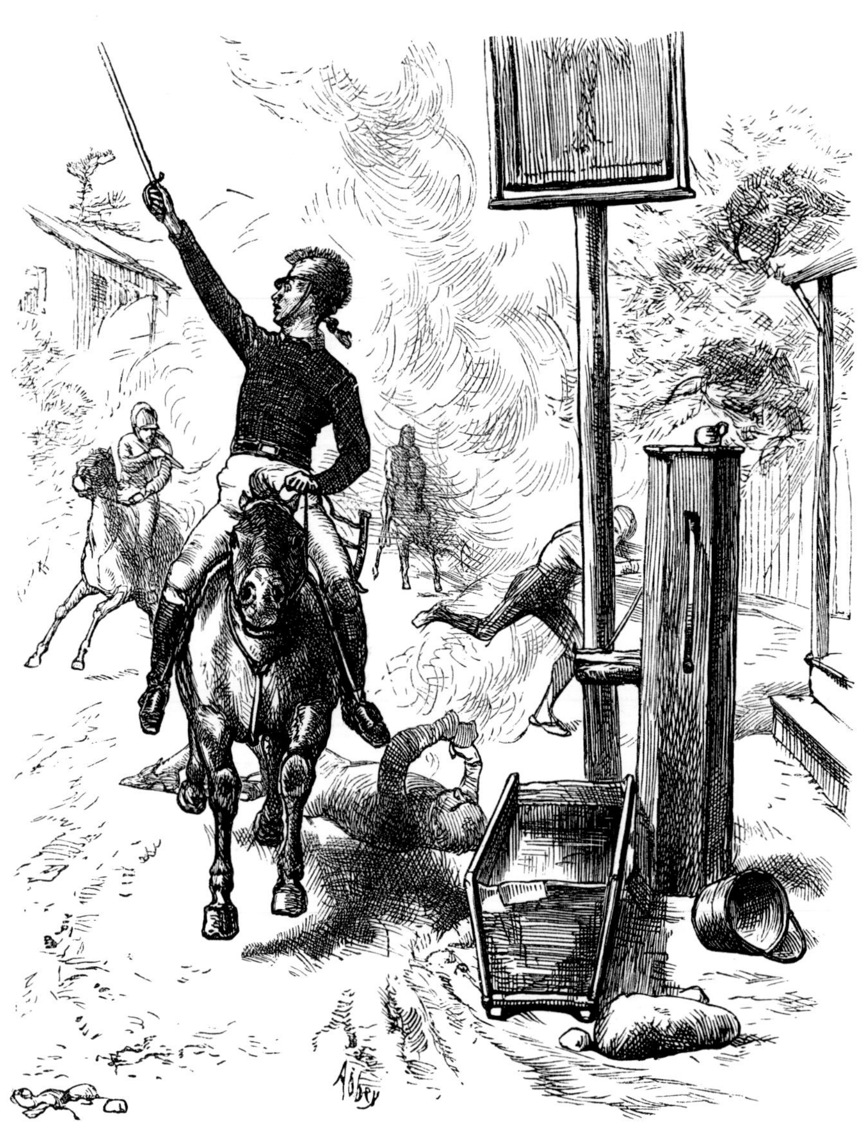

"Death, death to the redcoats!"

Harper's New Monthly Magazine, July 1876
"MacDonald's Raid—A.D. 1780"

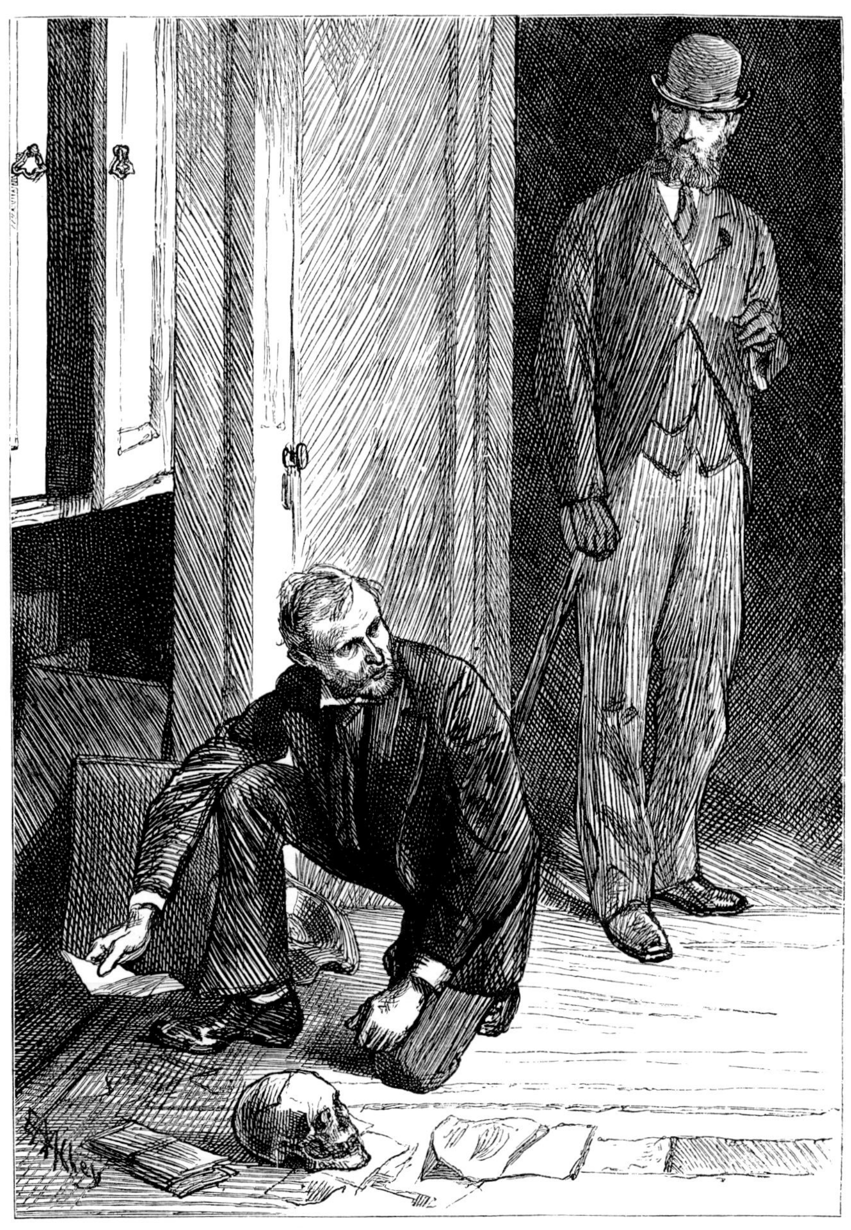

"I saw the figure of a man on his knees."

Harper's New Monthly Magazine, January 1877
"A Craniologist"

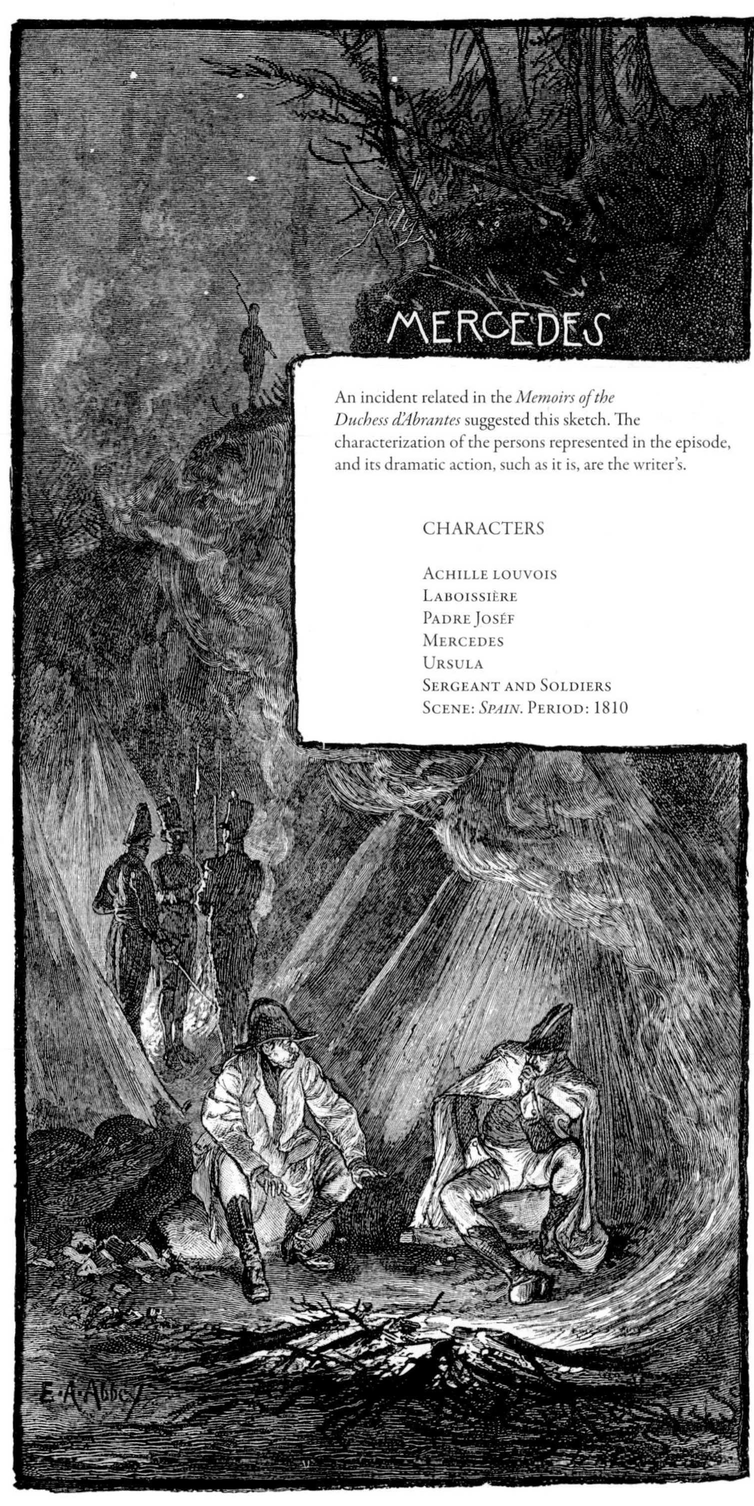

Harper's New Monthly Magazine, September 1878
"Mercedes"

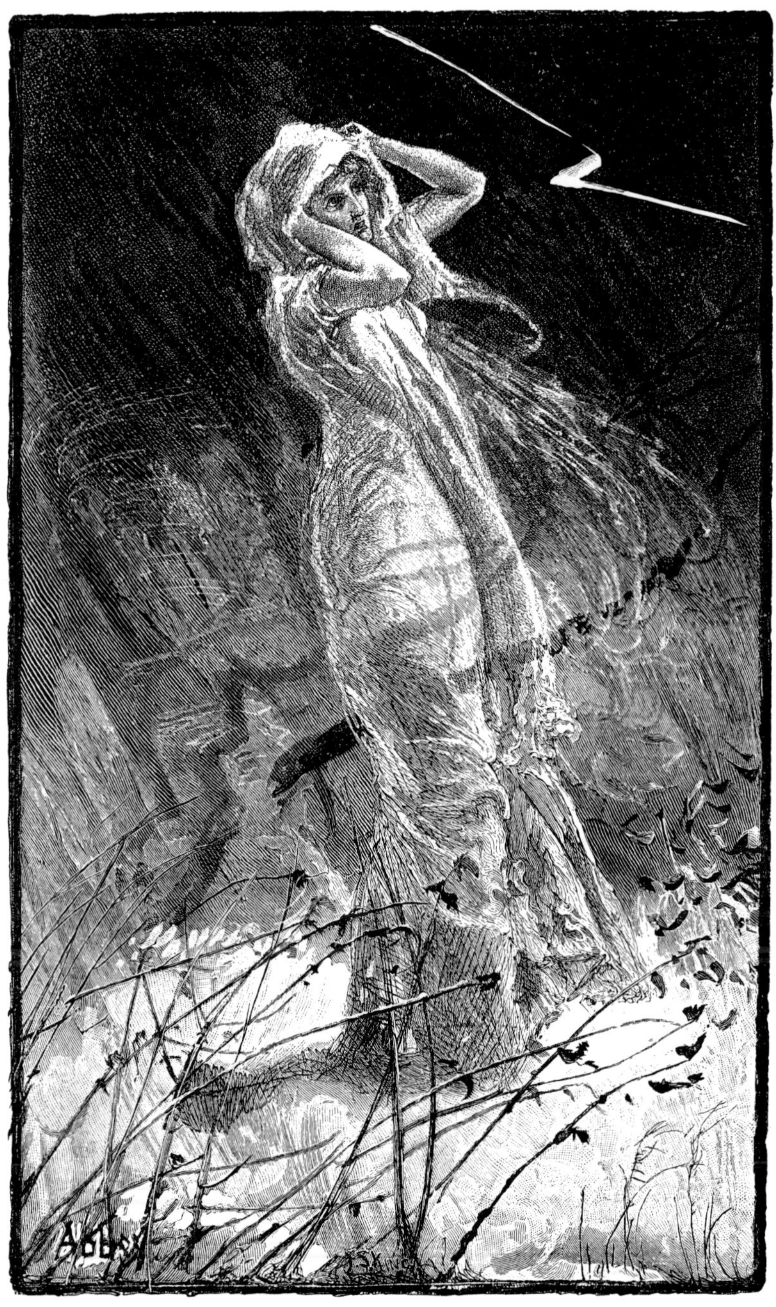

The white lady.

Harper's New Monthly Magazine, June 1879
"Rye, and Round There"

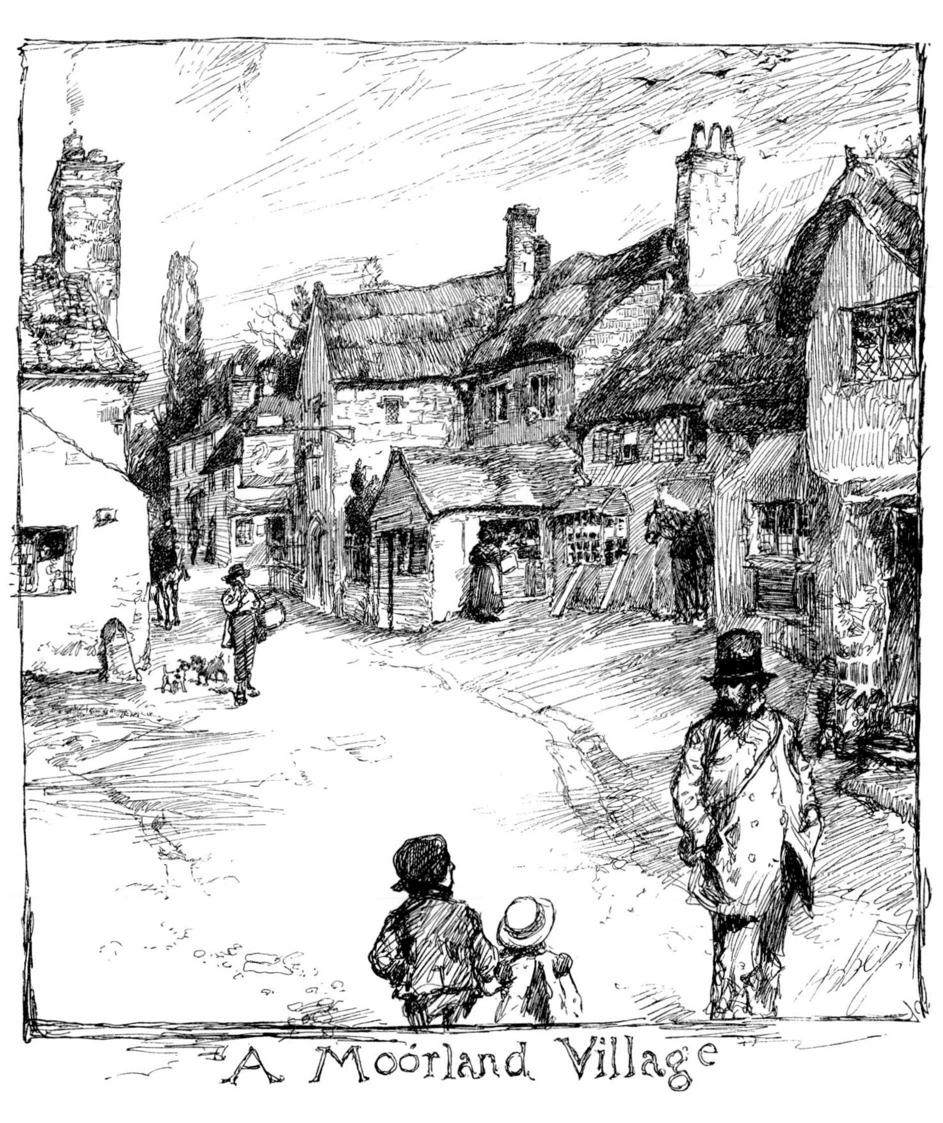

Harper's New Monthly Magazine, June 1880
"A Moorland Village"

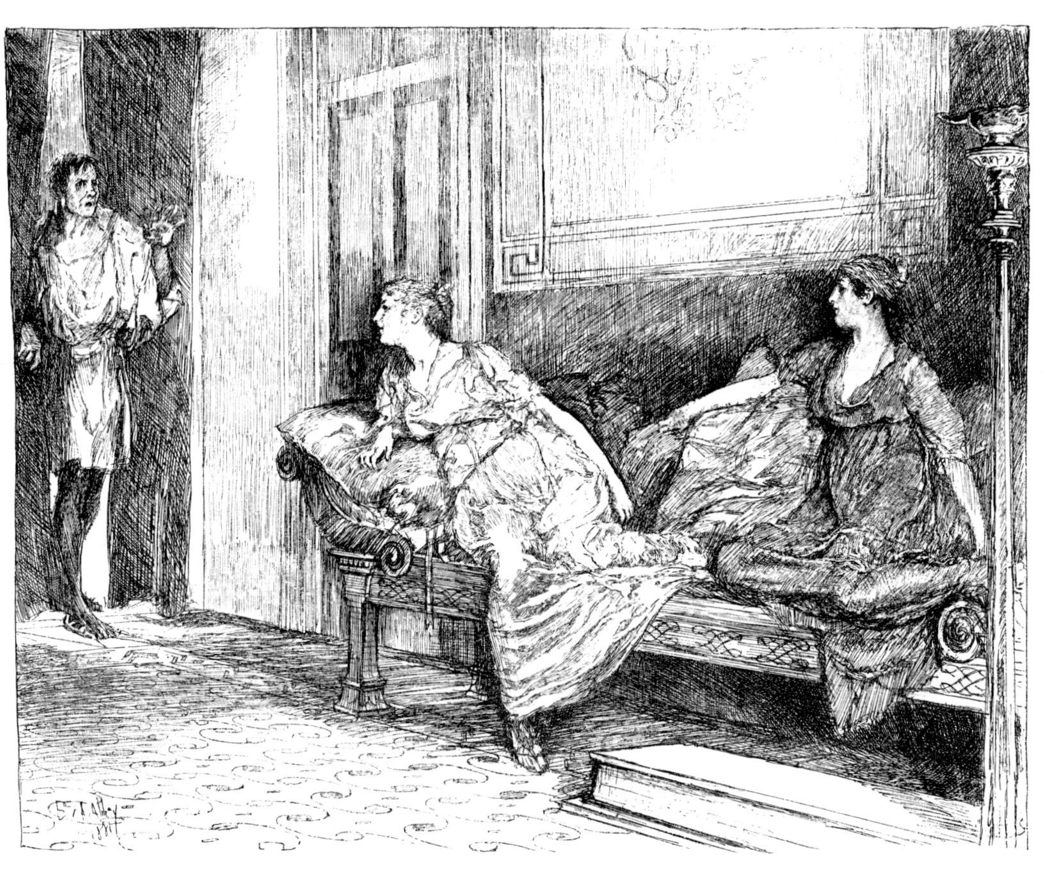

Dromio of Ephesus. "Why, mistress, sure my master is horn-mad."
Act II., Scene I.

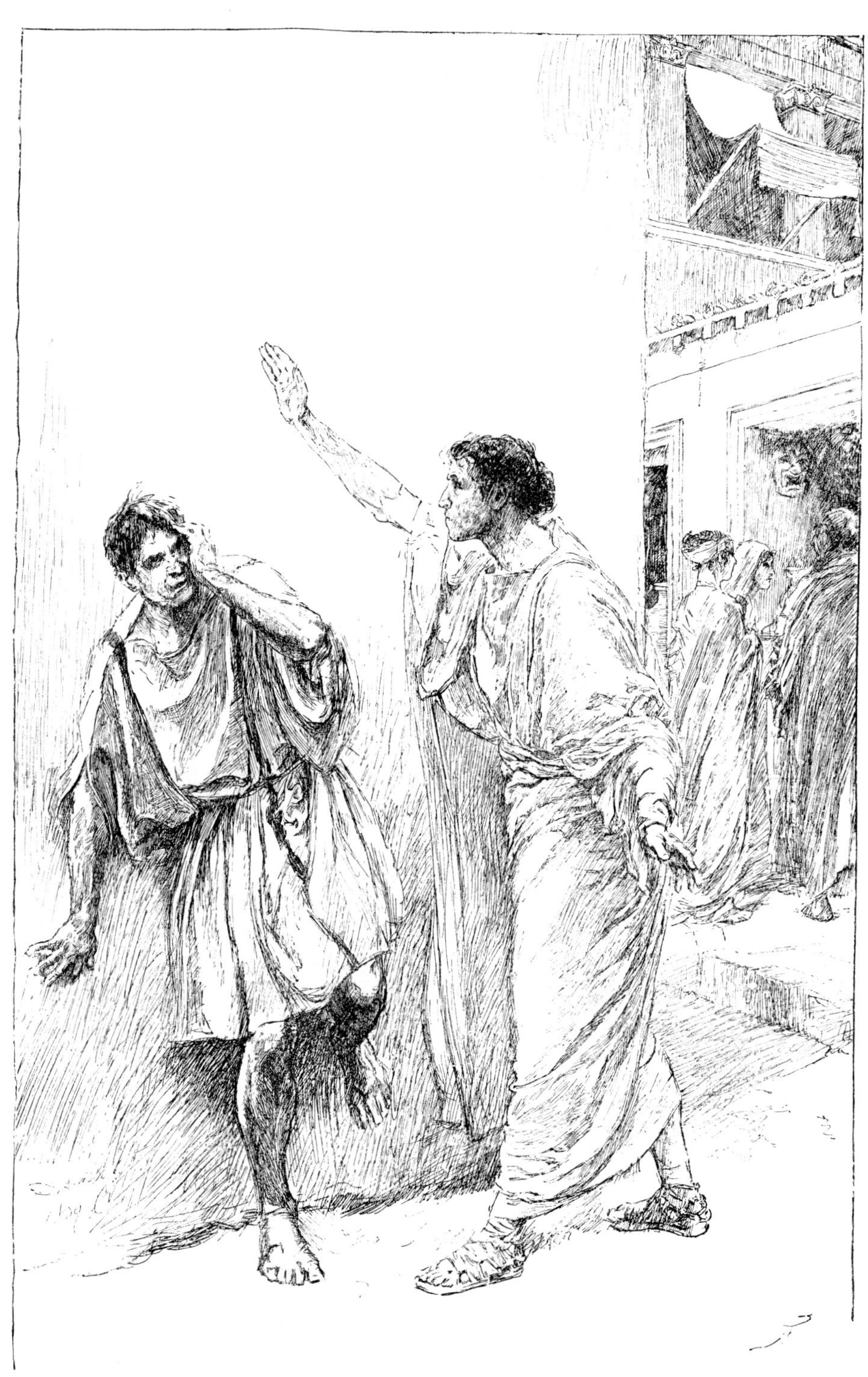

Dromio of Ephesus. "What mean you, sir."

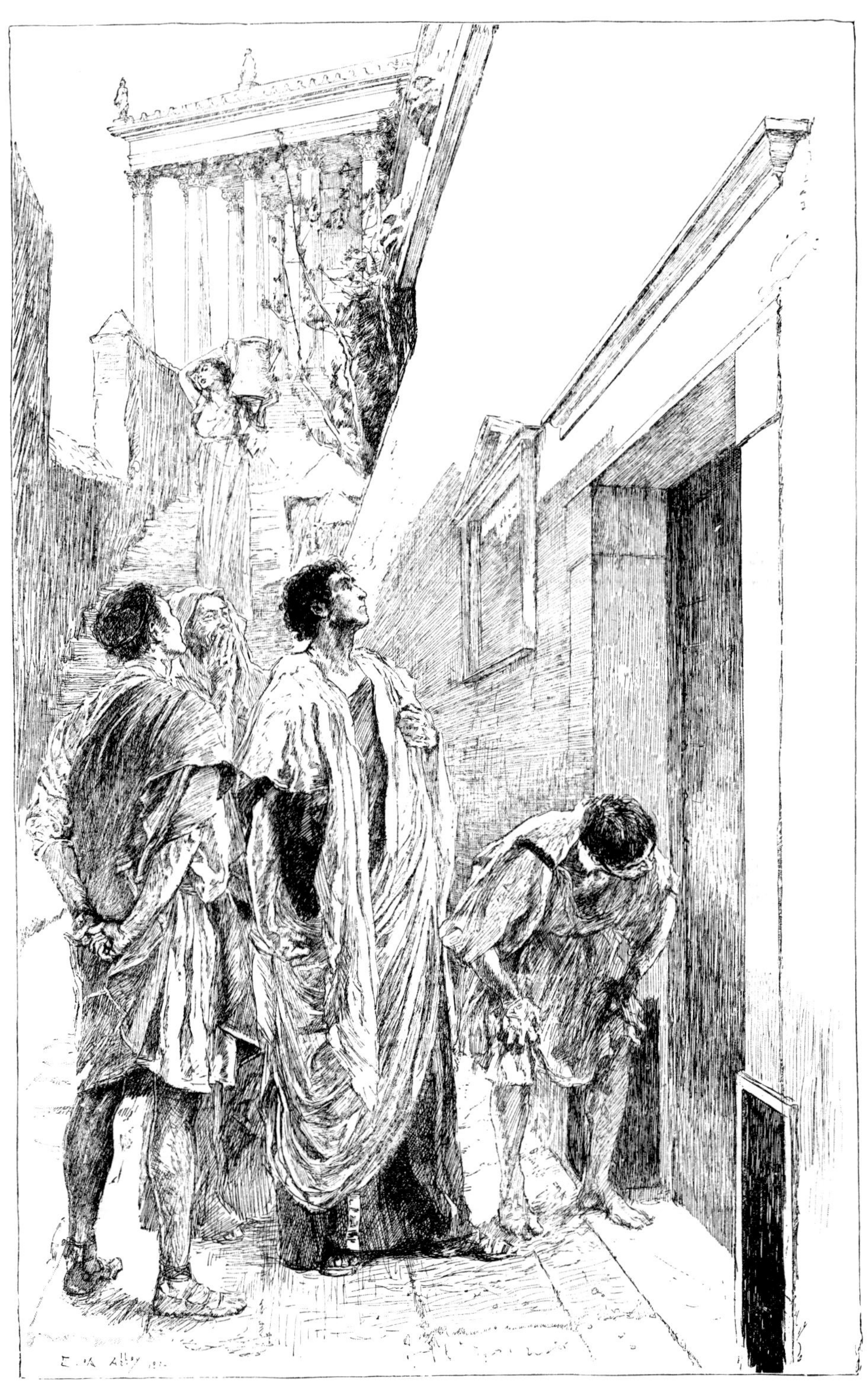

Dromio of Ephesus. "Let my master in, Luce."

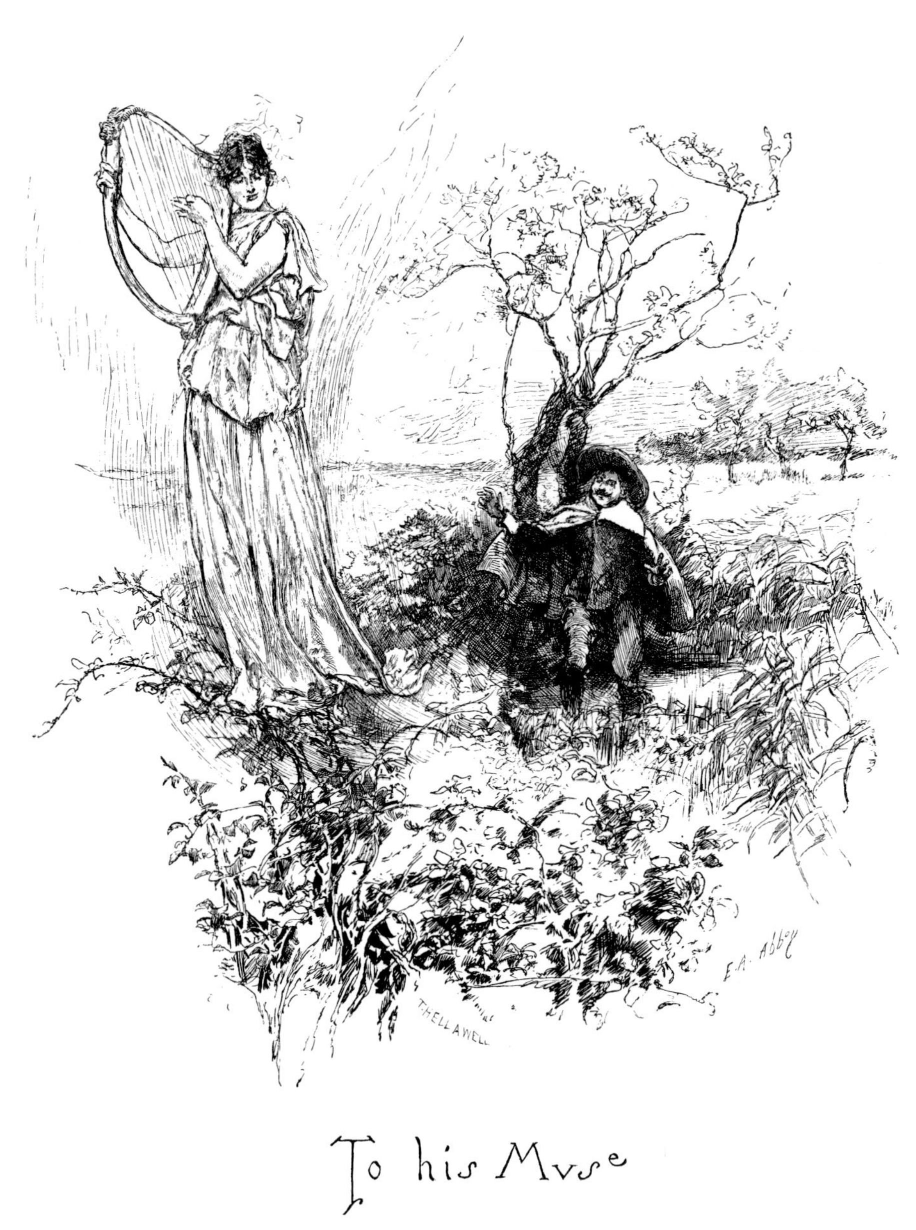

Selections From The Hesperides & Noble Numbers of Robert Herrick
"To his Muse," Harper & Brothers, 1882

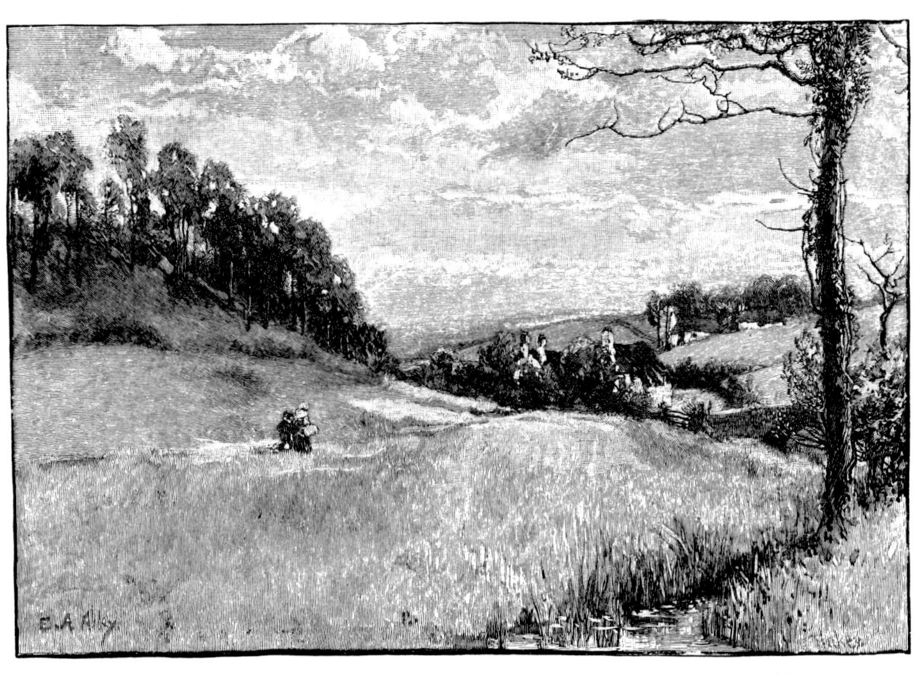

Selections From The Hesperides & Noble Numbers of Robert Herrick
"The Argument of His Book," Harper & Brothers, 1882

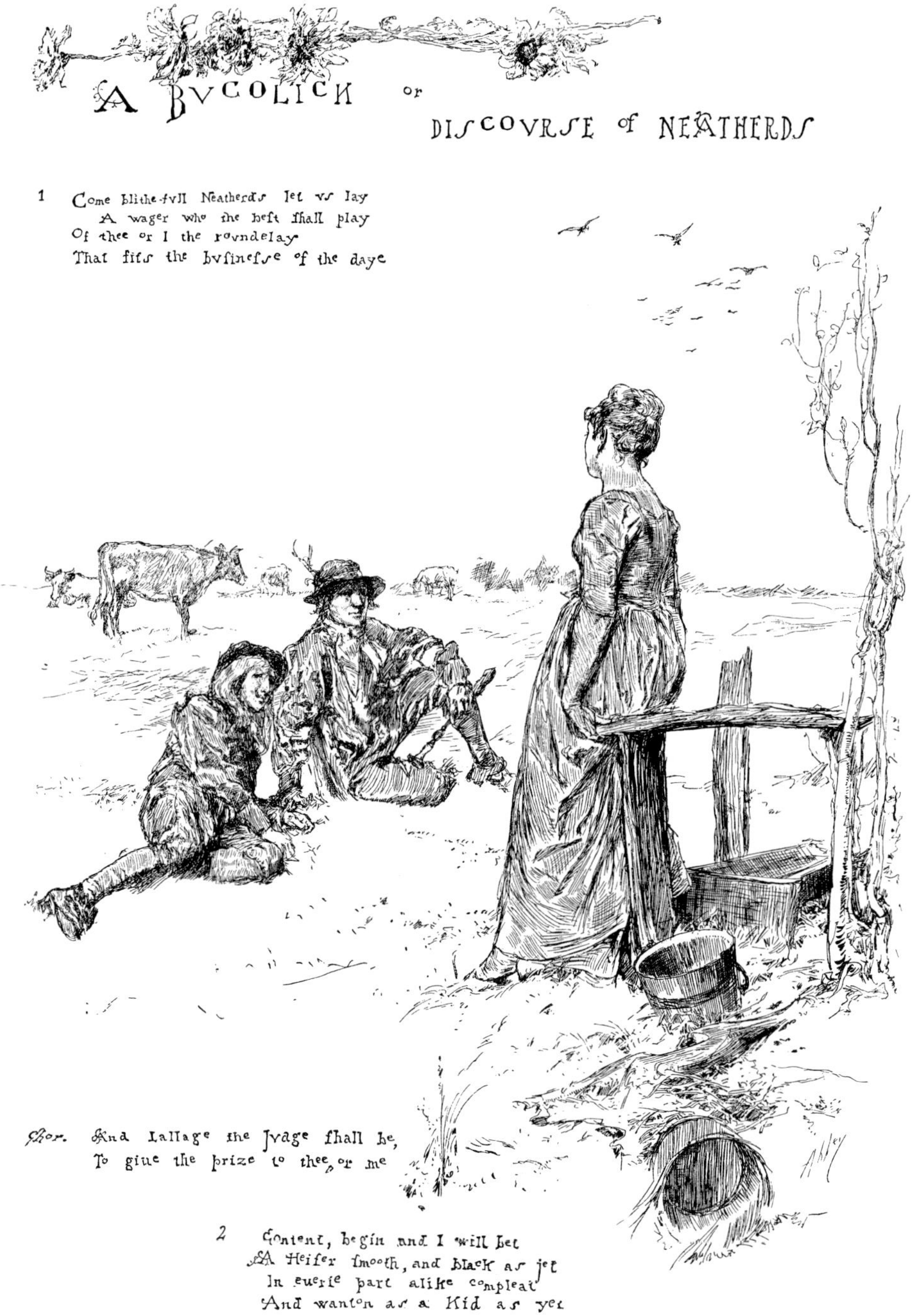

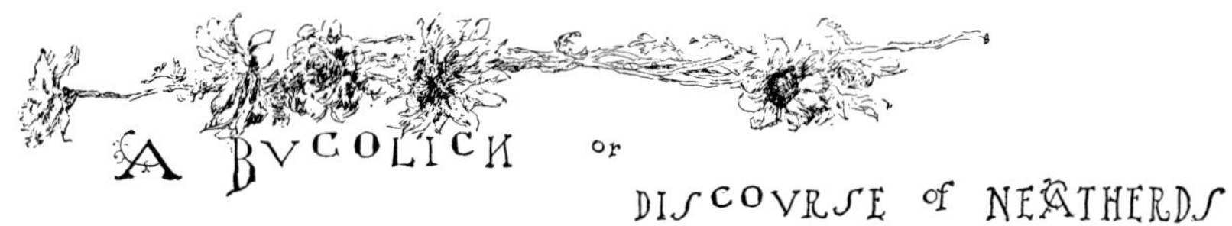

A BVCOLICK or DISCOVRSE of NEATHERDS

1 Come blithe-full Neatherds let vs lay
   A wager who the best shall play
   Of thee or I the roundelay
   That fits the bvsinesse of the daye

Chor. And Lallage the Jvdge shall be,
       To giue the prize to thee, or me

2 Content, begin and I will bet
   A Heifer smooth, and black as jet
   In euerie part alike compleat
   And wanton as a Kid as yet

Selections From The Hesperides & Noble Numbers of Robert Herrick
"A Beucolick, or Discourse of Neatherds," Harper & Brothers, 1882

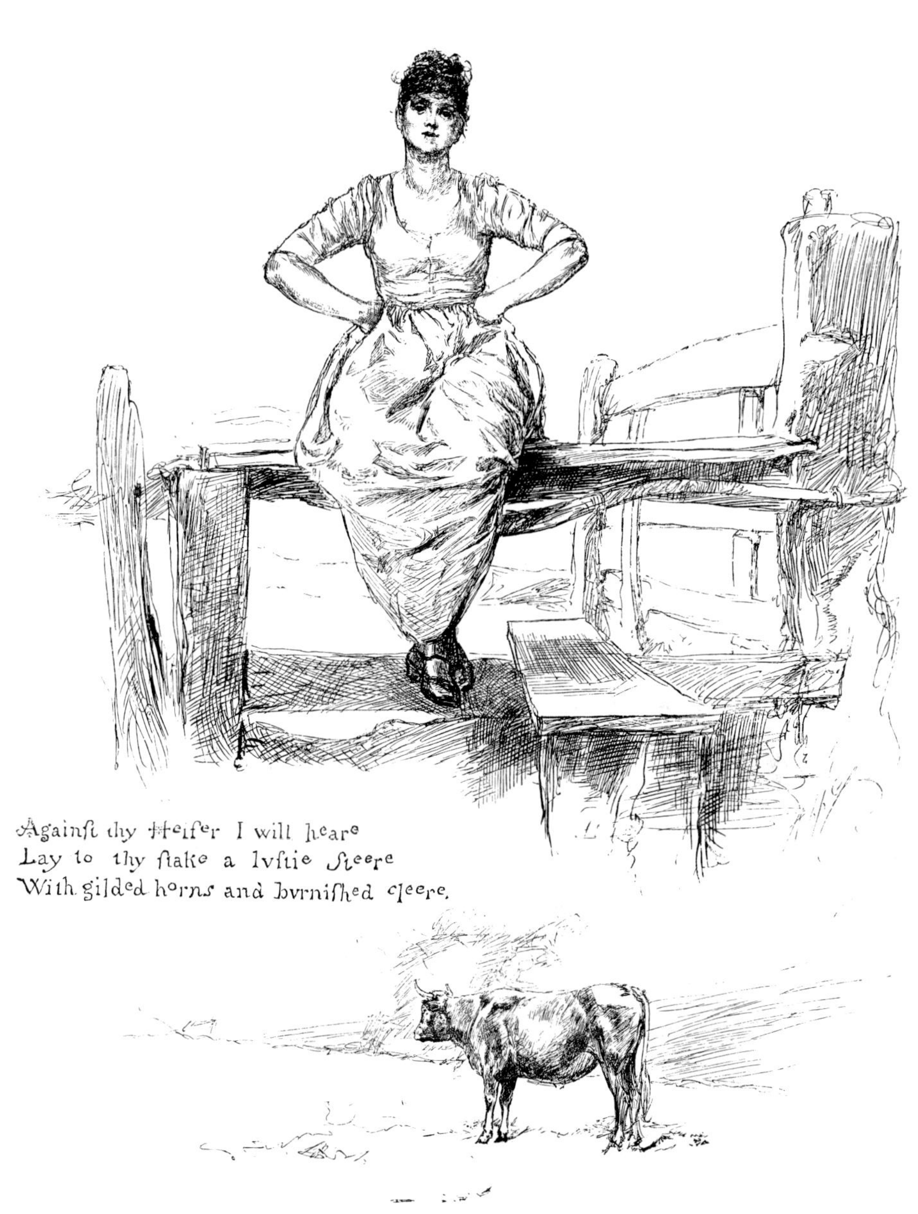

Selections From The Hesperides & Noble Numbers of Robert Herrick
"A Beucolick, or Discourse of Neatherds," Harper & Brothers, 1882

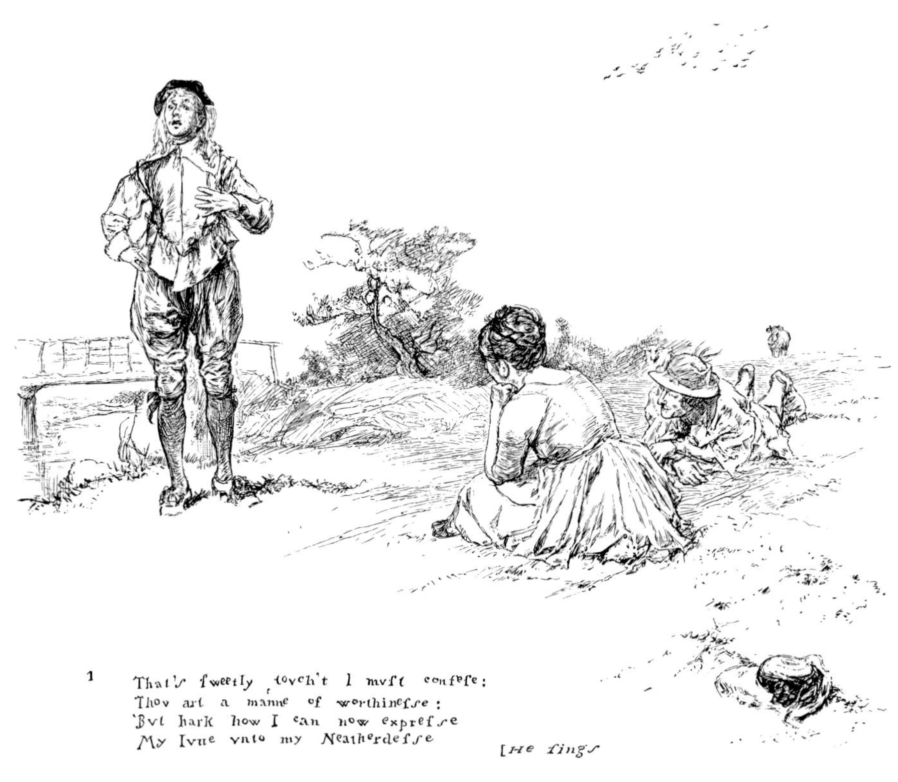

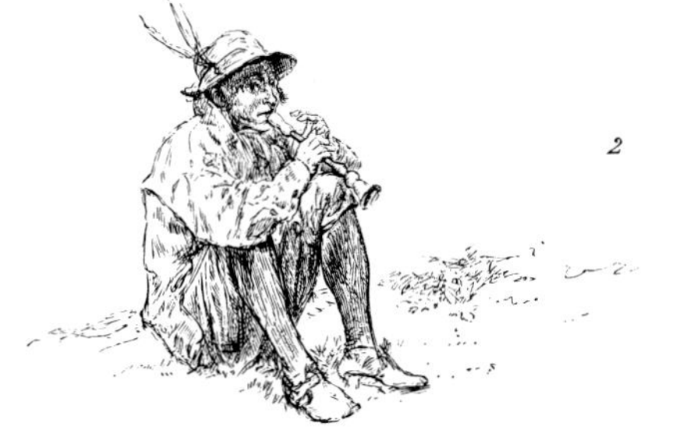

Selections From The Hesperides & Noble Numbers of Robert Herrick
"A Beucolick, or Discourse of Neatherds," Harper & Brothers, 1882

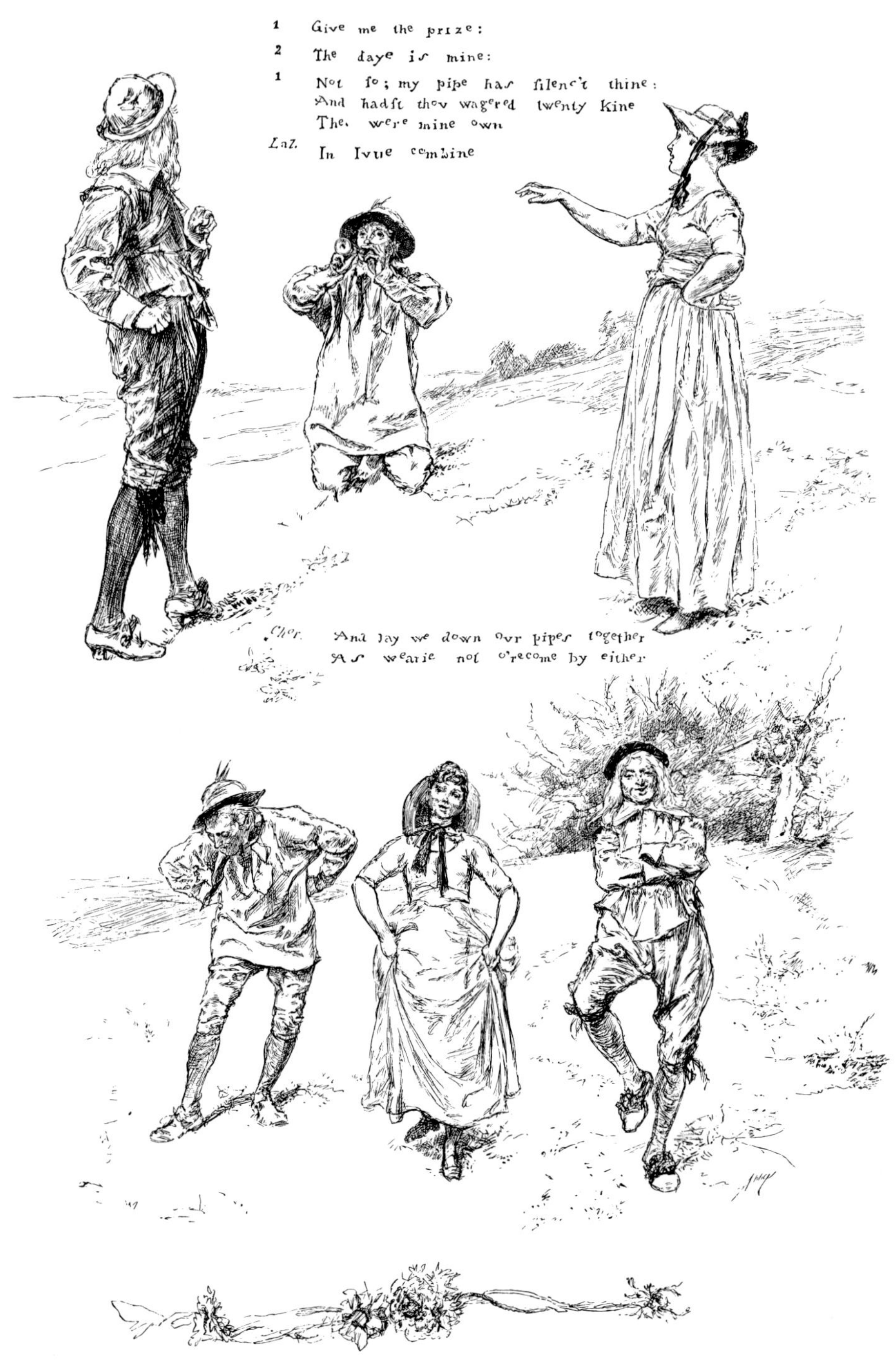

Selections From The Hesperides & Noble Numbers of Robert Herrick
"A Beucolick, or Discourse of Neatherds," Harper & Brothers, 1882

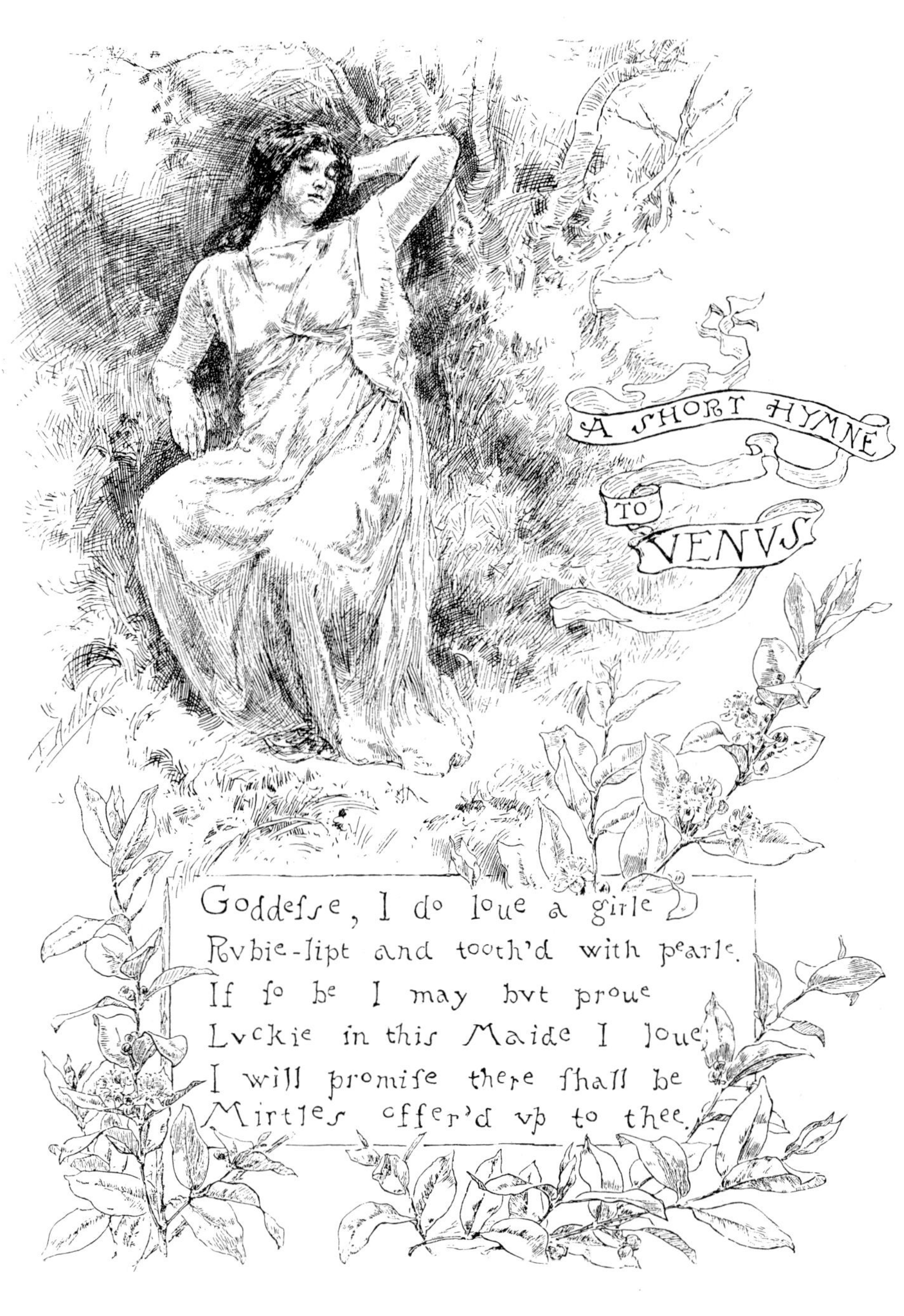

A SHORT HYMNE TO VENVS

Goddesse, I do loue a girle
Rvbie-lipt and tooth'd with pearle.
If so be I may bvt proue
Lvckie in this Maide I loue,
I will promise there shall be
Mirtles offer'd vp to thee.

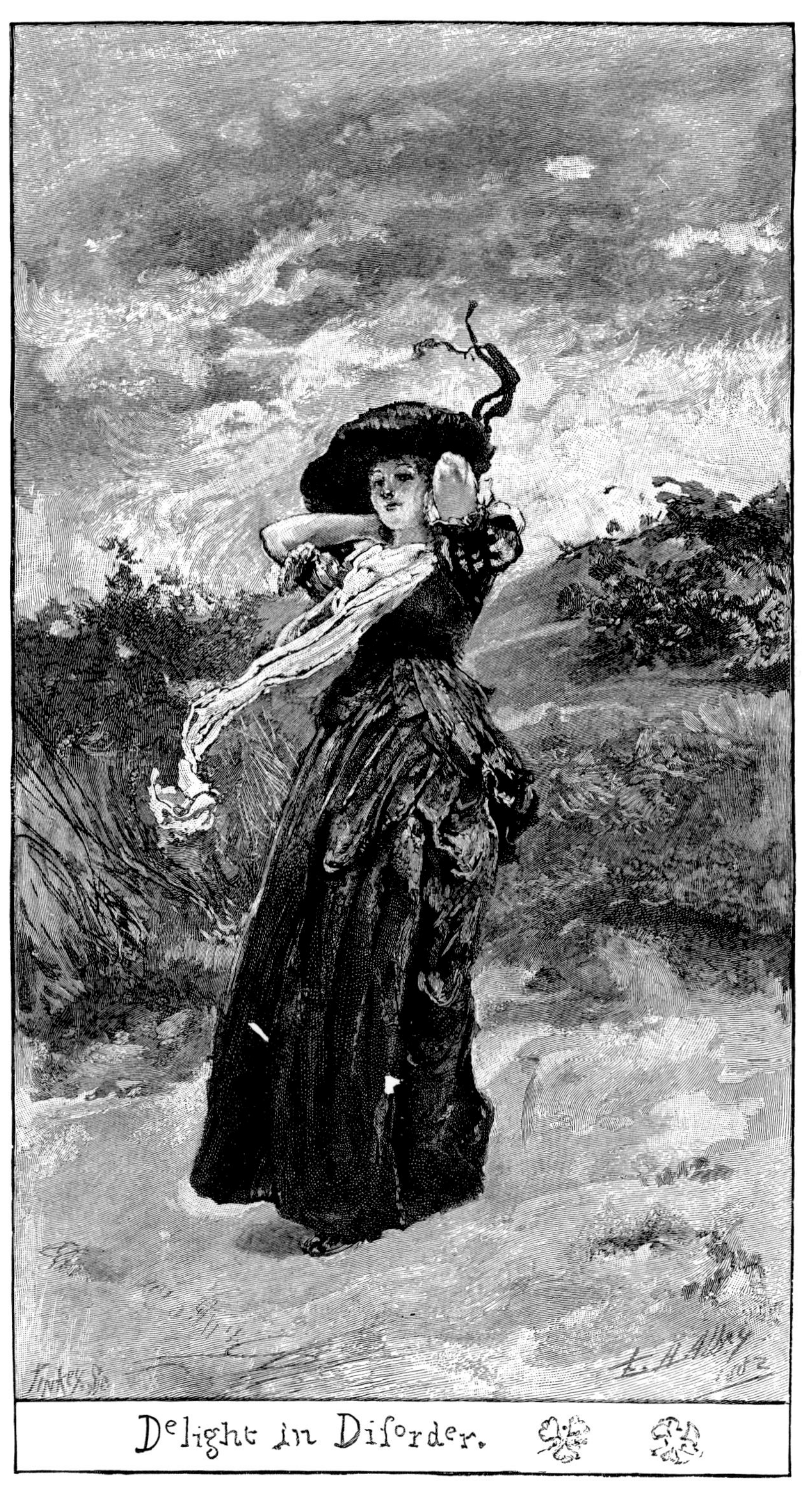

Selections From The Hesperides & Noble Numbers of Robert Herrick
"Delight in Disorder," Harper & Brothers, 1882

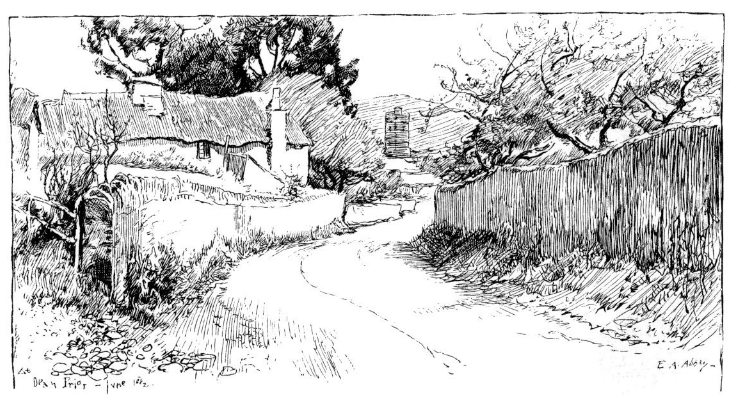

Selections From The Hesperides & Noble Numbers of Robert Herrick
"His Content in the Country," Harper & Brothers, 1882

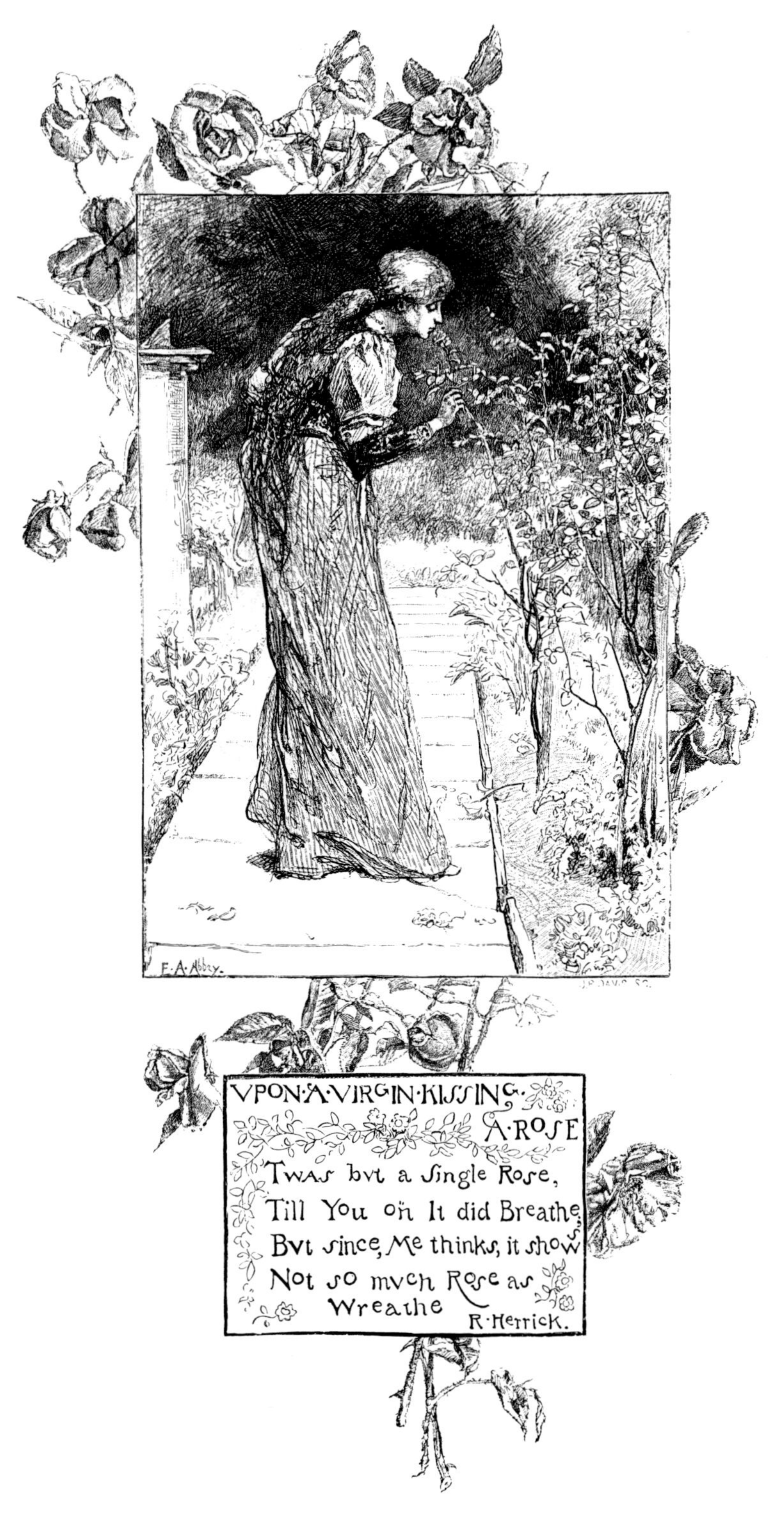

Selections From The Hesperides & Noble Numbers of Robert Herrick
"Upon a Virgin Kissing a Rose," Harper & Brothers, 1882

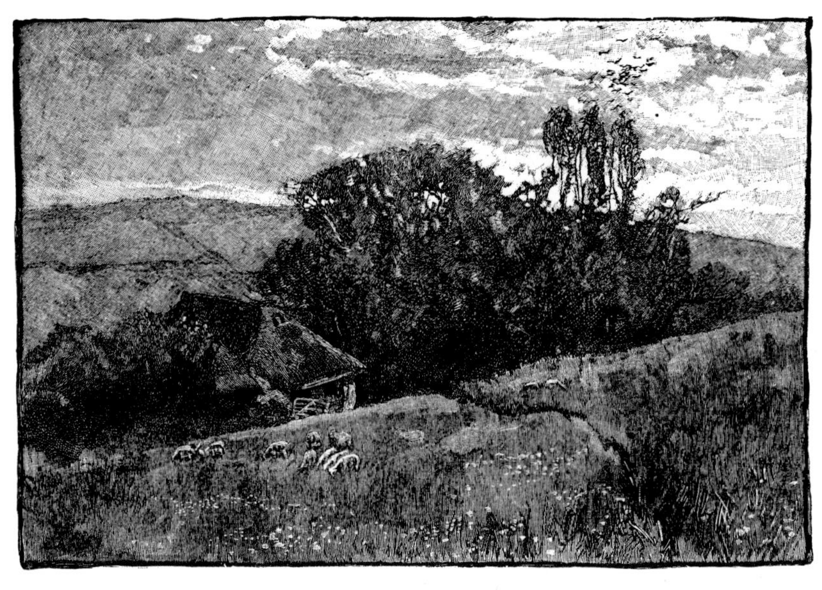

Selections From The Hesperides & Noble Numbers of Robert Herrick
"Discontent in Devon," Harper & Brothers, 1882

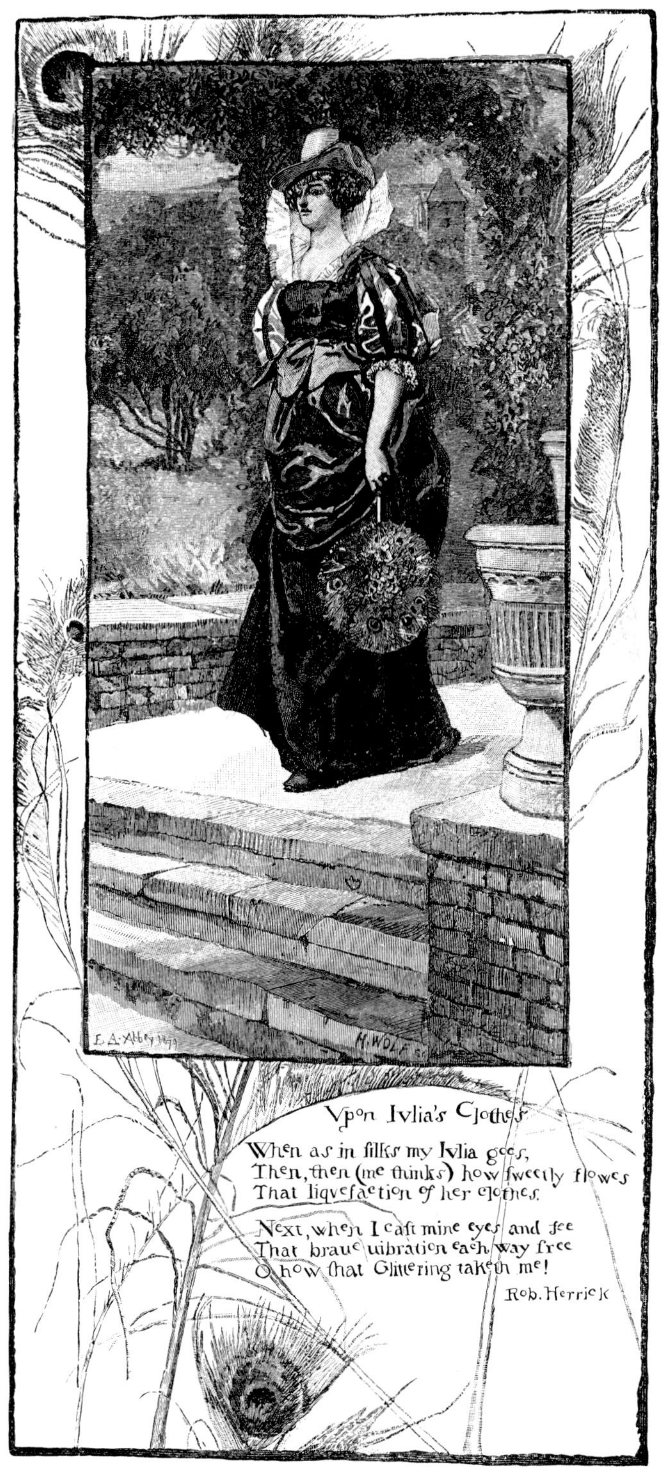

Selections From The Hesperides & Noble Numbers of Robert Herrick
"Upon Julia's Clothes," Harper & Brothers, 1882

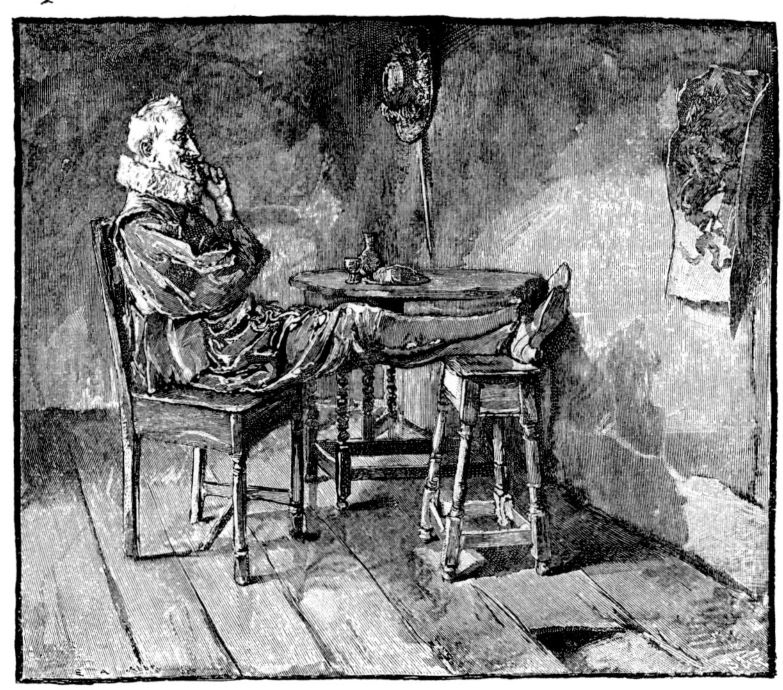

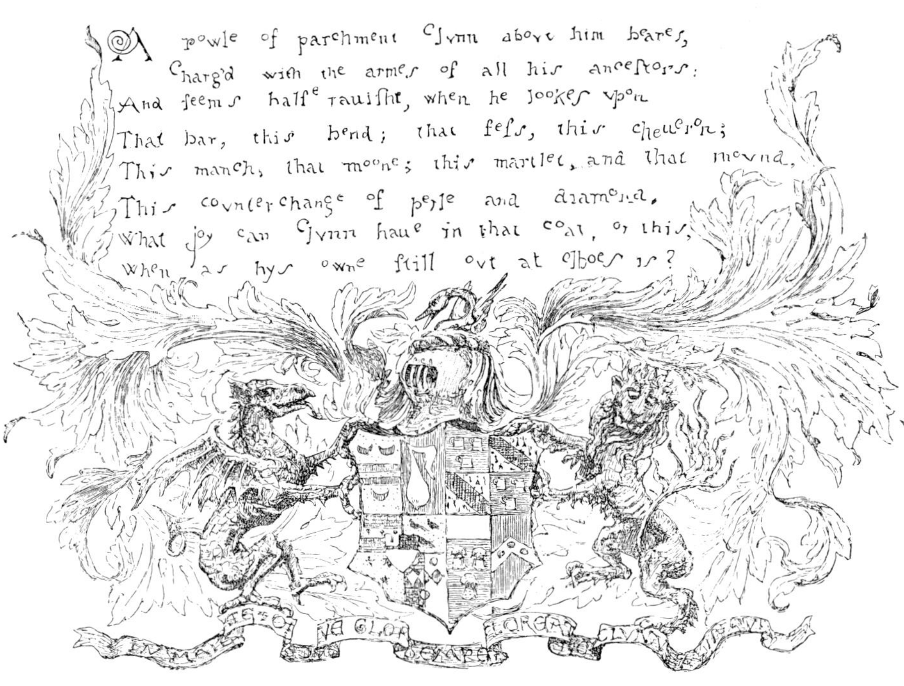

Selections From The Hesperides & Noble Numbers of Robert Herrick
"Upon Clunn," Harper & Brothers, 1882

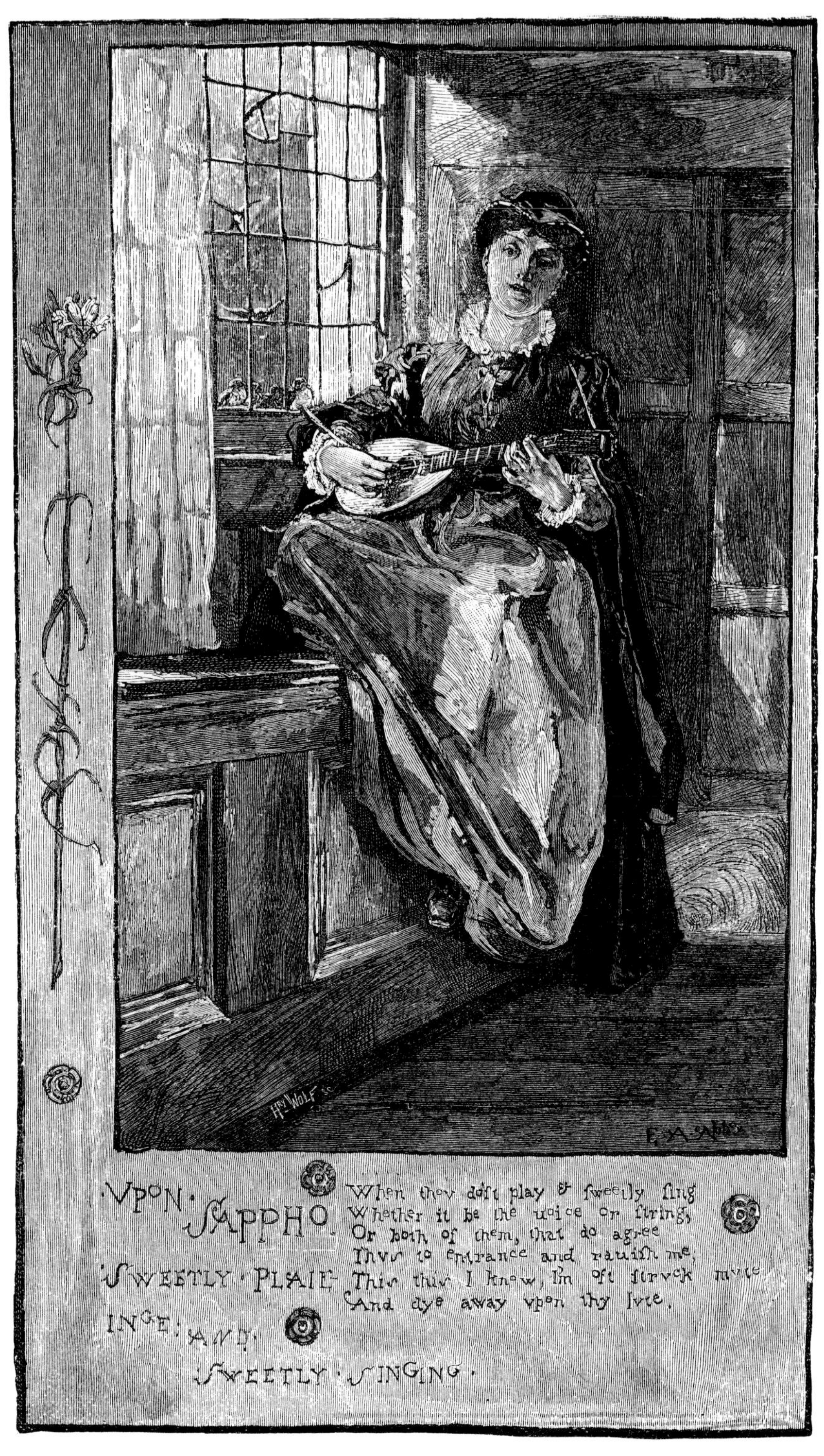

Selections From The Hesperides & Noble Numbers of Robert Herrick
"Upon Sapho, Sweetly Playing, and Sweetly Singing," Harper & Brothers, 1882

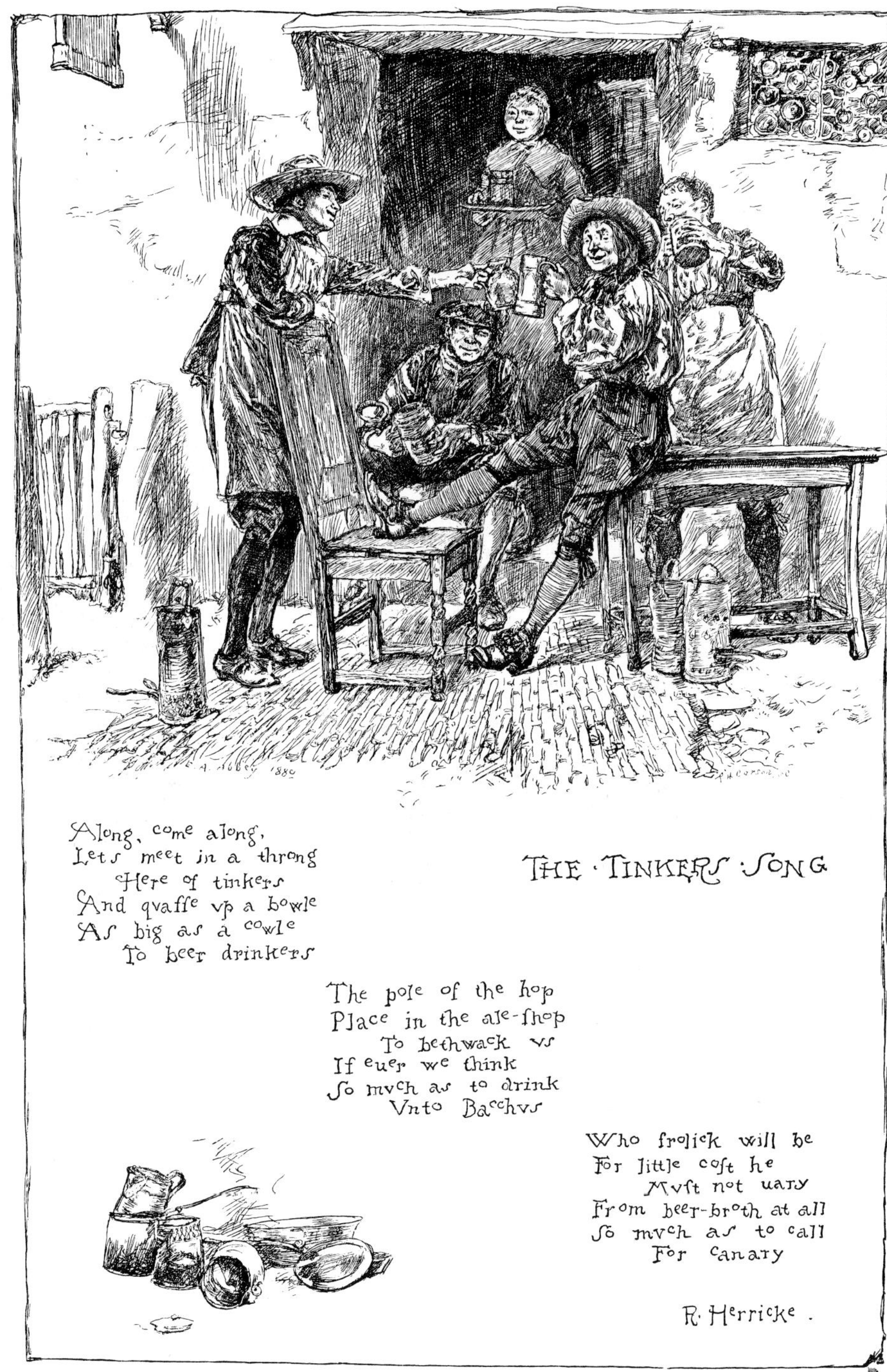

Selections From The Hesperides & Noble Numbers of Robert Herrick
"The Tinkers Song," Harper & Brothers, 1882

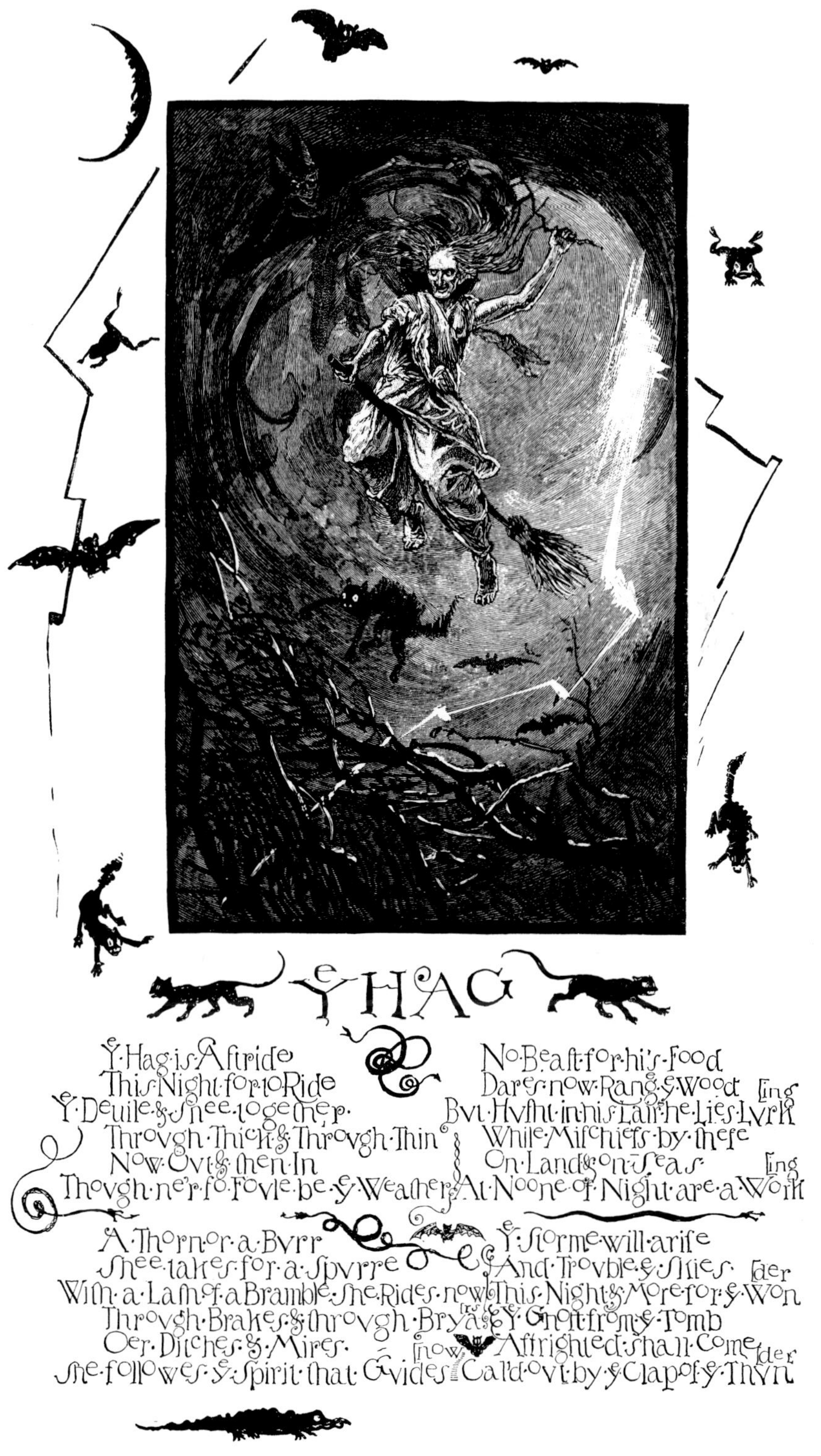

Selections From The Hesperides & Noble Numbers of Robert Herrick
"The Hag," Harper & Brothers, 1882

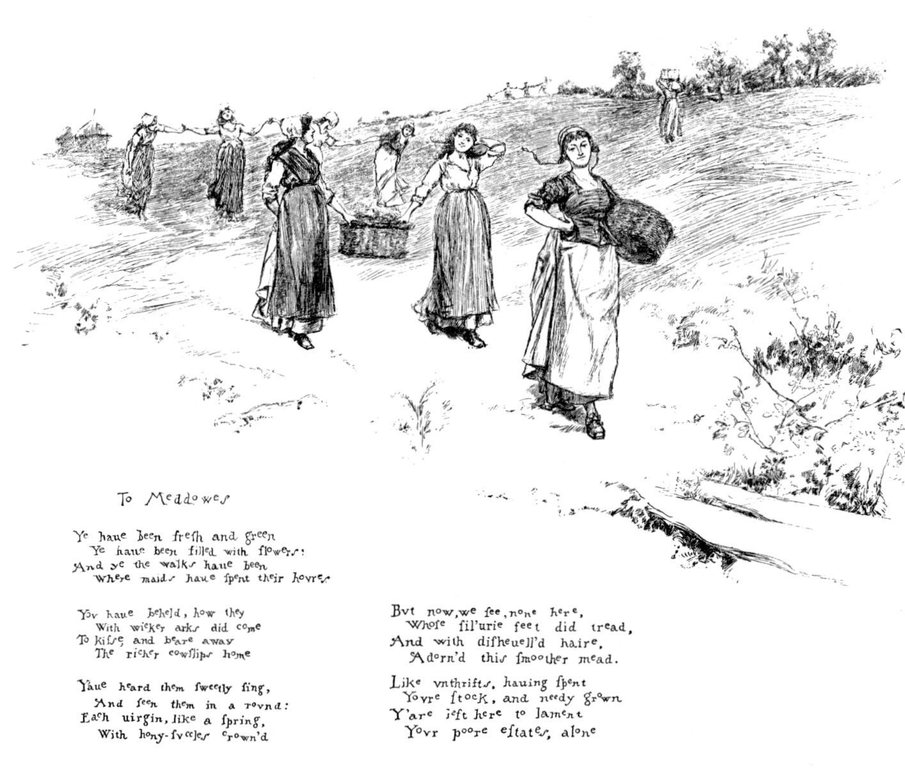

To Meddowes

Ye haue been fresh and green
  Ye haue been filled with flowers:
And ye the walks haue been
  Where maids haue spent their houres.

Yov haue beheld, how they
  With wicker arks did come
To kisse and beare away
  The richer cowslips home

Yaue heard them sweetly sing,
  And seen them in a rovnd:
Each uirgin, like a spring,
  With hony-svccles crown'd

Bvt now, we see, none here,
  Whose siluerie feet did tread,
And with disheuell'd haire,
  Adorn'd this smoother mead.

Like vnthrifts, hauing spent
  Yovre stock, and needy grown
Y'are left here to lament
  Yovr poore estates, alone

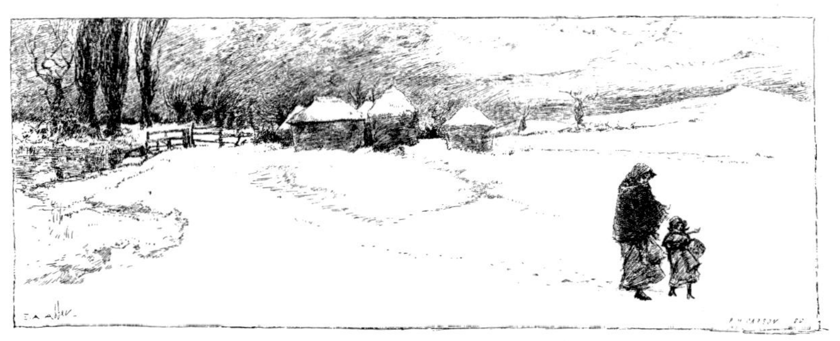

Selections From The Hesperides & Noble Numbers of Robert Herrick
"To Meddowes," Harper & Brothers, 1882

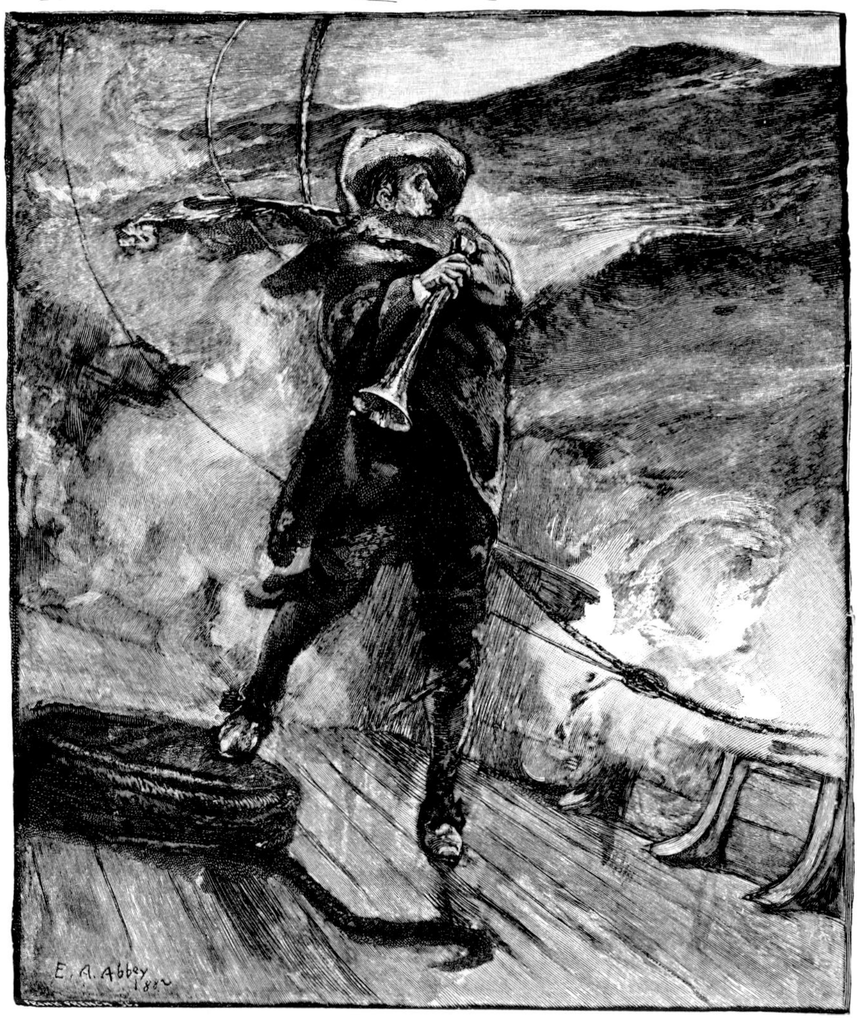

Selections From The Hesperides & Noble Numbers of Robert Herrick
"His Cavalier," Harper & Brothers, 1882

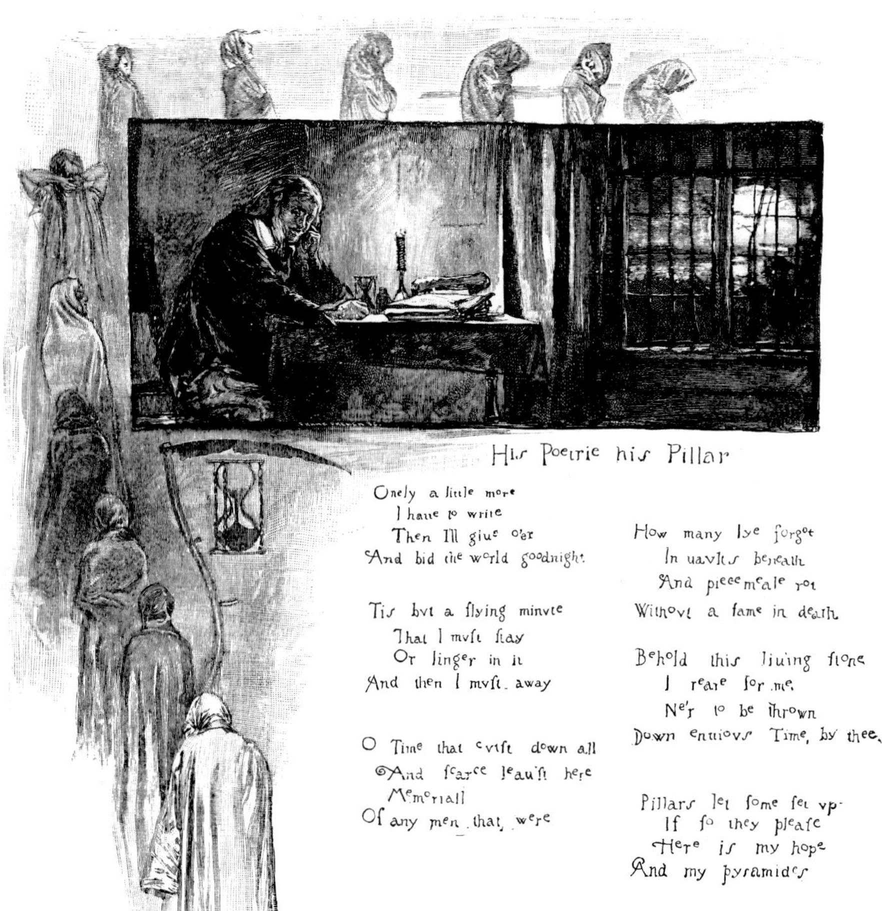

Selections From The Hesperides & Noble Numbers of Robert Herrick
"His Poetrie his Pillar," Harper & Brothers, 1882

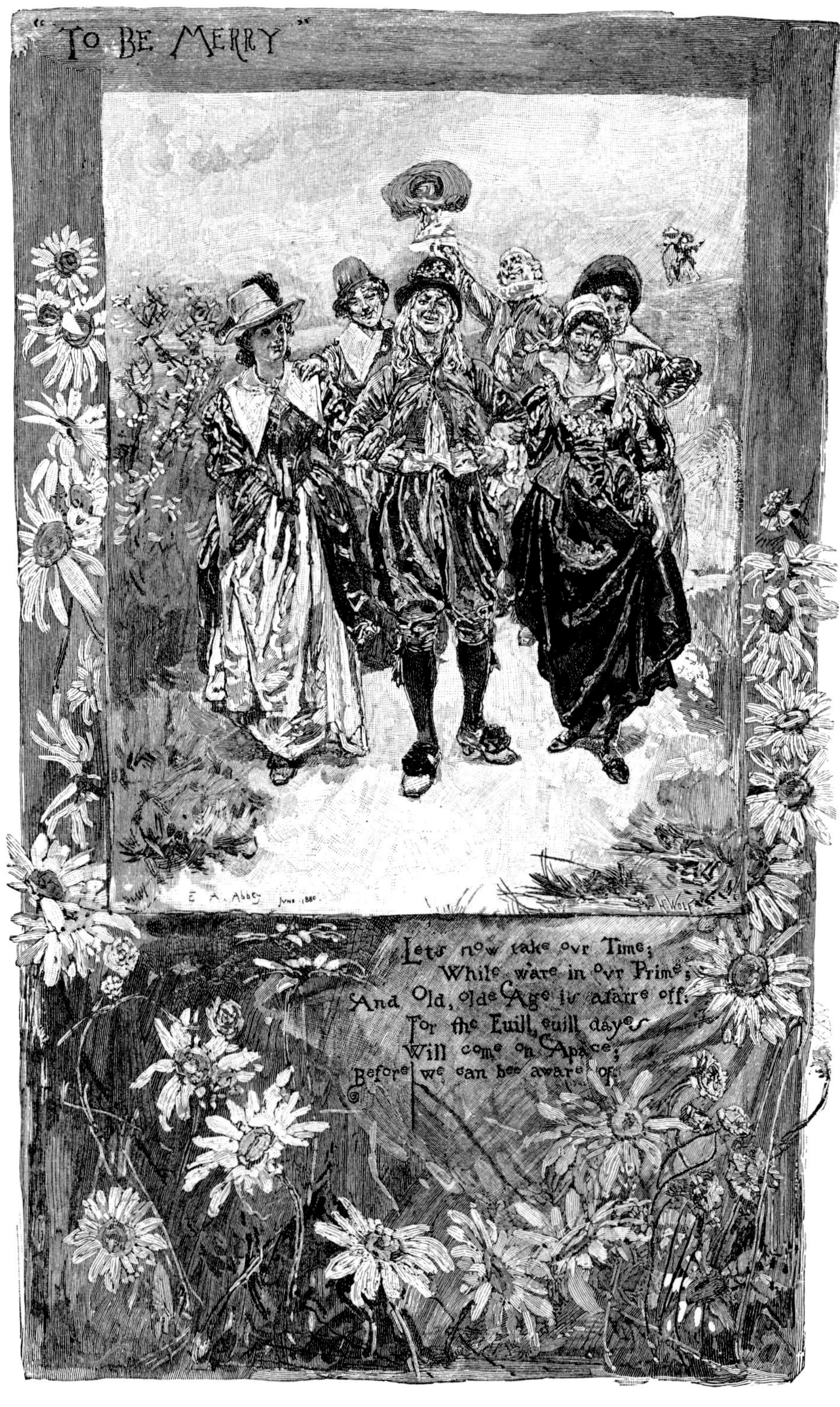

Selections From The Hesperides & Noble Numbers of Robert Herrick
"To be Merry," Harper & Brothers, 1882

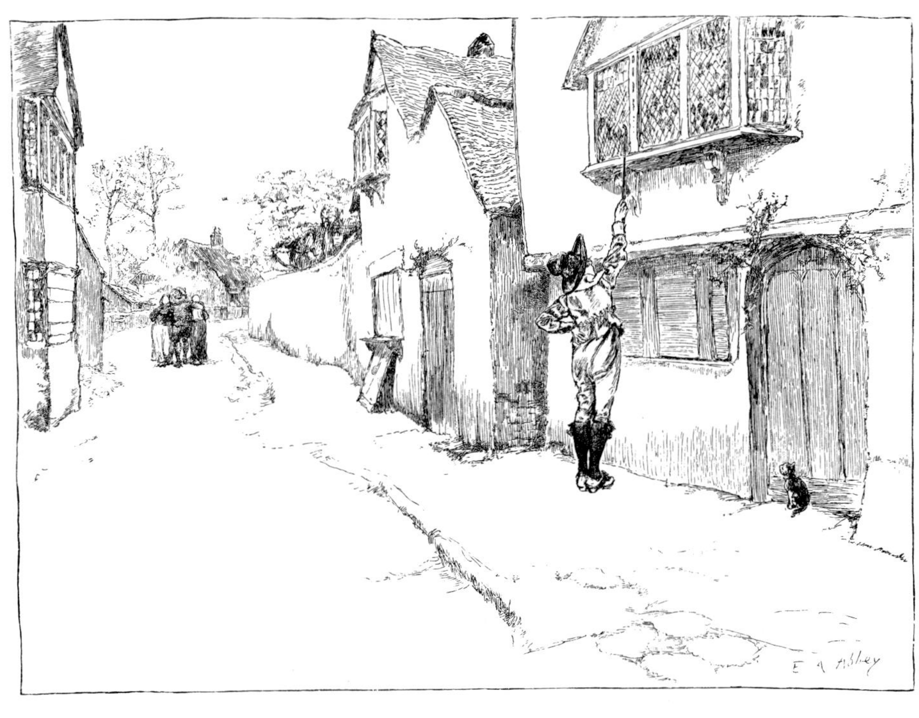

Selections From The Hesperides & Noble Numbers of Robert Herrick
"Corinna's Going a Maying," Harper & Brothers, 1882

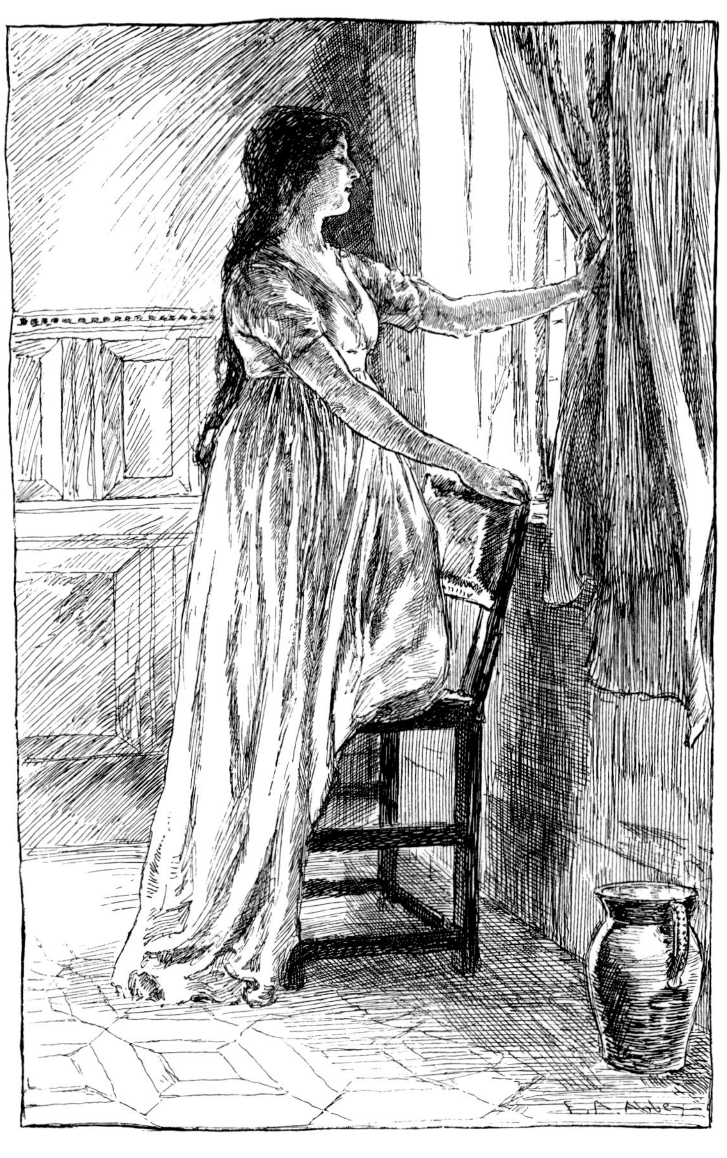

Selections From The Hesperides & Noble Numbers of Robert Herrick
"Corinna's Going a Maying," Harper & Brothers, 1882

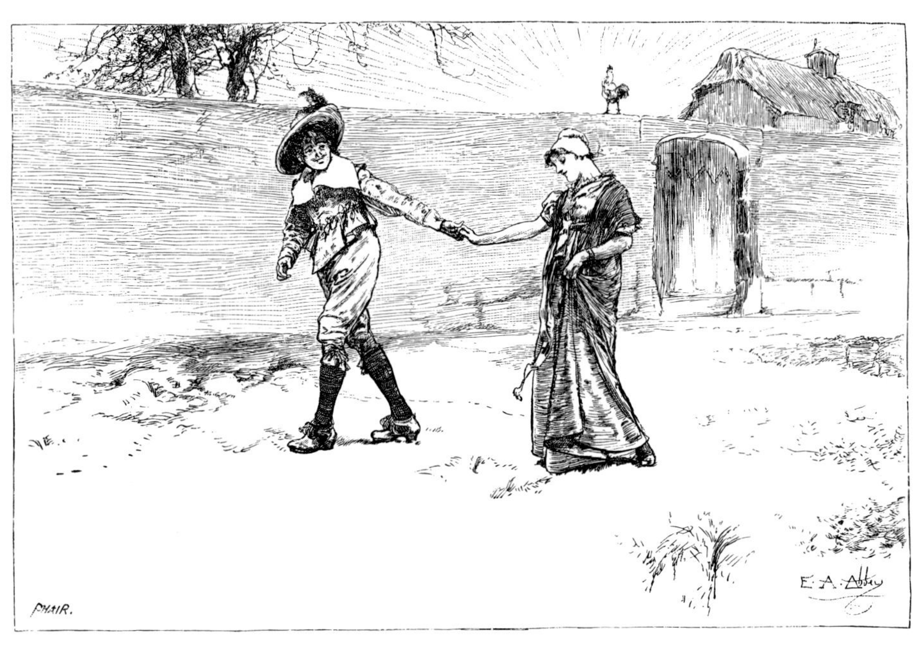

Selections From *The Hesperides & Noble Numbers of Robert Herrick*
"Corinna's Going a Maying," Harper & Brothers, 1882

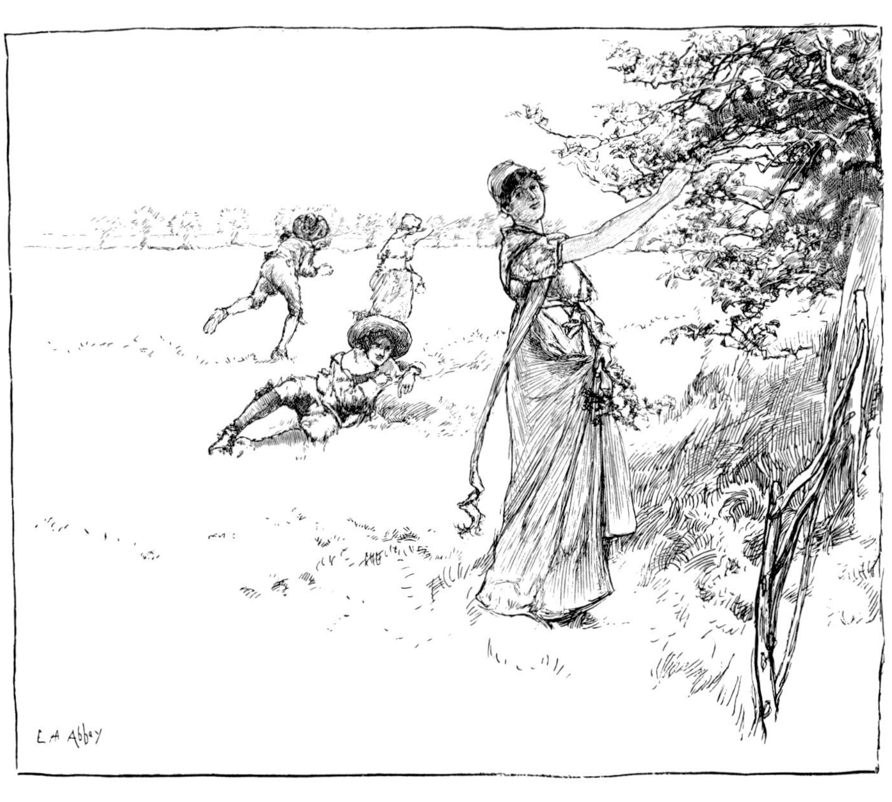

Selections From The Hesperides & Noble Numbers of Robert Herrick
"Corinna's Going a Maying," Harper & Brothers, 1882

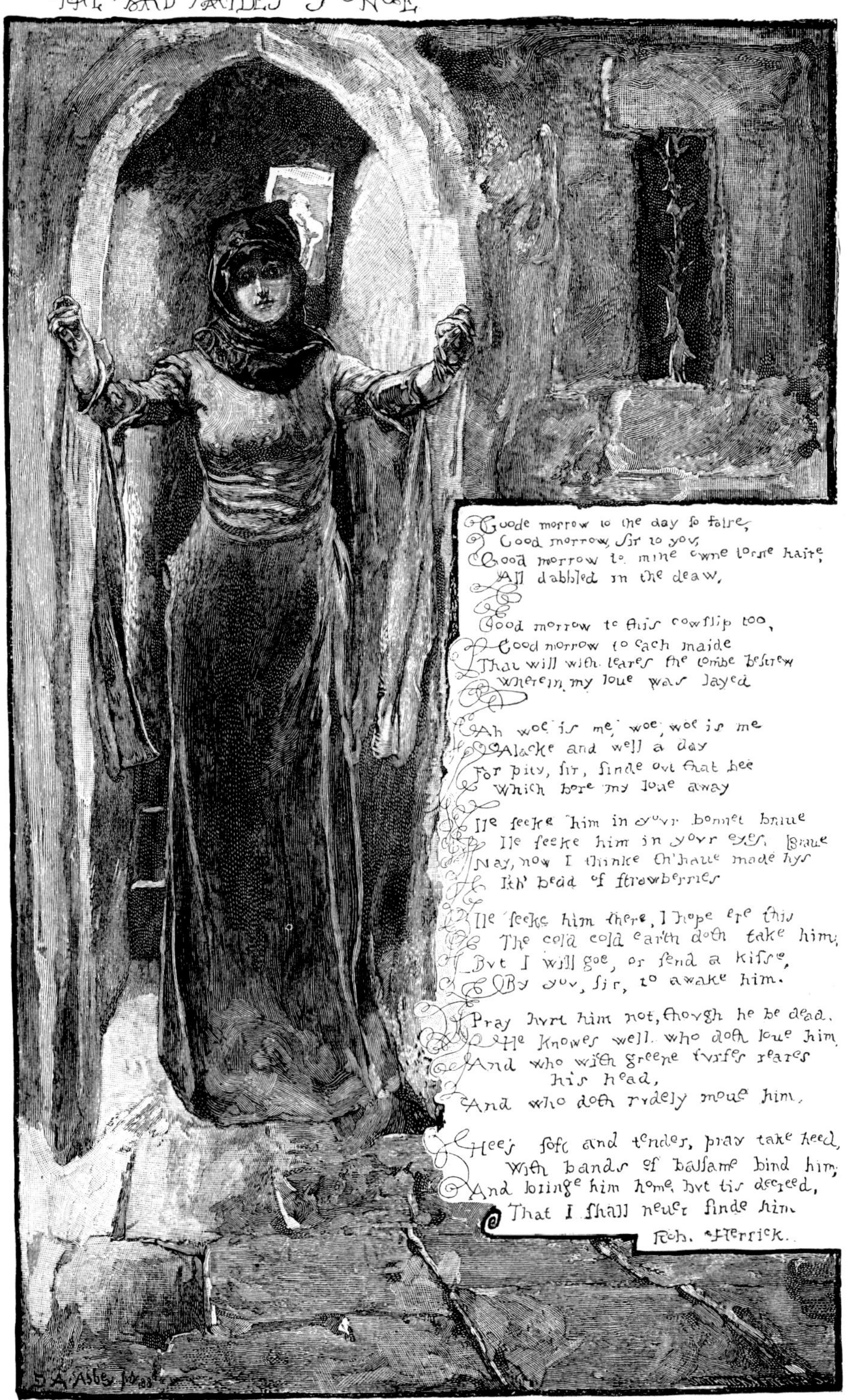

Selections From The Hesperides & Noble Numbers of Robert Herrick
"The Mad Maids Song," Harper & Brothers, 1882

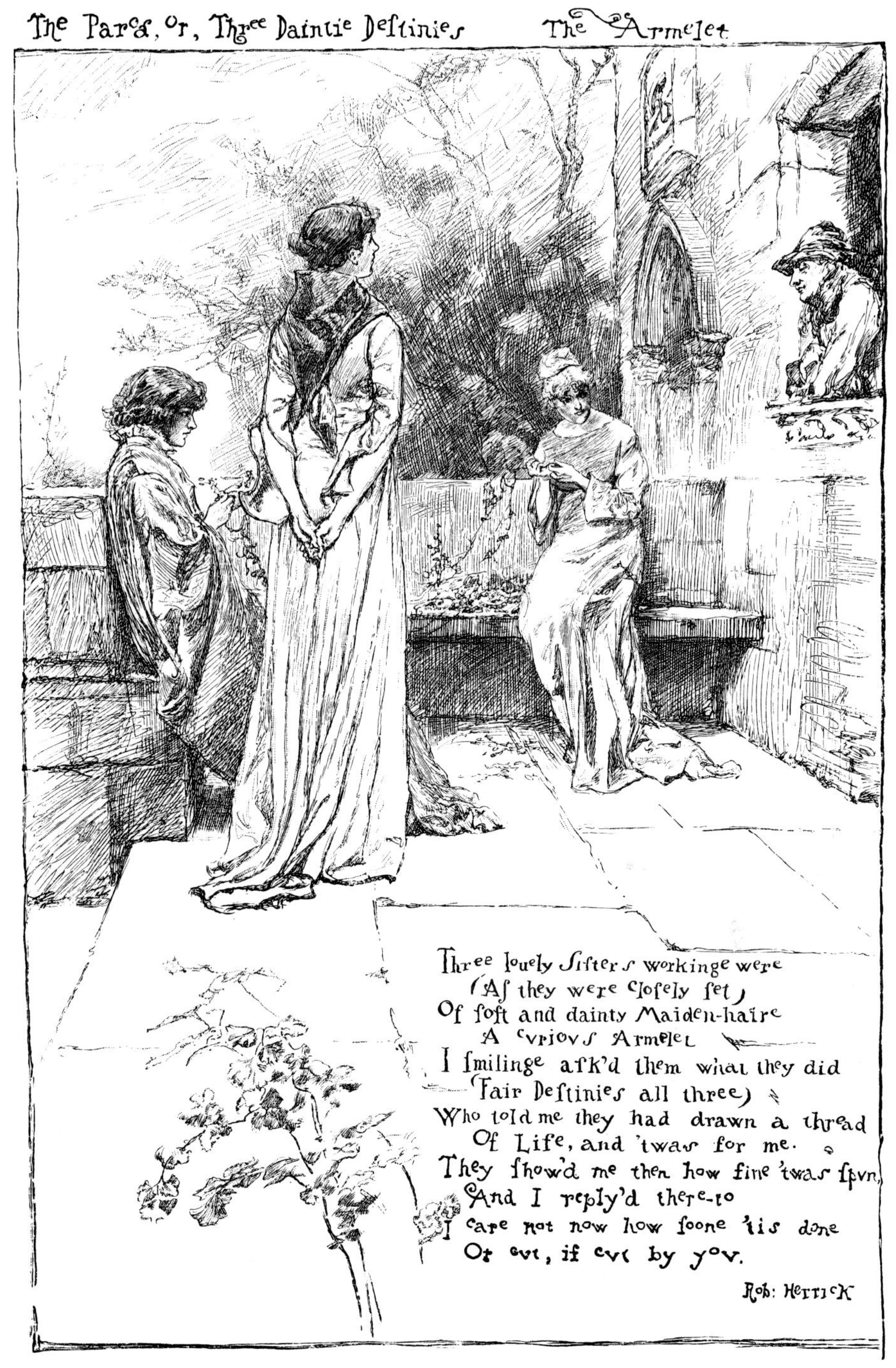

Selections From The Hesperides & Noble Numbers of Robert Herrick
"The Parcæ, or, Three Dainty Destinies: The Armilet," Harper & Brothers, 1882

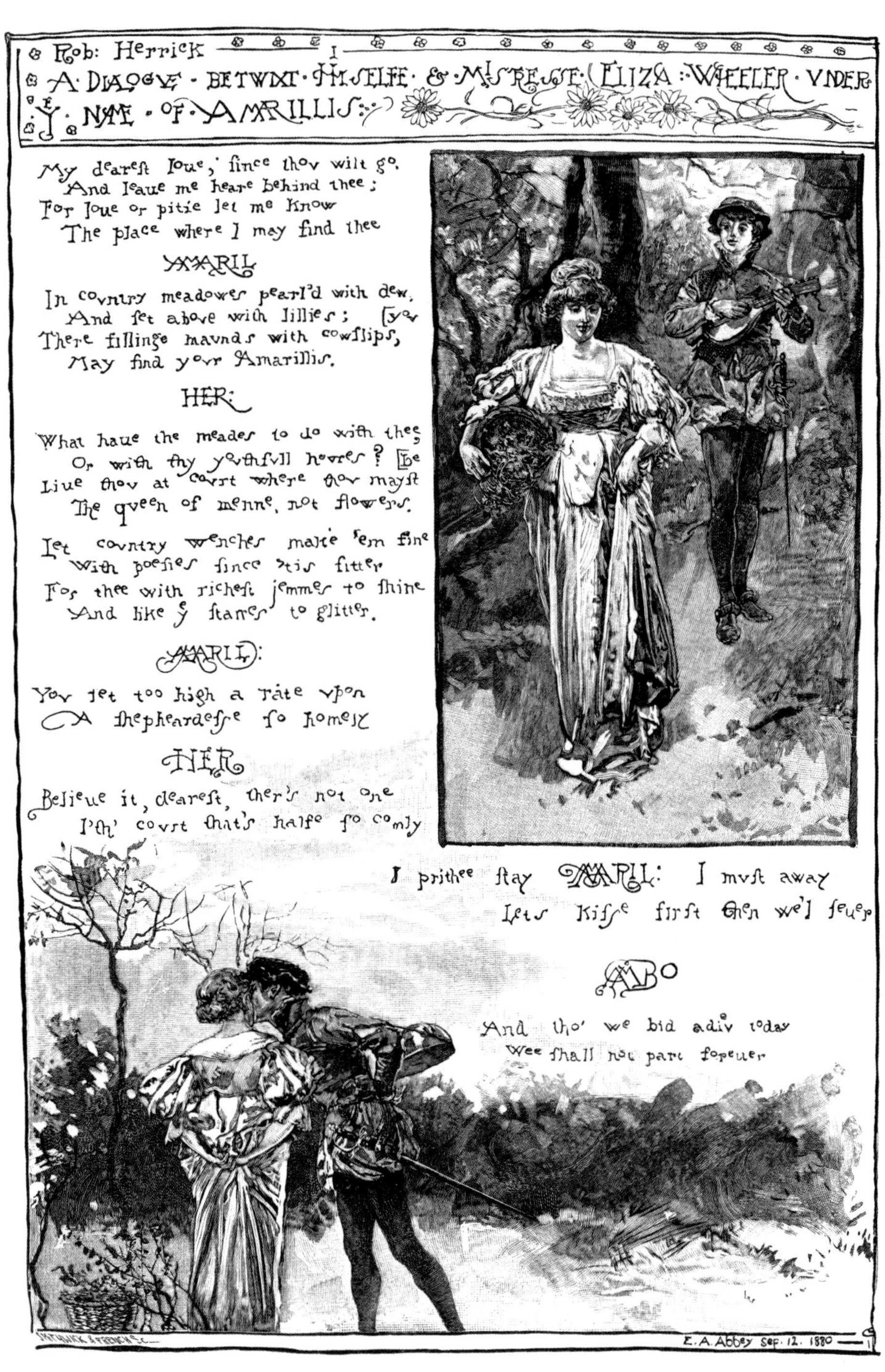

Selections From The Hesperides & Noble Numbers of Robert Herrick
"A Dialogue Betwixt Himselfe and Mistresse Eliza: Wheeler, under the Name of Amarillis,"
Harper & Brothers, 1882

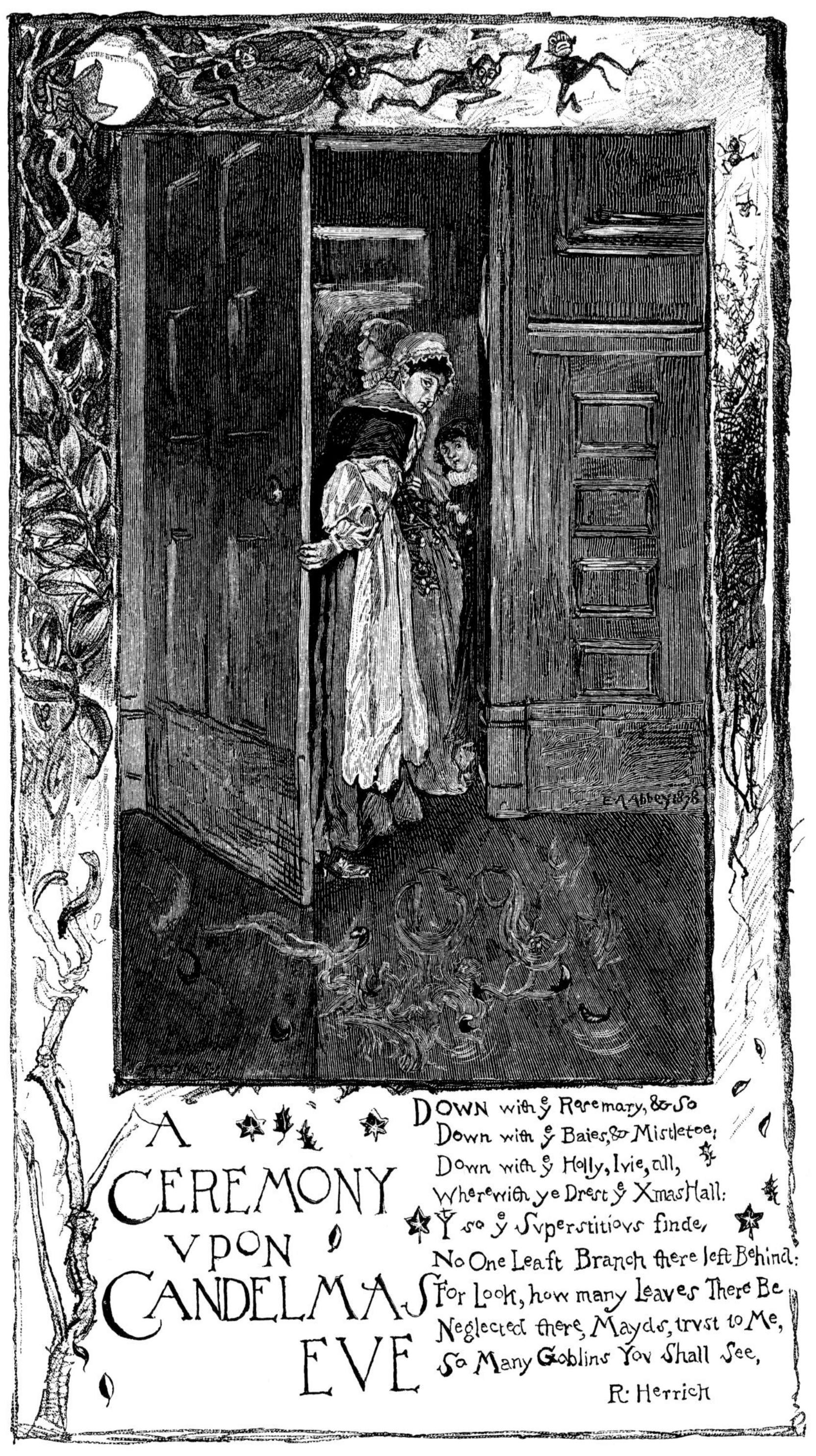

Selections From The Hesperides & Noble Numbers of Robert Herrick
"Ceremony upon Candlemas Eve," Harper & Brothers, 1882

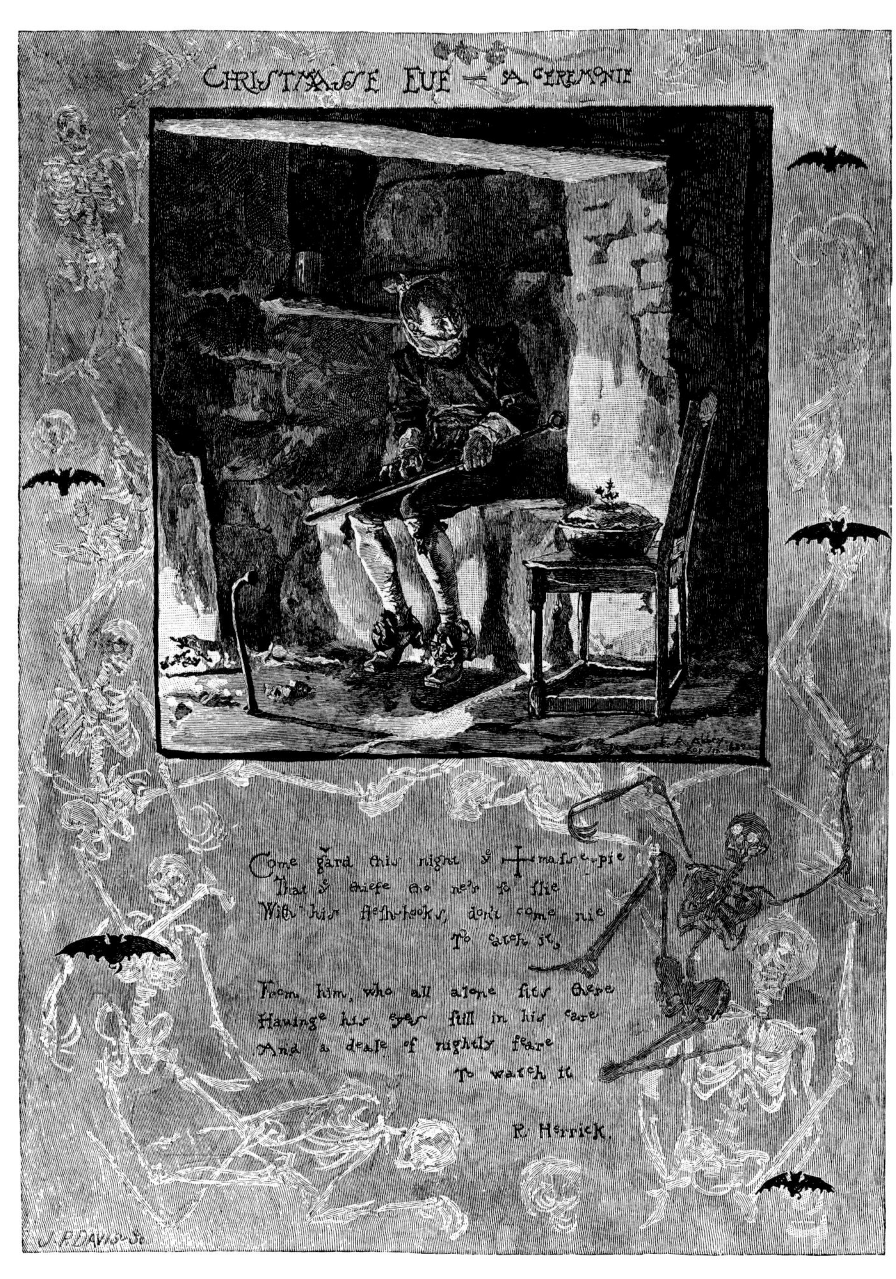

Selections From The Hesperides & Noble Numbers of Robert Herrick
"Christams Eve, another Ceremonie," Harper & Brothers, 1882

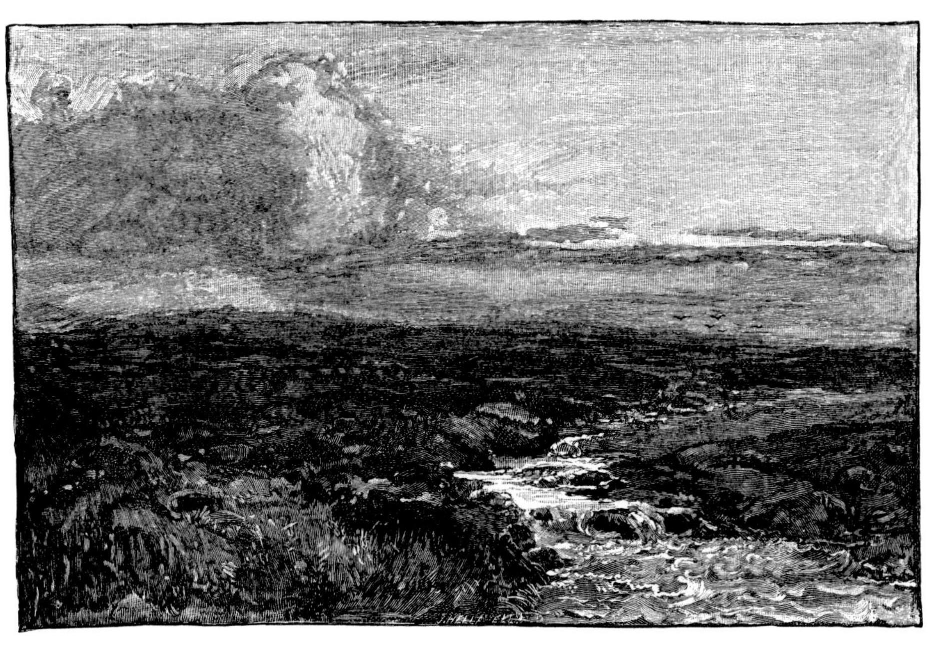

Selections From The Hesperides & Noble Numbers of Robert Herrick
"Dean-Bourn, a Rude River in Devon. By Which sometimes he lived," Harper & Brothers, 1882

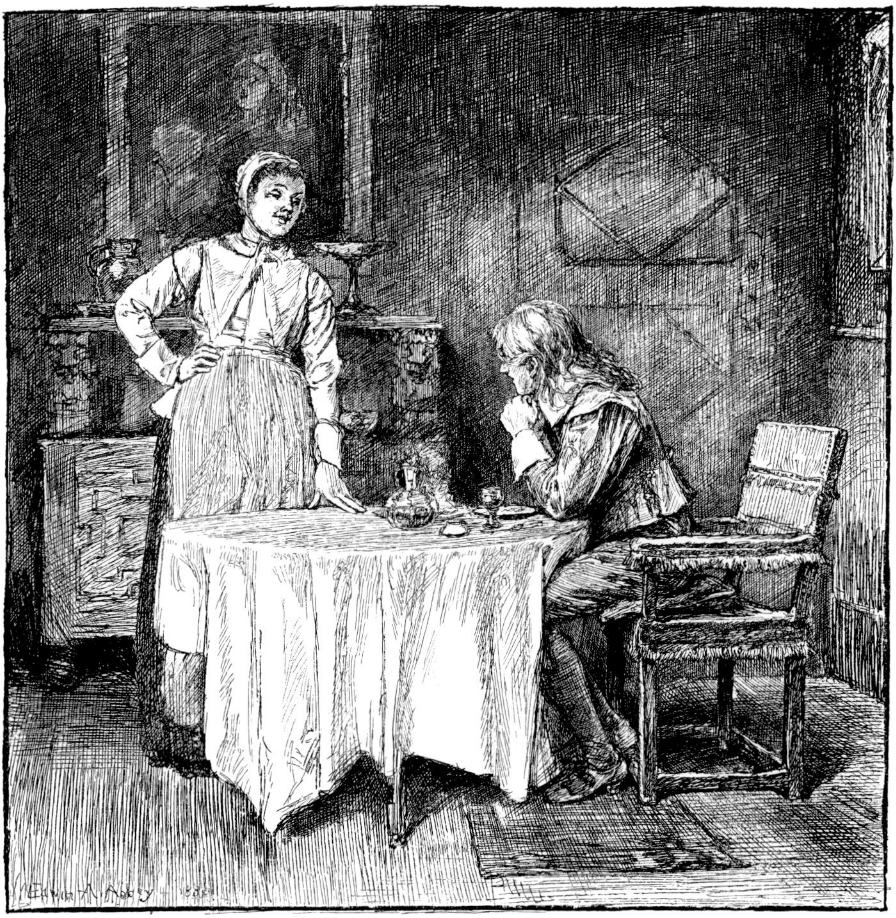

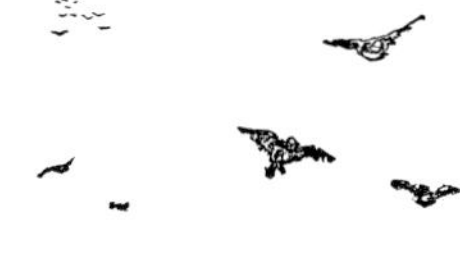

These ſvmmer-birds did with thy maſter ſtay
The times of warmth; bvt then they flew away;
Leaving their poet being now grown old
Expoſ'd to all the comming winters cold
Bvt thov, kind Prew, did'ſt with my fates abide
As well the winter's as the ſvmmer's tide
For which thy love, live with thy maſter here   R· Herrick
Not two bvt all the ſeaſons of the yeare

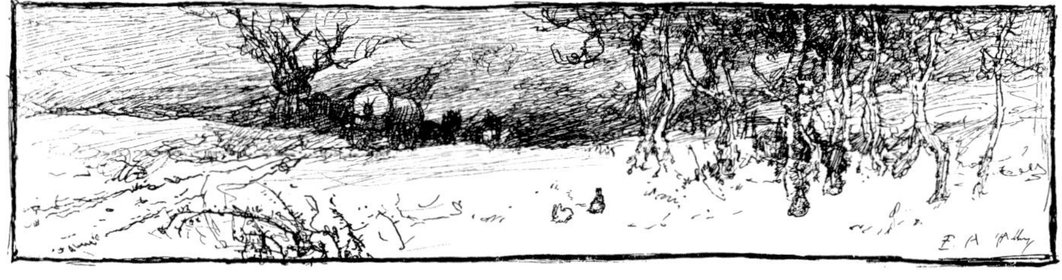

Selections From The Hesperides & Noble Numbers of Robert Herrick
"Upon Prew his maid," Harper & Brothers, 1882

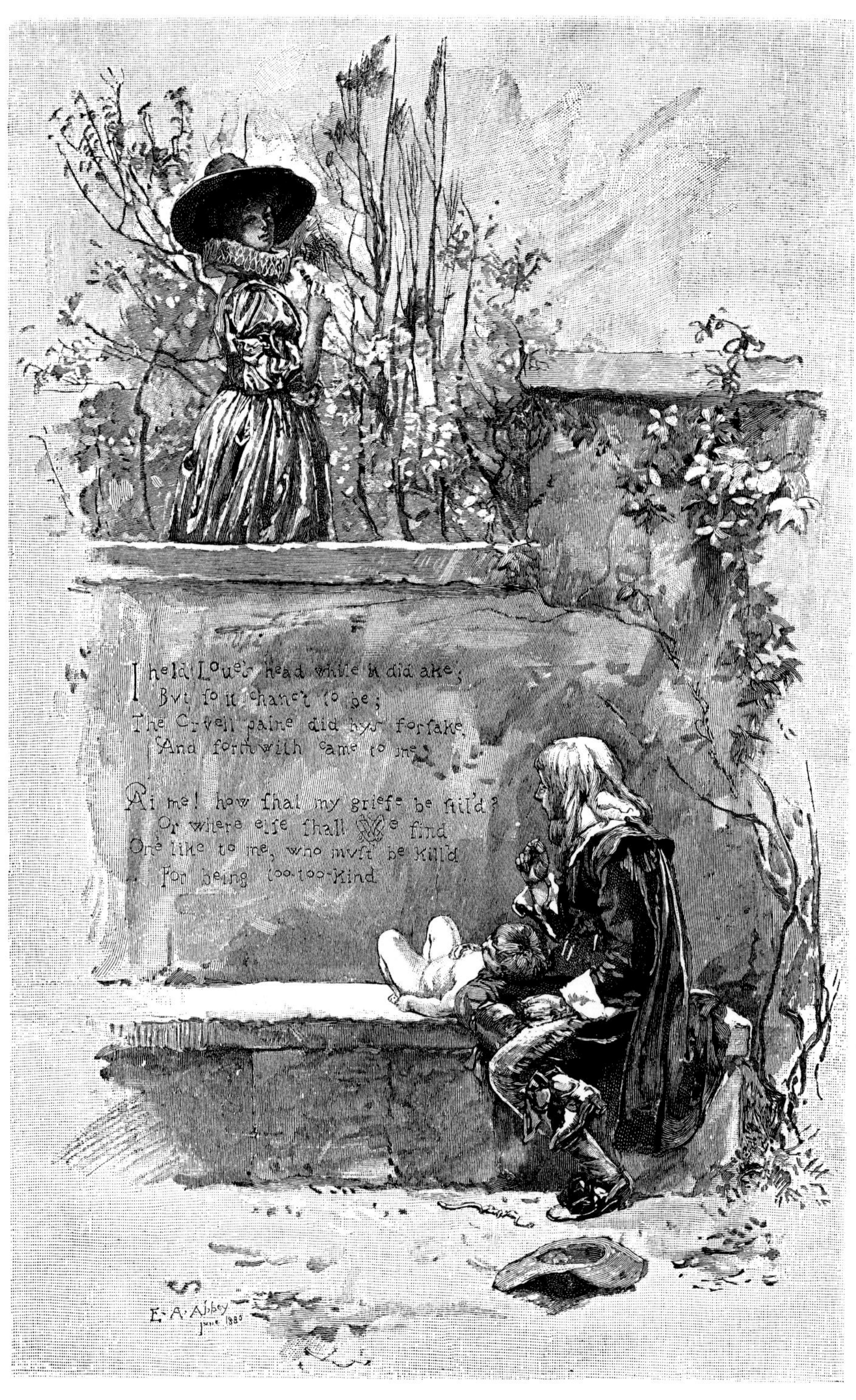

Selections From The Hesperides & Noble Numbers of Robert Herrick
"Upon Love," Harper & Brothers, 1882

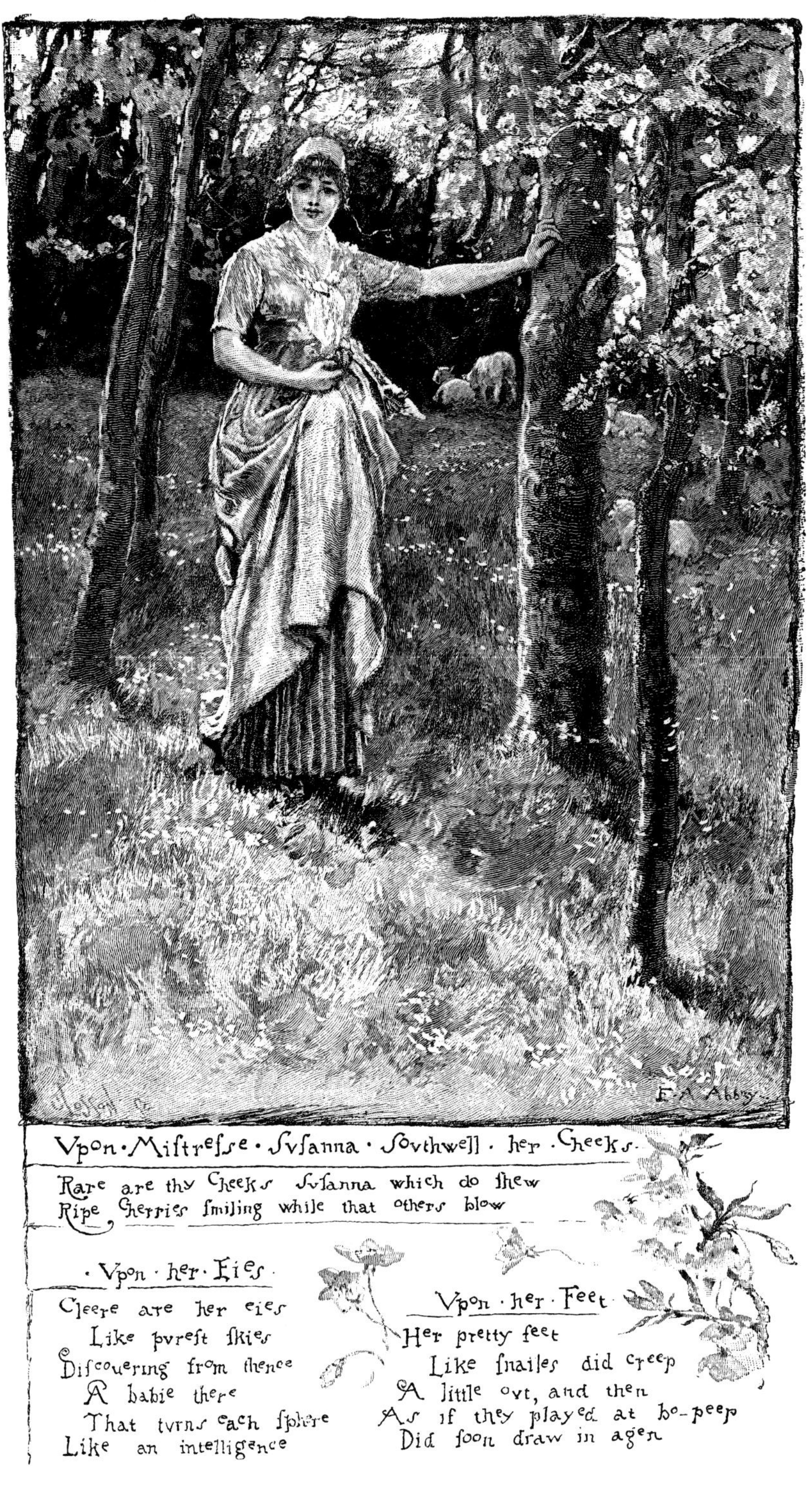

Selections From The Hesperides & Noble Numbers of Robert Herrick
"Upon Mistresse Susannah Southwell, Her Cheeks," Harper & Brothers, 1882

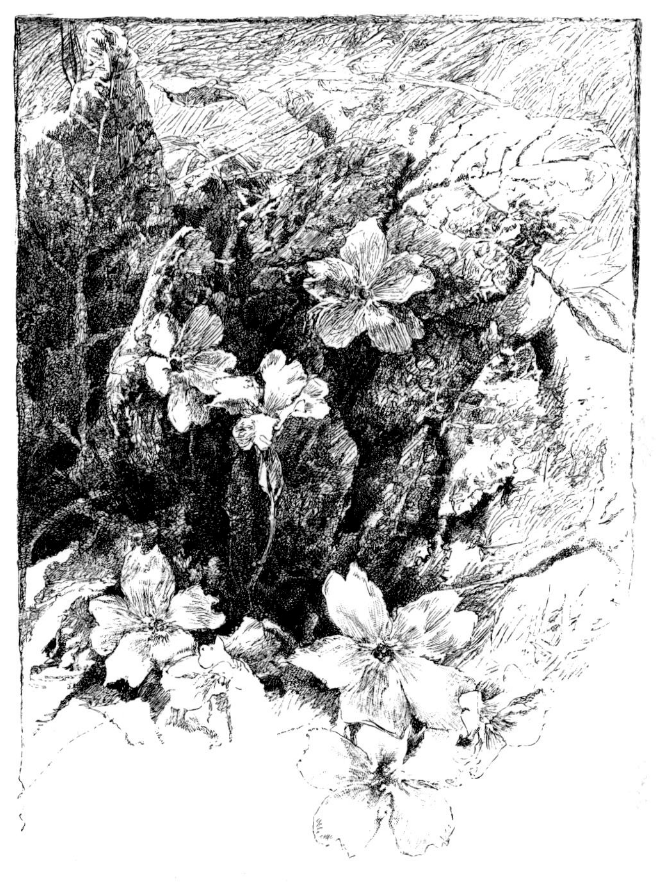

Selections From The Hesperides & Noble Numbers of Robert Herrick
"How Primroses came Green," Harper & Brothers, 1882

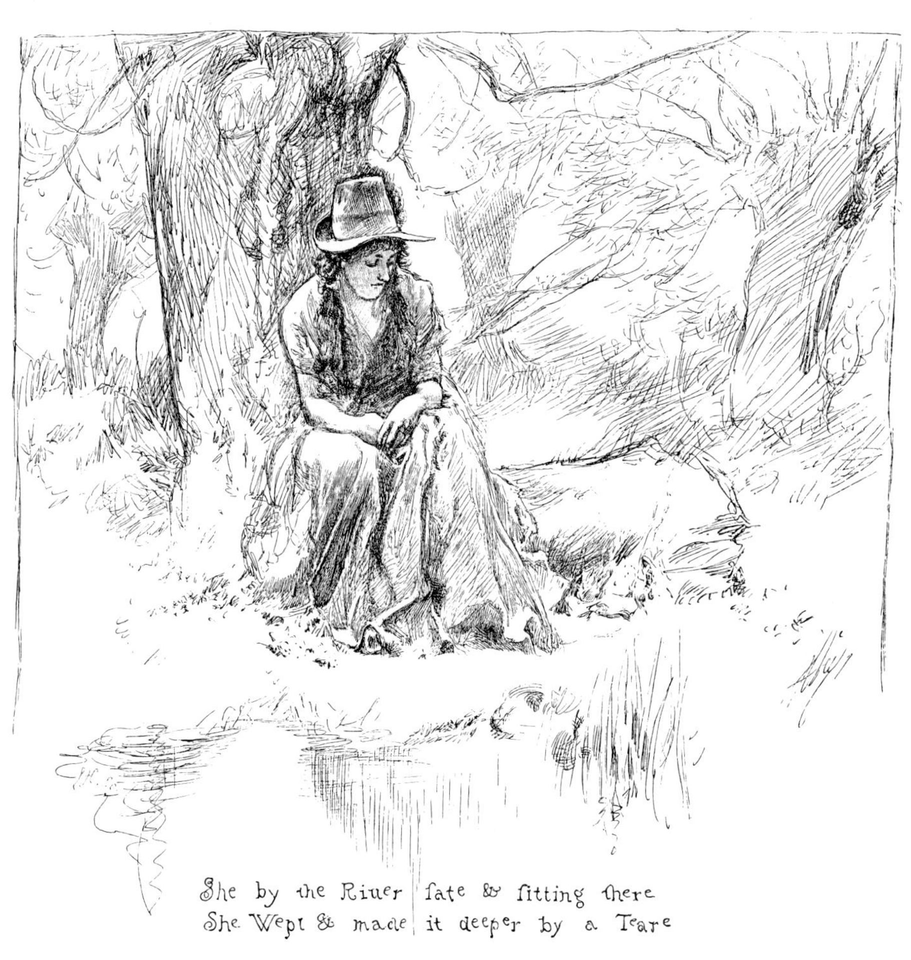

Selections From The Hesperides & Noble Numbers of Robert Herrick
"Another upon her Weeping," Harper & Brothers, 1882

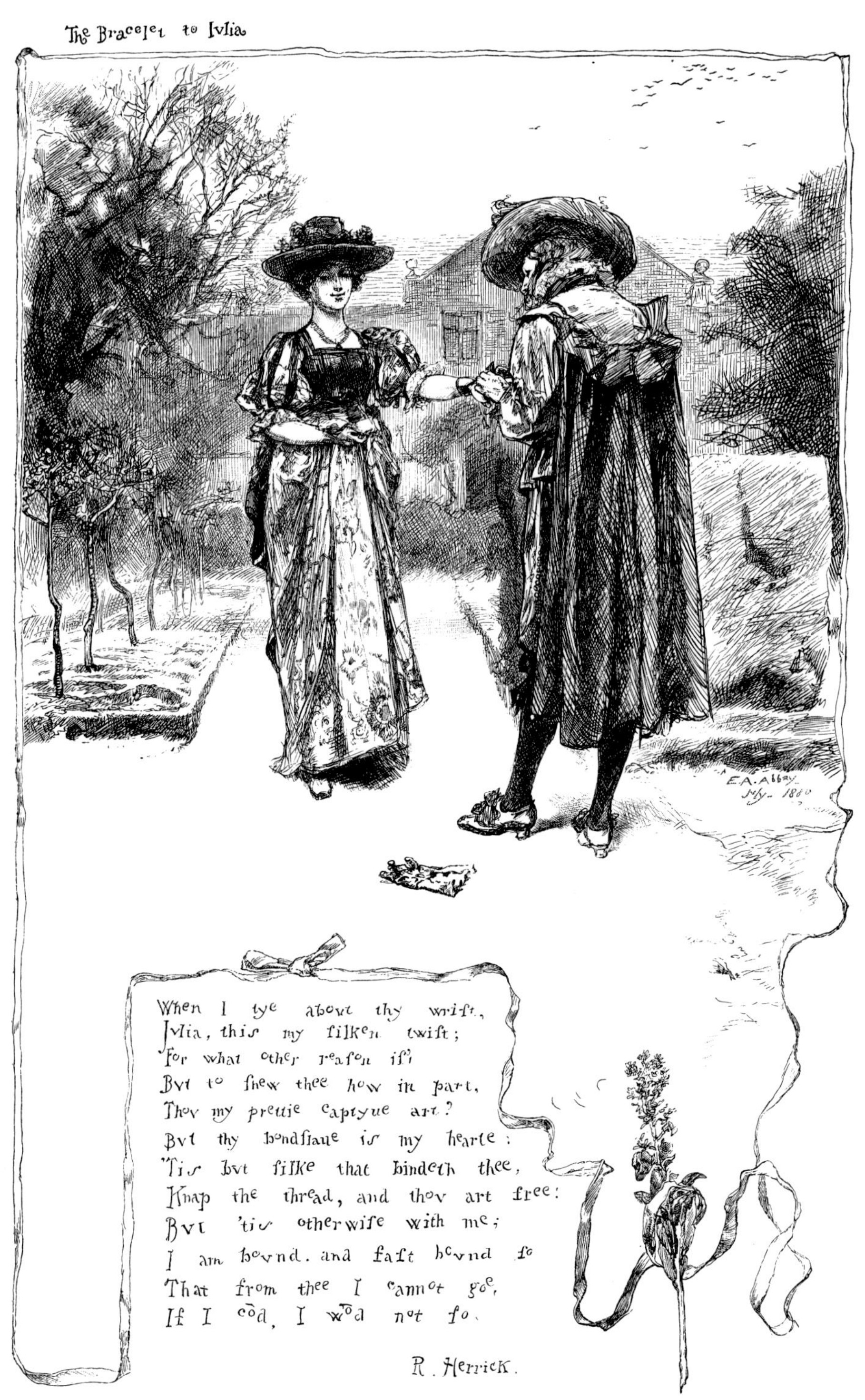

Selections From The Hesperides & Noble Numbers of Robert Herrick
"The Bracelet to Julia," Harper & Brothers, 1882
Originally published in *Harper's New Monthly Magazine*, July 1881

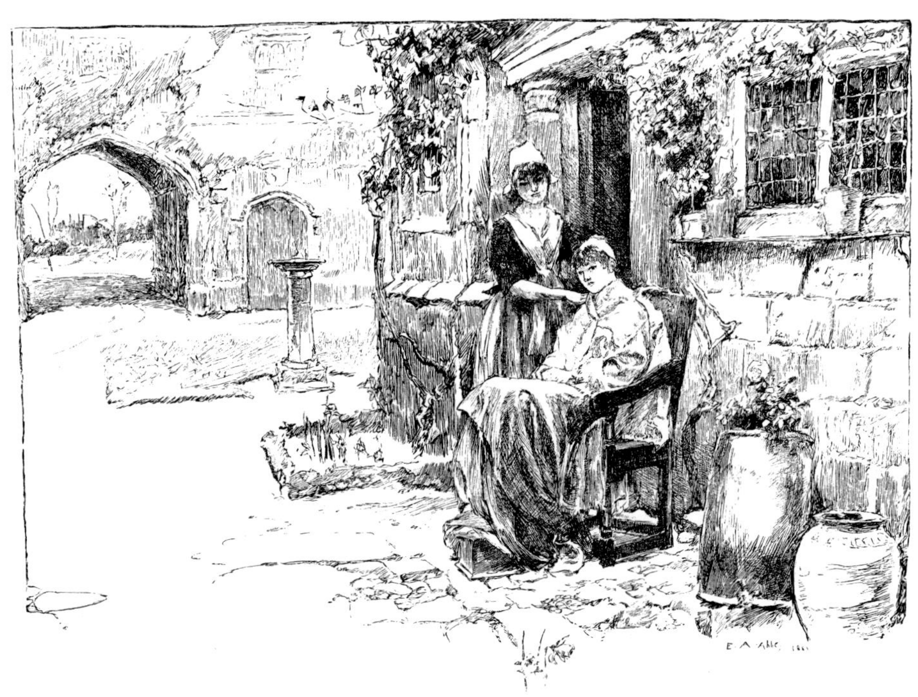

Sick is Anthea sickly is the Spring
The primrose sick, & sickly every thing
The while my deer Anthea do's but droop
The tulips lillies daffodills do stoops;
But when again sh'as got her healthfull houre
Each bending then, will rise a proper flower

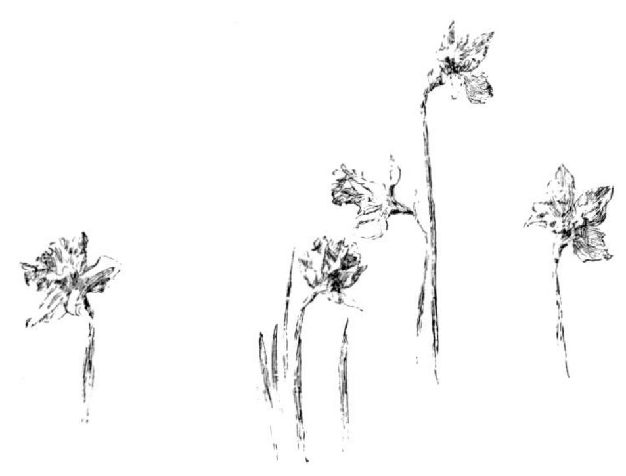

Selections From The Hesperides & Noble Numbers of Robert Herrick
"To Anthea," Harper & Brothers, 1882

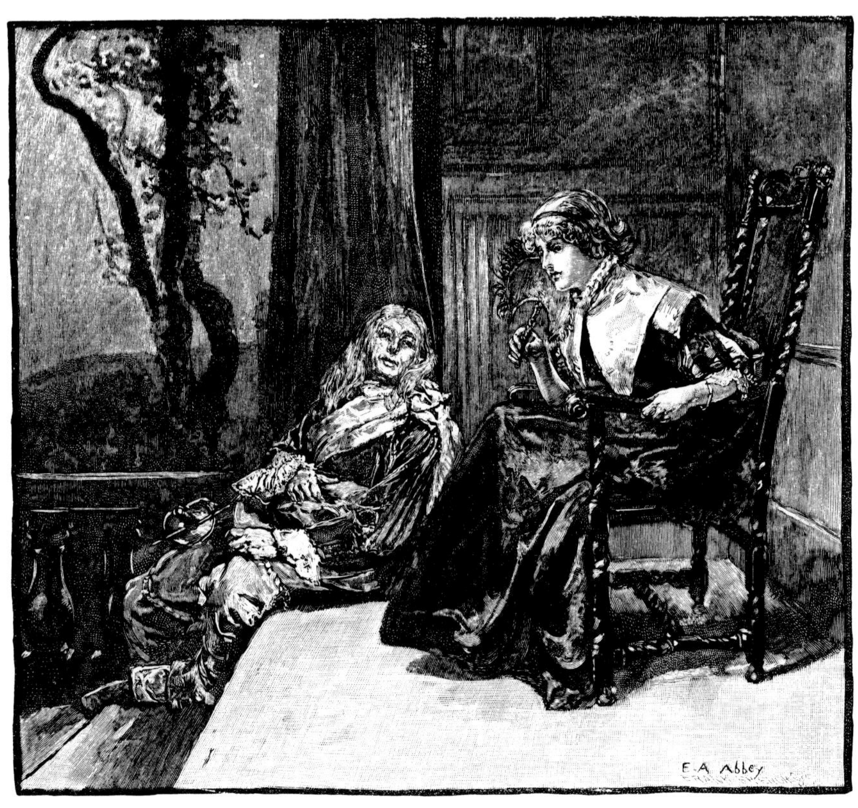

The Night-piece to Julia

Her eyes the glowe-worm lend thee
  The shootinge starres attend thee
    And the Elues also
    Whose little eyes glow
Like the sparkes of fire befriend thee

      No Will o' th' Wispe mis-light thee
      Nor Snake or Slowe worm bite thee
        But on, on thy way
        Not making a stay
    Since Ghost ther's none to affright thee

          Let not the darke thee cumber
          What thovgh the Moon do's slumber
            The starres of the night
            Will lend thee their light
        Like tapers cleare withovt nvmber

              Then Jvlia let me wooe thee
              Thvs, thvs to come vnto thee
                And when I shall meet
                Thy silu'ry feet,
            My sovle I'le povre into thee

Selections From The Hesperides & Noble Numbers of Robert Herrick
"The Night-Piece, to Julia," Harper & Brothers, 1882

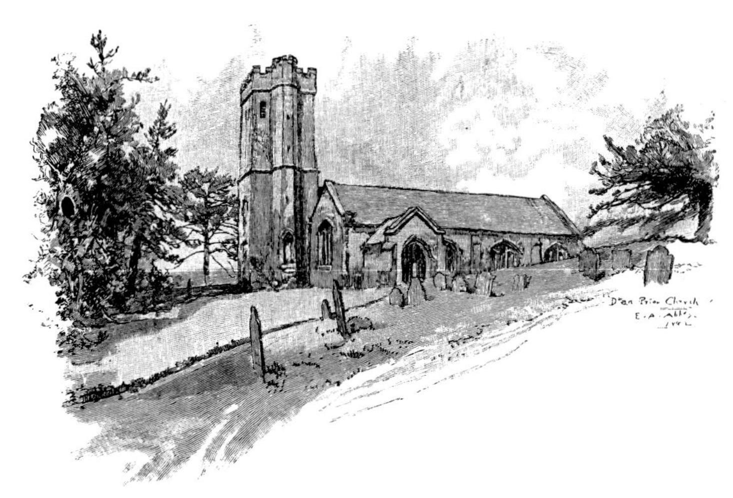

Selections From The Hesperides & Noble Numbers of Robert Herrick
"To Laurels," Harper & Brothers, 1882

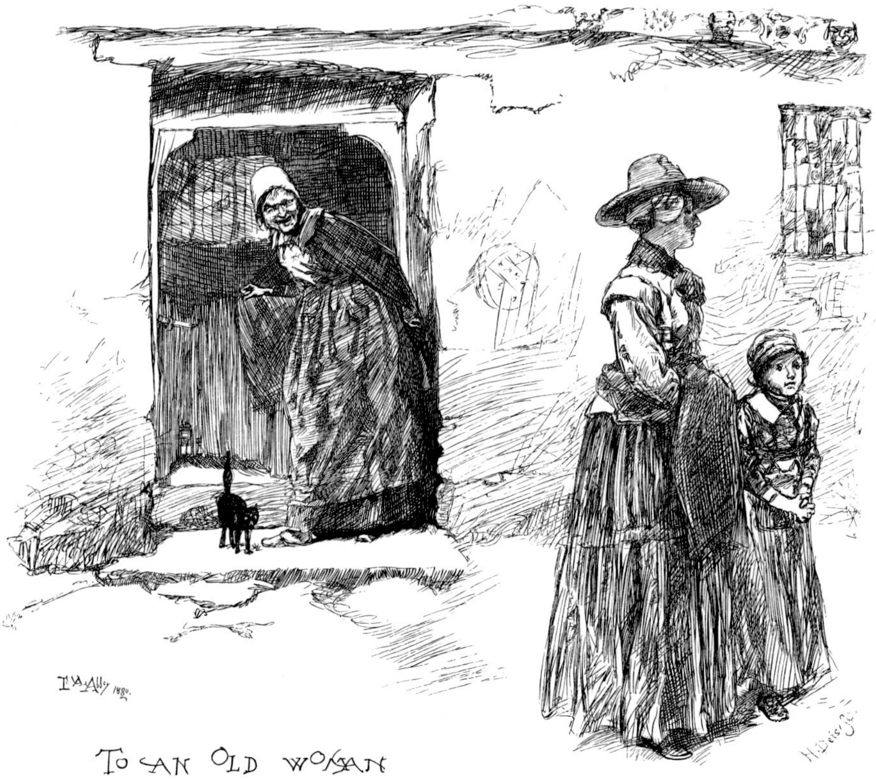

To an Old Woman

Old Widdow Prowse to do her neighbors
    euill
Wo'd gine some say her foul vnto yͤ
    deuill
Well when sh'as kild that pigge
    goose cocke or hen
What wo'd she giue to get that fowle
    againe

Rob: Hearicke.

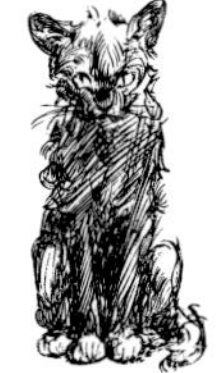

Selections From The Hesperides & Noble Numbers of Robert Herrick
"Upon an Old Woman," Harper & Brothers, 1882

Vpon Tap

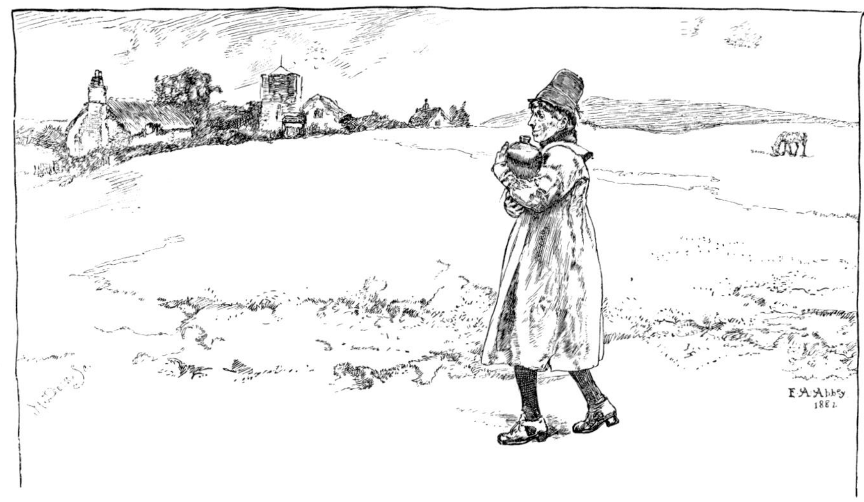

Tap (better known than trvsted) as we heare,
Sold his old Mother's spectacles for beere:
And not vnlikely; rather too than fail,
He'l sell her Eyes and Nose for Beer and Ale.

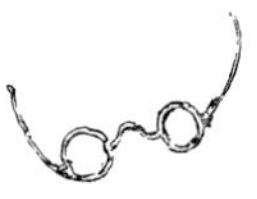

Selections From The Hesperides & Noble Numbers of Robert Herrick
"Upon Tap," Harper & Brothers, 1882

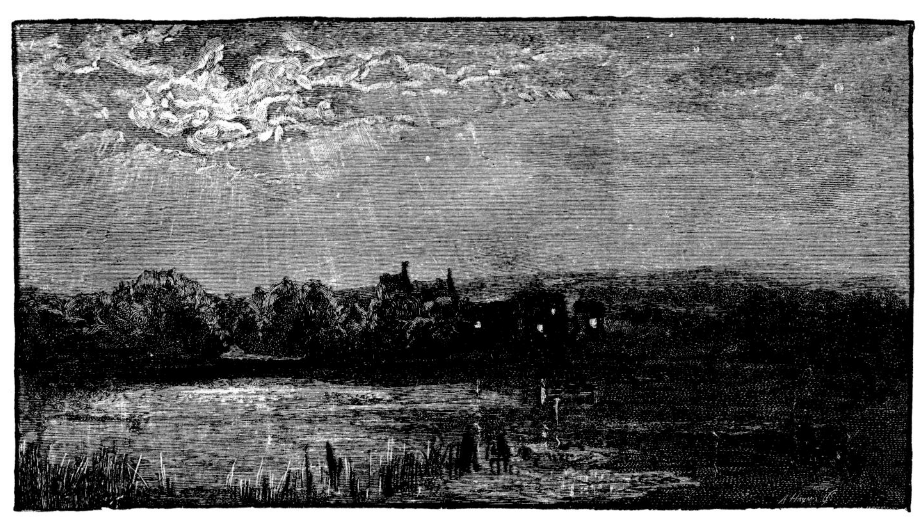

Selections From The Hesperides & Noble Numbers of Robert Herrick
"To Anthea," Harper & Brothers, 1882

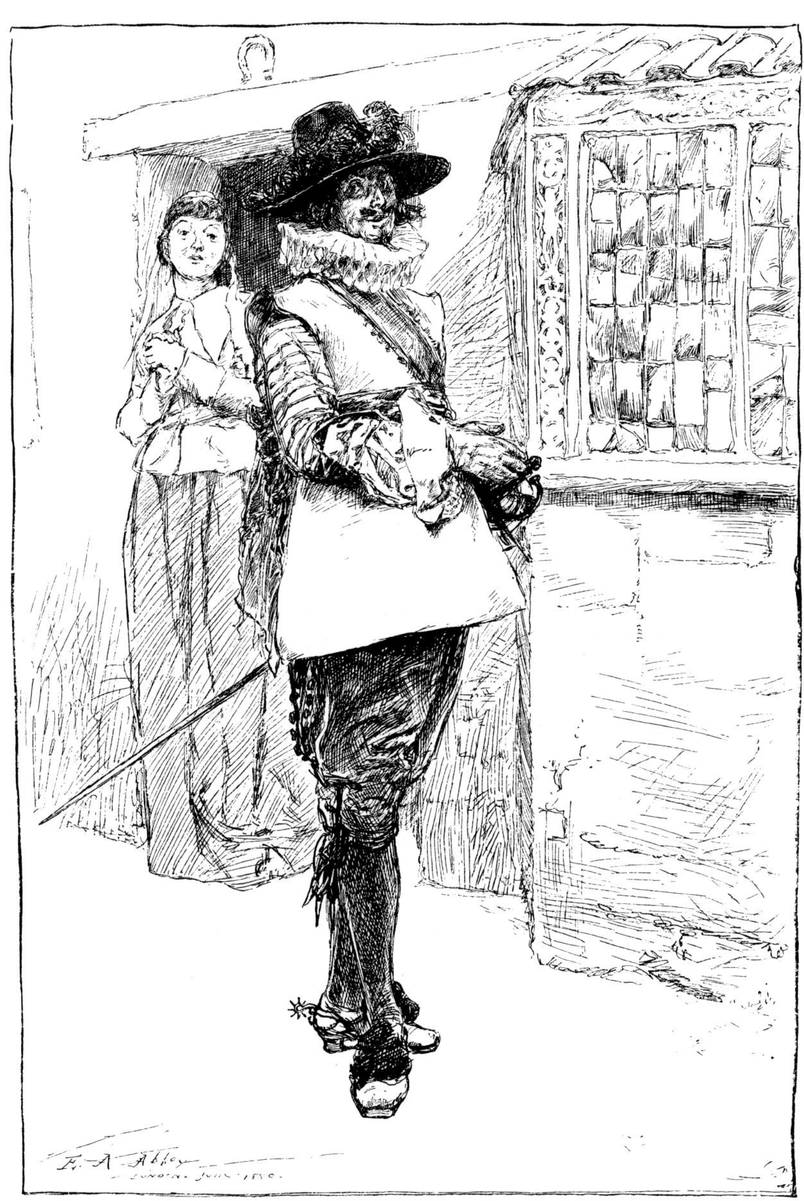

Selections From The Hesperides & Noble Numbers of Robert Herrick
"Upon Spur," Harper & Brothers, 1882

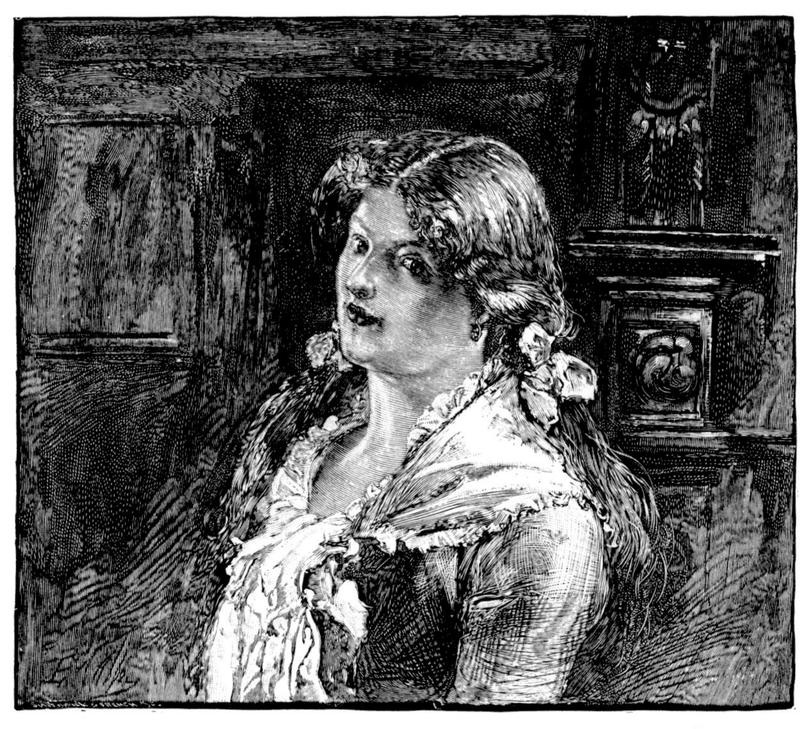

Selections From *The Hesperides & Noble Numbers of Robert Herrick*
"To Dianeme," Harper & Brothers, 1882

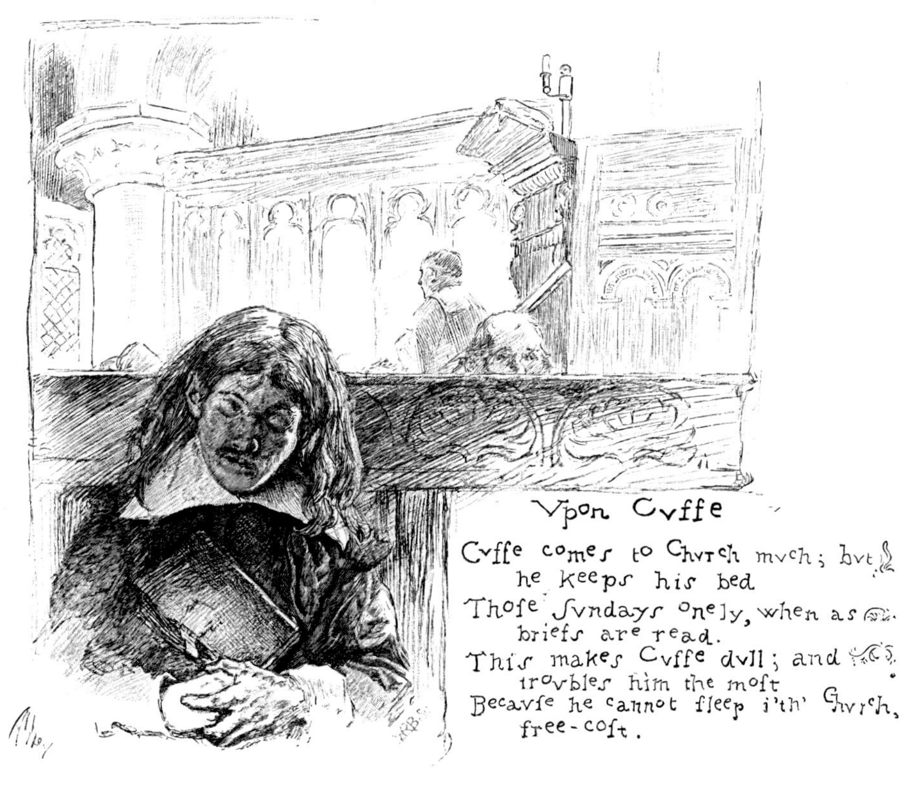

Selections From The Hesperides & Noble Numbers of Robert Herrick
"Upon Cuff. Epig.," Harper & Brothers, 1882

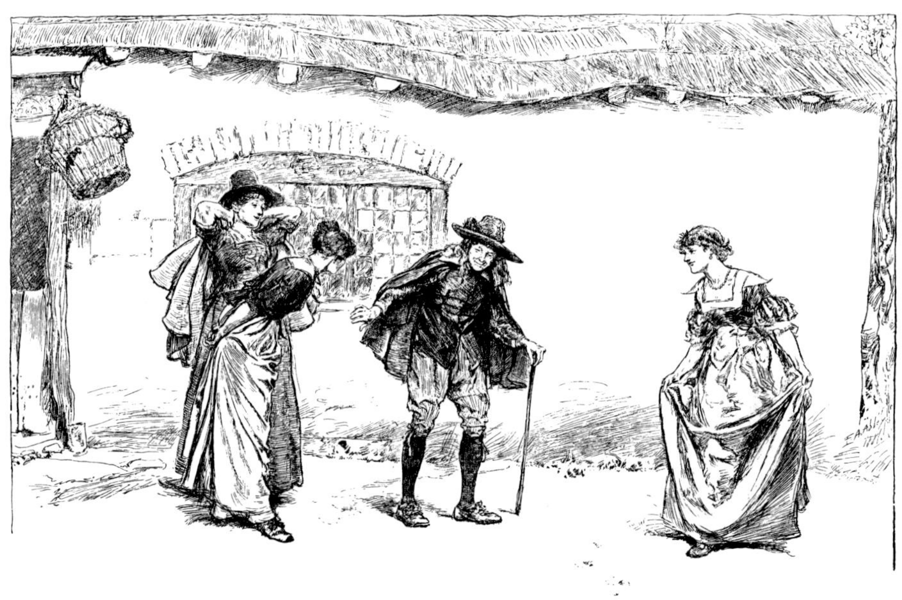

Selections From The Hesperides & Noble Numbers of Robert Herrick
"To his Girles who would have him Sportfull," Harper & Brothers, 1882

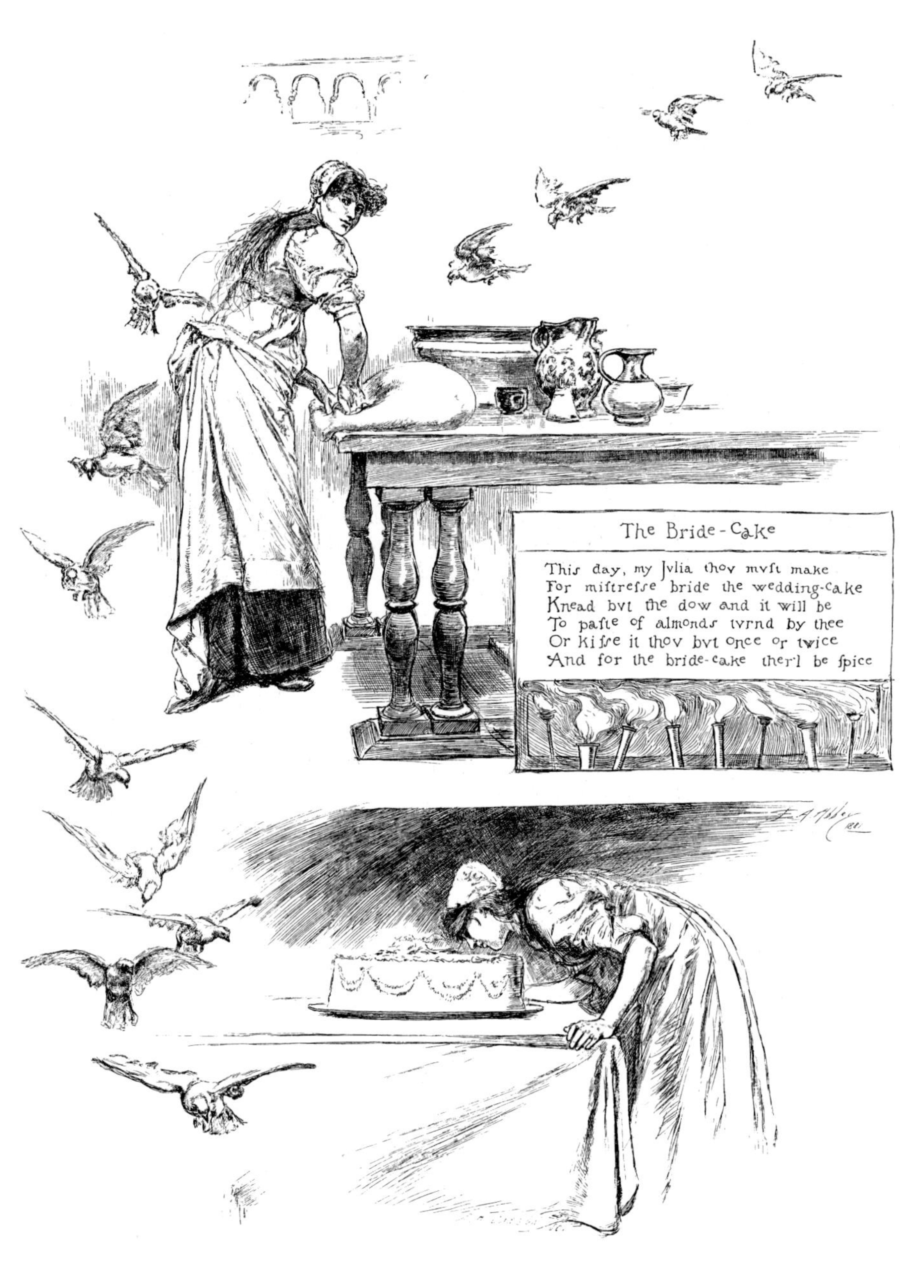

Selections From The Hesperides & Noble Numbers of Robert Herrick
"The Bride-Cake," Harper & Brothers, 1882

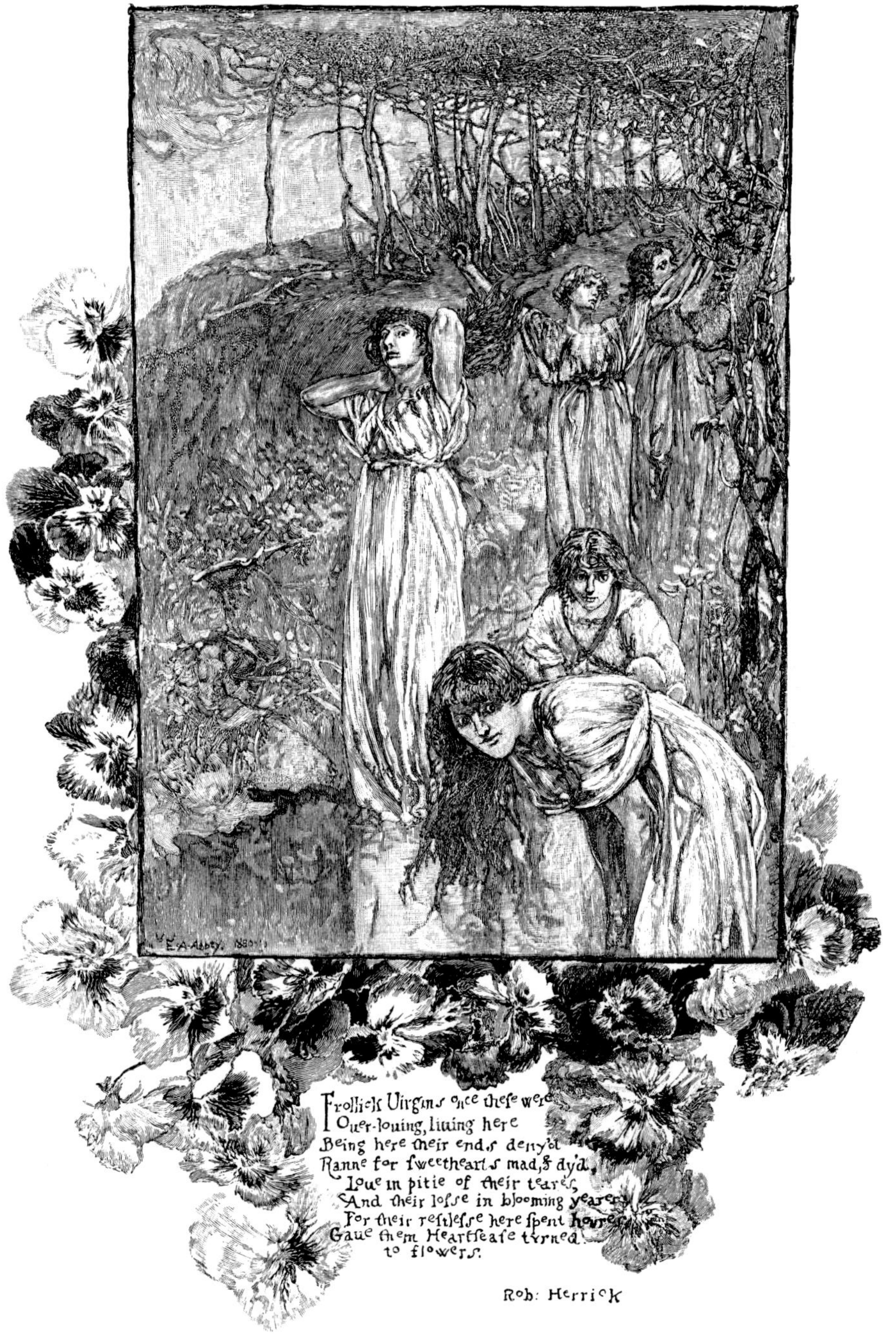

Selections From The Hesperides & Noble Numbers of Robert Herrick
"How Pansies or Heats-Esse came first," Harper & Brothers, 1882

On Chloris Walkinge in y̆ Snowe

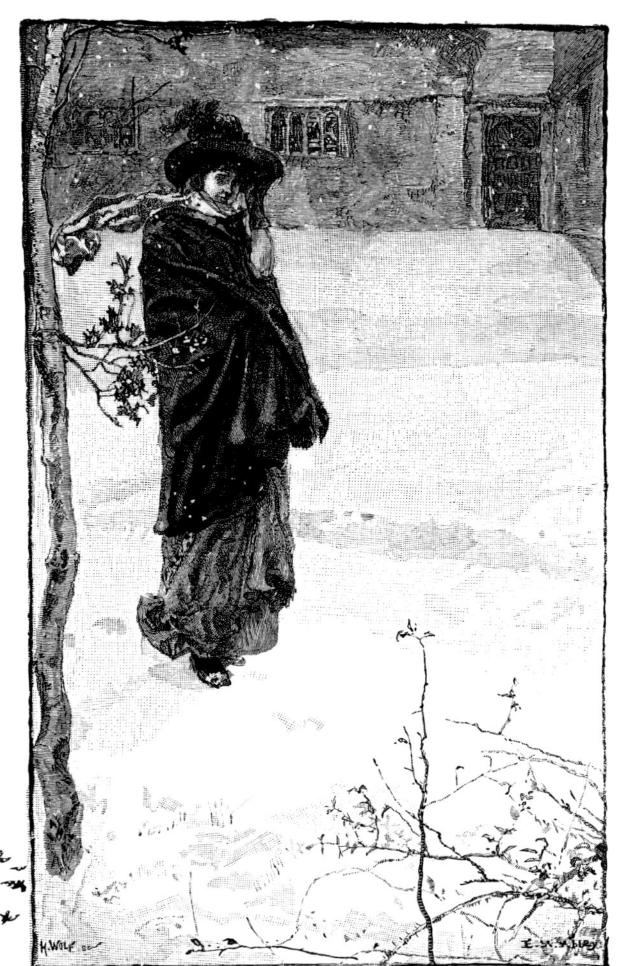

Selections From The Hesperides & Noble Numbers of Robert Herrick
"On Chloris Walking in the Snow," Harper & Brothers, 1882

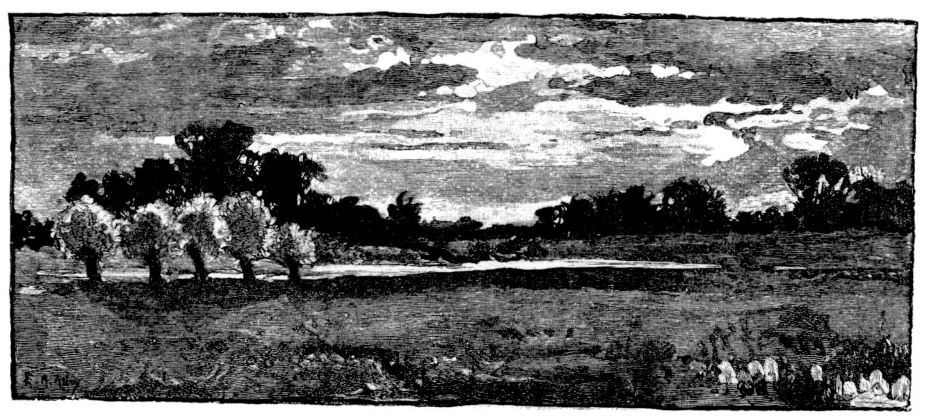

Selections From The Hesperides & Noble Numbers of Robert Herrick
"How Violets came Blew," Harper & Brothers, 1882

Upon Blanch

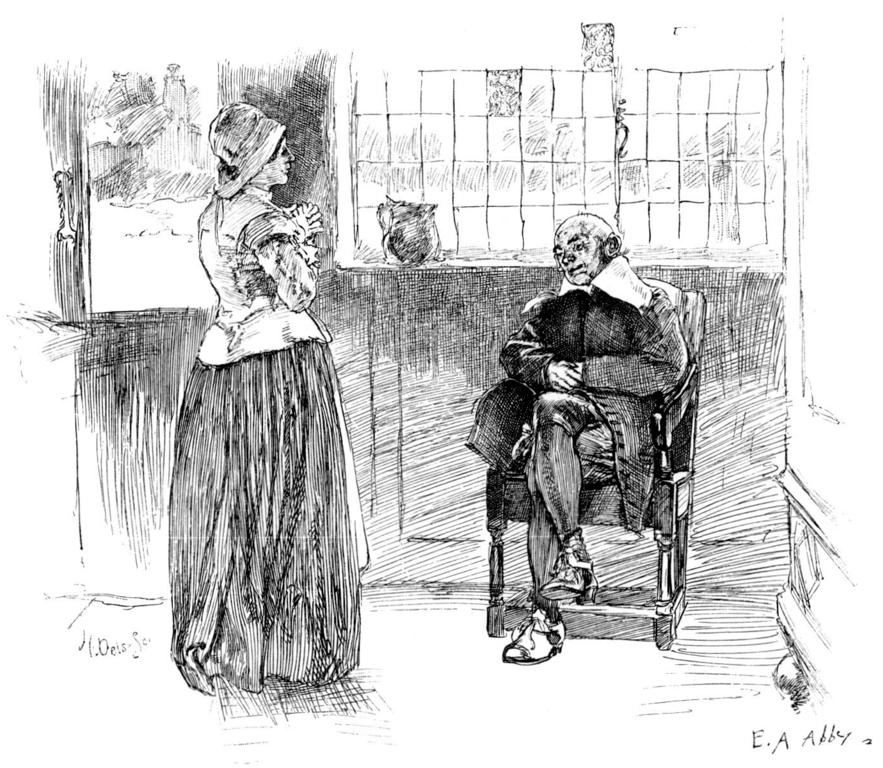

Blanch swears her Husbands lousy; when a scald
    Has blear'd his eyes: besides, his head is bald
Next, his wilde Eares like lethern wings full spread
Flutter to flie and beare away his head

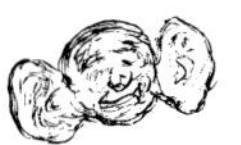

Selections From The Hesperides & Noble Numbers of Robert Herrick
"Upon Blanch," Harper & Brothers, 1882

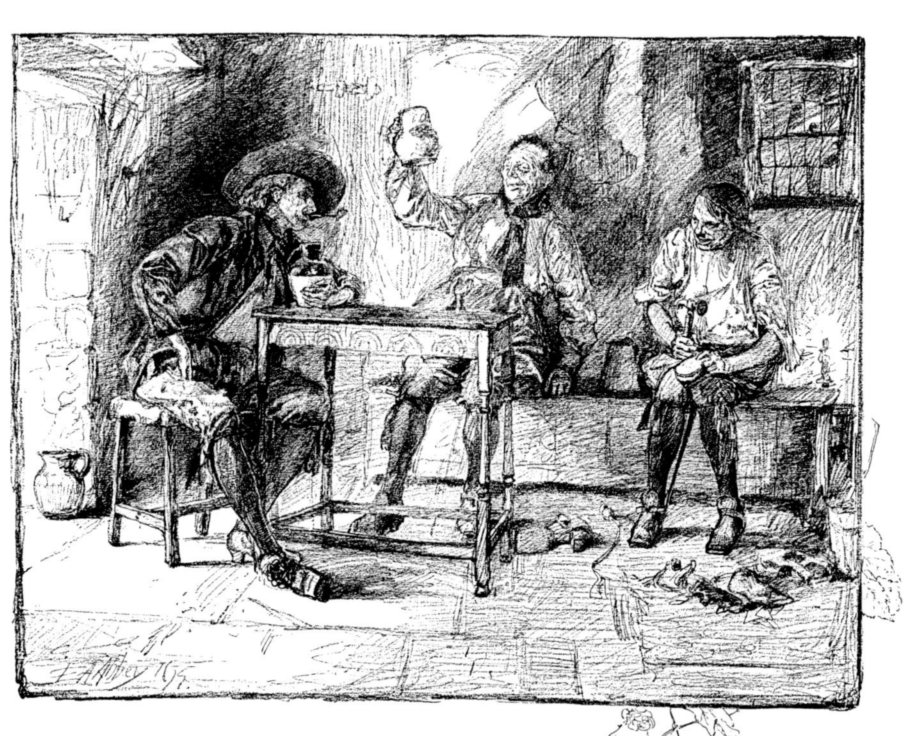

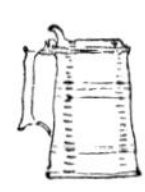

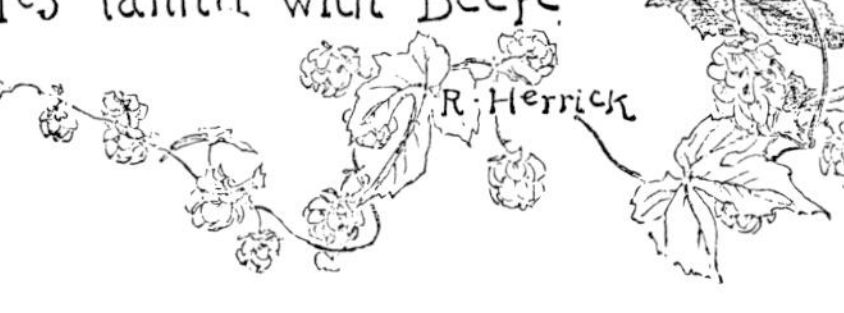

Selections From The Hesperides & Noble Numbers of Robert Herrick
"The Coblers Catch," Harper & Brothers, 1882

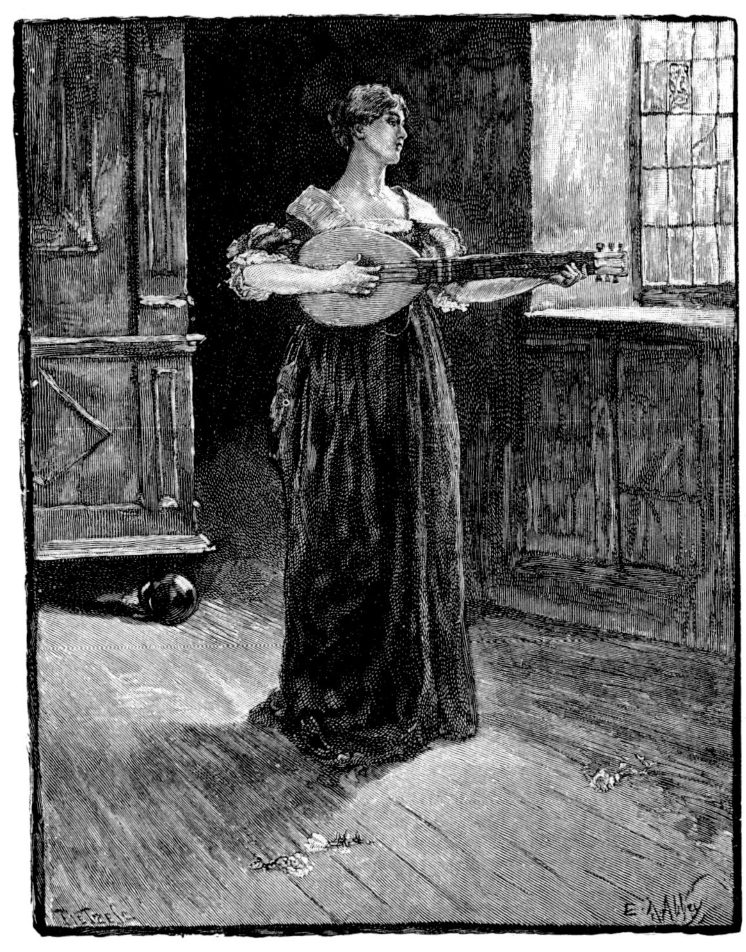

Selections From The Hesperides & Noble Numbers of Robert Herrick
"To Musique, to Becalme his Fever," Harper & Brothers, 1882

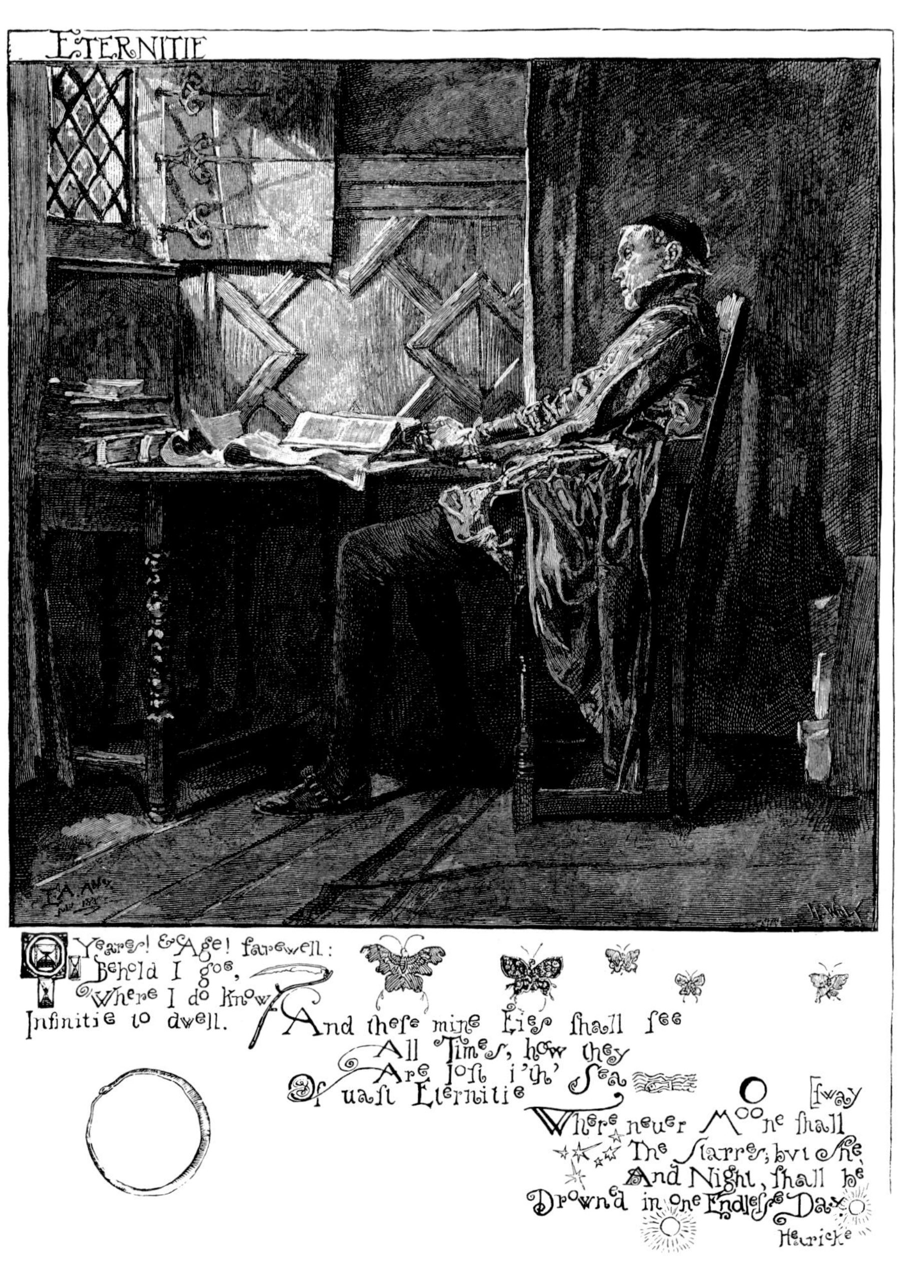

Selections From The Hesperides & Noble Numbers of Robert Herrick
"Eternitie," Harper & Brothers, 1882

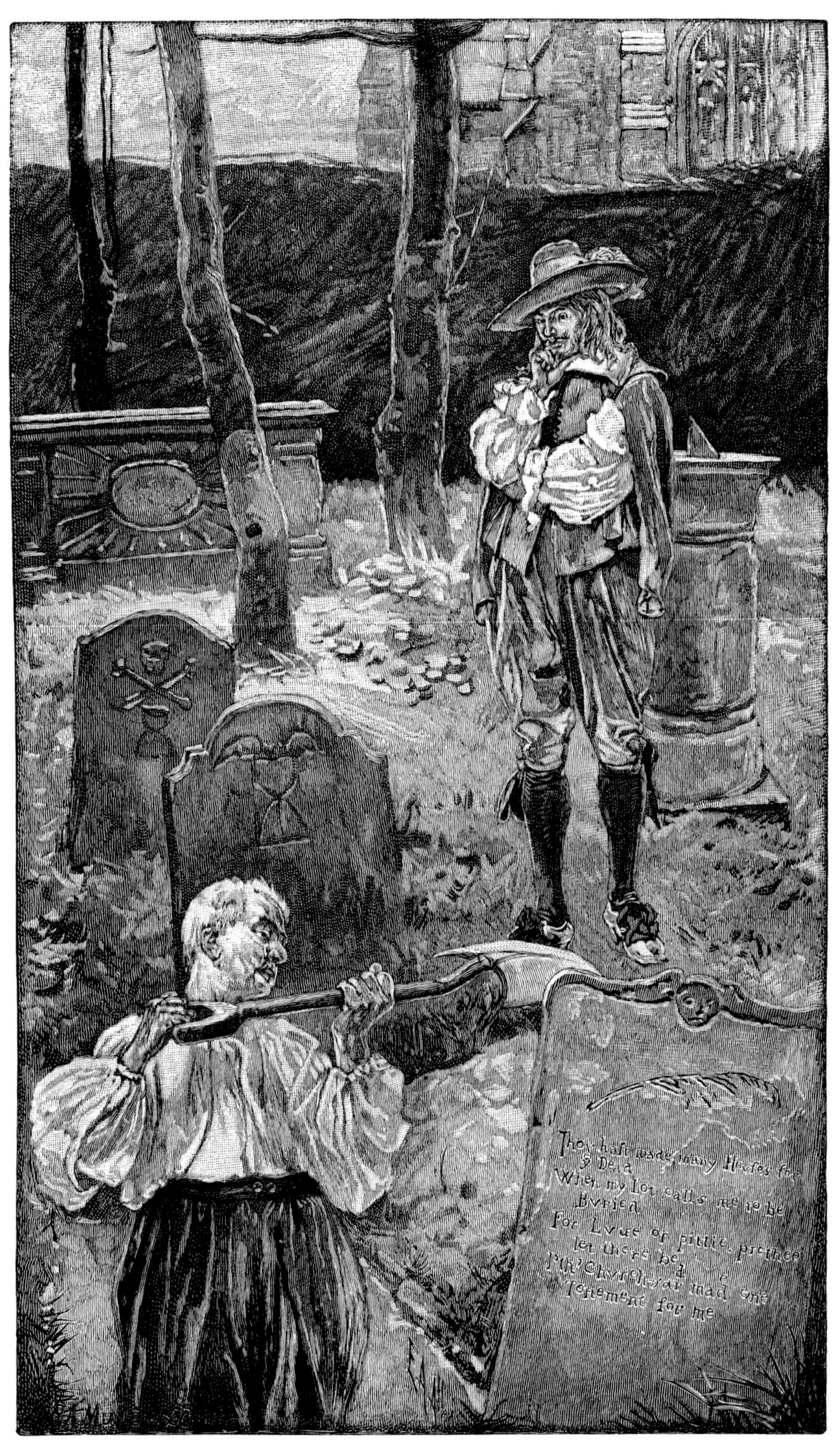

Selections From The Hesperides & Noble Numbers of Robert Herrick
"The Bed-man or Grave-Maker," Harper & Brothers, 1882

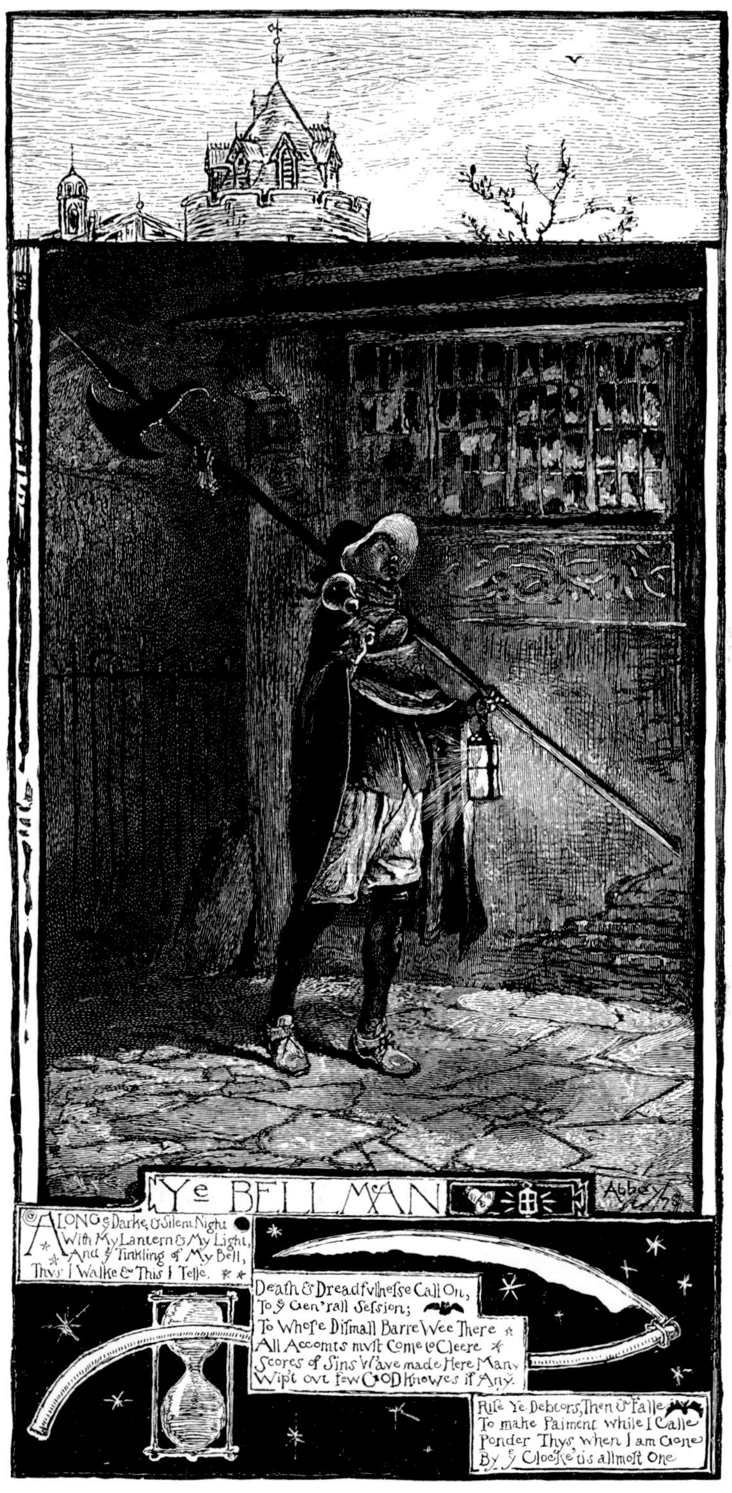

Selections From The Hesperides & Noble Numbers of Robert Herrick
"The Bell-Man," Harper & Brothers, 1882

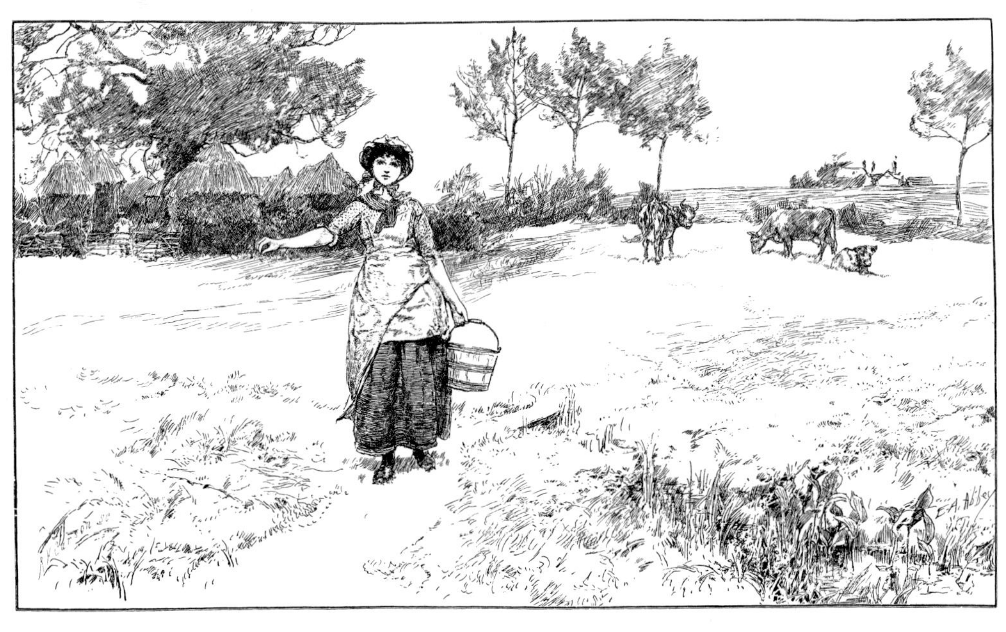

Harper's New Monthly Magazine, December 1883
"The Gossip about the West Highlanders — Milk Maid"

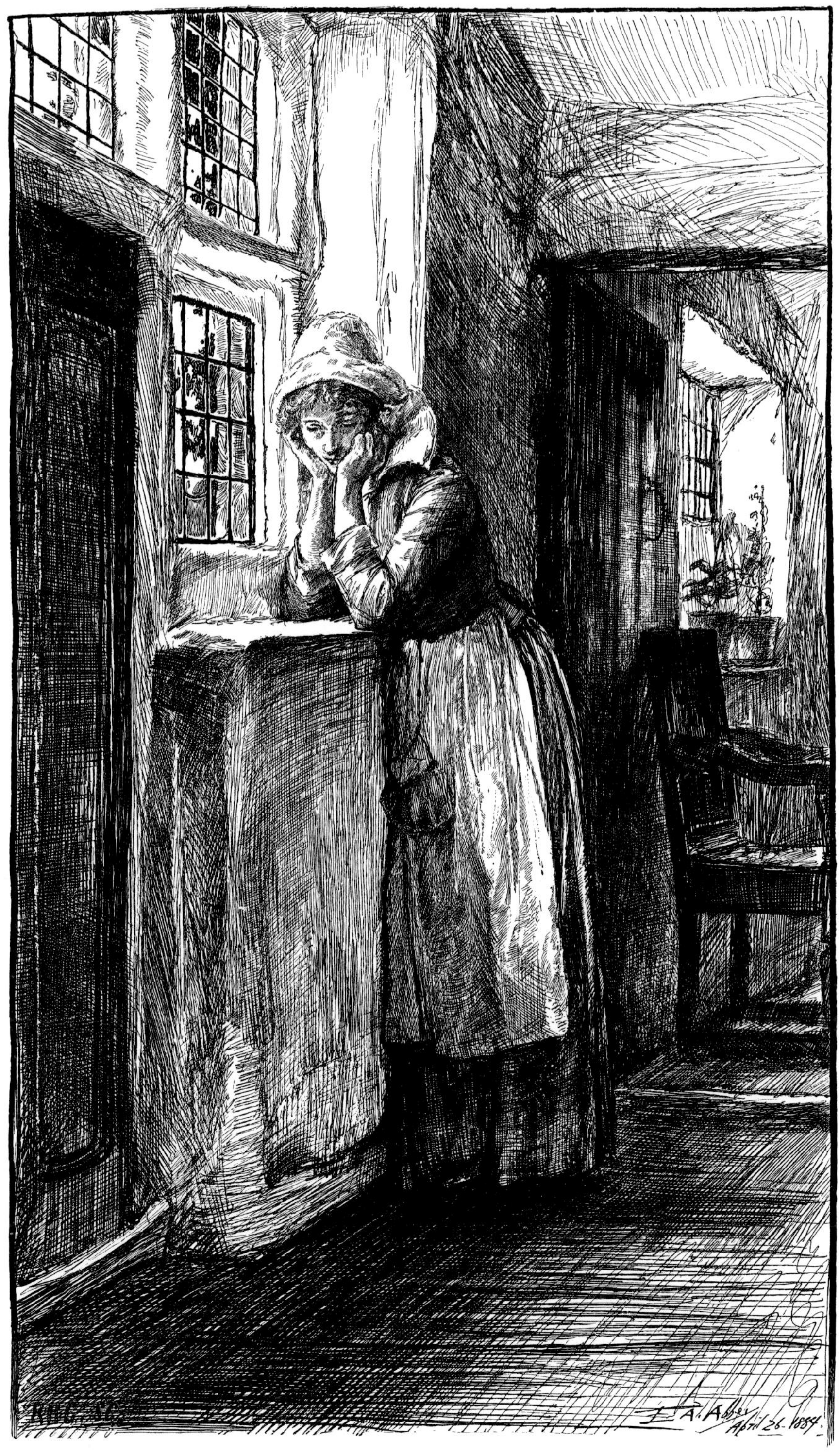

Judith.

Harper's New Monthly Magazine, October 1884
"Judith Shakespeare"

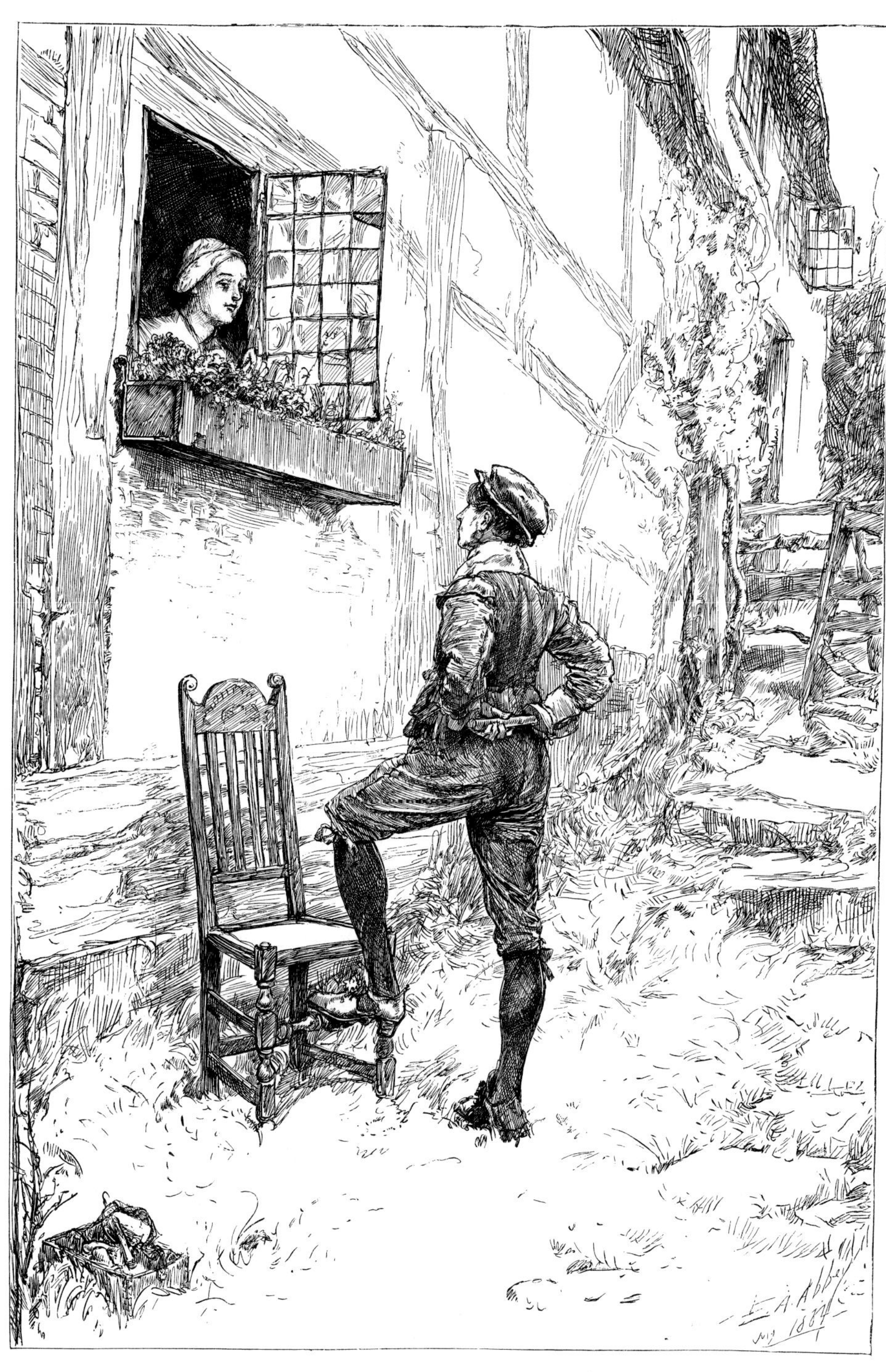

"'And her thanks to whom?' said Prudence, smiling."

Harper's New Monthly Magazine, November 1884
"Judith Shakespeare"

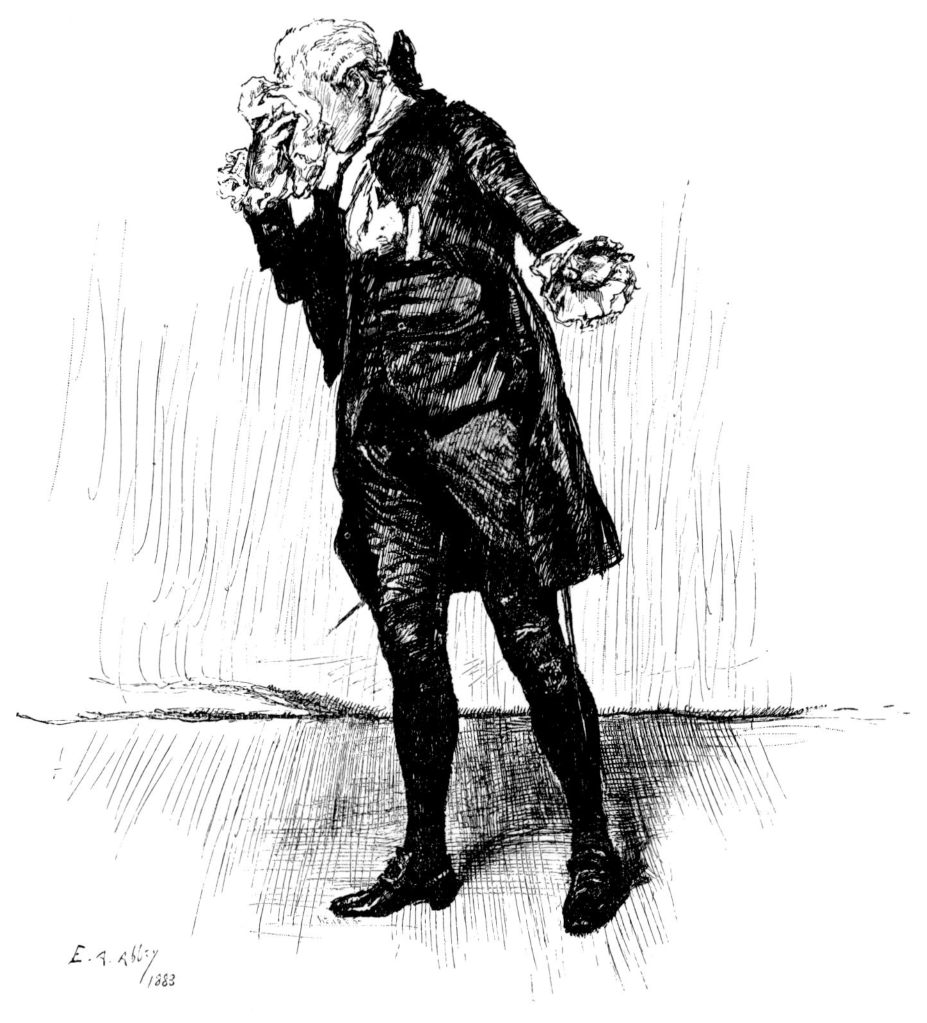

Prologue.

Harper's New Monthly Magazine, December 1884
"She Stoops to Conquer"

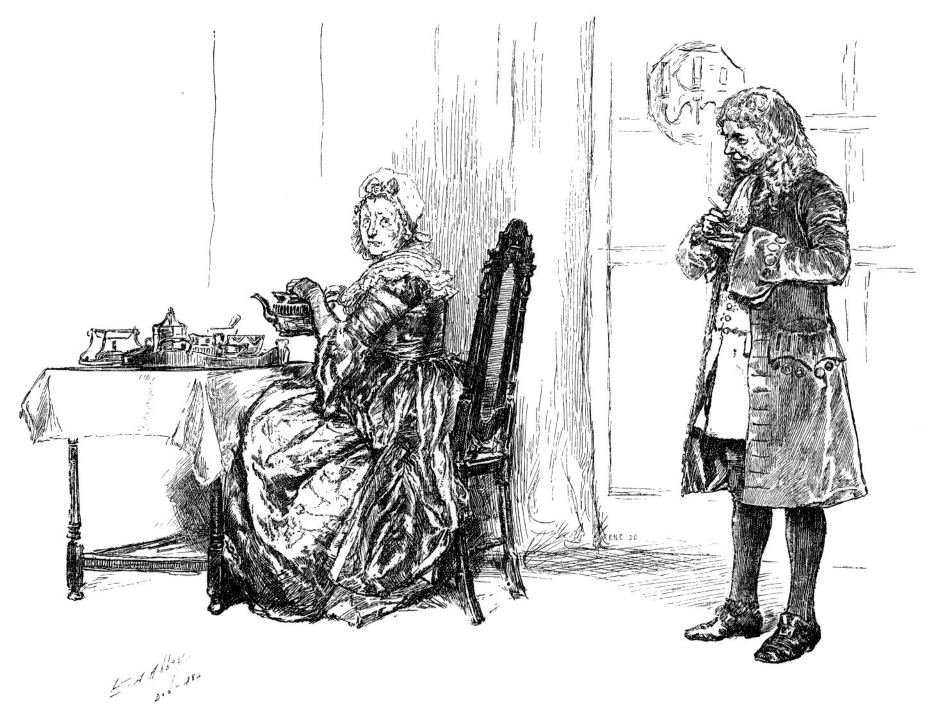

Act First.

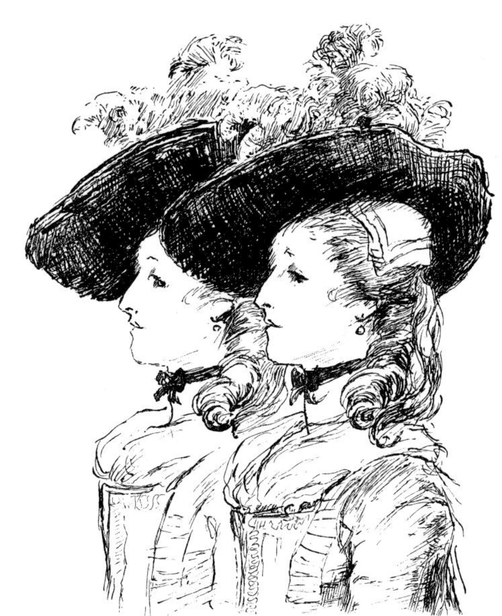

The Two Miss Hoggs.

Harper's New Monthly Magazine, December 1884
"She Stoops to Conquer"

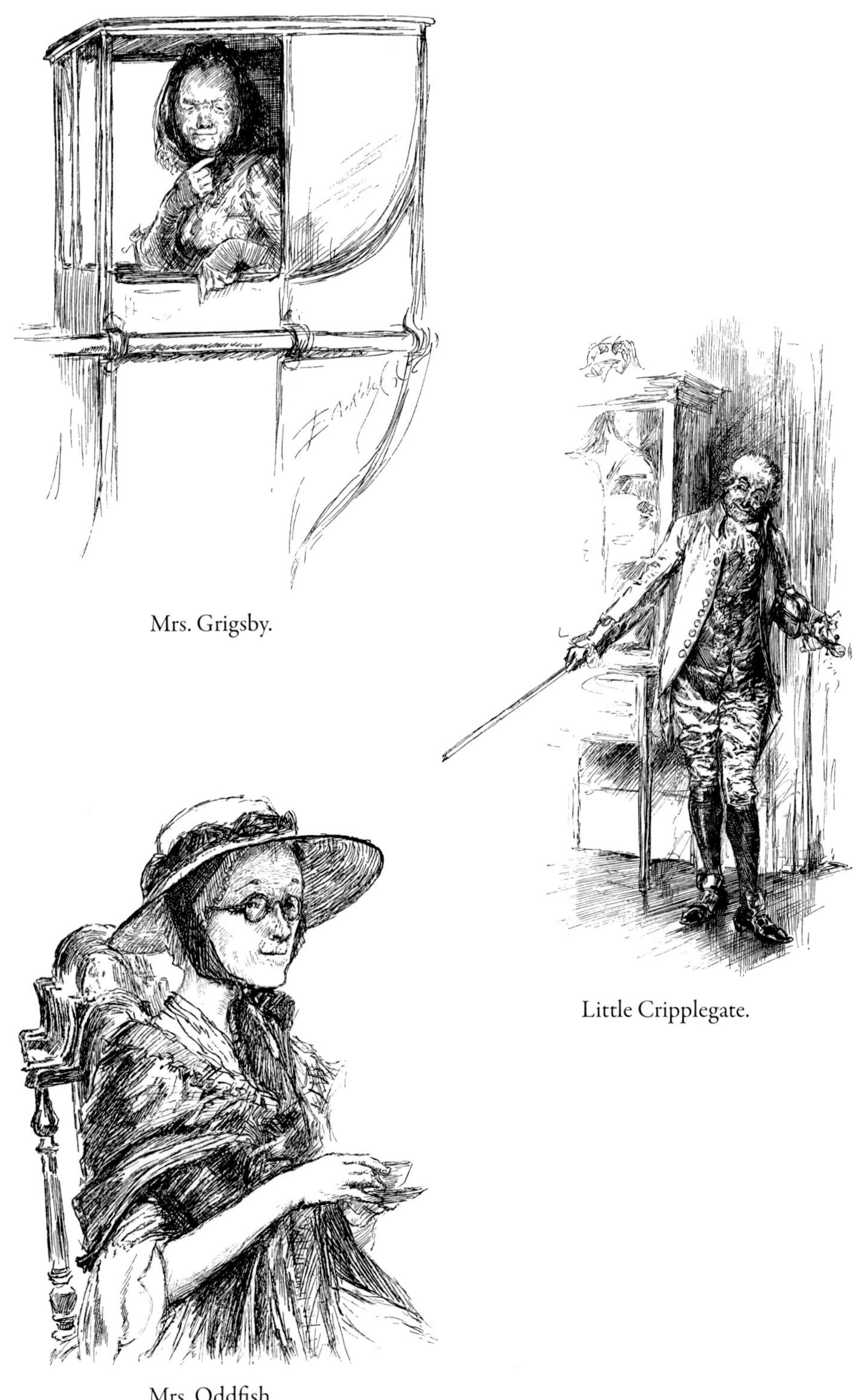

Mrs. Grigsby.

Little Cripplegate.

Mrs. Oddfish.

Harper's New Monthly Magazine, December 1884
"She Stoops to Conquer"

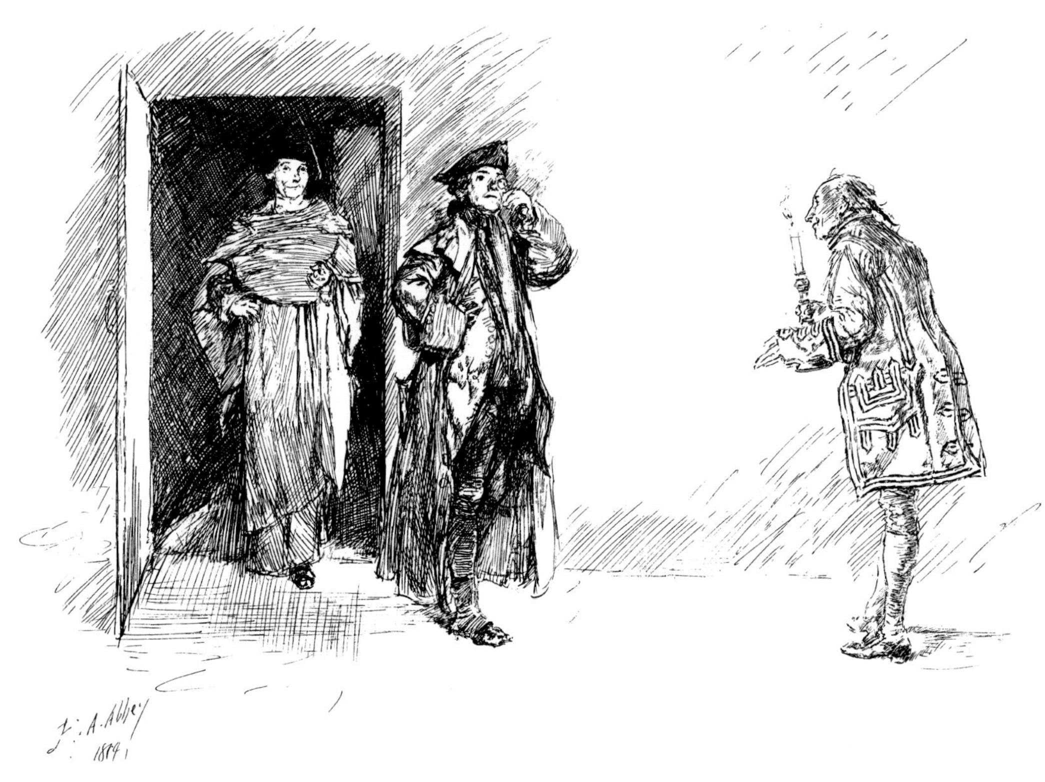

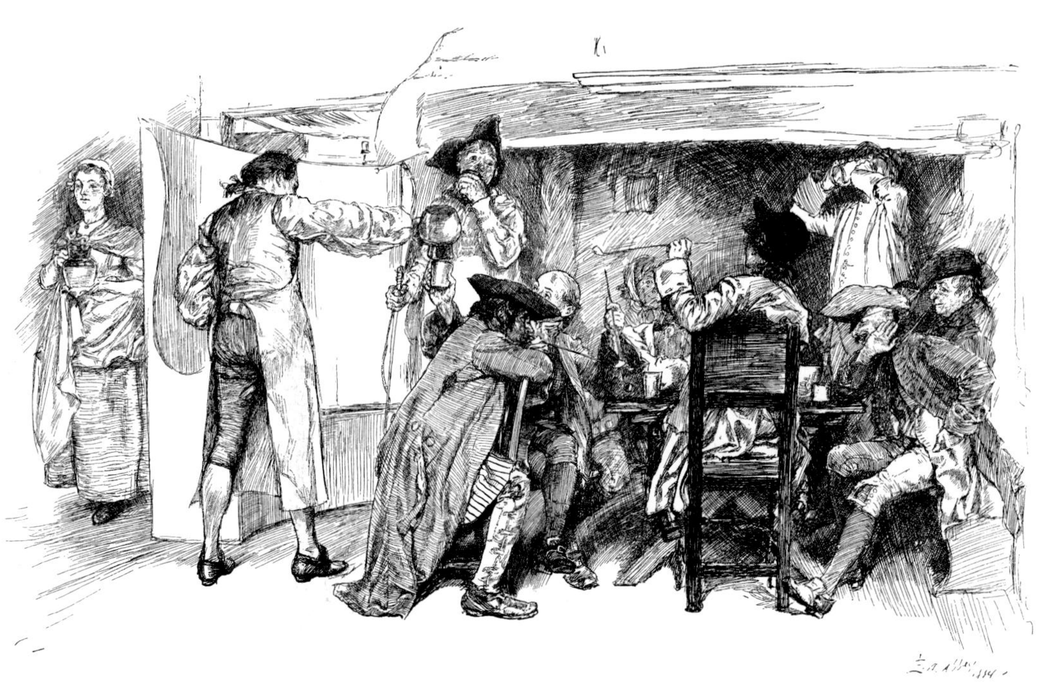

Ale-house Scene.

Harper's New Monthly Magazine, January 1885
"She Stoops to Conquer"

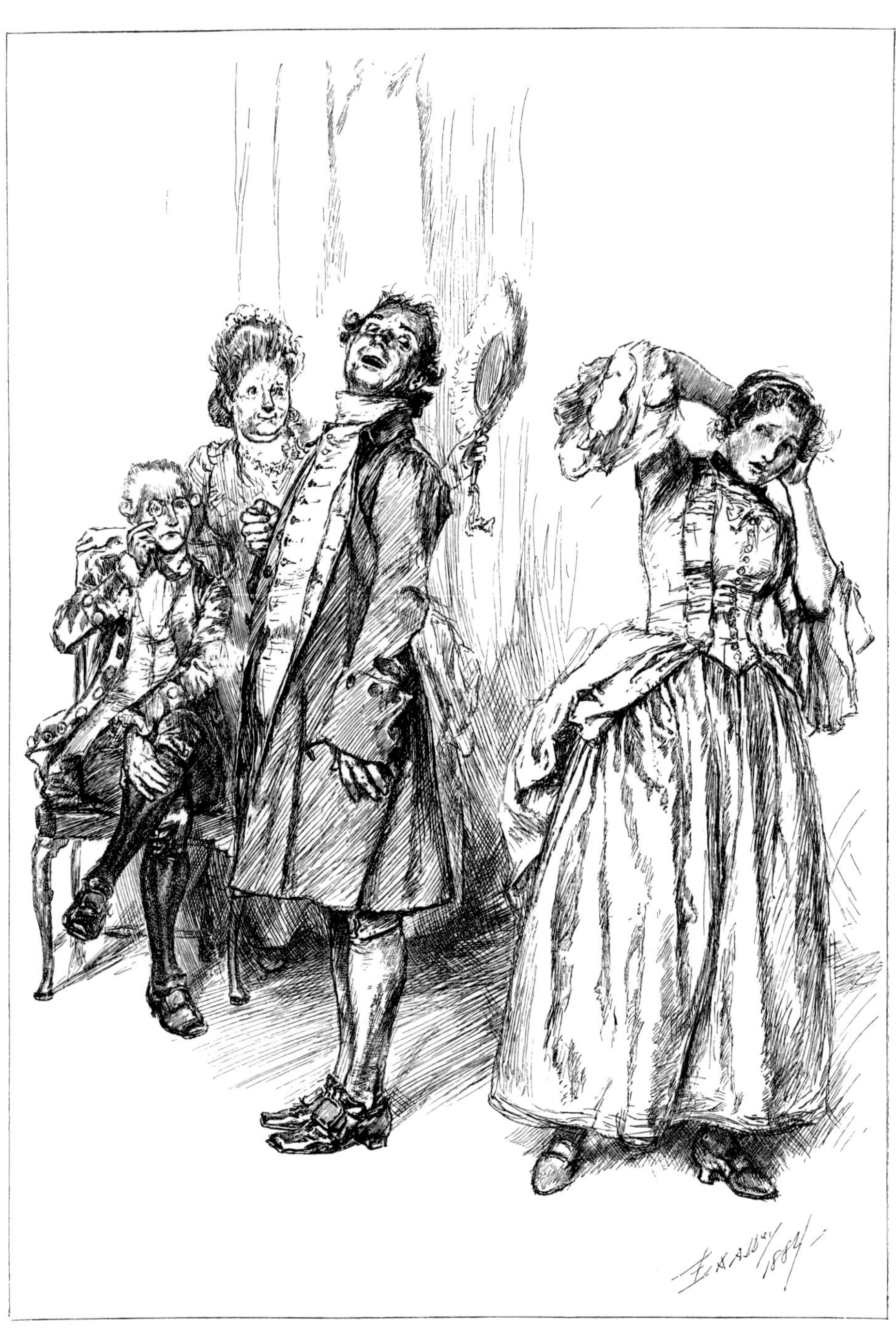

"O Lud! He has almost cracked my head."

Harper's New Monthly Magazine, November 1885
"She Stoops to Conquer"

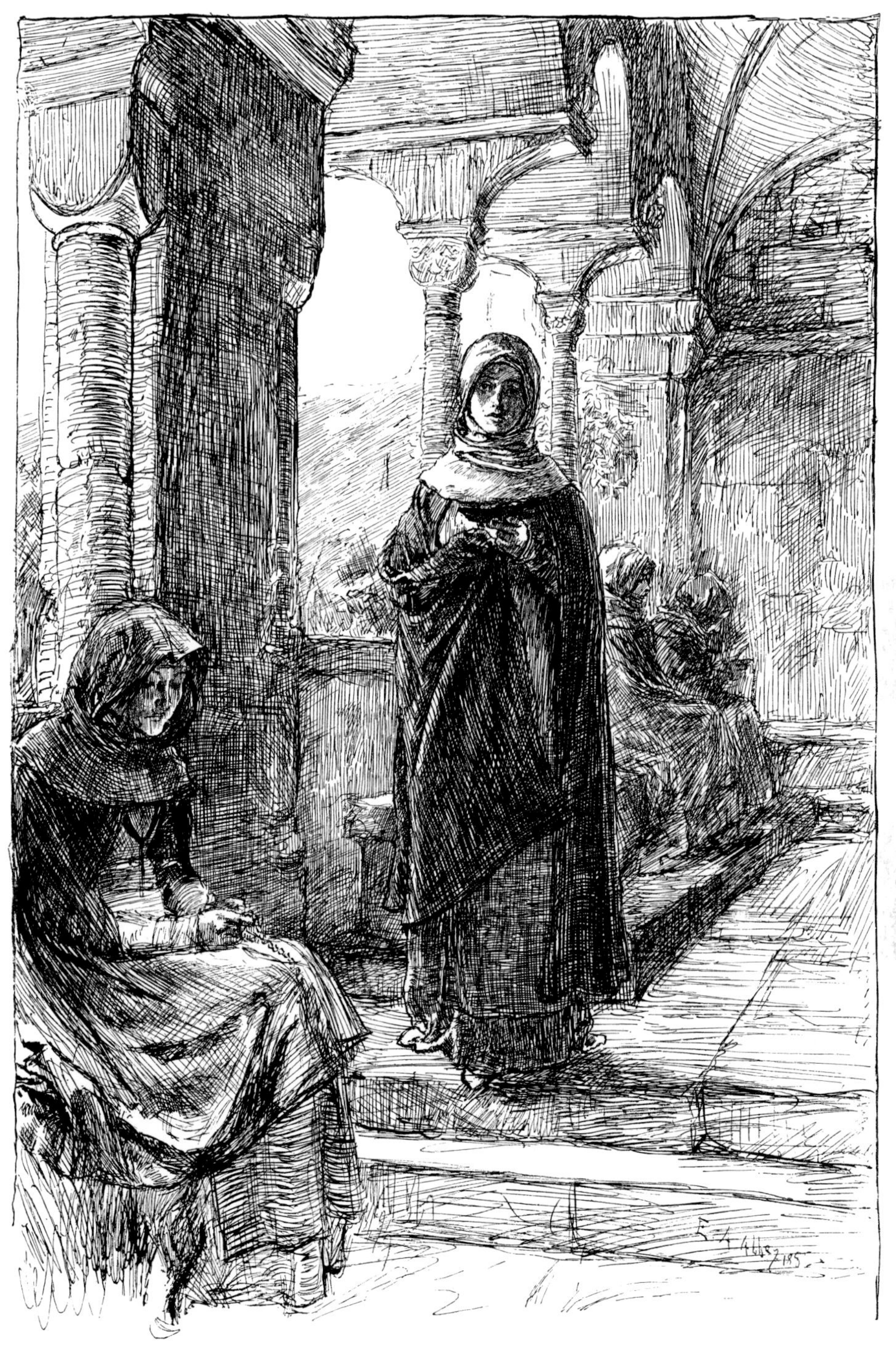

Harper's New Monthly Magazine, December 1885
"At Nonnenwerth"

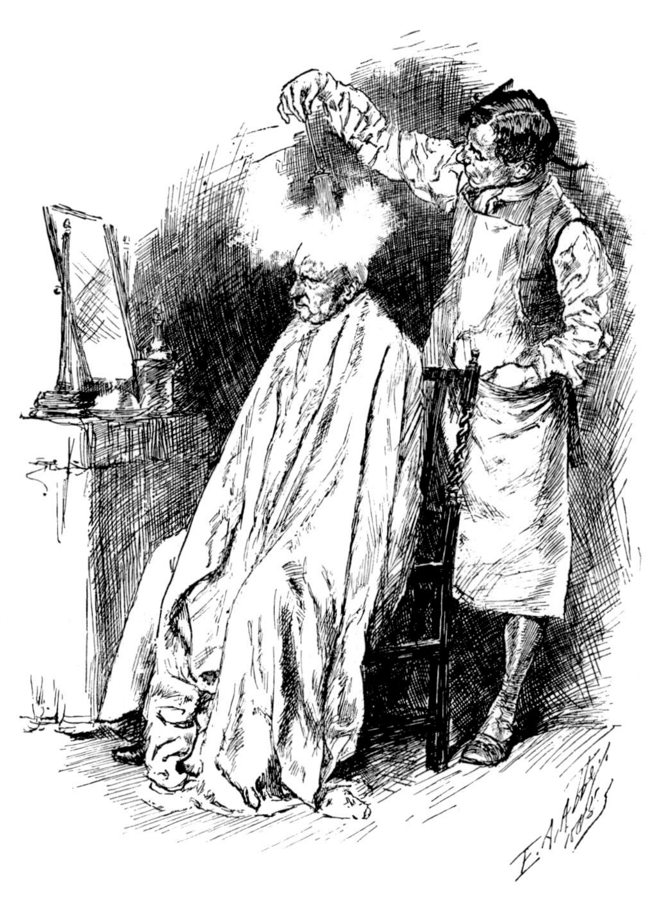

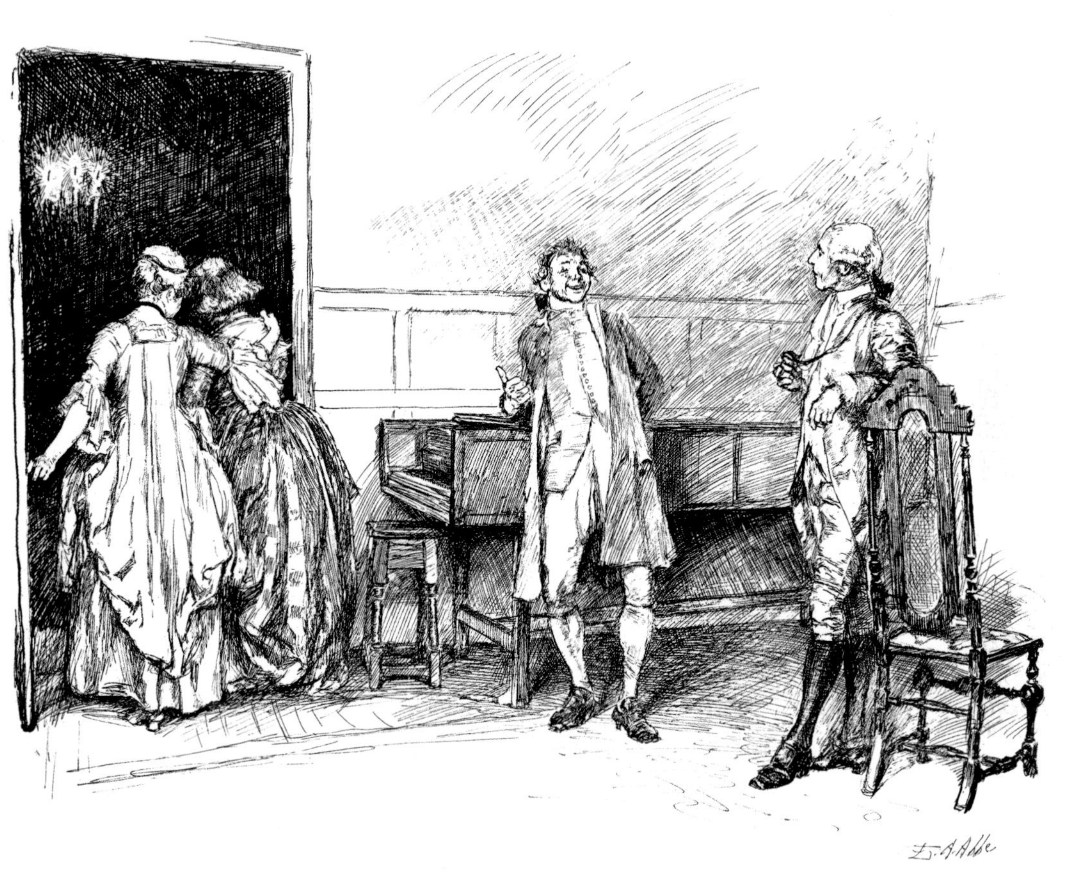

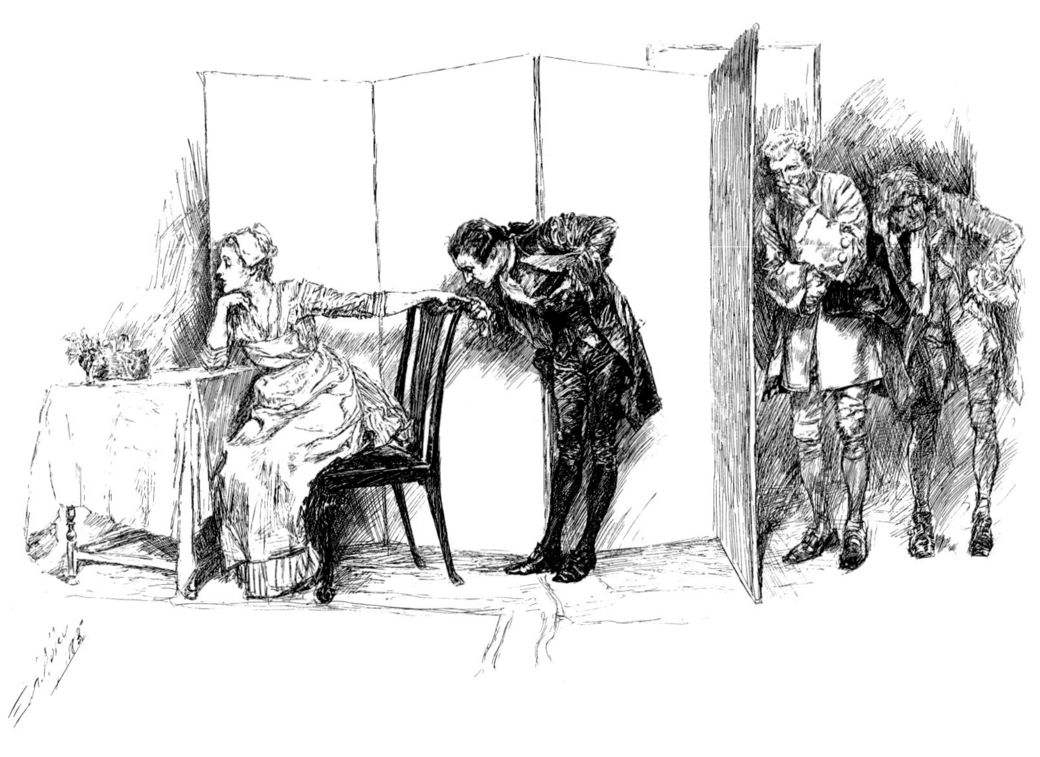

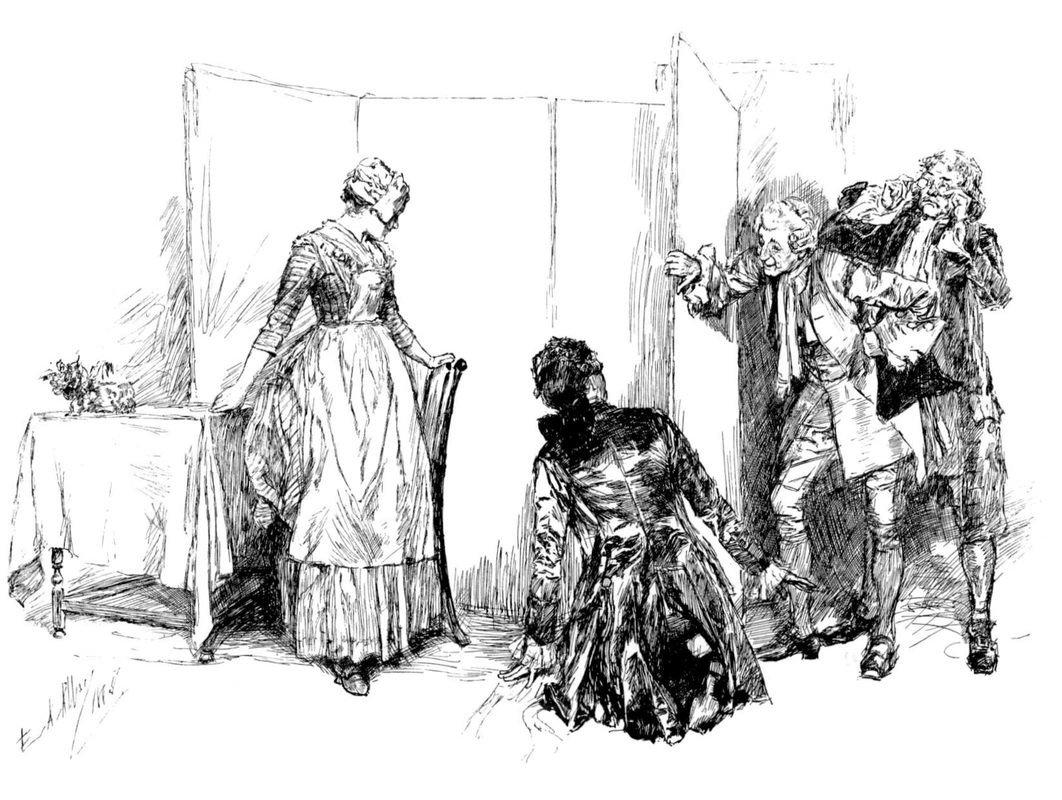

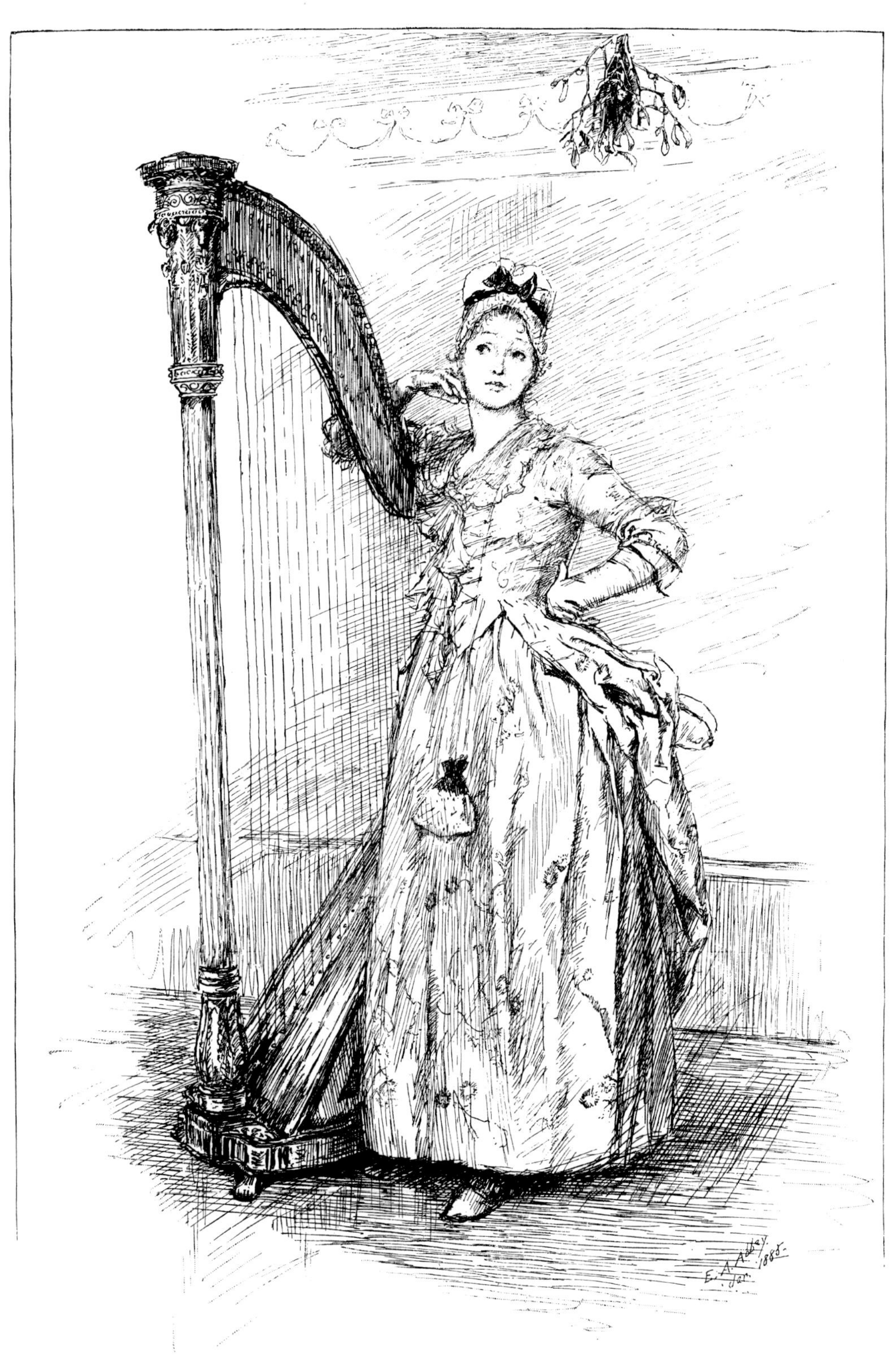

Harper's New Monthly Magazine, February 1886
"She Stoops to Conquer."

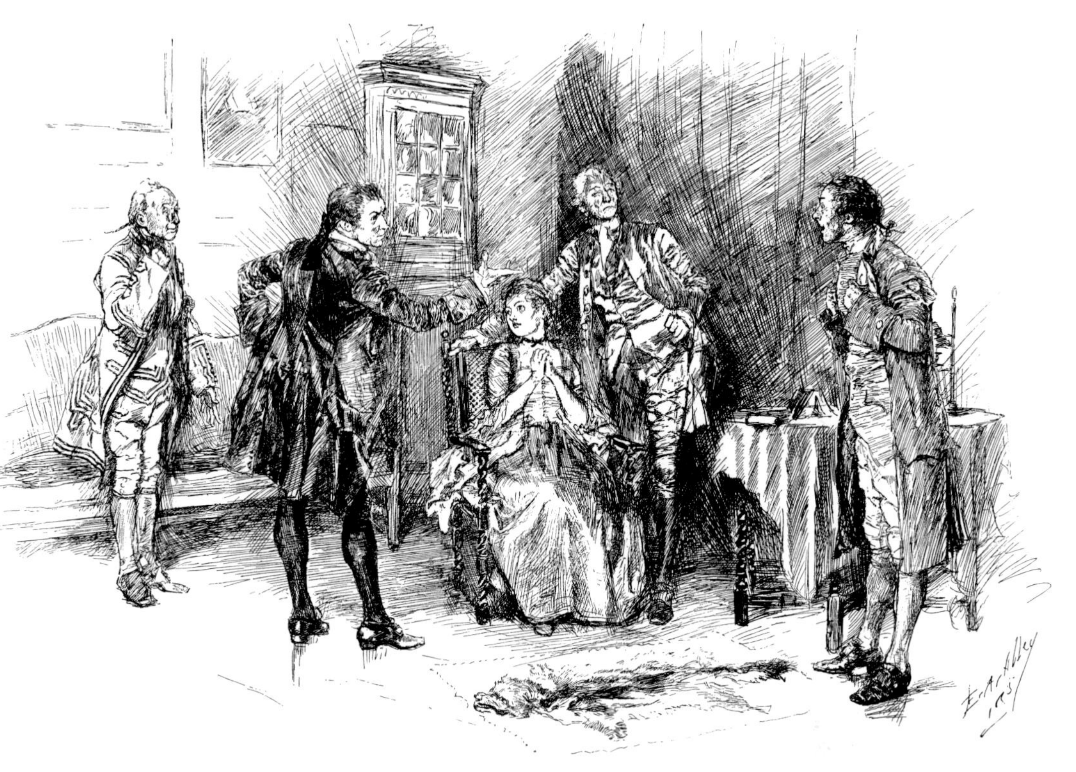

"Was it well done, Sir, to assist in rendering me ridiculous?"

Harper's New Monthly Magazine, April 1886
"She Stoops to Conquer"

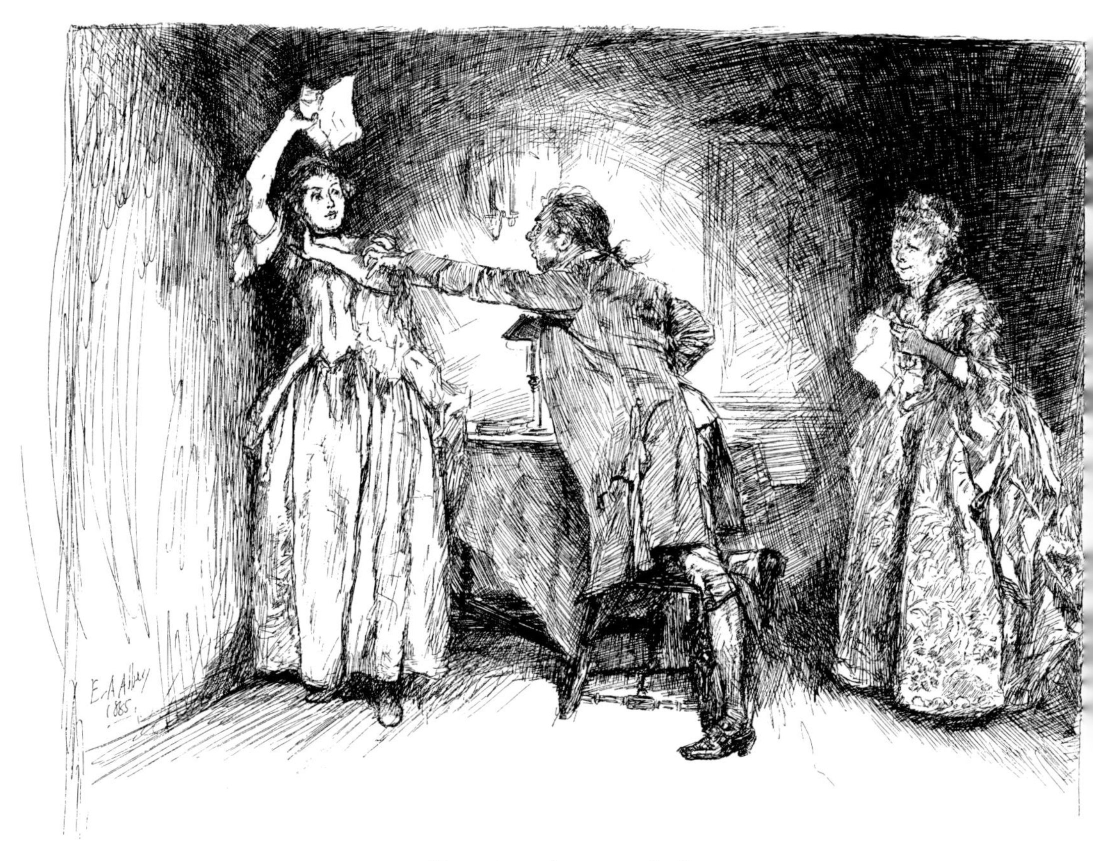

"Pray, Aunt, let me read it."

Harper's New Monthly Magazine, April 1886
"She Stoops to Conquer"

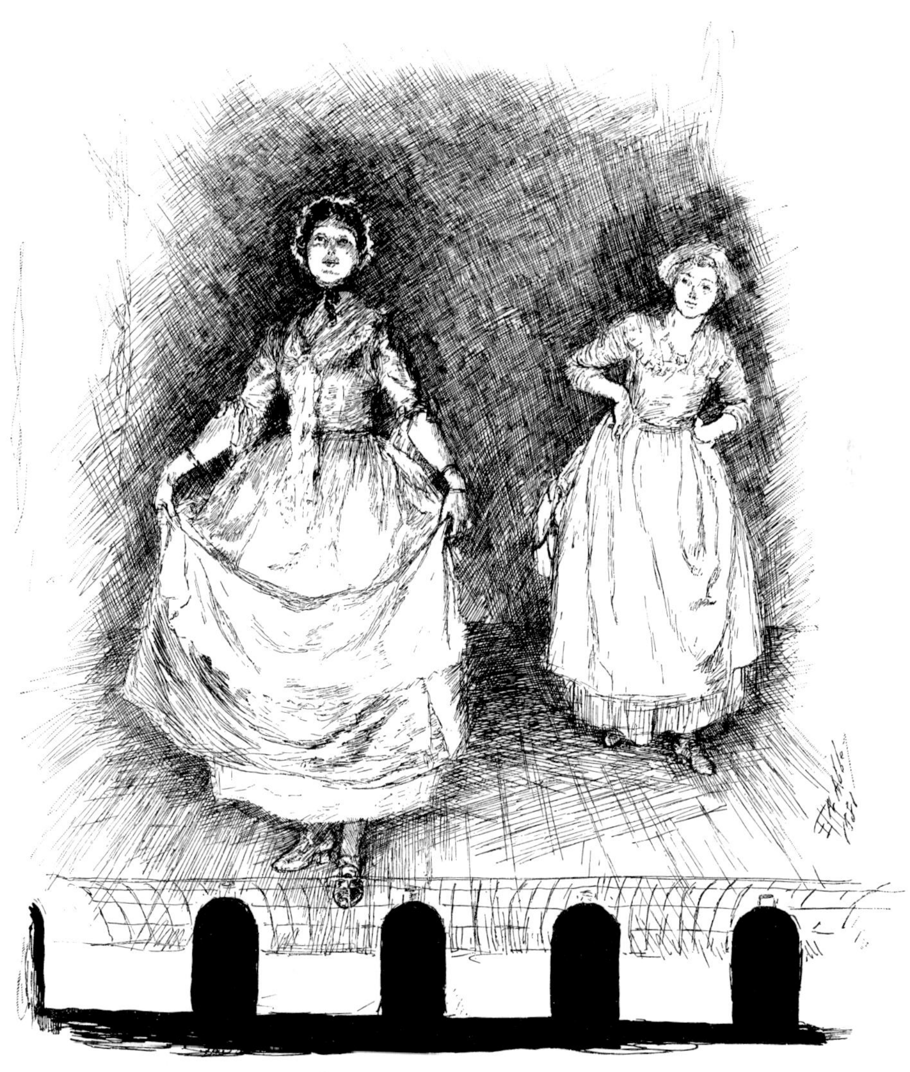

Epilogue to "She Stoops to Conquer."

Harper's New Monthly Magazine, August 1886
"She Stoops to Conquer"

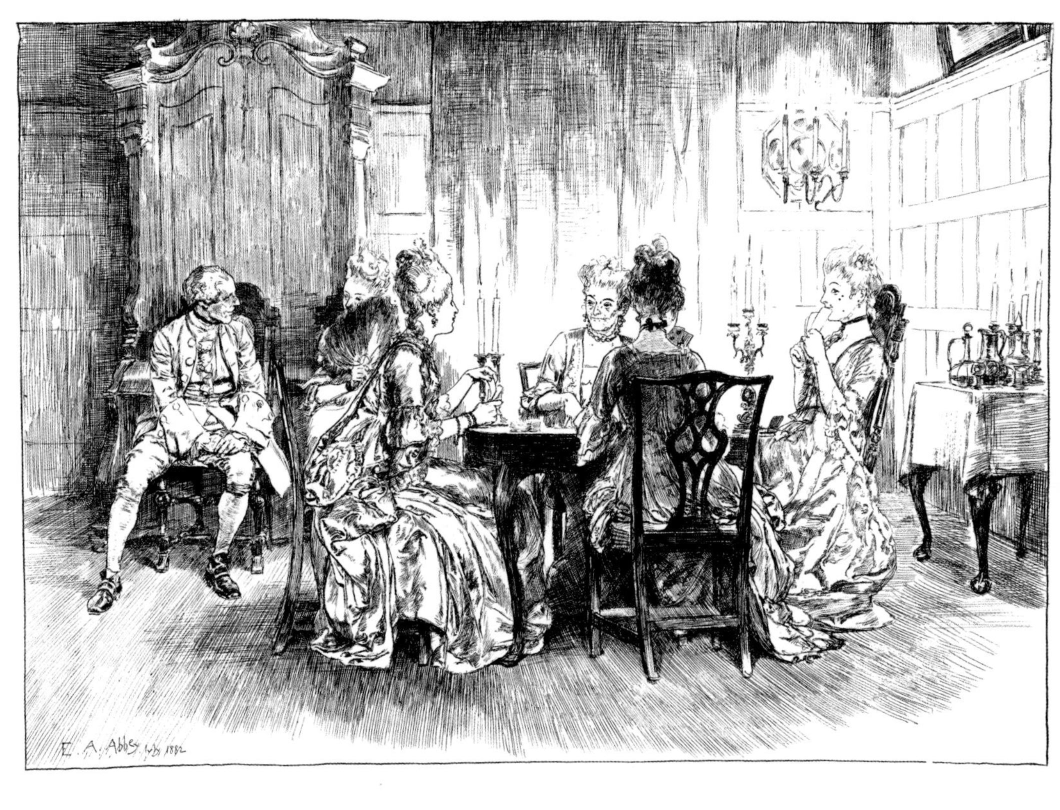

Harper's New Monthly Magazine
"She Stoops to Conquer"

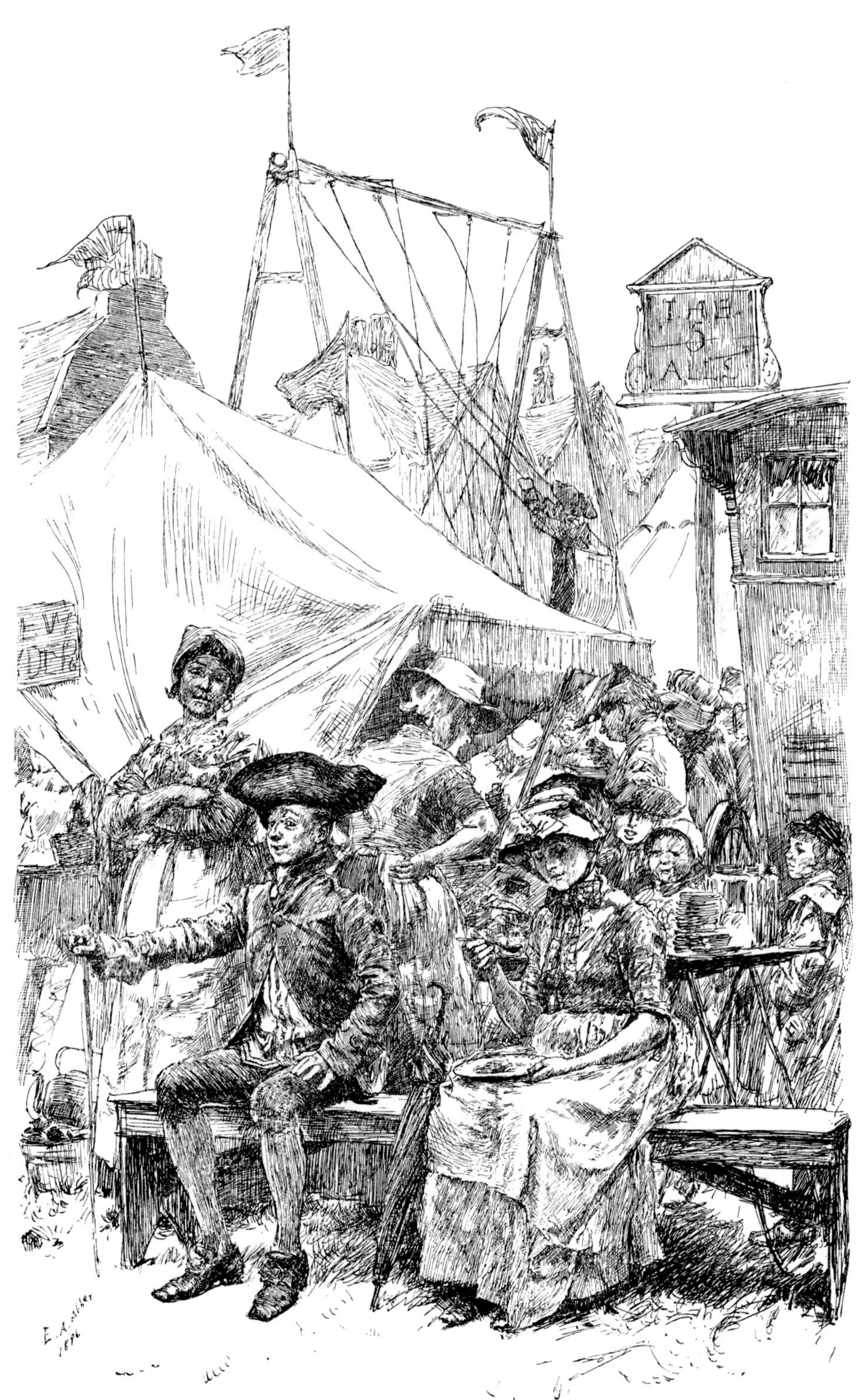

Harper's New Monthly Magazine, December 1886
"Sally in our alley."

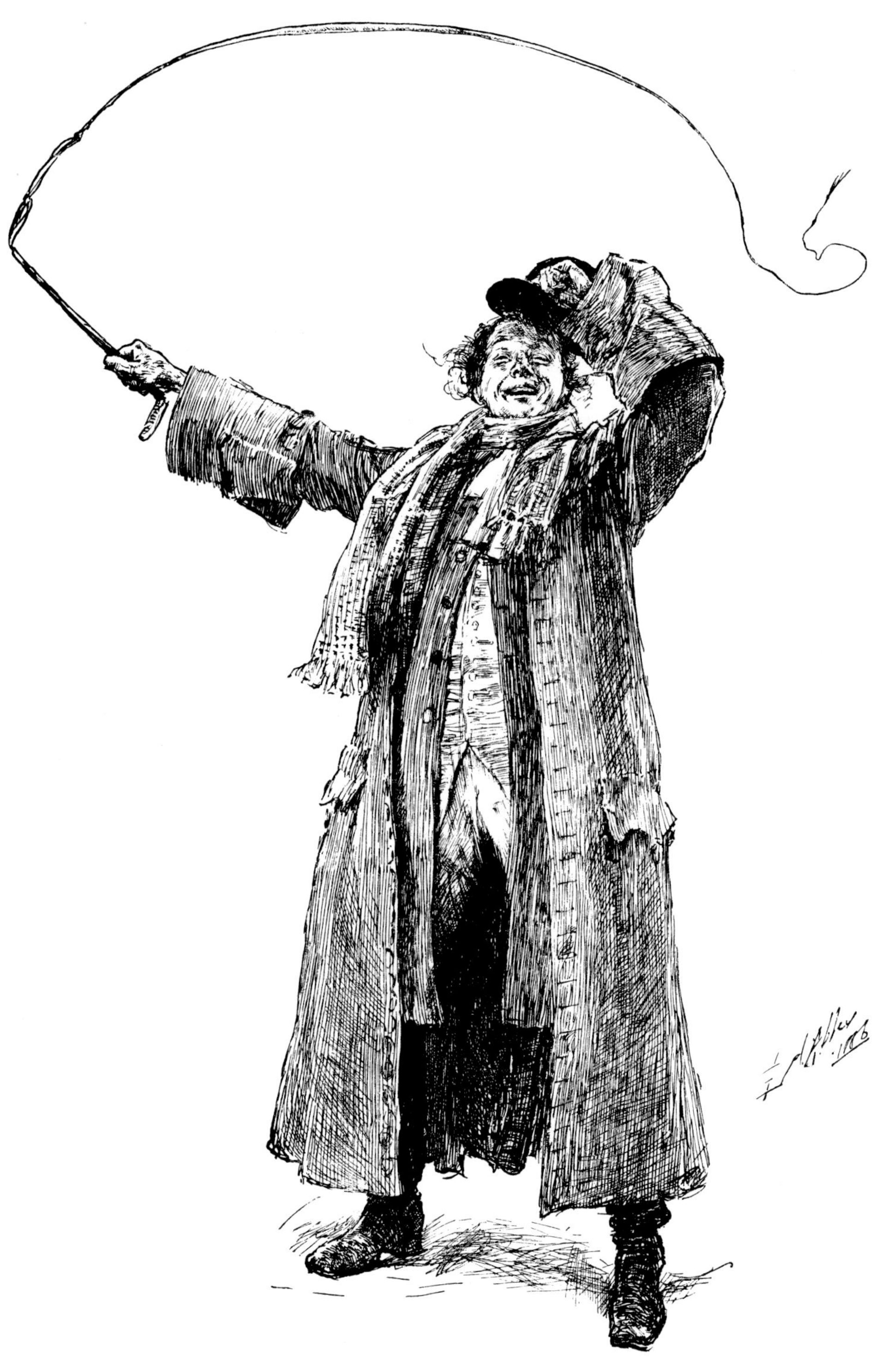

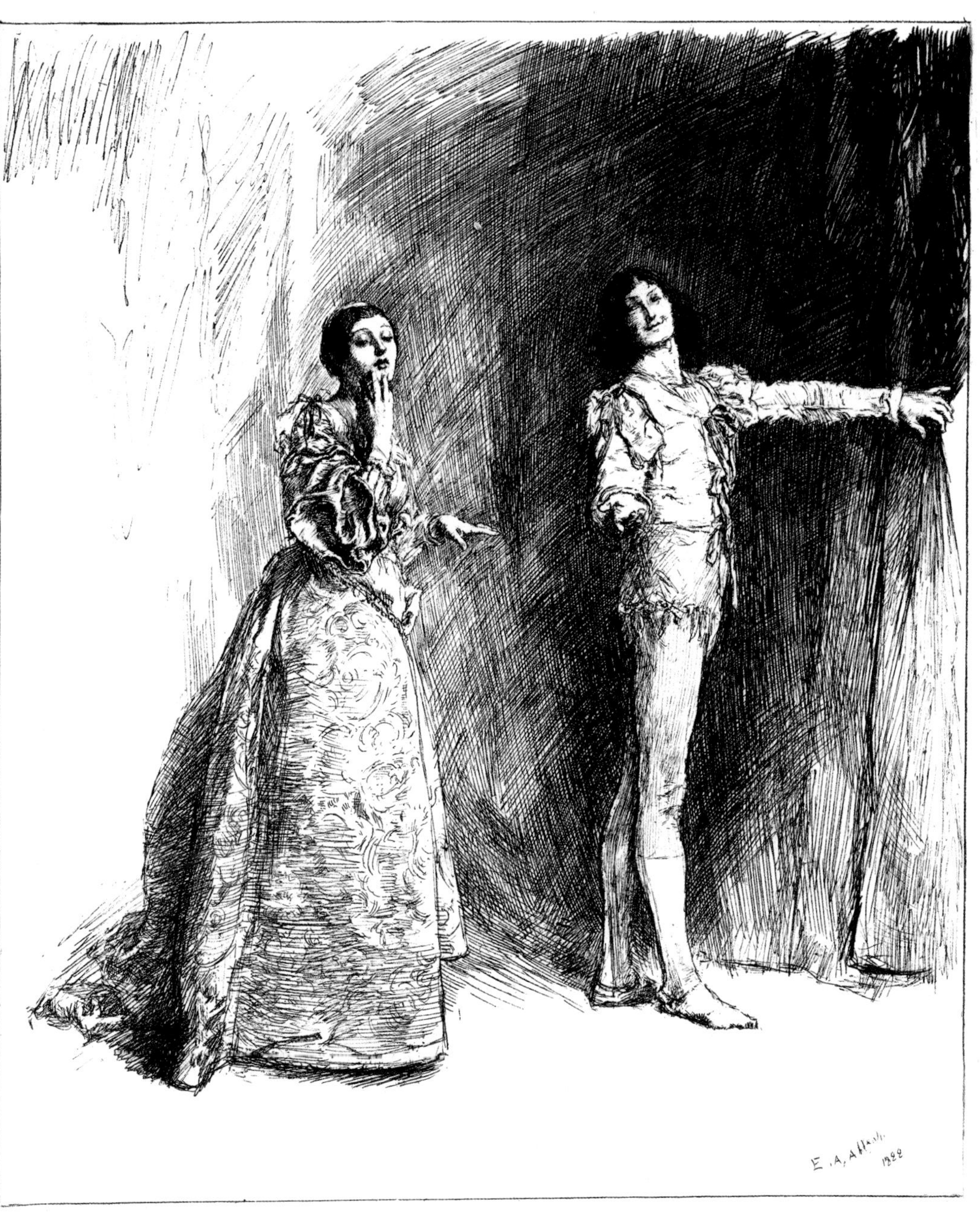

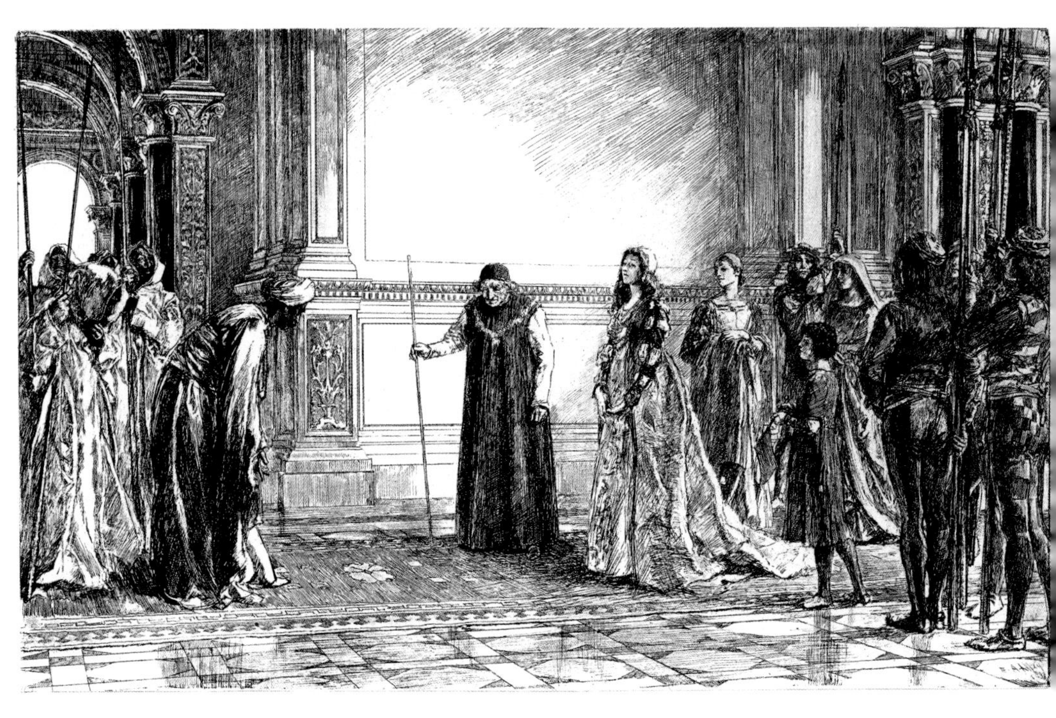

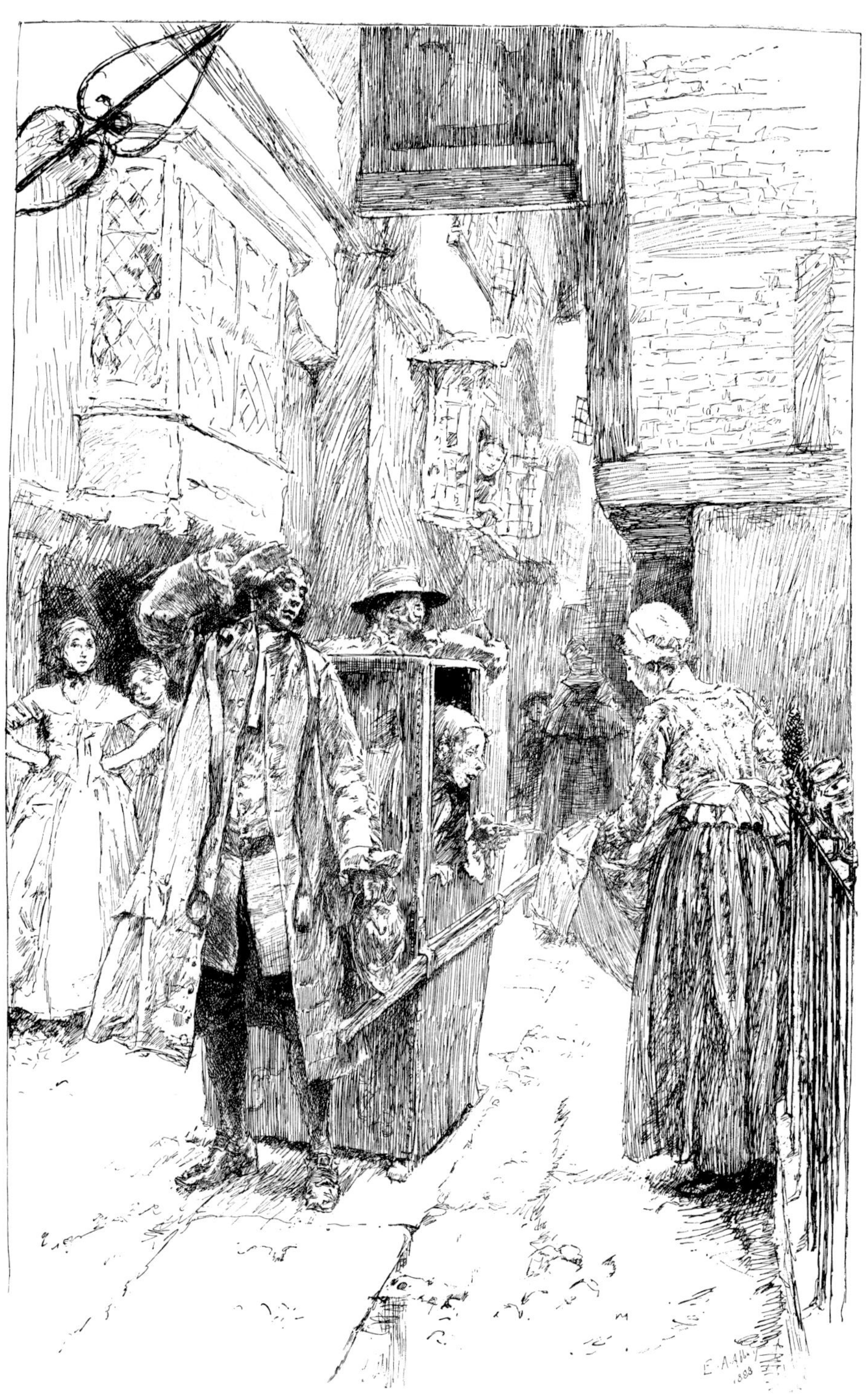

"He held a card: My lord, it said, would see the Bard."

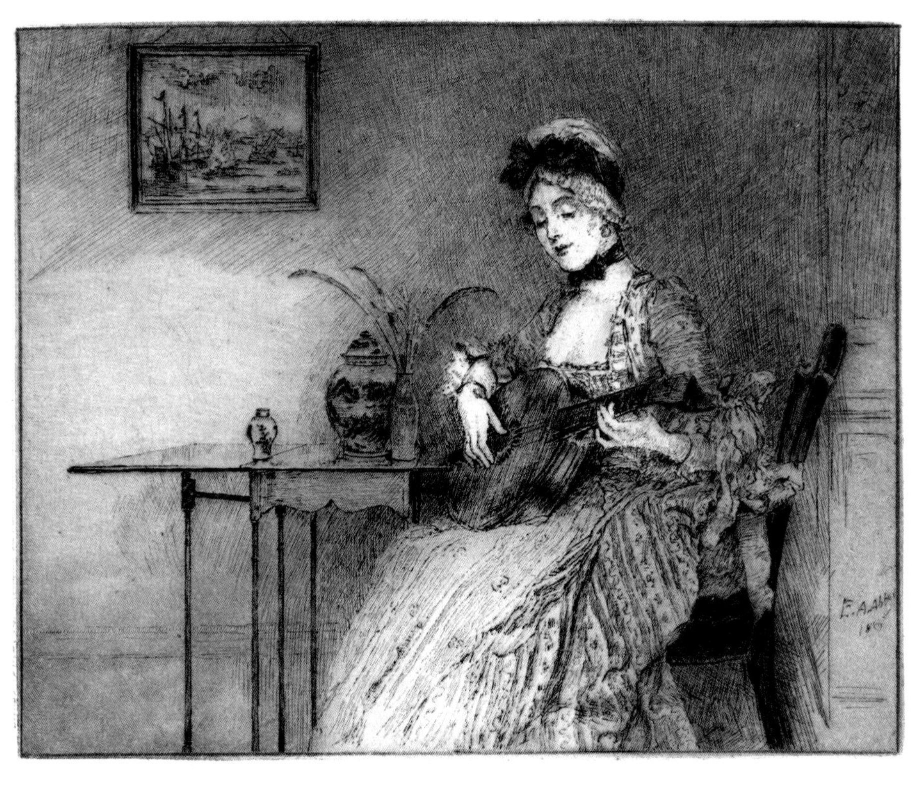

Old Songs
Harper & Brothers, 1888

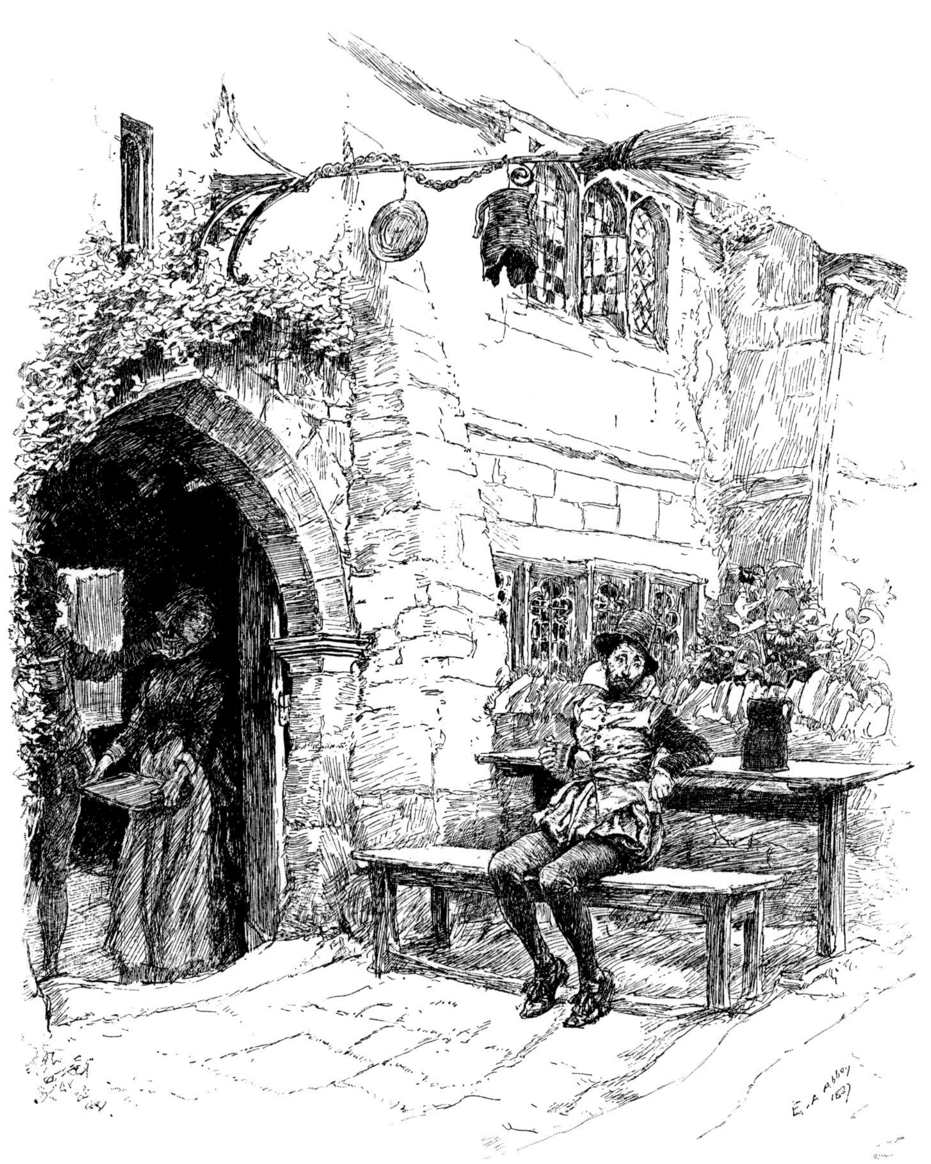

"But, now, alasse! Sh' as left me."

Old Songs
"A Love Song," Harper & Brothers, 1888
Originally published in *Harper's New Monthly Magazine*, October 1887

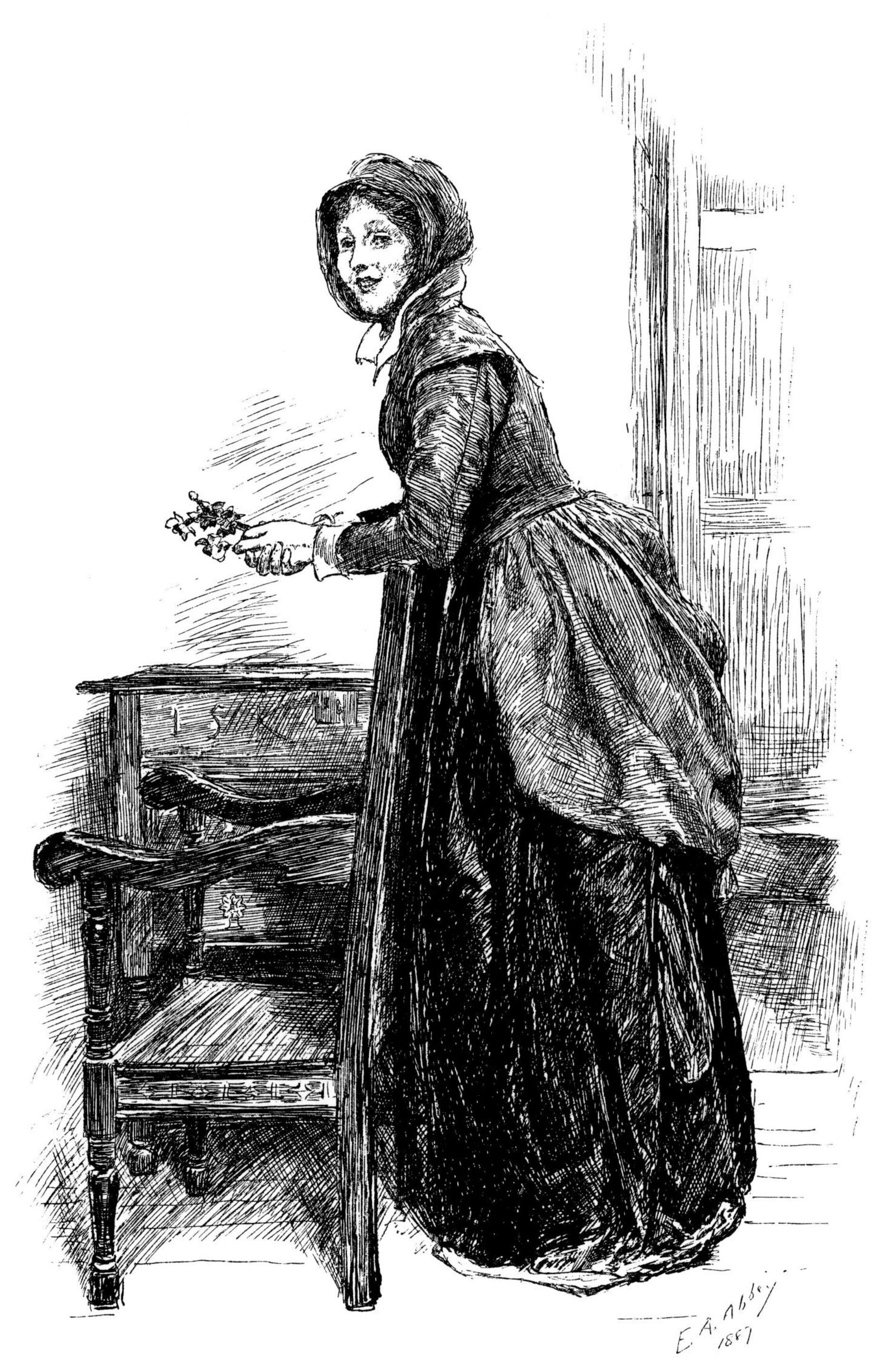

Her Sister.

Old Songs
"A Love Song," Harper & Brothers, 1888
Originally published in *Harper's New Monthly Magazine*, October 1887

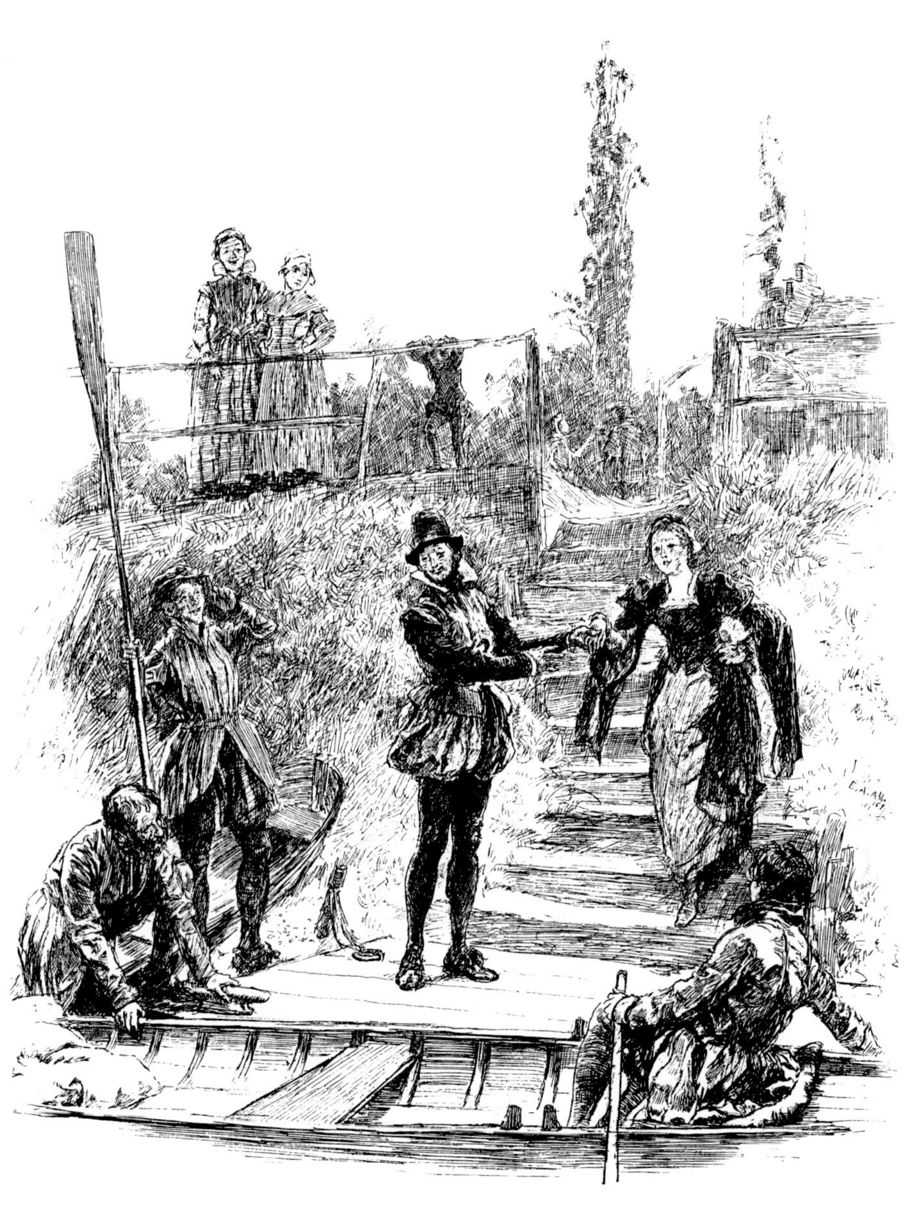

Old Songs
"A Love Song," Harper & Brothers, 1888

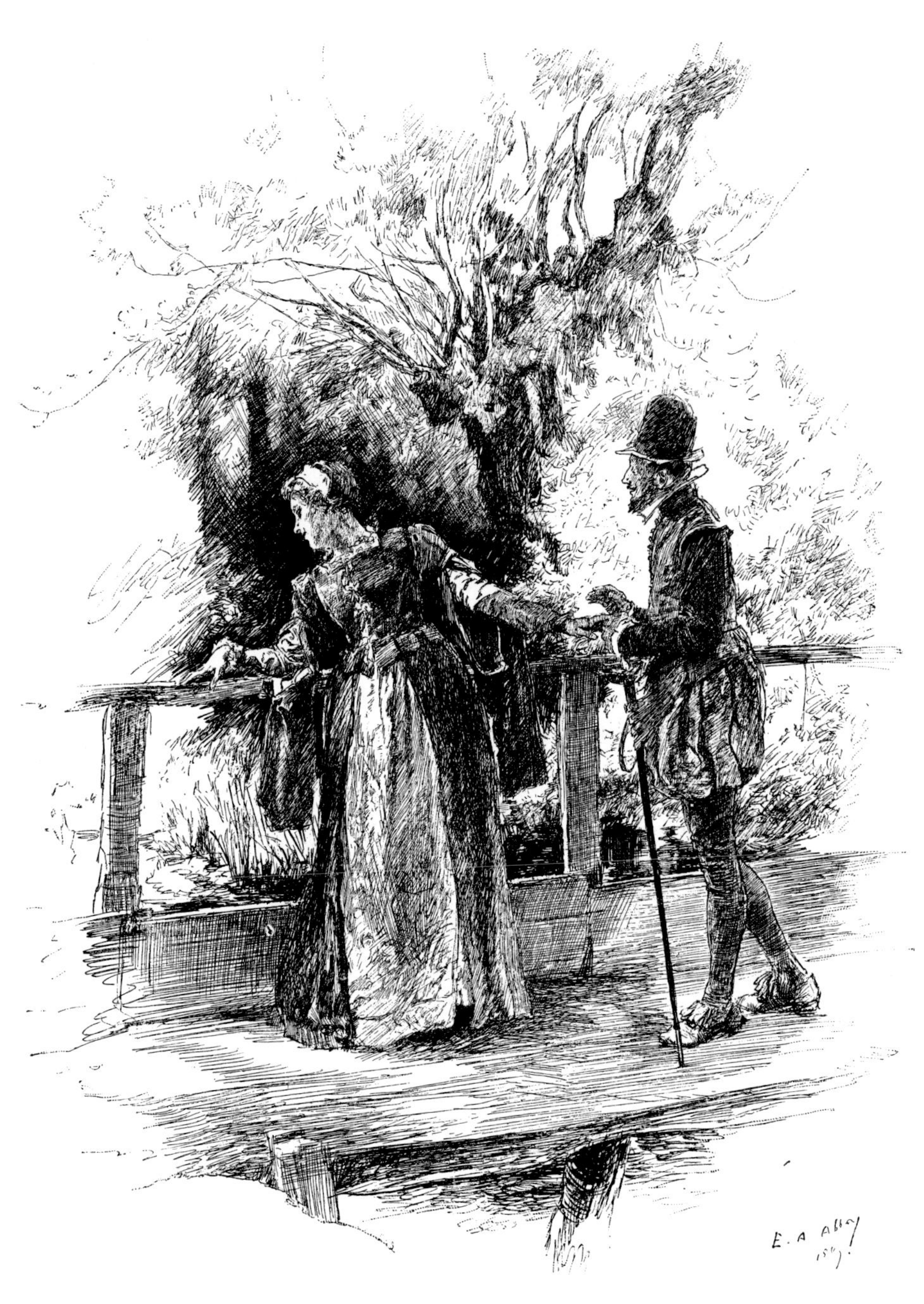

Old Songs
"A Love Song," Harper & Brothers, 1888
Originally published in *Harper's New Monthly Magazine*, October 1887

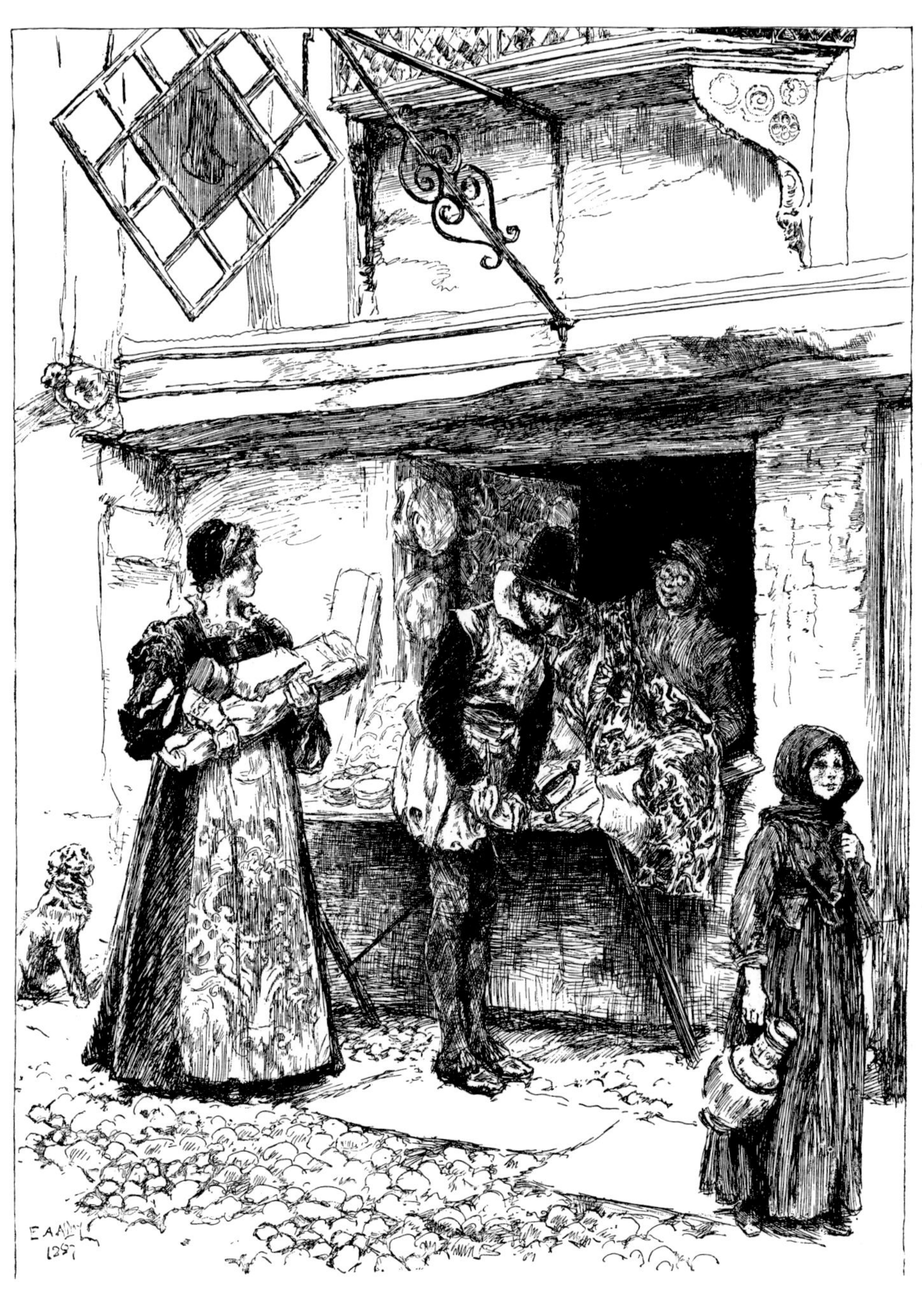

Old Songs
"A Love Song," Harper & Brothers, 1888
Originally published in *Harper's New Monthly Magazine*, October 1887

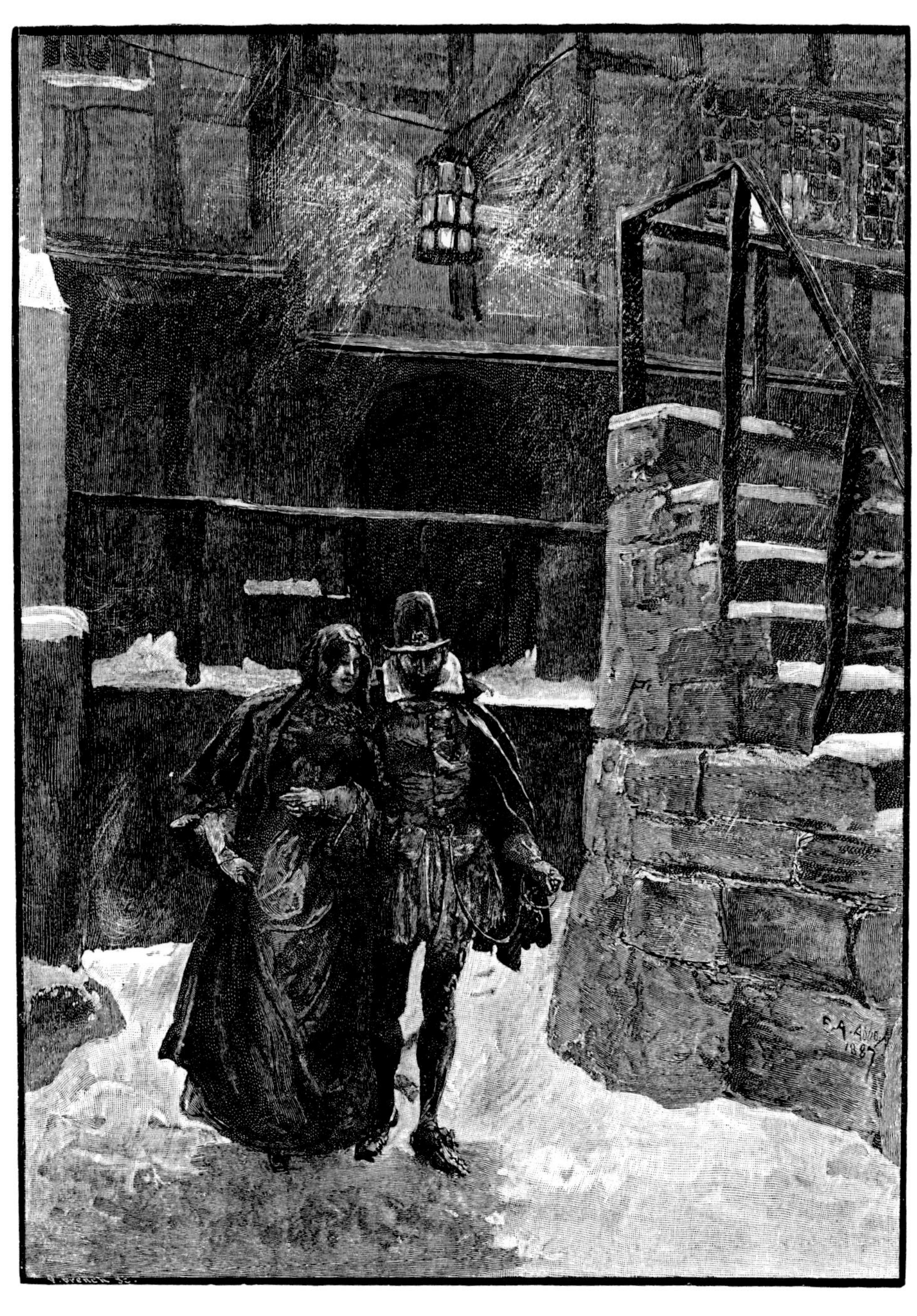

Old Songs
"A Love Song," Harper & Brothers, 1888

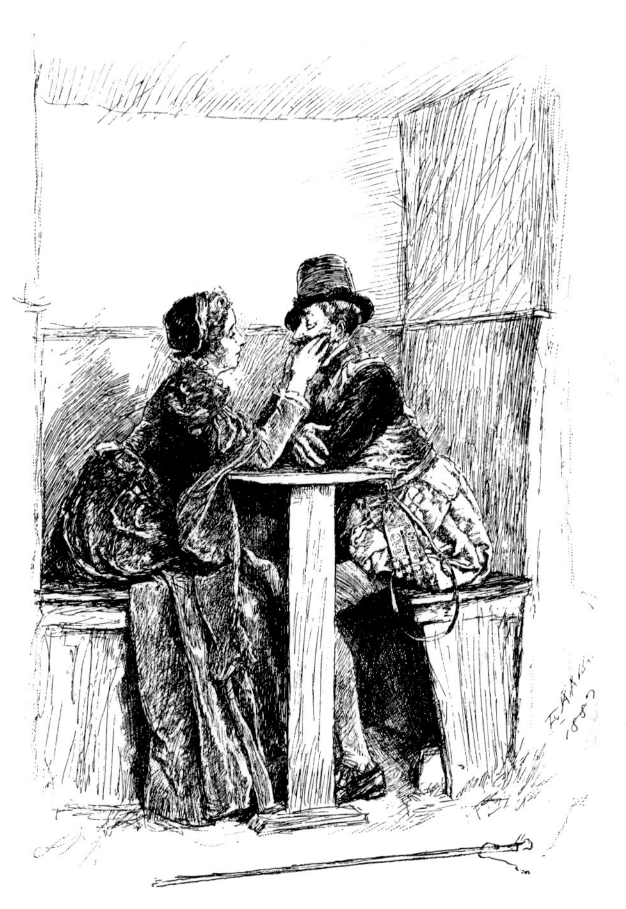

Old Songs
"A Love Song," Harper & Brothers, 1888

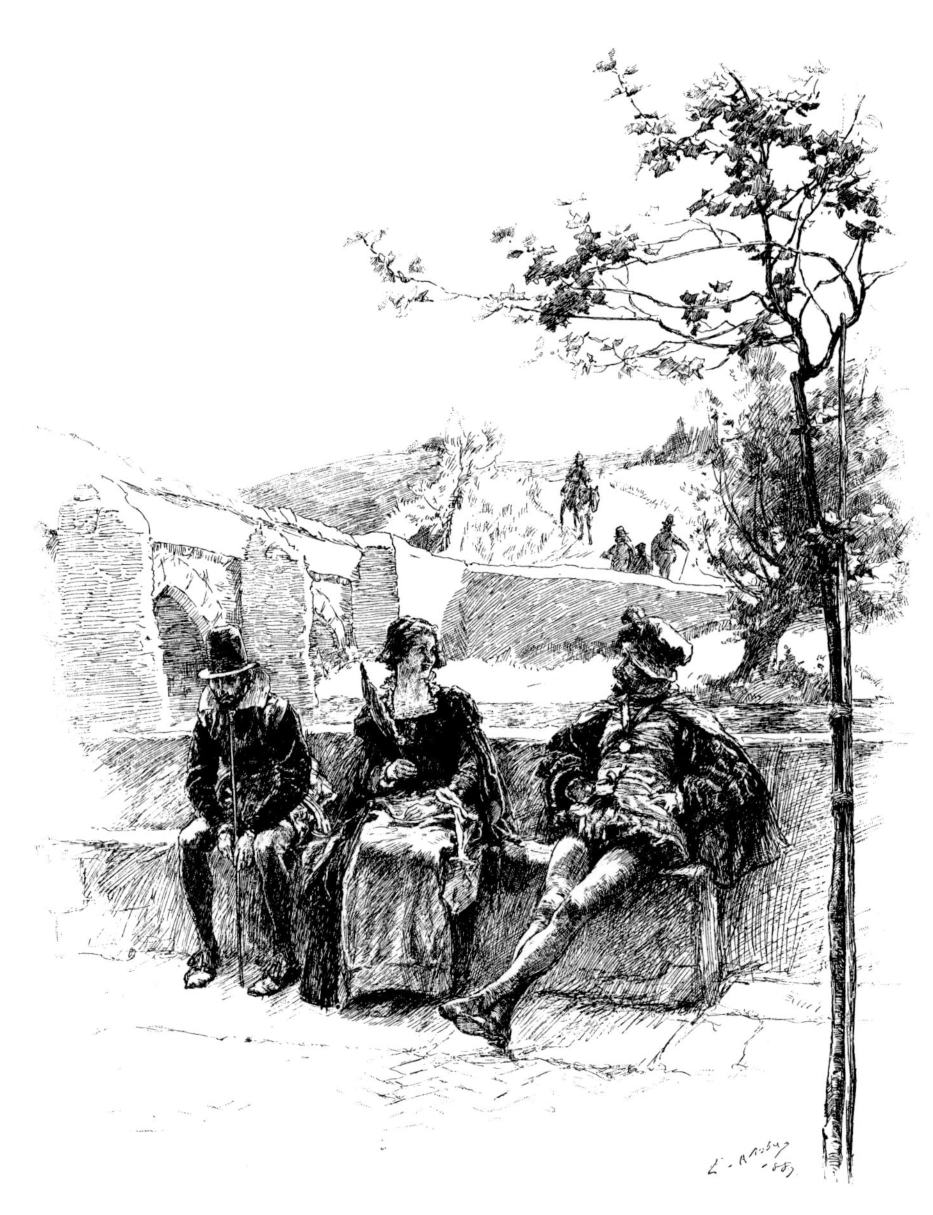

Old Songs
"A Love Song," Harper & Brothers, 1888

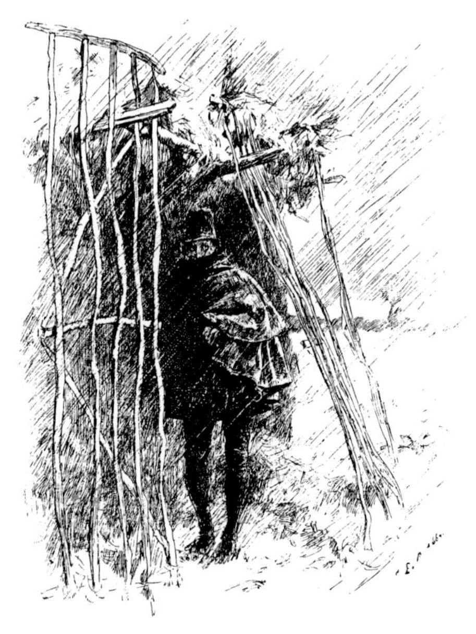

Old Songs
"A Love Song," Harper & Brothers, 1888

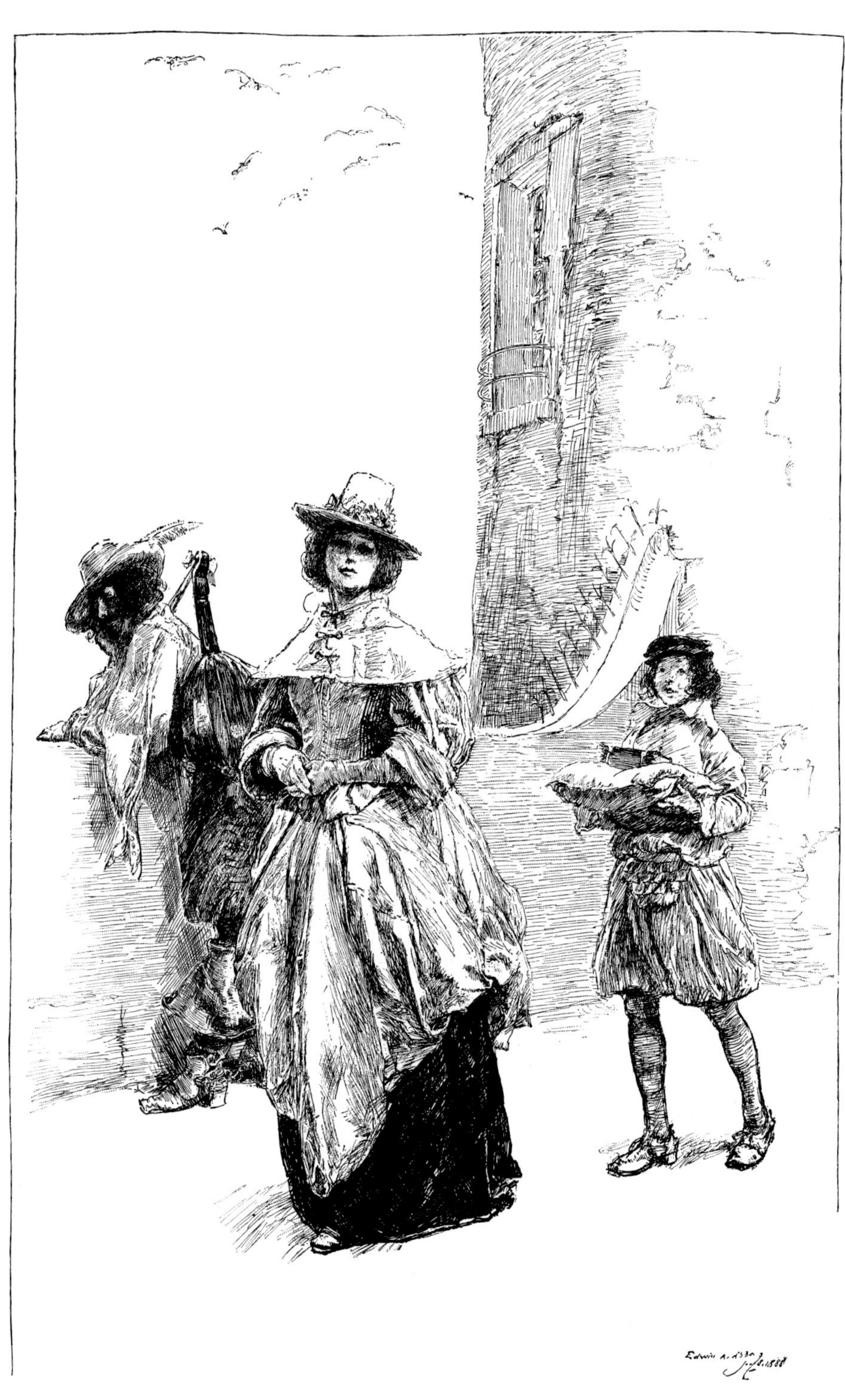

Old Songs
"Why canst Thou not, as Others do?" Harper & Brothers, 1888
Originally published in *Harper's New Monthly Magazine*, October 1888

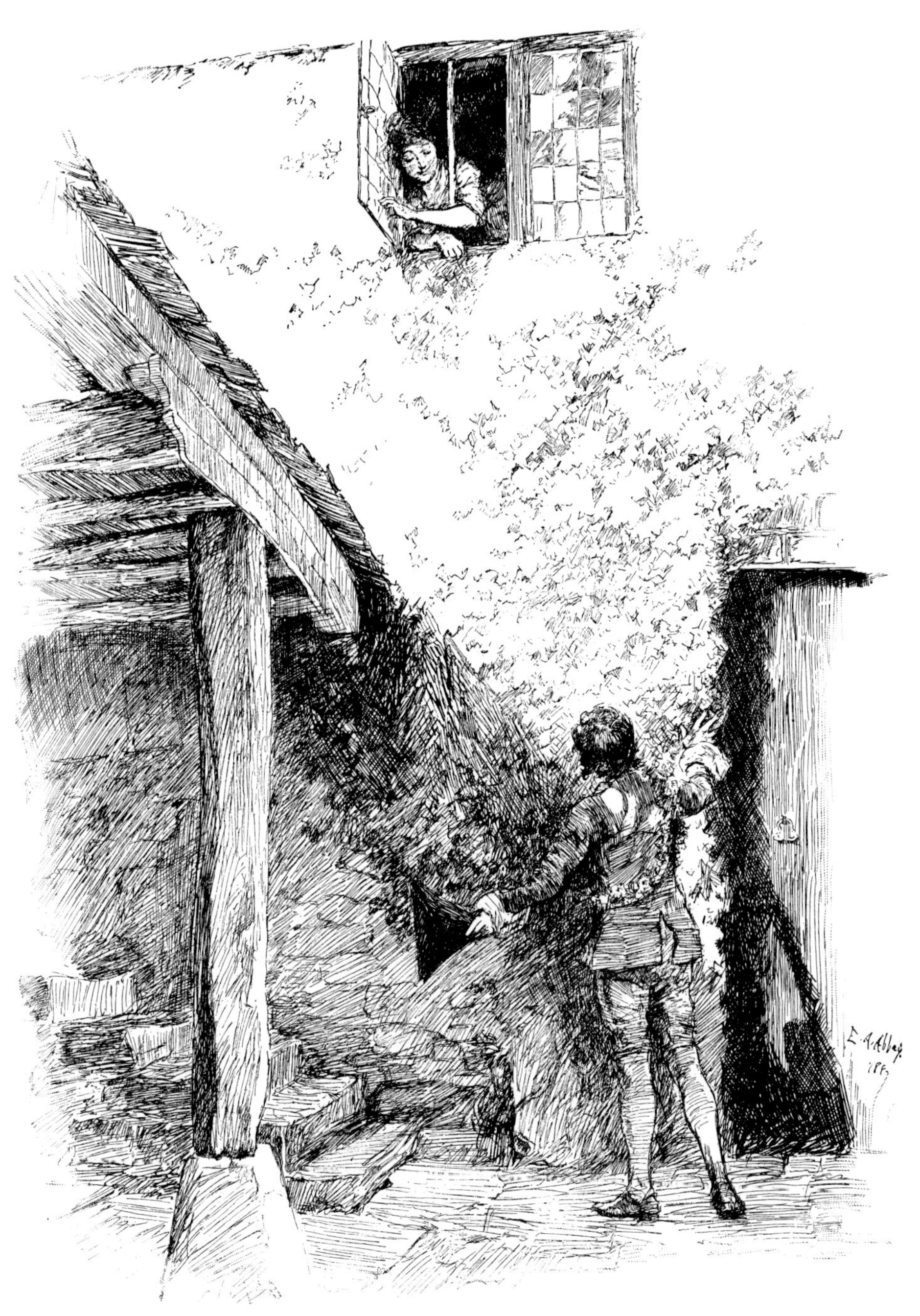

Old Songs
"With Jockey to the Fair," Harper & Brothers, 1888
Originally published in *Harper's New Monthly Magazine*, July 1888

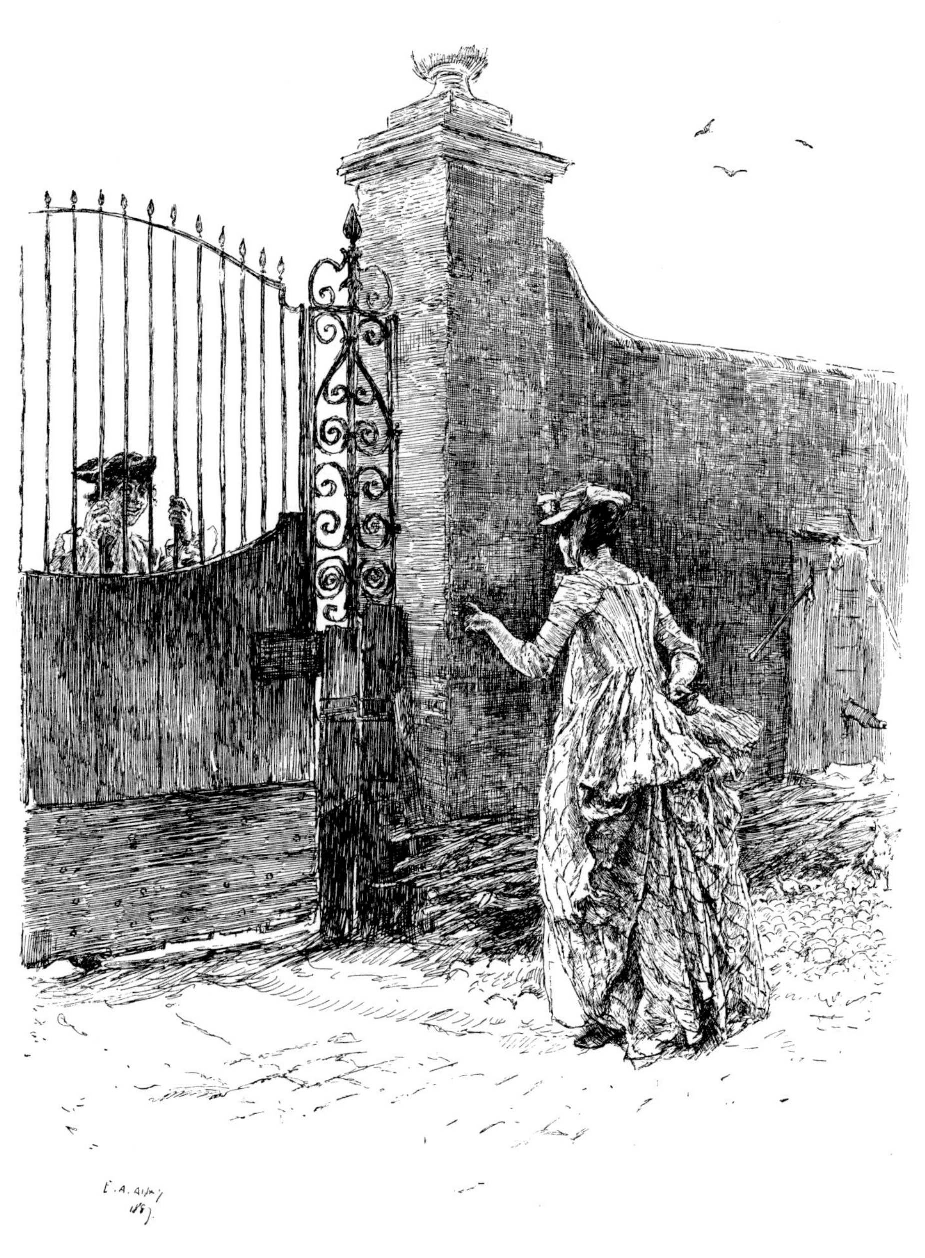

Old Songs
"With Jockey to the Fair," Harper & Brothers, 1888
Originally published in *Harper's New Monthly Magazine*, July 1888

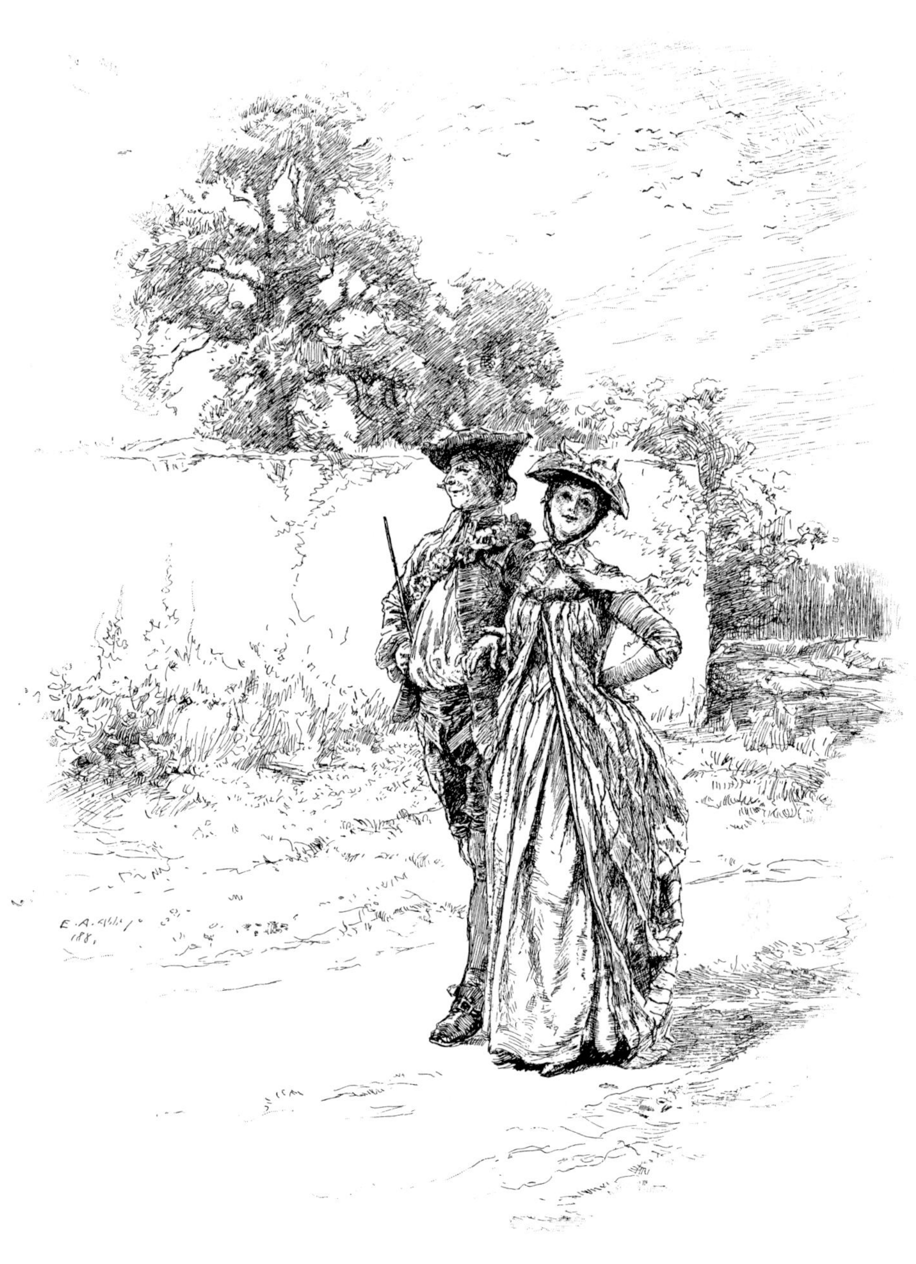

Old Songs
"With Jockey to the Fair," Harper & Brothers, 1888
Originally published in *Harper's New Monthly Magazine*, July 1888

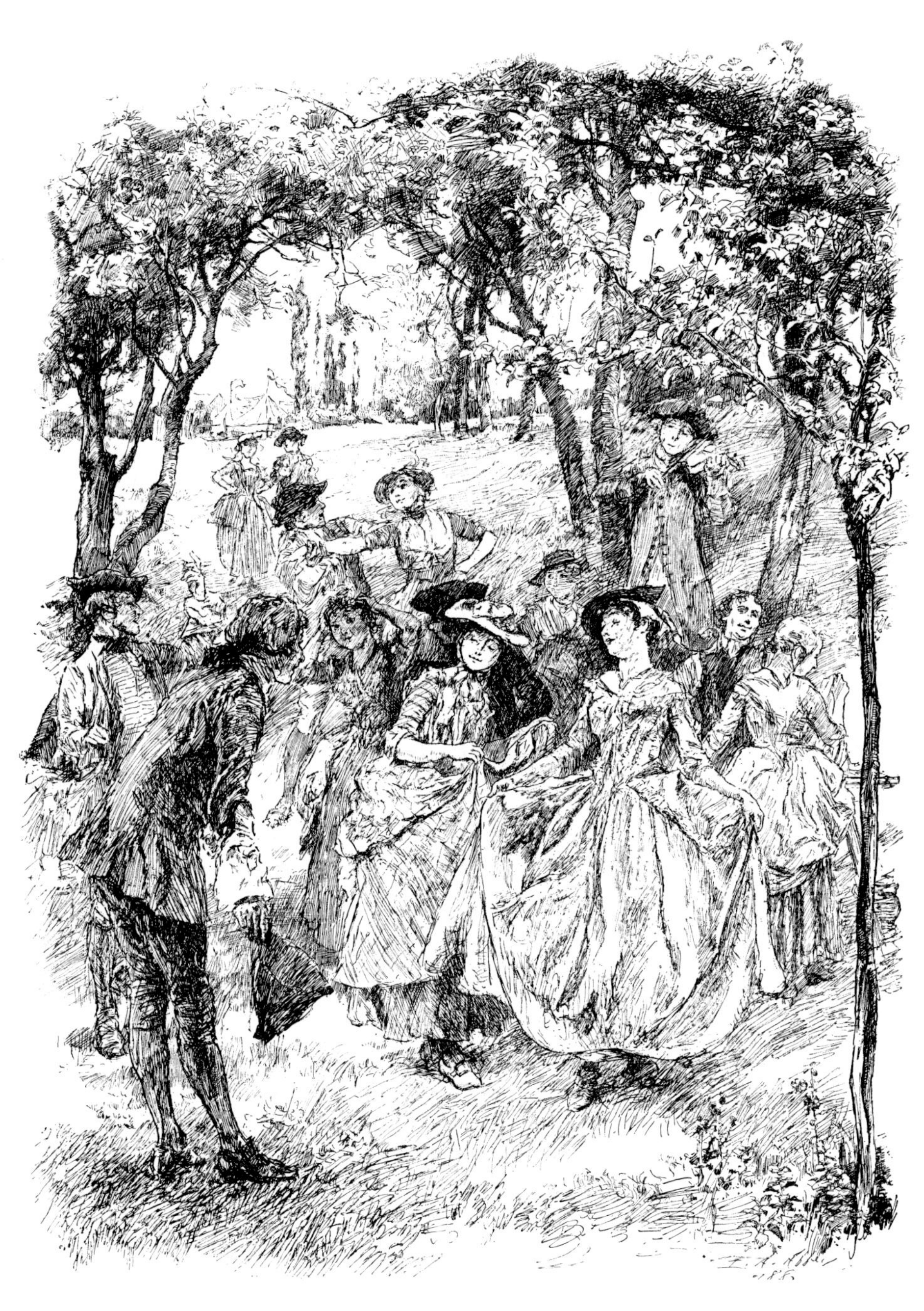

Old Songs
"With Jockey to the Fair," Harper & Brothers, 1888
Originally published in *Harper's New Monthly Magazine*, July 1888

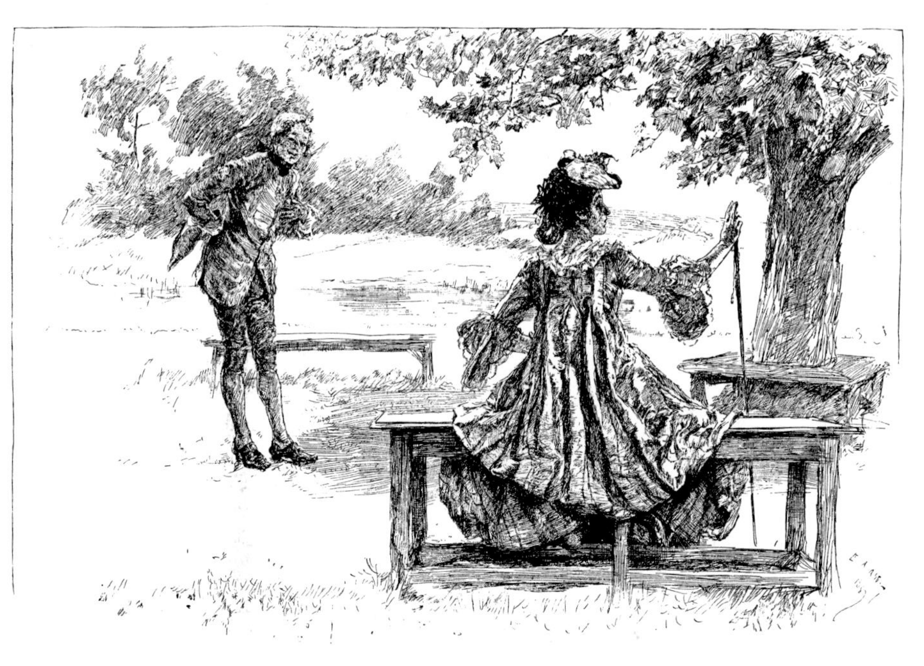

Old Songs
"Sweet Nelly, my Heart's Delight," Harper & Brothers, 1888

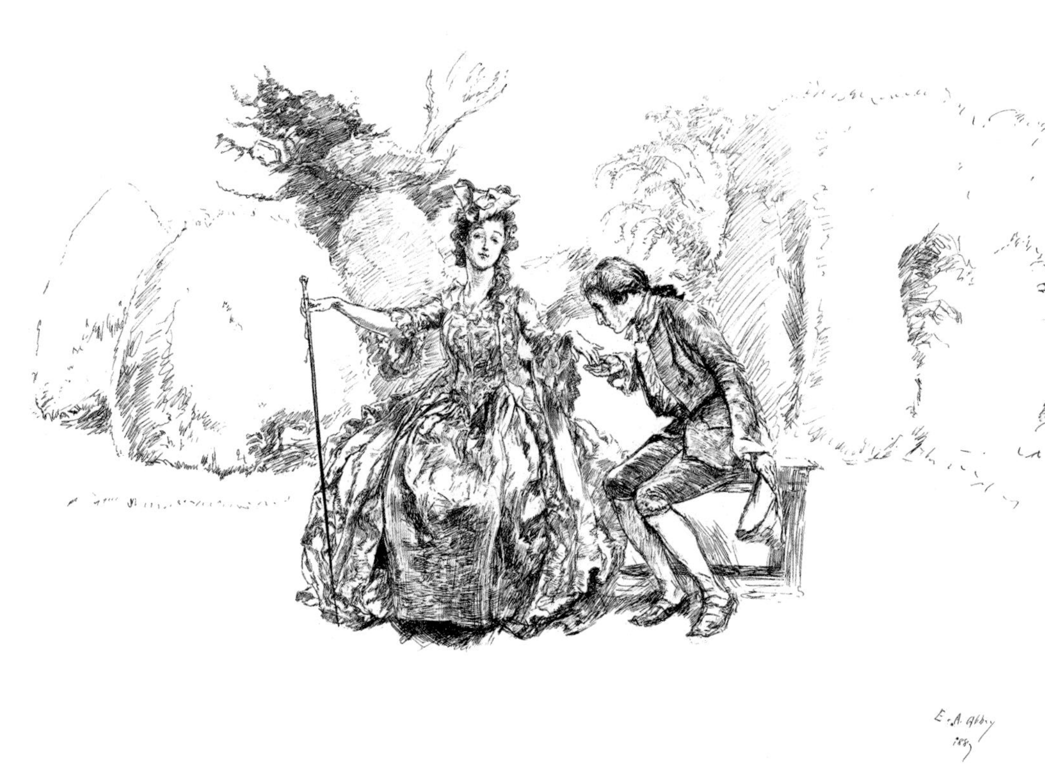

Old Songs
"Sweet Nelly, my Heart's Delight," Harper & Brothers, 1888

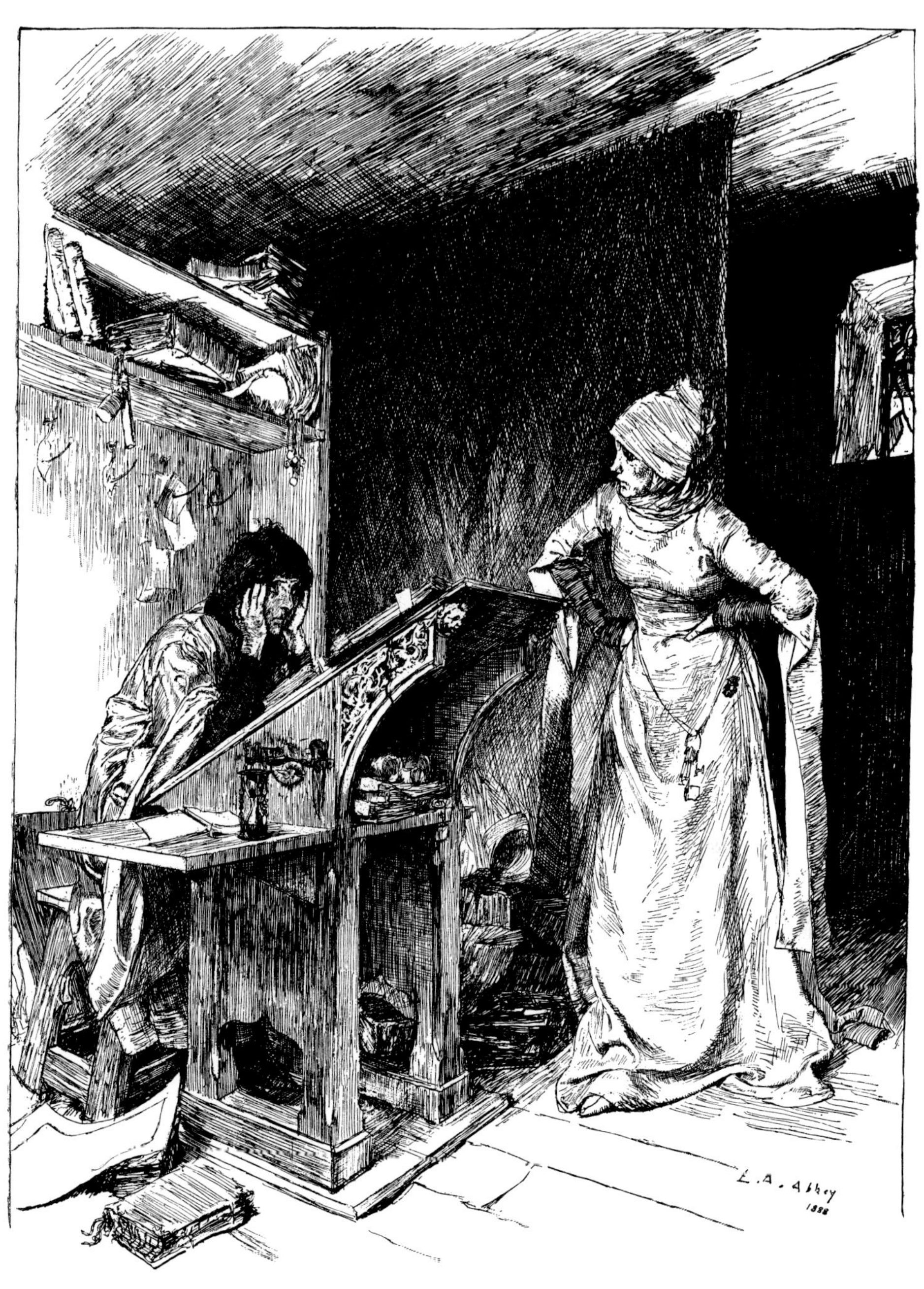

Old Songs
"What hap had I to marry a Shrow," Harper & Brothers, 1888
Originally published in *Harper's New Monthly Magazine*, October 1888

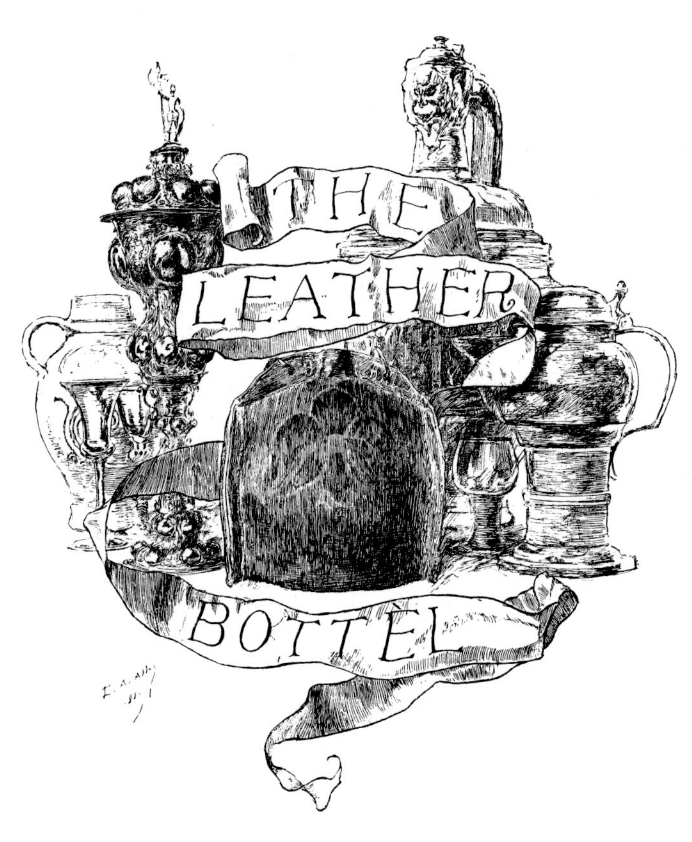

Old Songs
"The Leather Bottèl," Harper & Brothers, 1888

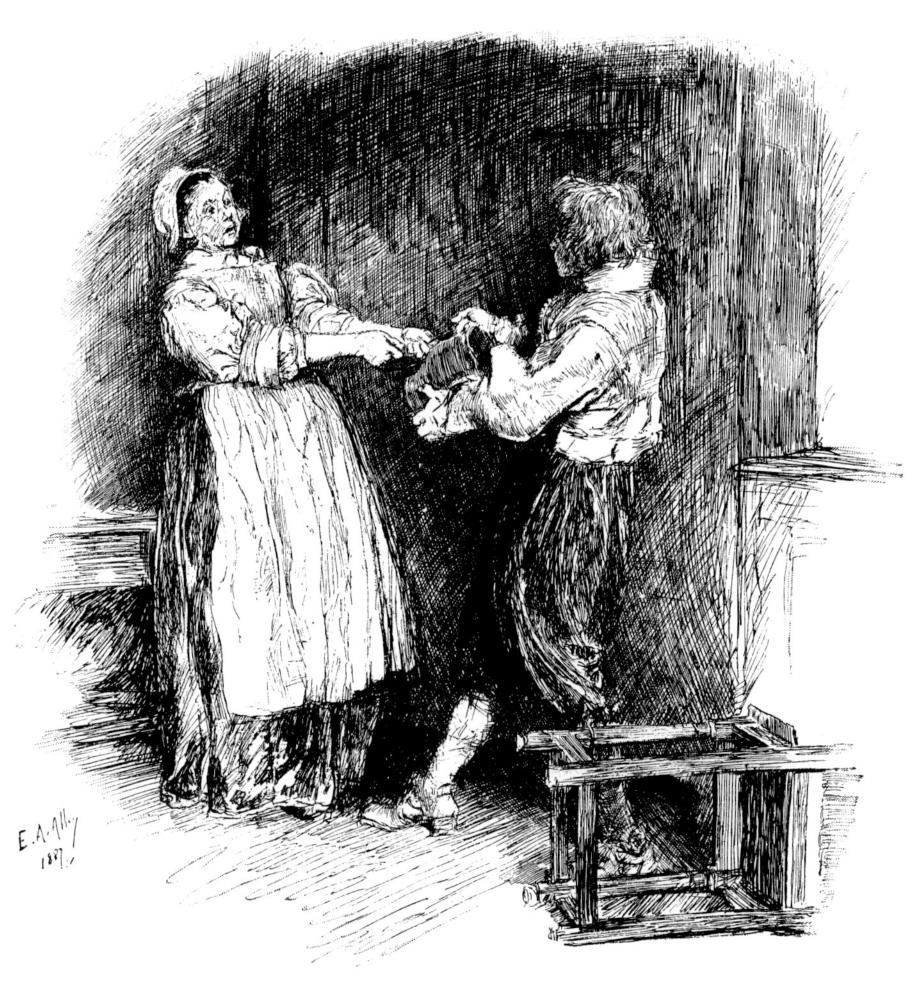

Old Songs
"The Leather Bottèl," Harper & Brothers, 1888

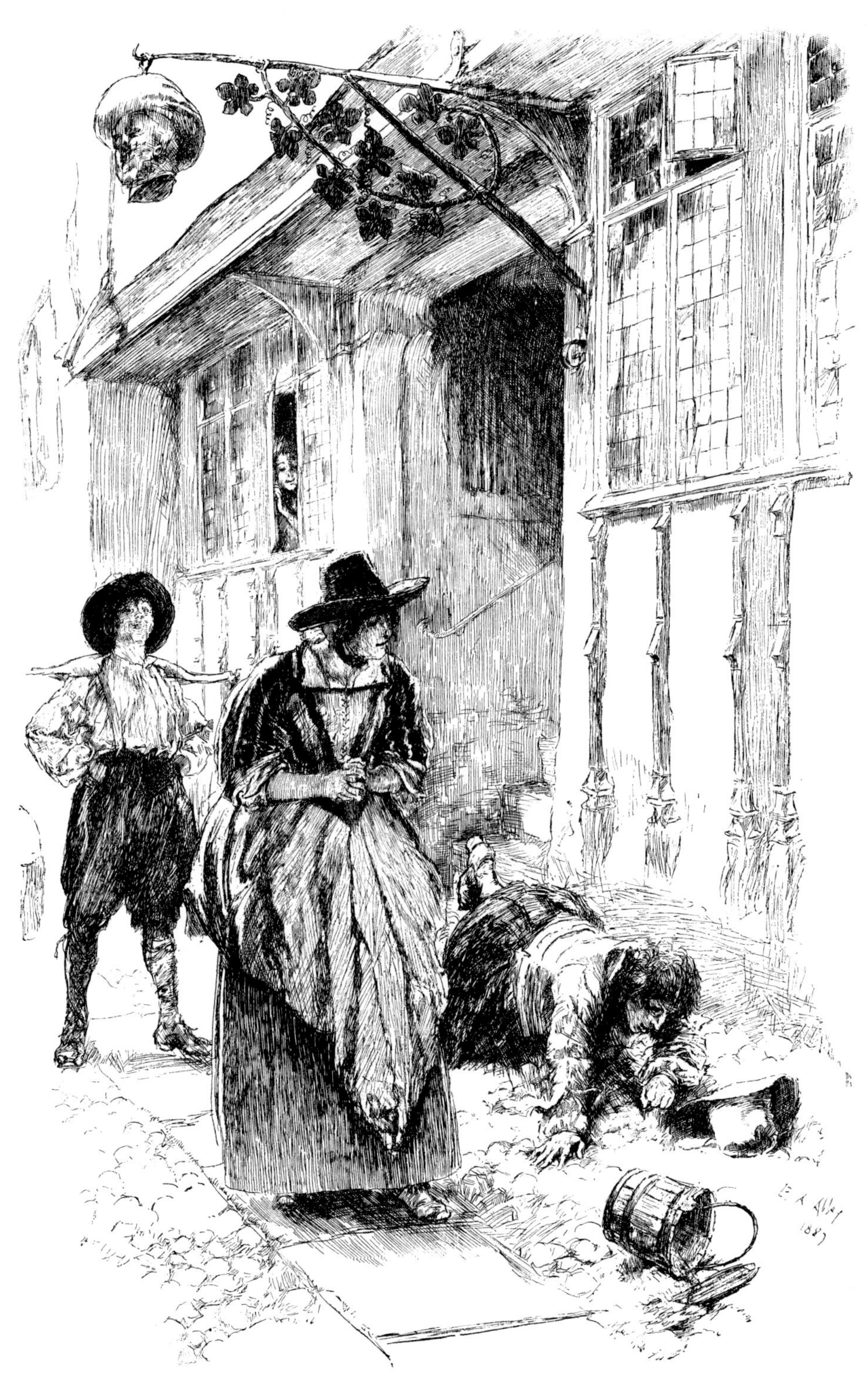

Old Songs
"The Leather Bottèl," Harper & Brothers, 1888
Originally published in *Harper's New Monthly Magazine*, August 1888

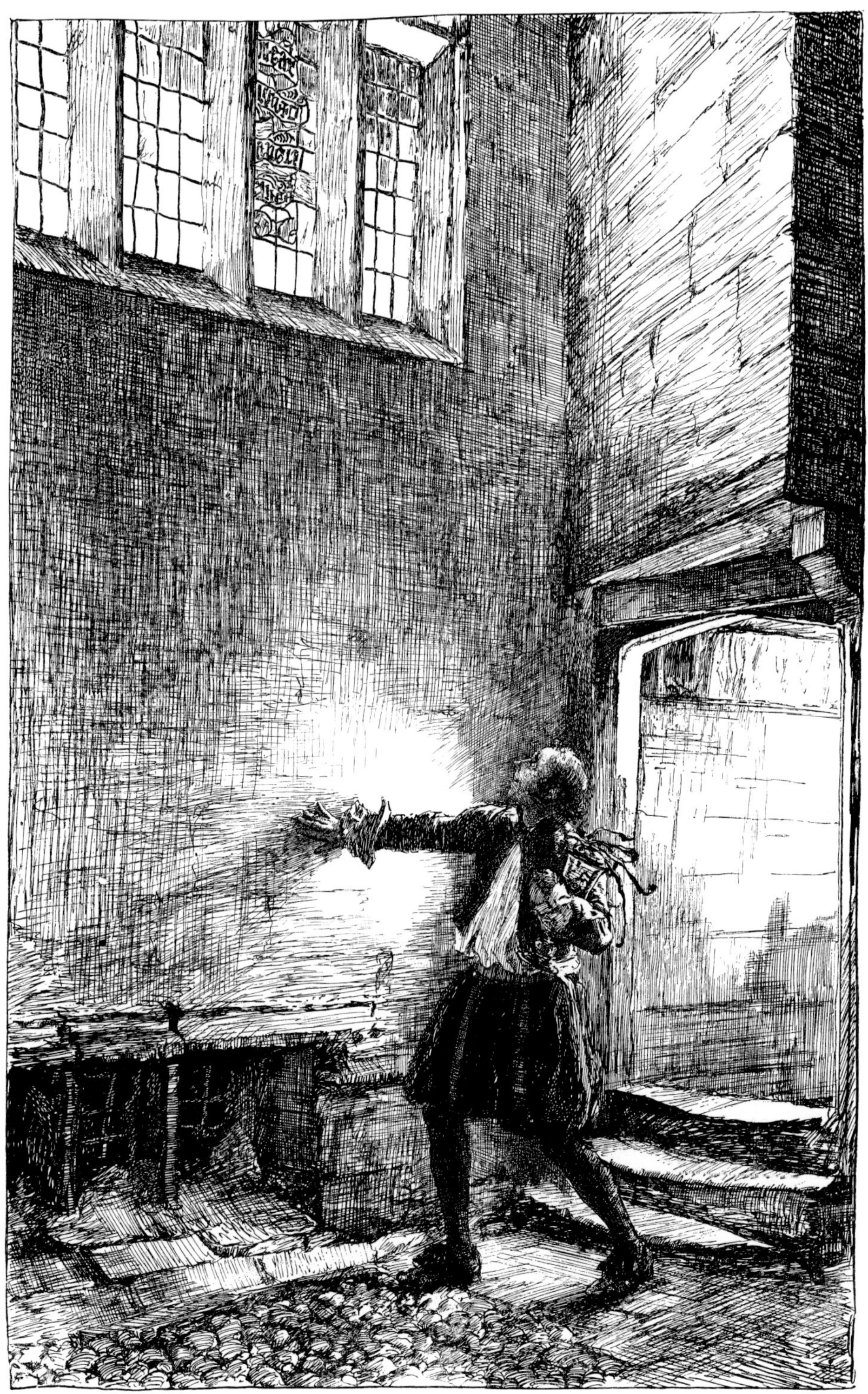

Old Songs
"The Leather Bottèl," Harper & Brothers, 1888
Originally published in *Harper's New Monthly Magazine*, August 1888

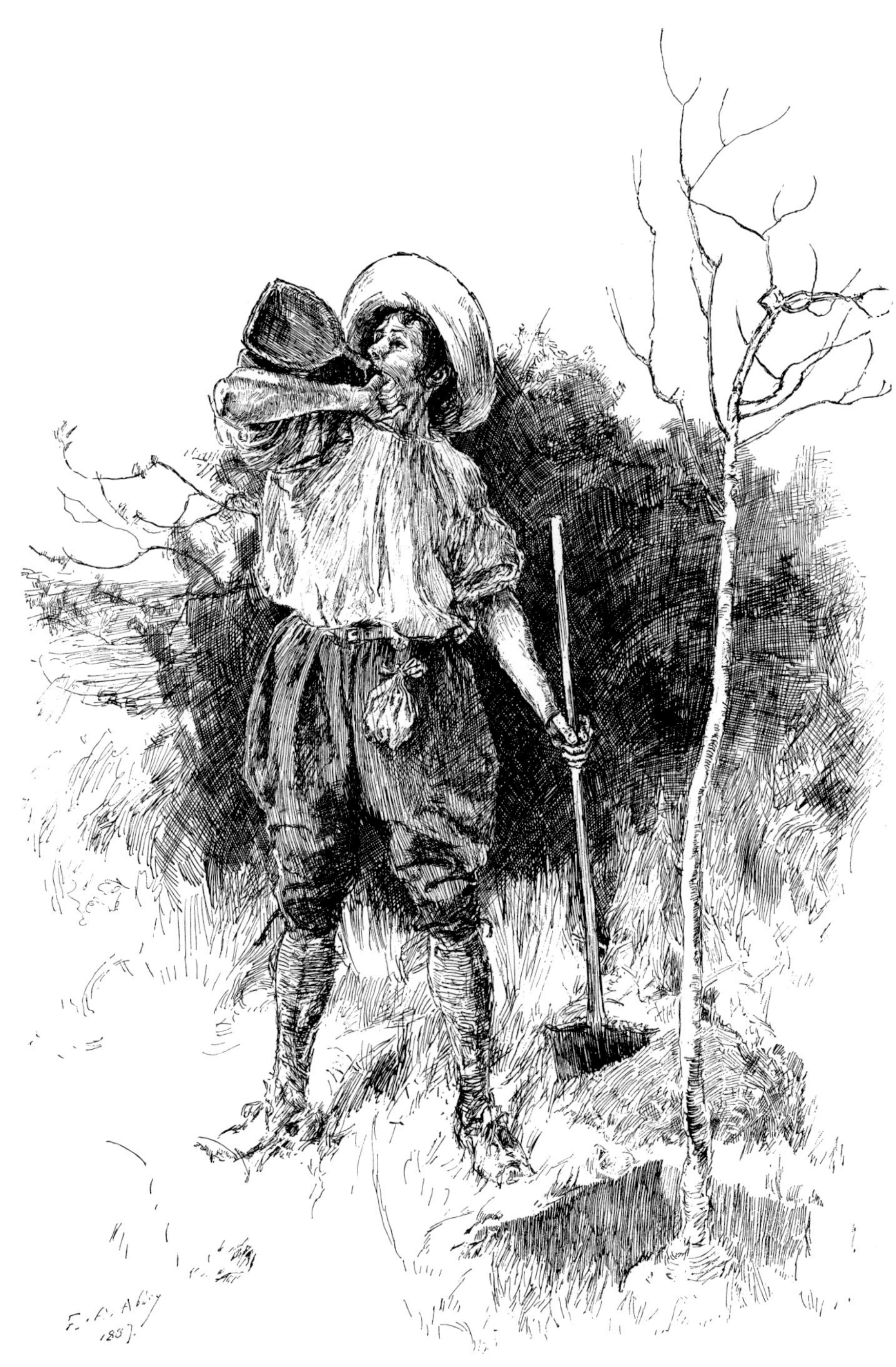

"The Leather Bottèl."

Old Songs
"The Leather Bottèl," Harper & Brothers, 1888

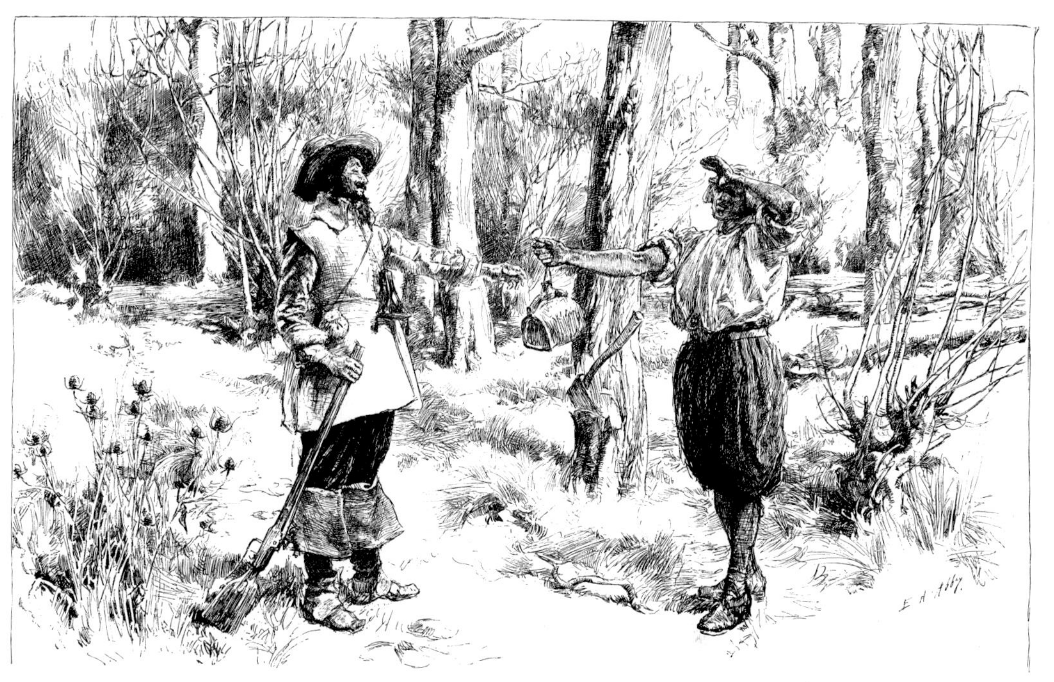

"For when he's hunting of the deer."

Old Songs
"The Leather Bottèl," Harper & Brothers, 1888

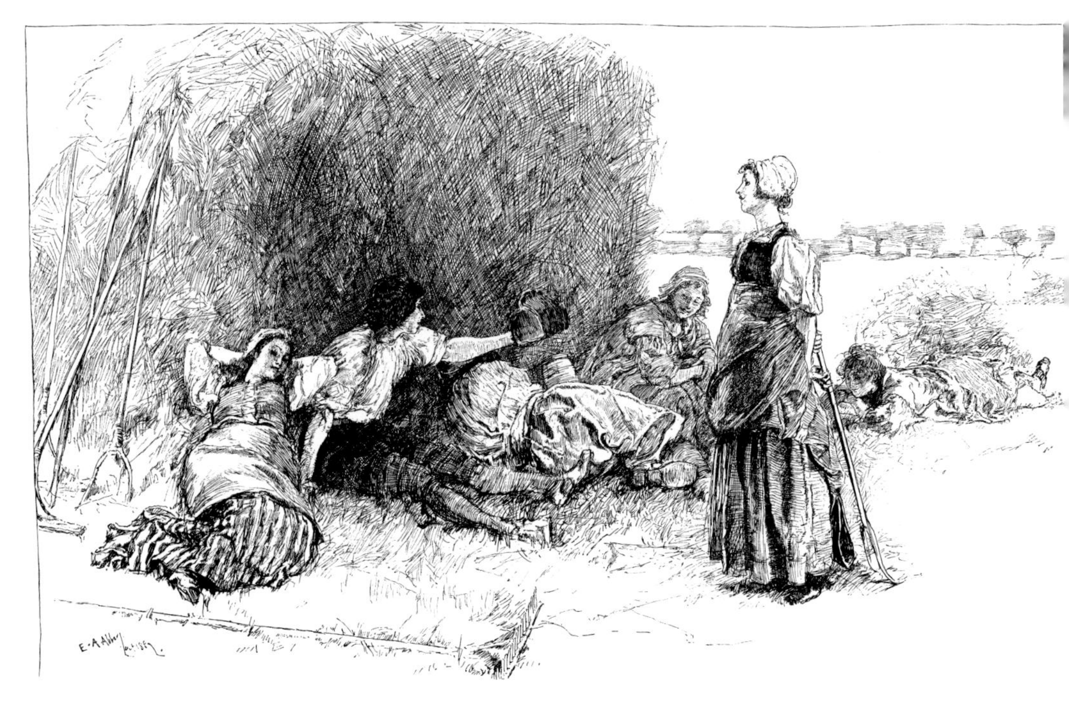

Old Songs
"The Leather Bottèl," Harper & Brothers, 1888
Originally published in *Harper's New Monthly Magazine*, August 1888

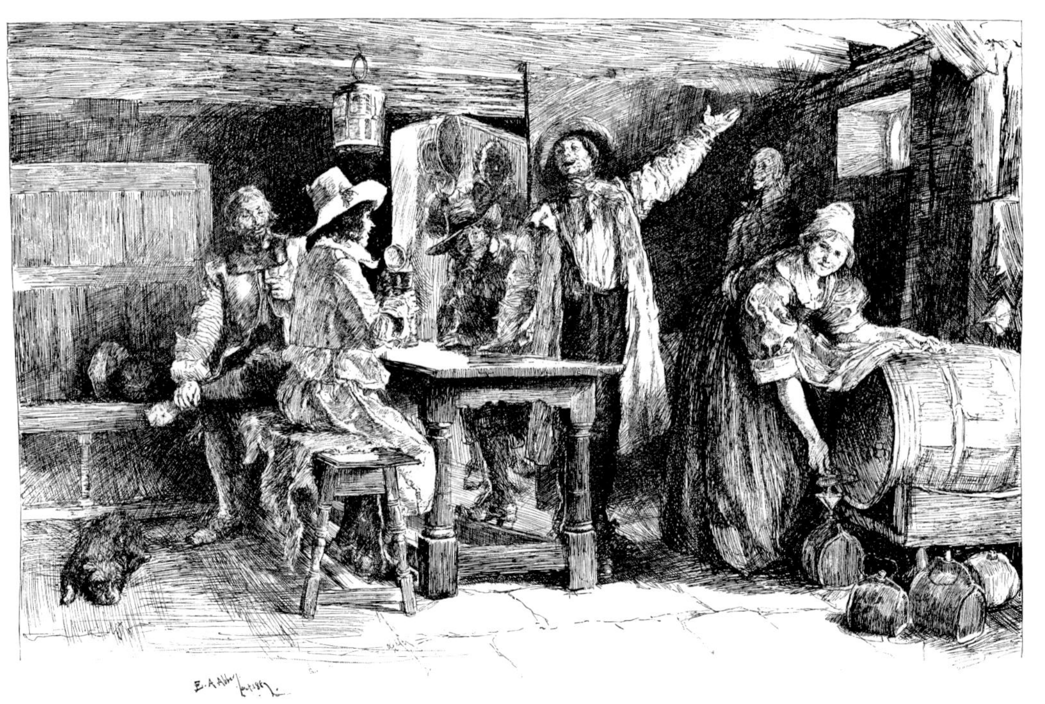

At the inn.

Old Songs
"The Leather Bottèl," Harper & Brothers, 1888

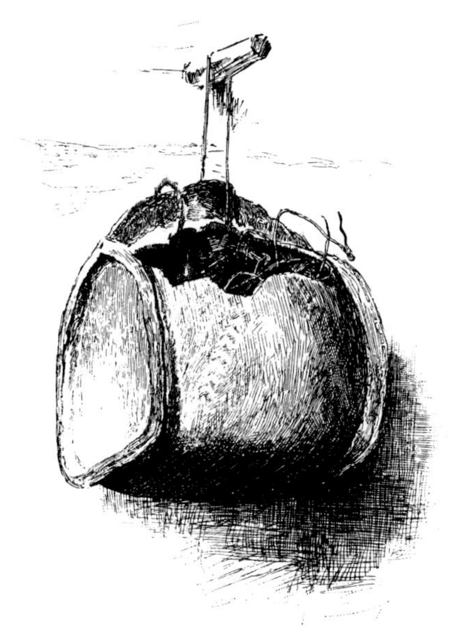

Old Songs
"The Leather Bottèl," Harper & Brothers, 1888

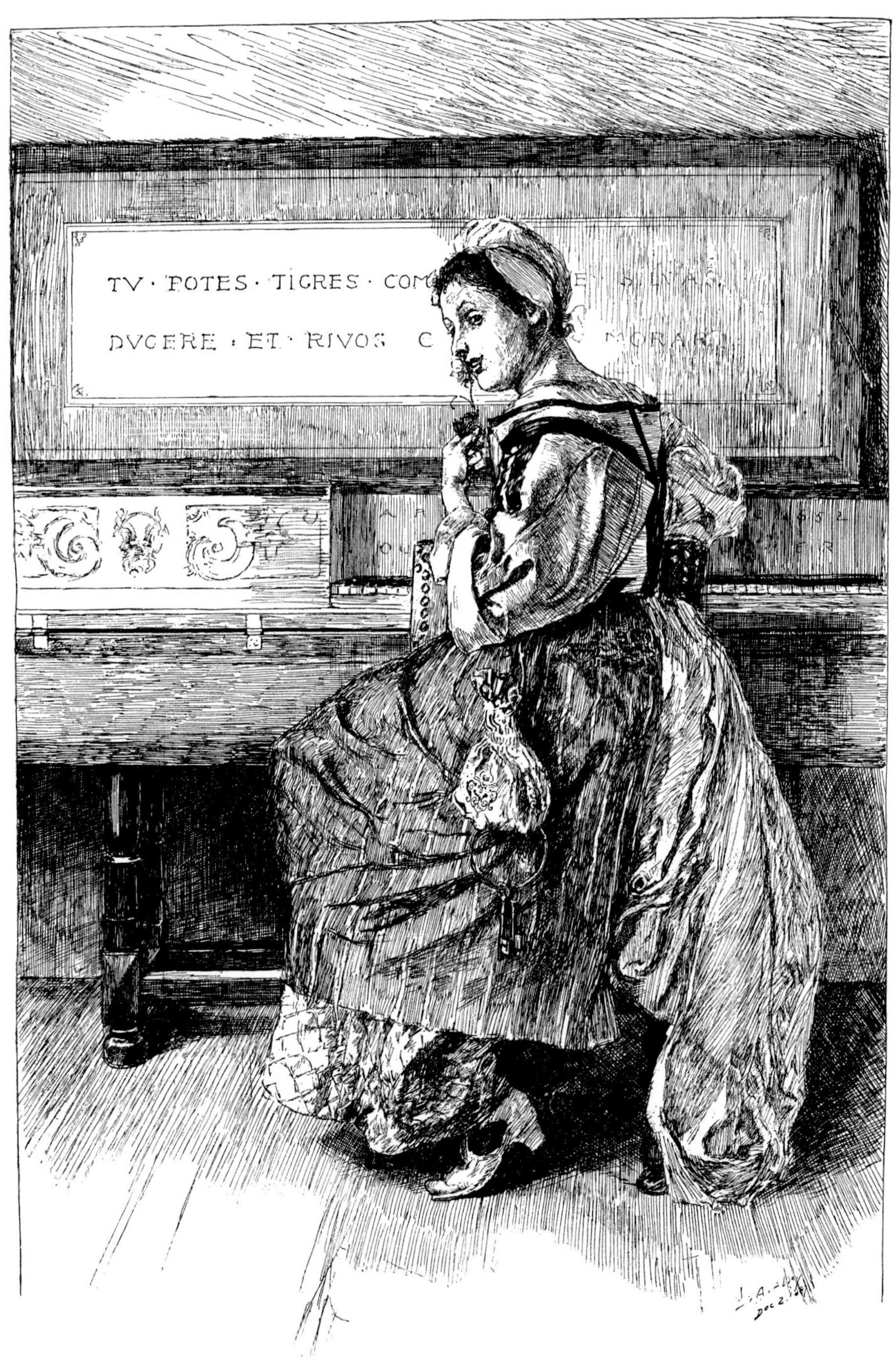

Old Songs
"Never Love Thee More," Harper & Brothers, 1888
Originally published in *Harper's New Monthly Magazine*, October 1888

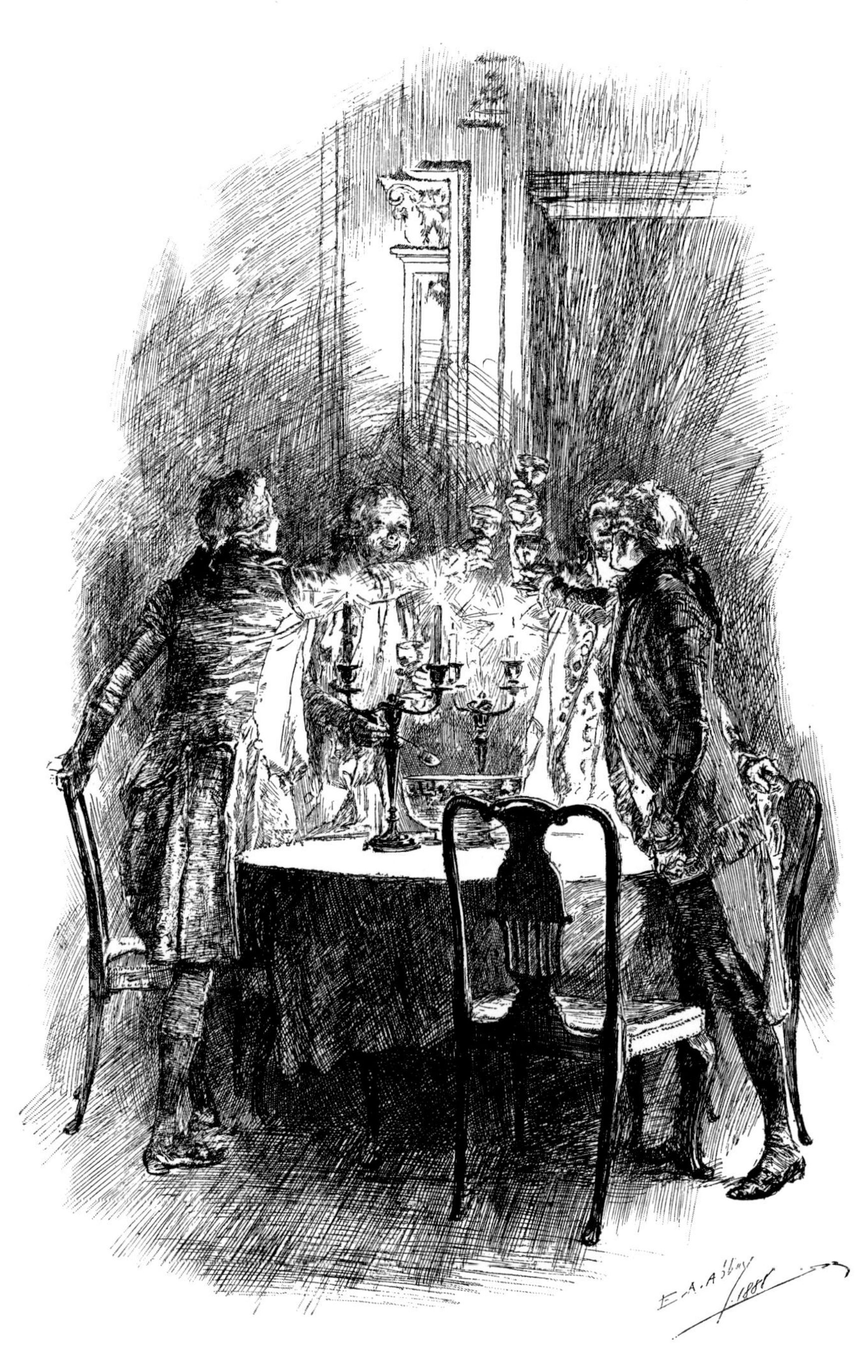

Old Songs
"Here's to the Maiden of Bathful Fifteen," Harper & Brothers, 1888
Originally published in *Harper's New Monthly Magazine*, October 1888

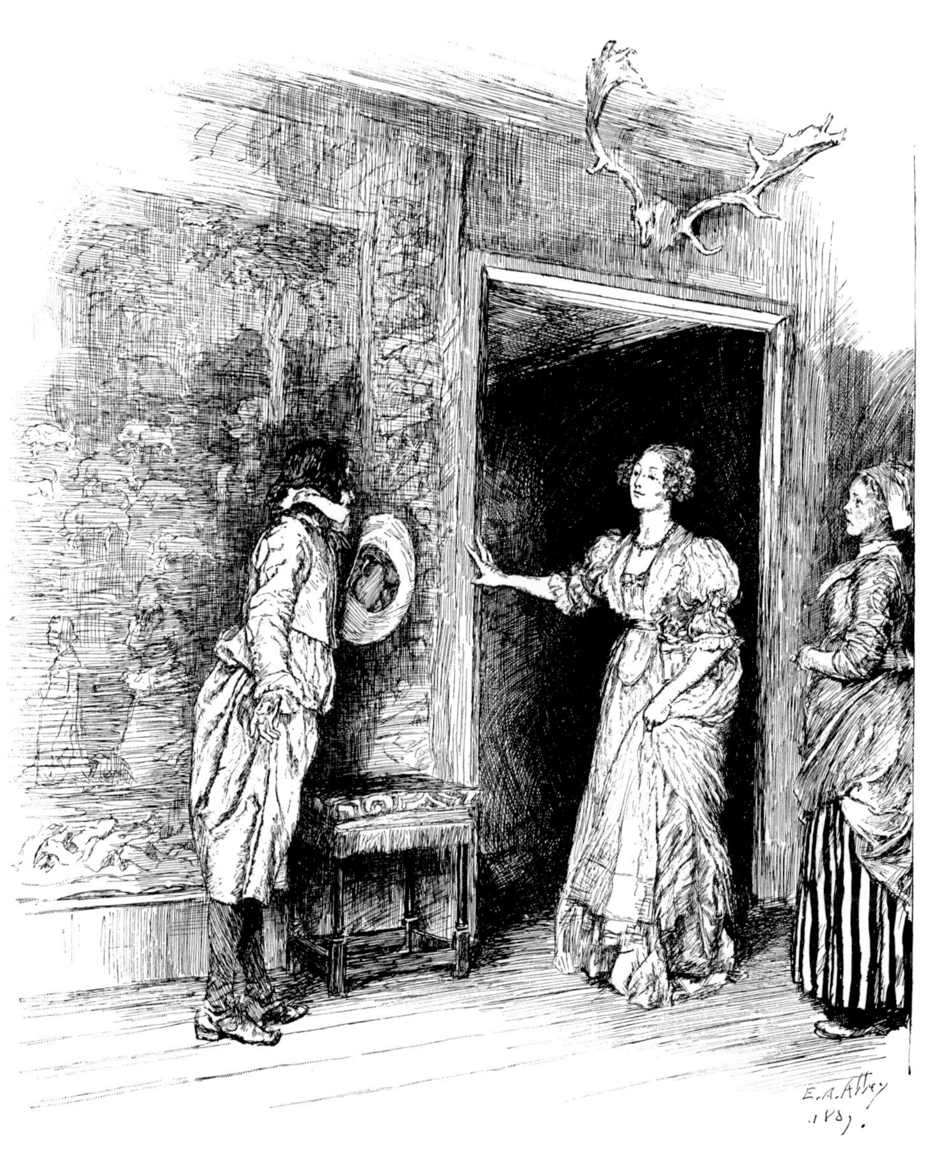

Old Songs
"Barbara Allen," Harper & Brothers, 1888

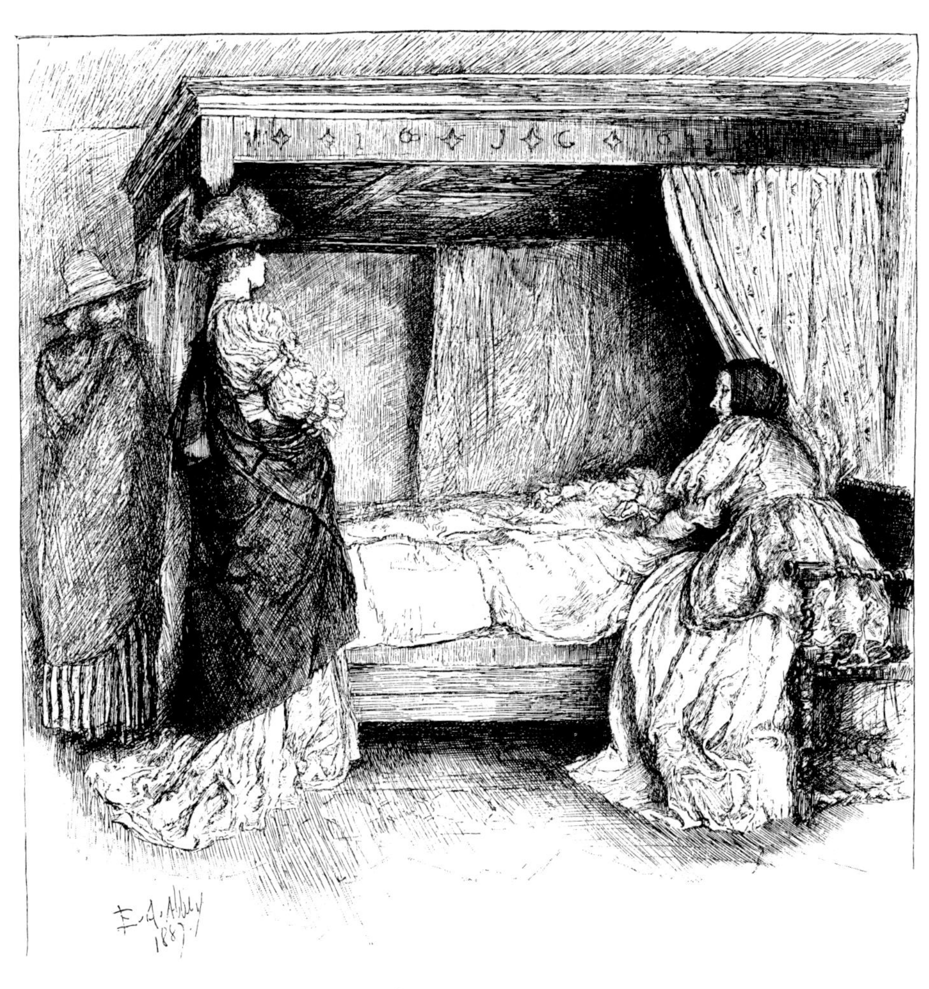

Old Songs
"Barbara Allen," Harper & Brothers, 1888

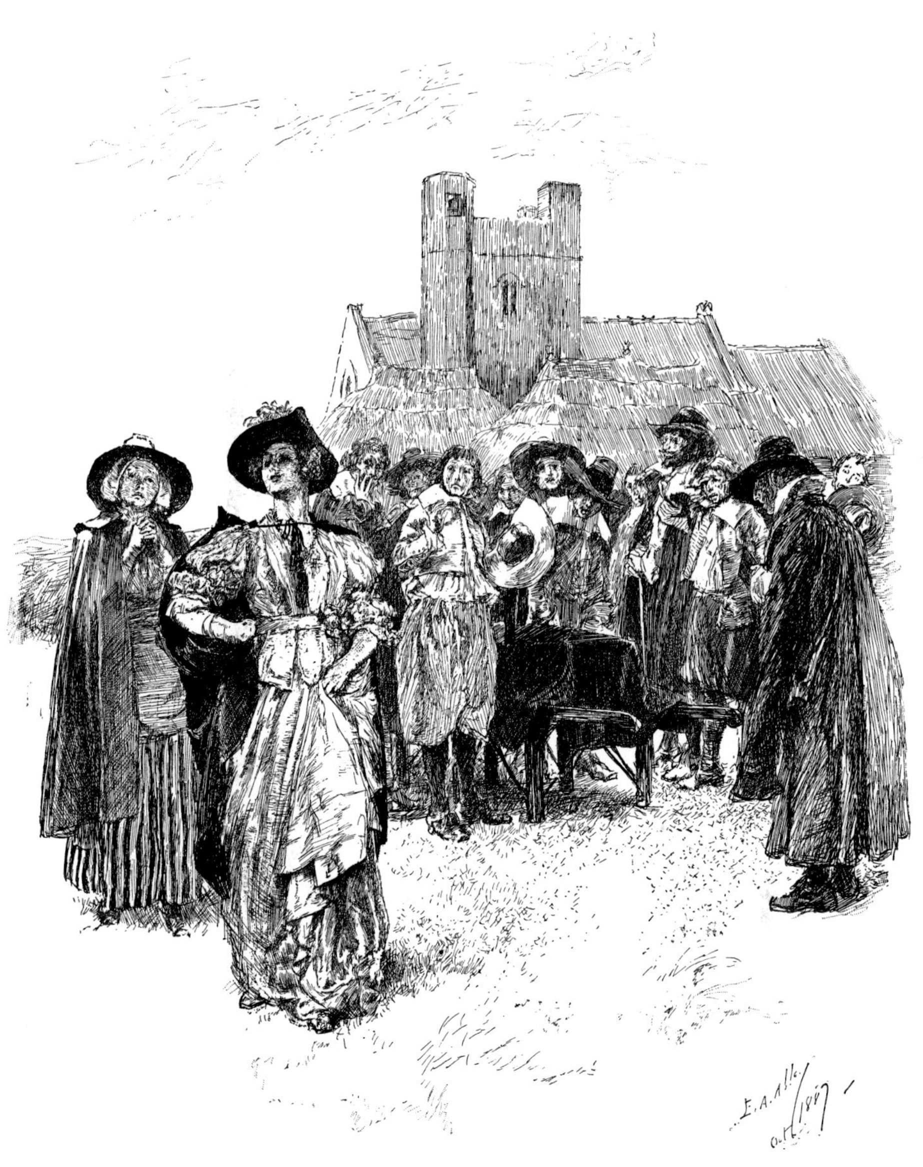

"And as she was walking on a day, she heard the bell a ringing."

Old Songs
"Barbara Allen," Harper & Brothers, 1888

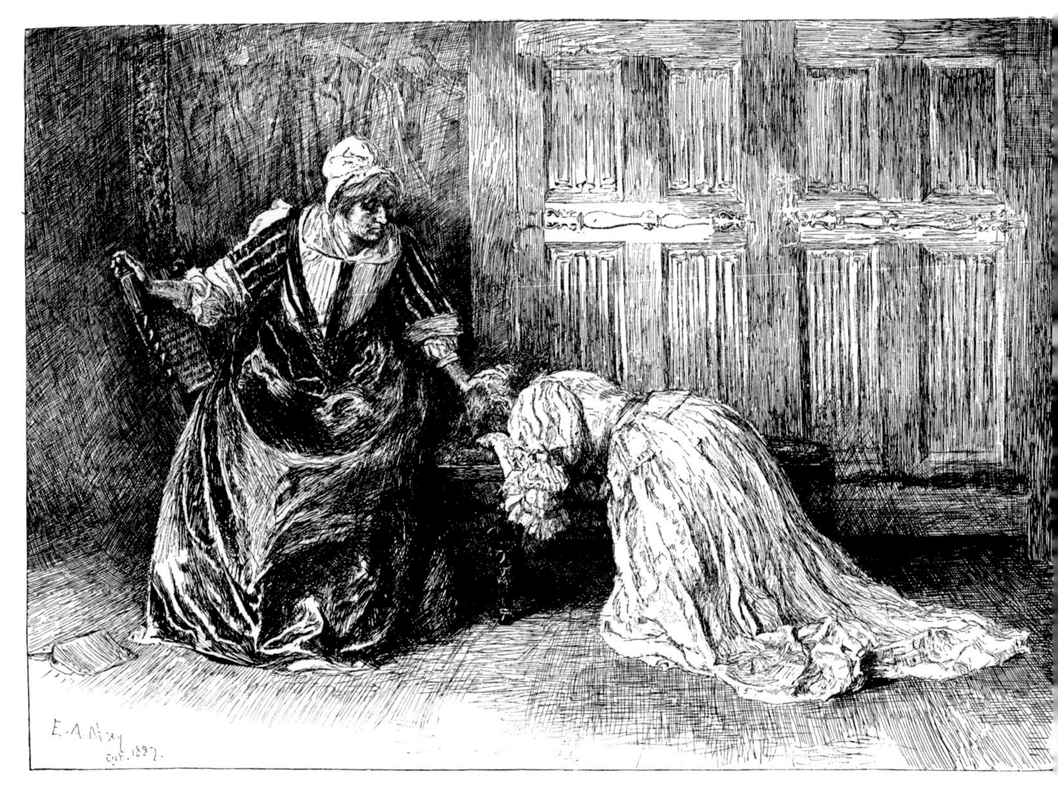

"O Mother! Mother! Make my bed, for his death hath quite undone me."

Old Songs
"Barbara Allen," Harper & Brothers, 1888

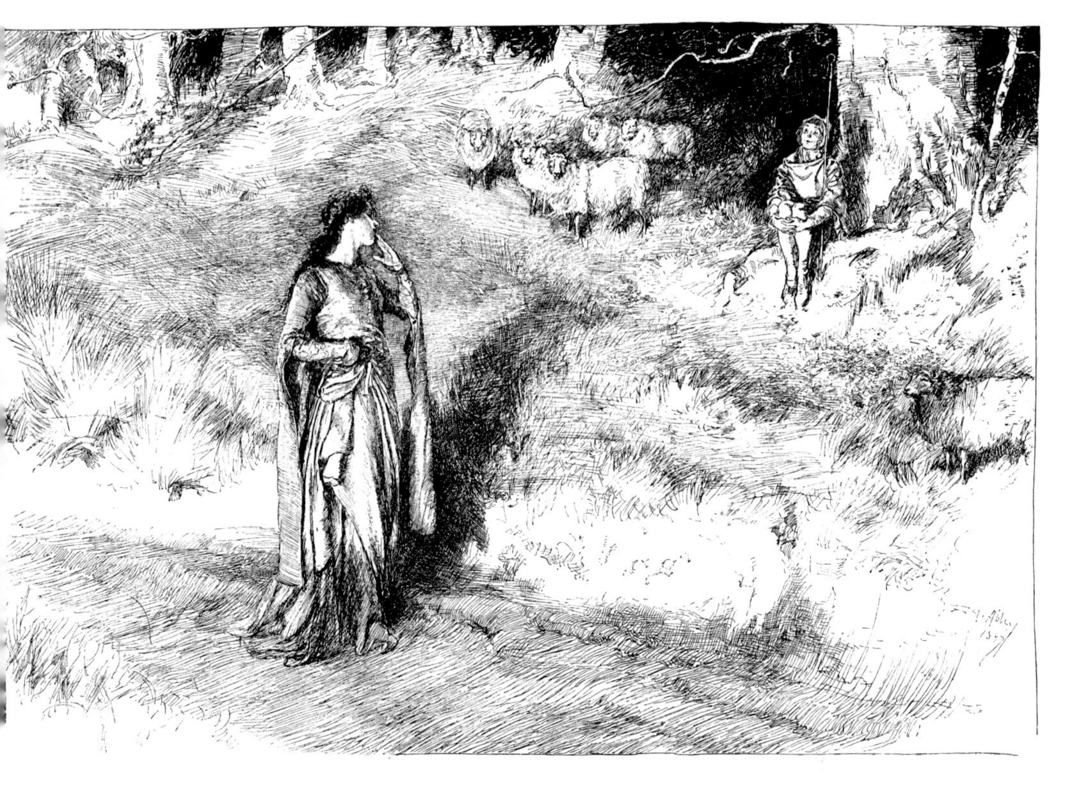

Old Songs
"Perigot & Cuddy's Roundelay," Harper & Brothers, 1888
Originally published in *Harper's New Monthly Magazine*, October 1888

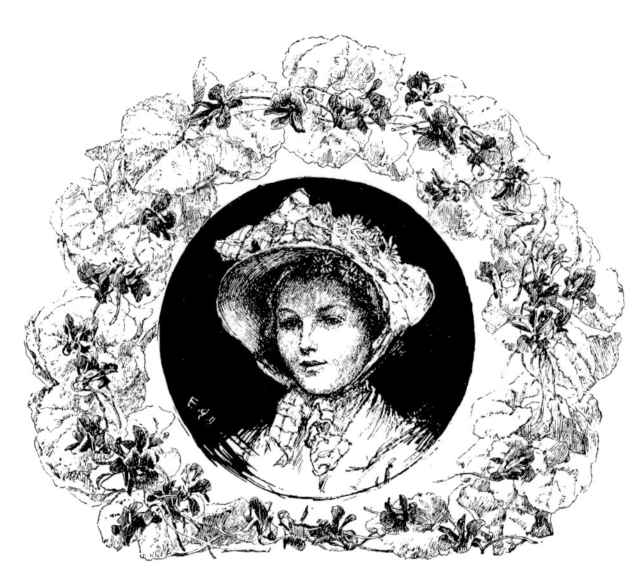

Old Songs
"Sally in Our Alley," Harper & Brothers, 1888

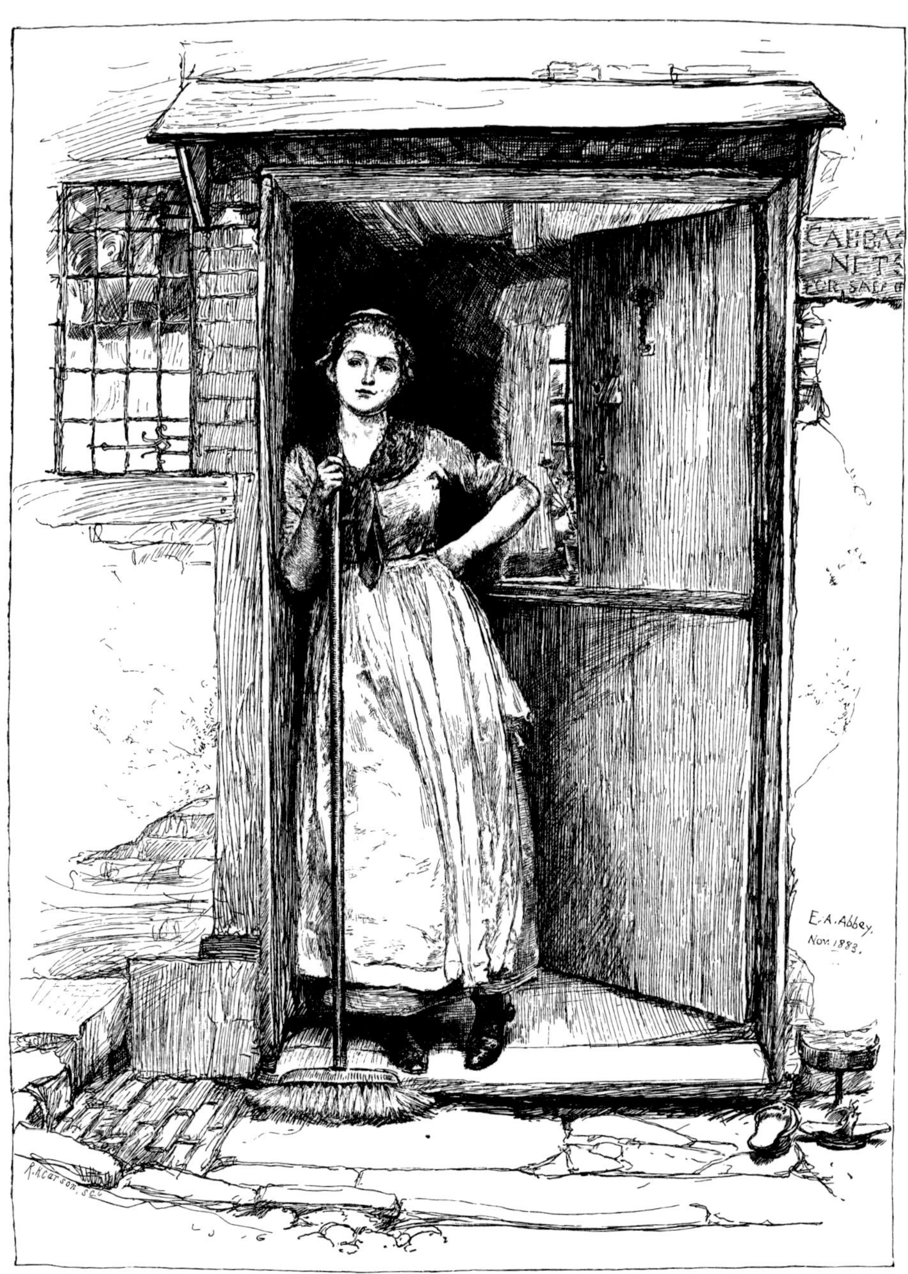

"There's none like pretty Sally."

Old Songs
"Sally in Our Alley," Harper & Brothers, 1888
Originally published in *Harper's New Monthly Magazine*, December 1886

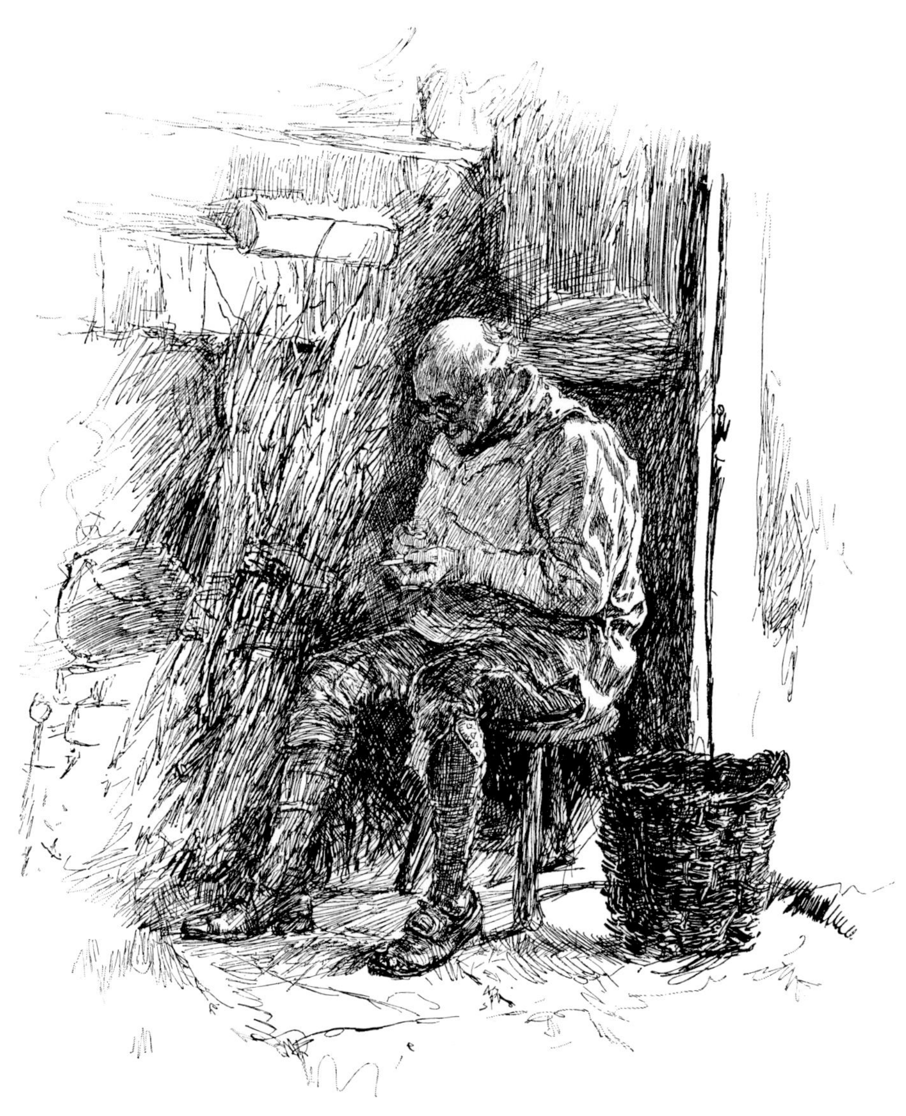

"Her father he makes cabbage-nets."

Old Songs
"Sally in Our Alley," Harper & Brothers, 1888
Originally published in *Harper's New Monthly Magazine*, December 1886

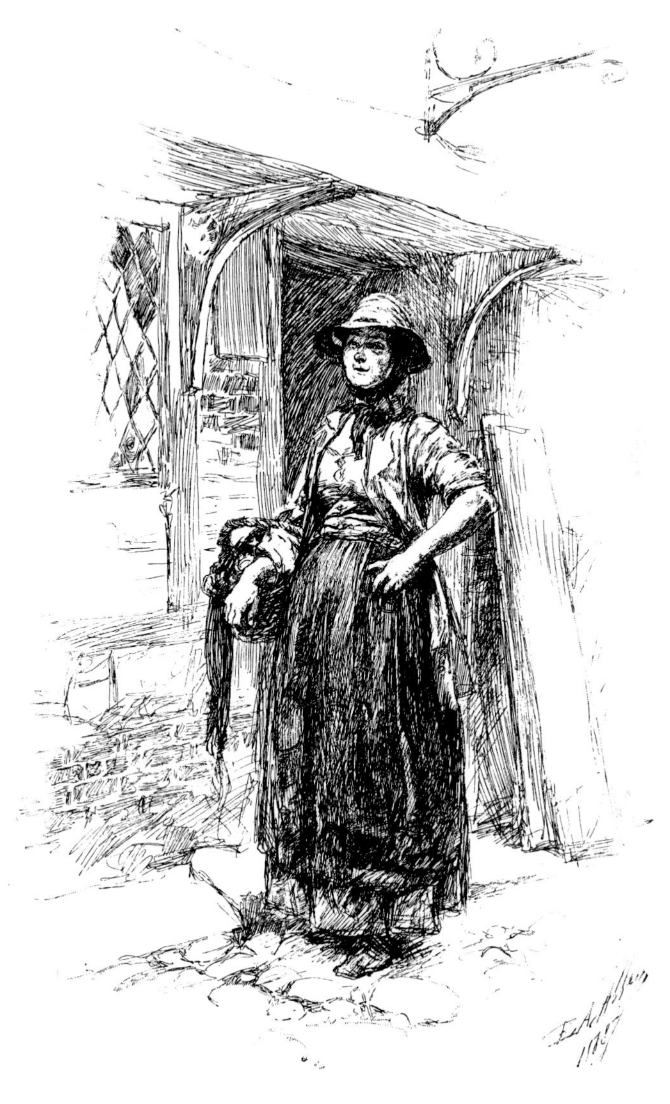

Old Songs
"Sally in Our Alley," Harper & Brothers, 1888

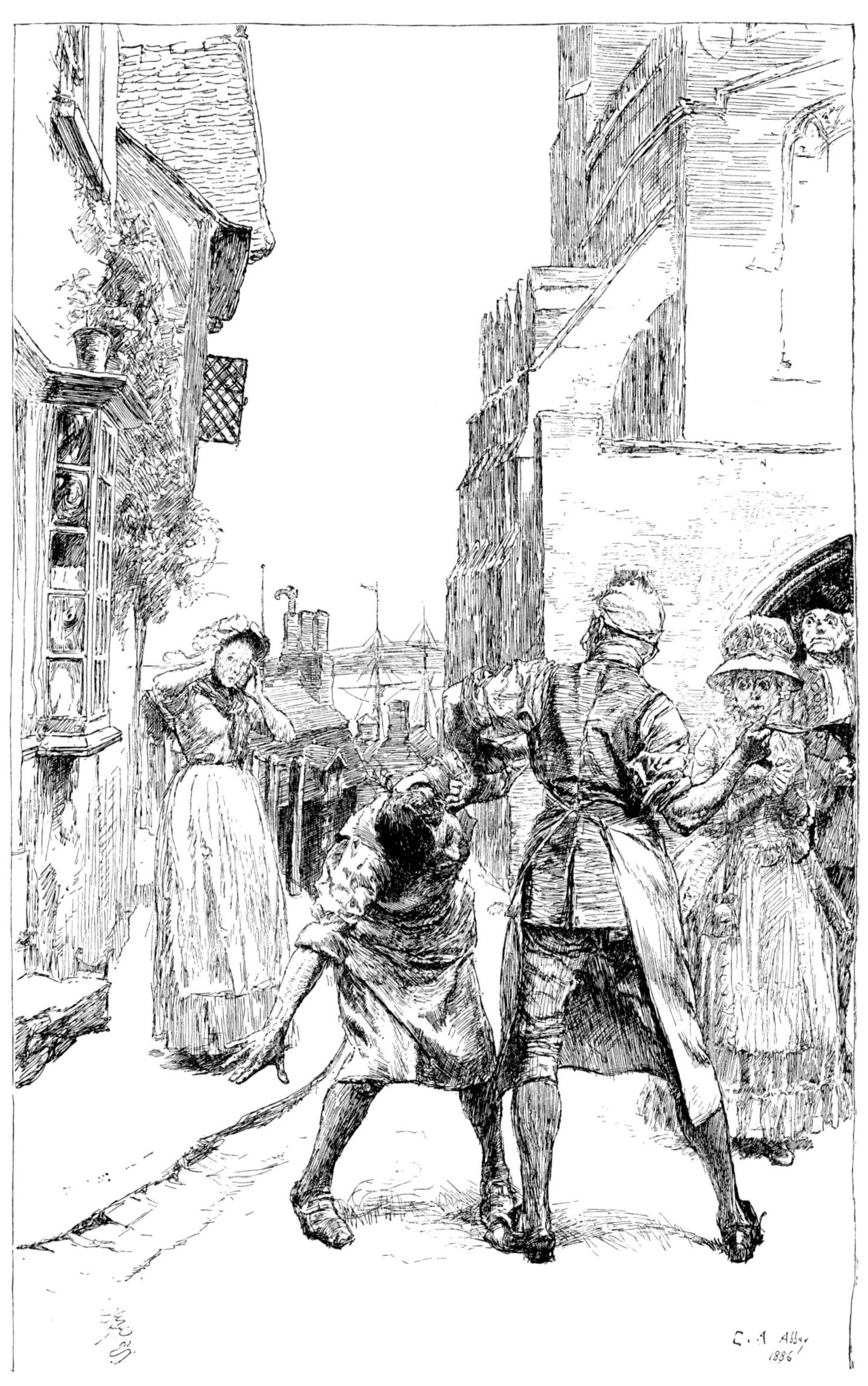

Old Songs
"Sally in Our Alley," Harper & Brothers, 1888

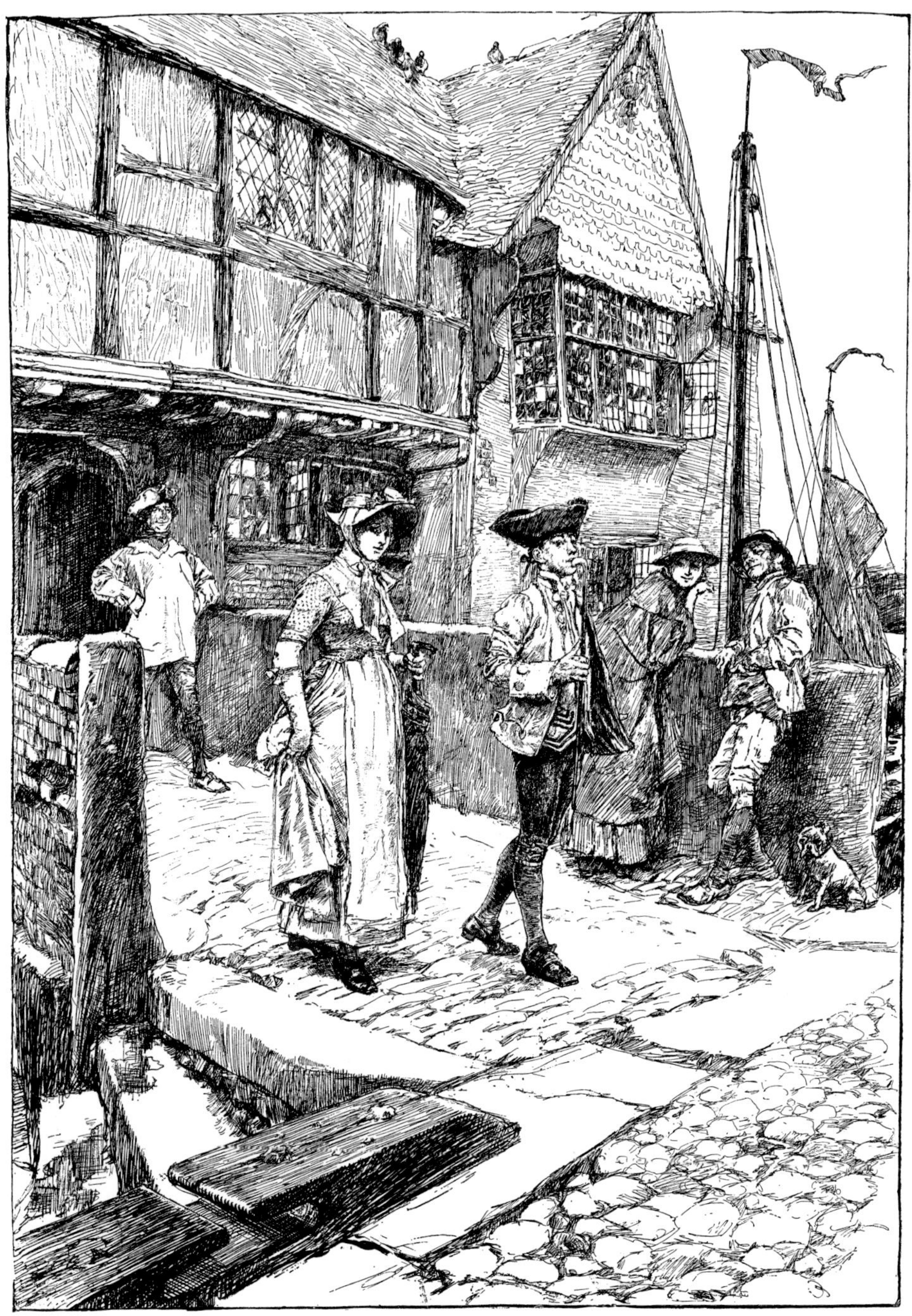

"To walk abroad with Sally."

Old Songs
"Sally in Our Alley," Harper & Brothers, 1888
Originally published in *Harper's New Monthly Magazine*, December 1886

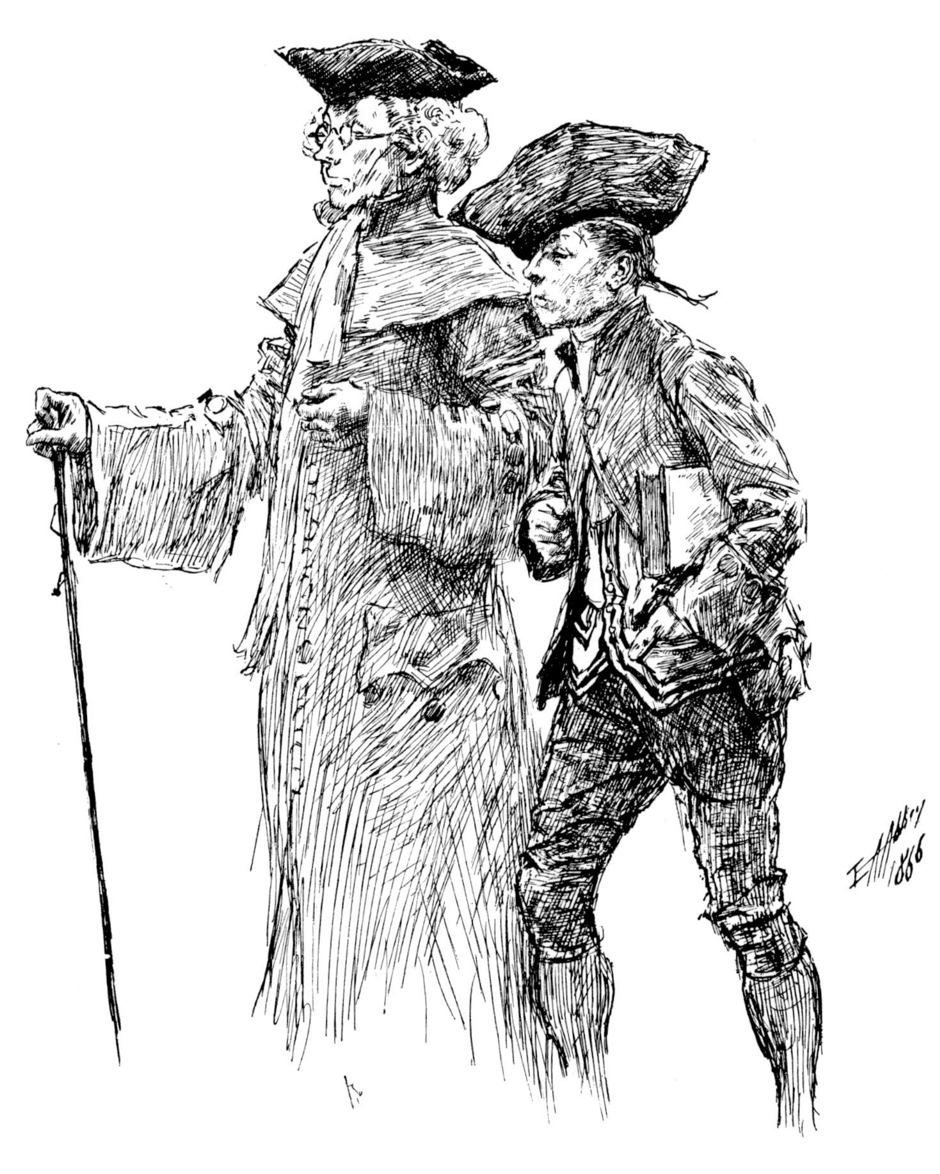

Old Songs
"Sally in Our Alley," Harper & Brothers, 1888

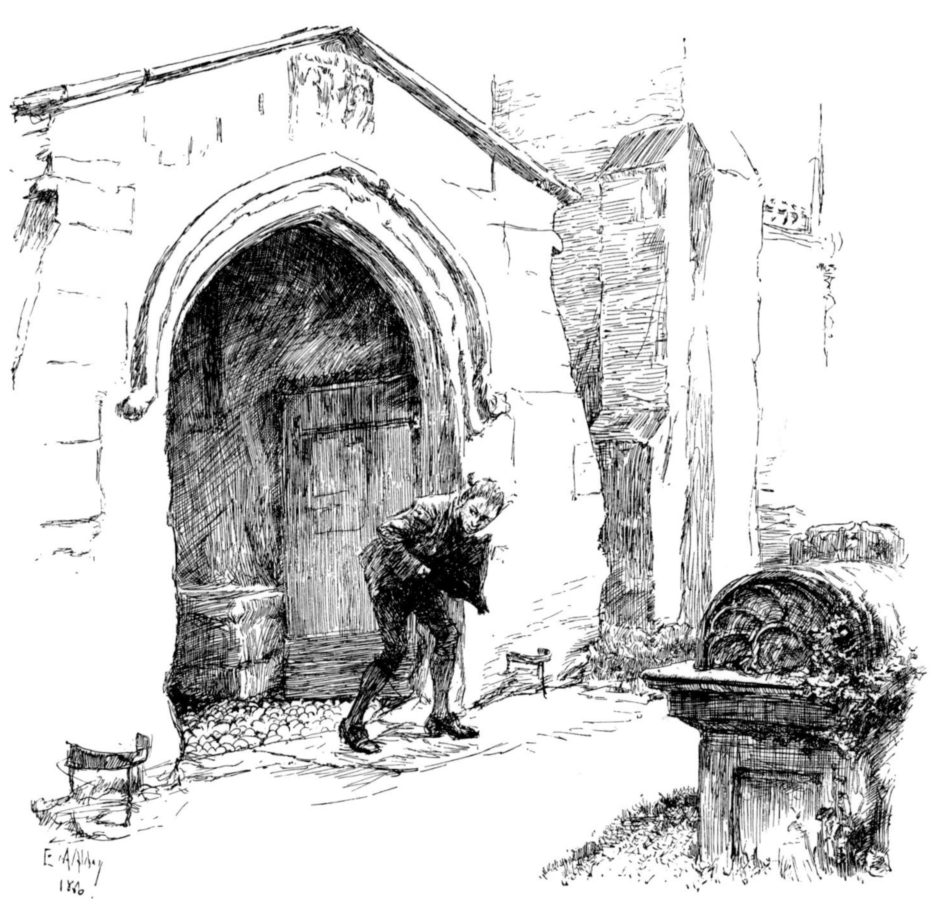

"I leave him in the lurch."

Old Songs
"Sally in Our Alley," Harper & Brothers, 1888
Originally published in *Harper's New Monthly Magazine*, December 1886

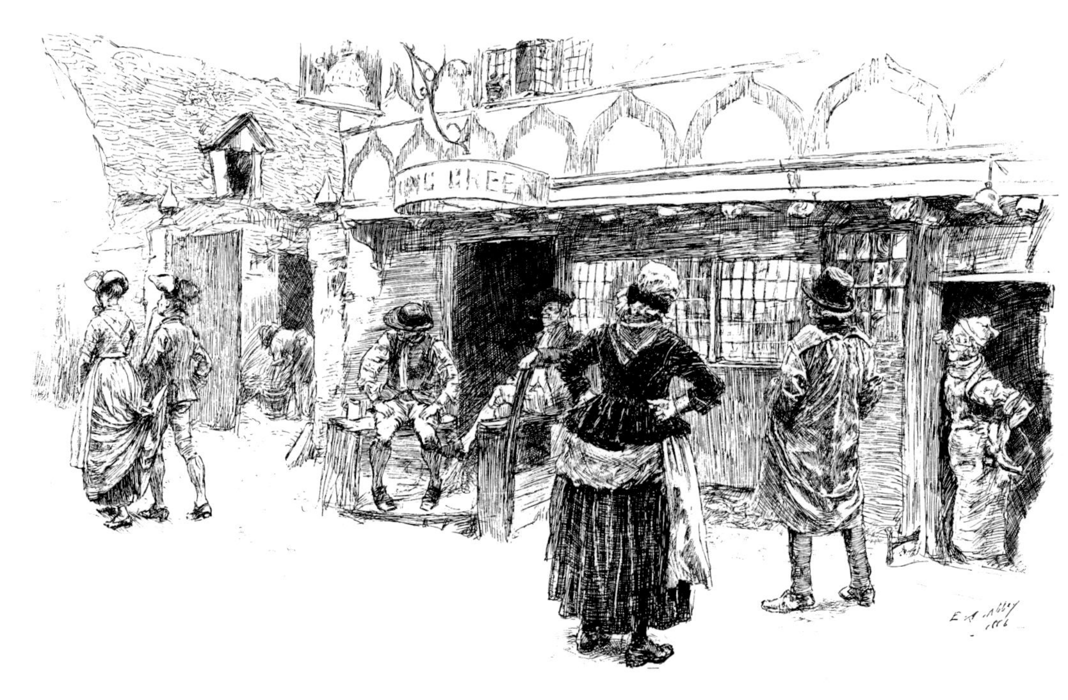

Old Songs
"Sally in Our Alley," Harper & Brothers, 1888

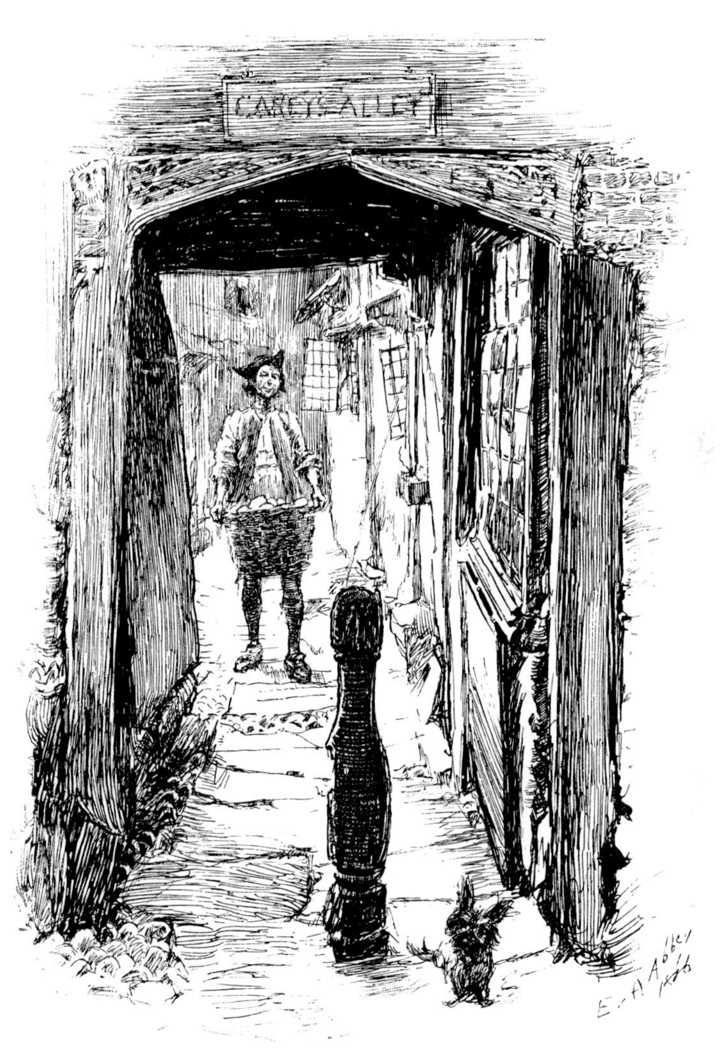

Old Songs
"Sally in Our Alley," Harper & Brothers, 1888

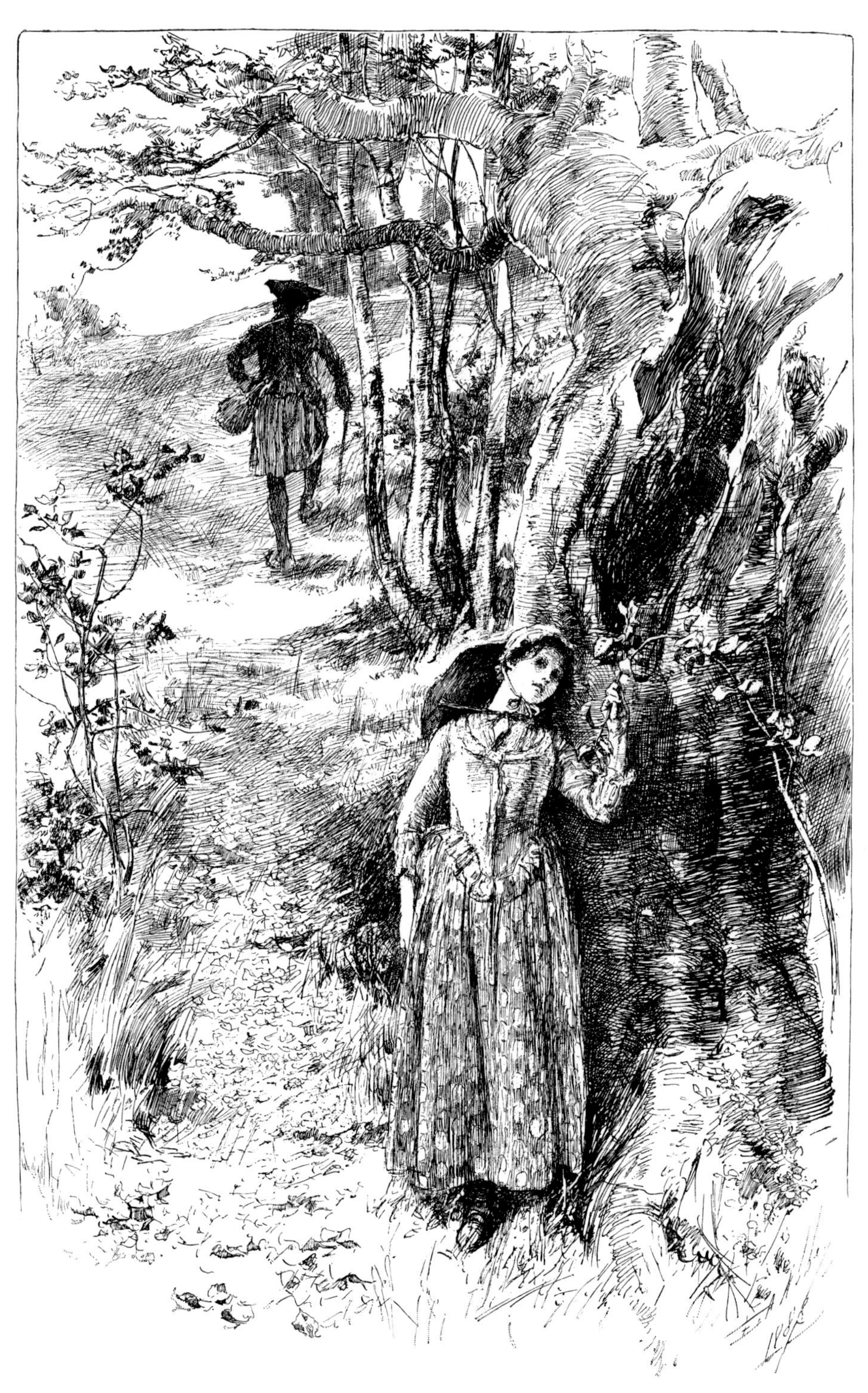

Old Songs
"Early One Morning," Harper & Brothers, 1888
Originally published in *Harper's New Monthly Magazine*, October 1888

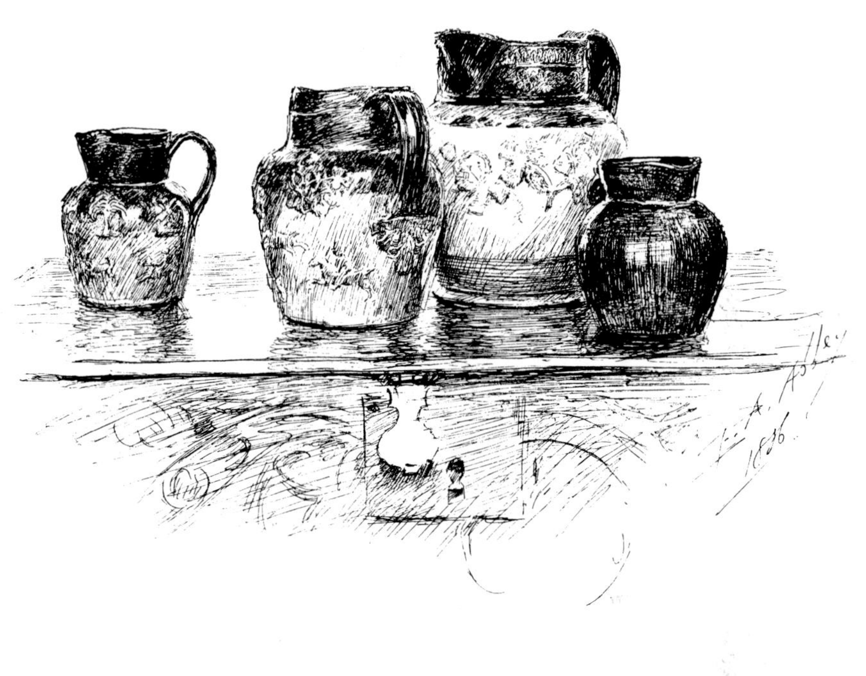

Old Songs
"Kitty of Coleraine," Harper & Brothers, 1888

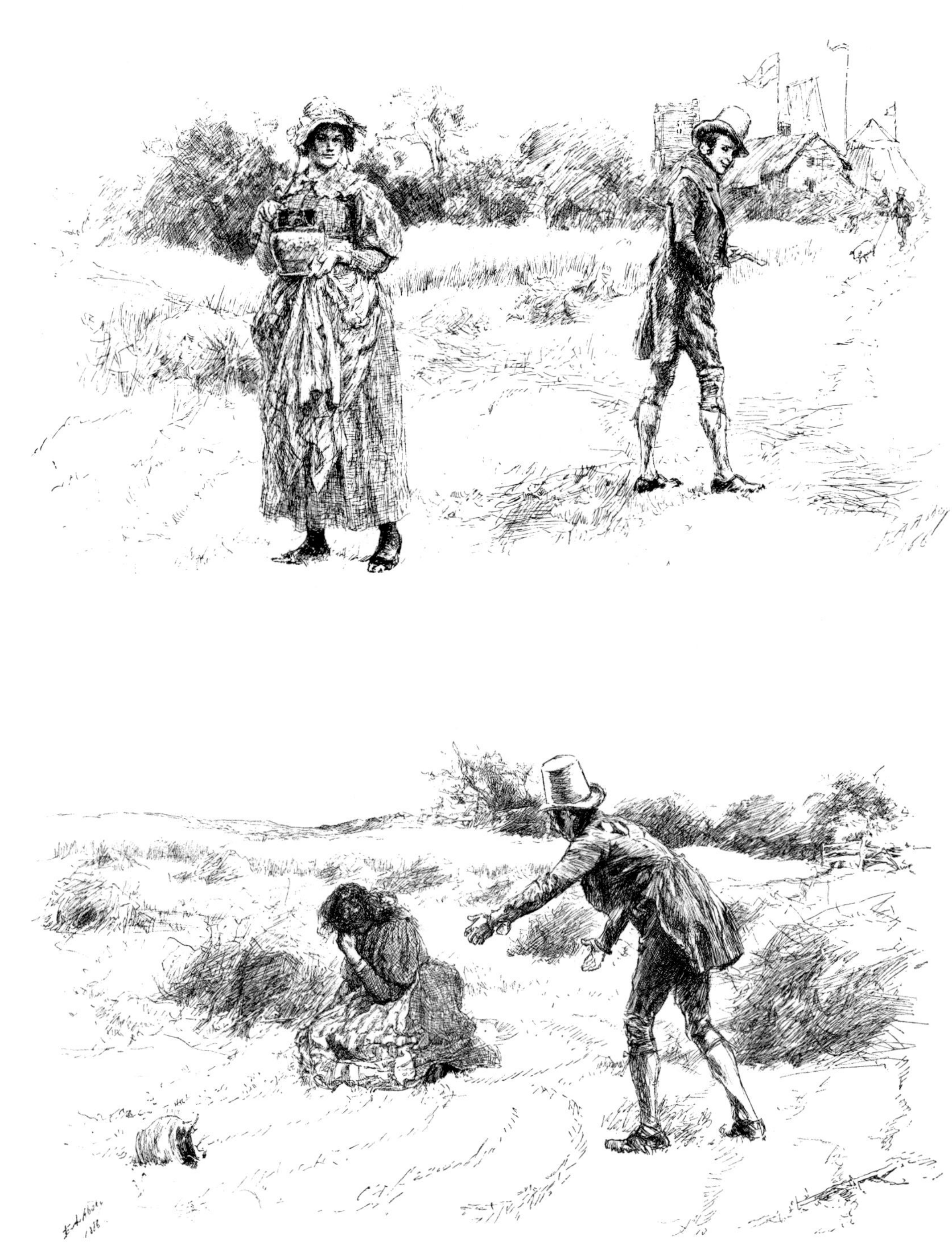

Old Songs
"Kitty of Coleraine," Harper & Brothers, 1888

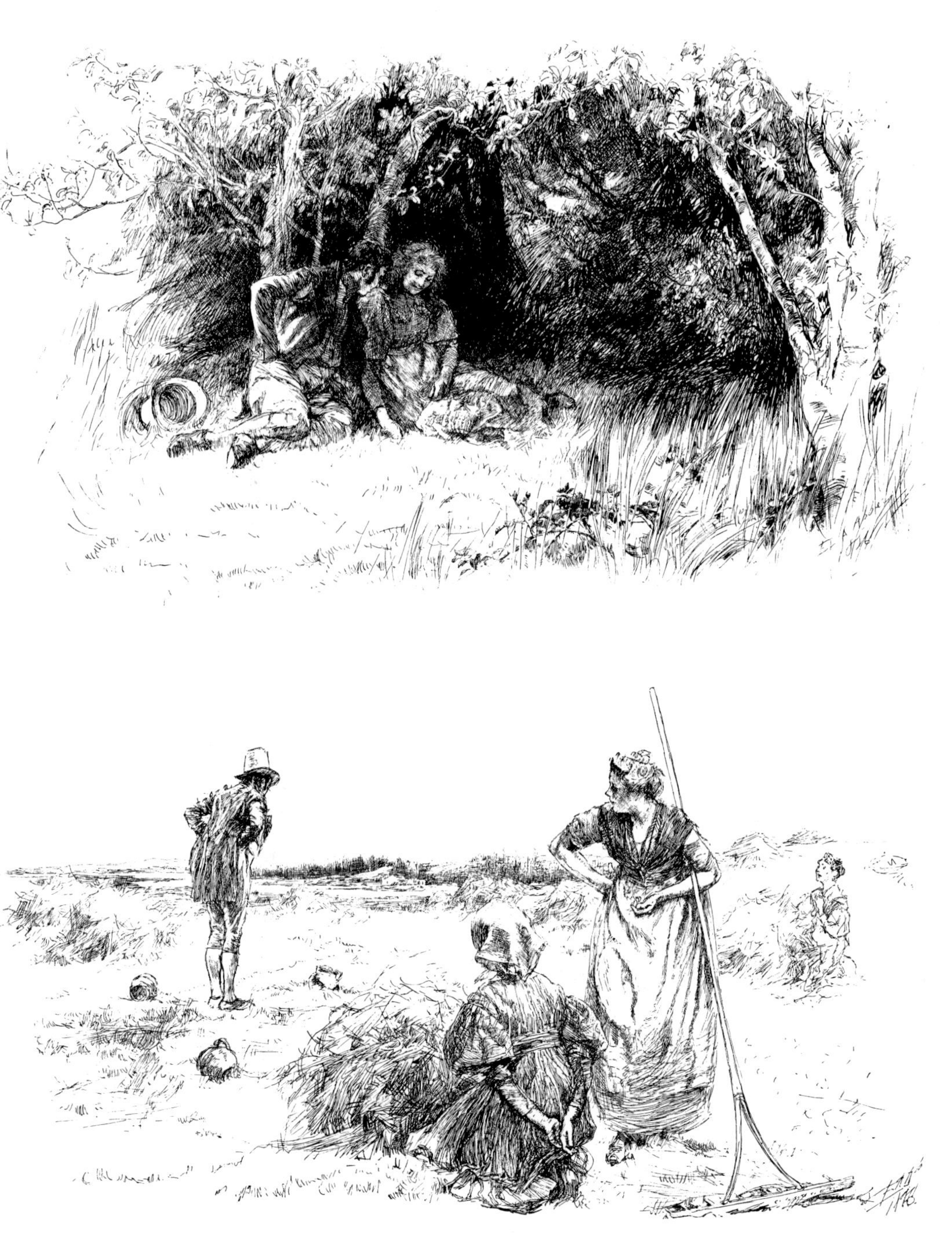

Old Songs
"Kitty of Coleraine," Harper & Brothers, 1888

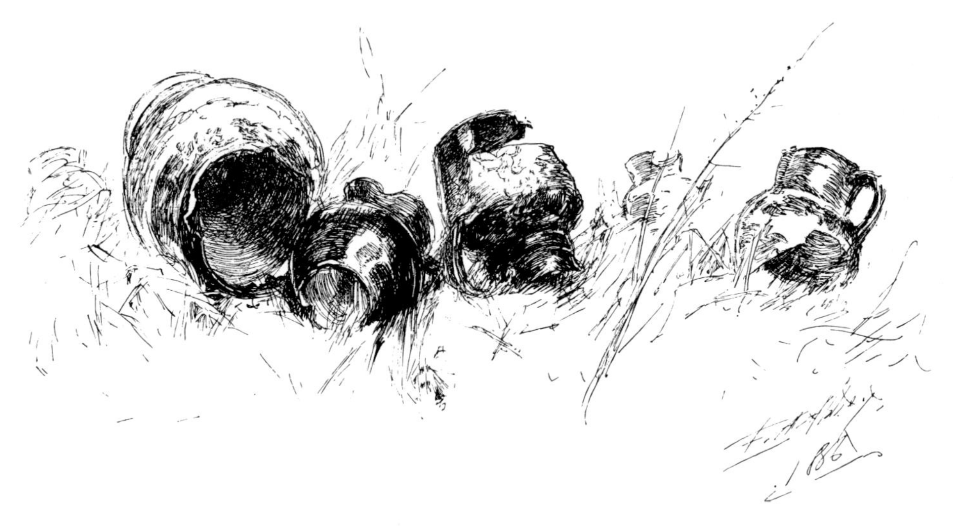

Old Songs
"Kitty of Coleraine," Harper & Brothers, 1888

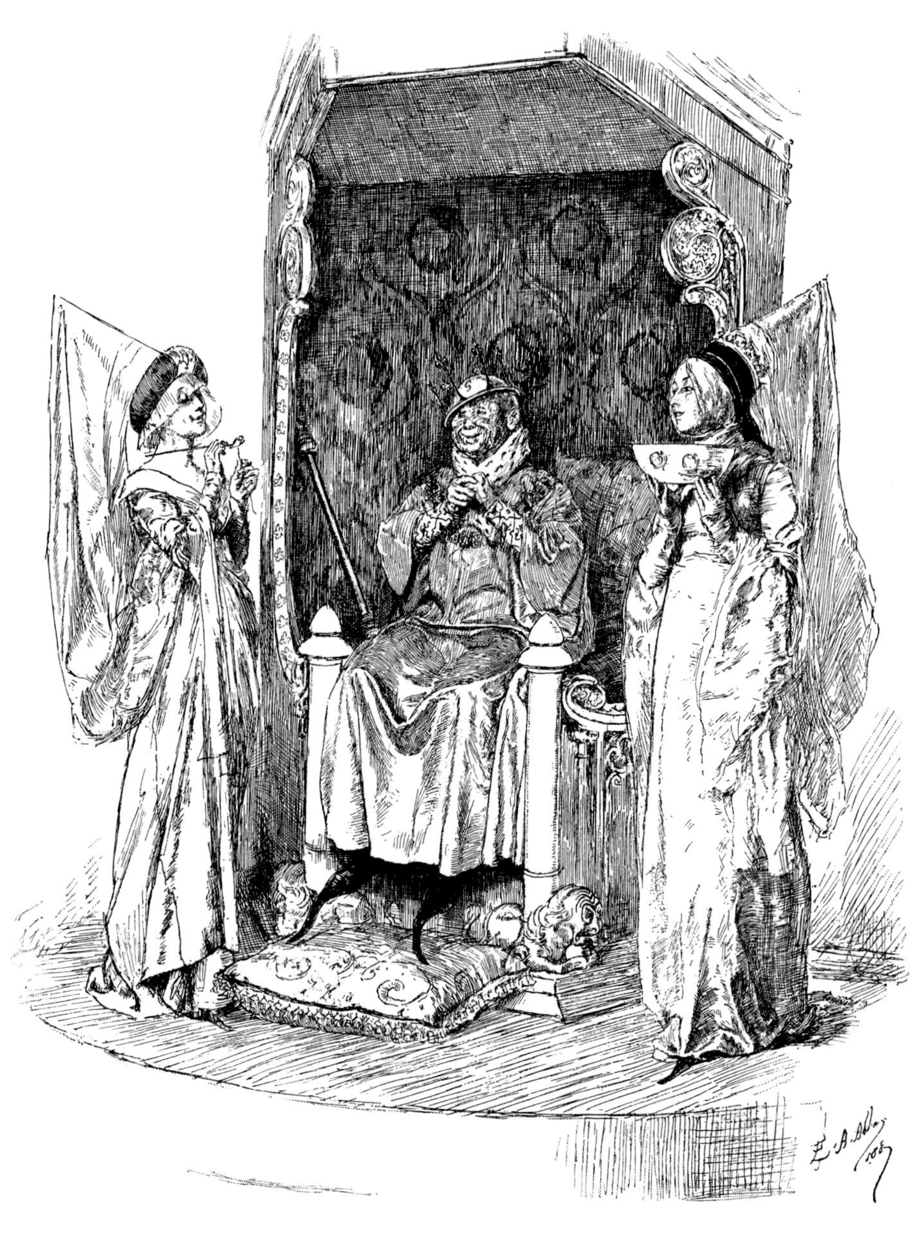

Old Songs
"Old King Cole," Harper & Brothers, 1888
Originally published in *Harper's New Monthly Magazine*, October 1888

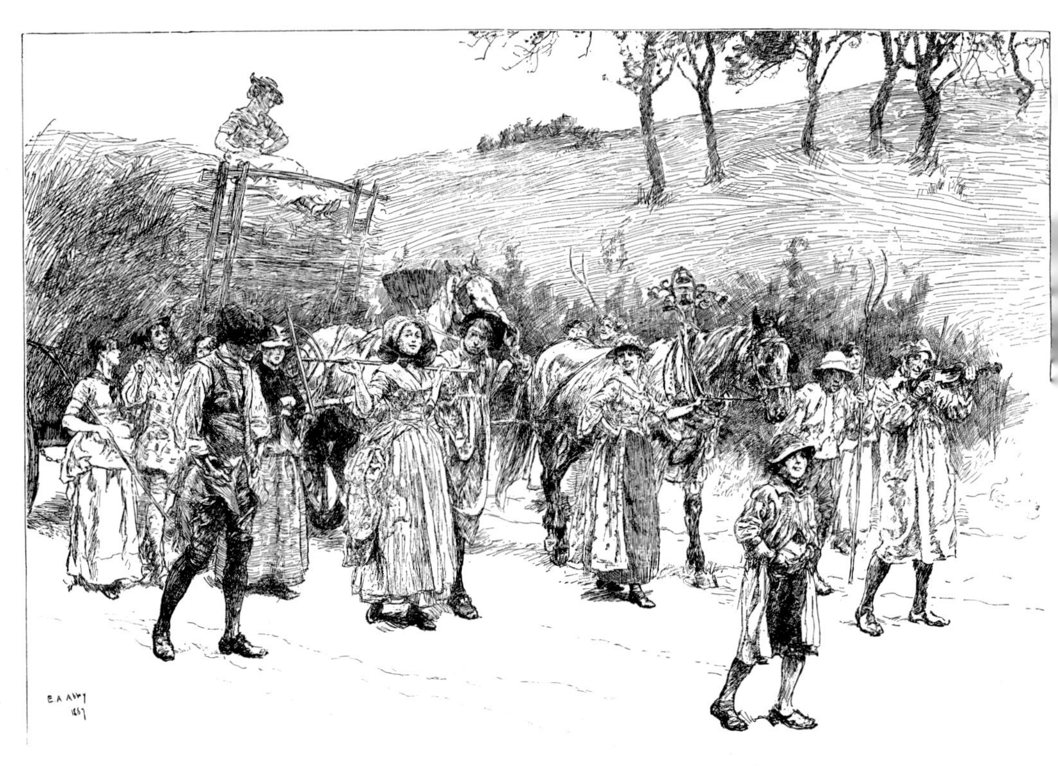

Old Songs
"Harvest-Home," Harper & Brothers, 1888

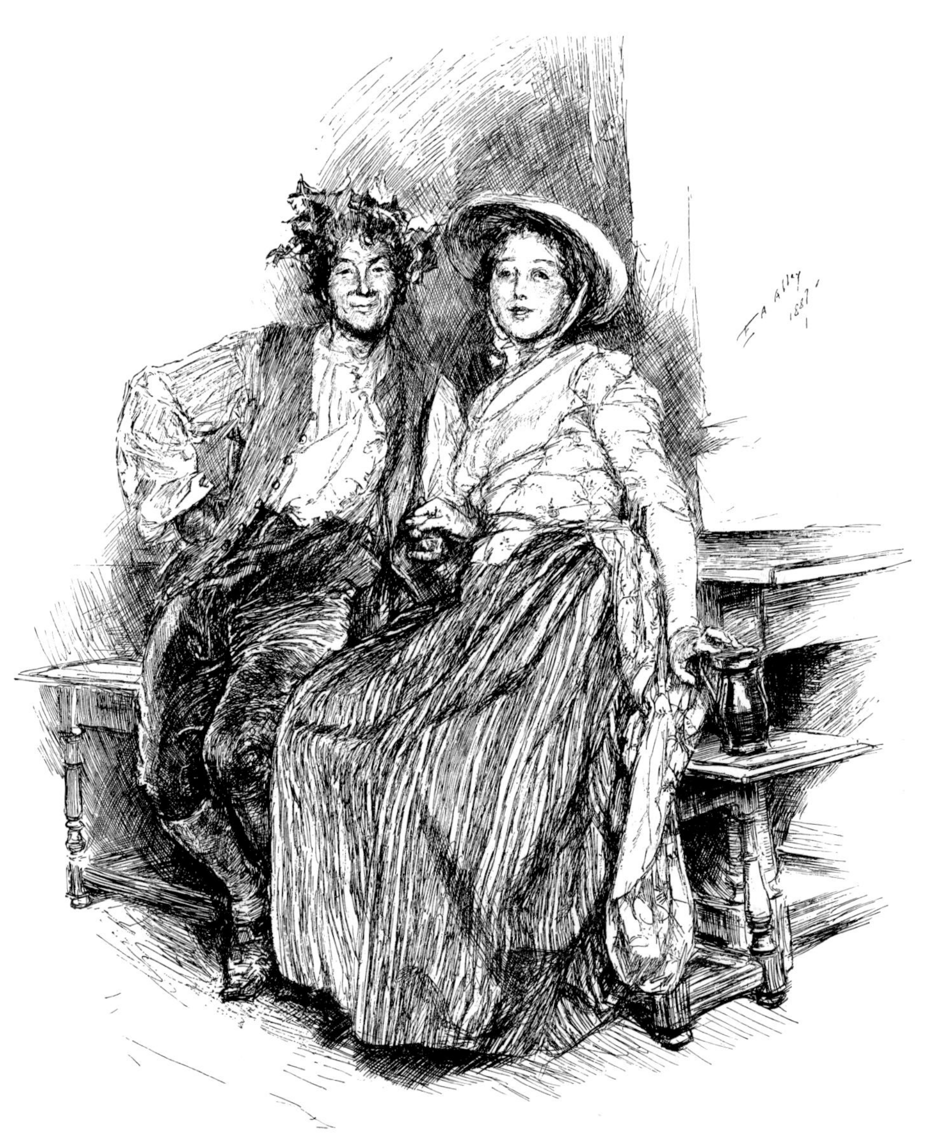

'Tis Ceres bids play
And keep holiday
To celebrate harvest-home.

Old Songs
"Harvest-Home," Harper & Brothers, 1888

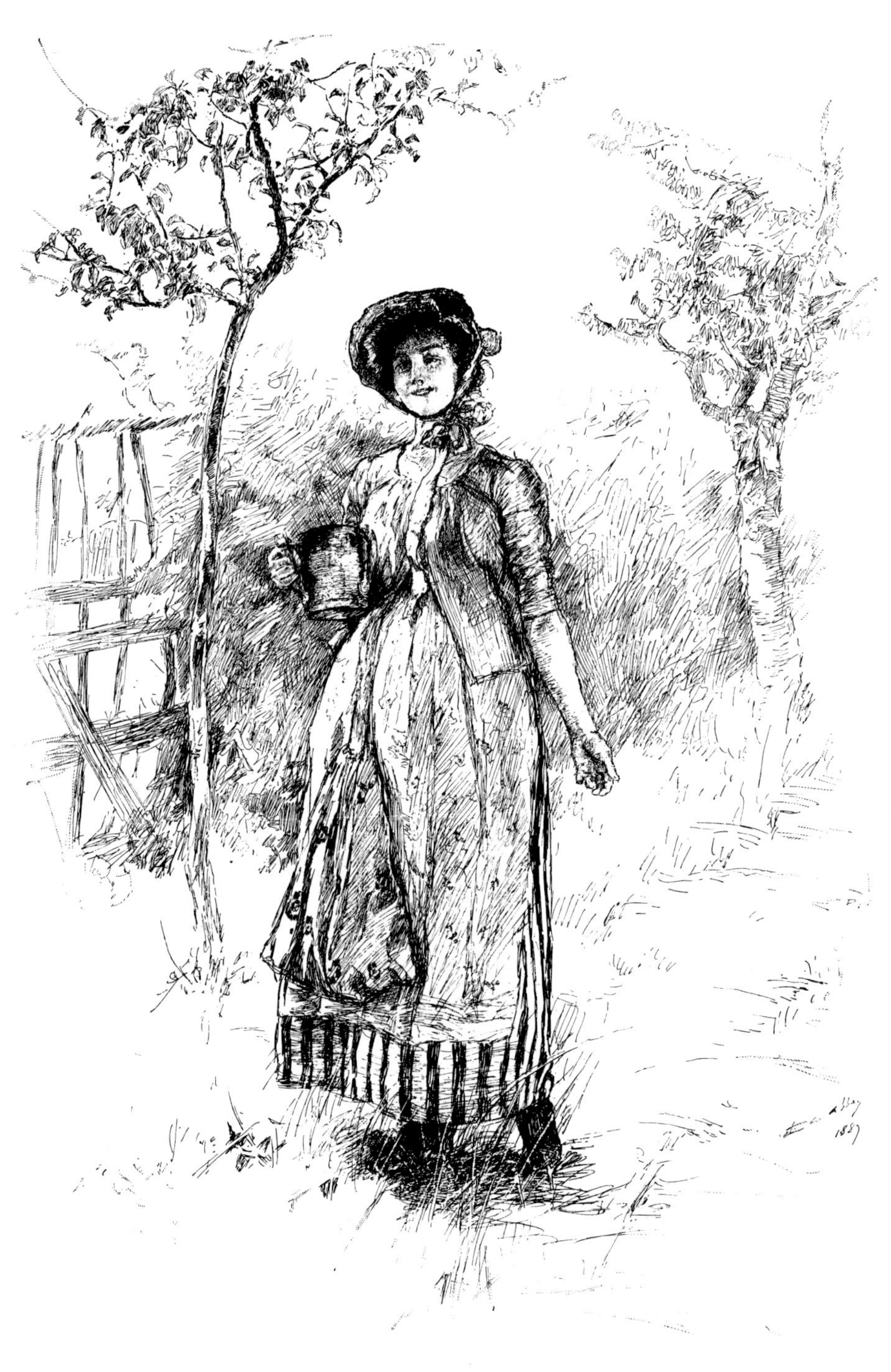

Old Songs
"Harvest Home," Harper & Brothers, 1888

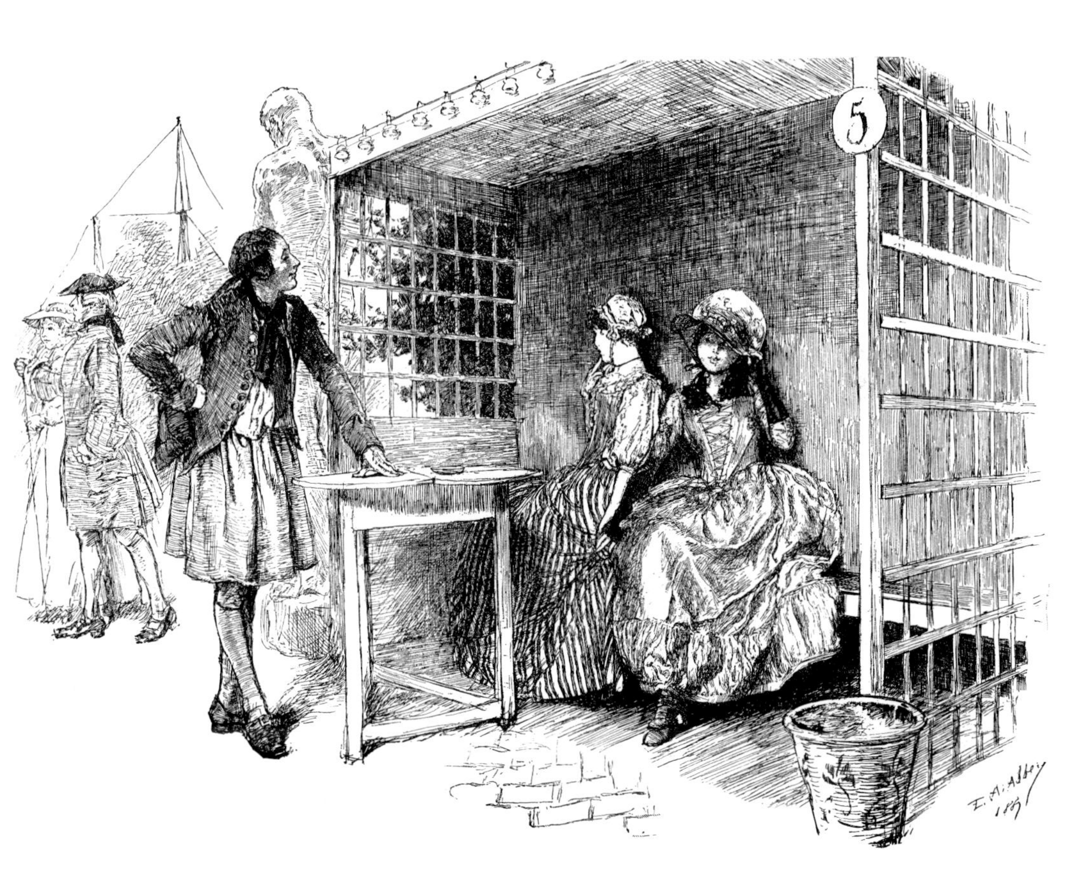

Old Songs
"Down in Cupid's Garden," Harper & Brothers, 1888

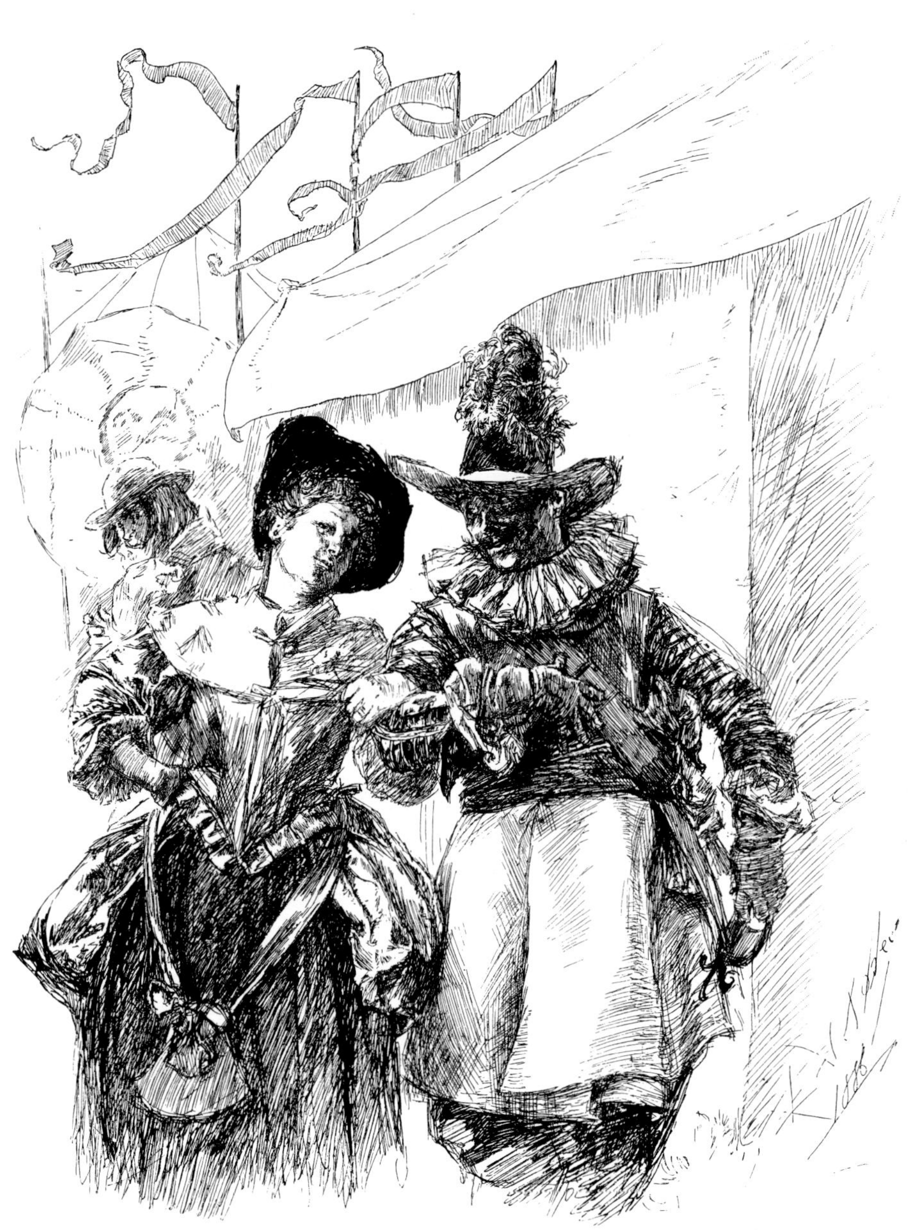

"All the fair yesterday she did pass by me."

Old Songs
"Phillada Flouts Me," Harper & Brothers, 1888
Originally published in *Harper's New Monthly Magazine*, July 1887

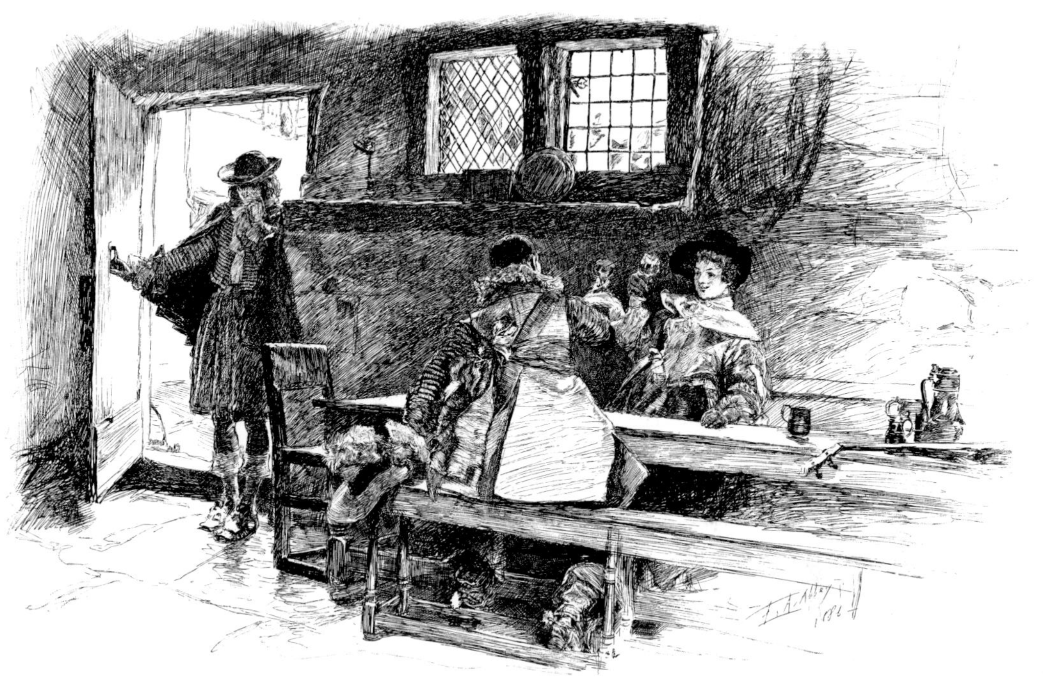

"Will had her to the wine."

Old Songs
"Phillada Flouts Me," Harper & Brothers, 1888

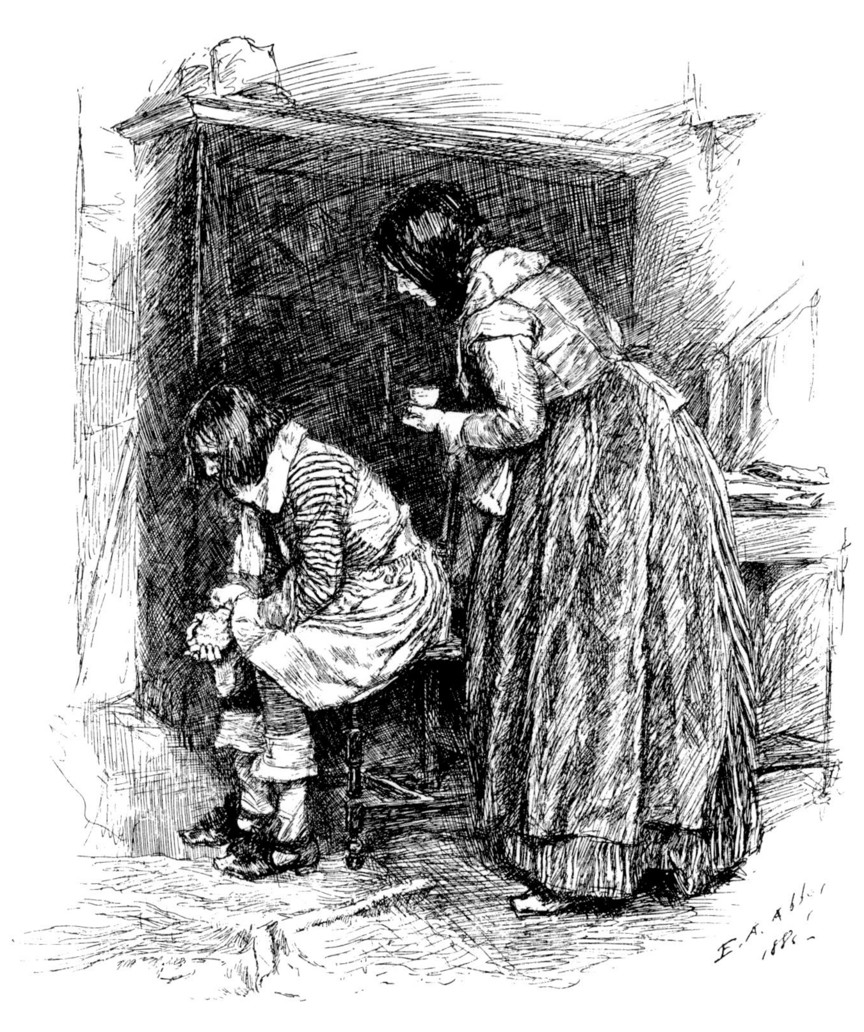

Old Songs
"Phillada Flouts Me," Harper & Brothers, 1888

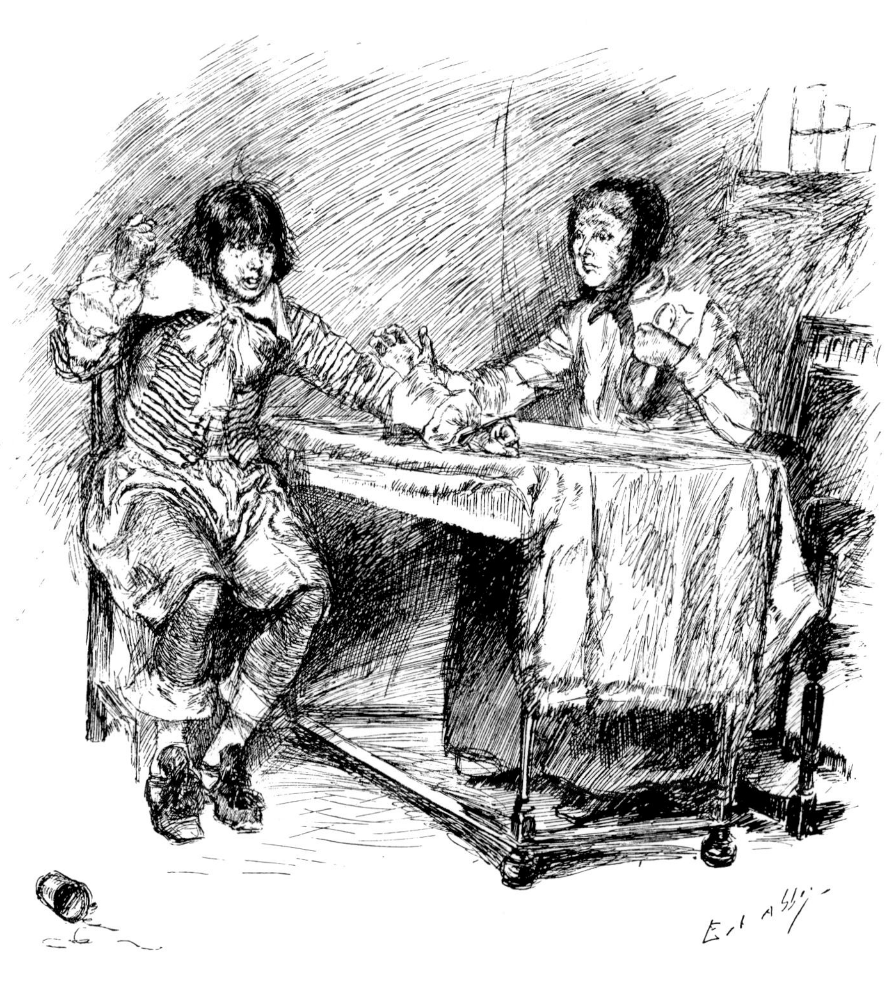

Old Songs
"Phillada Flouts Me," Harper & Brothers, 1888

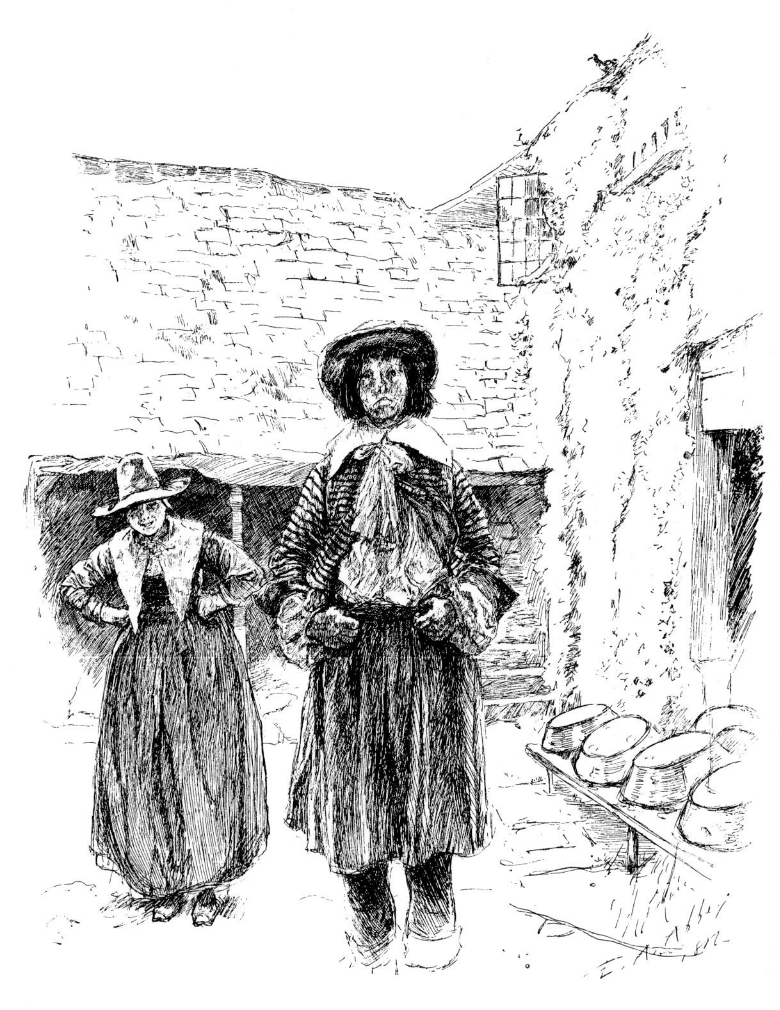

Old Songs
"Phillada Flouts Me," Harper & Brothers, 1888

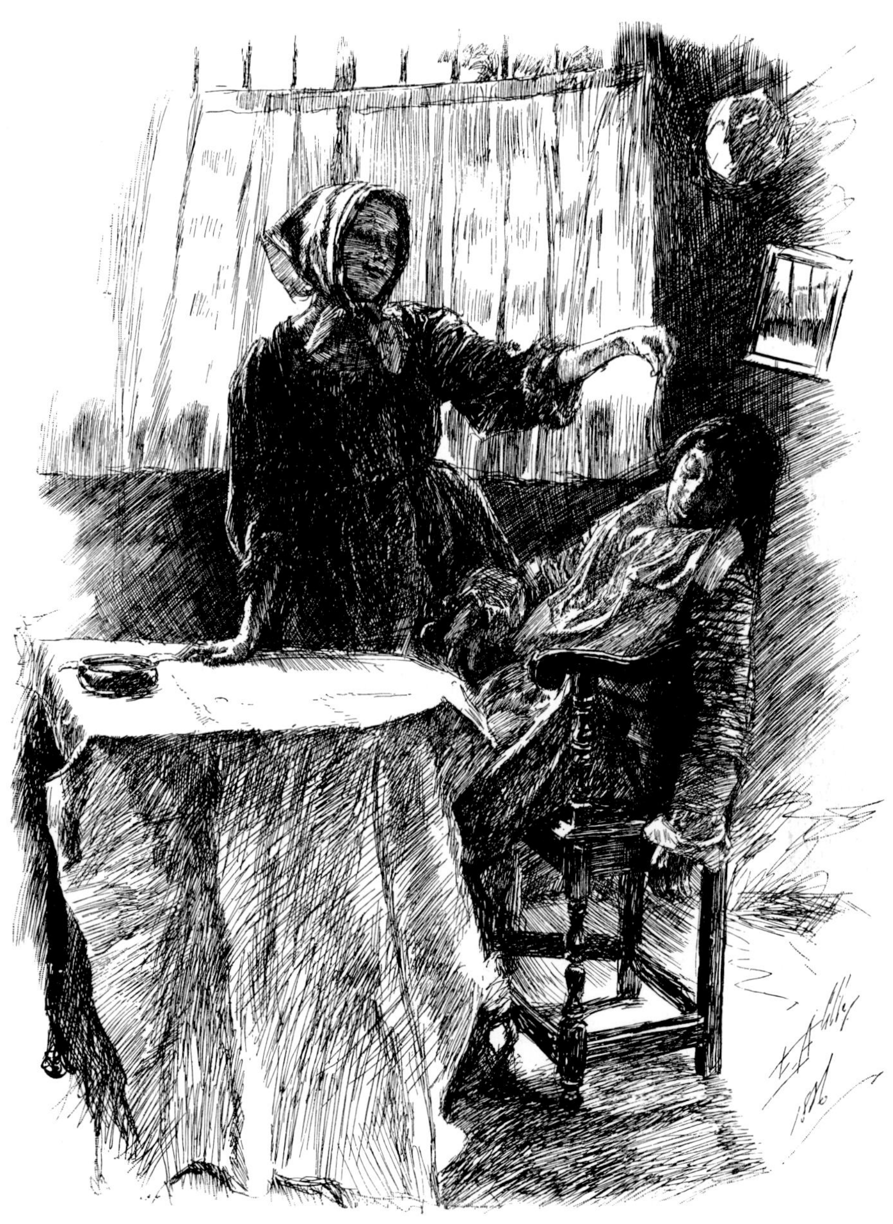

"T'other plays with my nose."

Old Songs
"Phillada Flouts Me," Harper & Brothers, 1888
Originally published in *Harper's New Monthly Magazine*, July 1887

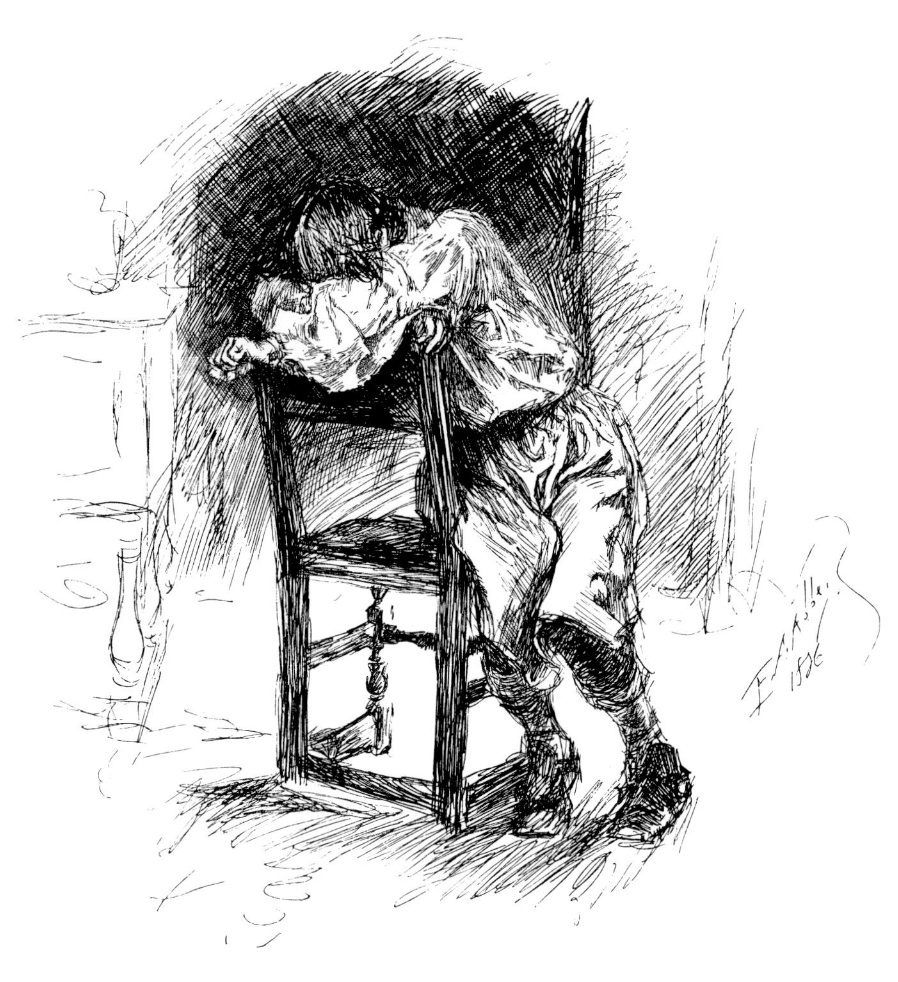

Old Songs
"Phillada Flouts Me," Harper & Brothers, 1888

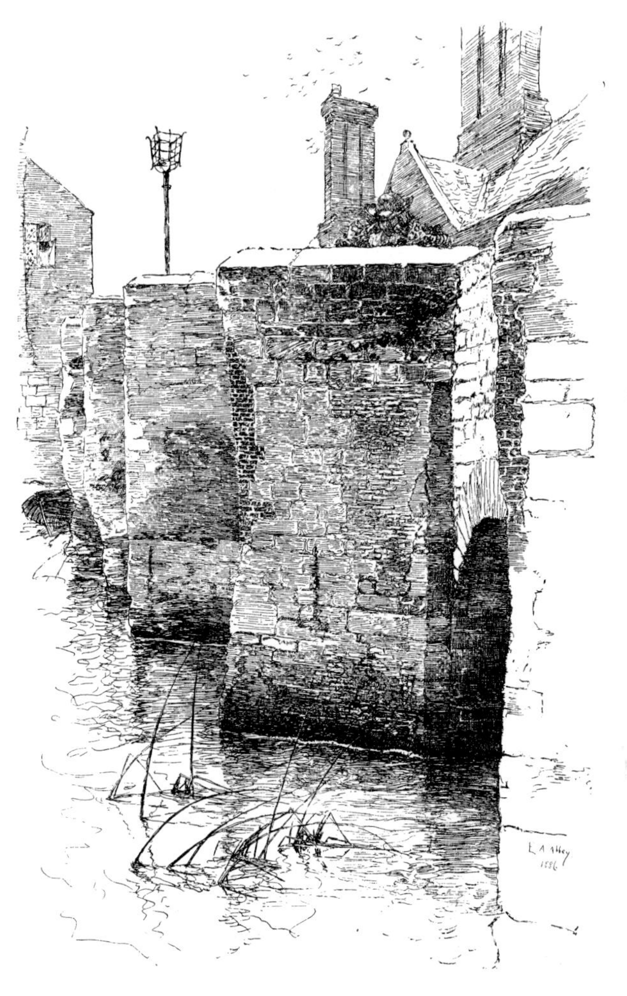

Old Songs
"Phillada Flouts Me," Harper & Brothers, 1888

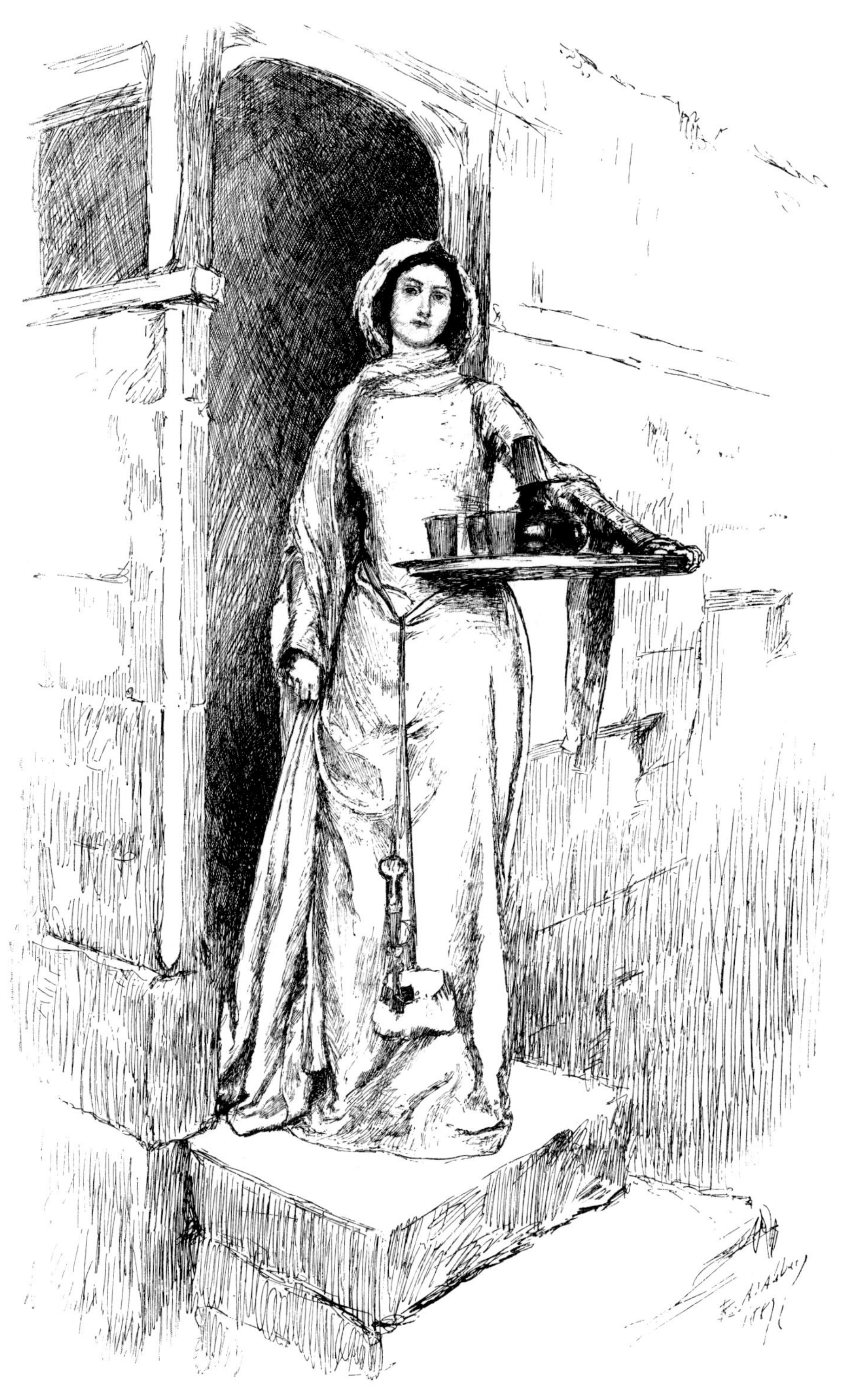

Harper's New Monthly Magazine, June 1889
The Comedies of Shakespeare — "Merry Wives of Windsor."
Act I., Scene I. — Enter Mistress Anne Page with Wine.

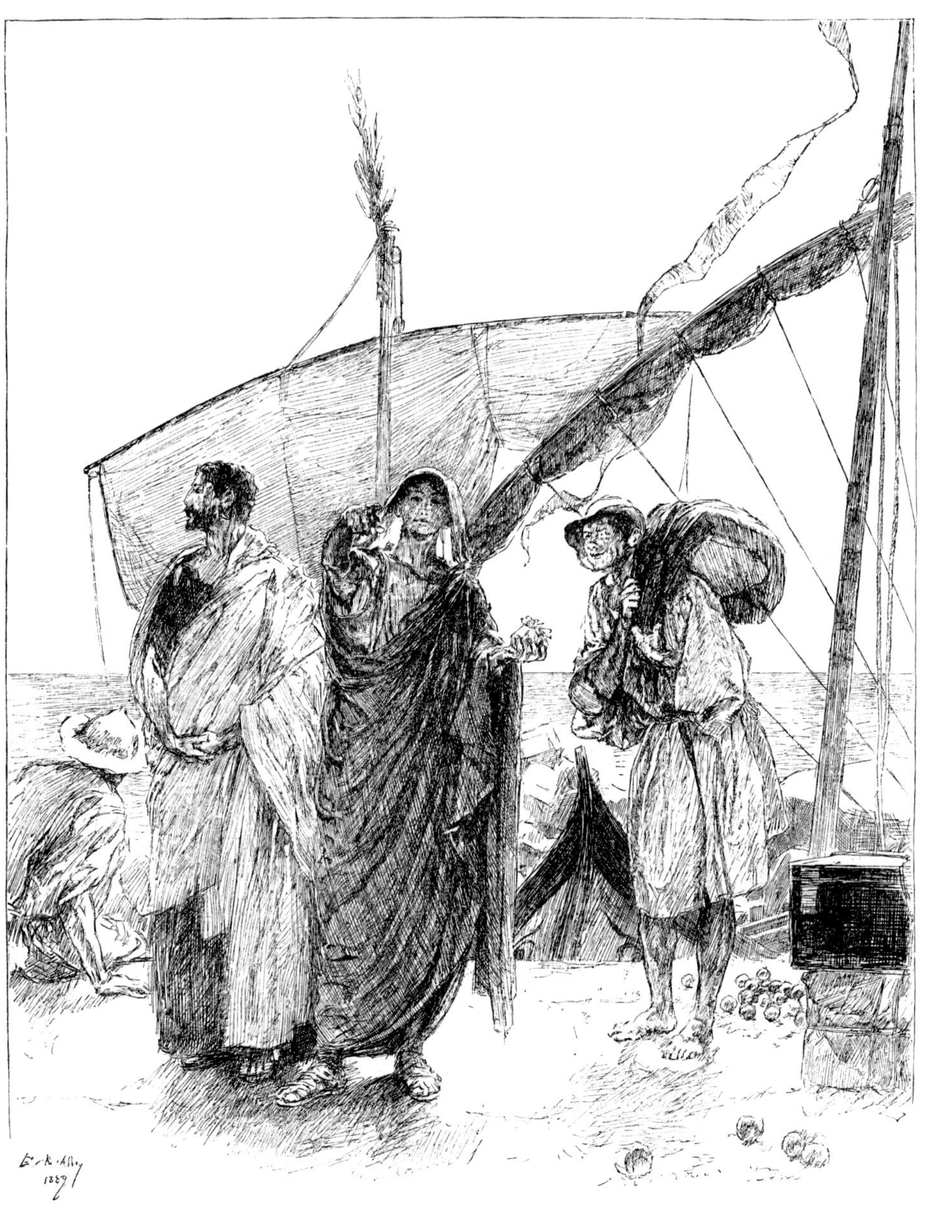

Antipholus of Syracuse. "Go, bear it to the Centaur."

Harper's New Monthly Magazine, August 1889
"The Comedy of Errors."
Act I., Scene II. — The Mart.

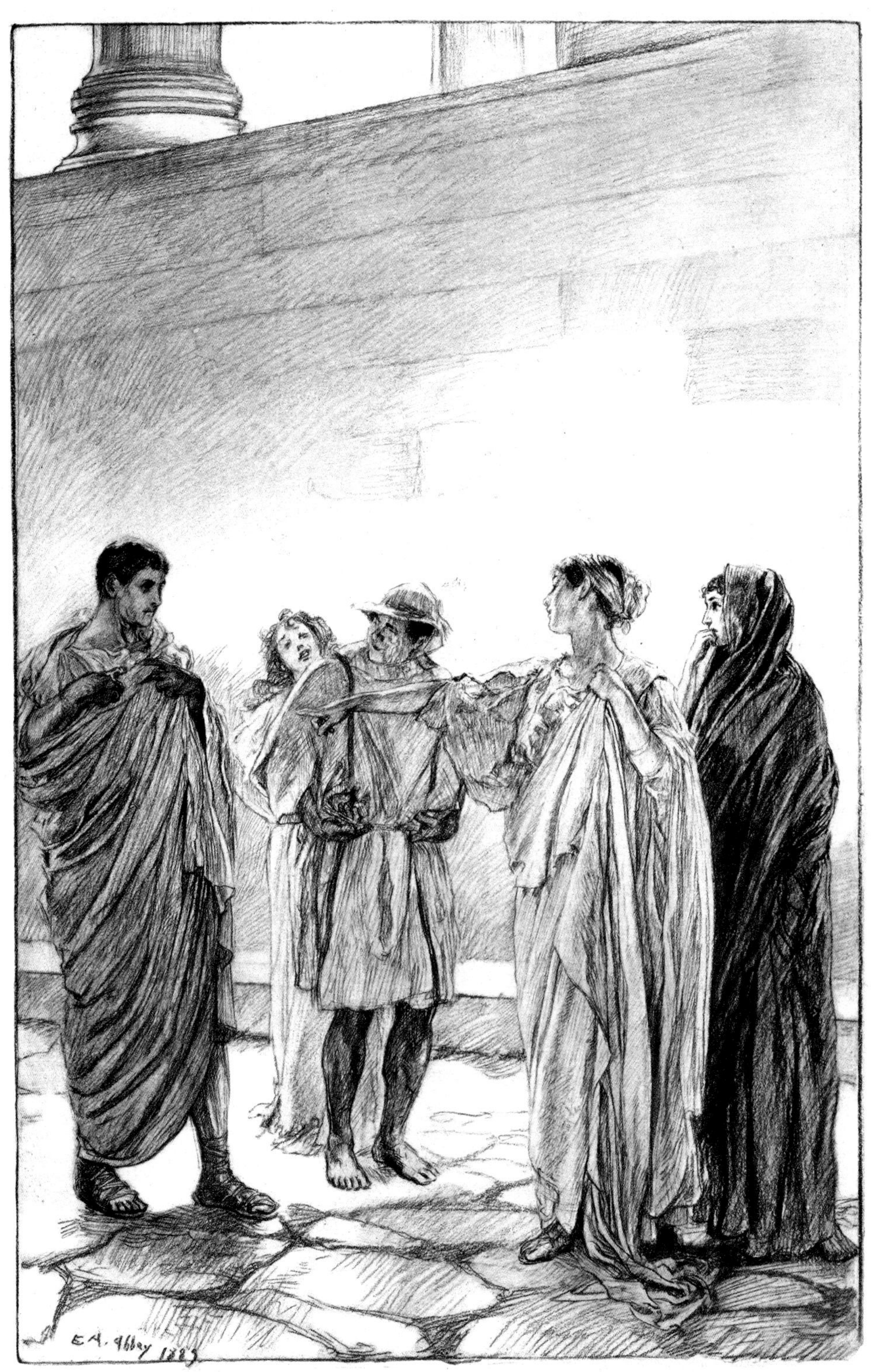

Adrina. "Ay, ay, Antipholus, look strange and frown."

Harper's New Monthly Magazine, August 1889
"The Comedy of Errors."
Act II., Scene II. — Adriana, Luciana, Antipholus and Dromio of Syracuse.

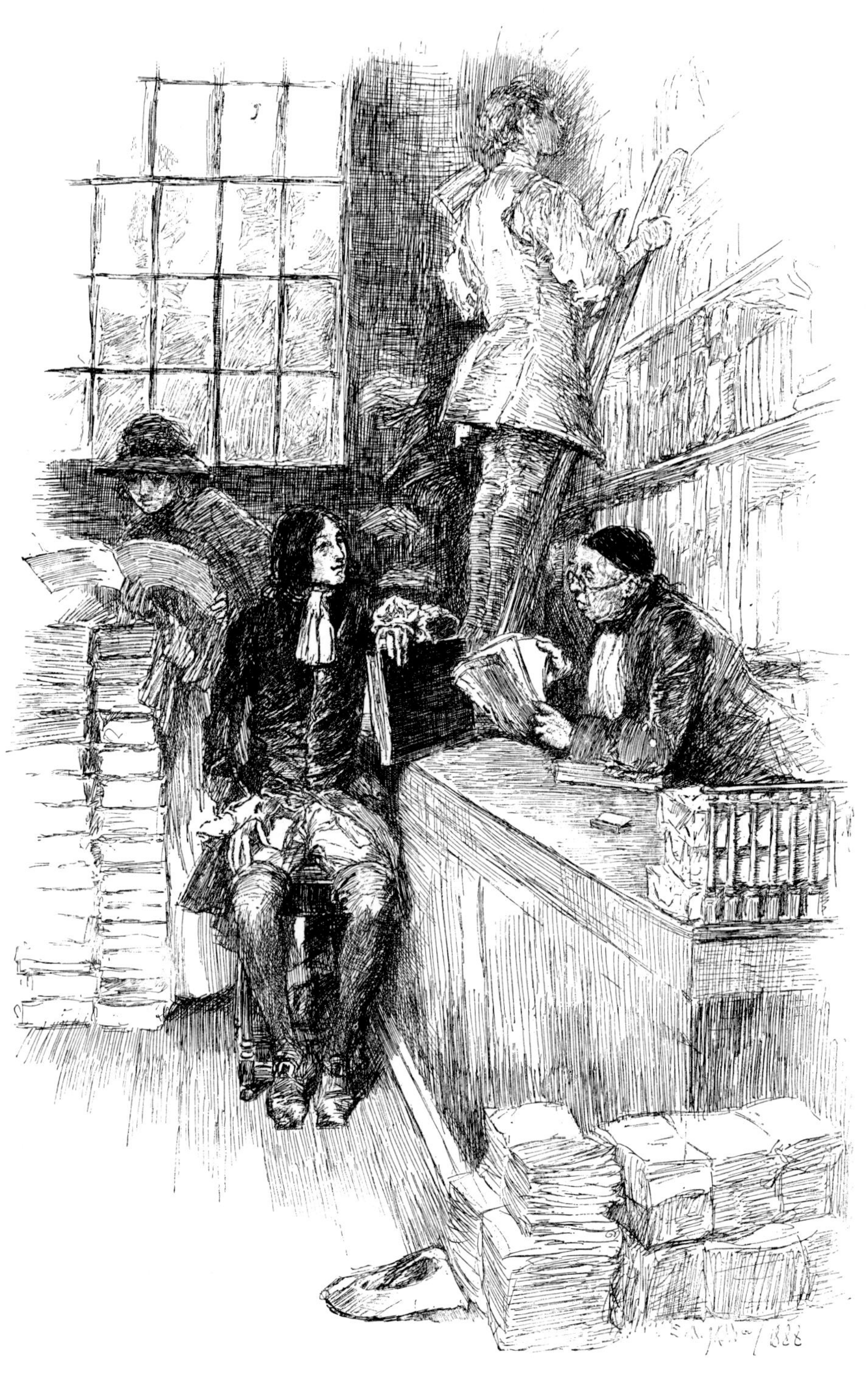

Harper's New Monthly Magazine, November 1889
"The Noble Patron."

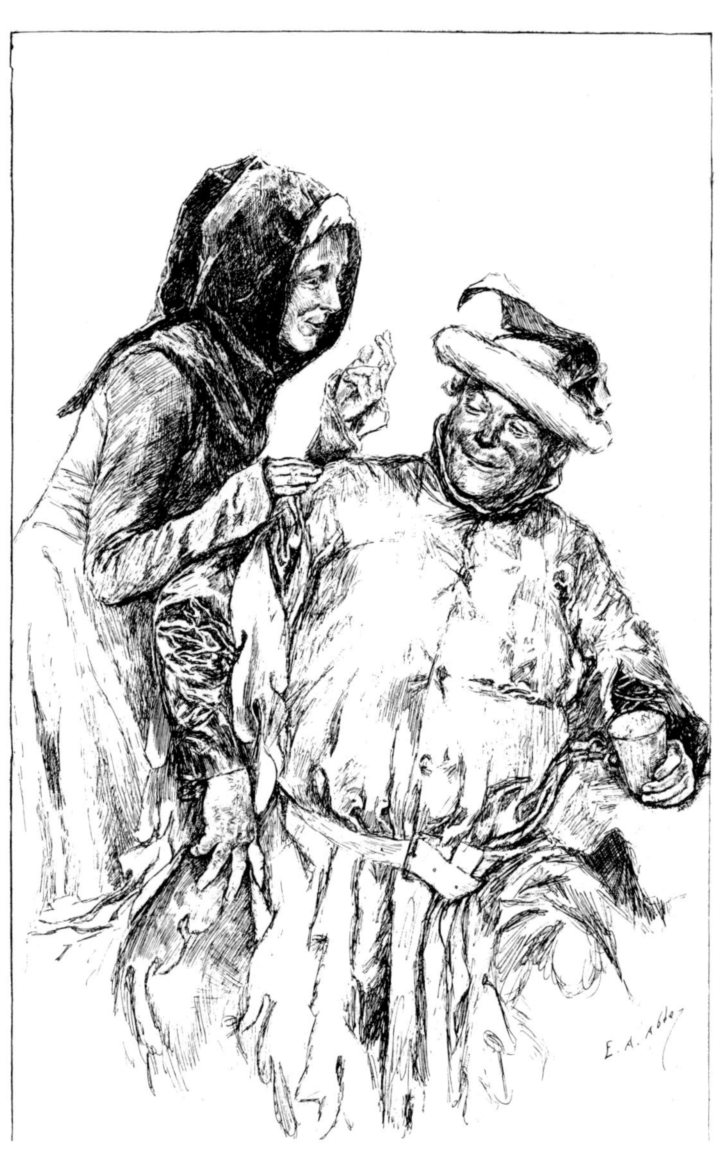

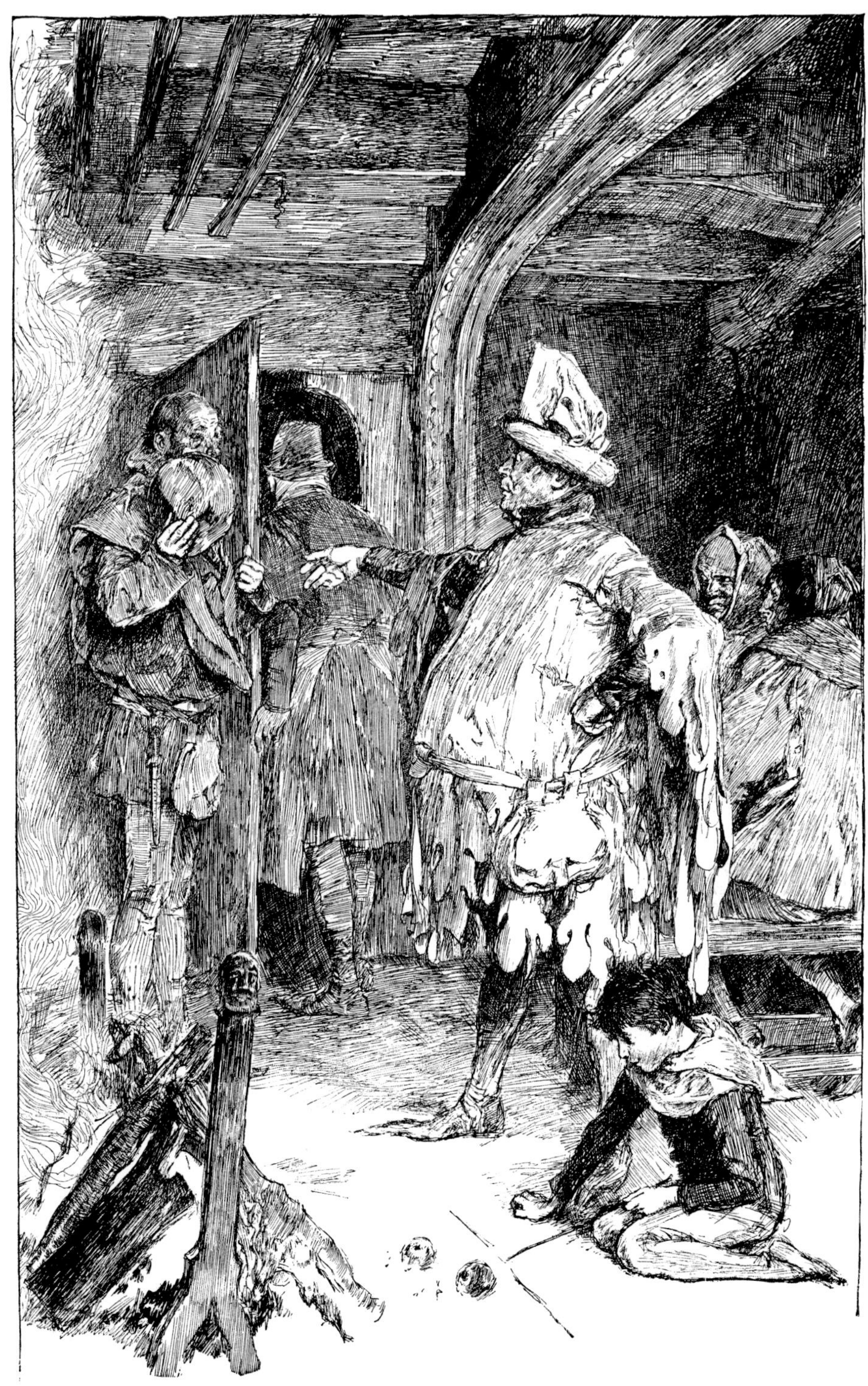

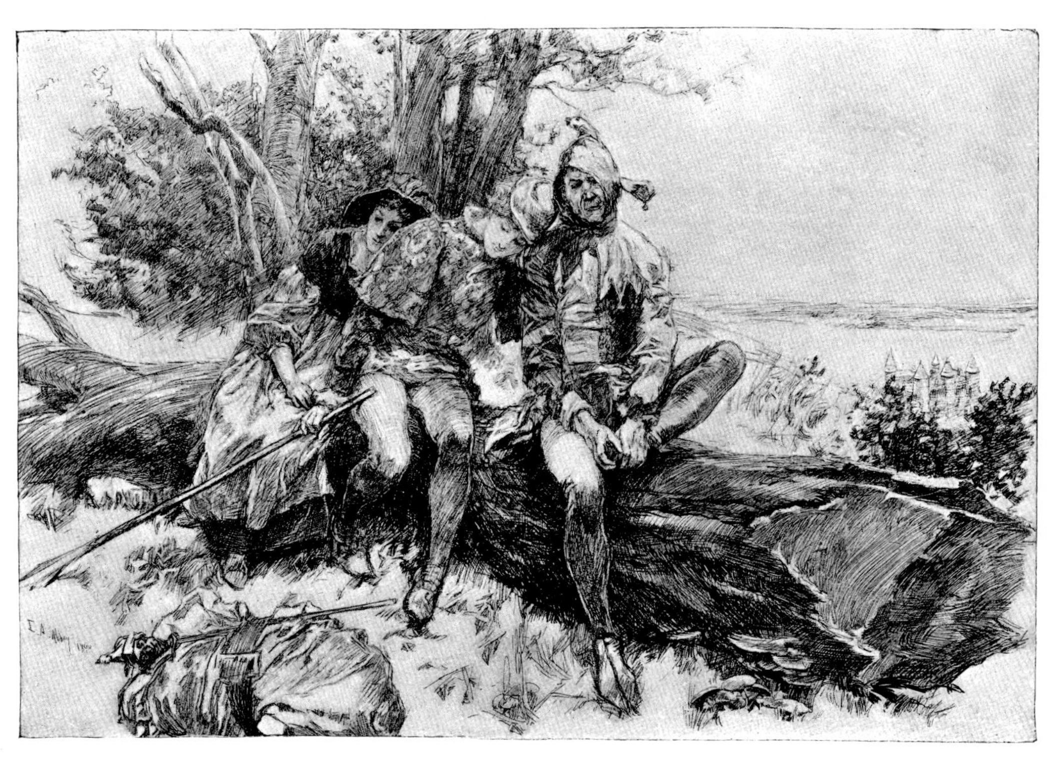

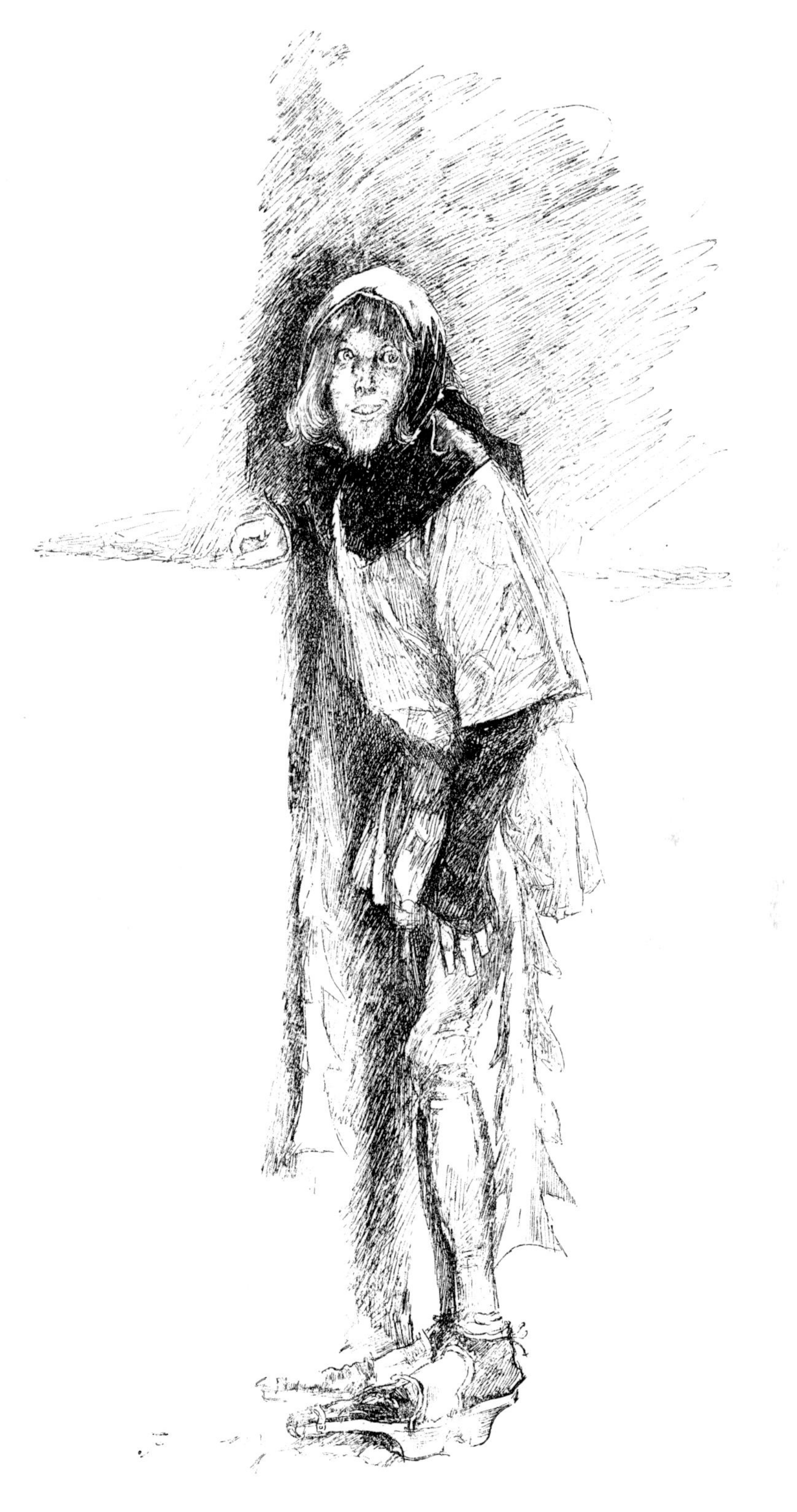

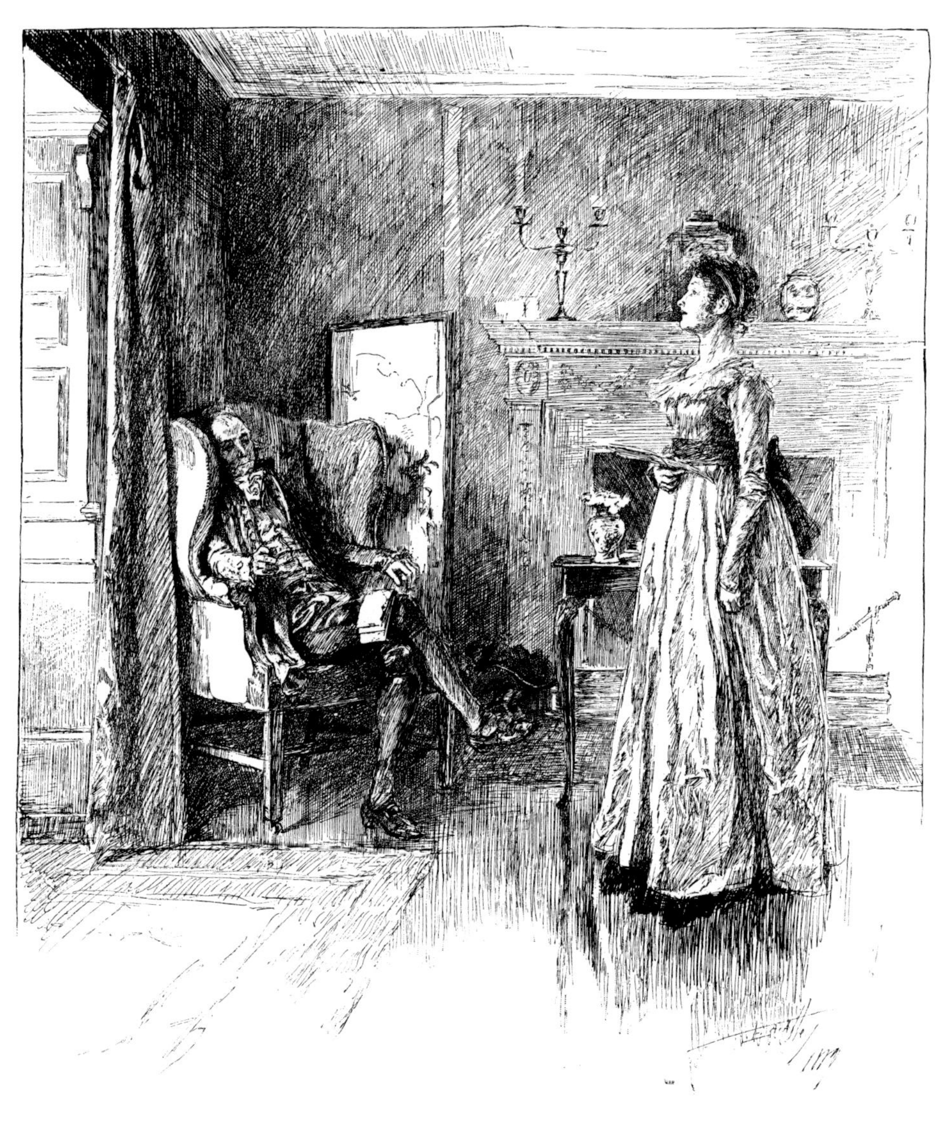

The Quiet Life
Harper & Brothers, 1889
Originally published in *Harper's New Monthly Magazine*, August 1889

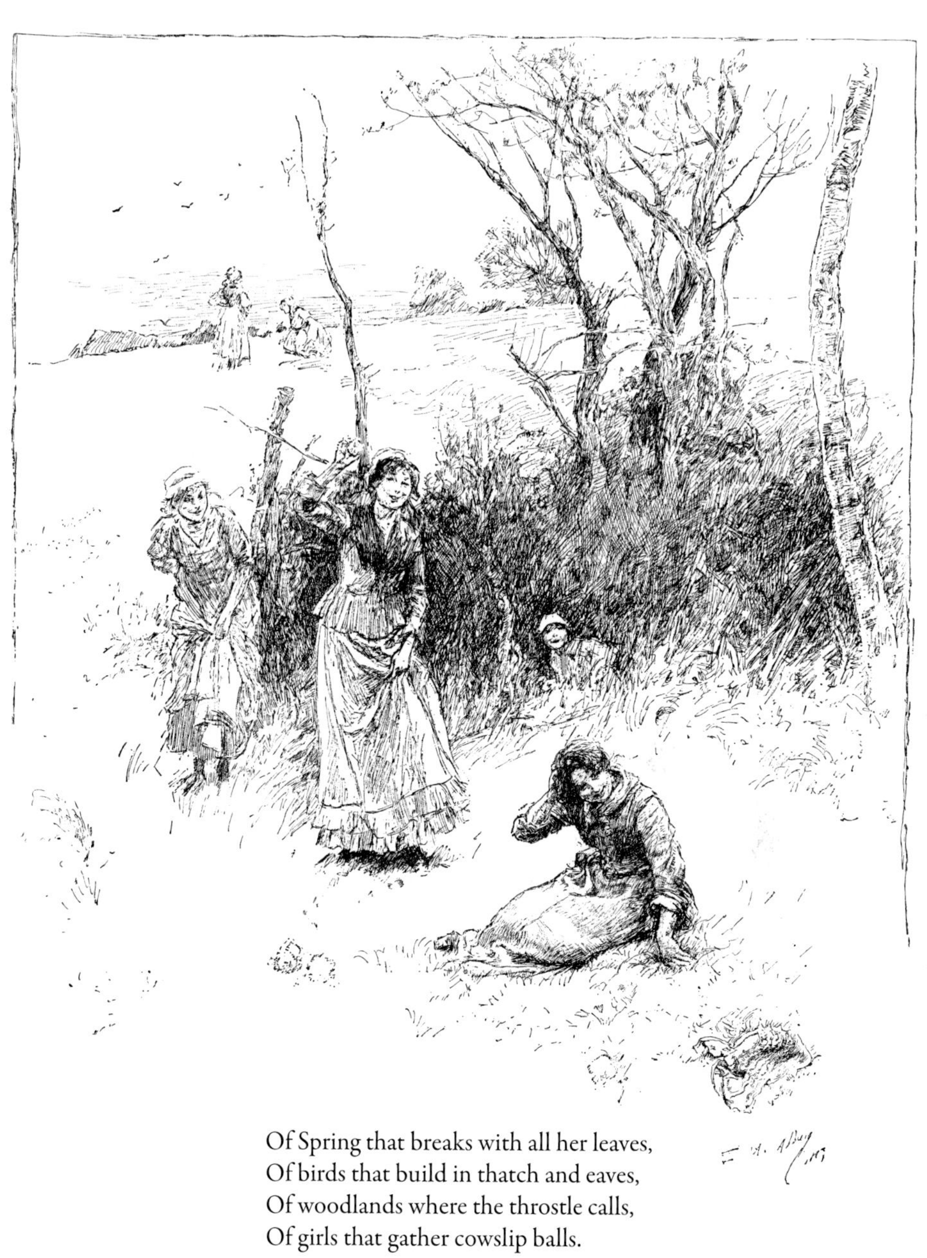

Of Spring that breaks with all her leaves,
Of birds that build in thatch and eaves,
Of woodlands where the throstle calls,
Of girls that gather cowslip balls.

The Quiet Life
"Prologue," Harper & Brothers, 1889

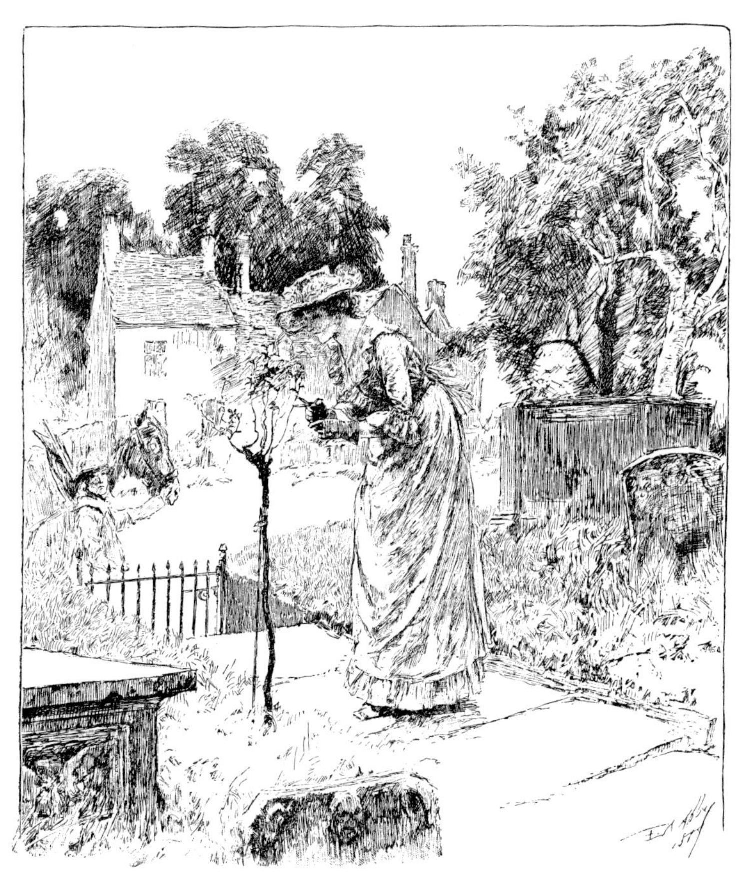

Of kine that low and lambs that cry,
Of wains that jolt and rumble by.

The Quiet Life
"Prologue," Harper & Brothers, 1889

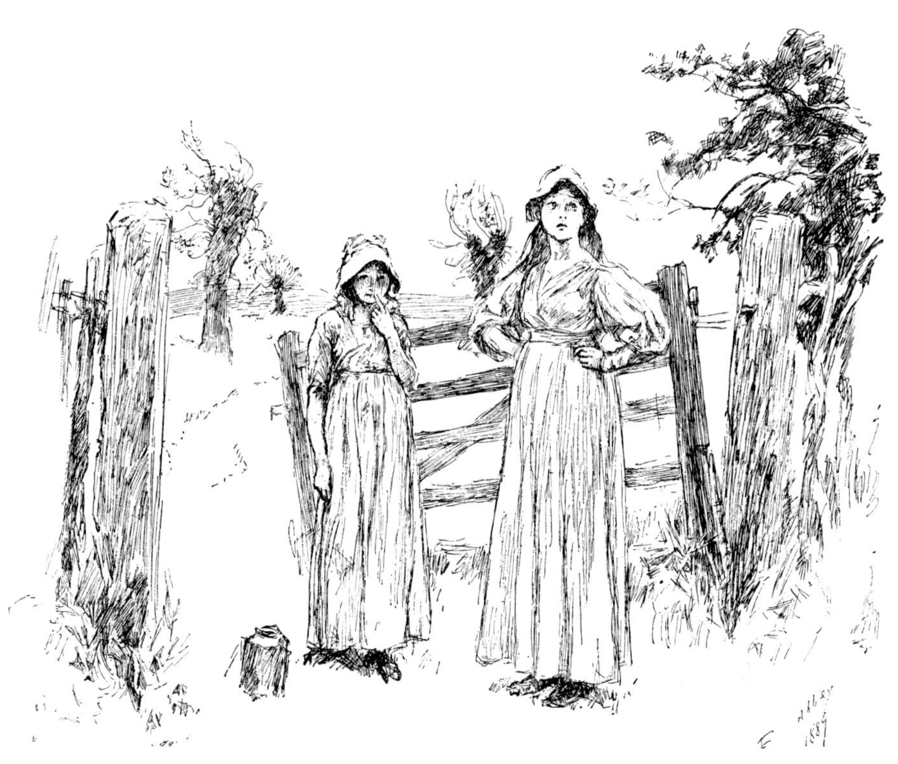

Of brooks that sing by brambly ways,
Of sunburned fold that stand at gaze.

The Quiet Life
"Prologue," Harper & Brothers, 1889

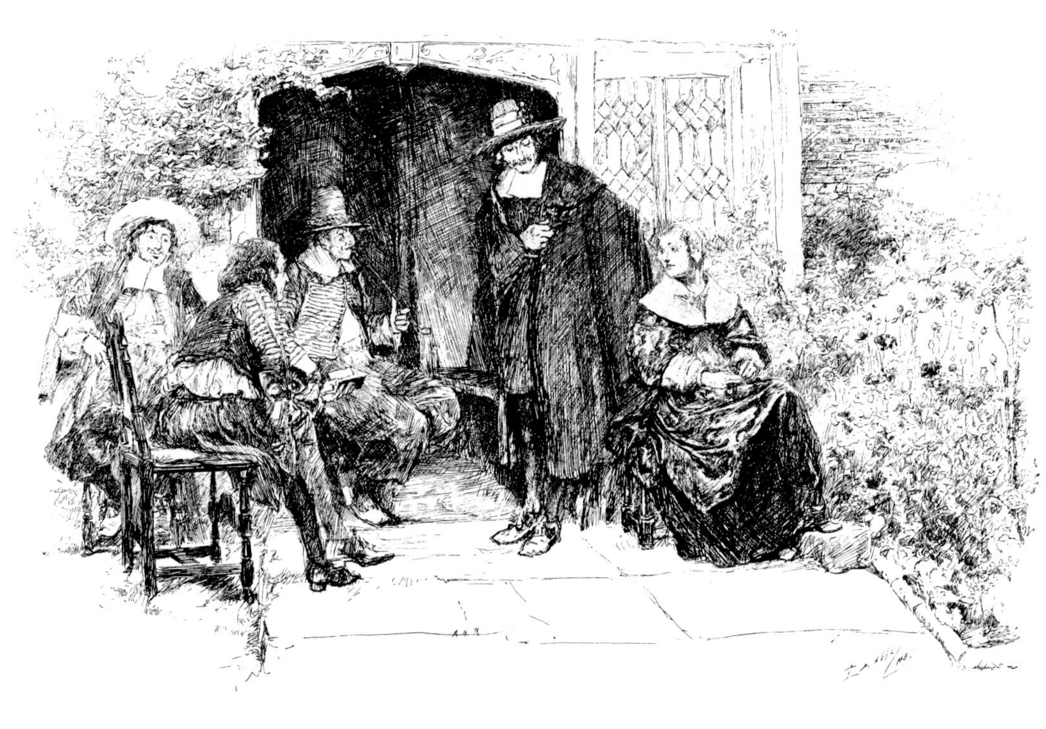

The Quiet Life
"The Wish," Harper & Brothers, 1889

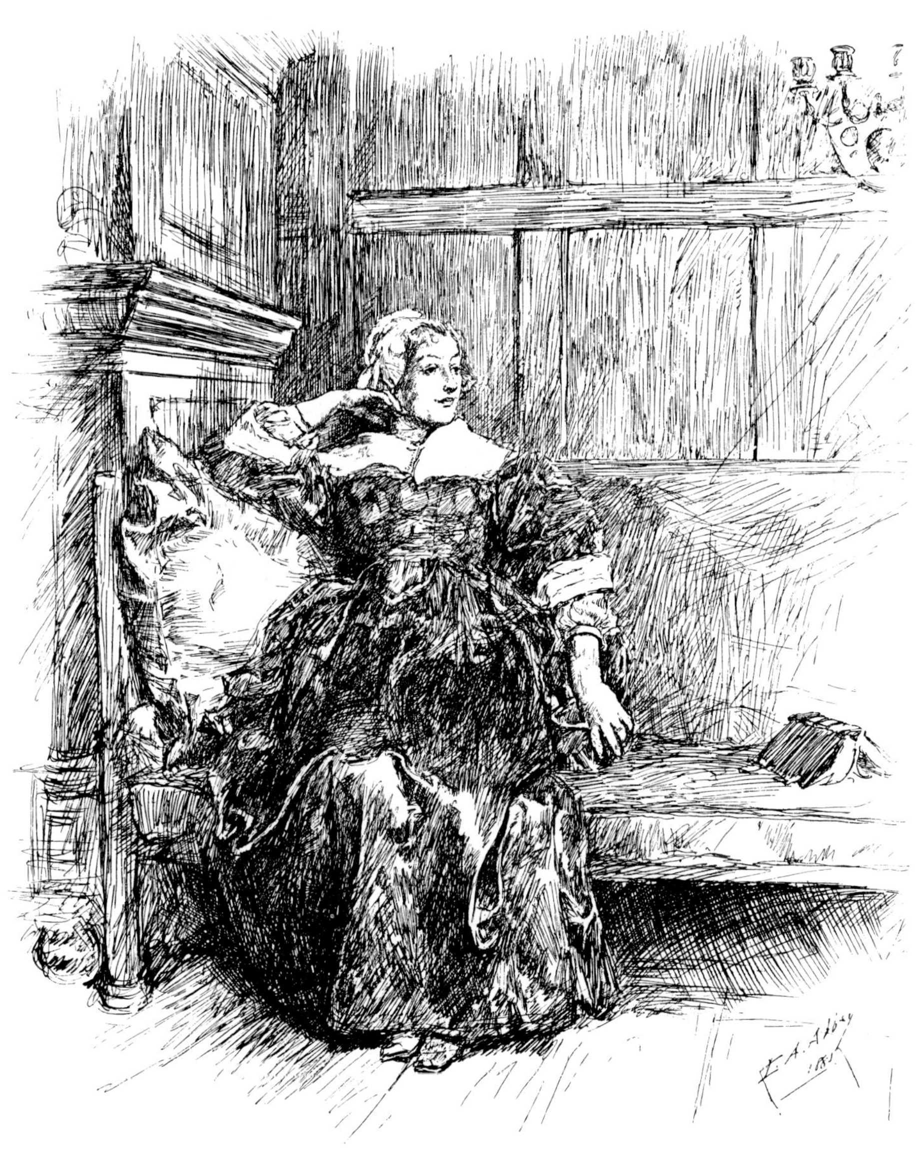

The Quiet Life
"The Wish," Harper & Brothers, 1889

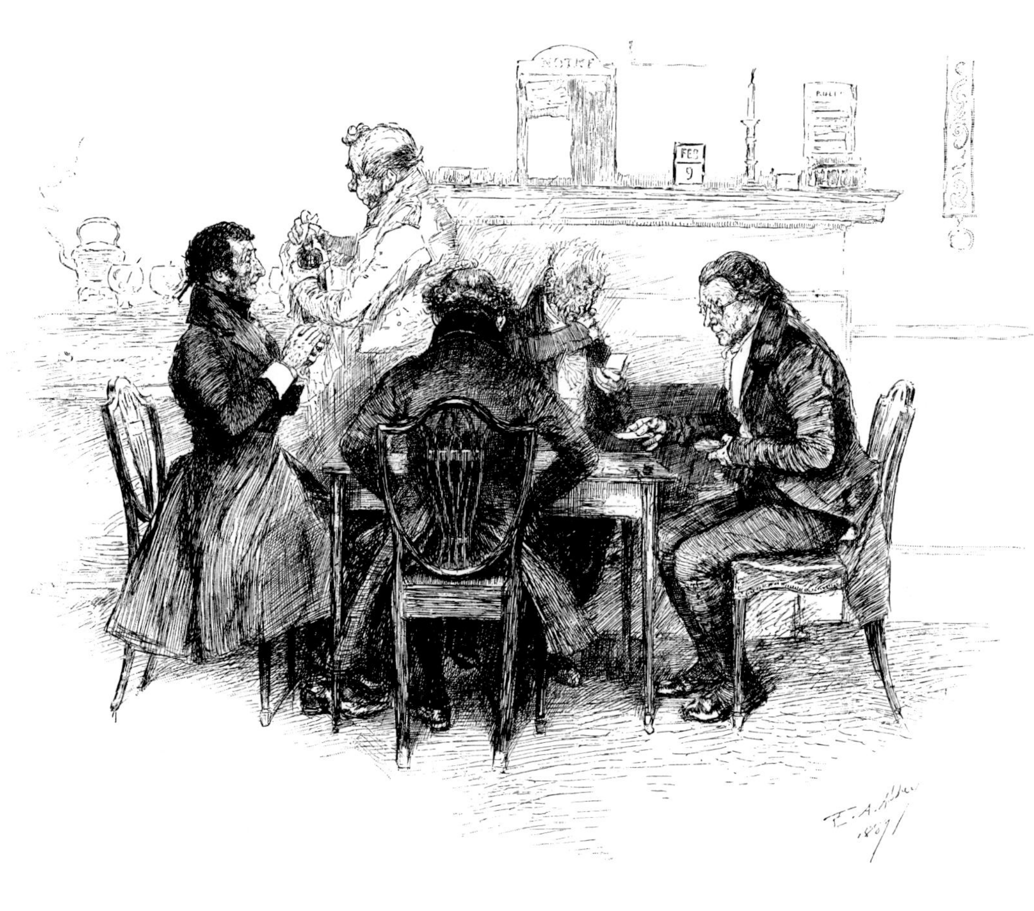

The Quiet Life
"Quince," Harper & Brothers, 1889

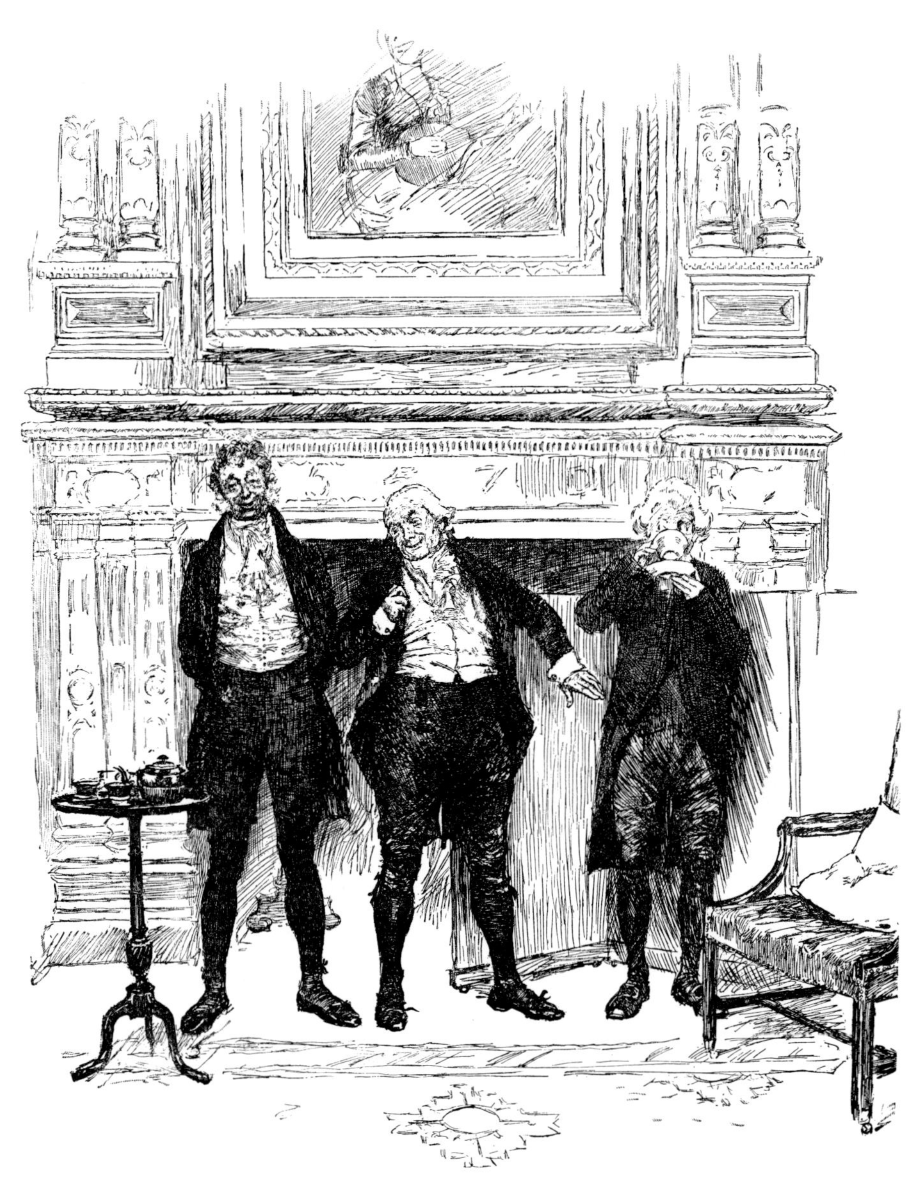

The Quiet Life
"Quince," Harper & Brothers, 1889

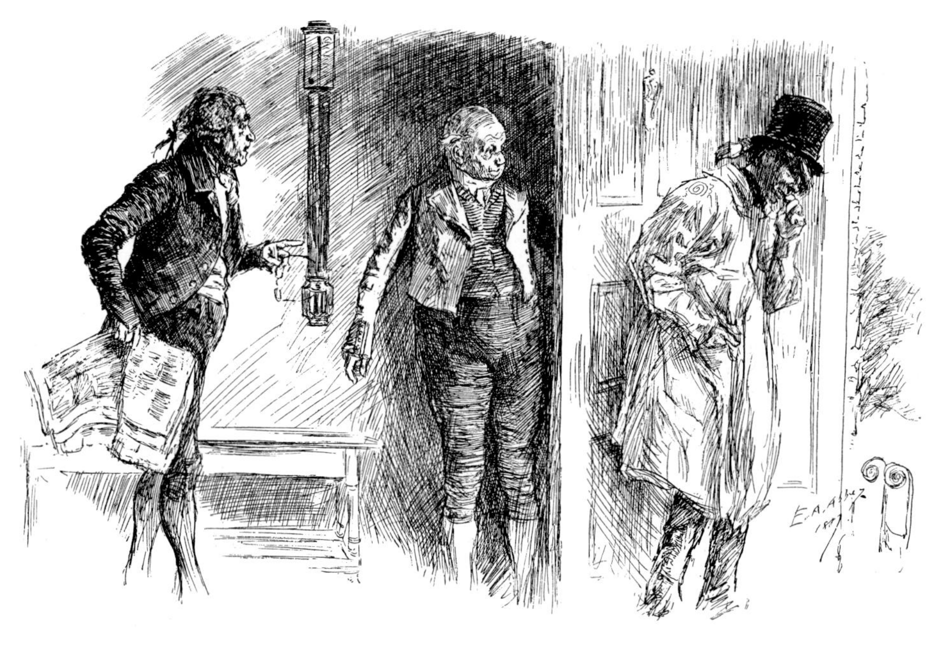

The Quiet Life
"Quince," Harper & Brothers, 1889

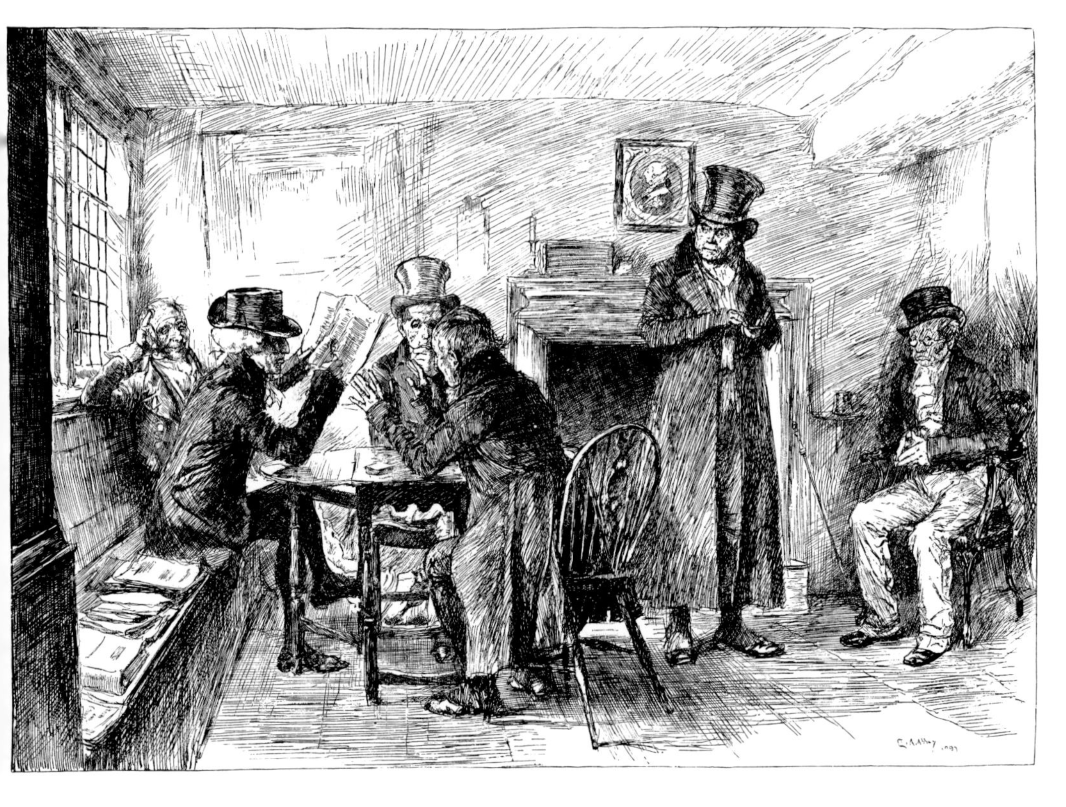

The Quiet Life
"Quince," Harper & Brothers, 1889

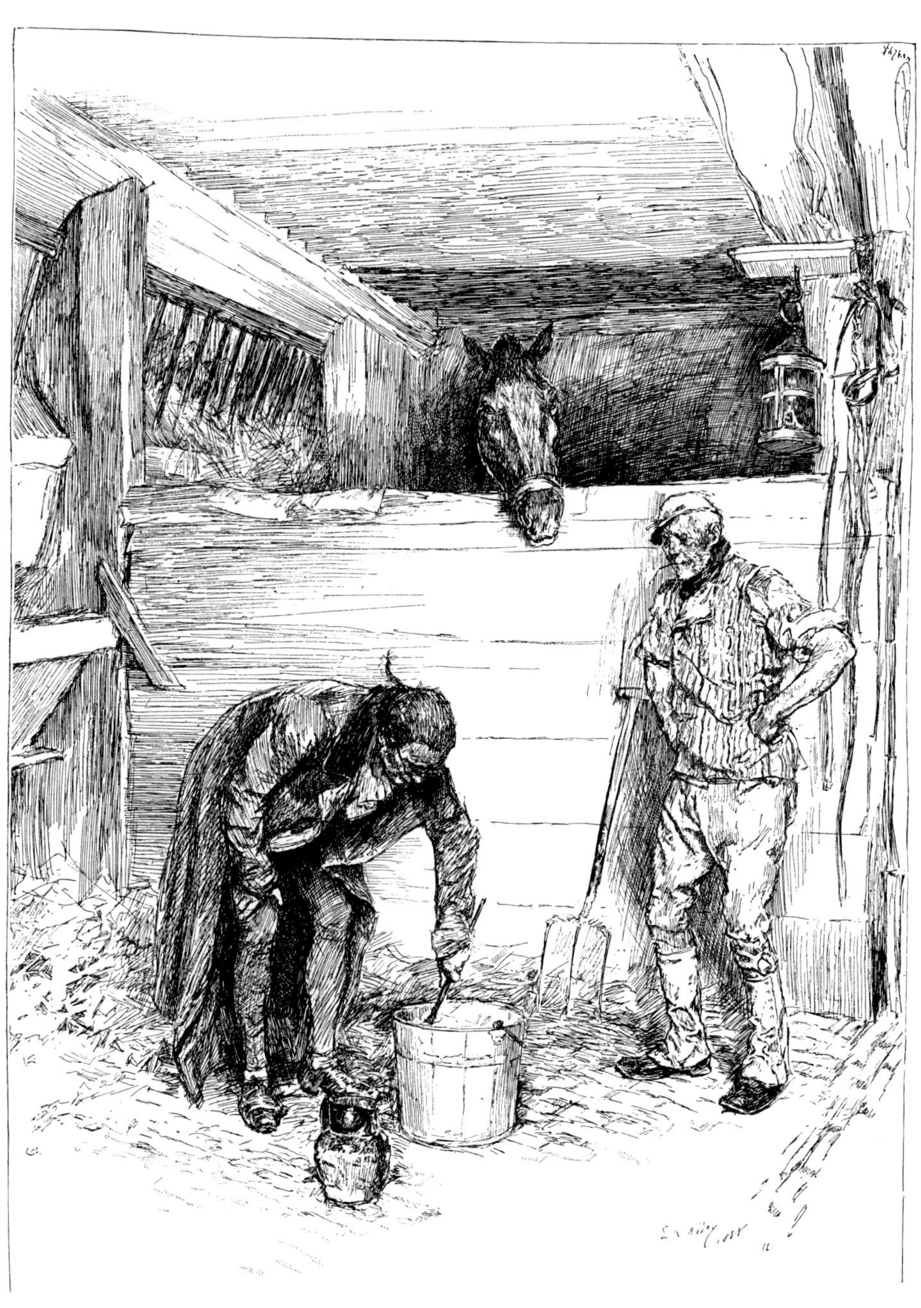

"And None knew why he fed them both with his own hands six days in seven."

The Quiet Life
"Quince," Harper & Brothers, 1889
Originally published in *Harper's New Monthly Magazine*, June 1889

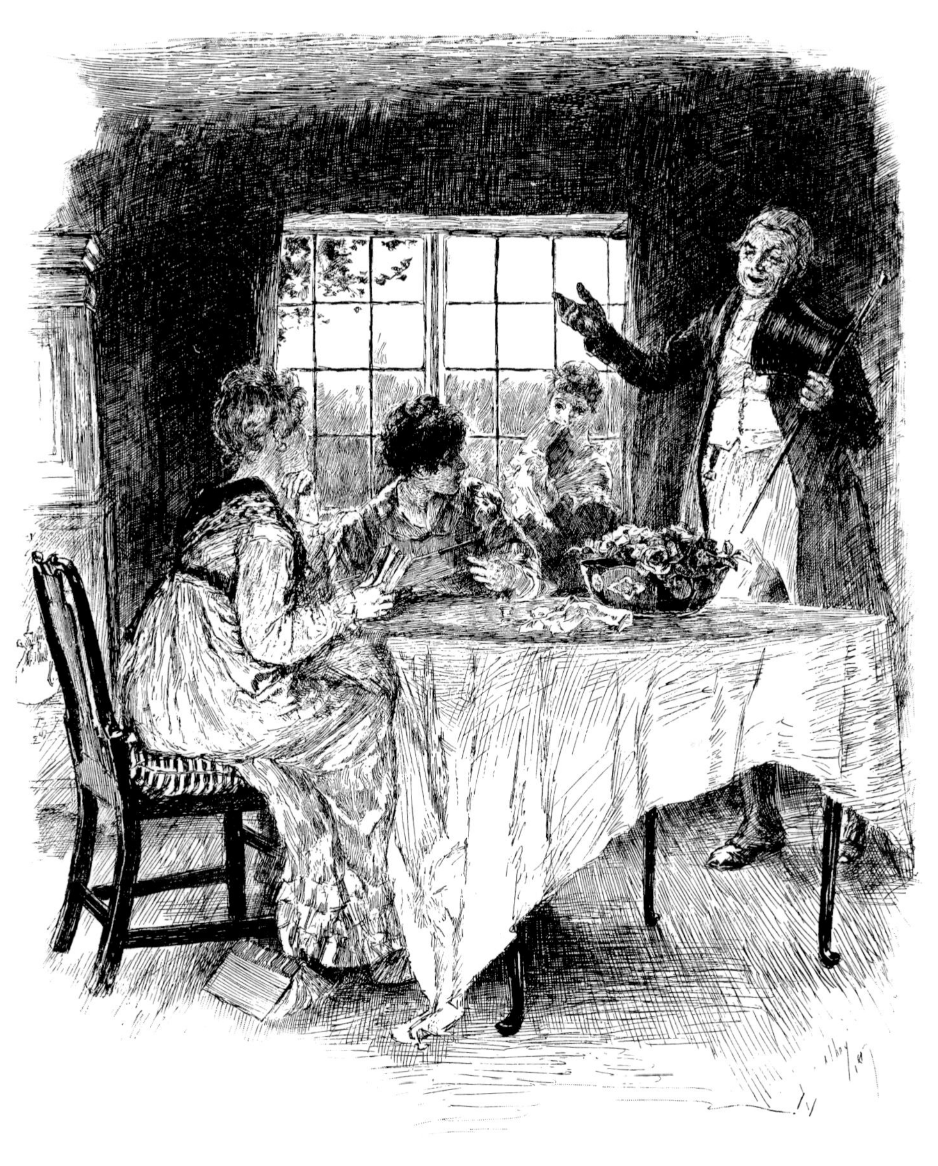

The Quiet Life
"Quince," Harper & Brothers, 1889

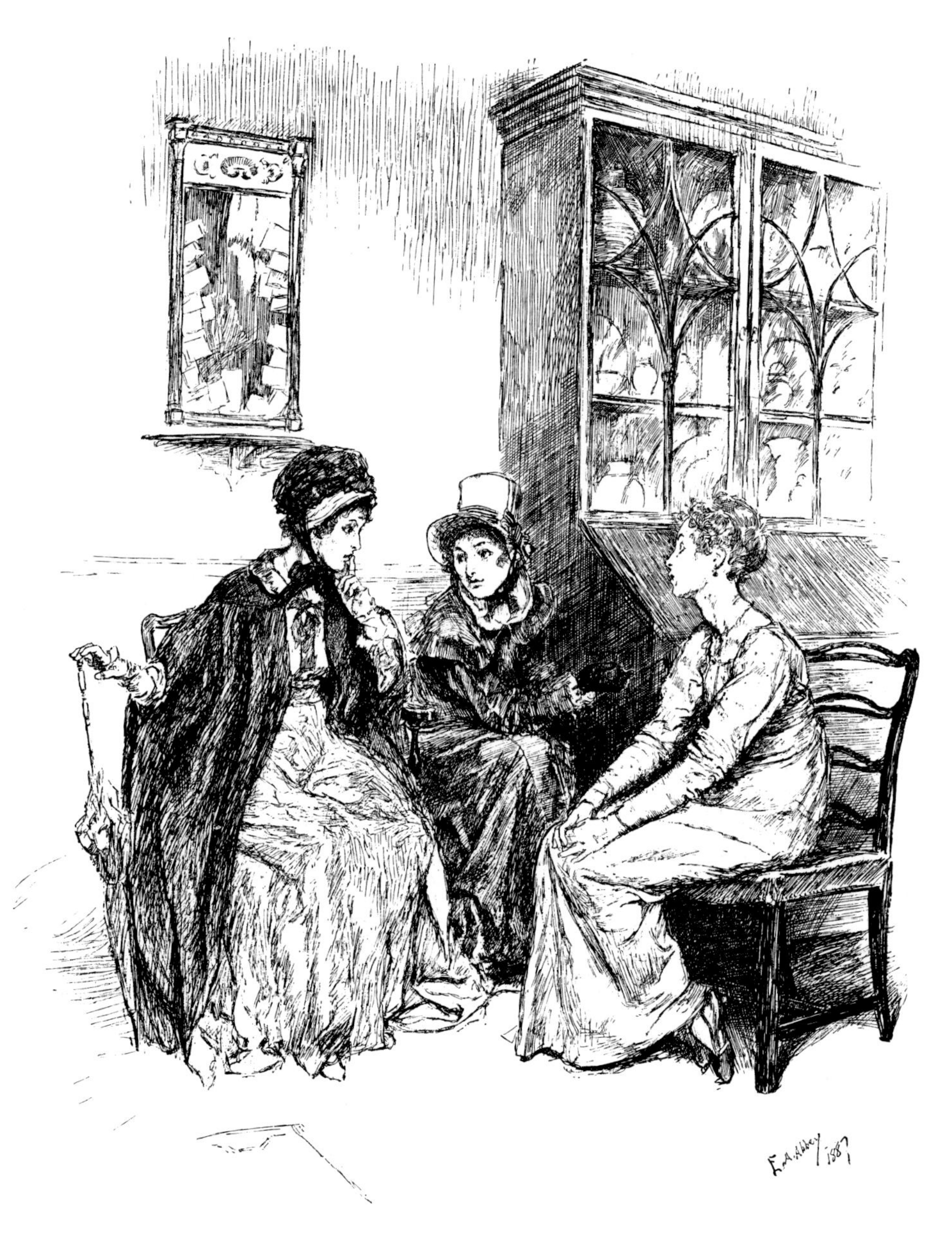

The Quiet Life
"Quince," Harper & Brothers, 1889

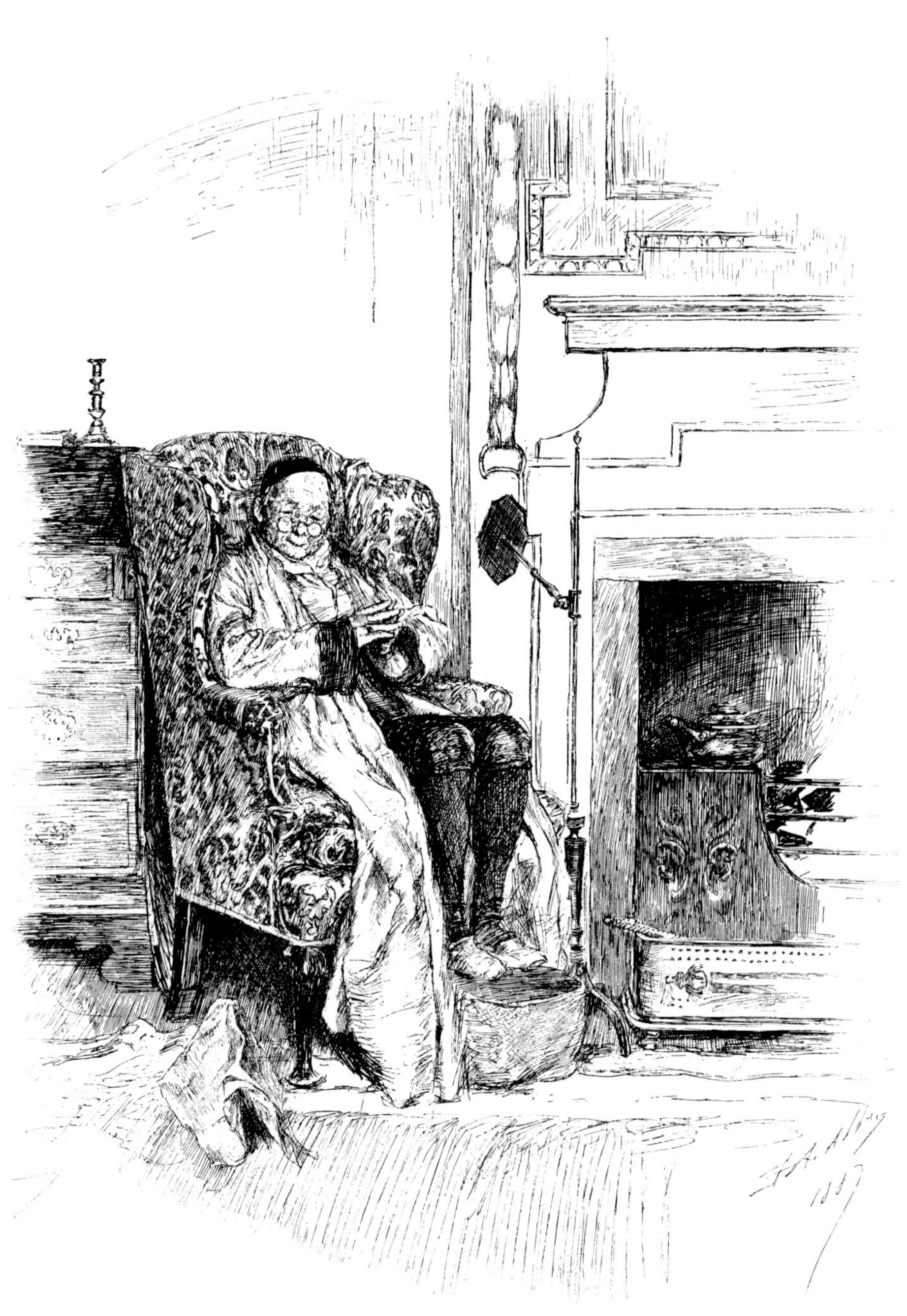

The Quiet Life
"Quince," Harper & Brothers, 1889

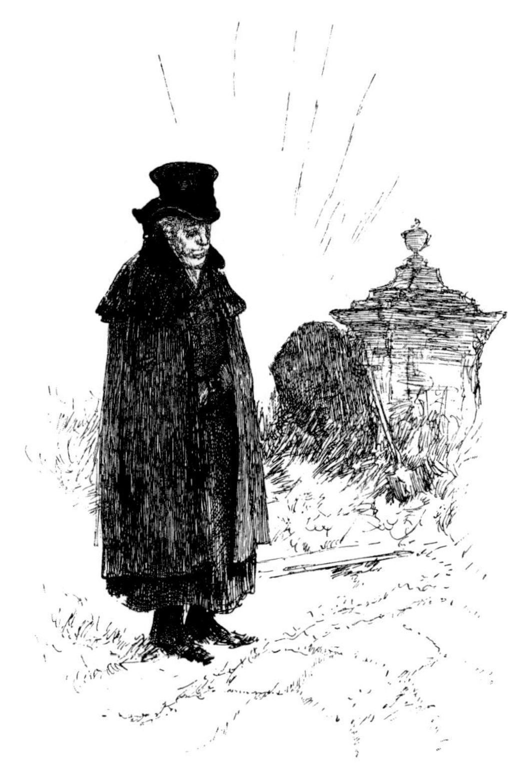

The Quiet Life
"The Vicar," Harper & Brothers, 1889

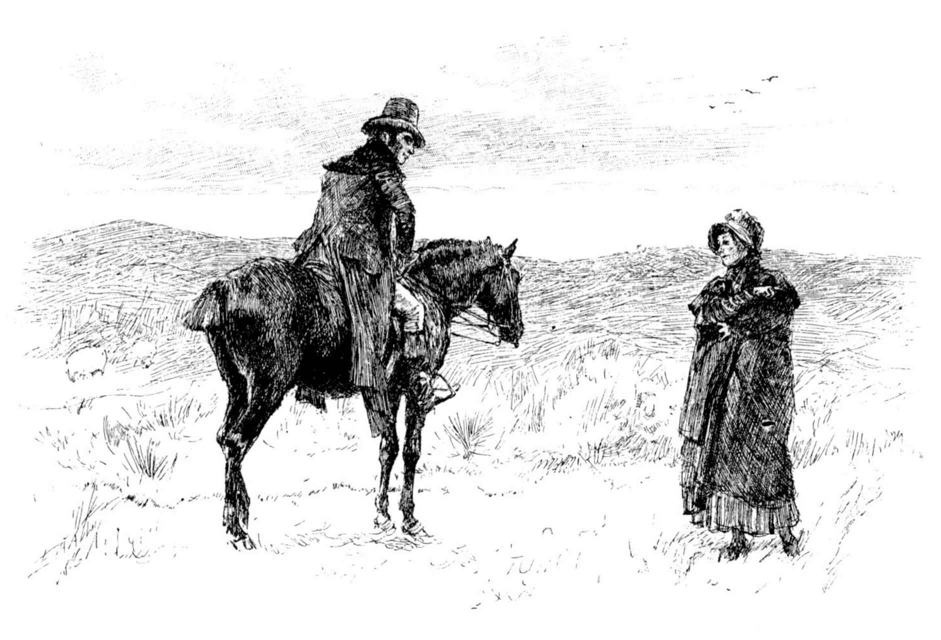

The Quiet Life
"The Vicar," Harper & Brothers, 1889

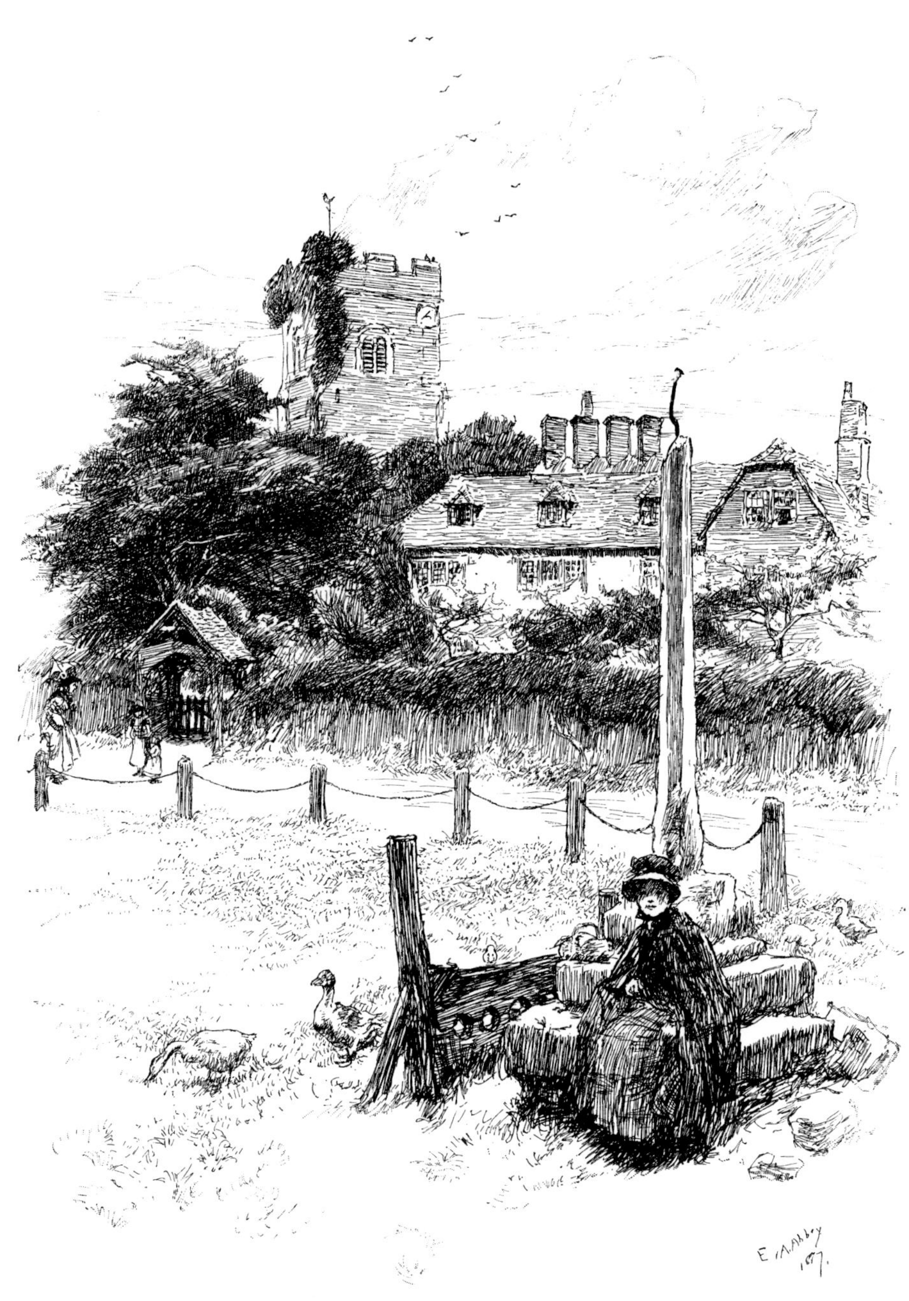

"The Parson's Wicket."

The Quiet Life
"The Vicar," Harper & Brothers, 1889
Originally published in *Harper's New Monthly Magazine*, December 1887

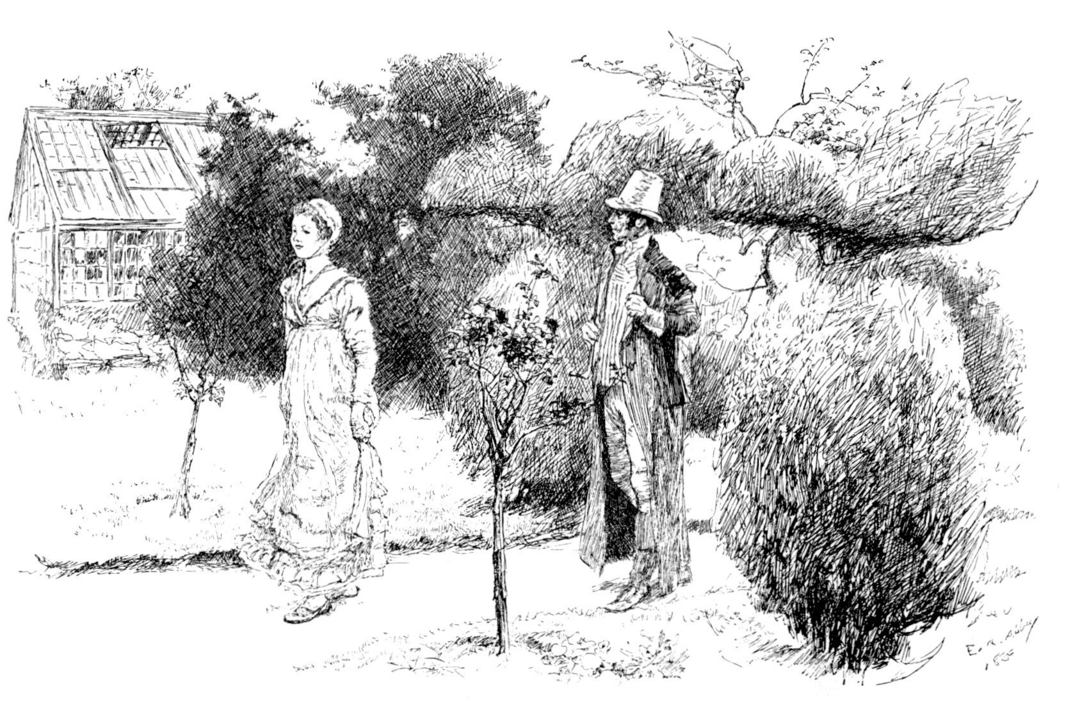

The Quiet Life
"The Vicar," Harper & Brothers, 1889

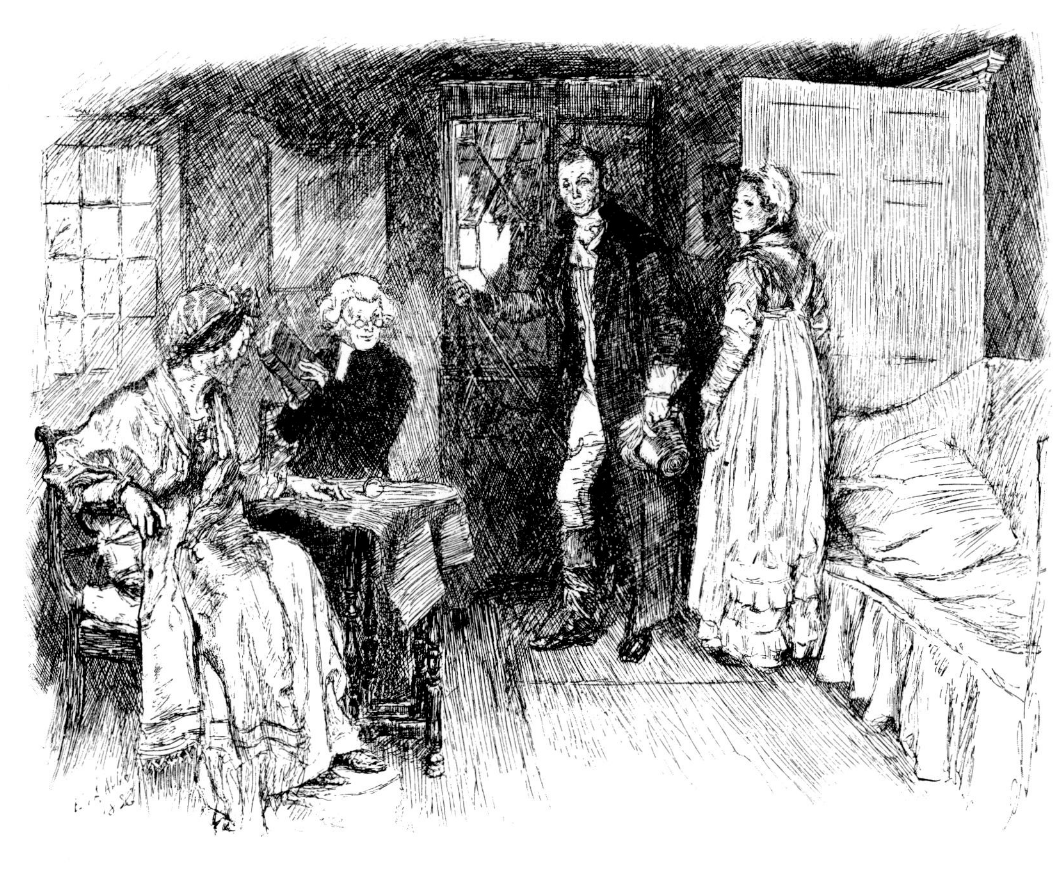

The Quiet Life
"The Vicar," Harper & Brothers, 1889

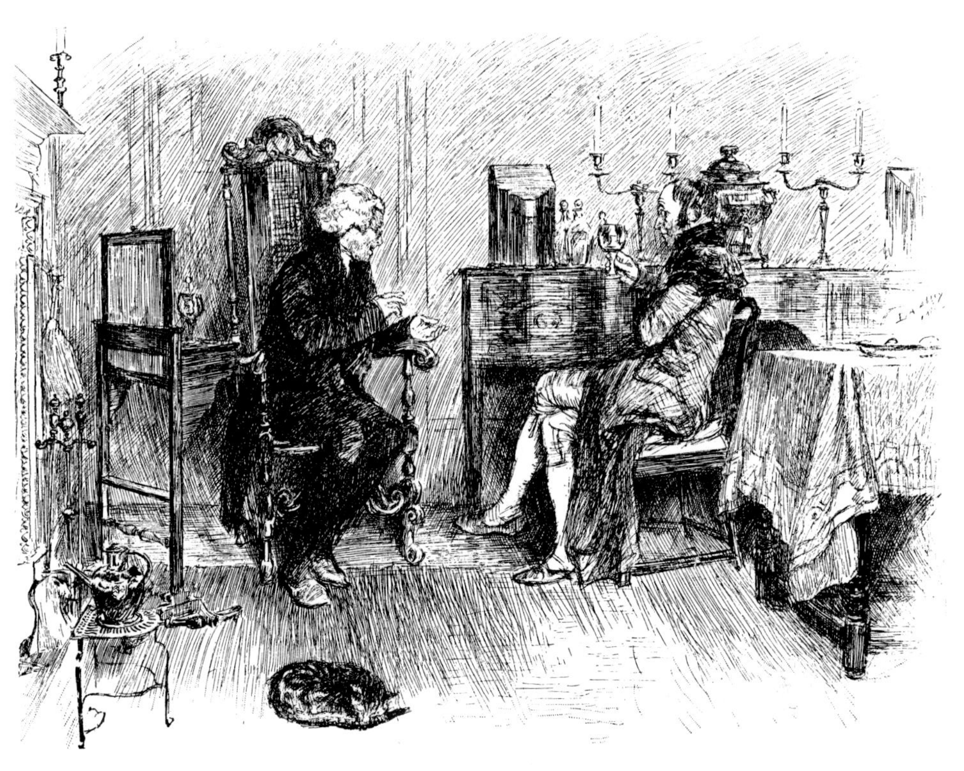

The Quiet Life
"The Vicar," Harper & Brothers, 1889

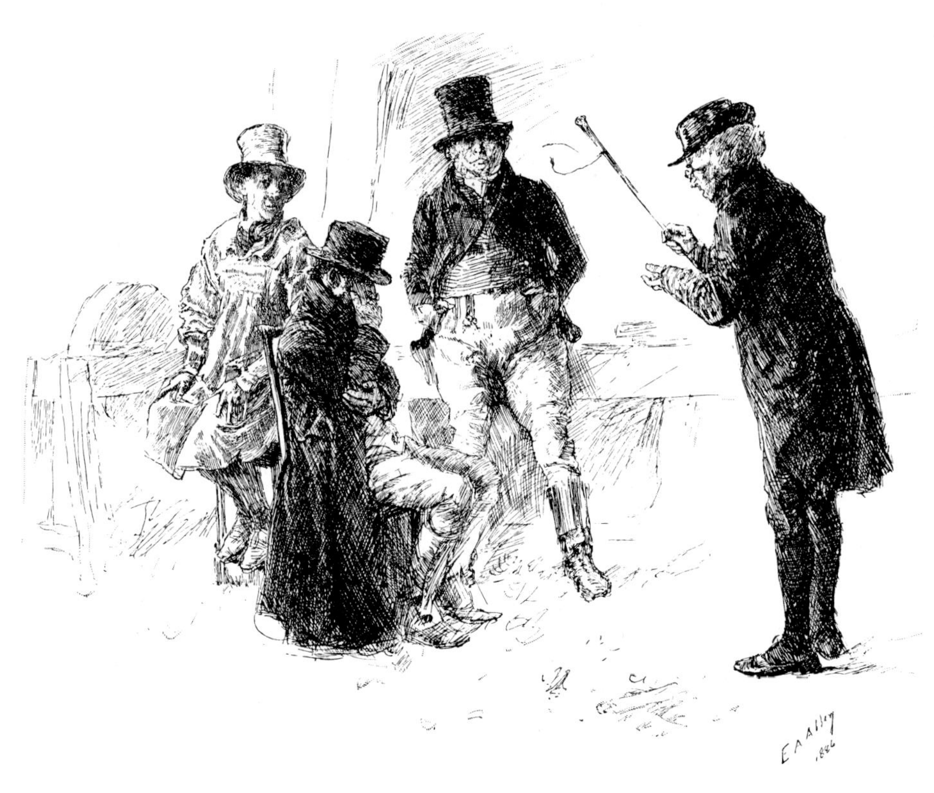

The Quiet Life
"The Vicar," Harper & Brothers, 1889

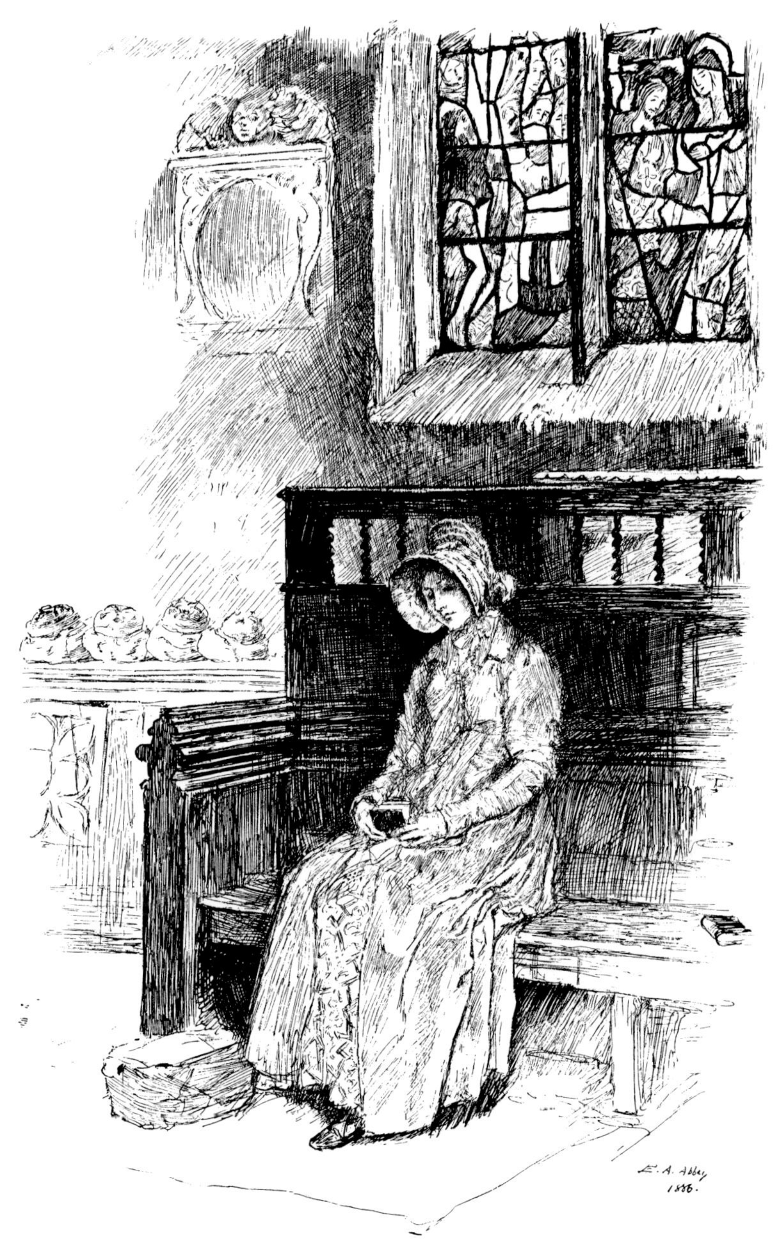

The Quiet Life
"The Vicar," Harper & Brothers, 1889

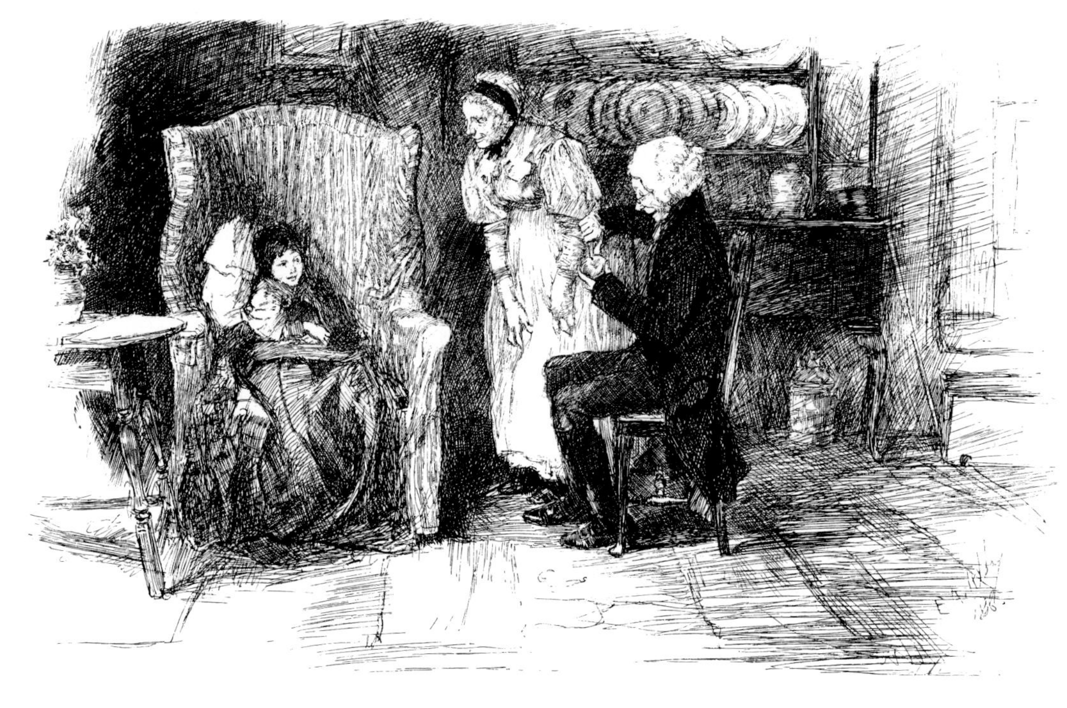

The Quiet Life
"The Vicar," Harper & Brothers, 1889

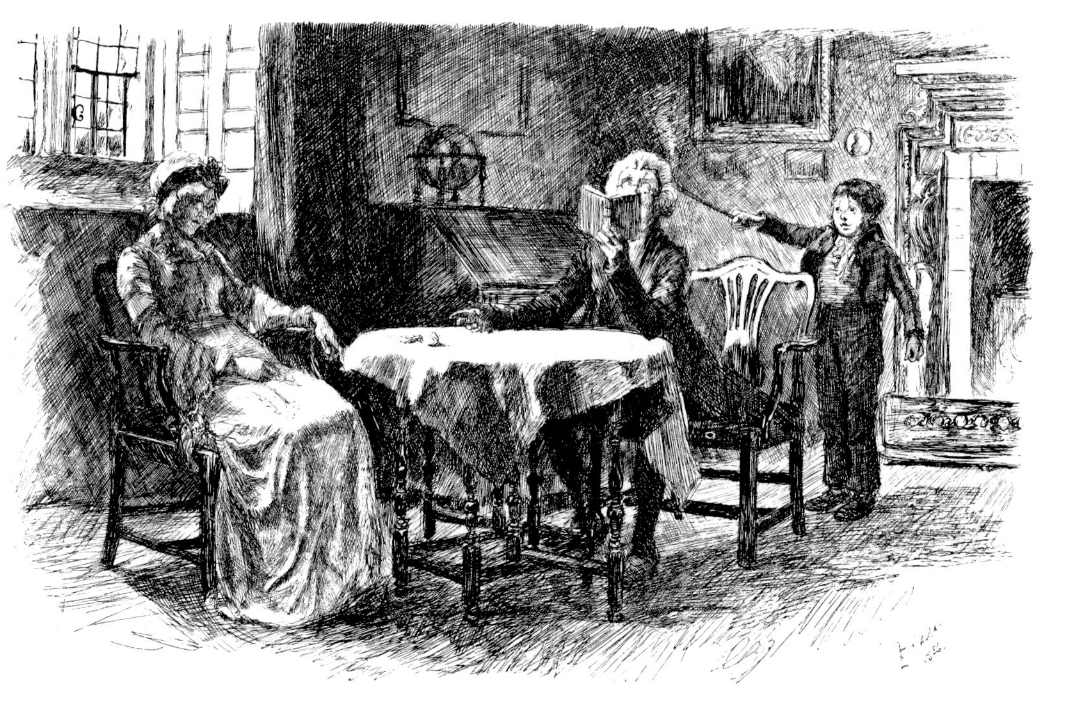

The Quiet Life
"The Vicar," Harper & Brothers, 1889

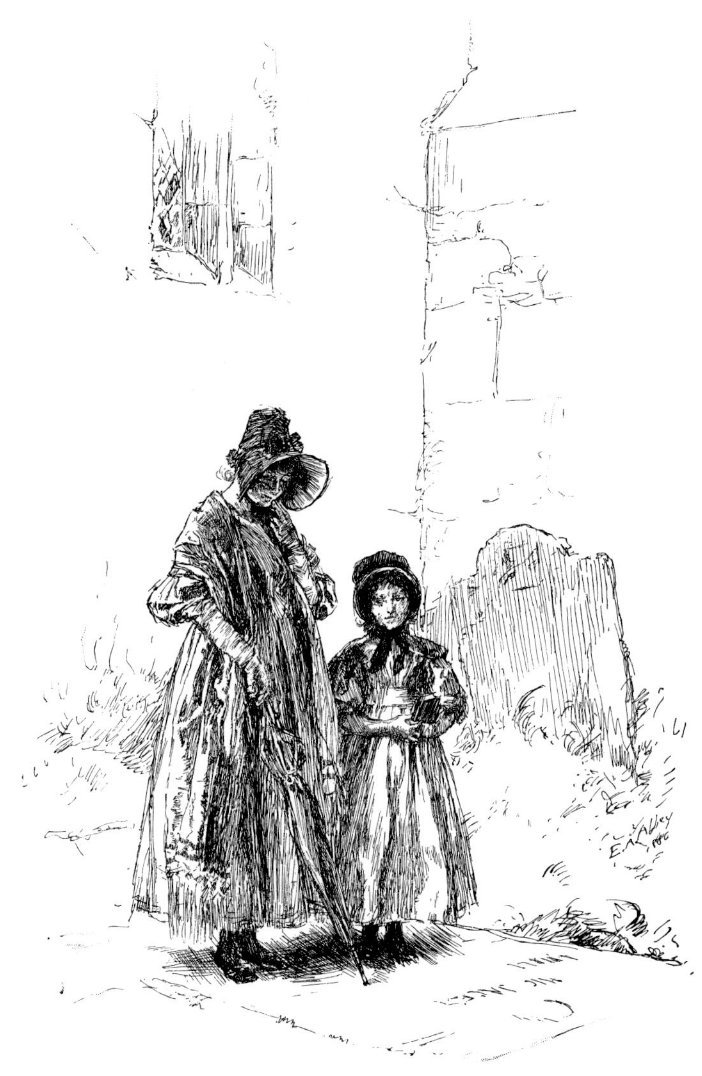

"Hic Jacket Gvlielmvs Brown."

The Quiet Life
"The Vicar," Harper & Brothers, 1889
Originally published in *Harper's New Monthly Magazine*, December 1887

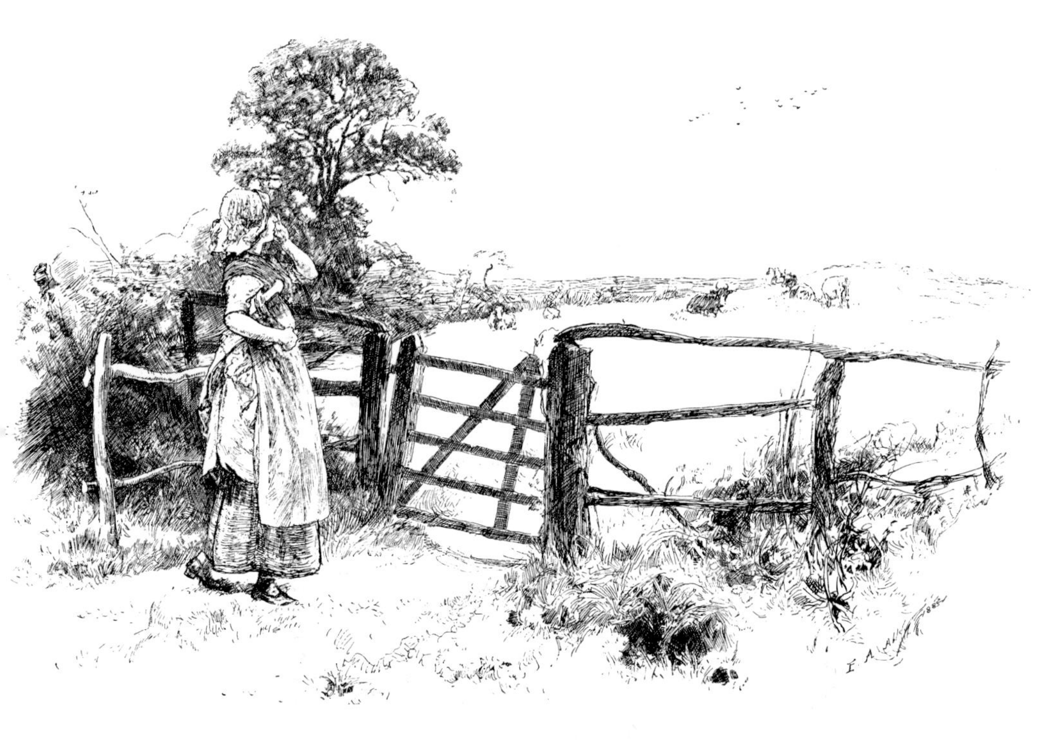

The Quiet Life
"Ode to Solitude," Harper & Brothers, 1889

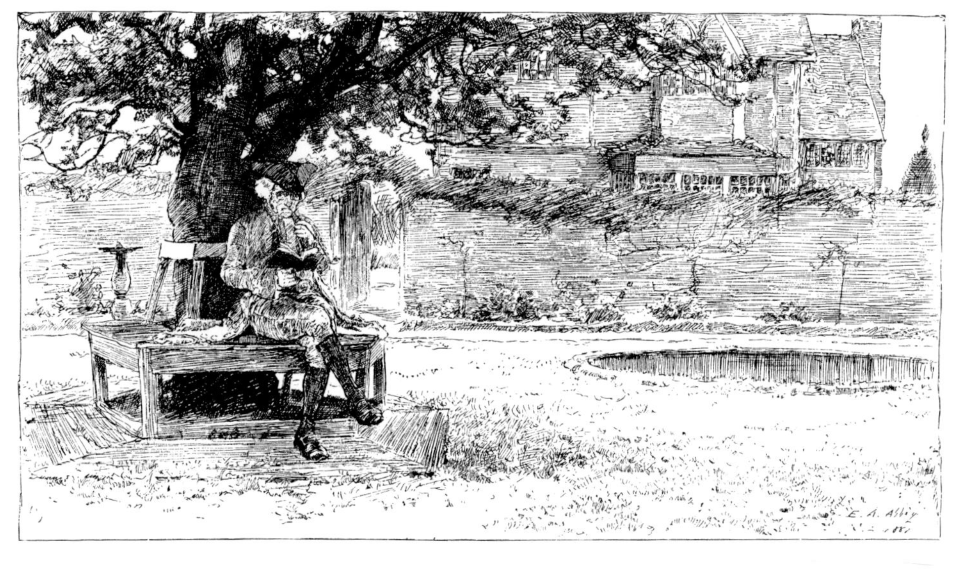

The Quiet Life
"Ode to Solitude," Harper & Brothers, 1889

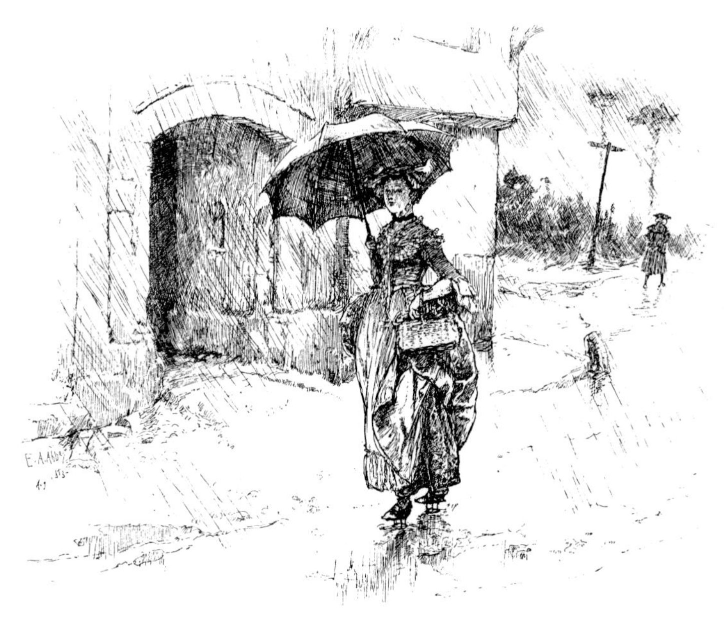

The Quiet Life
"Ode to Solitude," Harper & Brothers, 1889

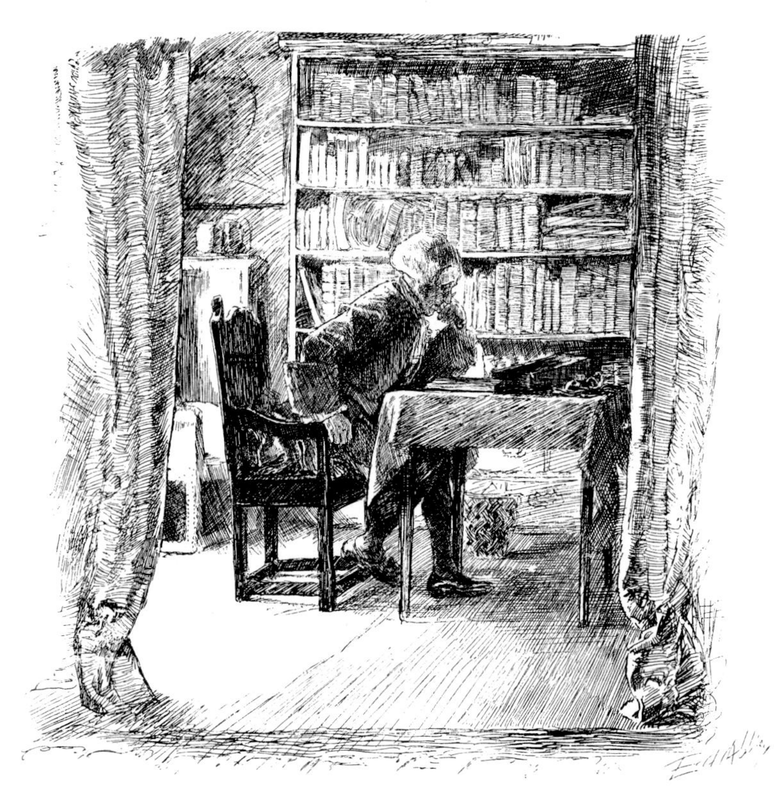

The Quiet Life
"Ode to Solitude," Harper & Brothers, 1889

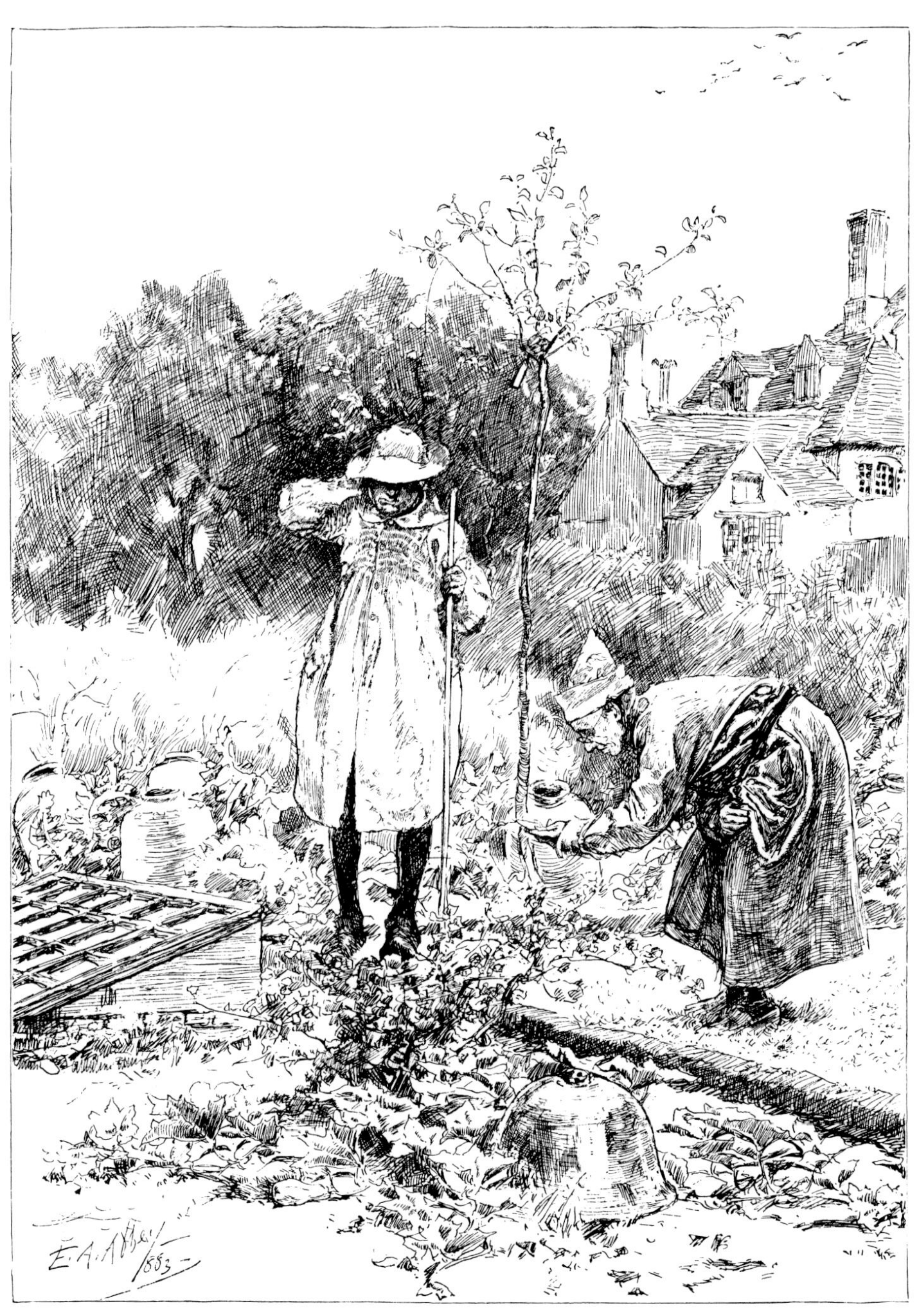

The Quiet Life
"Ode to Solitude," Harper & Brothers, 1889

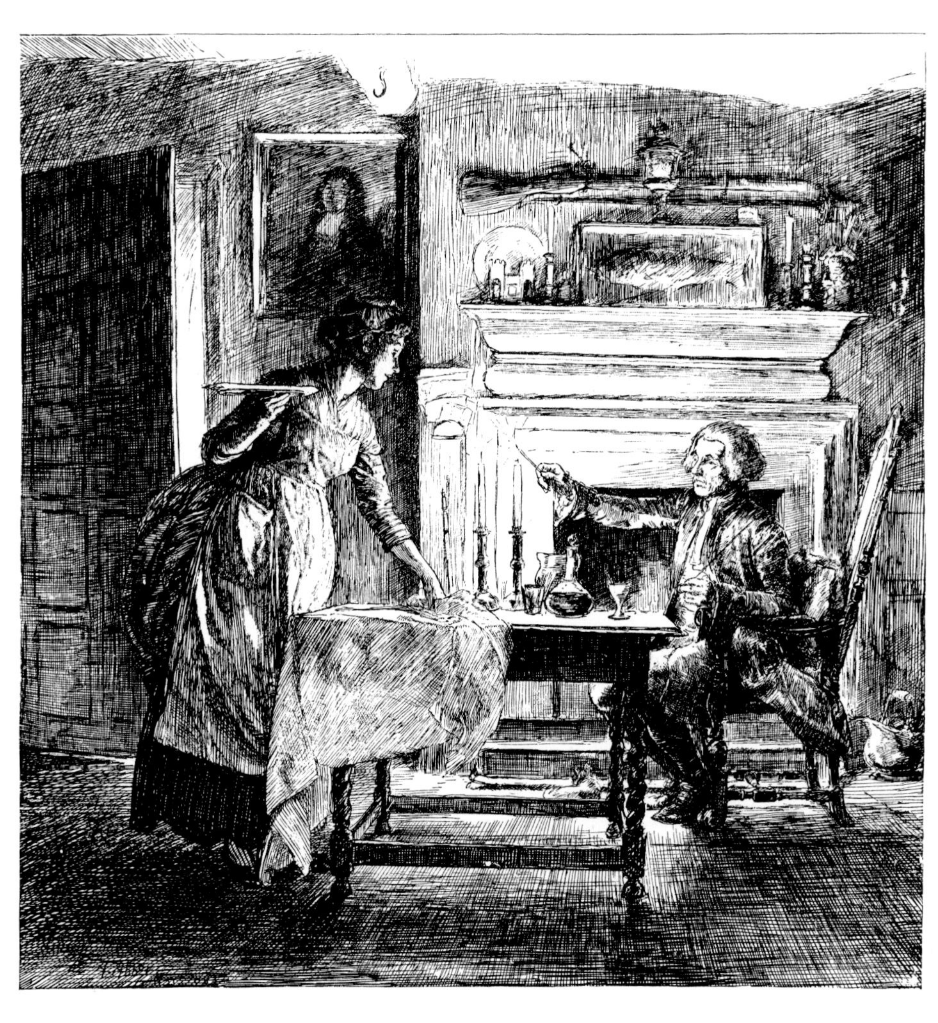

The Quiet Life
"Ode to Solitude," Harper & Brothers, 1889

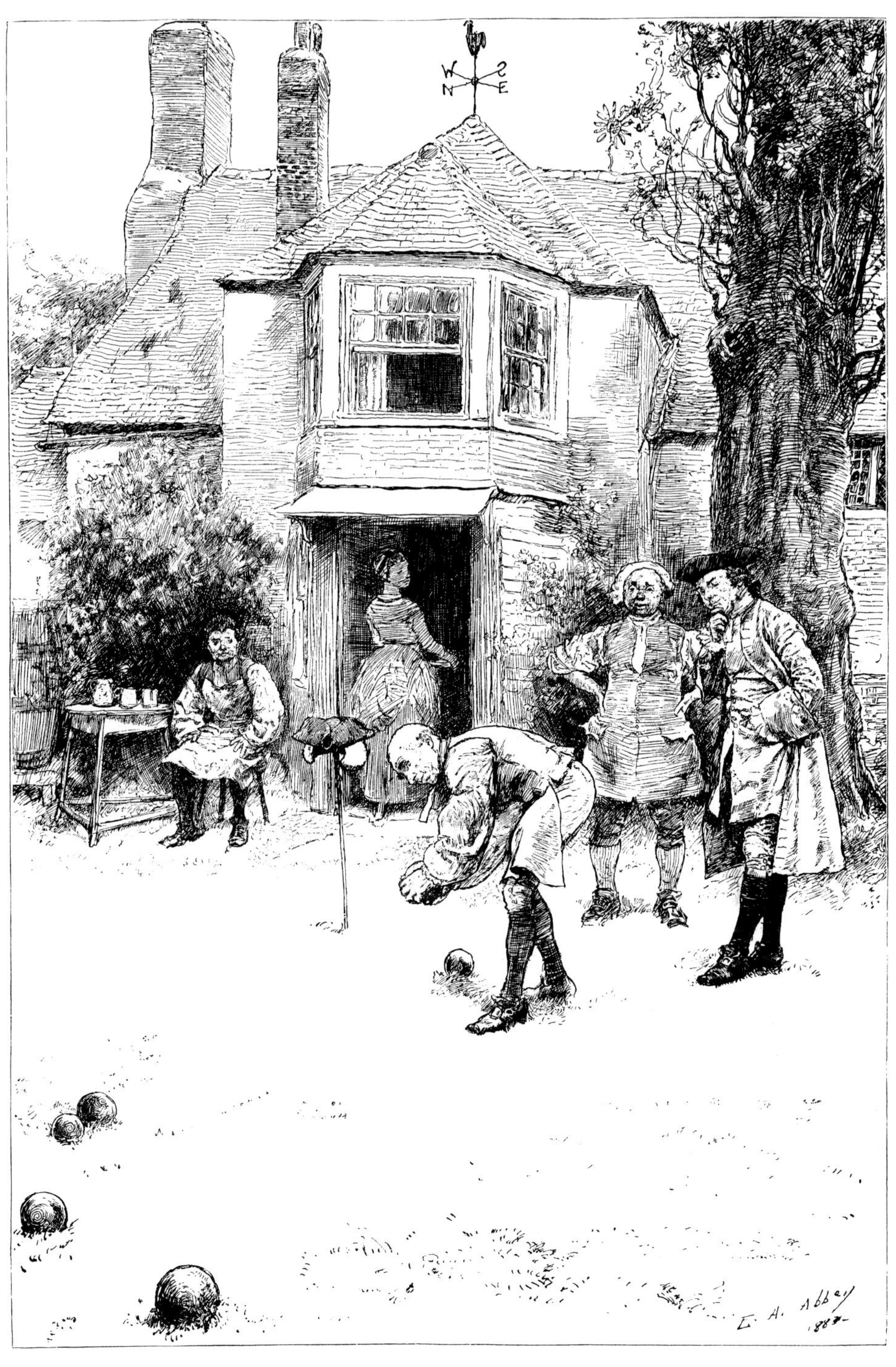

The Quiet Life
"Ode to Solitude," Harper & Brothers, 1889

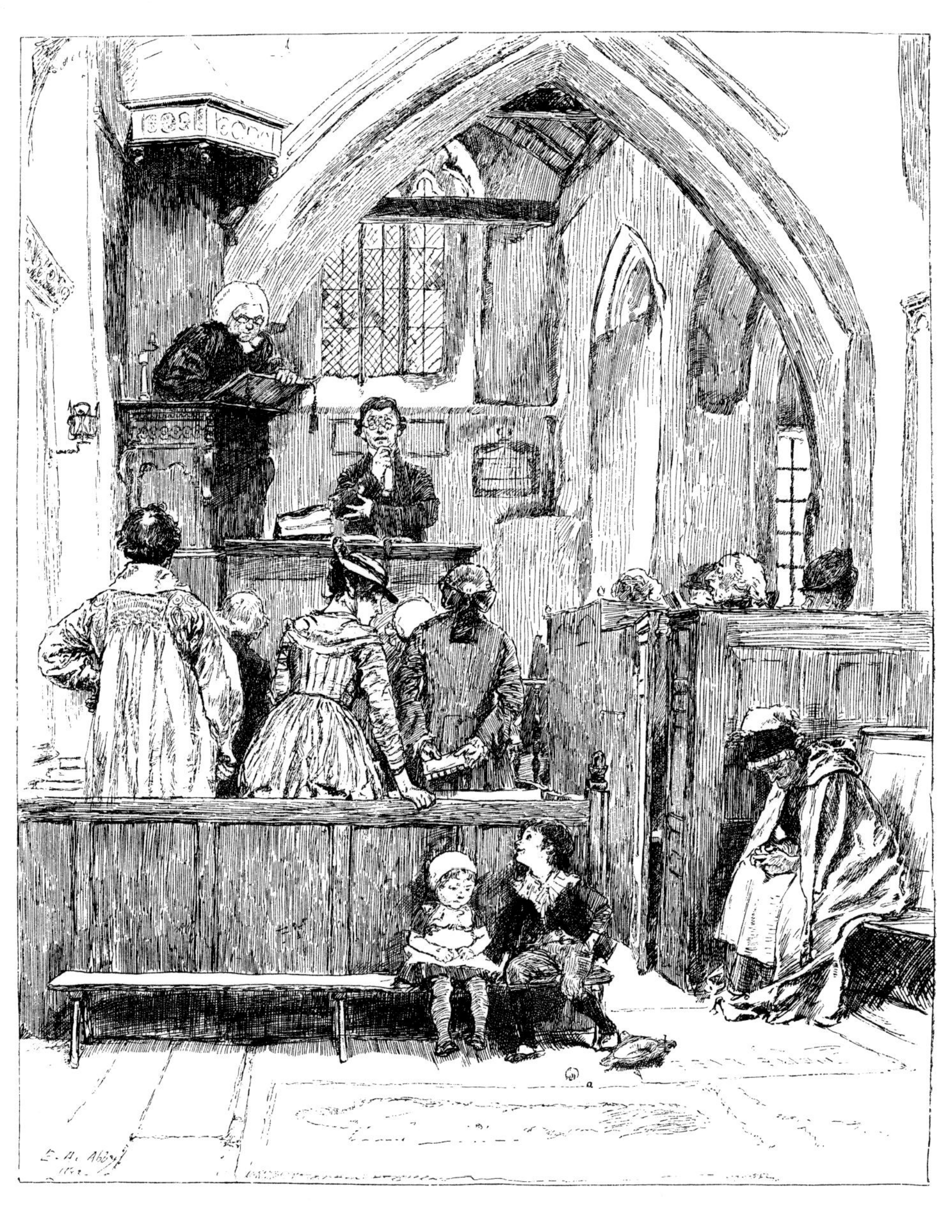

The Quiet Life
"Ode to Solitude," Harper & Brothers, 1889
Originally published in *Harper's New Monthly Magazine*, December 1883

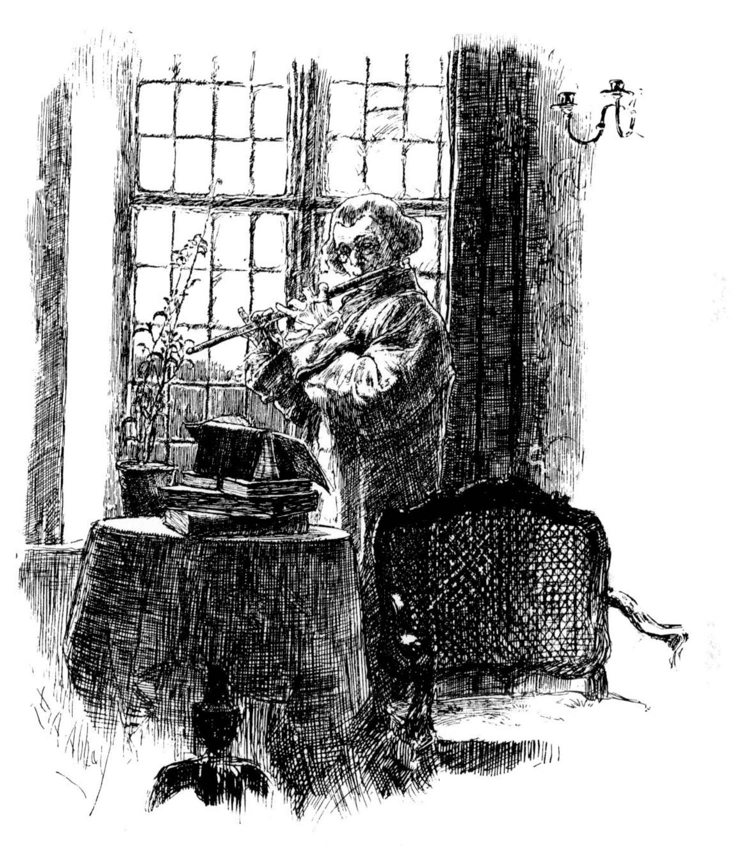

The Quiet Life
"Ode to Solitude," Harper & Brothers, 1889

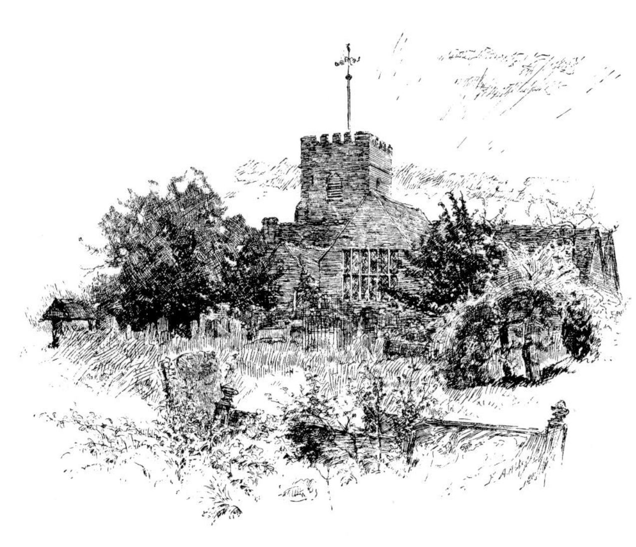

The Quiet Life
"The Married Man," Harper & Brothers, 1889

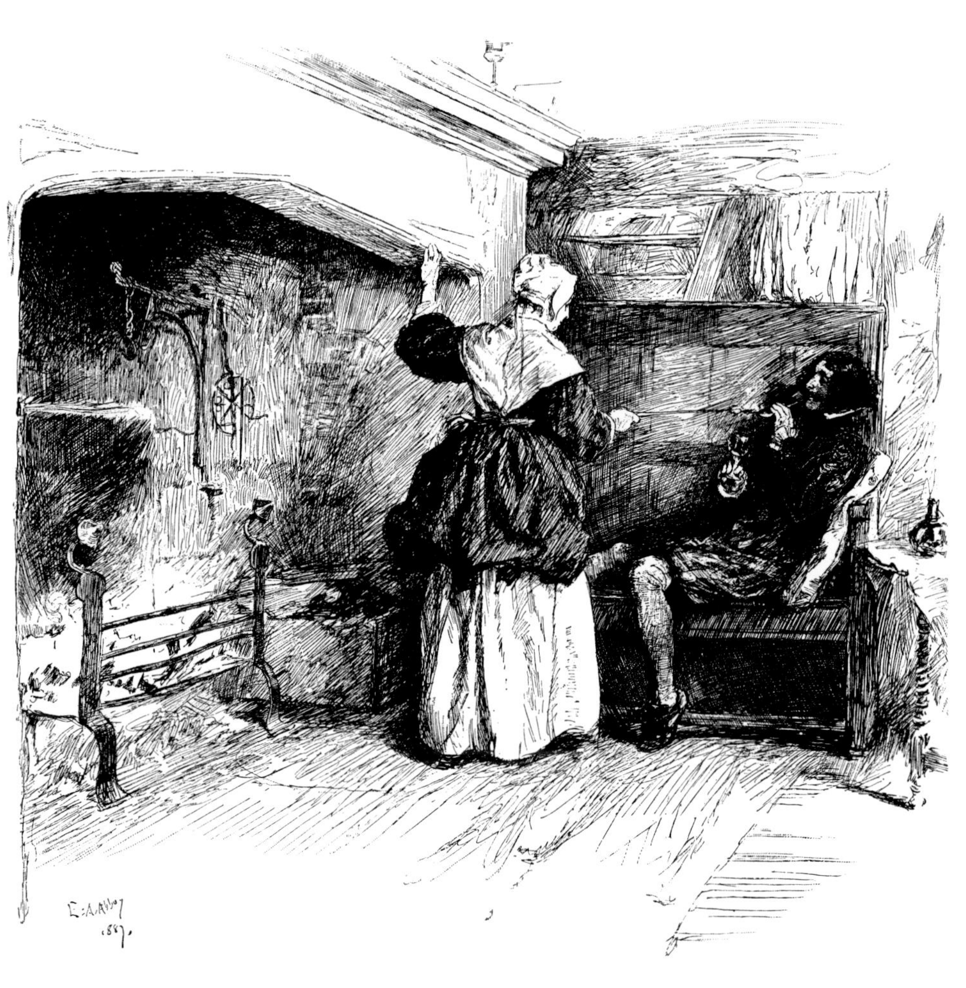

The Quiet Life
"The Married Man," Harper & Brothers, 1889
Originally published in *Harper's New Monthly Magazine*, May 1888

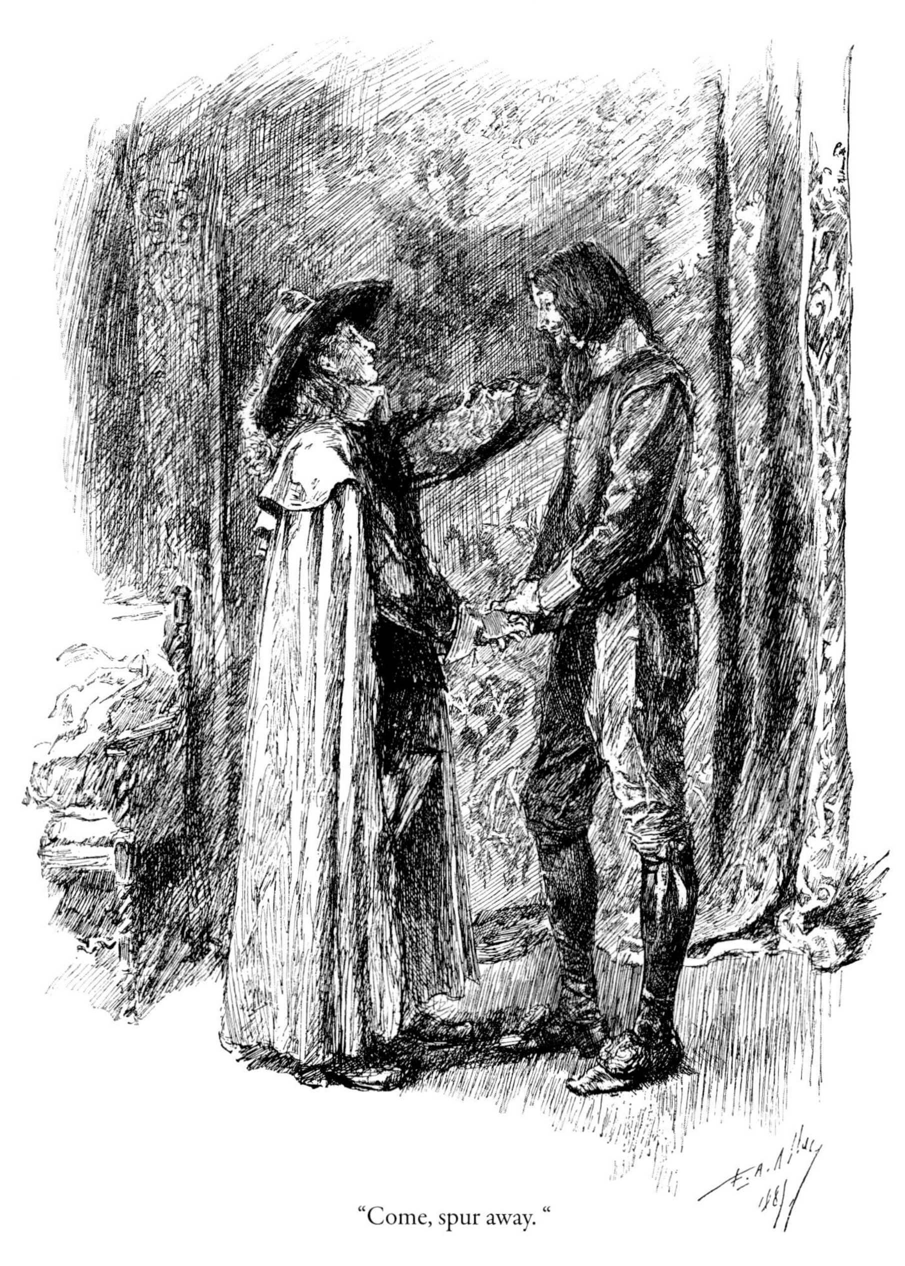

The Quiet Life
"To Master Anthony Stafford," Harper & Brothers, 1889

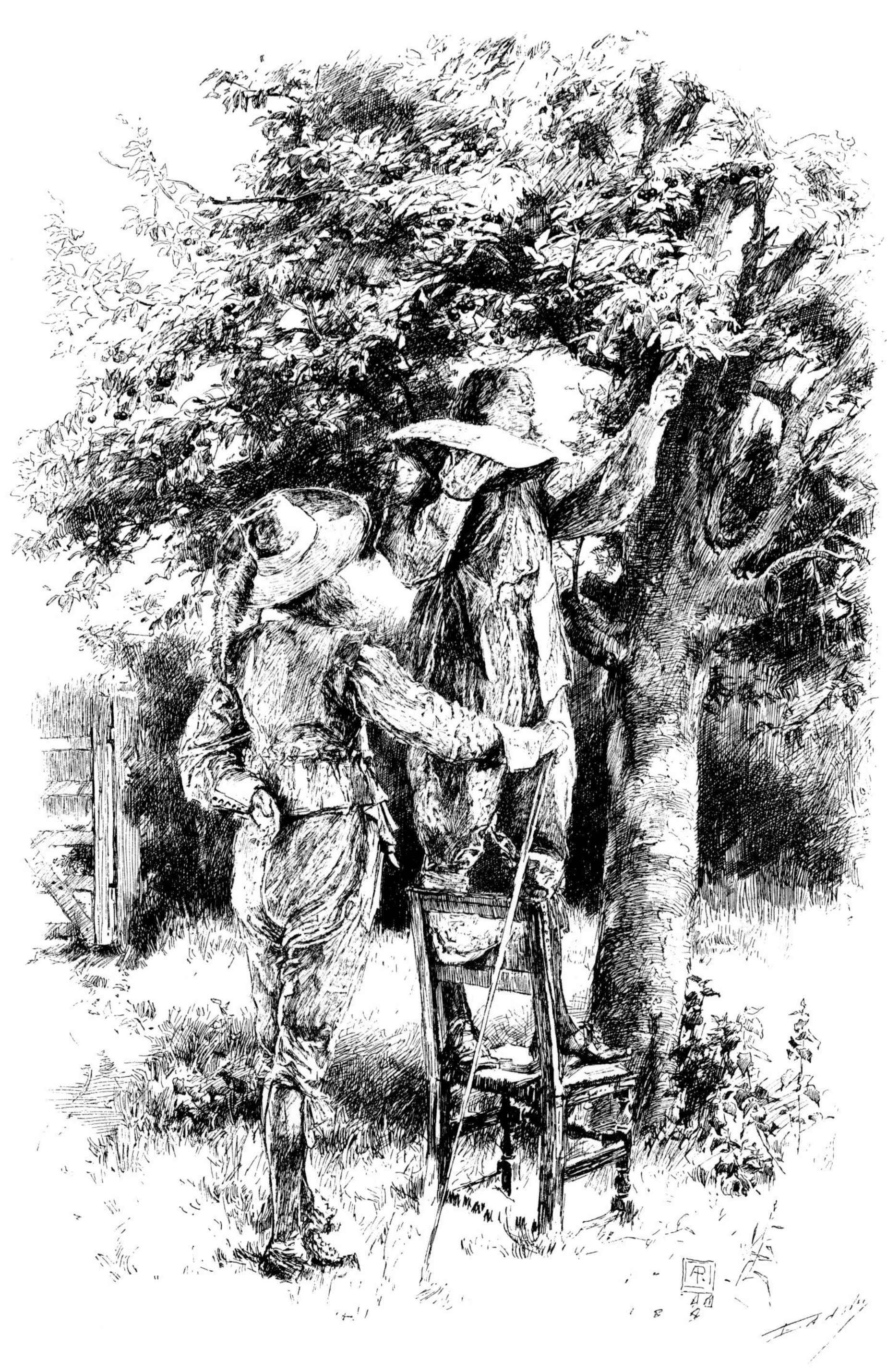

The Quiet Life
"To Master Anthony Stafford," Harper & Brothers, 1889
(Figures by E.A. Abbey, background by Alfred W. Parsons)

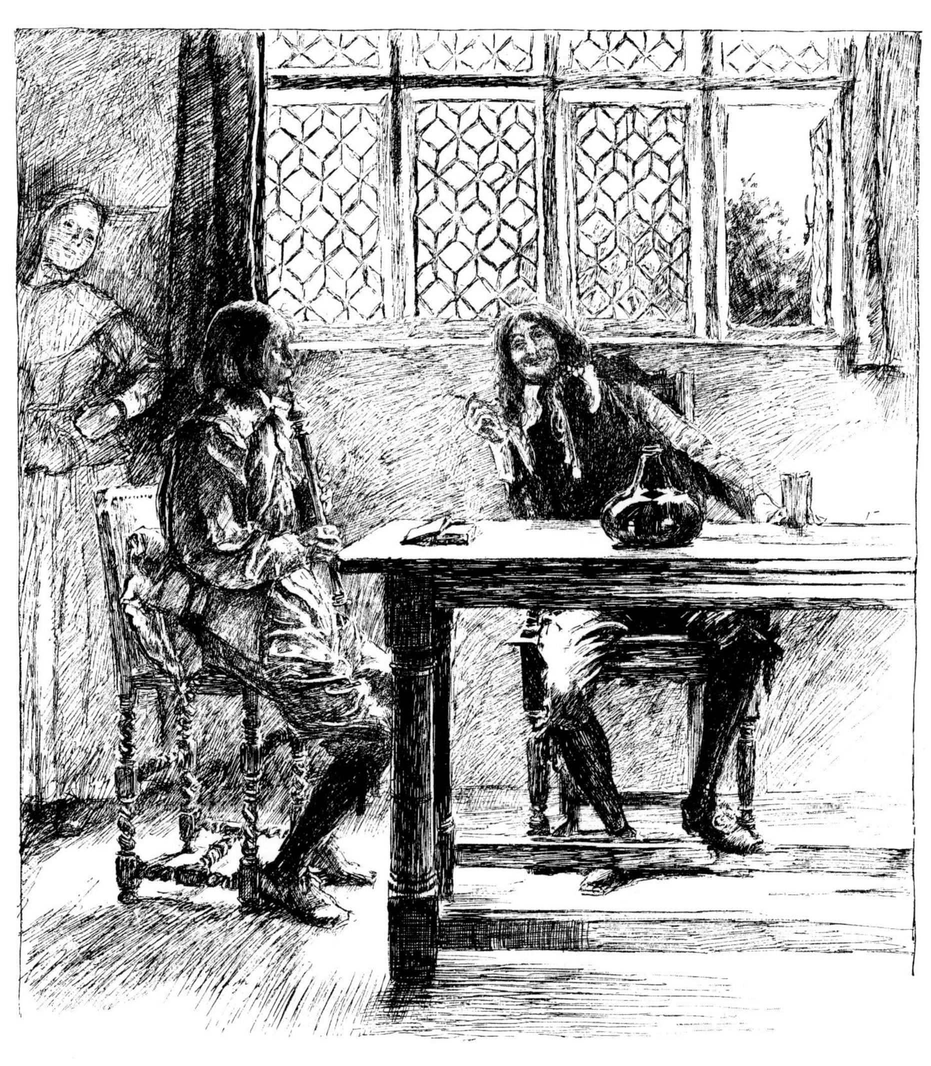

The Quiet Life
"To Master Anthony Stafford," Harper & Brothers, 1889

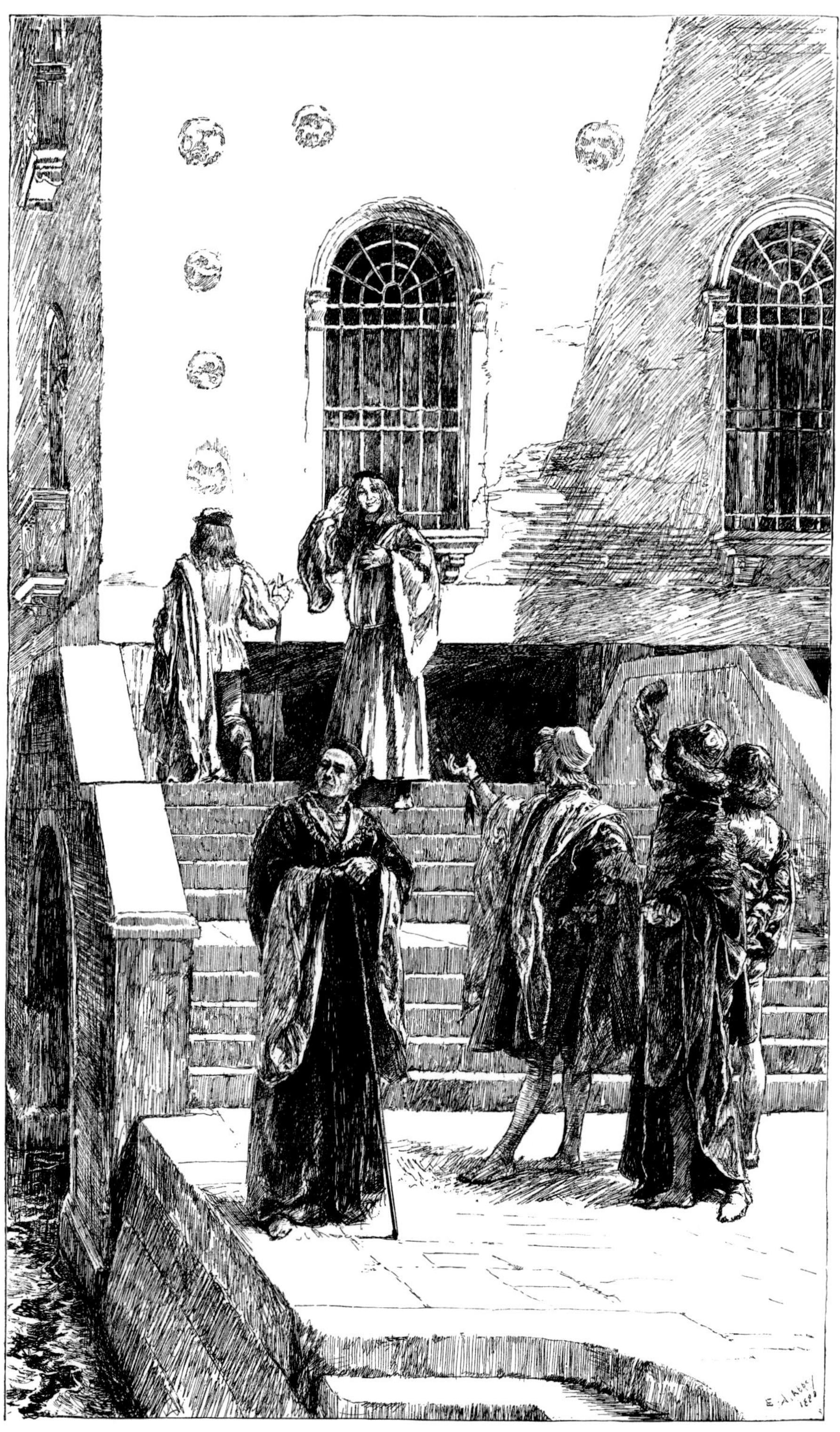

Harper's New Monthly Magazine, April 1890
The Comedies of Shakespeare — "The Merchant of Venice"
Act I., Scene I. — Enter Salarino and Salanio.

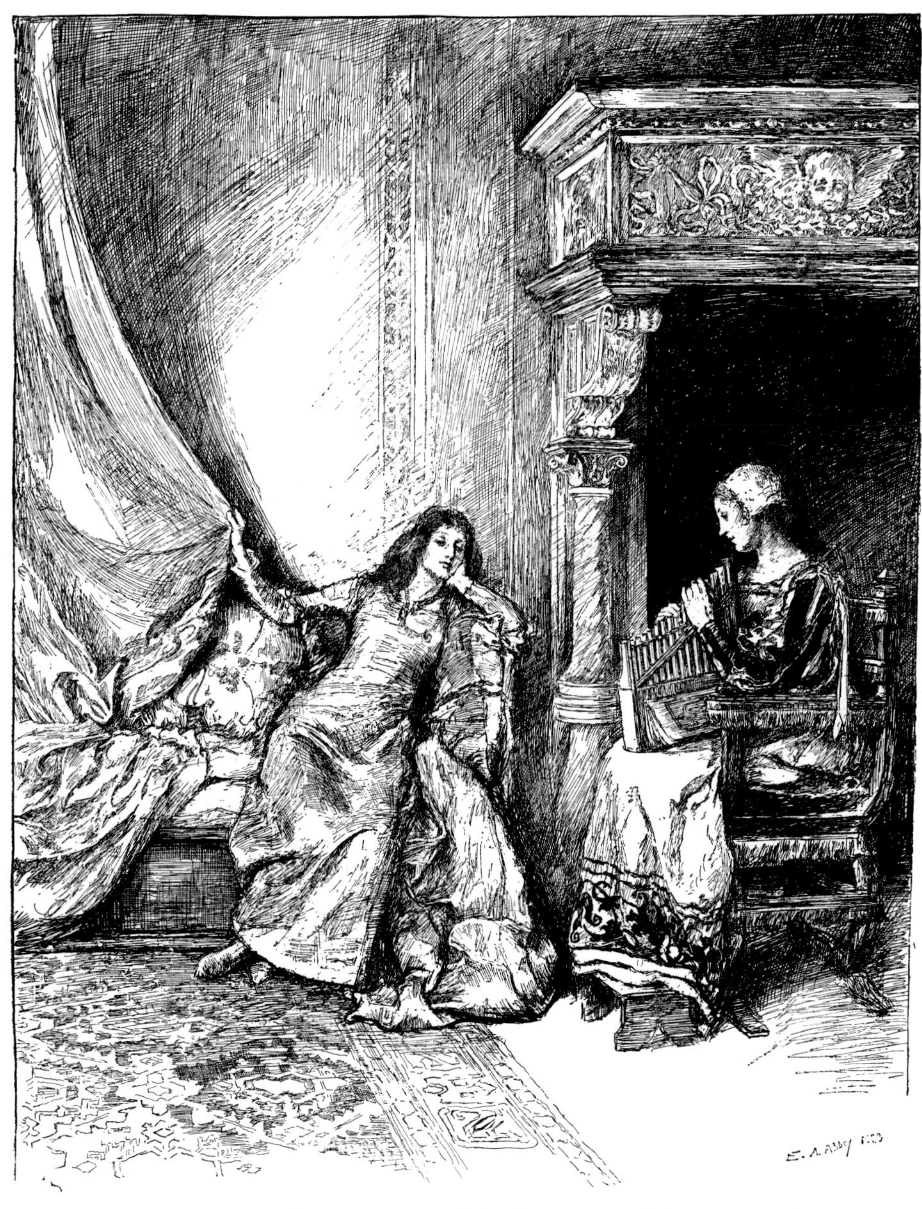

Portia. "By my troth, Nerissa, my little body is aweary of this great world."

Harper's New Monthly Magazine, April 1890
The Comedies of Shakespeare — "The Merchant of Venice"
Act I., Scene II. — Belmont. A room in Portia's house.

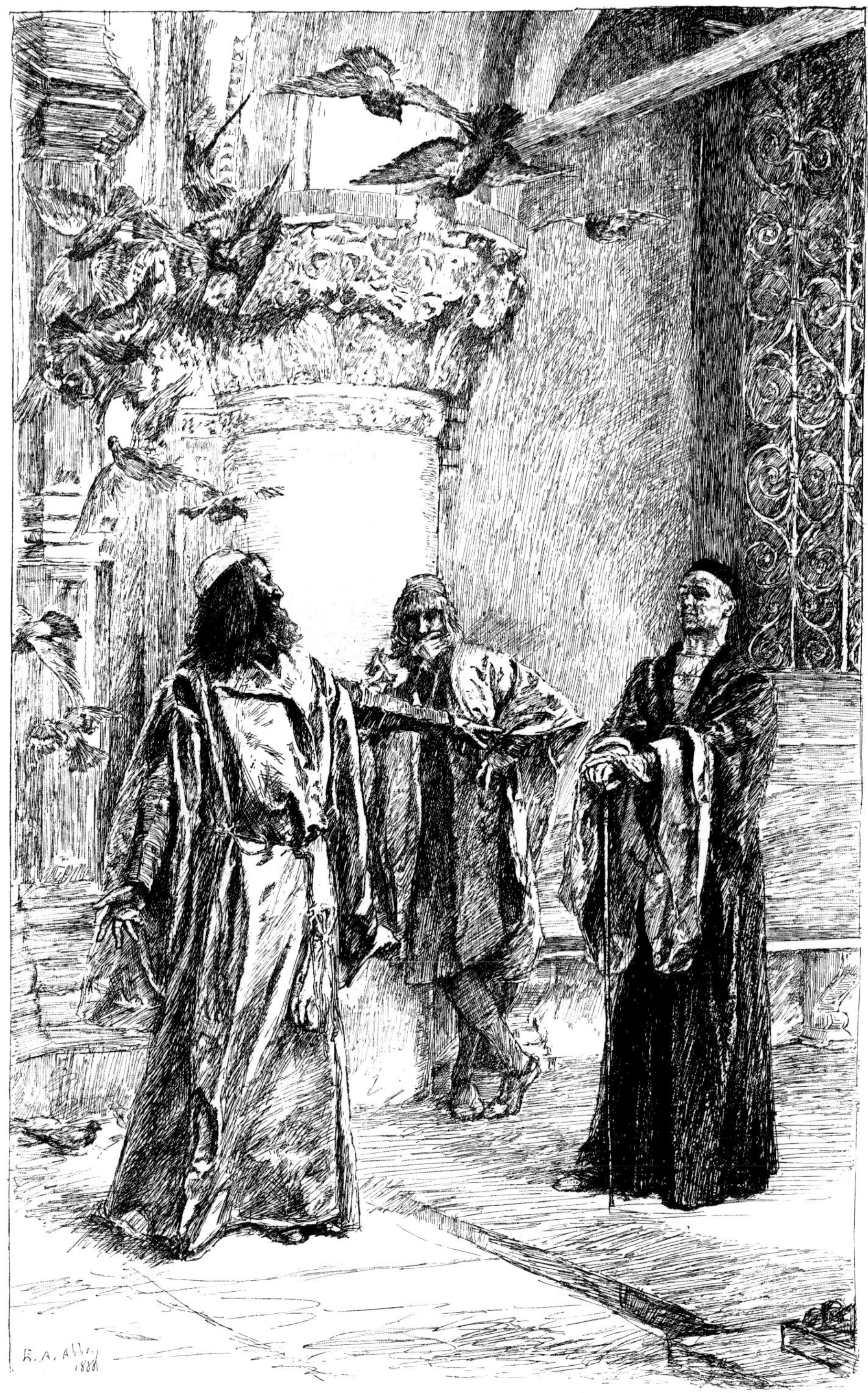

Shylock. "And for these courtesies I'll lend you thus much monies!"

Harper's New Monthly Magazine, April 1890
The Comedies of Shakespeare — "The Merchant of Venice"
Act I., Scene III. — Venice. A public place.

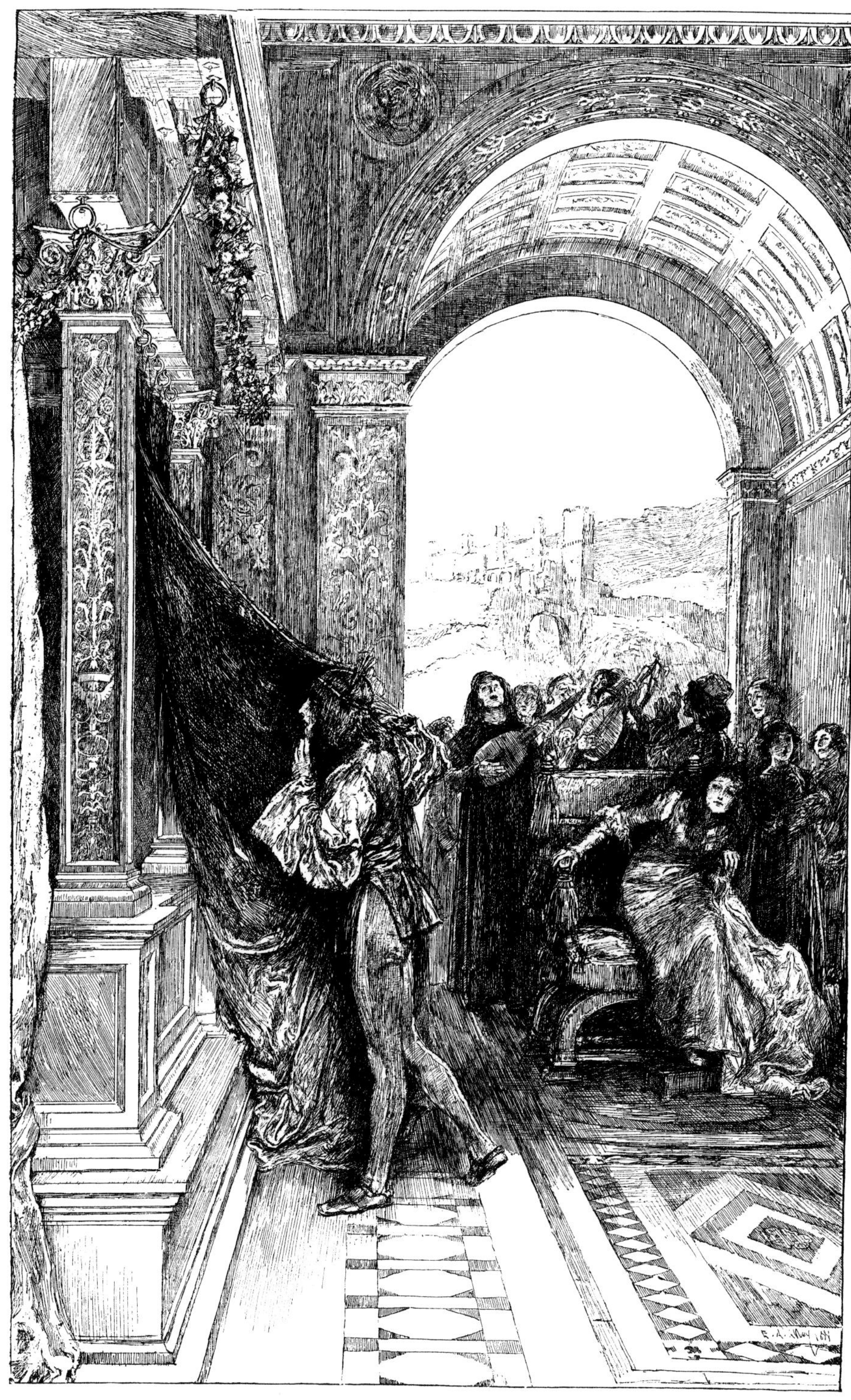

Portia. "Away then: I am lock'd in one of them; if you do love me, you will find me out."

Harper's New Monthly Magazine, April 1890
The Comedies of Shakespeare — "The Merchant of Venice"
Act III., Scene II. — Belmont. A room in Portia's house.

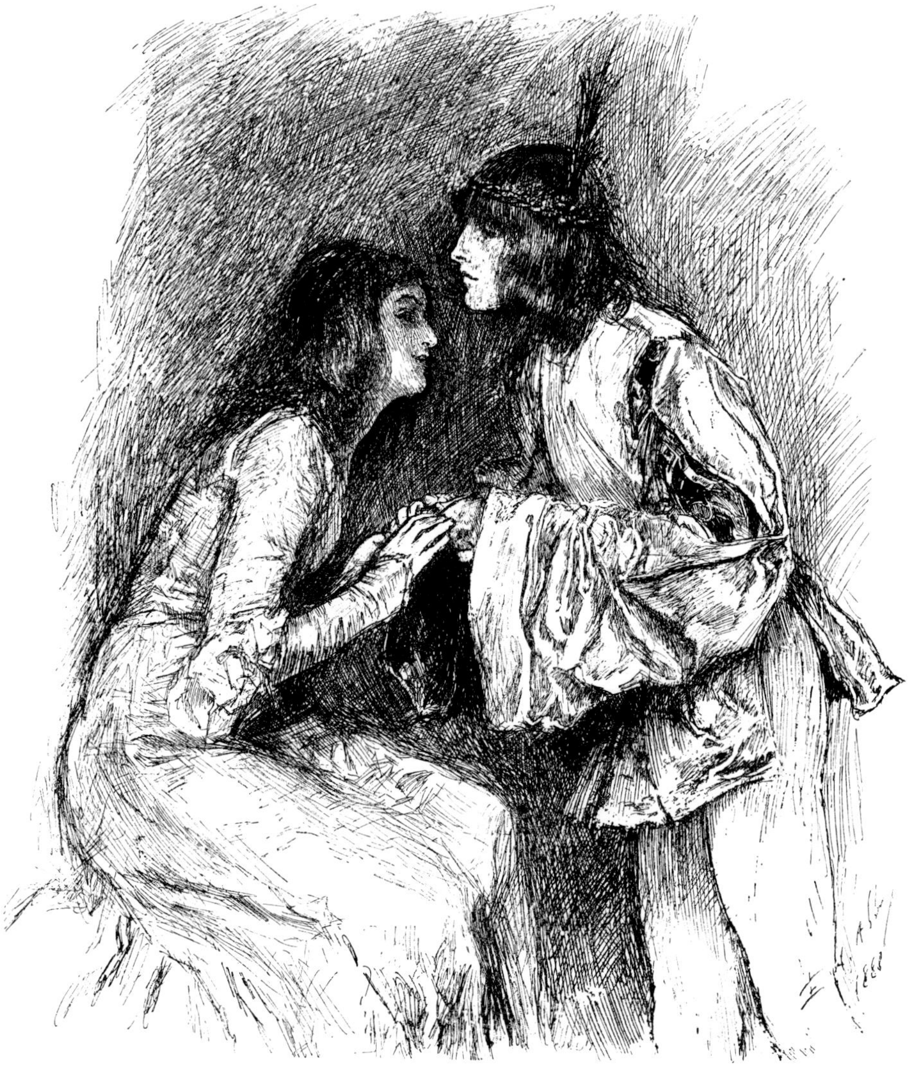

Bassanio. "A gentle scroll; —Fair lady, by your leave." *[Kissing her]*

Harper's New Monthly Magazine, April 1890
The Comedies of Shakespeare — "Merchant of Venice."
Act III., Scene II. — Belmont.

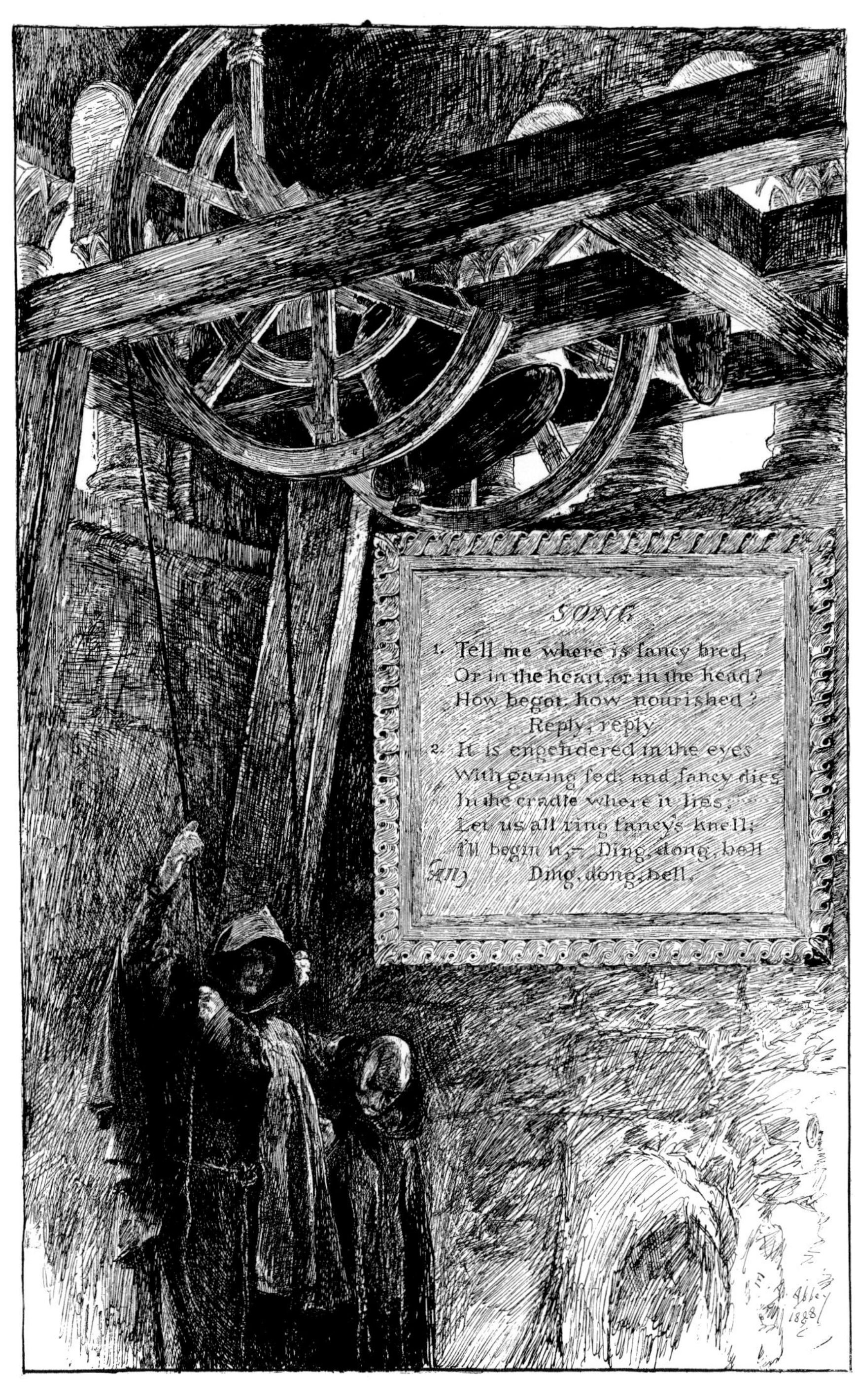

Harper's Bazar, April 1890
Act III., Scene II. — Song in the "Merchant of Venice"

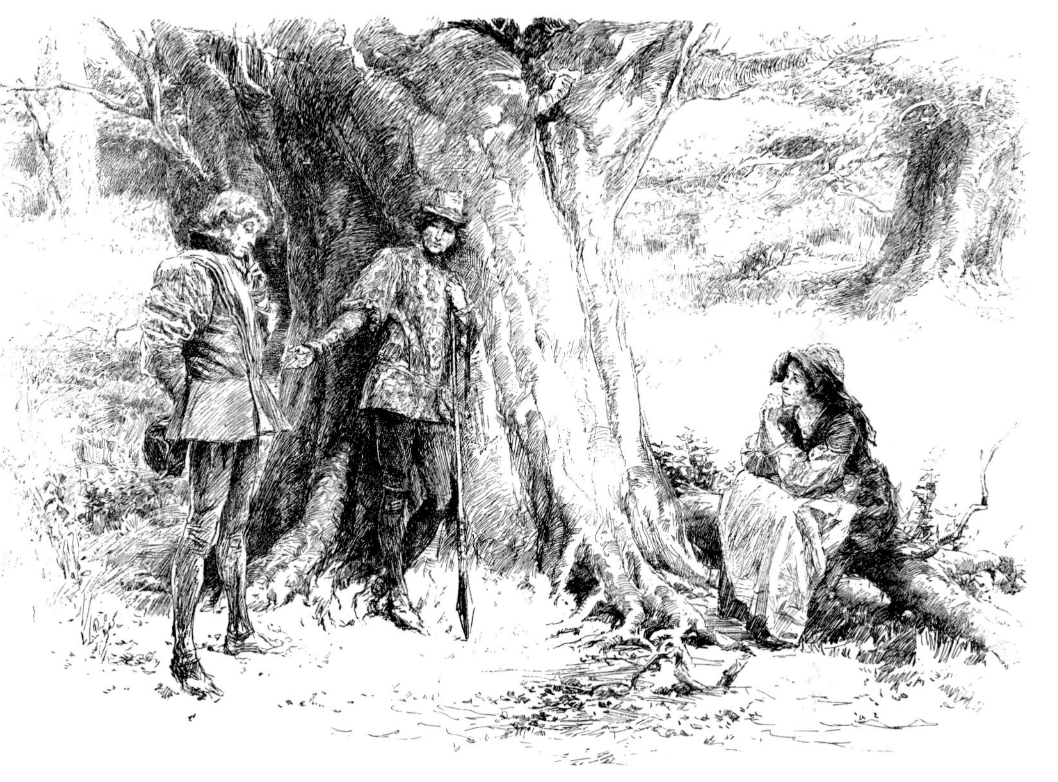

Rosalind. "...Give me your hand, Orlando."

Harper's New Monthly Magazine, December 1890
The Comedies of Shakespeare — "As You Like It"
Act IV., Scene I. — The forest.

Ay, these be clever folk indeed
That make the pictures in the books,
So he who runs, but doth not read,
May see the story as it looks.
Give praise to each in his degree—
Comparisons, I'm told, are shabby—
I simply say that as for me,
The king of all is one E. Abbey.

I too have somewhat of a taste
In print and cut, in plate and etching;
Had other things been otherwise
I too had turned this had to sketching.
In London ways, by Paris quais,
I've gathered many a sacred scrawl
Of Dürer, Keene, and Rembrandt e'en,
But Abbey is a match for all.

Yes, Hogarth knew a thing or two,
If one may judge from the collections;
Gavarni's store of worldly lore
Was great in much the same directions;
Bayard did well for L'Immortel;
Vierge is clever, Parsons able:
I keep them all upon my shelves,
But keep my Abbey on my table.

His is the hand for dimpled chins,
For fresh young cheeks and dainty waists;
And his the eye for shrunken shins,
Fore wigs and ruffs and old-time tastes.
He draws at will with equal skill,
Nor doubts the lesson that it teaches,
The patch that mars my lady's face,
Or haply mends some bumpkin's breeches.

I never knew a neater touch
For doublets, hose, and peaked shoes,
For parsons, ploughmen, peers, and such,
For milkmaids, and for morning dews;
And when he shows us Julia's "cloathes,"
Or Barbara Allen's pretty face,
I pin my faith to furbelows,
And preach the gewgaw's saving grace.

And, Master Abbey, for the rest,
You'll never make me really think
You work on common Whatman's best,
Or Bristol-board, with Indian-ink!
Nay, I do hold there's witchcraft in't
Nor mean to do you any harm
When I protest that in each tint
You put some private potent charm.

VALENTINE ADAMS.

Harper's New Monthly Magazine, October 1890
Upon Abbey, His Illustrious Illustrations.

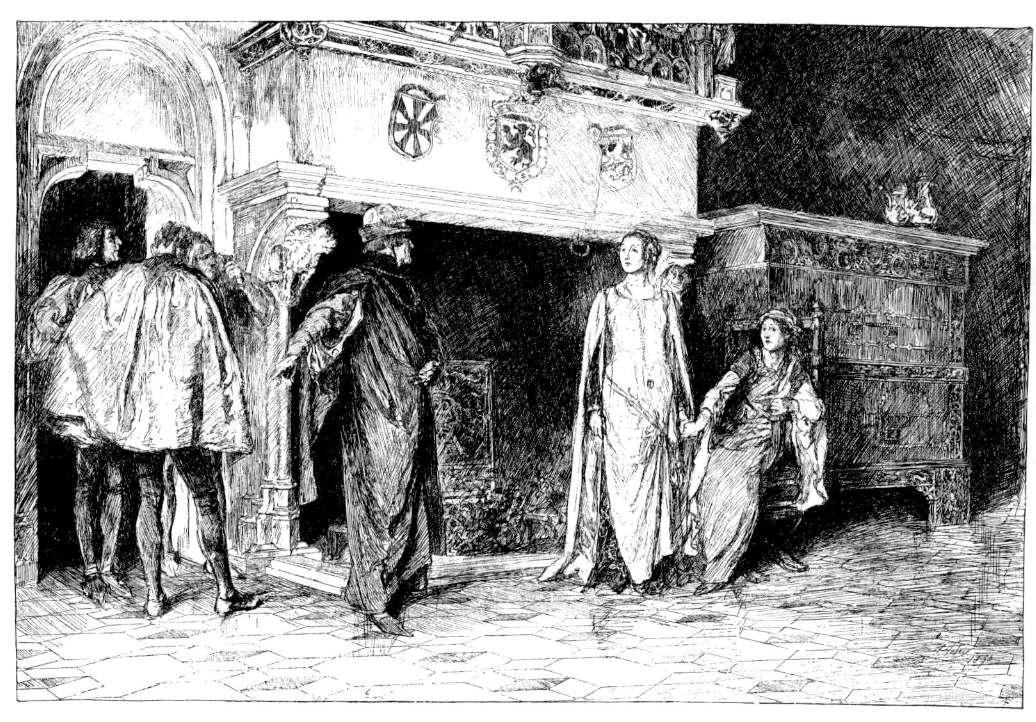

Duke Frederick. "Mistress, despatch you with your safest haste."

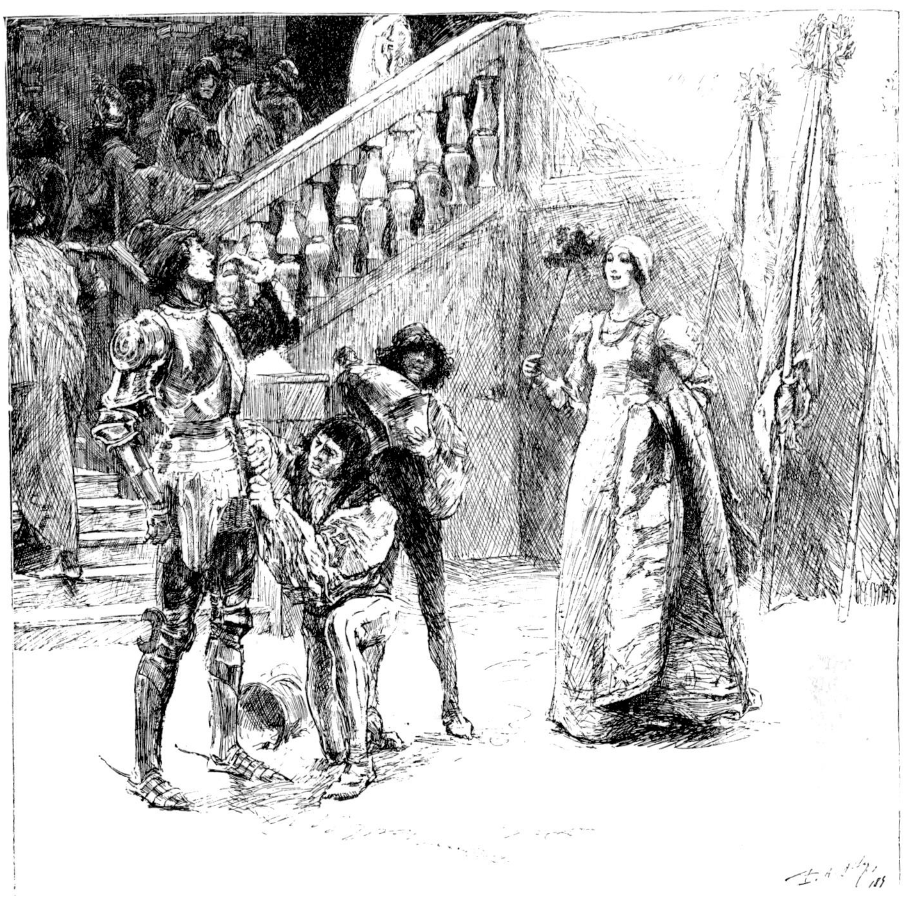

Benedick. "What my dear Lady Disdain! Are you yet living?"

Harper's New Monthly Magazine, September 1891
The Comedies of Shakespeare — "Much Ado About Nothing"
Act I., Scene I. — Before Leonato's House.

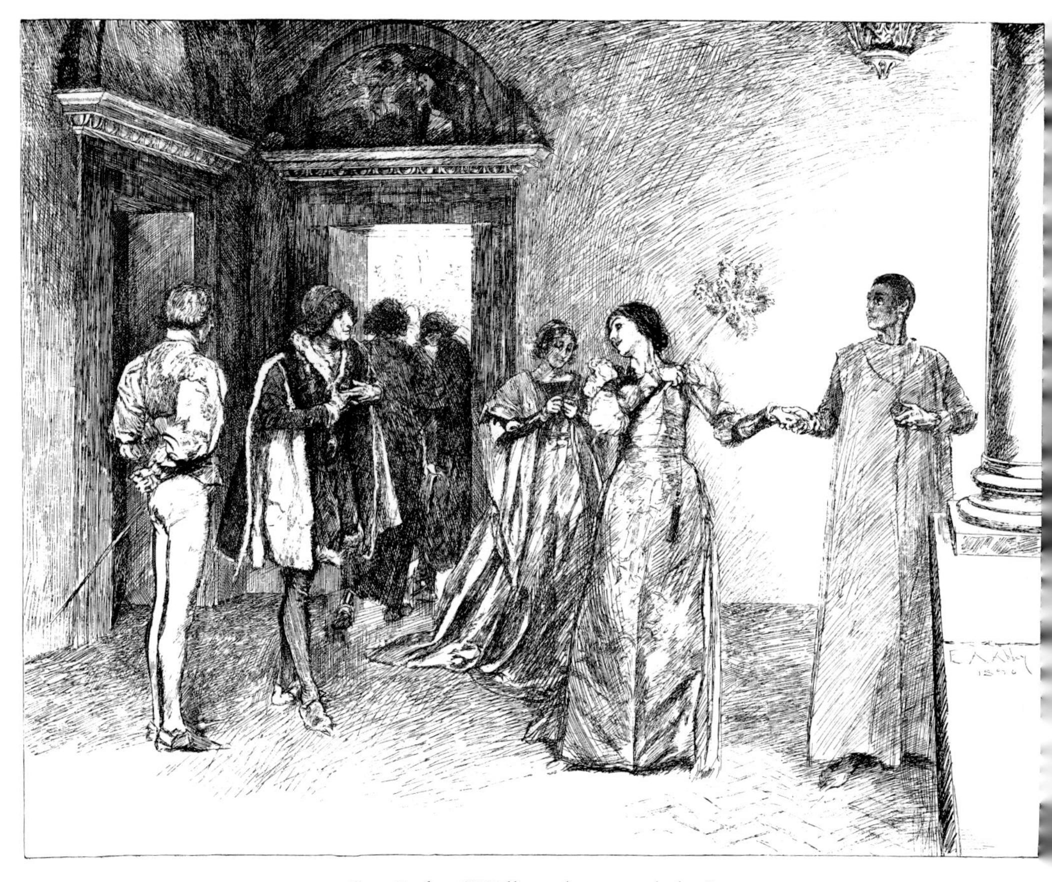

Don Pedro. "Will you have me, lady?"

Harper's New Monthly Magazine, September 1891
The Comedies of Shakespeare — "Much Ado About Nothing"
Act II., Scene I. — A Hall in Leonato's House.

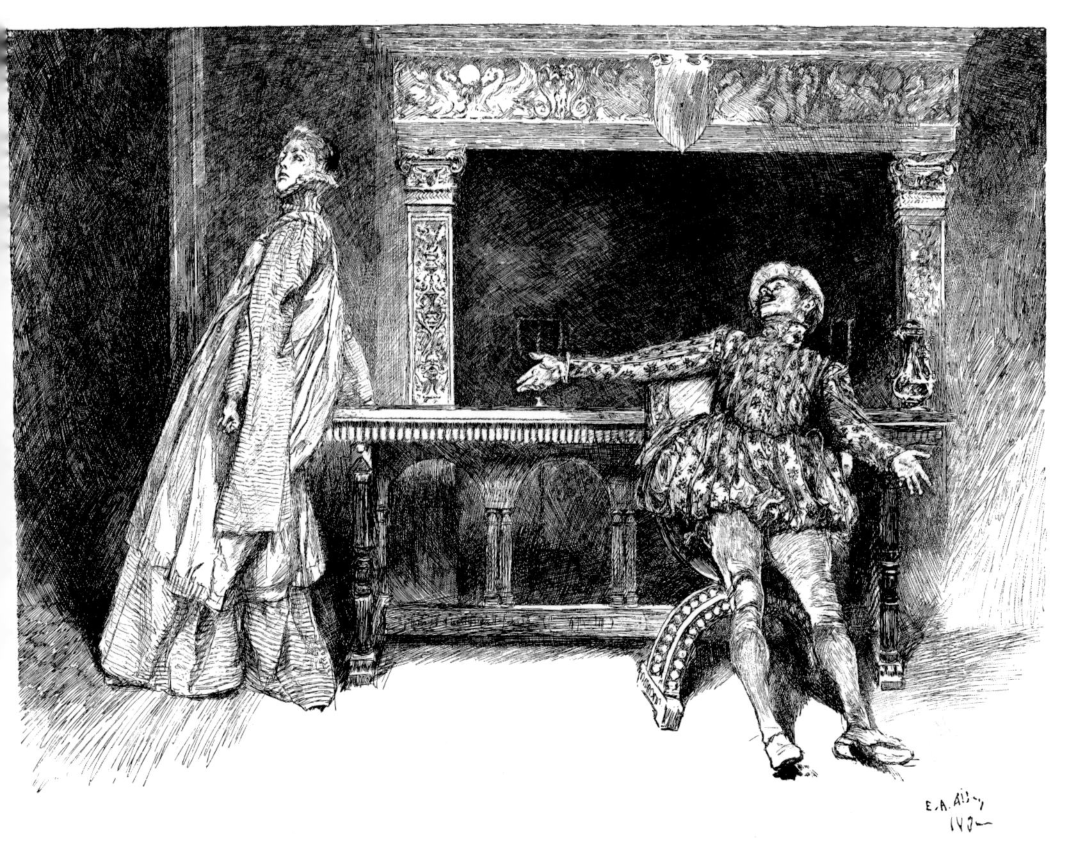

Harper's New Monthly Magazine, September 1891
The Comedies of Shakespeare — "Much Ado About Nothing"
Act II., Scene I. — Petruchio Banters Katharina

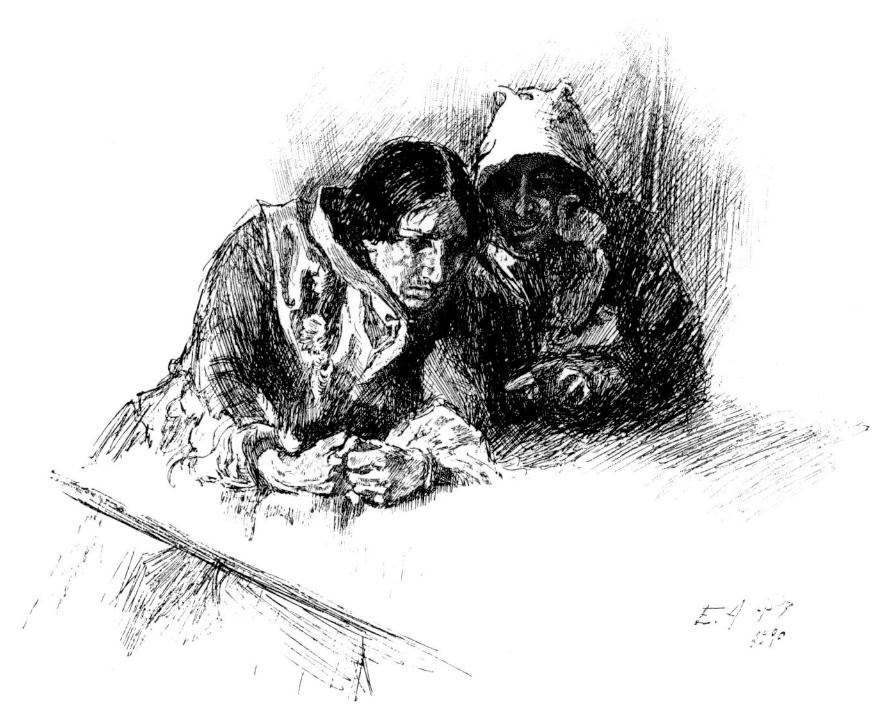

Don John. "Only to despite them, I will endeavor anything."

Harper's New Monthly Magazine, September 1891
The Comedies of Shakespeare — "Much Ado About Nothing"
Act II., Scene II. — Another Room in Leonato's House.

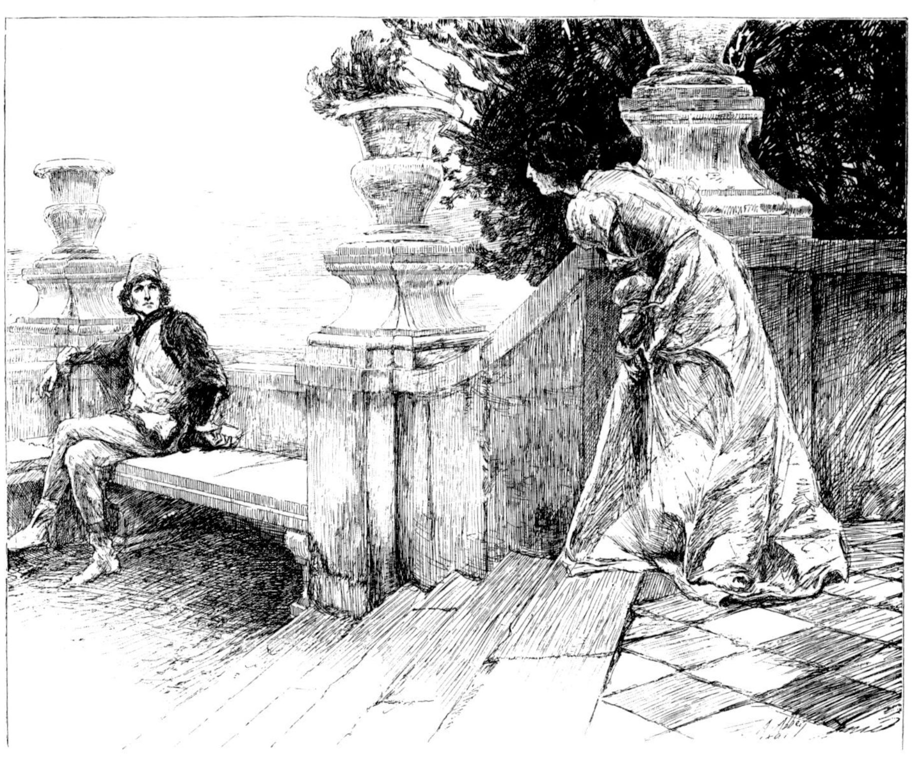

Beatrice. "Against my will, I am sent to bid you come into dinner."

Harper's New Monthly Magazine, September 1891
The Comedies of Shakespeare — "Much Ado About Nothing"
Act II., Scene III. — Leonato's Garden.

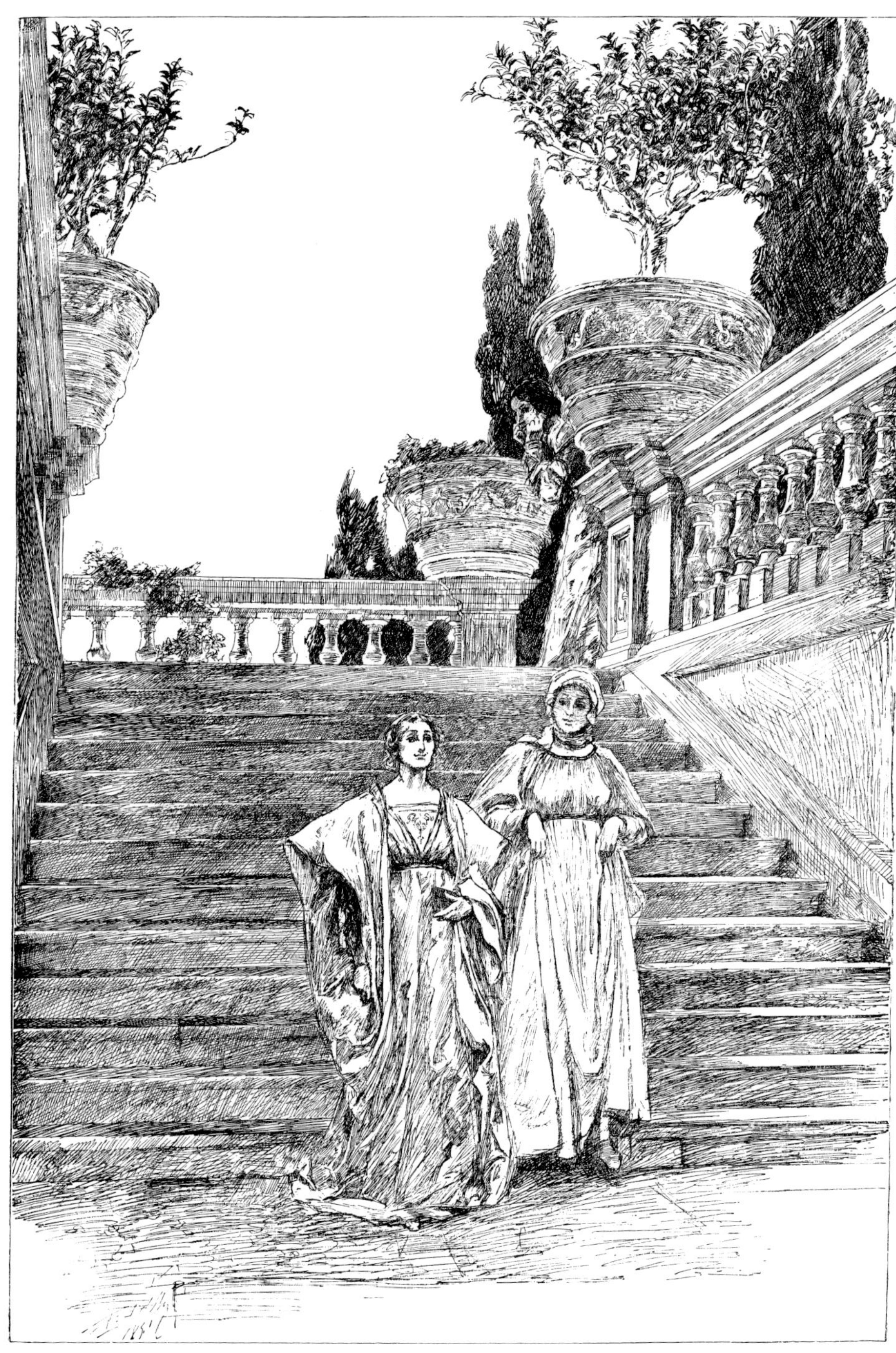

Ursula. "She's lim'd, I warrant you; we have caught her, madam."
Hero. "If it prove so, then loving goes by haps:
Some Cupid kills with arrows, some with traps."

Harper's New Monthly Magazine, September 1891
The Comedies of Shakespeare — "Much Ado About Nothing"
Act III., Scene I. — Leonato's garden.

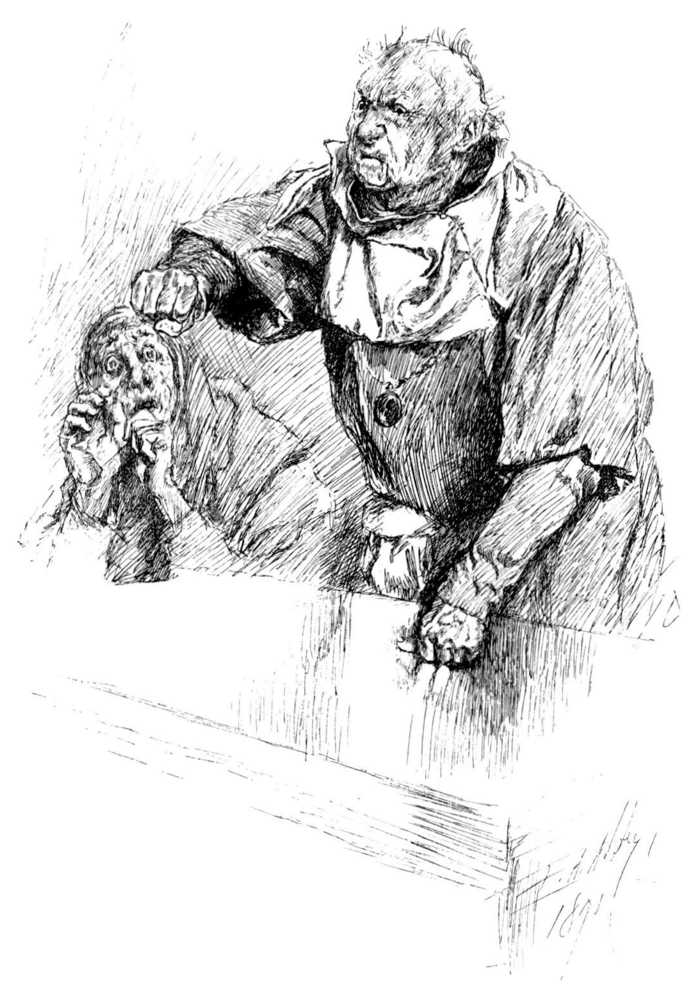

Dogberry. "Dost thou not suspect my place?
Dost thou not suspect my years?
—O that he were here to write me down an ass!"

Harper's New Monthly Magazine, September 1891
The Comedies of Shakespeare — "Much Ado About Nothing"
Act IV., Scene II. — A Prison.

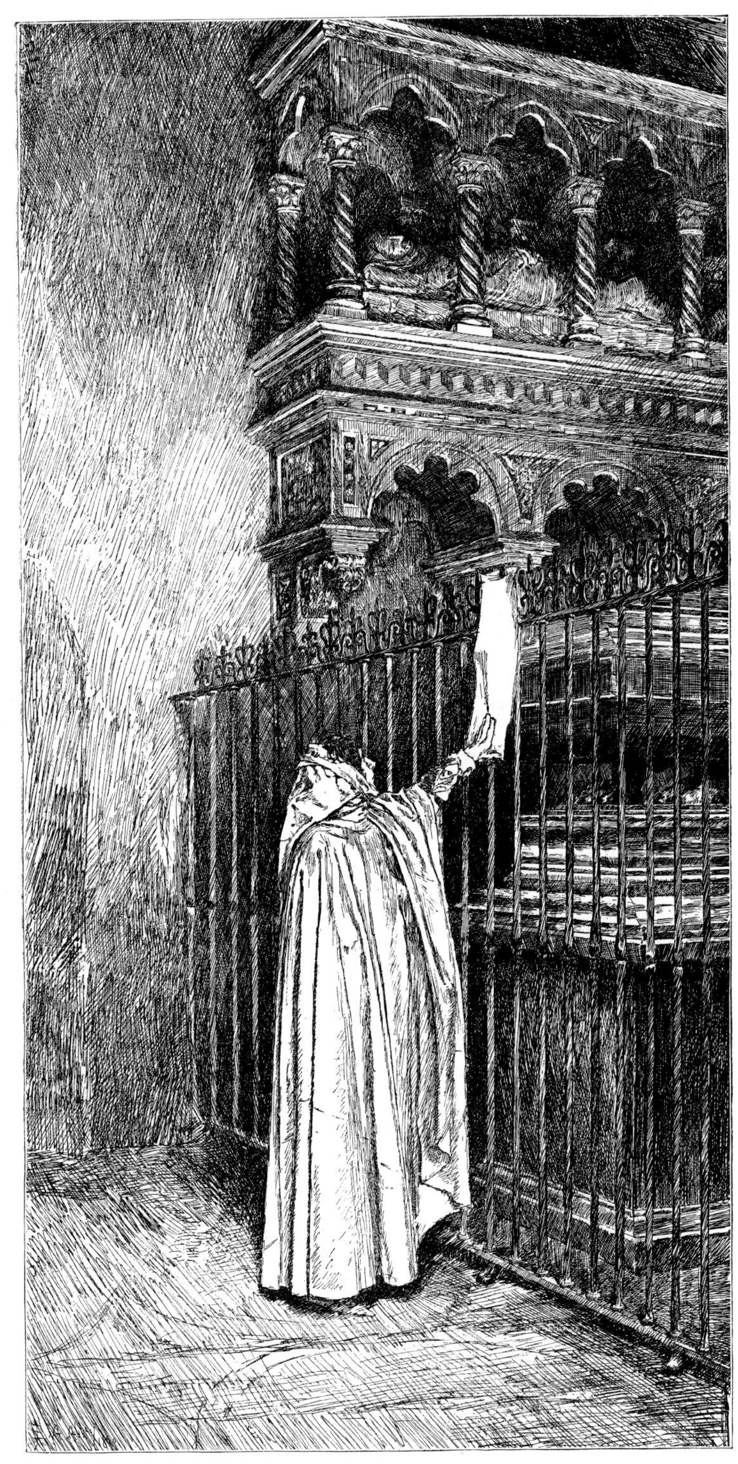

Claudio *(reads from a scroll)*. "Done to death by slanderous
tongues Was the Hero that here lies."

Harper's New Monthly Magazine, September 1891
The Comedies of Shakespeare — "Much Ado About Nothing"
Act V., Scene III. — A Church.

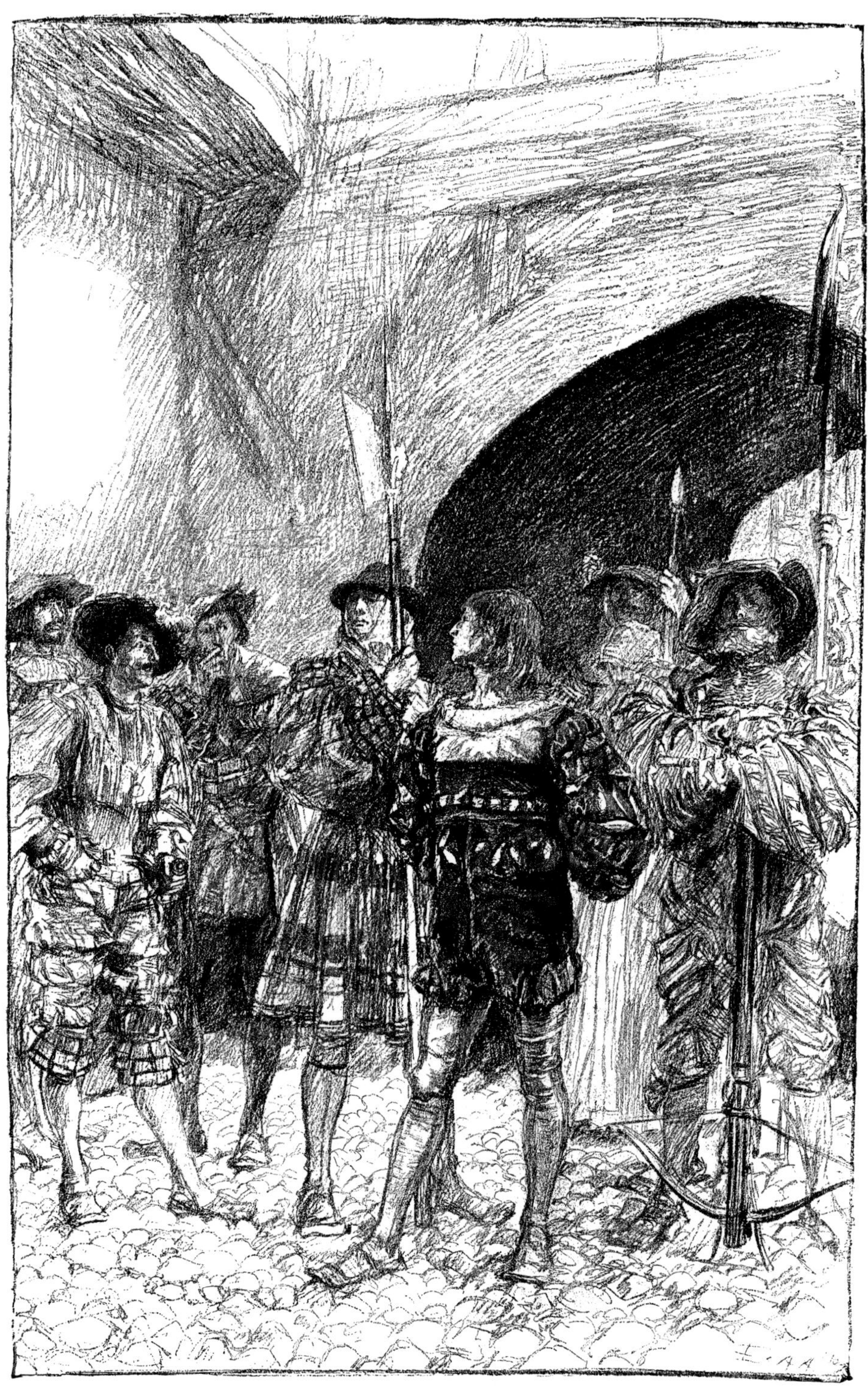

Harper's New Monthly Magazine, December 1891
The Comedies of Shakespeare — "Measure for Measure."
Act I., Scene II. — Lucio and Claudio.

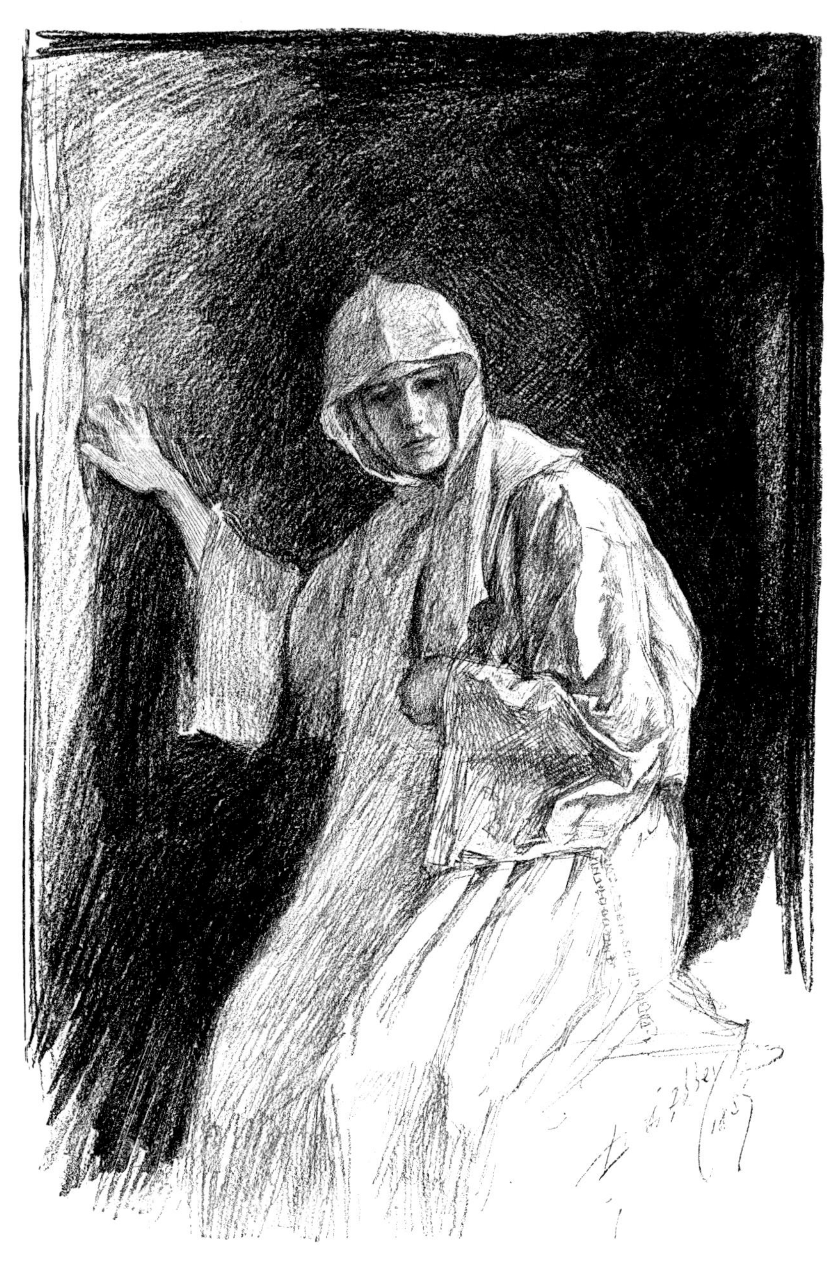

Harper's New Monthly Magazine, December 1891
The Comedies of Shakespeare — "Measure for Measure."
Act I., Scene IV. — Isabella at the nunnery.

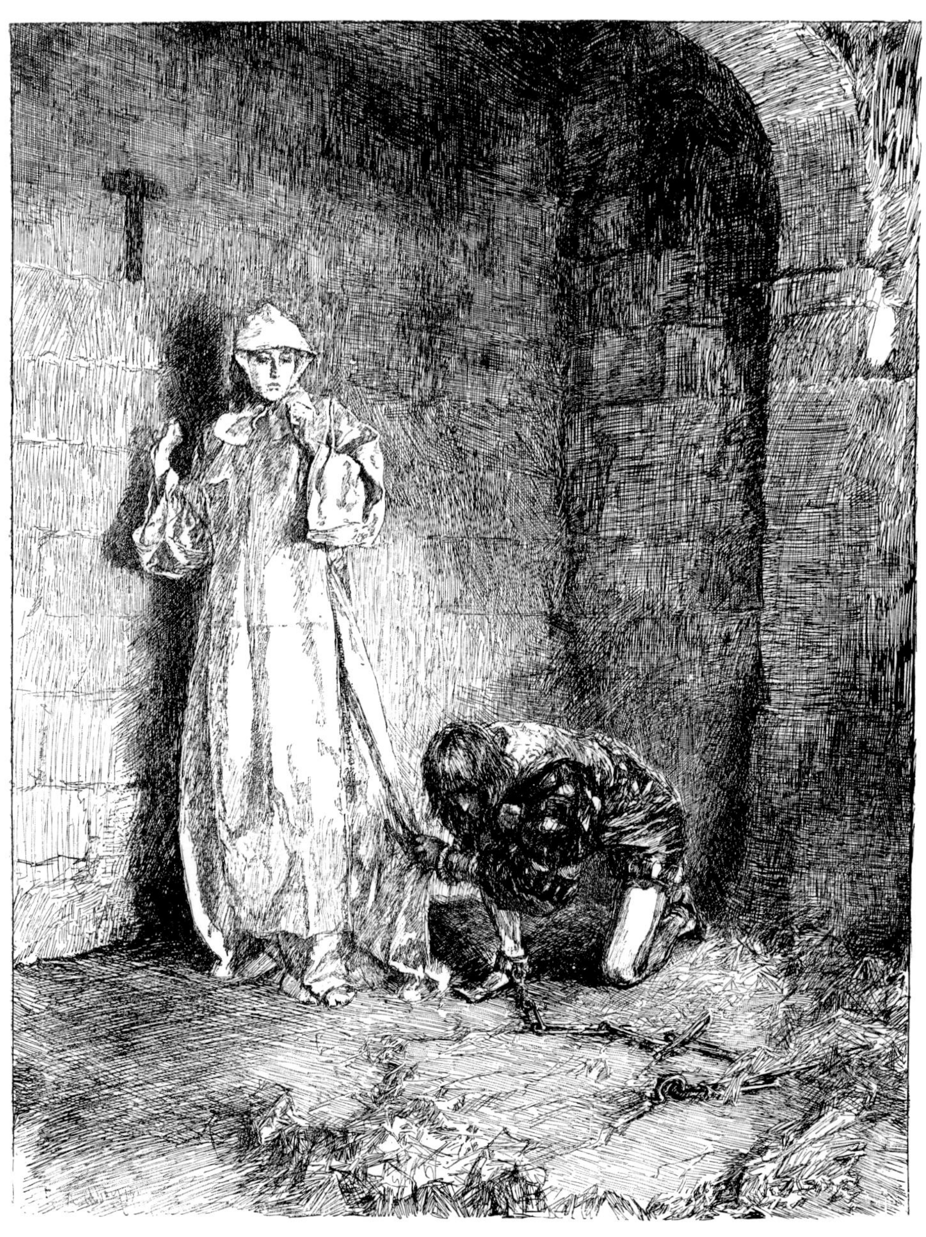

Harper's New Monthly Magazine, December 1891
The Comedies of Shakespeare — "Measure for Measure."
Act III., Scene I. — Claudio and Isabella.

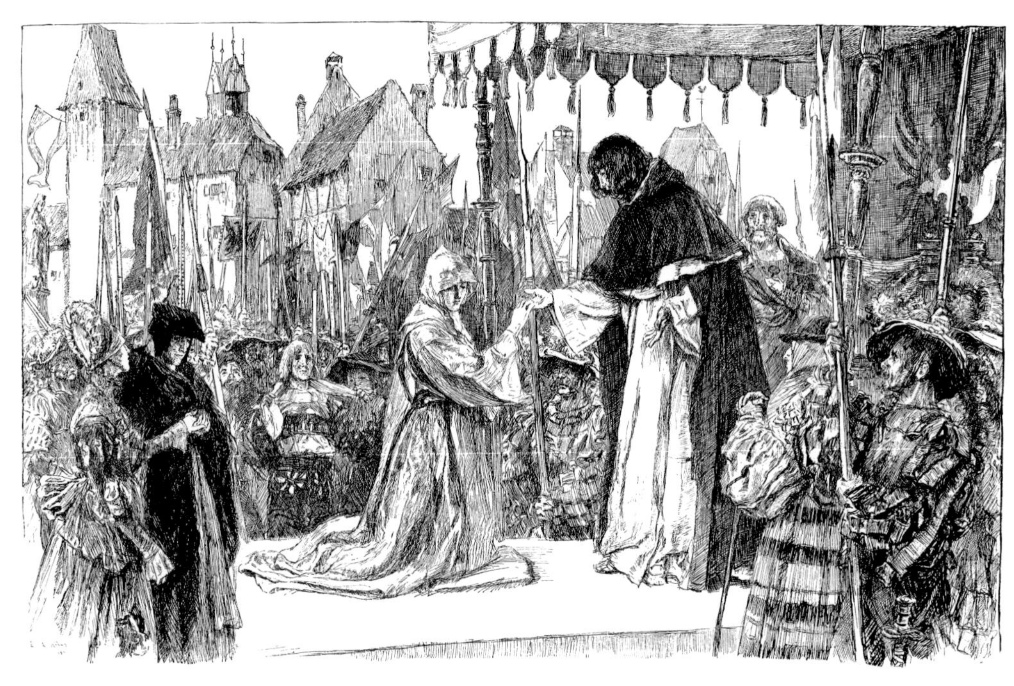

Harper's New Monthly Magazine, December 1891
The Comedies of Shakespeare — "Measure for Measure."
Act V., Scene I. — Isabella and the Duke.

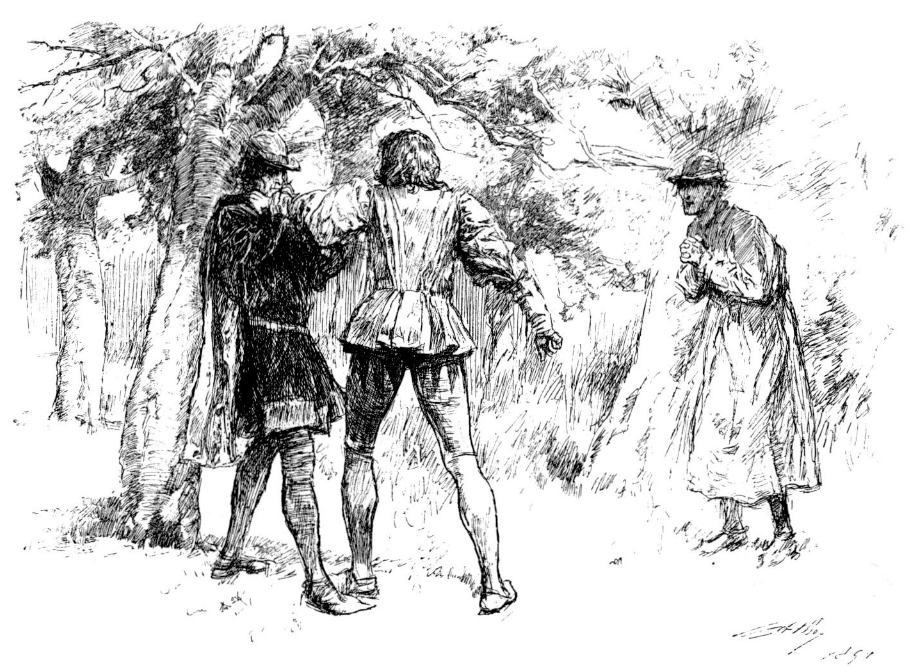

Oliver. "Wilt thou lay hands on me, villain?"

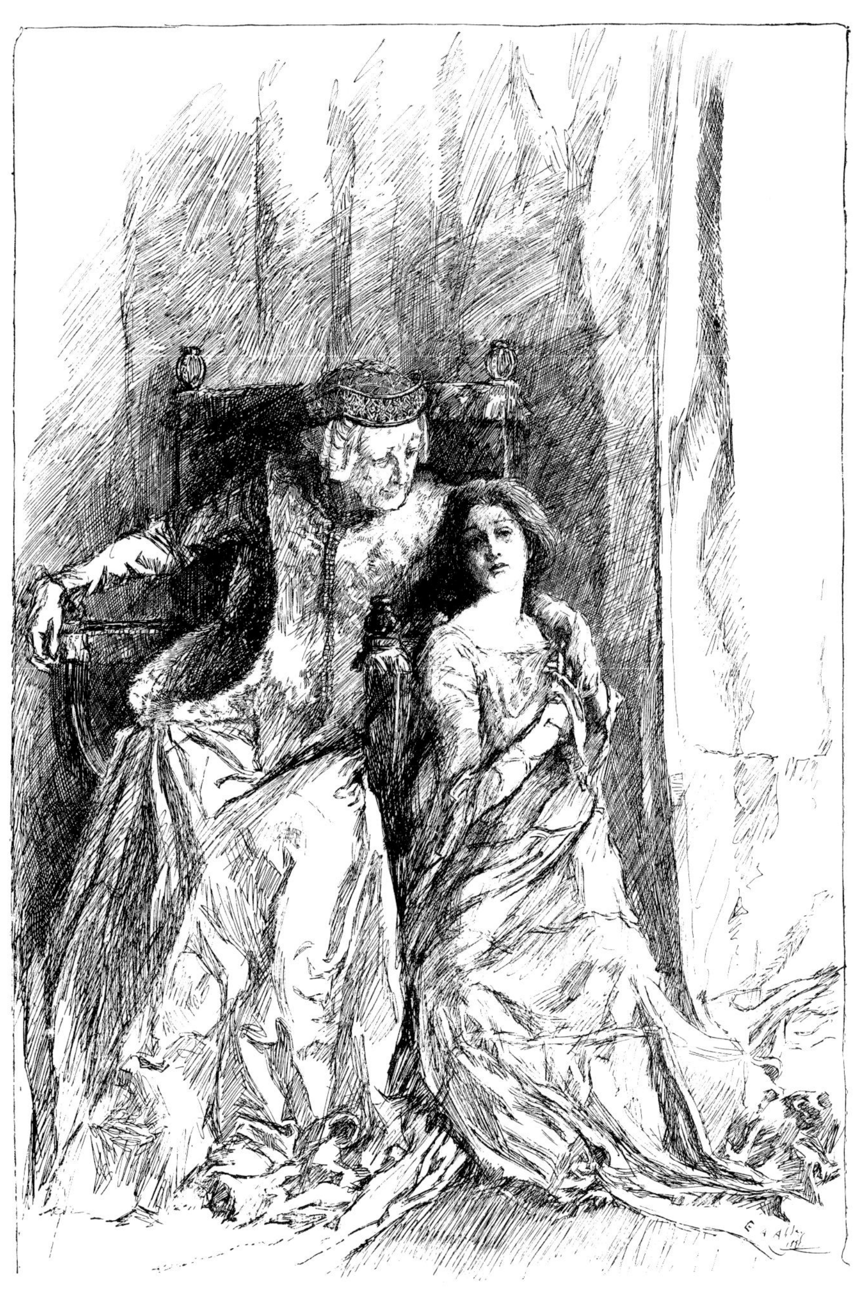

Helena. "Pardon, madam; the Count Rousillon cannot be my brother."

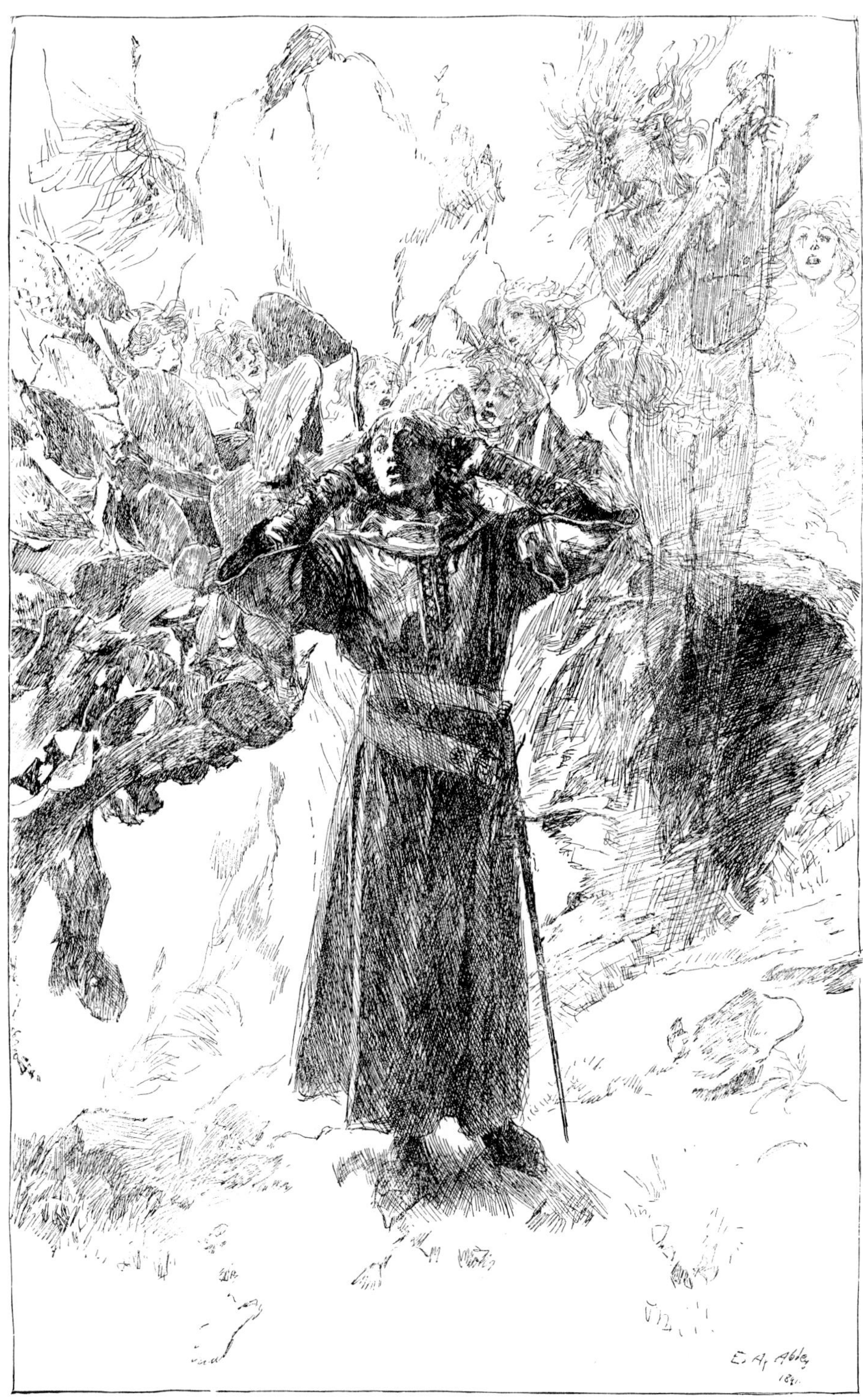

Ferdinand. "Where should this music be? I' th' air or th' Earth?"

Harper's New Monthly Magazine, April 1892
The Comedies of Shakespeare — "The Tempest"
Act I., Scene II. — Ferdinand and Ariel.

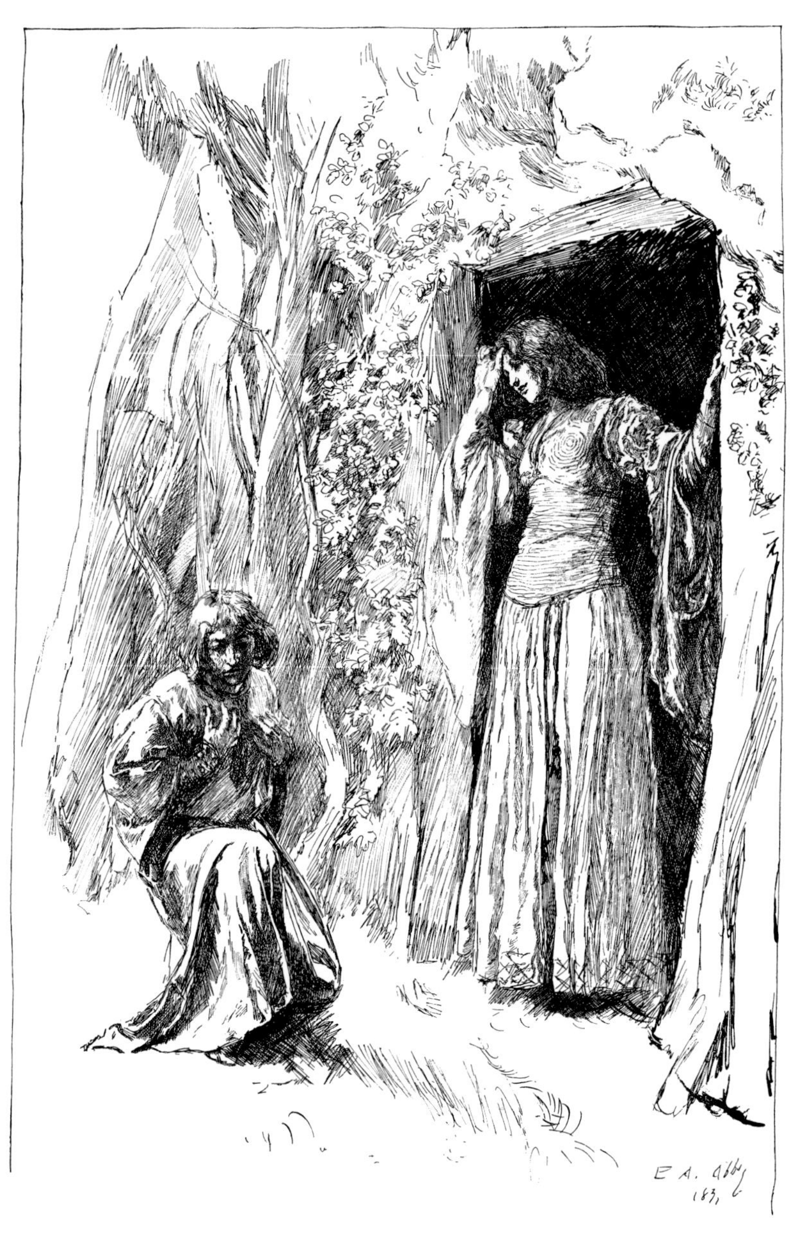

Harper's New Monthly Magazine, April 1892
The Comedies of Shakespeare — "The Tempest"
Act III., Scene I. — Ferdinand meets Miranda.

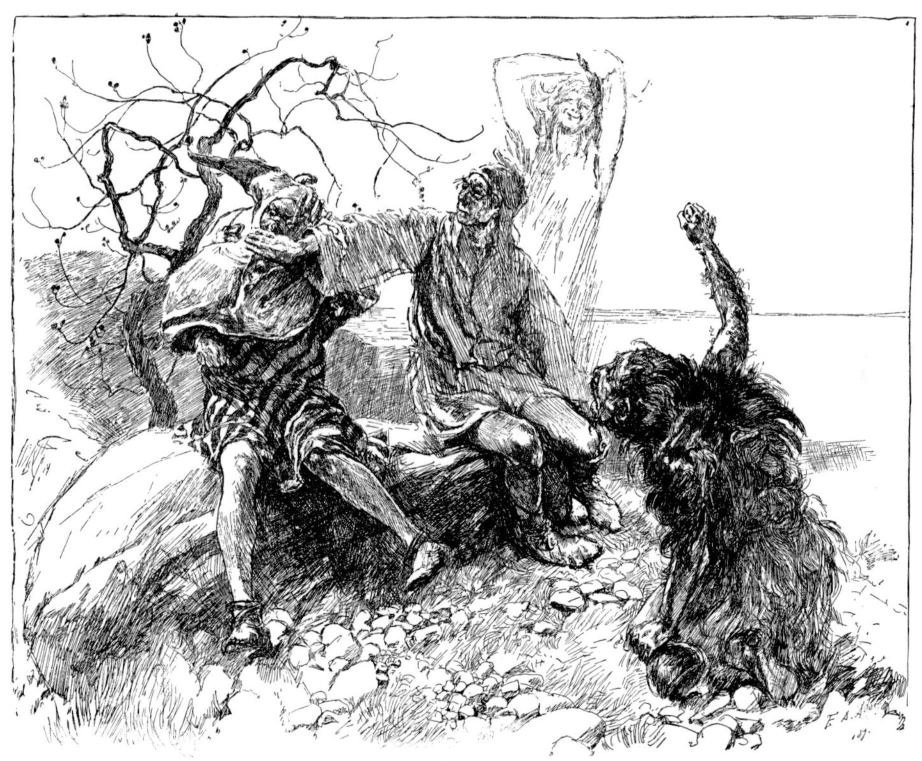

Caliban, Stefano, and Trinculo (Ariel Inveisible).

Harper's New Monthly Magazine, April 1892
The Comedies of Shakespeare — "The Tempest"
Act III., Scene II. — Another part of the island.

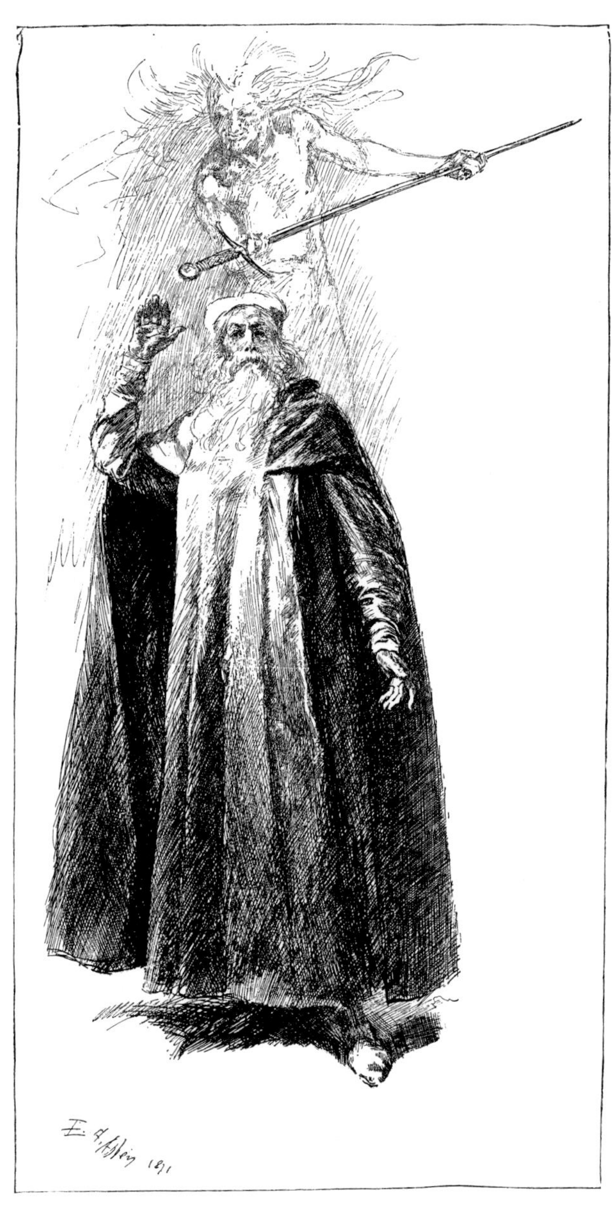

Harper's New Monthly Magazine, April 1892
The Comedies of Shakespeare — "The Tempest"
Act V., Scene I. — Prospero and Ariel.

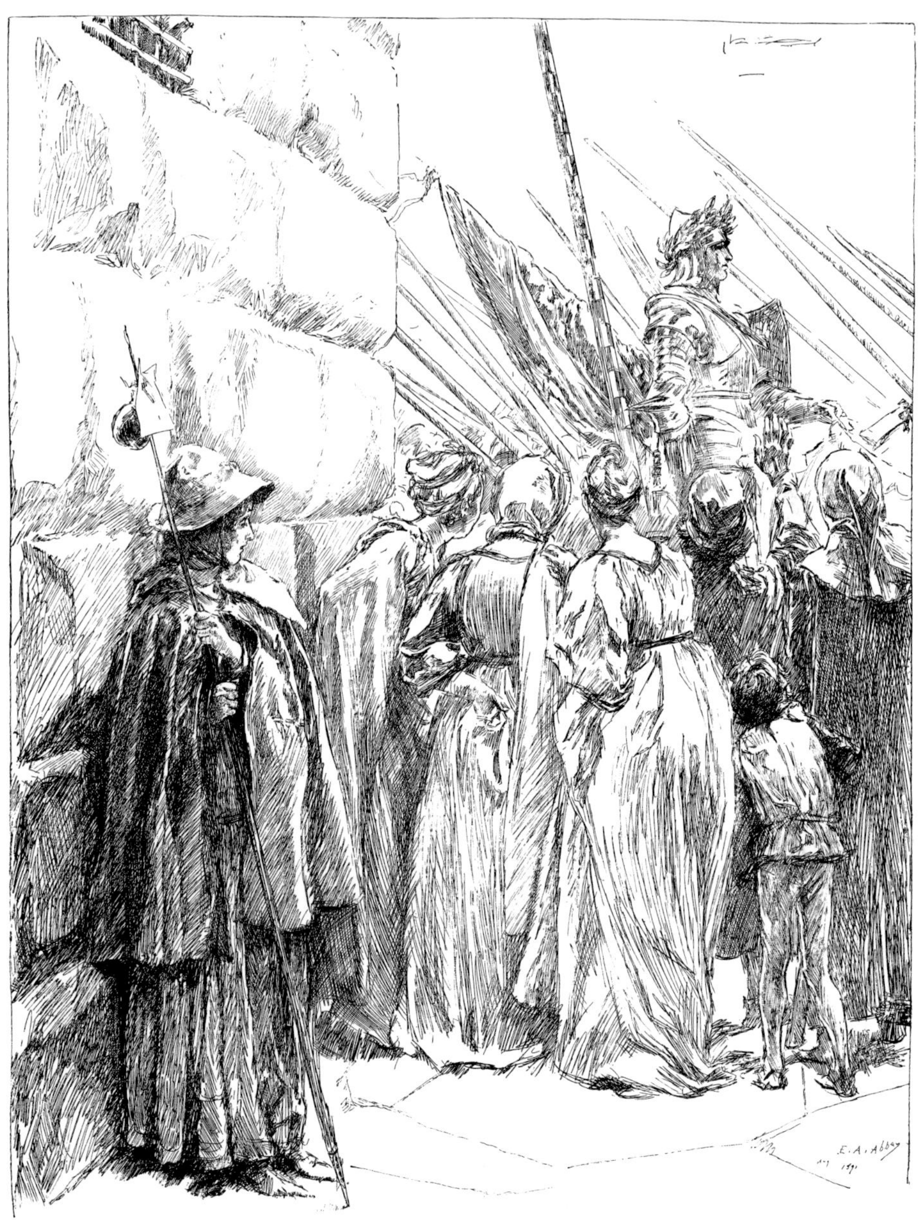

Enterance of Florentine Army.

Harper's New Monthly Magazine, July 1892
The Comedies of Shakespeare — "All's Well That Ends Well"
Act III., Scene V. — Florence. Without the walls. A tucket afar off.

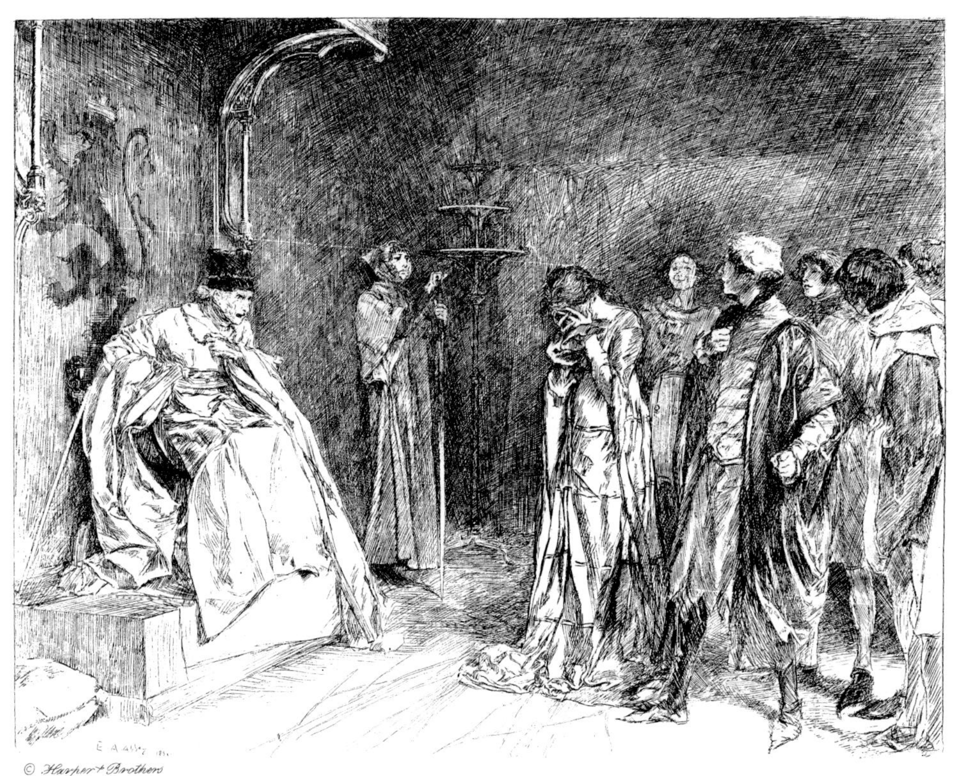

King. "Why, then, young Bertram, take her; she's thy wife."
Bertram. "My wife, my Liege? I shall beseech your highness in such a business,
give me leave to use the help of mine own eyes."
King. "Know'st thou not, Bertram, what she has done for me?"

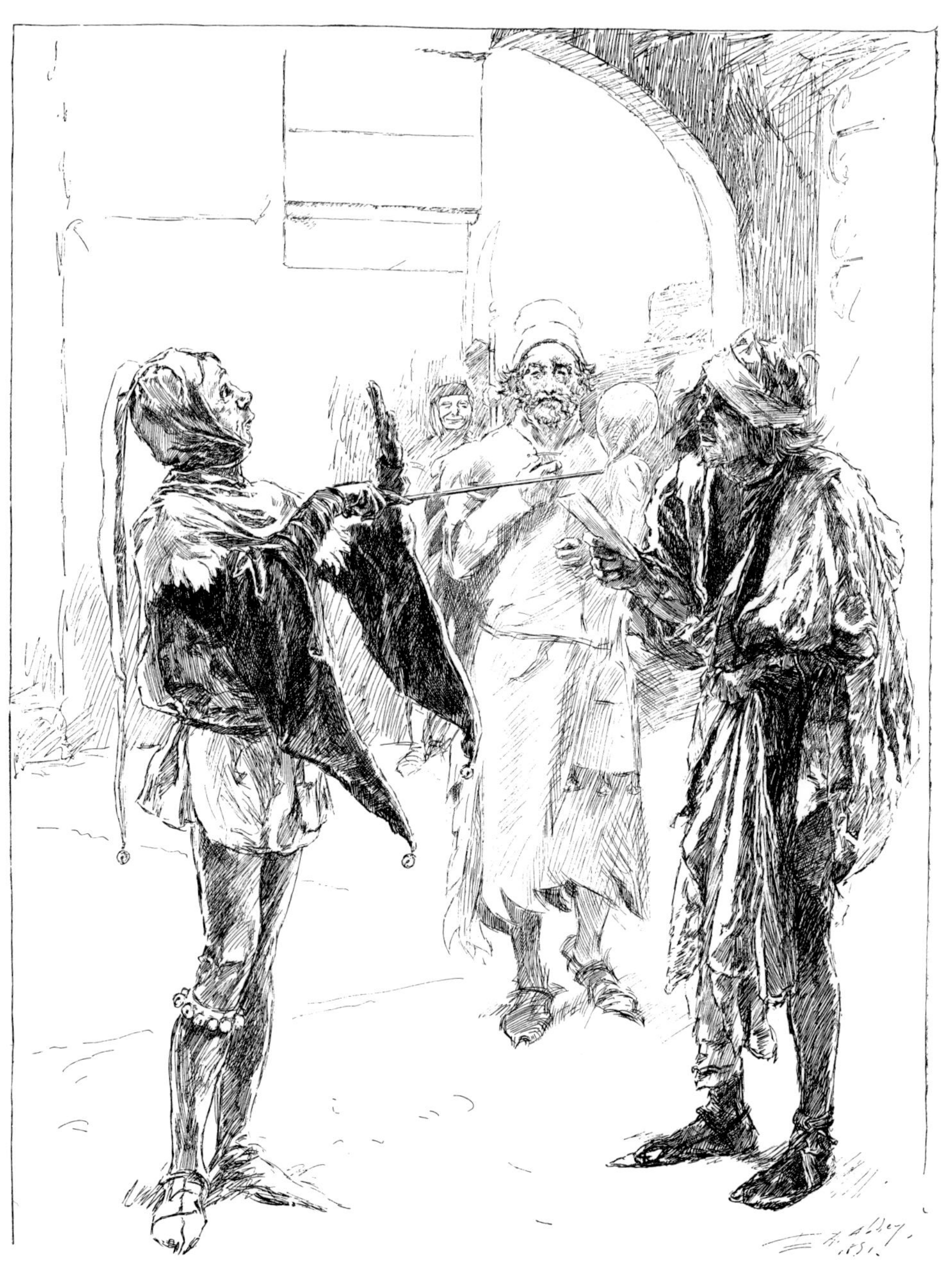

Clown. "Foh! prithee, stand away."

Harper's New Monthly Magazine, July 1892
The Comedies of Shakespeare — "All's Well That Ends Well"
Act V., Scene II. — Rousillon. Before the Count's palace.

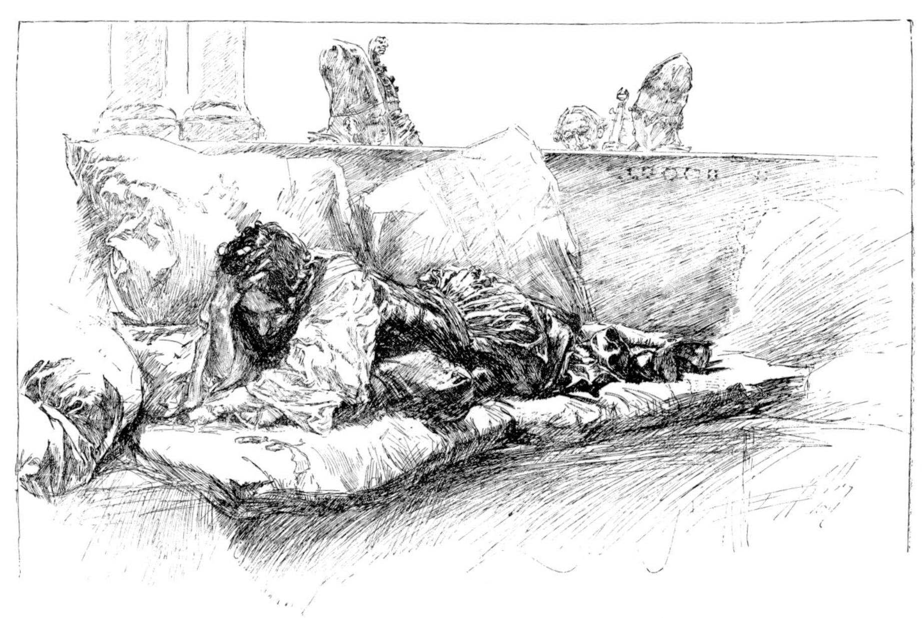

Duke. "If music be the food of love, play on."

Harper's New Monthly Magazine, February 1893
The Comedies of Shakespeare — "The Twelfth Night; or, What You Will"
Act I., Scene I. — The Duke and the musicians.

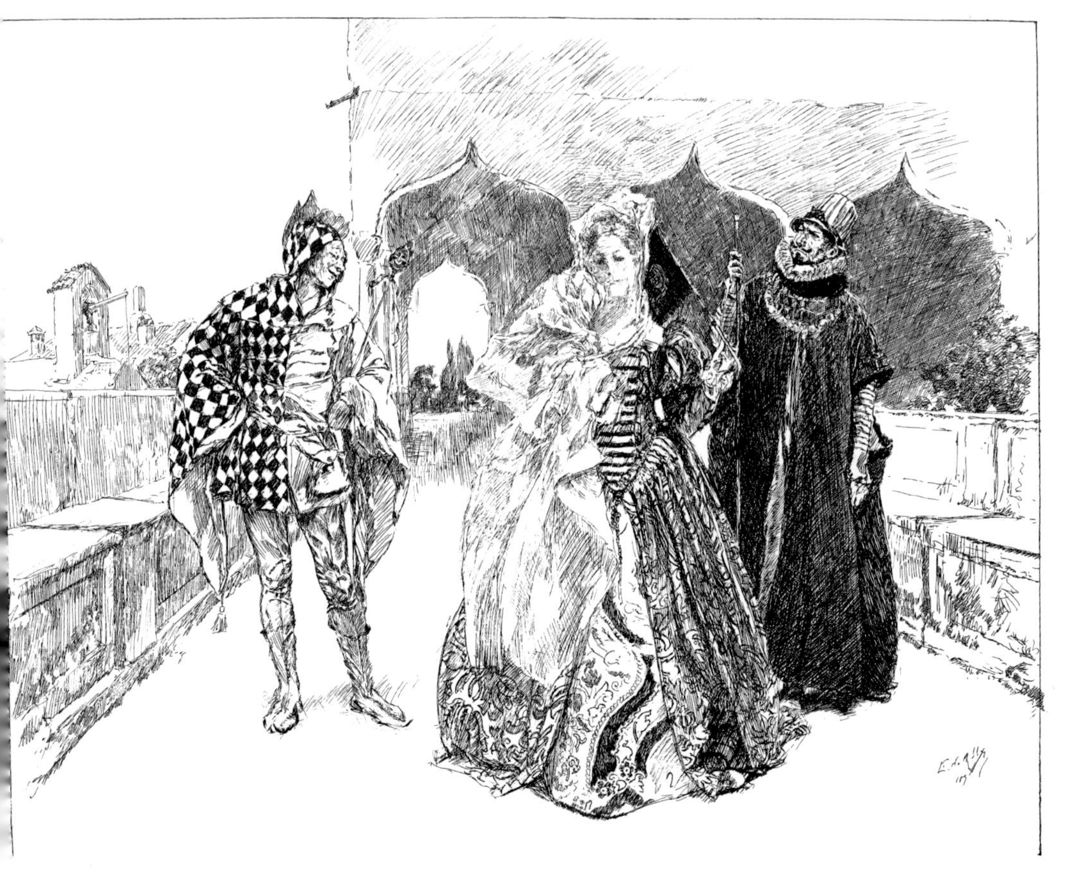

Malvolio. "I marvel your ladyship takes delight in such a barren rascal."

Harper's New Monthly Magazine, February 1893
The Comedies of Shakespeare — "The Twelfth Night; or, What You Will"
Act I., Scene V. — Olivia, The Clown and Malvolio.

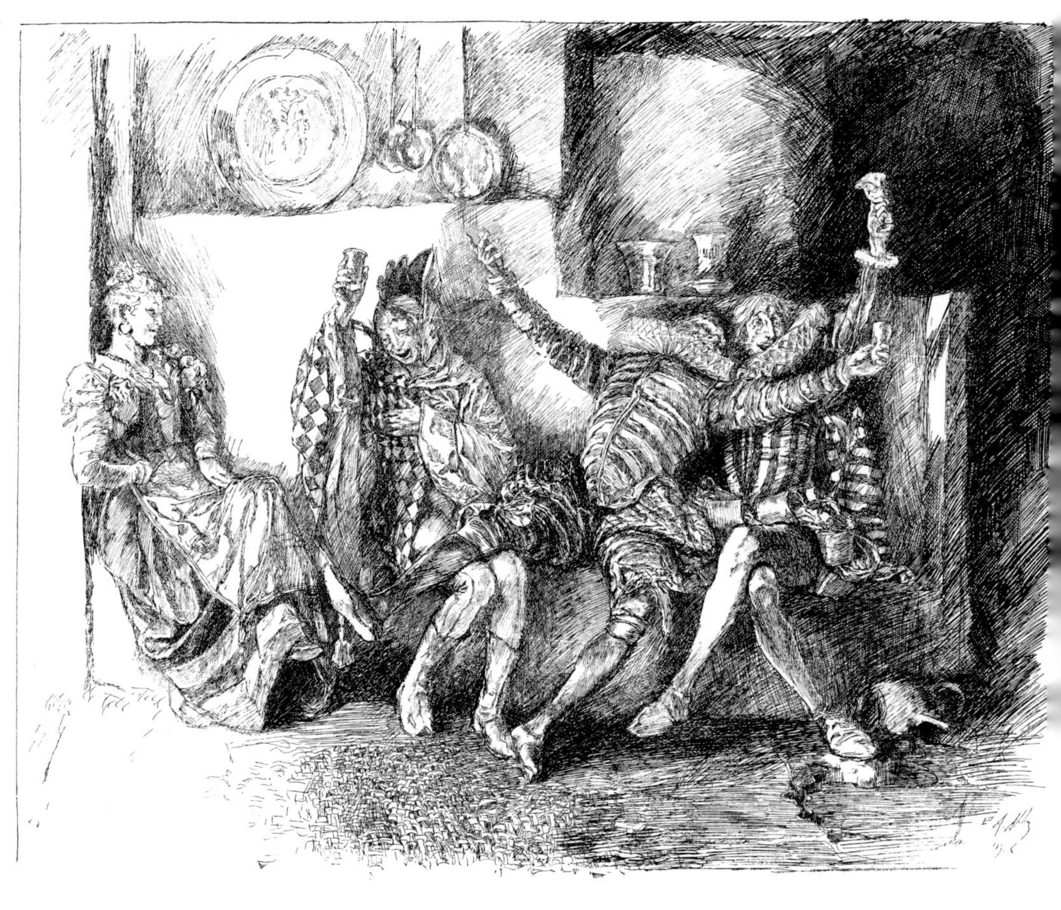

Harper's New Monthly Magazine, February 1893
The Comedies of Shakespeare — "The Twelfth Night; or, What You Will"
Act II., Scene III. — Sir Toby and his Companions.

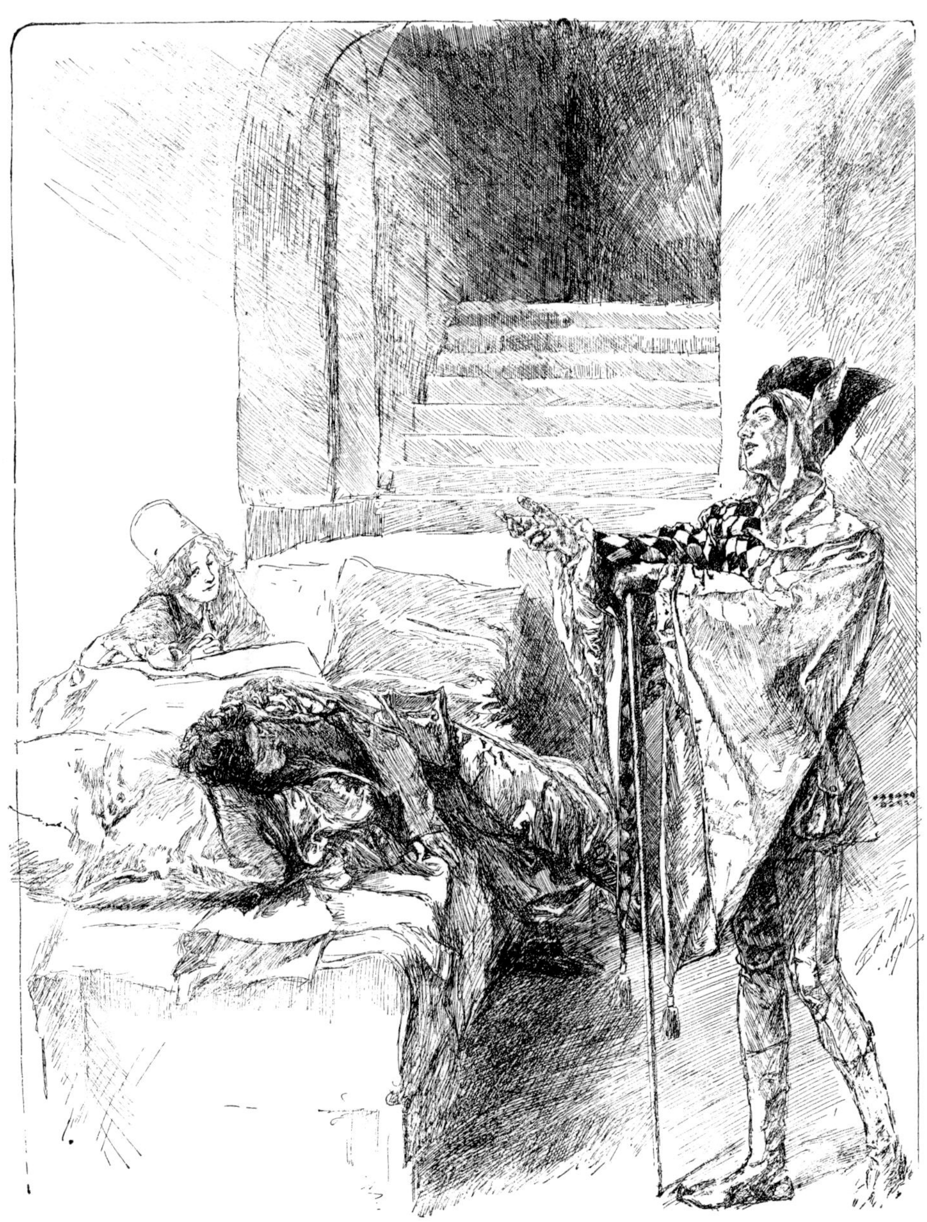

Clown sings. "Come Away, come away, Death,..."

Harper's *New Monthly Magazine*, February 1893
The Comedies of Shakespeare — "The Twelfth Night; or, What You Will"
Act II., Scene IV. — The Duke, Viola and clown.

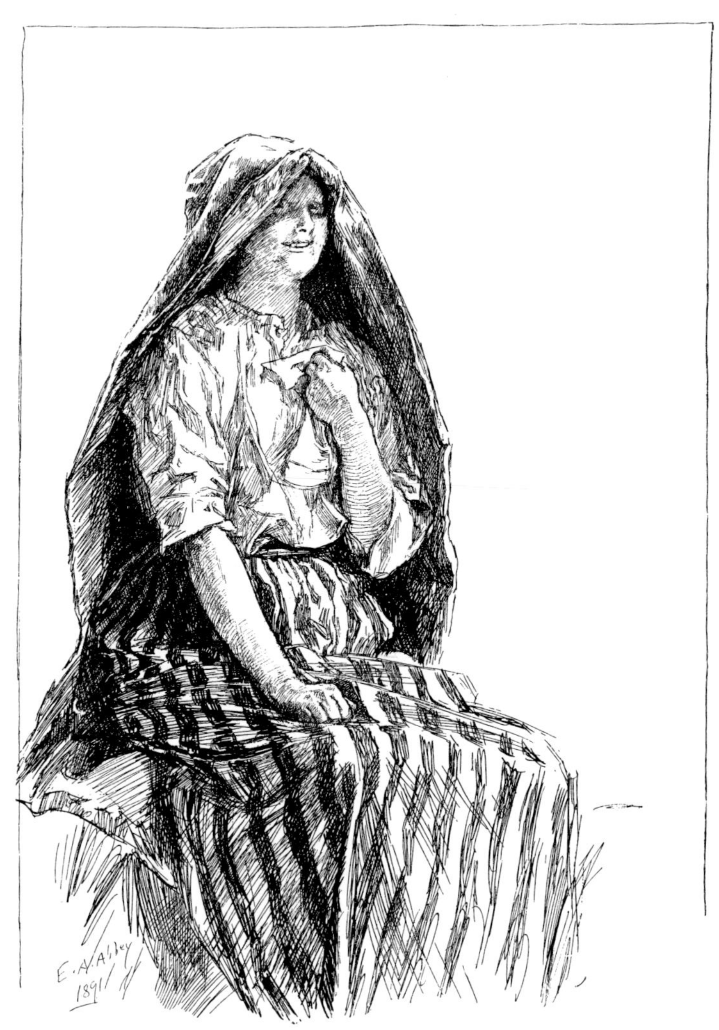

Jaquenetta.

Harper's New Monthly Magazine, May 1893
The Comedies of Shakespeare — "Love's Labor's Lost"

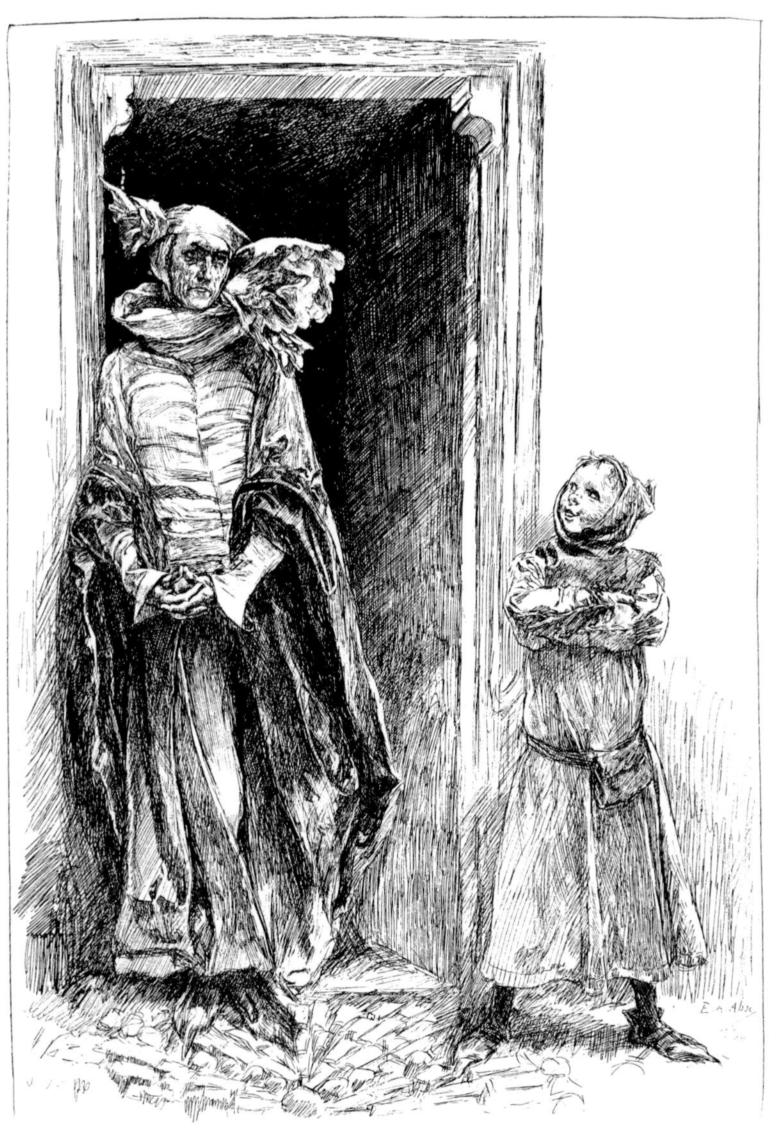

Armado. "What wilt thou prove?"
Moth. "A man, if I live; and this by, in and without, upon the instant."

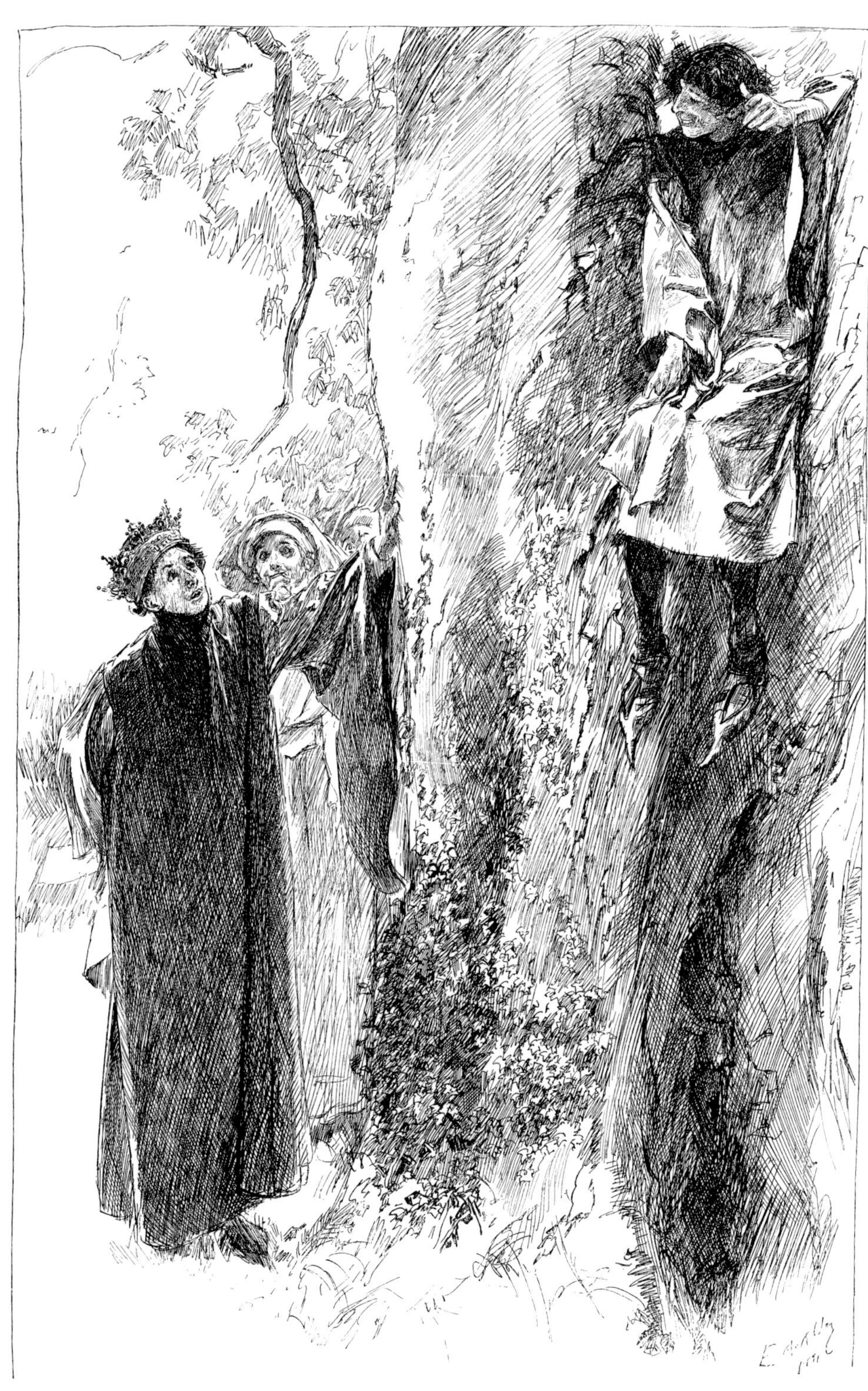

Harper's New Monthly Magazine, May 1893
The Comedies of Shakespeare — "Love's Labor's Lost"
Act IV., Scene III. — Biron and the King.

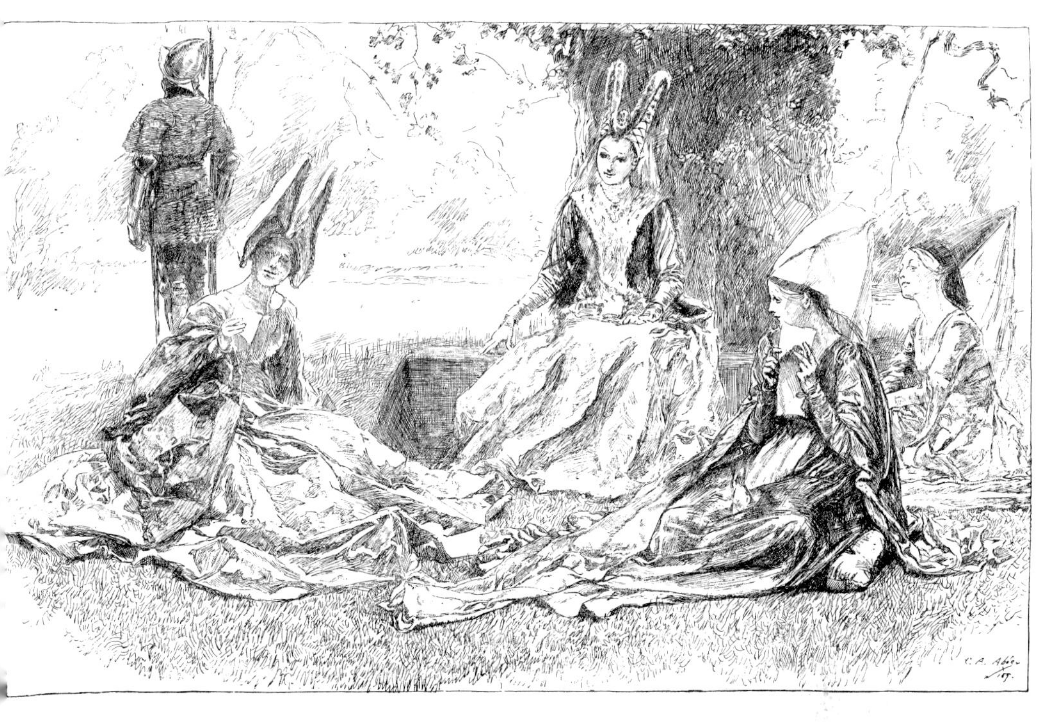

Harper's New Monthly Magazine, May 1893
The Comedies of Shakespeare — "Love's Labor's Lost"
Act V., Scene II. — Before the princess's pavilion.

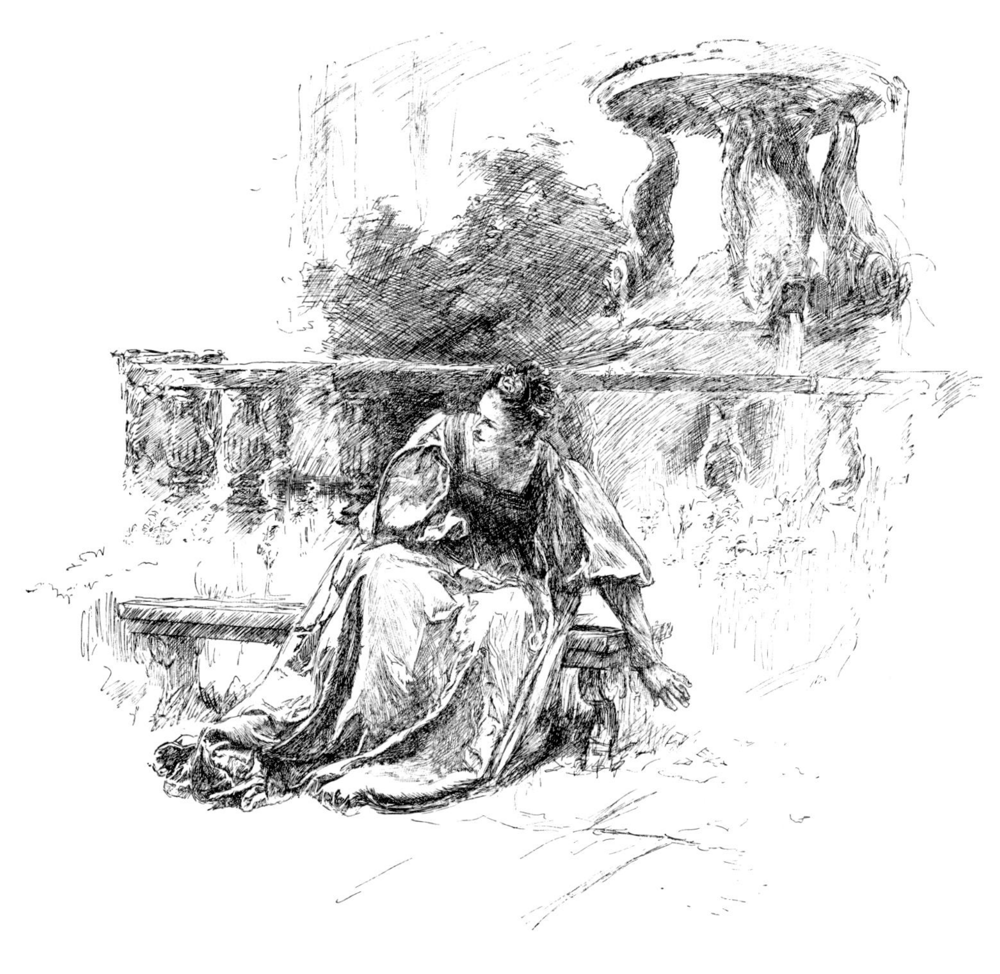

Harper's New Monthly Magazine, September 1893
The Comedies of Shakespeare — "Two Gentlemen of Verona."
Act I., Scene II. — The Torn Letter.

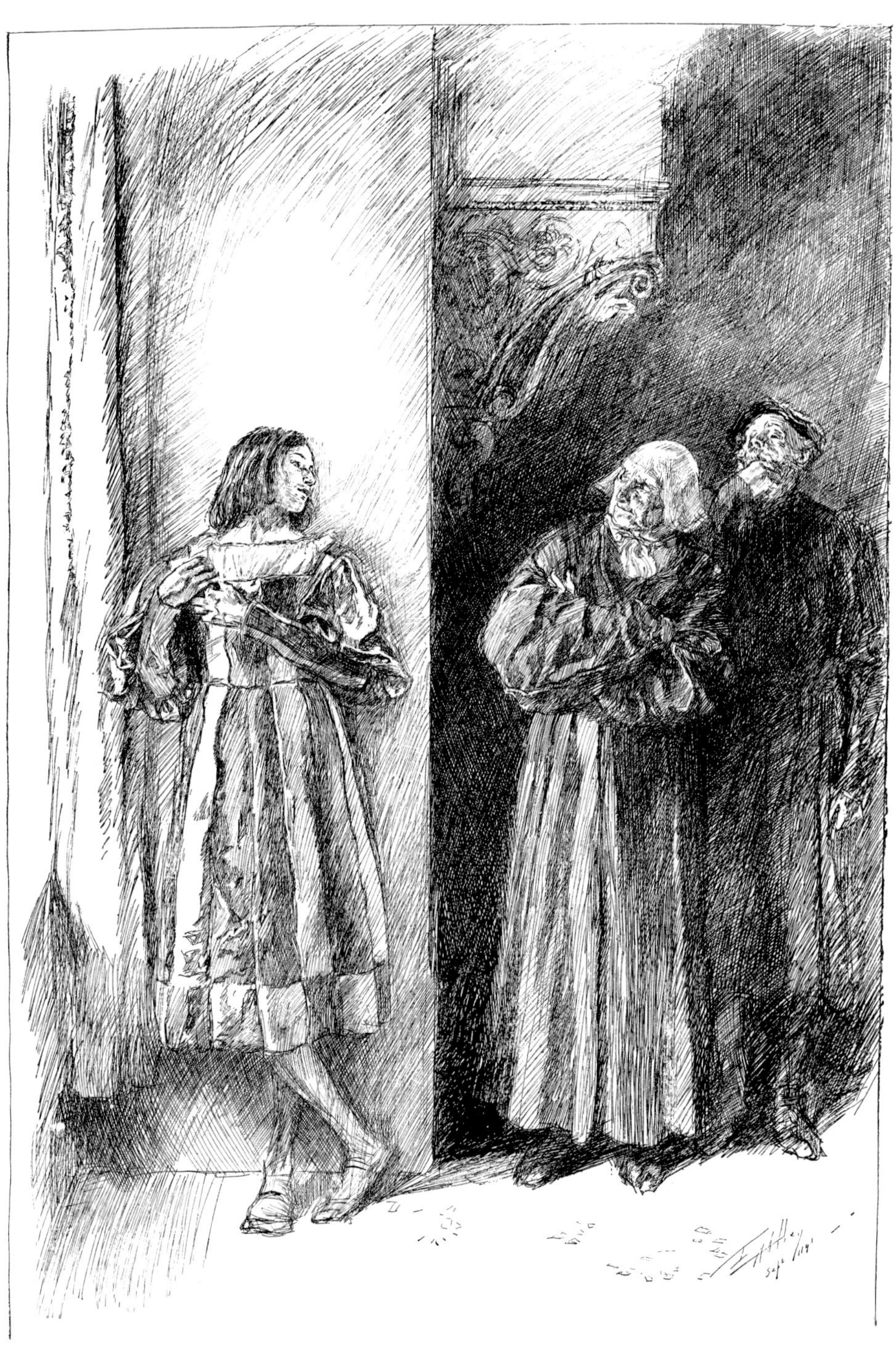

Harper's New Monthly Magazine, September 1893
The Comedies of Shakespeare — "Two Gentlemen of Verona."
Act I., Scene III. — Proteus and his father.

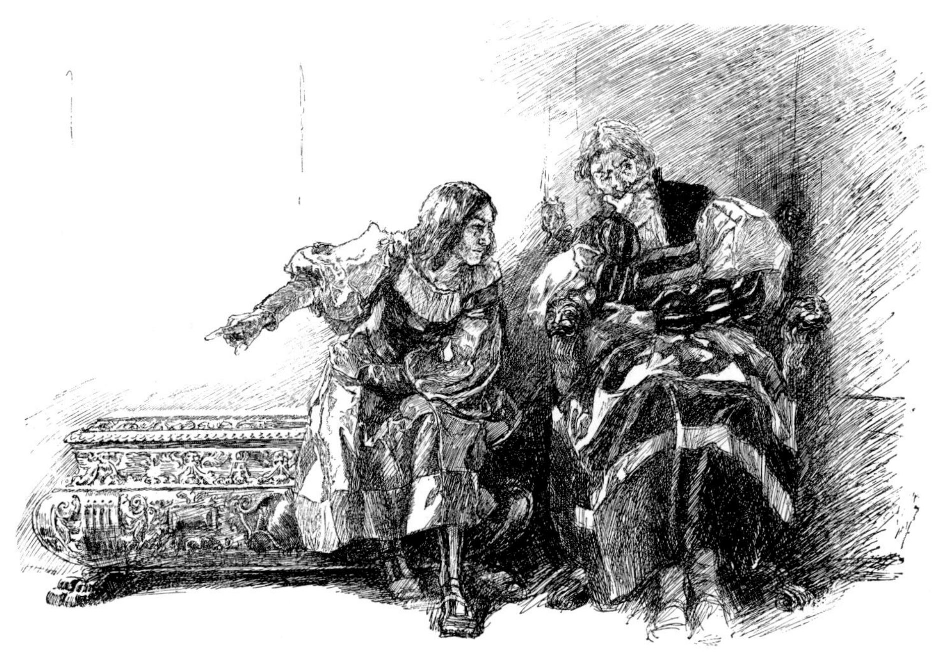

Harper's New Monthly Magazine, September 1893
The Comedies of Shakespeare — "Two Gentlemen of Verona."
Act III., Scene I. — Proteus and the Duke.

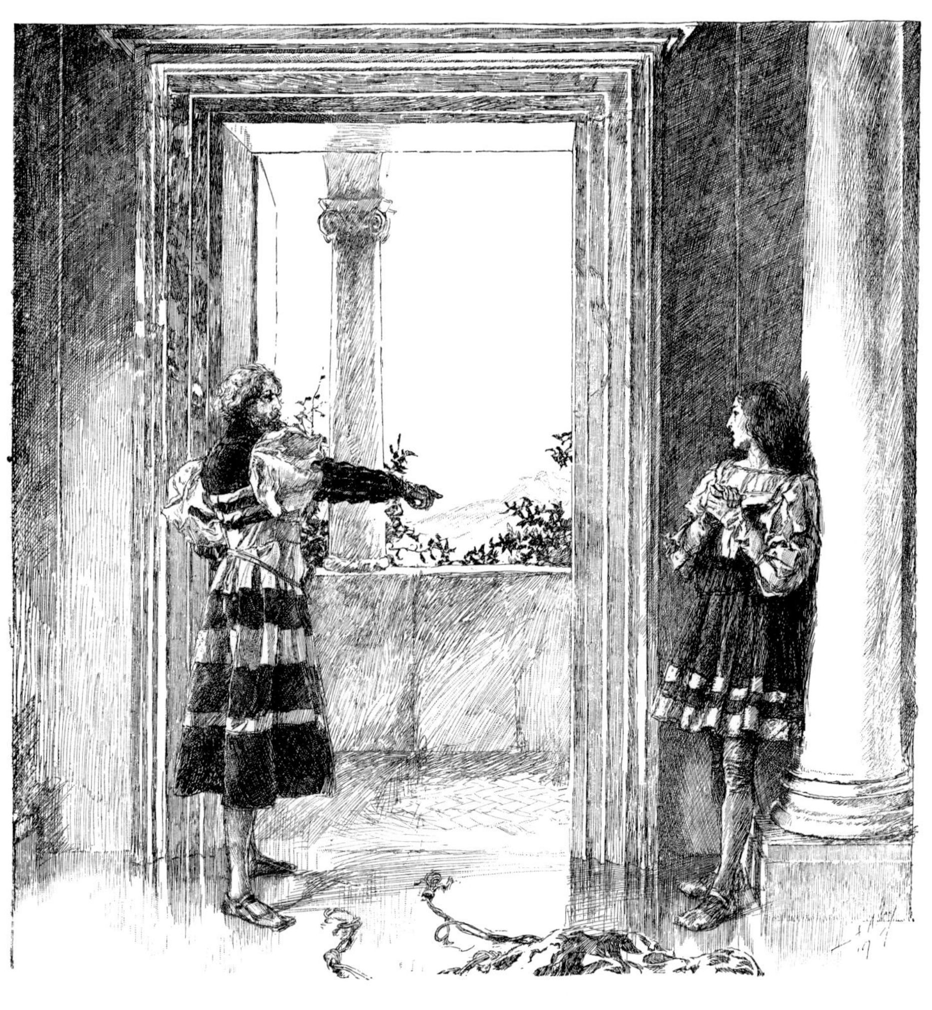

Harper's New Monthly Magazine, September 1893
The Comedies of Shakespeare — "Two Gentlemen of Verona."
Act III., Scene I. — The Duke expels Valentine.

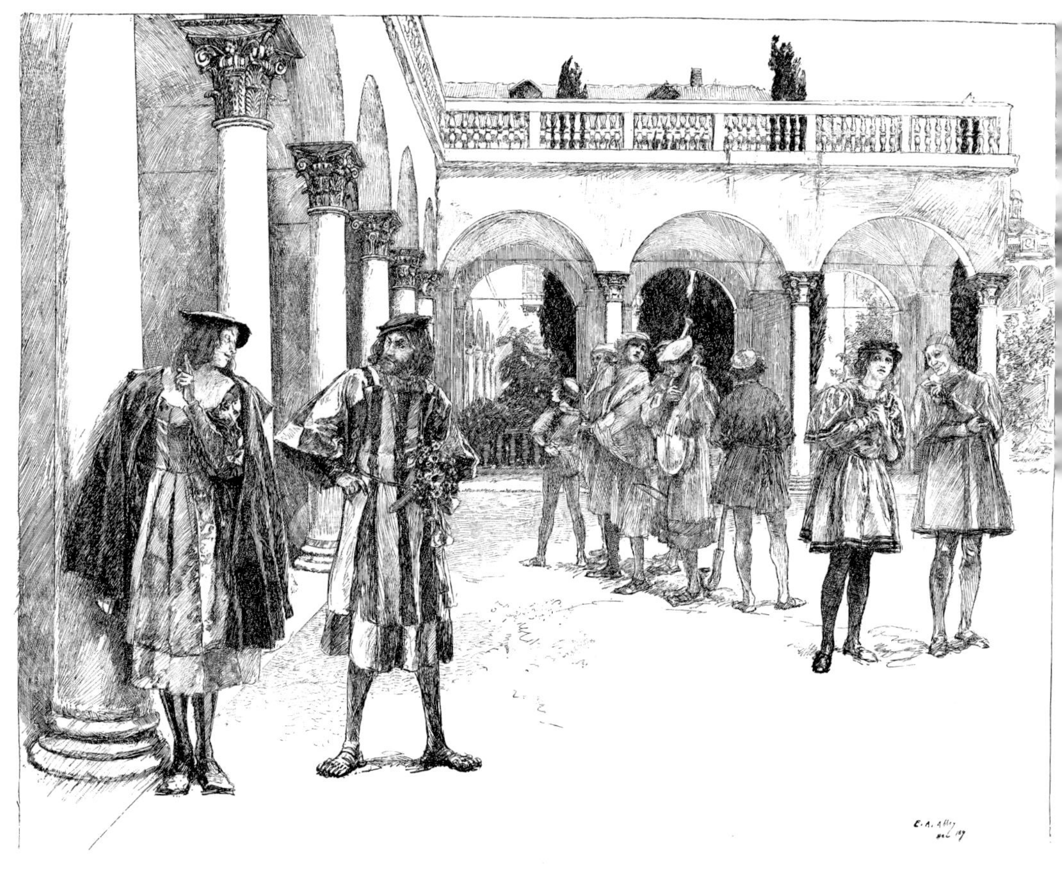

Thurio. "Who is Silvia? What is she that all out swains commend her?"

Harper's New Monthly Magazine, September 1893
The Comedies of Shakespeare — "Two Gentlemen of Verona."
Act IV., Scene II. — The Court of the palace.; under Silvia's window.
Poteus, Thurio and Musicians, host and Julia dressed as a boy.

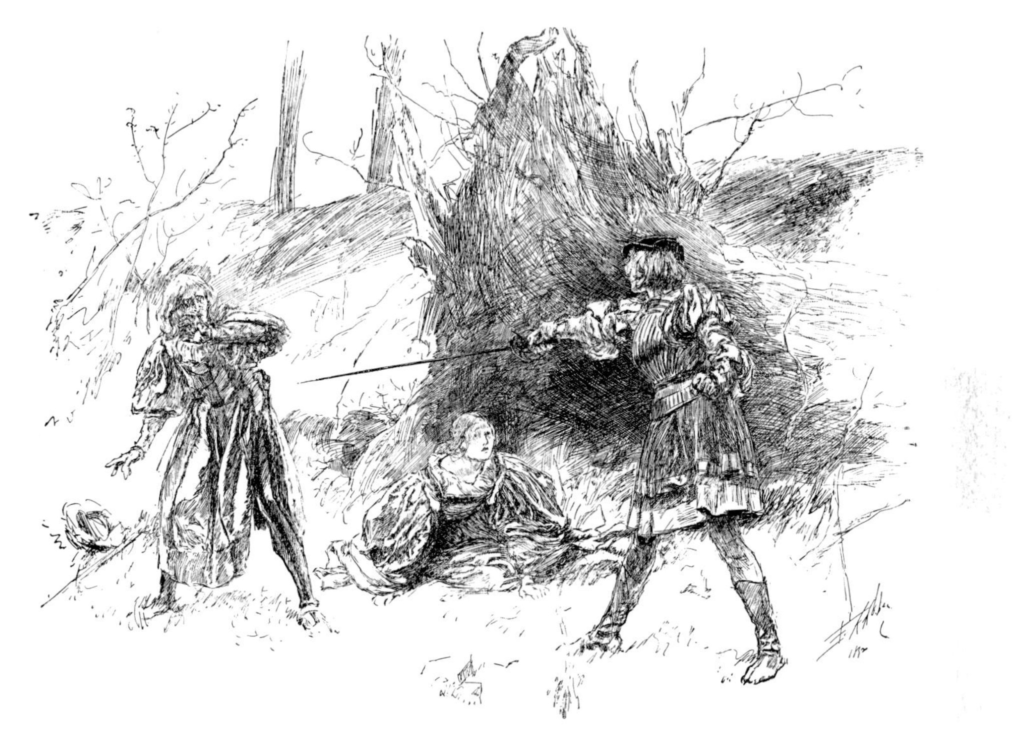

Harper's New Monthly Magazine, September 1893
The Comedies of Shakespeare — "Two Gentlemen of Verona."
Act V., Scene IV. — Valentine rescues Silvia.

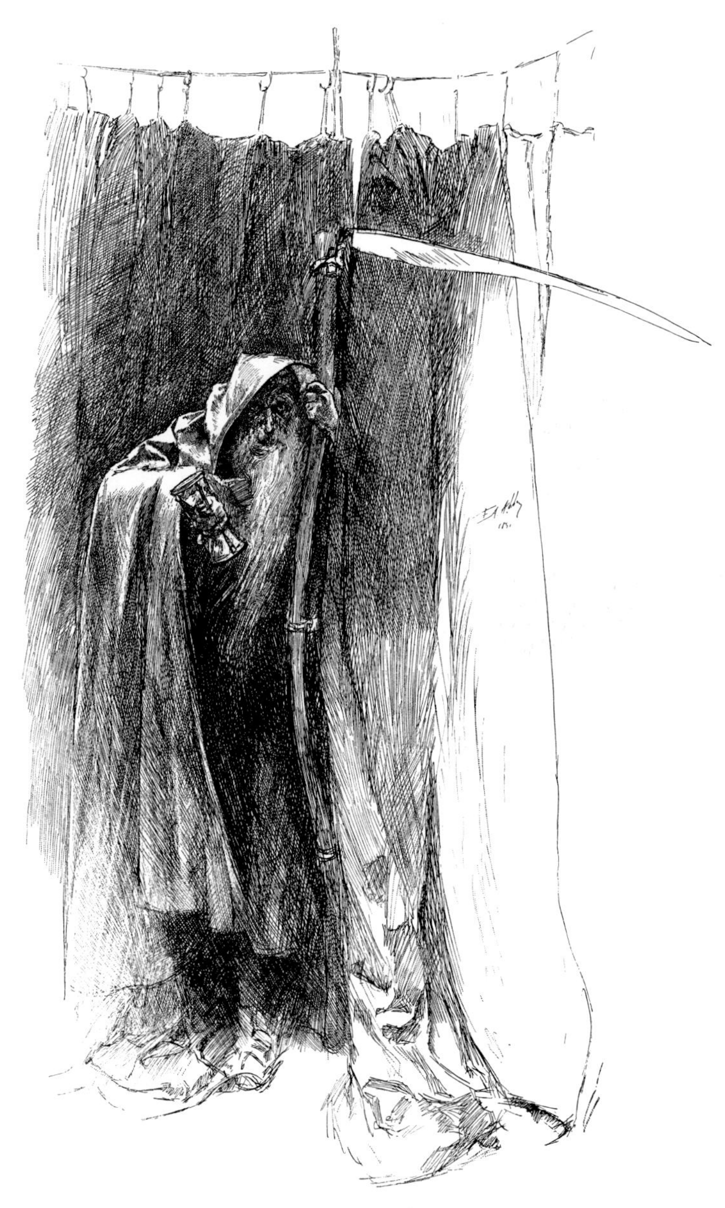

Enter Time, as chorus.

Harper's New Monthly Magazine, April 1894
The Comedies of Shakespeare — "Winter's Tale."

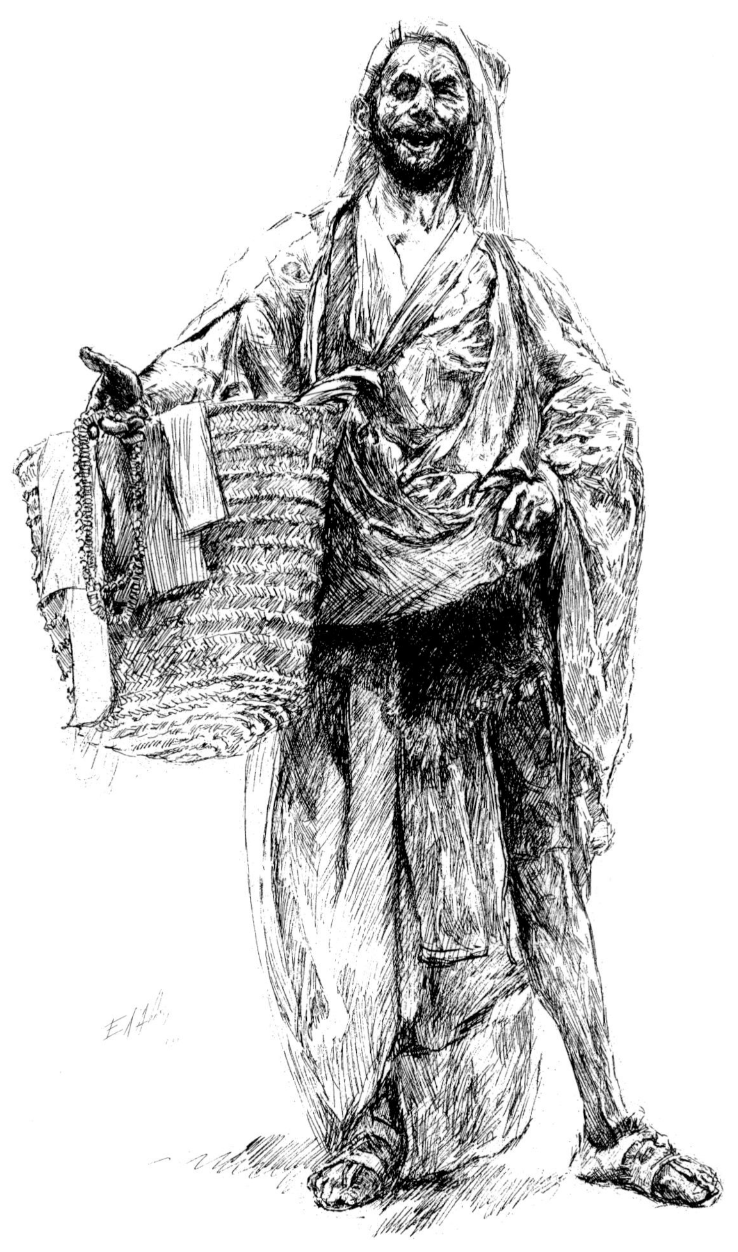

Autolycus.

Harper's New Monthly Magazine, April 1894
The Comedies of Shakespeare — "Winter's Tale."

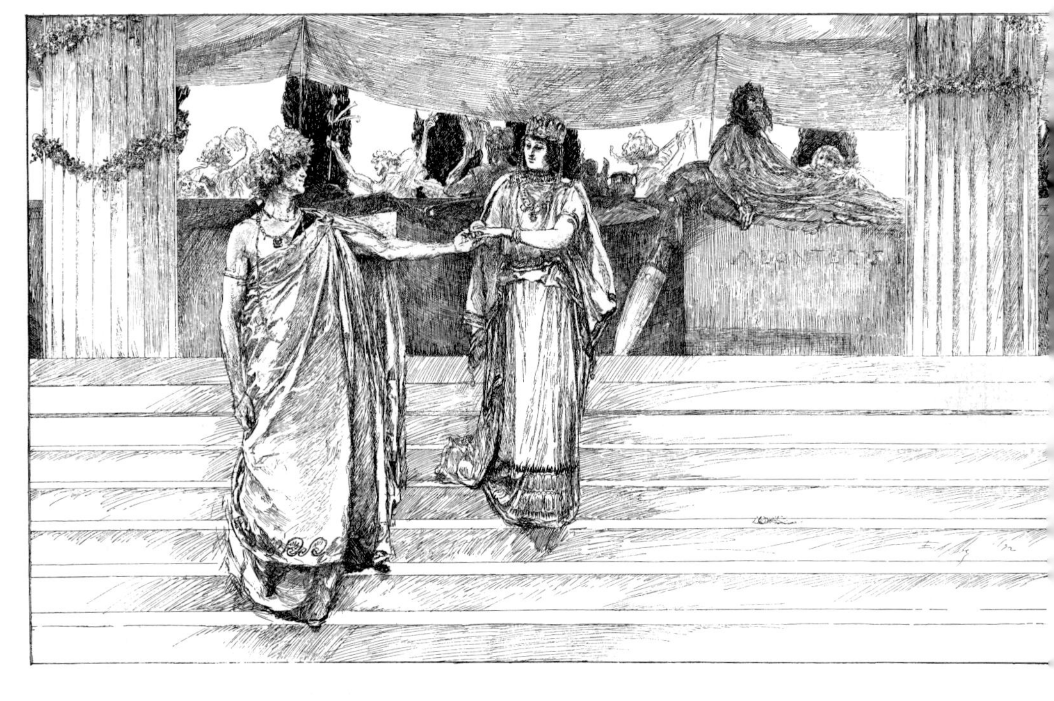

Harper's New Monthly Magazine, April 1894
The Comedies of Shakespeare — "Winter's Tale."
Act I., Scene II. — Hermione entreats Polixenes.

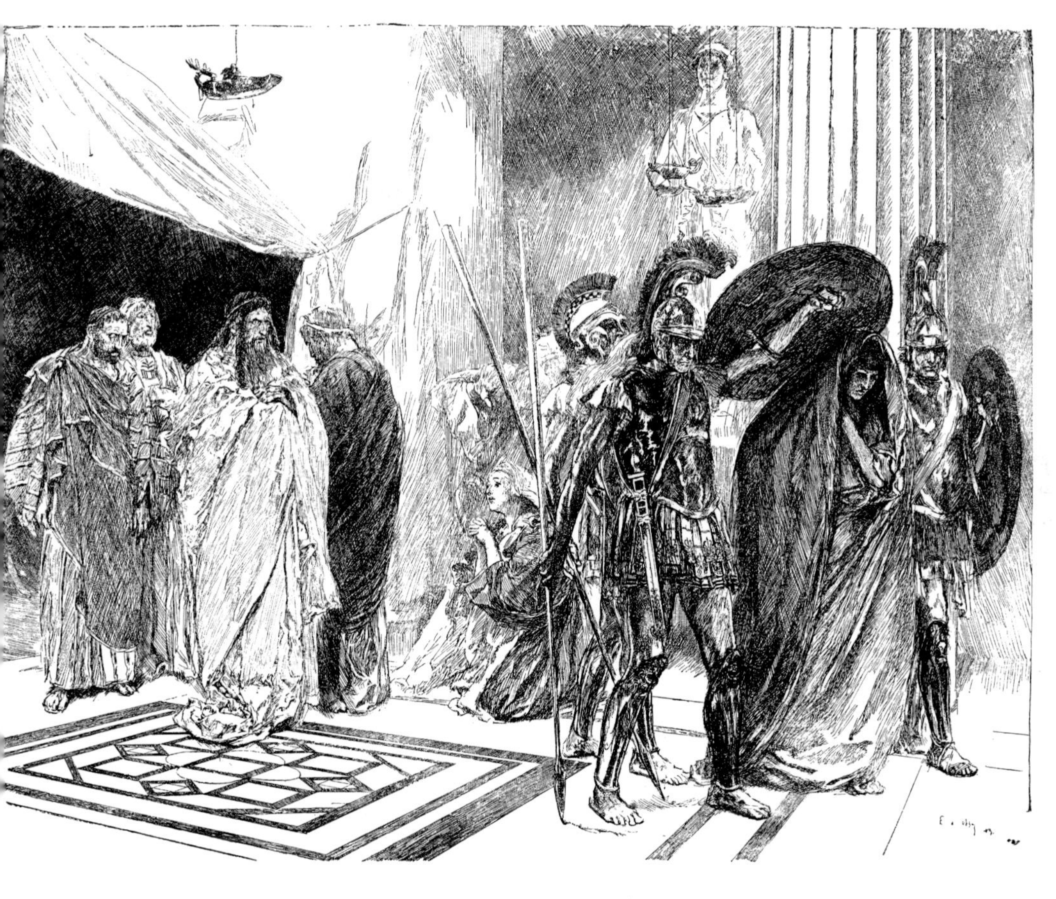

Harper's New Monthly Magazine, April 1894
The Comedies of Shakespeare — "Winter's Tale."
Act II., Scene I. — The Imprisonment of the Queen.

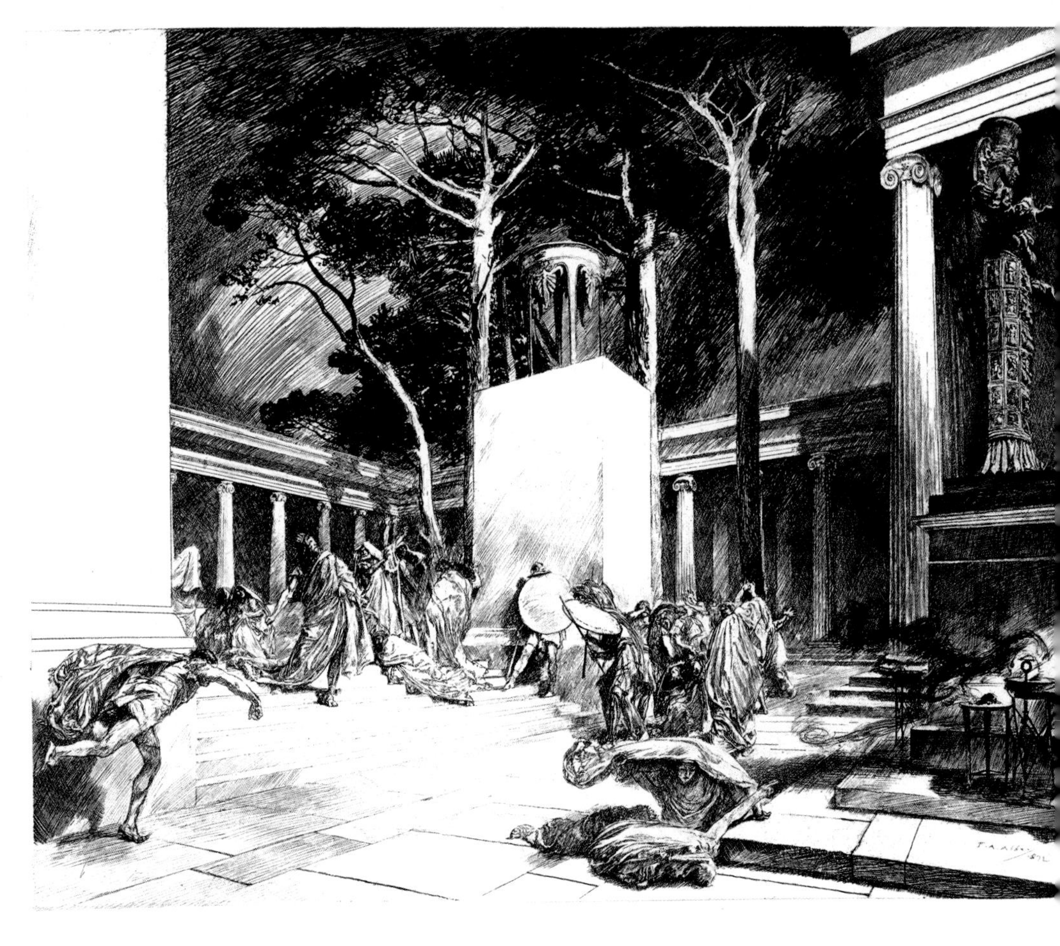

Harper's New Monthly Magazine, April 1894
The Comedies of Shakespeare — "Winter's Tale."
Act III., Scene II. — The Oracle defied.

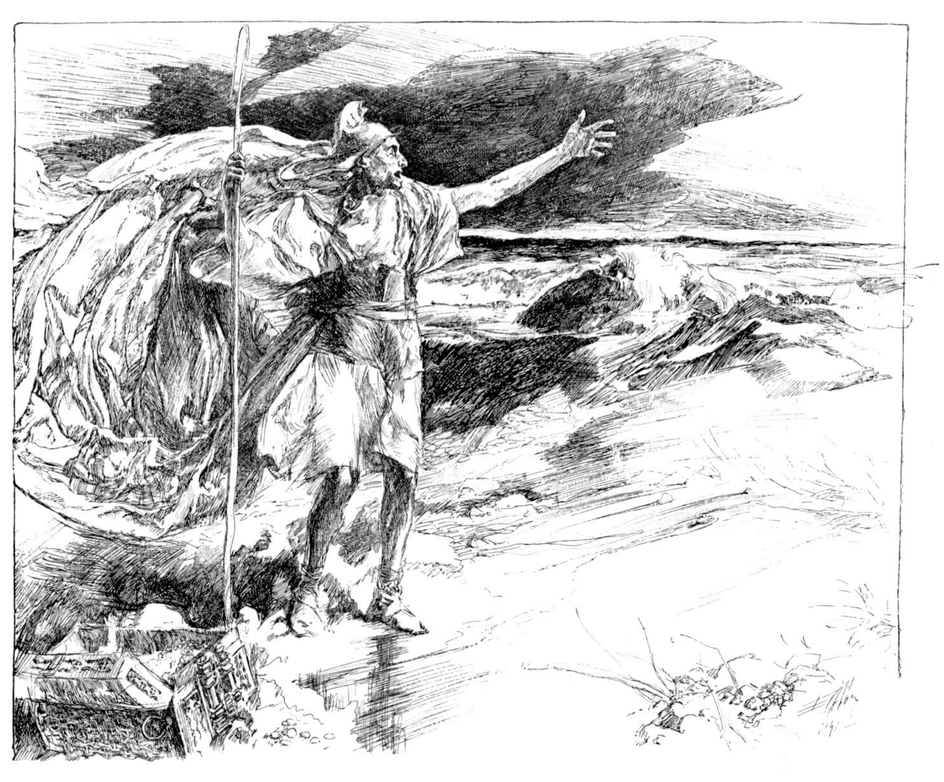

Harper's New Monthly Magazine, April 1894
The Comedies of Shakespeare — "Winter's Tale."
Act III., Scene III. — Perdita Discovered

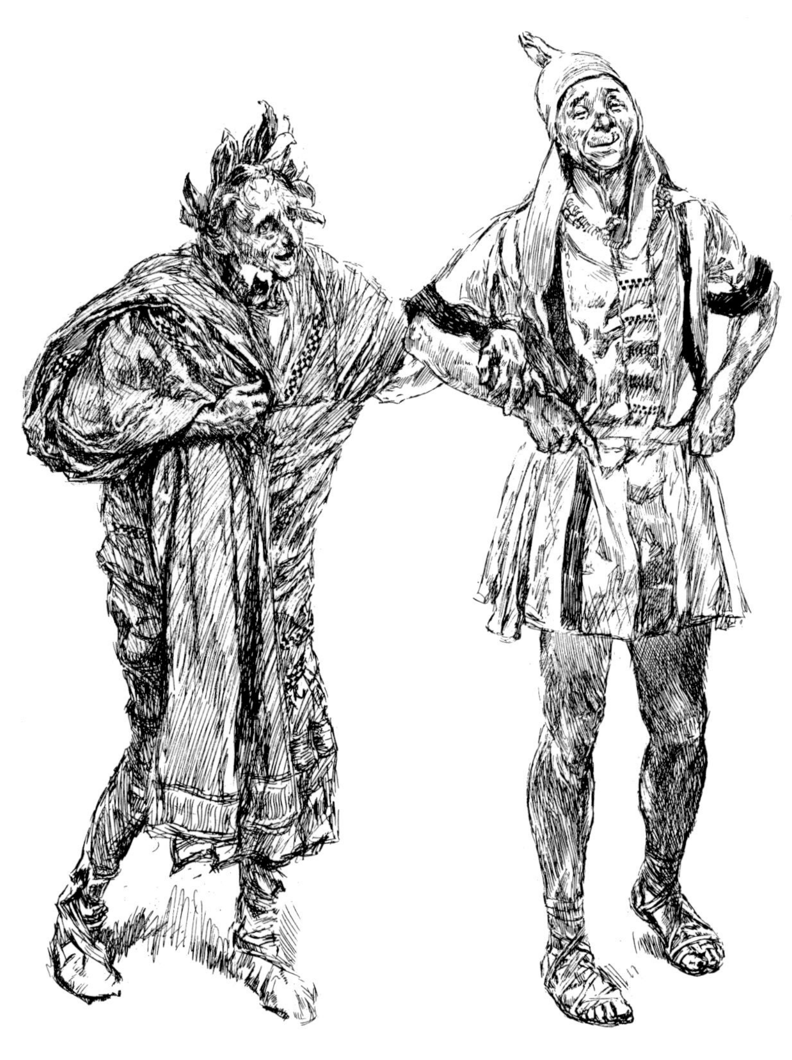

Harper's New Monthly Magazine, April 1894
The Comedies of Shakespeare — "Winter's Tale."
Act IV., Scene II. — Perdita's foster-relatives.

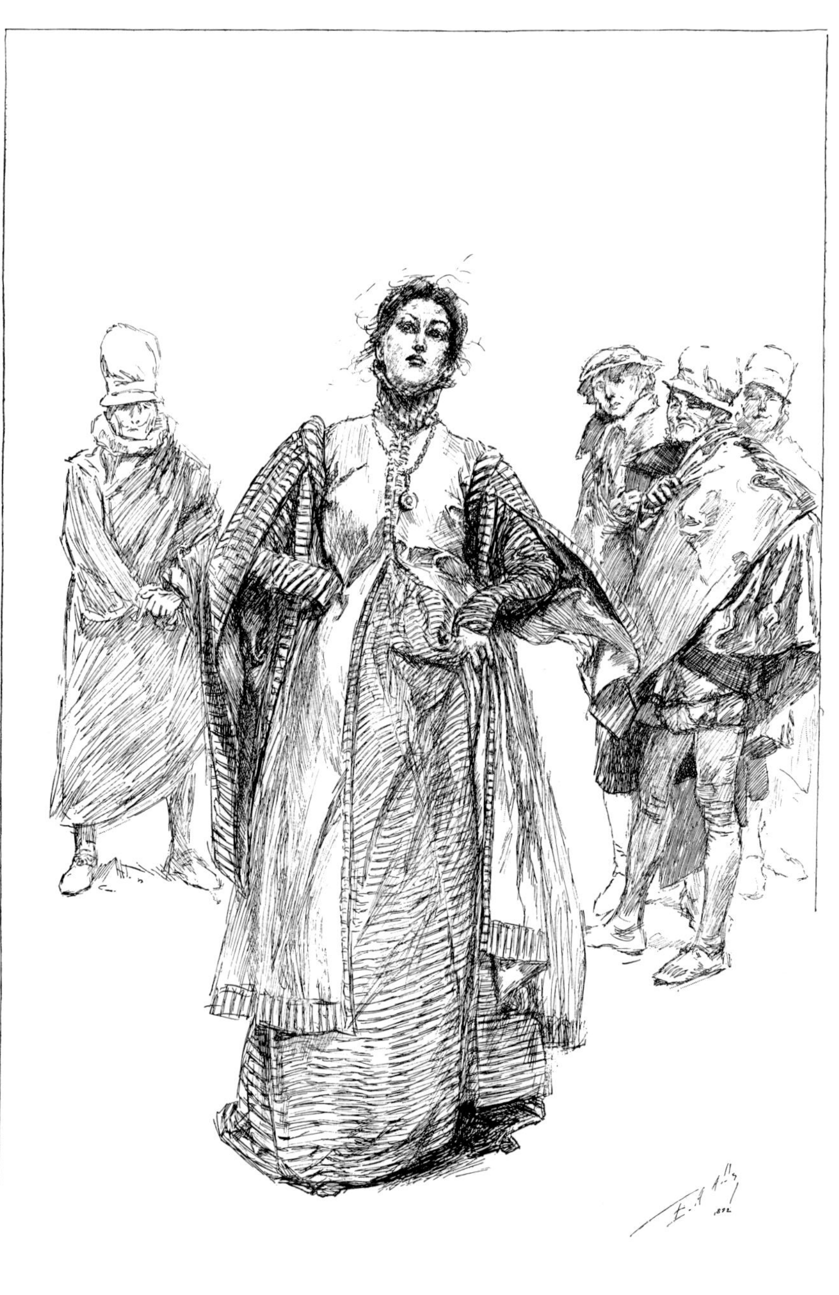

Harper's New Monthly Magazine, December 1894
The Comedies of Shakespeare XIII. — "Taming of the Shrew"
Act I., Scene I. — Katherina.

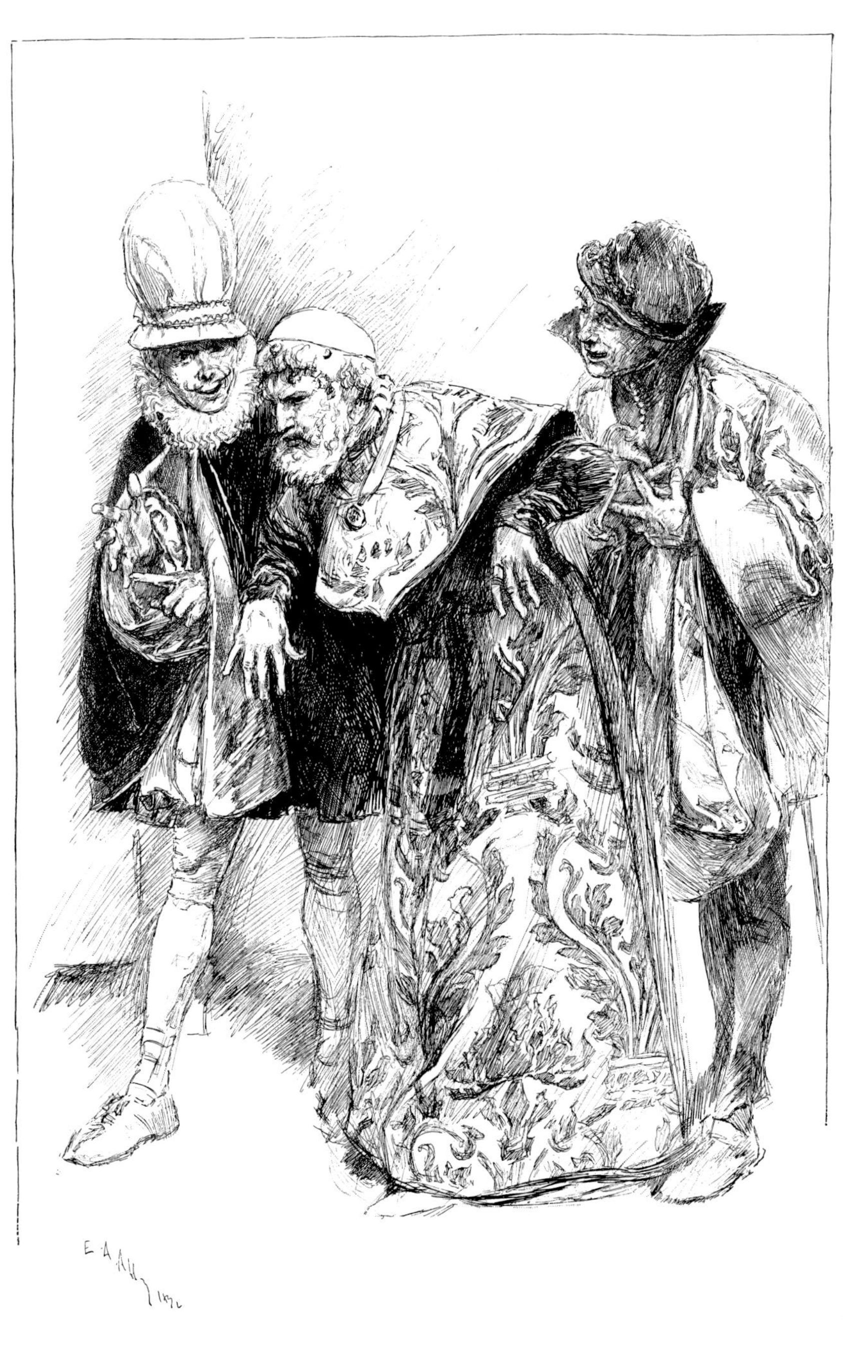

Harper's New Monthly Magazine, December 1894
The Comedies of Shakespeare XIII. — "Taming of the Shrew"
Act I., Scene I. — Baptista Protests.

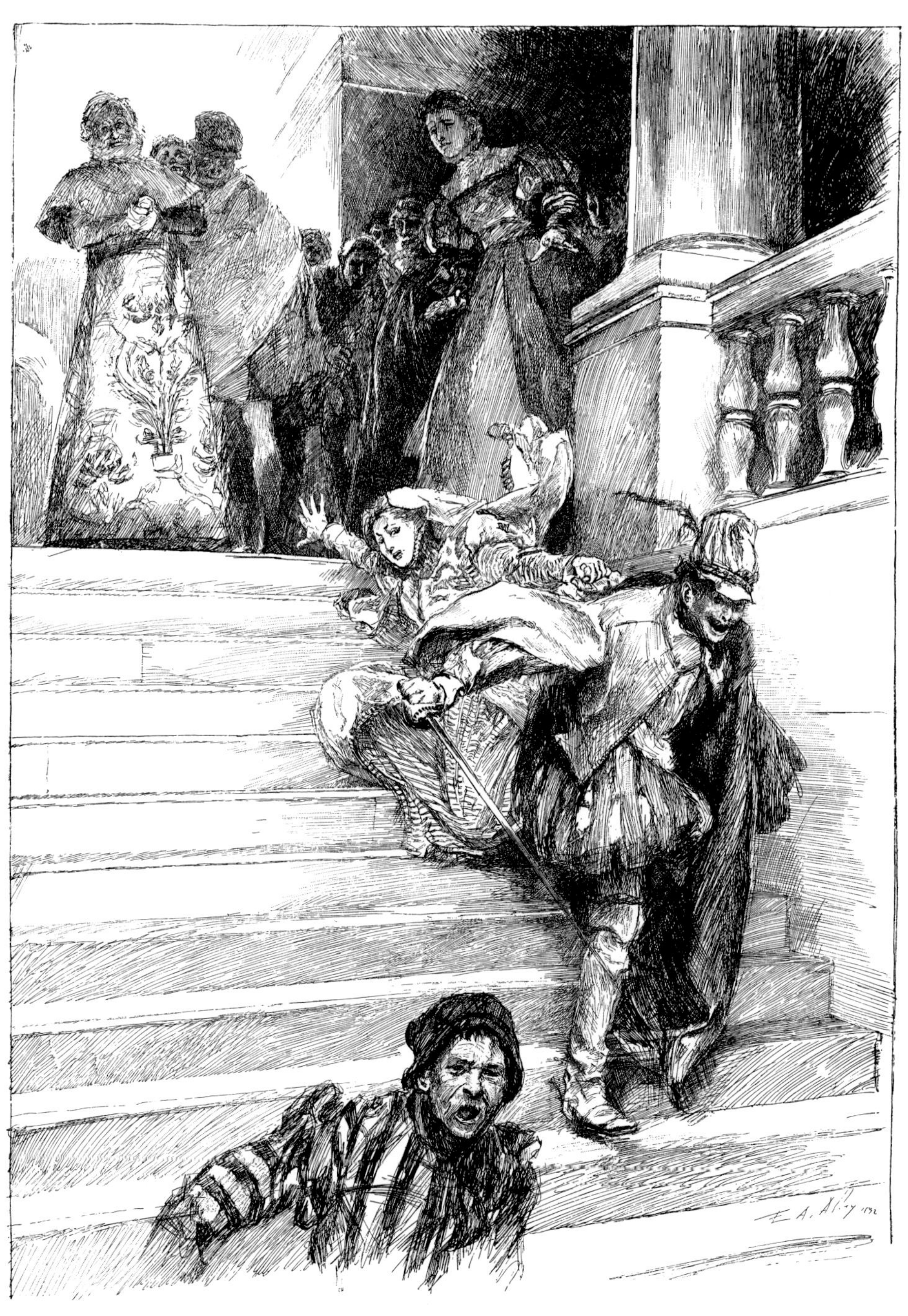

Harper's New Monthly Magazine, December 1894
The Comedies of Shakespeare XIII. — "Taming of the Shrew"
Act III., Scene II. — Petruchio bears of his bride.

311

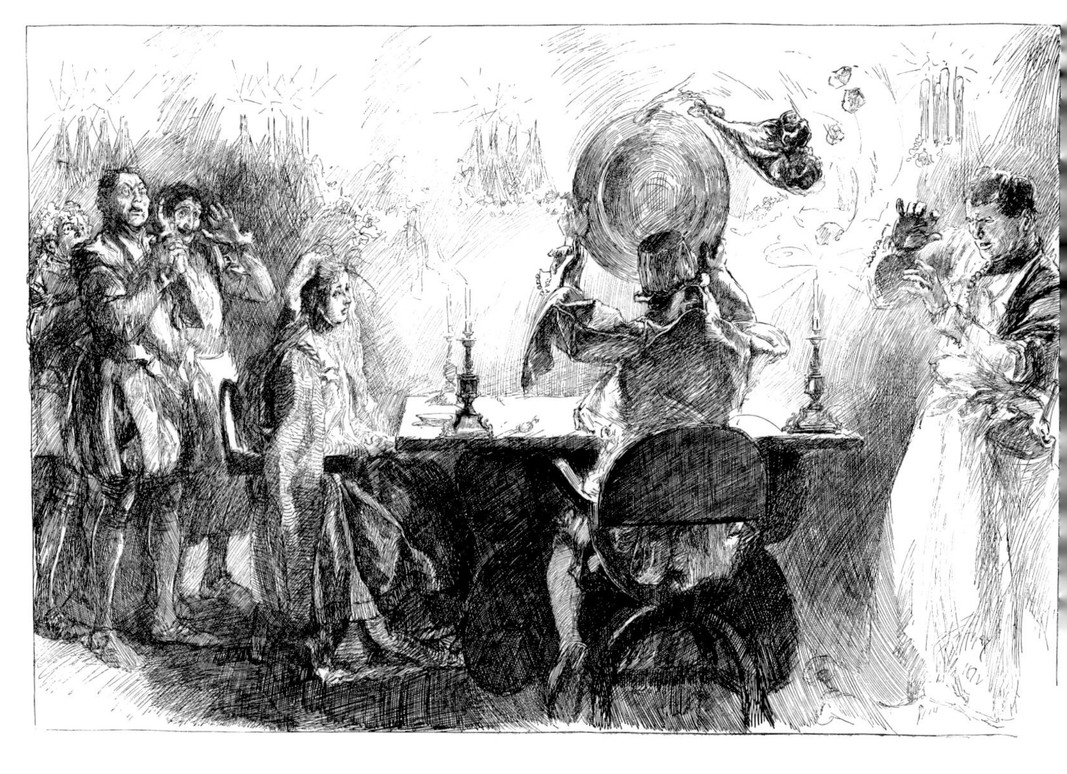

Harper's New Monthly Magazine, December 1894
The Comedies of Shakespeare XIII. — "Taming of the Shrew"
Act IV., Scene I. — Petruchio overturns the trencher.

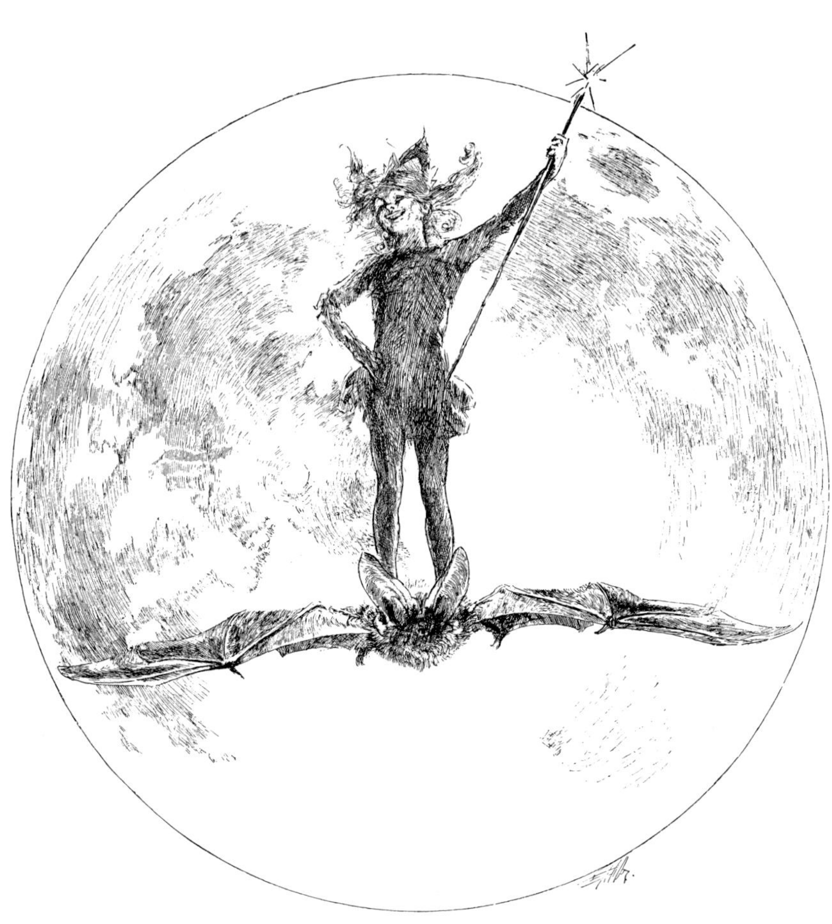

Harper's New Monthly Magazine, August 1895
The Comedies of Shakespeare XIV. — "Midsummer-Night's Dream."

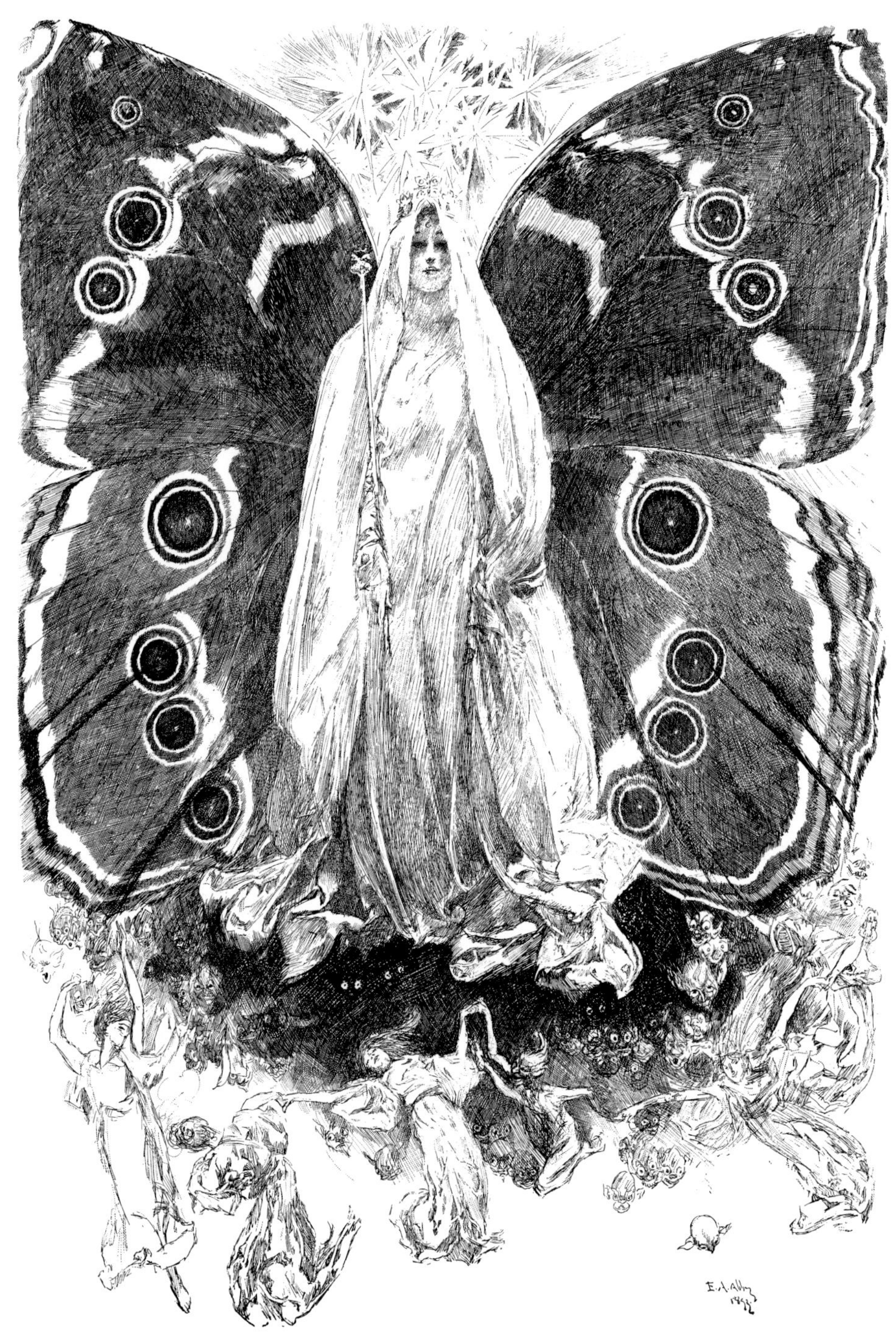

Titania.

Harper's New Monthly Magazine, August 1895
The Comedies of Shakespeare XIV. — "Midsummer-Night's Dream."

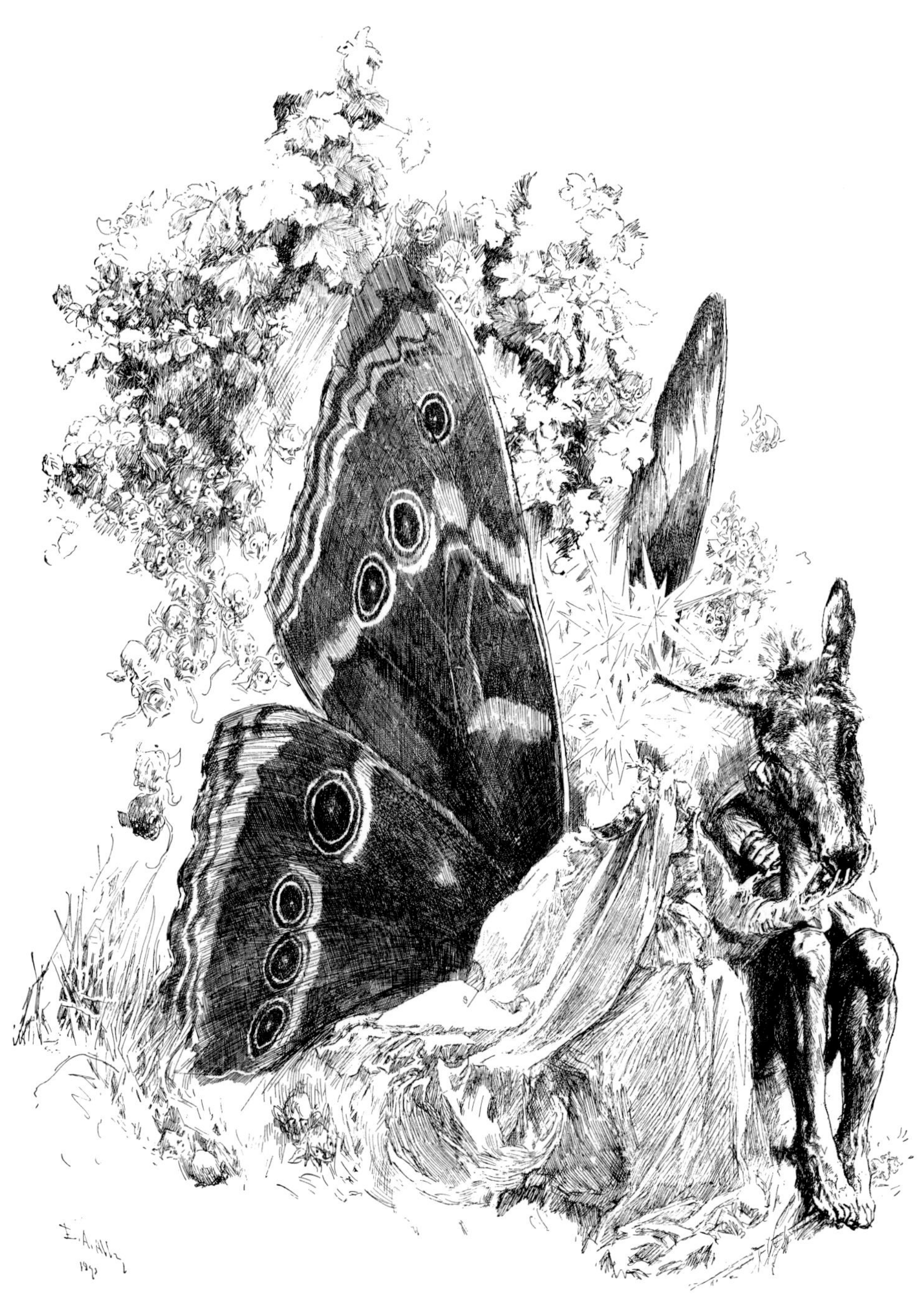

Bottom and Titania.

Harper's New Monthly Magazine, August 1895
The Comedies of Shakespeare XIV. — "Midsummer-Night's Dream."

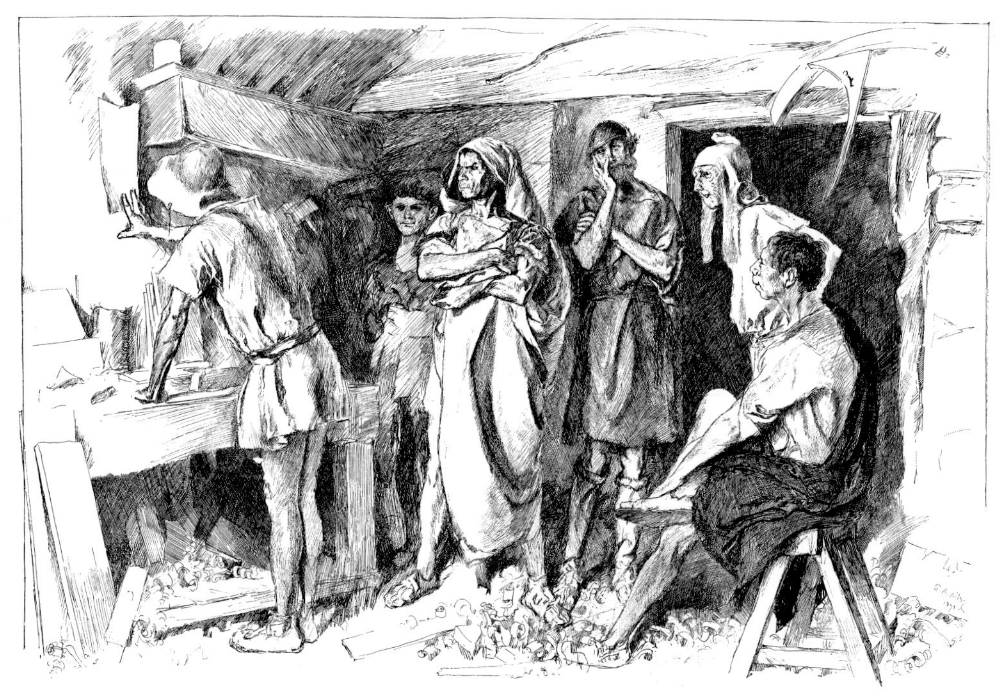

In Quince's Shop.

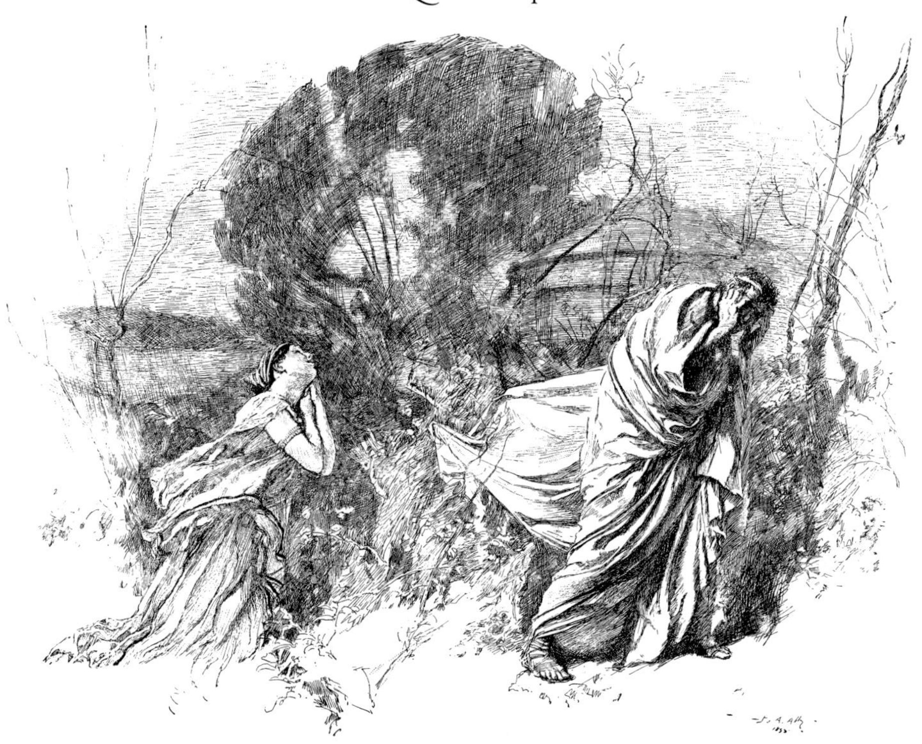

Helena pursues Demetrius.

Harper's New Monthly Magazine, August 1895
The Comedies of Shakespeare XIV. — "Midsummer-Night's Dream."
Bottom: *Act II., Scene II.*

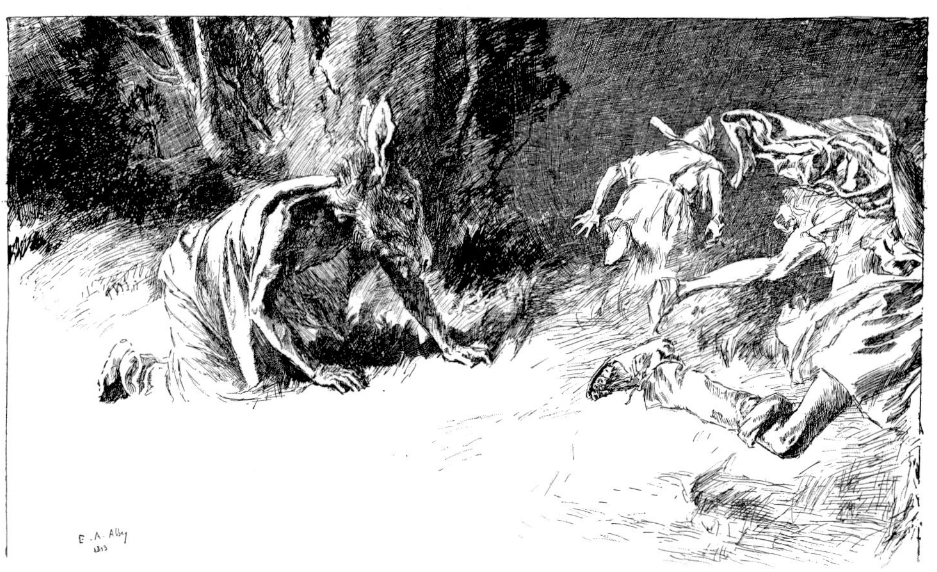

The Transformation of Bottom.

Harper's New Monthly Magazine, August 1895
The Comedies of Shakespeare XIV. — "Midsummer-Night's Dream."
Act III., Scene I. — The wood. Titania lying asleep.

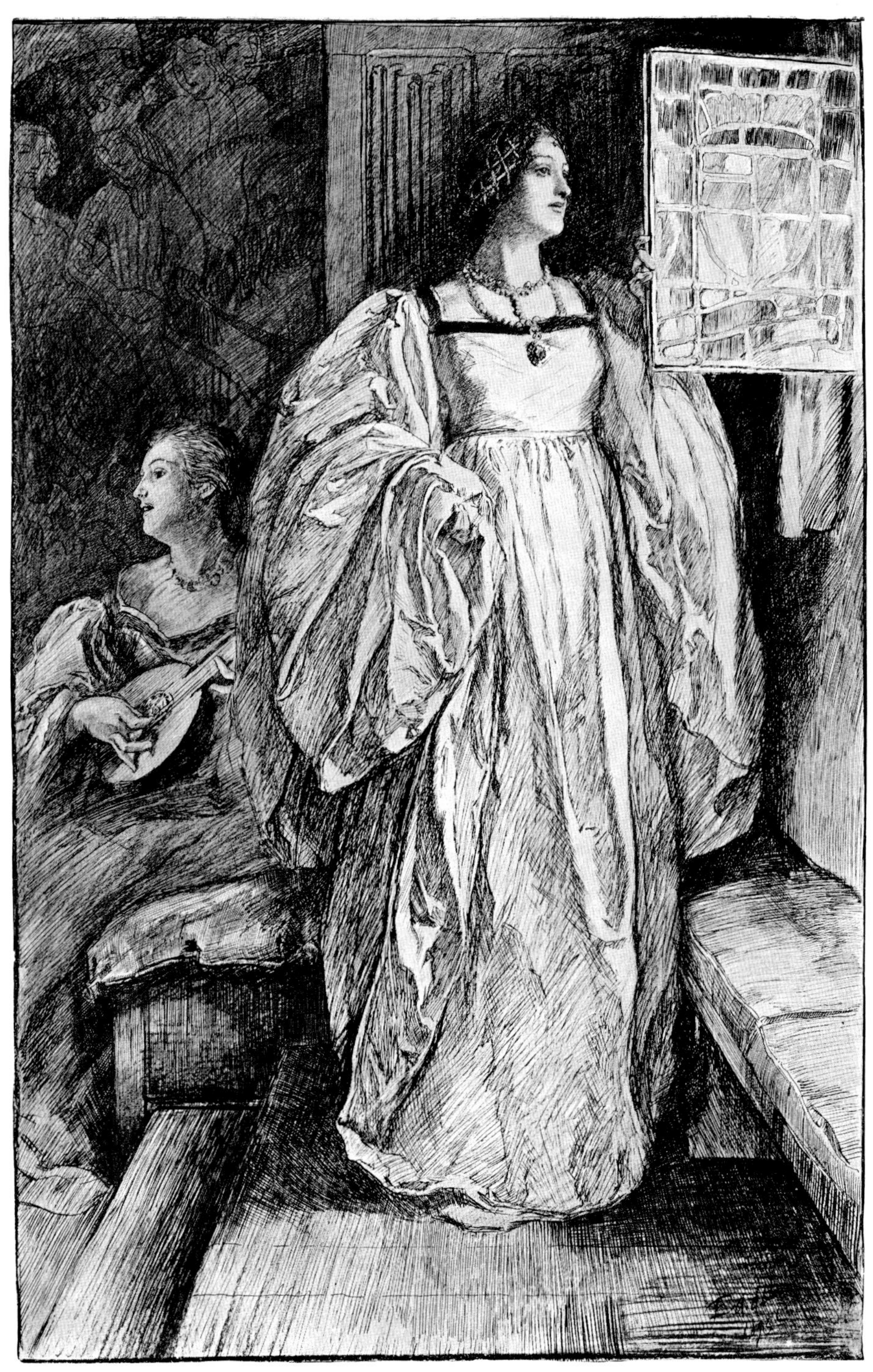

At the Window.

Harper's New Monthly Magazine, August 1896
"The Silent Voice."

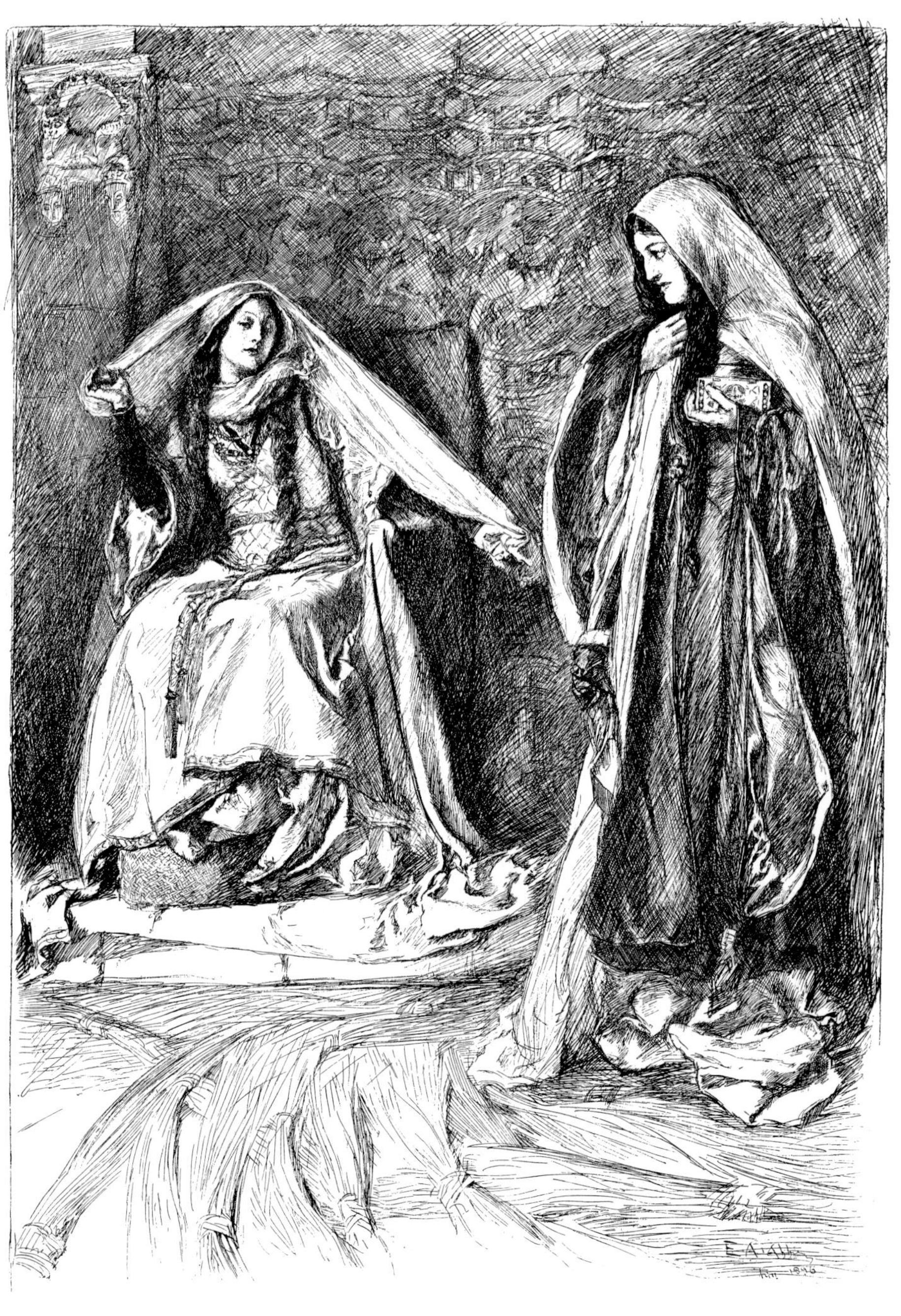

Scribner's Magazine, February 1897
"Scenes from the great novels—II; Ivanhoe."

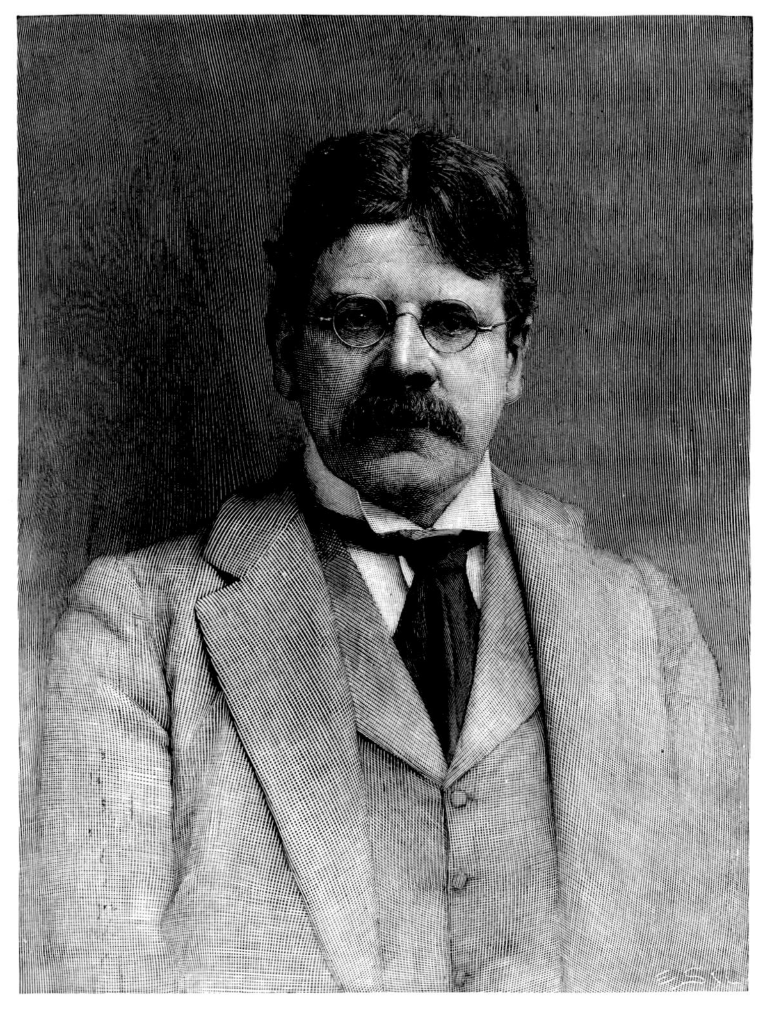

Harper's New Monthly Magazine, May 1900.

THE ART OF
E.A. ABBEY, R.A.

by

Henry Strachey

To describe Mr. Abbey as a "costume-painter" would be essentially false as it would be superficially correct. The "costume-painter" is he who delights in the quaint fashions and lovely materials of our ancestors' clothes. His aim is to construct a picture which will bring in a curious and beautiful bit of armor and gorgeously colored slashed doublet which he happens to have about him, and which, being pretty to look at, are nice to paint. If any little incident, such as a Cavalier lover or a Puritan rival, can be thrown in, so much the better. The Academy-going public will be pleased, and so the chances increased of the picture being favorable hung. An archæological sauce is not without its uses: it attracts all the learned who like pictures, but who have no feeling for art. How all these ingredients of a typical costume picture by themselves will not make a work of serious art, however good may be the execution of the painting. Something else must be present. What this something else is has ben the aim of writers on art to define. Each critic considers that he has arrived at the truth, and often the result is plausible enough, till the next prophet demonstrates the falsity of the theory, and proposes a new one of his own instead.

It is sad that this soul of art should be so indefinite, for people are led to disbelieve in its existence. But really, it is intangible only when verbal description is attempted. People who possess the appreciation of art are seldom in doubt when confronted by and example; the doubts arise when they try to give reasons. Mr. Raskin was sometimes driven to prove that pictures he sincerely admired were false in principle because they did not fit his last gospel. How many of his irritating paradoxes would have been unnecessary if he had recognized that true art cannot by forced into a formula! The best thing ever said on this subject is a sentence by Jean François Millet: "*L'art ne vit que de passion, et on ne peut pas de passionner pour rien.*"* Here is no hard-and-fast definition, but the recognition of the larger meanings of art. Neither costumes, nor mountains and trees, nor

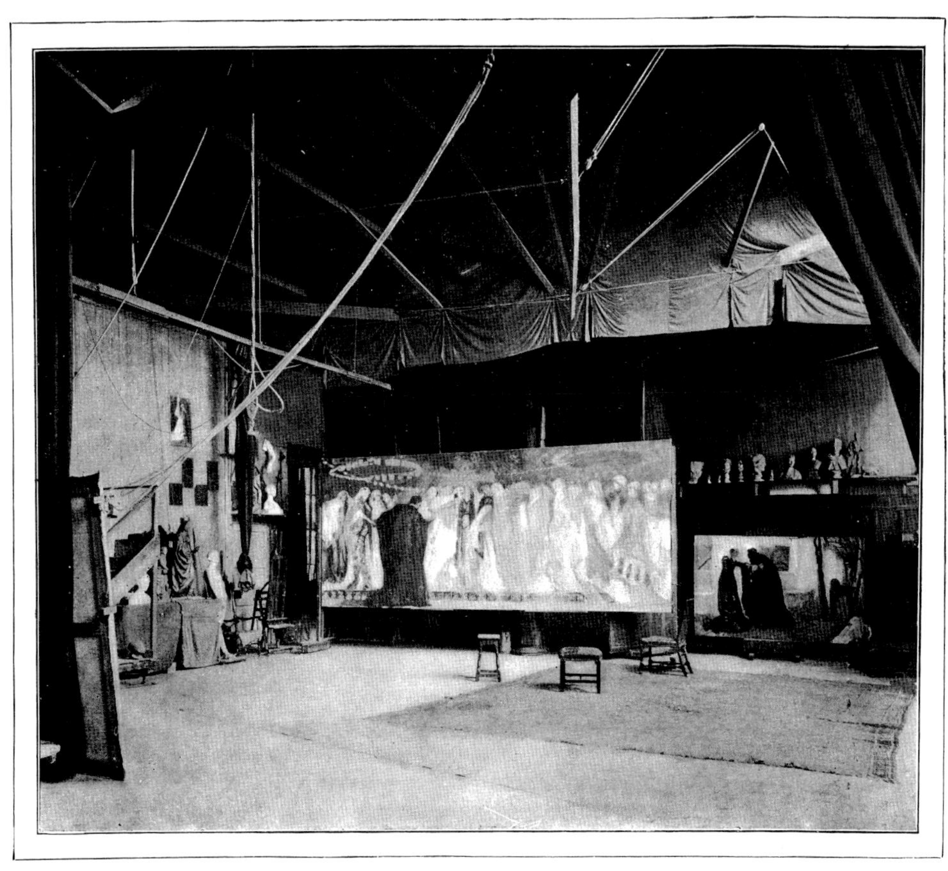

Abbey's studio in 1895.

lovely faces alone will make real pictures; the "consecration and the poet's dream" must be there as well. How this consecration shall manifest itself must be left to the genius of each different painter.

To understand Mr. Abbey's pictures we much realize his mental standpoint. It is an entire misapprehension of his art if we assume, because he works through the medium of costume, that costume is this inspiration or his end. The vague poetic impulse at the back on an artist's mind has to find a concrete form to express itself. In the present instance the expression of Mr. Abbey's matured art has been by means of the dresses of the Middle Ages. But because the painter has shown such delight in the various garments of man, we must not say, with the Quaker lady whose husband had left off knee-breeches with a change of opinions, "Friend, does thy religion consist of trousers?" Rather we must consider what motive has guided Mr. Abbey into his present course.

Art lives by passion alone, and one cannot become impassioned about nothing.

Mr. Berenson, in his book on the *Central Italian Painters*, in a most interesting chapter on "Illustration," sums up in the following words what he means by the term: "Illustration is everything which in a work of art appeals to us, not for any intrinsic quality, as of color or form or composition, contained in the work of art itself, but for the value the thing represented has elsewhere, whether in the world outside or in the mind within." And again: Great art would be defined not as the blind imitation of nature, but as the reproduction of visual images haunting great minds." Images haunt most minds when they read literature or history, but the interest of these images depends on the quality of the mind that calls them up. Therefore Mr. Abbey's picture of Richard III. wooing the Lady Anne is not in the least made of a work of art because of the elaborate setting of the stage, and the accuracy of the dresses and heraldry, and all the trappings of a mediæval state funeral. It is interesting because the scene in Shakespeare's play called up, in a mind of exceptional visualizing power, images which were beautiful and expressive in themselves. Add to this, great capacity of form and color, and also execution, and the result is the striking picture we saw at the Academy in 1896. Mr. Abbey is an illustrator of the greatest power and originality. Of course the word illustrator is here used in the special sense of Mr. Berenson, and not in the ordinary way, which means that a picture of drawing has direct reference to a book. Mr. Abbey has the power of calling up an endless series of mental pictures, and these he puts on canvas, and thus lets the world share in his visions. And what visions this painter has given us! The black procession attending the bier of Henry VI. in the *Richard III.* picture is one of those things which the ordinary imagination is dimly conscious of when fired by romantic poetry, but which is too vague to leave any distinct impression. But the painter not only sees the vision, but can make us see it too. And here we come to the question of the presentment. The object of primary importance is that the spectator's imagination should be fired: but to do this the painter's also must be kindled. He must choose shapes and colors that are intensely interesting to him, or else his work will be cold. Practically it matters very little to the right-minded spectator what the nature of the objects is out of which the painter chooses to fashion the conduit-pipe for his imagination.

If mediæval costume touches the painter deeply enough to heat

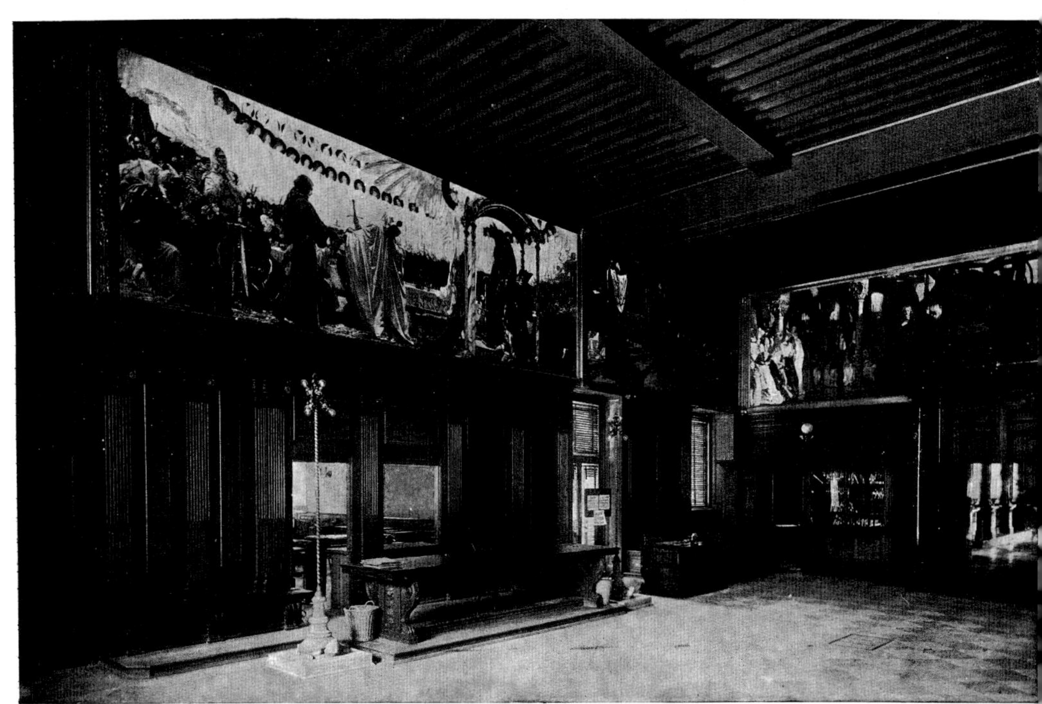

A Section of Mr. Abbey's "Holy Grail" in the Boston Public Library in 1895.

his imagination to that point at which it communicates warmth to others, the desired result has been attained. He who looks at the picture receives pleasurable sensations, not from the costumes, be they never so accurately studied, but from the contact with a mind which has the power of communicating the warmth with which it glowed when under the enthusiasm of visualized forms of beauty. Pictures such as Mr. Abbey's are often as stumbling-block to those who really possess the artistic sense, and for like reason too often, alas, to those who have no pictorial appreciation, but whose delight in painting is merely that of archæological studies and museum reminiscences. These people, when they find their favorite things represented, judge of the picture merely by its accuracy. So it happens that when the experts in mediæval tailoring and armory rejoice over a picture, the lover of art is apt to pass by, because these museum qualities are generally found in works in which learning has stifled the spirit. But to treat Mr. Abbey so would be to do a great injustice. His mind works in a particular way, and if the finds that the reconstruction of past ages gives scope to his imagination, it is neither a reason for praise nor for blame. What is essentially interesting is not the outward form, but "the passion and the life, whose fountains are within."

"O lady, we receive but what we give,
And in our life alone does nature live."

It is because Mr. Abbey puts this passion and life into his pictures that they are true works of art, and not because they are monuments of careful study.

This careful study is, no doubt, to some pictorially right-minded people, a great charm, and there is no reason why it should not be, just as other people will be interested in the actual manipulation of the paint.

To the present writer the question of what paints and ground were employed to produce the beautiful red of the Duke of Gloster's cloak is of more interest than whether the cloak is cut exactly to the fashion of 1438. But these are personal matters, and wholly outside the region of art. Not so, however, is the question of the actual painting of pictures—the finished surface of paint which meets the eye. This question of the painting, the technique, is of the utmost importance, for by it the painter

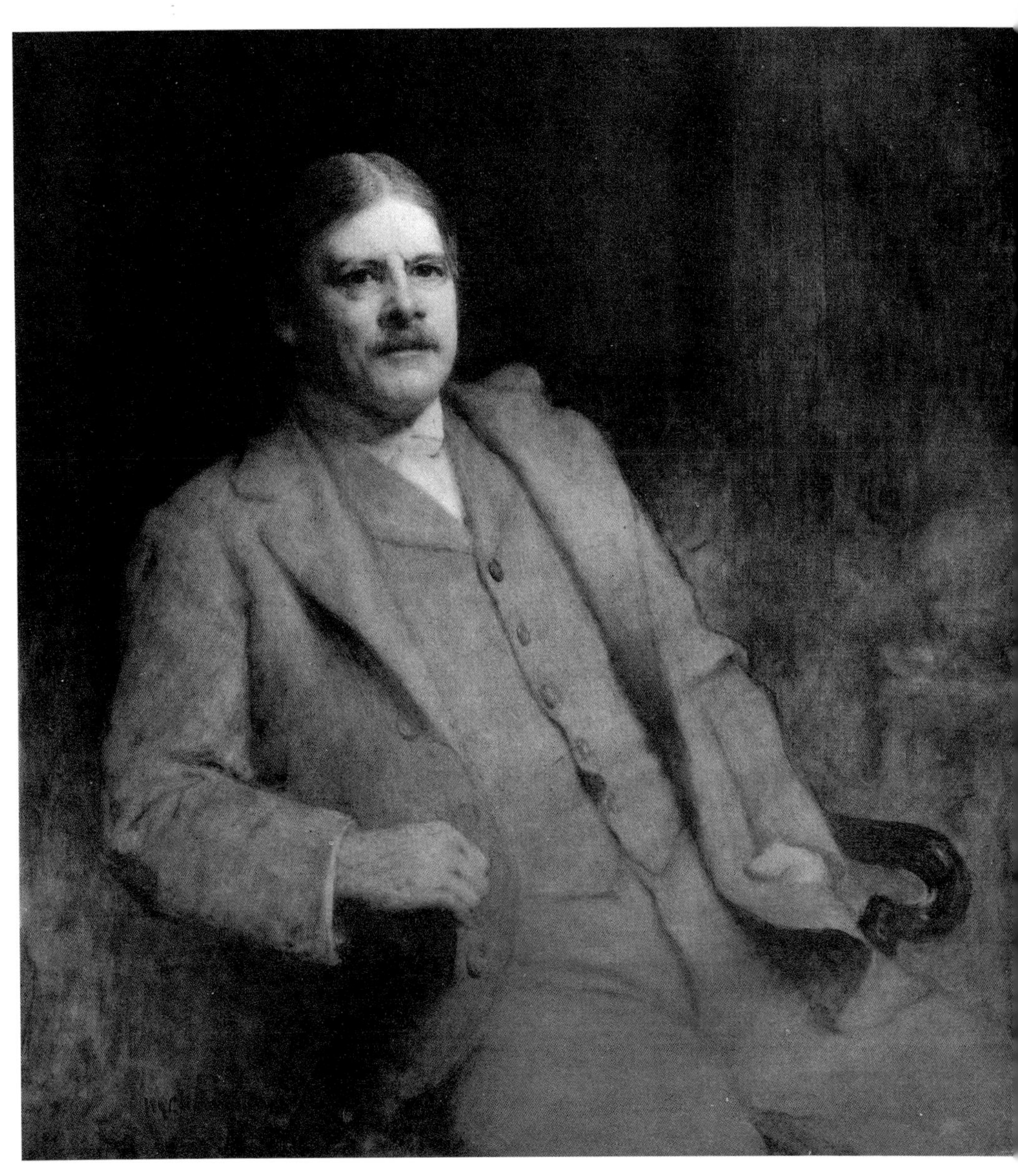

Edwin Austin Abbey portrait by unknown artist.

speaks to us in a more subtle language than that of reason. The arguments, the incidents, and the imagery of "Paradise Lost" might all be reproduced in different language from that which was used by the poet. But what a difference! Take away from the argument the incomparable splendor and beauty of the Miltonic verse, and how different would be its effect! The verbal harmonies of the lines are needed to make us feel the greatness and majesty of the thoughts. So in a picture we must, to appreciate it truly, be mindful of the way in which the painter has expressed himself in his painting.

The world was for long accustomed to think of Mr. Abbey only as a master of black and white, as especially of pen drawing, and in this branch of art his technical power was conspicuous. His most important works in this direction were the illustration of Shakespeare's comedies, which appeared in *Harper's Magazine*. The originality of these illustrations was great—the artist visualized the familiar scenes of the plays in quite a different way from anything that had gone before. Instead of the conventional stage costume founded on Elizabethan dress, we saw Shakespeare's people put back into an earlier time. The style of the clothes and accessories was much less familiar. The fantastic dresses of the period chosen by the artist—that of pre-Tudor times—gave scope for the marvelous ingenuity of the designer. For Mr. Abbey is remarkable for the wealth of his invention and research in details. These illustrations are undoubtedly of great charm; they are revelations of character, and they show insight into the plays. Yet somehow they do not entirely convince us that we are looking at the real people we have always known. Somehow the deep humanity does not seem to be there. There is almost an air of masquerade. The grace, the energy, and the vivacity are there, but not quite the depth of feeling. The illustrations of the *Tempest* may be quoted as an example; in them Prospero is too much the wizard and too little the philosopher. If one were inclined to push such objections, it would be possible to point out that in the picture of *King Lear*, hung in the Academy of 1898, Regan and Goneril are more impish demons of mischief than tragic incarnations of evil. But it would be going too far not to admit that Mr. Abbey has in this really splendid work created two figures of extraordinarily active malice, even if we feel that they have not quite the weight we are accustomed to expect in the two most terrible of Shakespeare's creations. With the figure of Cordelia, who wishes to find fault? In it Mr. Abbey has corrected a common fault in our visual conception of this heroine. Too often people are wont to consider her to be Ophelia's twin sister. But Cordelia was made of sterner stuff, and it is difficult to conceive of a more appropriate figure than the one in the picture we are discussing. Admirable, too, is the figure of Lear; only his back is seen, but the bent form tells of the collapse after the cyclone of denunciation of his favorite daughter.

Mr. Abbey devoted himself for long to black and white work, but it was not on account of any lock of color sense that he did so. Few things are more remarkable about this artist than his sudden transition from an able black and white draughtsman to a painter of unusual accomplishment.

To paint in oils is easy; but to be able to use oil paint so as to get out of it the peculiar power of expression the medium is capable of comes to few artists. Young ladies generally paint in oils, believing that it is easier to do so than to paint in water-colors. There is a certain truth in this, as in most fallacies. It is easy to bury preliminary blunders under thick coats of sticky paint. But this is not oil-painting in the sense of Titian.

If we look attentively at the surface of a picture by Titian, we find a wonderful variety in the way in which the actual paint is varied in its applications to the canvas. This prince of painters did not consider that it was enough to color his canvas to the right hue in patches of given shapes. Rather he sought and found the right kind of touch necessary for every part of the pictures, so that such a part might have its full and proper effect. Hazlitt said that words should be so chosen as to produce the "exact extreme characteristic impression." So it was with Titian. He was not satisfied merely to paint the flesh of Bacchus of a different color from that of the man with the snakes round his body on the right of the picture in the National Gallery. He gave a completely different consistency to the paint as well; its substance, as well as its color and shape, he made expressive. It must not be thought that mere differentiation of surface is all that is required, or else most of the Academicians would have to be pronounced painters in this highest sense. There are many people who can draw well, have a good feeling for color, can suggest the surfaces of the objects they represent, but still are not painters in this special

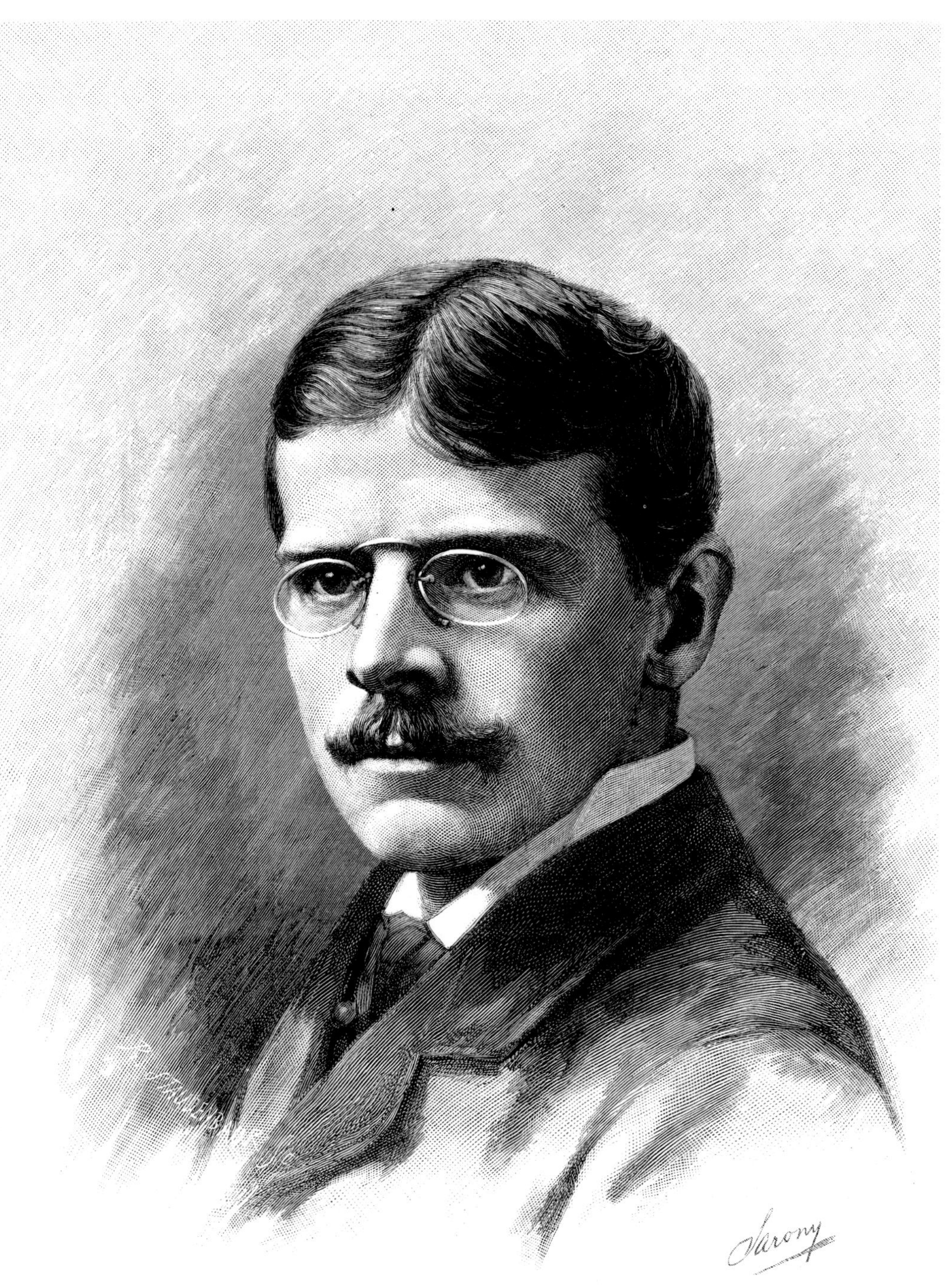

Harper's Weekly cover
December 4, 1886
Edwin Austin Abbey drawn by Napoleon Sarony

application of the word. In no school of painting was the possession of this gift so common as in the Venetian. The Florentines rarely attained it. Velasquez, of course, was a master of this art, and so were Rembrandt and Holbein. If the reader has realized the significance of this subtle quality, he will also realize that it may exist in styles which in every other quality are wide asunder.

Mr. Abbey is conspicuous by the possession of this gift; he knows how to wield the magic of the brush so that his painting, apart from its color or form, is eloquent. Without this power, the characterization of Cordelia would not have been as impressive as it is. There is something in the very way her figure and those of Regan and Goneril are painted that makes us realize the absolute division between her and her sisters. The miracle is that mere oil paint should be capable of such power of expression. William Hunt, in his admirable talks on art, says:

"Then the material in which they work is of a nature so impossible! Imagine! You have never tried it? This undertaking to render sunlight, life, air, flowers, with the same tarry, unguent substance which you employ to keep wood from water-soak, or which you avoid for fear of having clothes soiled. For the sign 'Look out for PAINT' is hung up with the same universal conscience and has almost as much power as the sign 'Smallpox here.'"

No doubt many pictures, in spite of other qualities, always keep something of this freshly painted railings effect. But the true painter is he who can transmute the "tarry substance" into something which is in itself a joy to behold. From this question of paint to that of color is but a step. What is a colorist? He may use the most sober hues and yet be one; or, on the contrary, he may employ all the brilliant colors at once and still be one. Probably the least inaccurate definition of a colorist is this: he who so arranges colors that they shall be at once harmonious and effective. A number of sober grays may be put together by one who has no color sense so that they will look merely dull. But a colorist will arrange equally sober grays so that the beauty of their sobriety strikes us at once. But the test of a painter's capacity for harmony is when he comes to deal with strong and even violent colors. A master will place the most glaring hue so that it melts into the general scheme, and although it may dominate the picture, it is never isolated. Many painters use bright colors and yet do not produce that glowing effect which delights us in some works. Their colors seem hard and stiff; there is no reaction one upon another. But in such a work as the matchless "Concert," by Giorgione, in the Louvre, every color seems to belong to and be in harmony with every other, so that from top to bottom the pictures glows as with golden sunlight. Mr. Abbey is too fond of accentuating individual patches of color to ever reach the supreme point of the art achieved by Giorgione and Titian. Nevertheless, in his own way, he is a remarkable colorist; for it seems an easy thing for him to assemble together all the colors which usually are looked upon as jarring, and then by the alchemy of his art turn them into harmony.

This was notably the case in the picture of *Hamlet*, where, surrounded by red, dull green, and black, a purple flashed out with startling daring and success. It was in the background of this picture, which represents the King and Queen looking on at the play, that Mr. Abbey perhaps nearest approached to the ideal of coloring—that is, the perfect union of colors which presents to the eye a resplendent effect without the prominence of any particular hue. In this background green, red and black were welded into a perfectly satisfactory harmony. It would be quite unjust to say that Mr. Abbey's pictures were anything but extremely harmonious; yet it is the salience of the colors that first strikes us, and after we have realized their brightness we recognize their harmony. The opposite is the care with the great Venetians. We are struck by the harmony first and the brightness of the colors afterwards.

When Mr. Abbey turned his attention from black and white to painting, he began a no less ambitious work than the decoration of a room in the Boston Library. The subject chosen, that of the Holy Grail, was one admirably adapted to the artist's special faculty of illustration— using this word in the special sense referred to at the beginning of this article. Of the finished half of the decorations the present writer can only judge from photographs, never having seen the originals, though he has seen the second half of the series now awaiting the finishing-touches in the artist's studio. This great series of wall-paintings reveals qualities of design which the artist had not made use of before he embarked on this work. There is a largeness of style combined with the wealth of detail that is new. This breadth of style, which, it may be said, might have been pushed still further without hurt, is indeed the essential quality of wall-decoration. Foremost among the modern masters of this noble branch of art stands Puvis de Chavannes, whose death in the plenitude of his powers European art deplores. The whole secret of the art of this great man, as he has told us himself, consists in elimination. In some autobiographical notes he has said, in reference to the difference between his system of wall-decoration and that usually practiced in France:

"I have striven that every gesture should express something, and that the color, instead of contrasting, as in the past, with the whiteness of its frame, should harmonize with it. Instead of making holes in the wall, as do pictures which are too much forced, I have contented myself with simply decorating it."

Perhaps when Mr. Abbey undertakes another scheme of wall-decoration he will add still greater severity to his style; if he does, we need not fear that he will do so at the sacrifice of charm. In the designs of the Holy Grail decorations one cannot help being struck with the wonderful felicity and appropriateness of the artist's invention. What could be happier in its arrangement than the first of the series, where the kneeling nun holds up the baby Galahad before the angel bearing the Grail? The design of this angel is of the greatest beauty; in no other single figure has the artist exceeded the grace and felicity of arrangement of this "divine bird." The angel floats in the air; the bottom of its long white drapery is supported by fluttering doves, while the grate wings, seen only in part, make an aureole to this bearer of the Hold Grail. Throughout this series Mr. Abbey has been at enormous pains to hunt up archæological details, and has laid the round-arched architecture of southern France under contribution. If contact with actual monuments and relics of the past stimulates the painter's imagination, let him be as learned as he pleases. But those who look on painting as a language of the emotions, and not as a means of conveying information as to actual things, will pay more attention to the striking effect produced by the assemblage of upright lances of the knights as they kneel in the chapel than to the date of the round arches. It must not be supposed for a moment that Mr. Abbey attaches any undue importance to the learned details of his work; he is much too sounds a critic and true an artist to make any confusion between the flesh and the spirit of a picture. Mr. Abbey is by nature a scholar; he has a wide and at the same time a minute acquaintance with art, and his taste is of the most catholic description. While he occupies himself with the intricacies of form revealed in the elaborate mediæval dresses he loves to paint, he is keenly alive to the grandeur and severe majesty of Byzantine art.

He can appreciate to the full those glowing Venetian idyls of which the Giorgione "Concert" in the Louvre is the archetype, while he is no less sensitive to the subtleties of a profile by Piero della Francesca. It is always interesting to speculate as to who were the artistic ancestors of a painter. Probably it would not be far wrong to trace many of Mr. Abbey's predilections in form and style to Holbein, Botticelli, and Carpaccio. It is to their love of grace, fancy and exquisite taste that the modern painter is akin, more than to the deeply reflective poetry and passionate inspiration of such men as Michelangelo and Tintoretto. This may be exemplified in the peculiarities of form noticeable in the work of Mr. Abbey. He inclines to thin, supple bodies, and delicate, sensitive faces and hands, rather than to statuesque of monumental ideal of form. His draperies, too, wind and twist into endless graceful folds, and are curious in pattern and rich in material. A heraldic feeling is often present, giving at once a quaintness and decorative charm not easy to describe, but easy to feel. These leanings show that the artist is more in accord with the joyous poetry of the early Renaissance than with the passion of the later part of that period, more in sympathy with the May morning of Benozzo Gozzoli than with the dawn of Giotto or the sunset of Titian. It is without slightest wish to depreciate that these comparisons have been made, but simply with the desire to understand. It is not the business of the writer on art to be a judge who sets up a standard and then condemns all who do not come up to it. Better that the critic should try to enter into the mind of him he writes about. His work of criticism is best accomplished by trying to realize what is the peculiar nature and bent of the mind of the man whose art is under consideration. If the point of view of the artist is truly set forth, the judgement will come of itself. It is in this spirit that the present study of the art of Mr. Abbey has been written, and its work will have been accomplished if the reader by its means may be brought to what De Quincey called the sympathy of comprehension; for this is the true road to the higher sympathy of approbation.

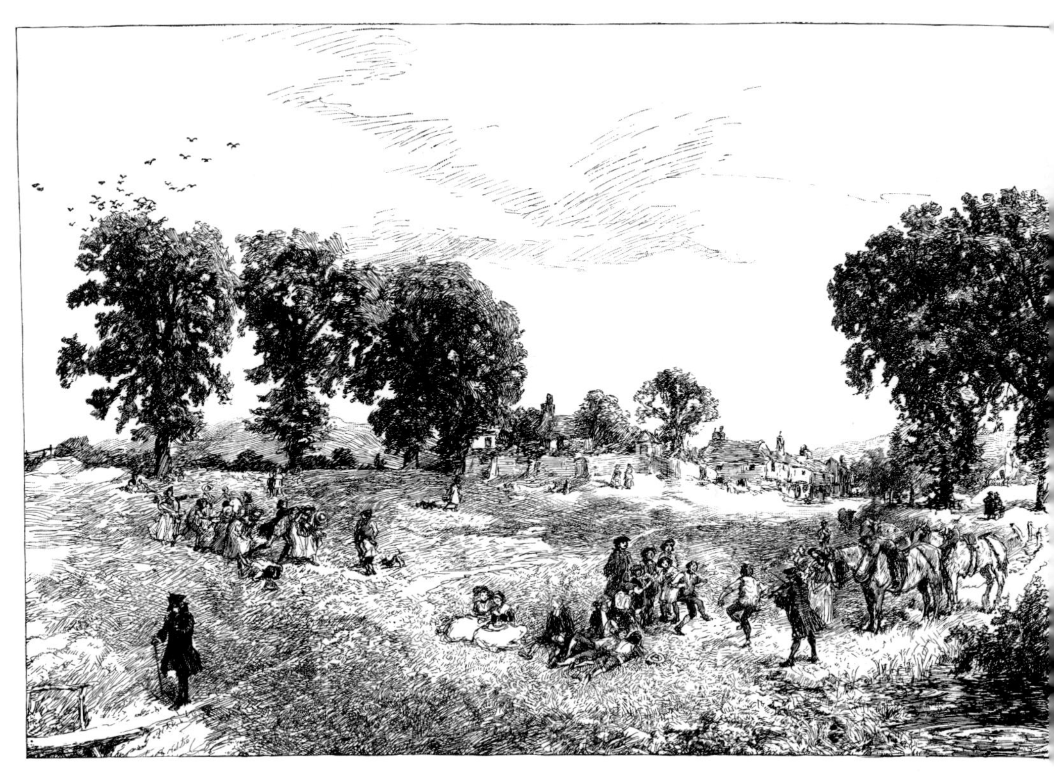

"How often have I loiter'd o'er thy green."

The Deserted Village
Harper & Brothers, October 1902
Originally published in *Harper's New Monthly Magazine*, February 1902

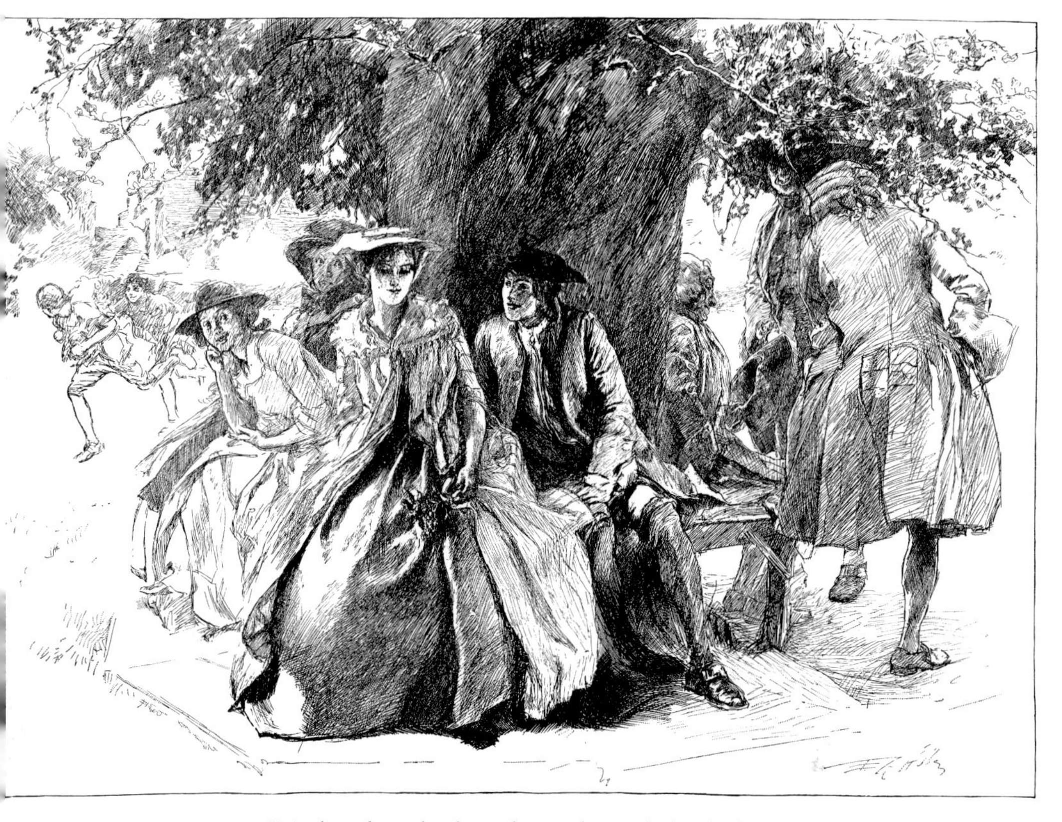

"The hawthorn bush, with seats beneath the shade."

The Deserted Village
Harper & Brothers, October 1902
Originally published in *Harper's New Monthly Magazine*, February 1902

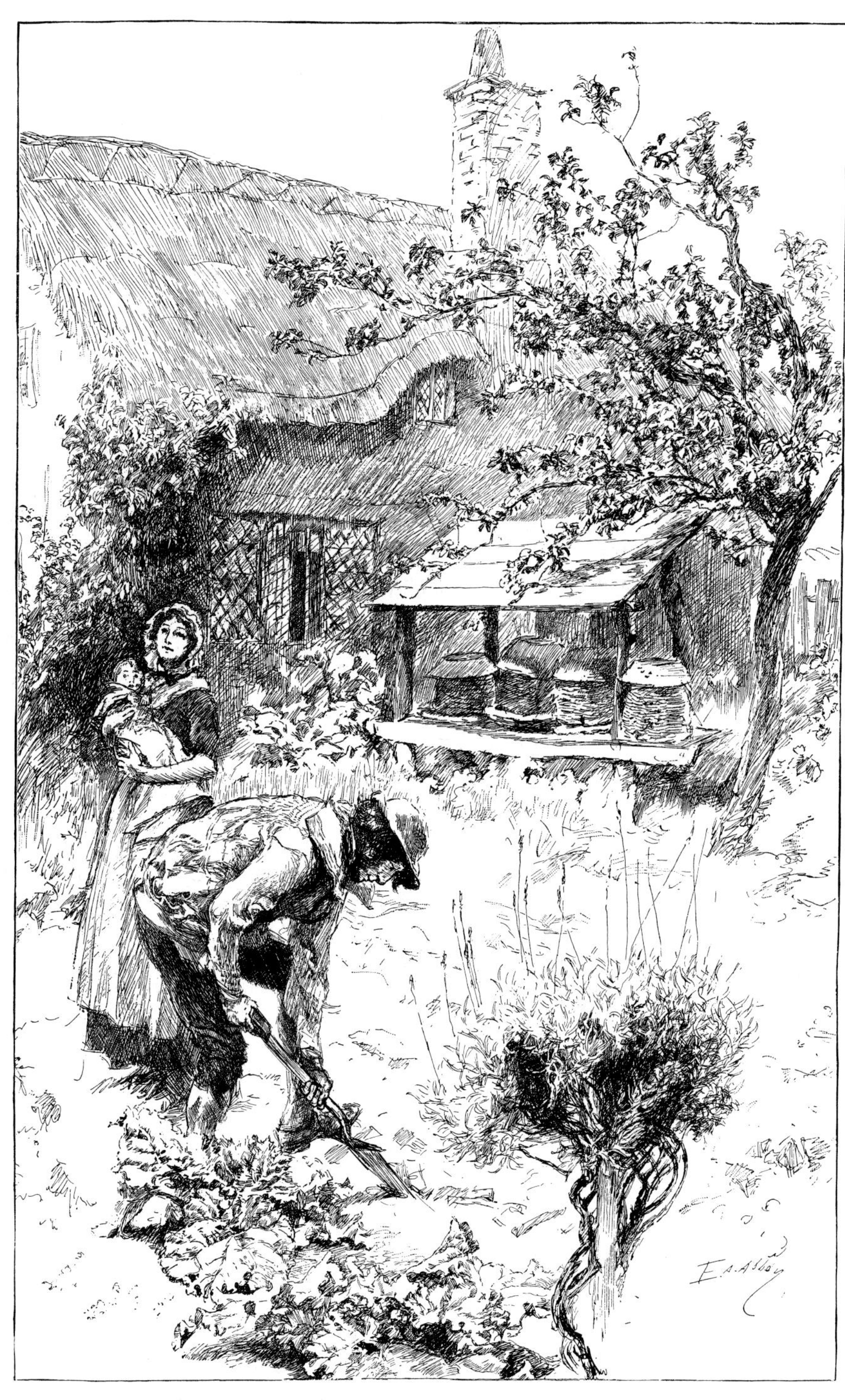

"When every rood of ground maintain'd its man."

The Deserted Village
Harper & Brothers, October 1902
Originally published in *Harper's New Monthly Magazine*, February 1902

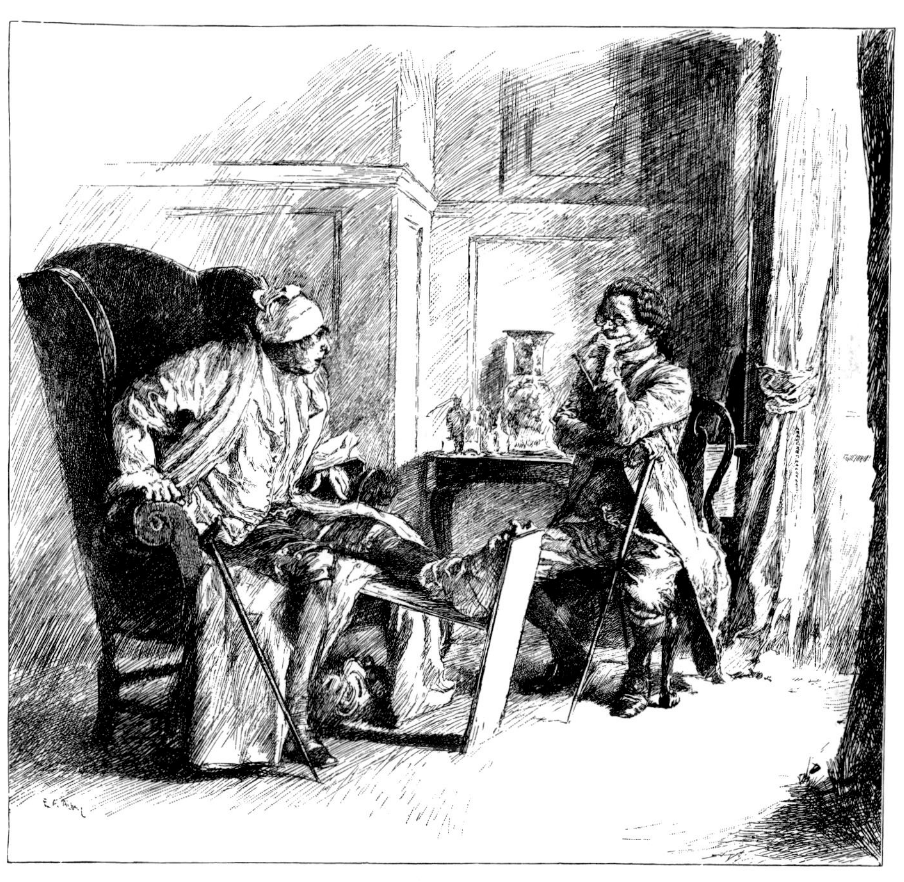

"And every pang that folly pays to pride."

The Deserted Village
Harper & Brothers, October 1902

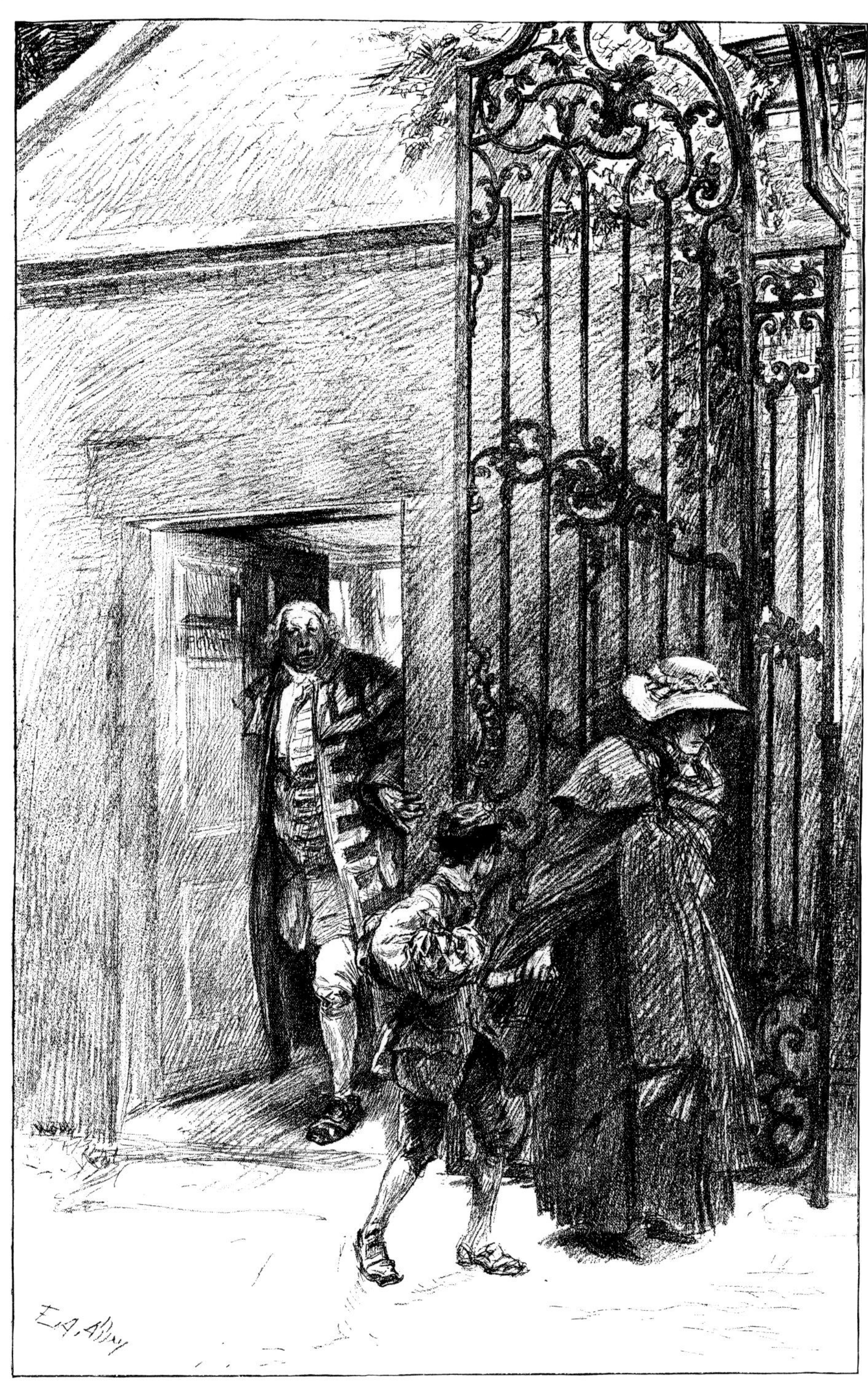

"Nor surly porter stands in guilty state."

The Deserted Village
Harper & Brothers, October 1902
Originally published in *Harper's New Monthly Magazine*, February 1902

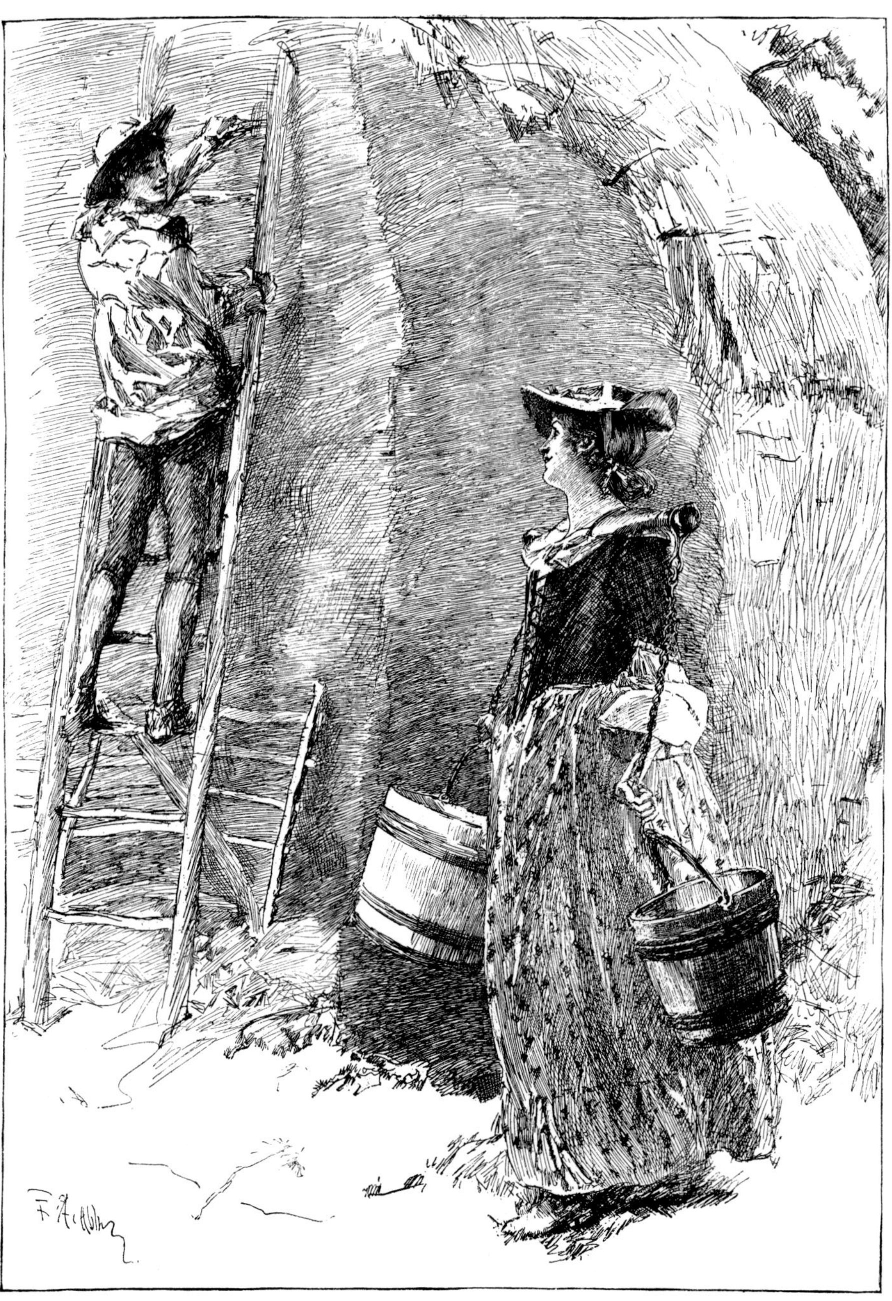

"The swain responsive as the milkmaid sung."

The Deserted Village
Harper & Brothers, October 1902
Originally published in *Harper's New Monthly Magazine*, January 1902

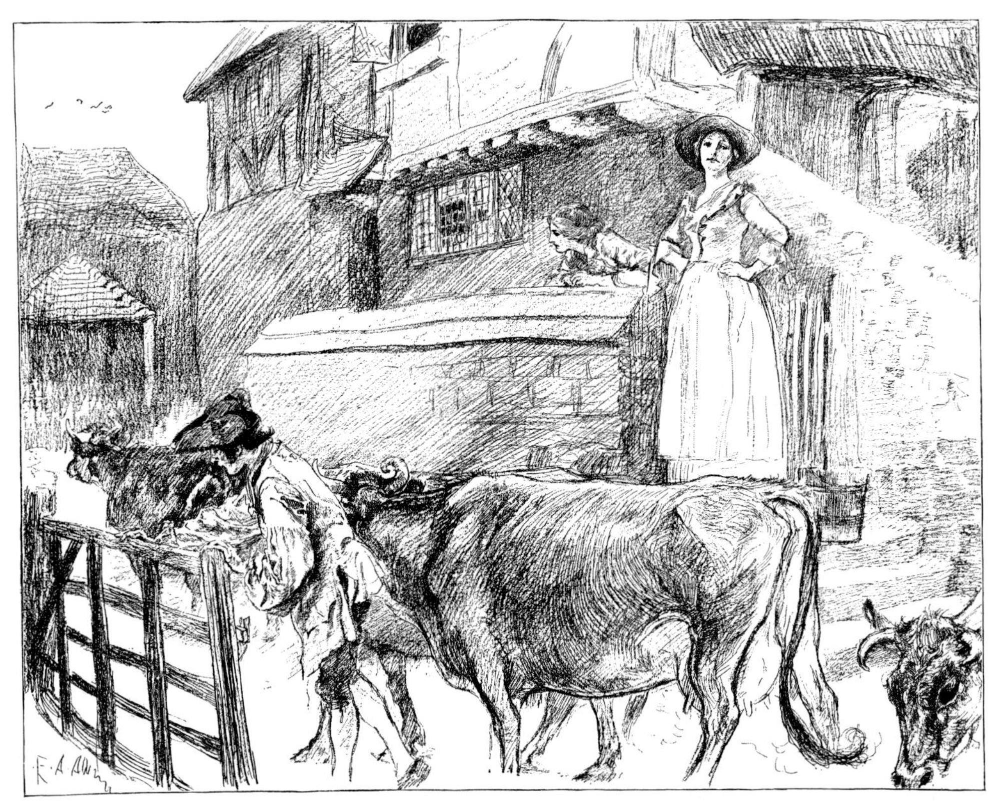

"The sober heard that low'd to meet their young."

The Deserted Village
Harper & Brothers, October 1902
Originally published in *Harper's New Monthly Magazine*, March 1902

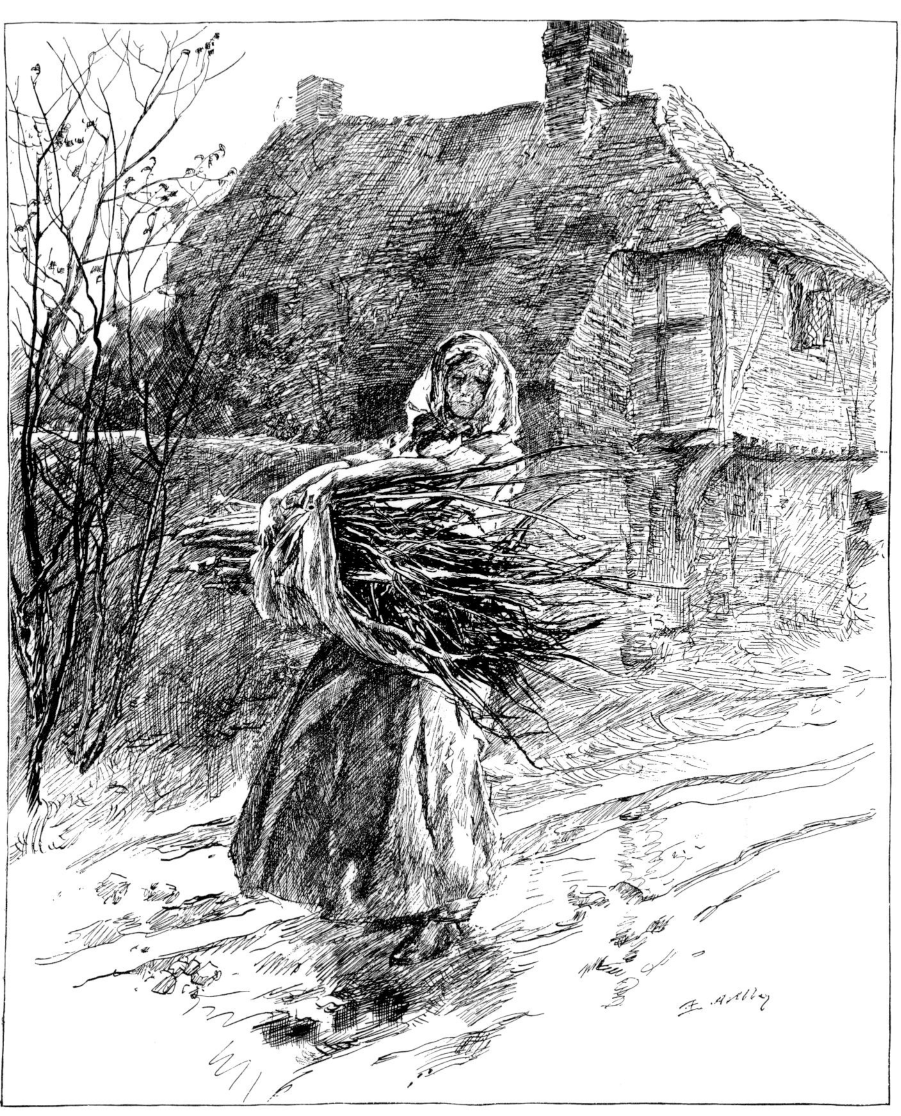

"The sad historian of the pensive plain."

The Deserted Village
Harper & Brothers, October 1902
Originally published in *Harper's New Monthly Magazine*, March 1902

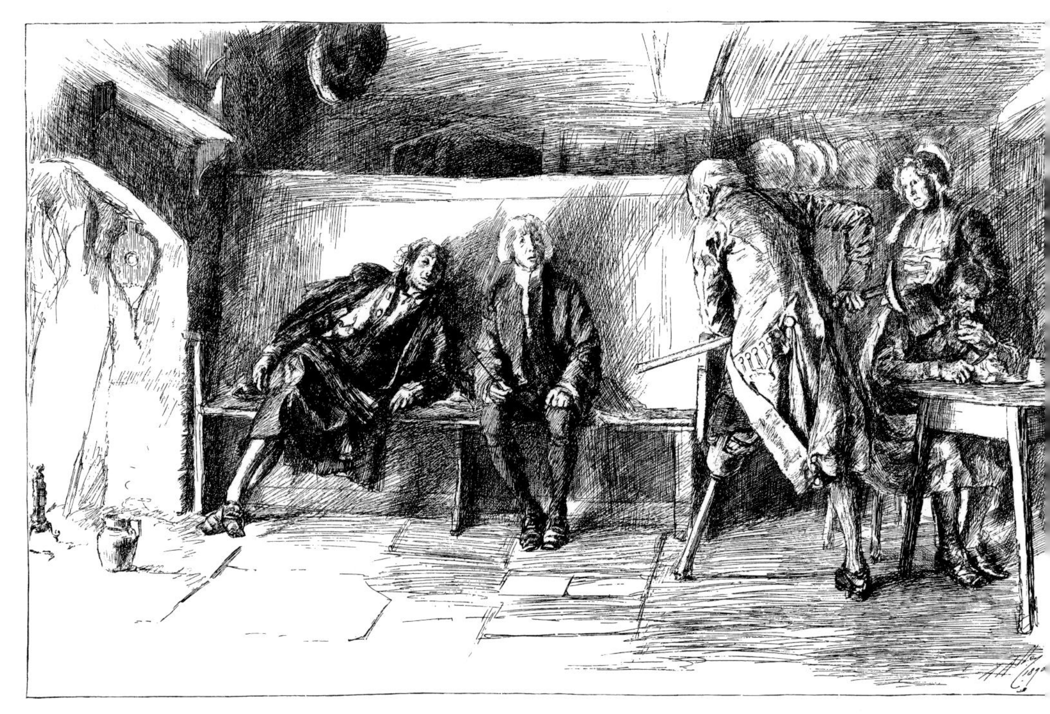

"His house was known to all the vagrant train."

The Deserted Village
Harper & Brothers, October 1902

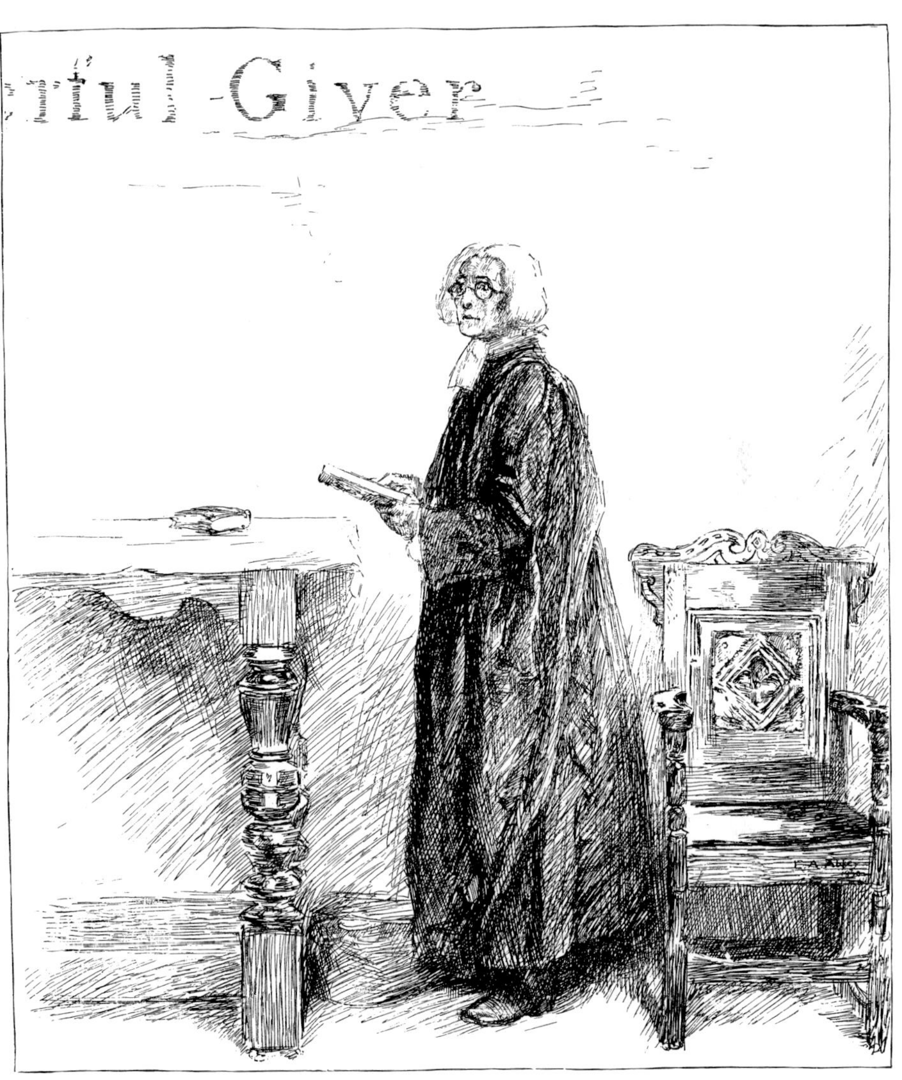

"His looks adorn'd the venerable place."

The Deserted Village
Harper & Brothers, October 1902

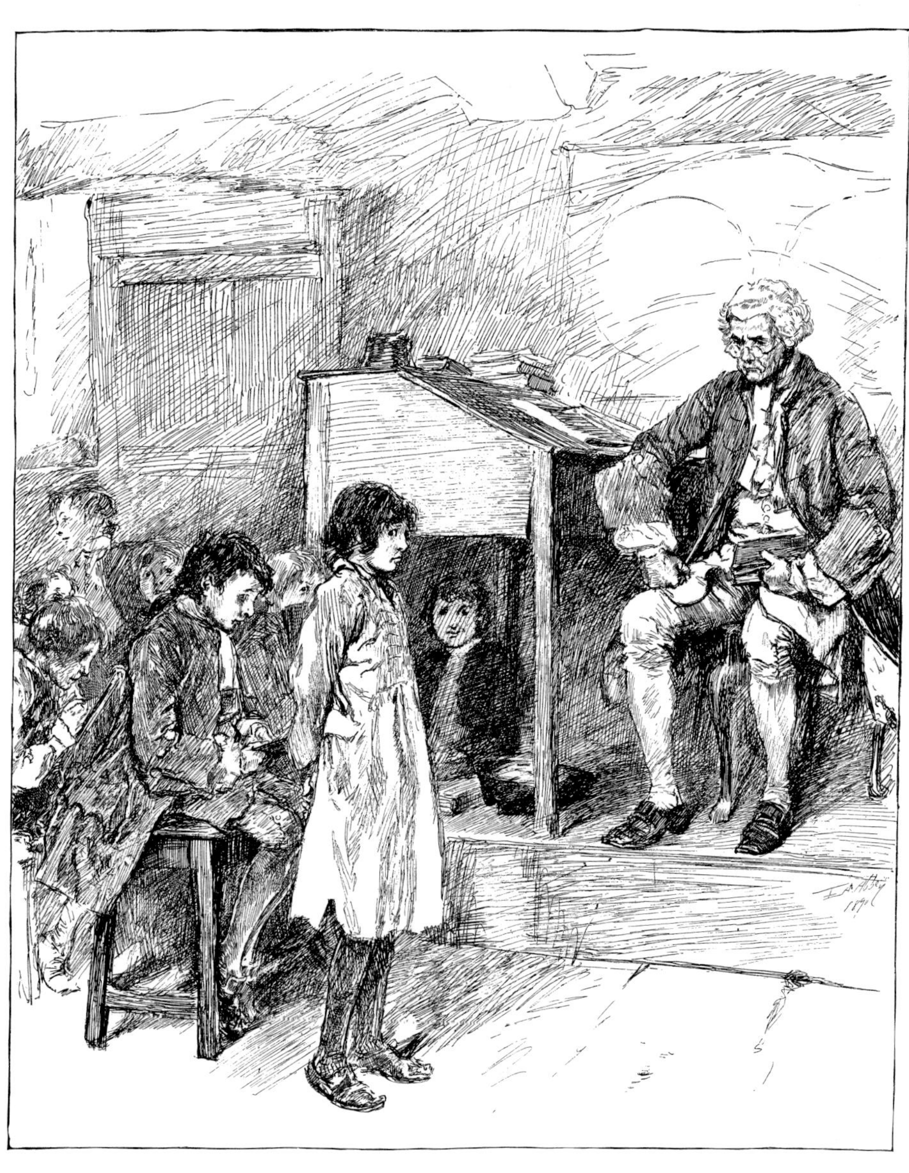

"A man severe he was, and stern to view."

The Deserted Village
Harper & Brothers, October 1902
Originally published in *Harper's New Monthly Magazine*, April 1902

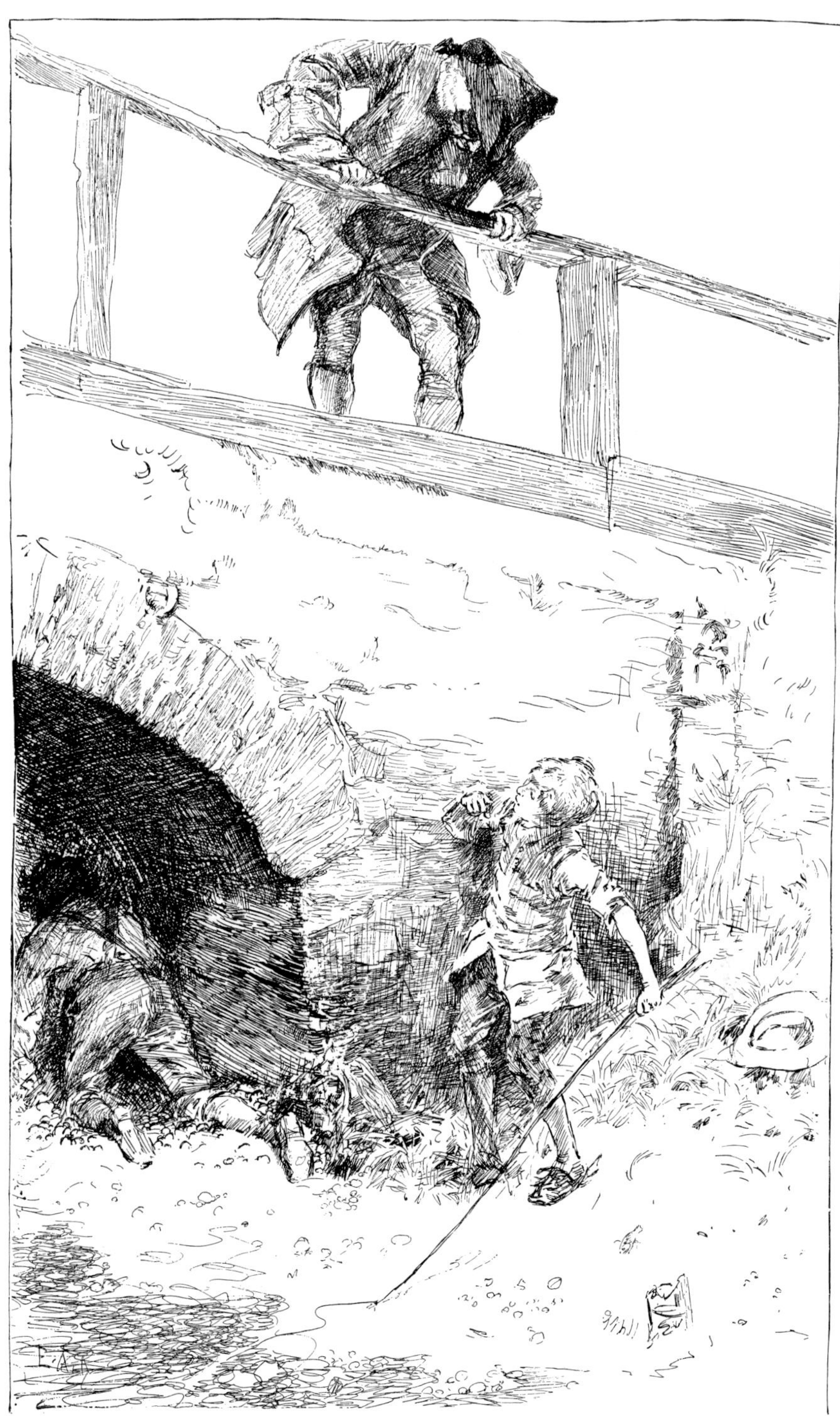

The Deserted Village
Harper & Brothers, October 1902
Originally published in *Harper's New Monthly Magazine*, April 1902

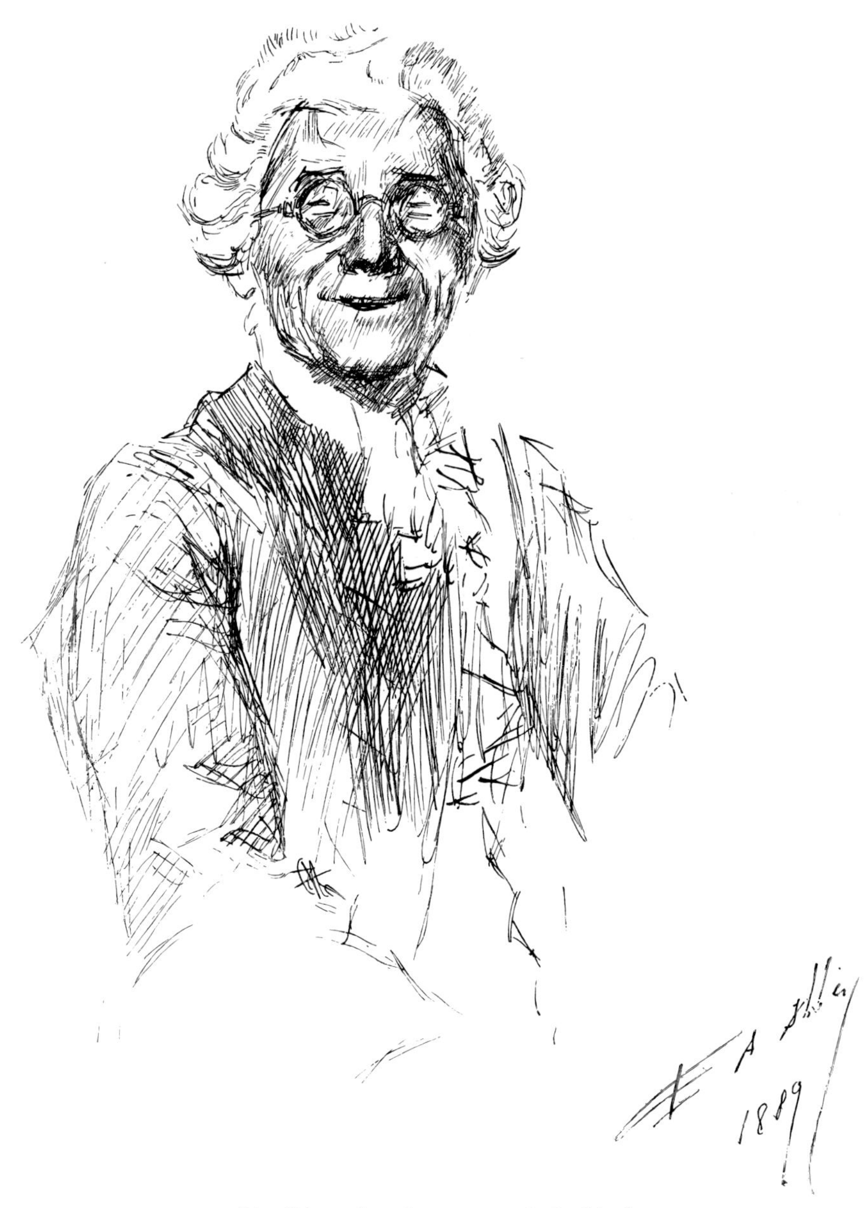

"At all his jokes, for many a joke had he."

The Deserted Village
Harper & Brothers, October 1902

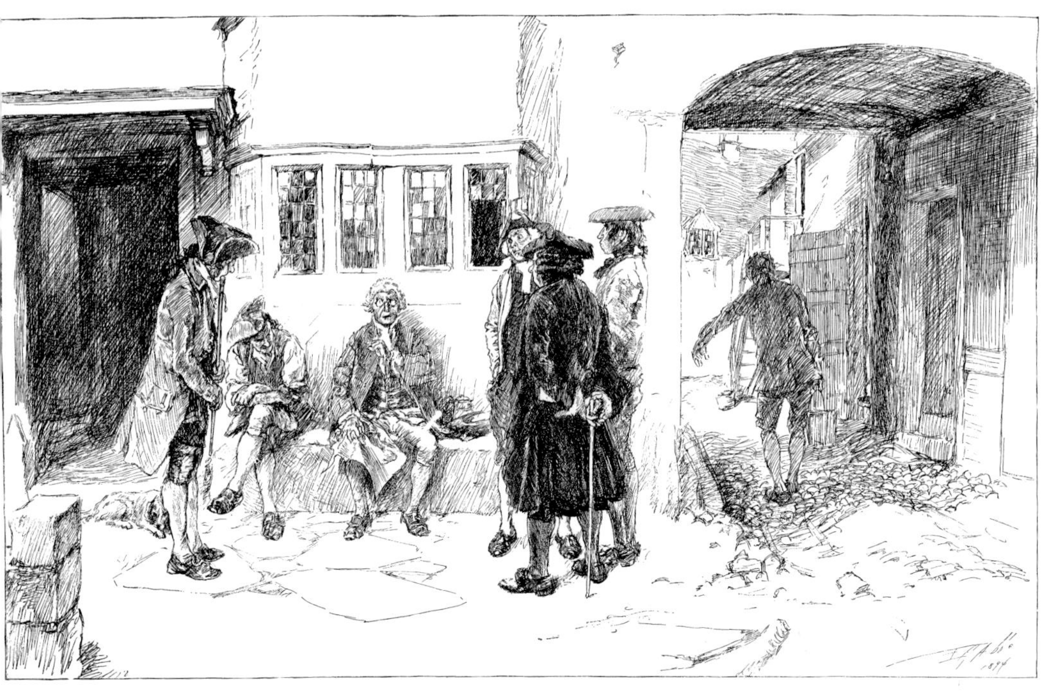

"While words of learned length and thundering sound."

The Deserted Village
Harper & Brothers, October 1902
Originally published in *Harper's New Monthly Magazine*, April 1902

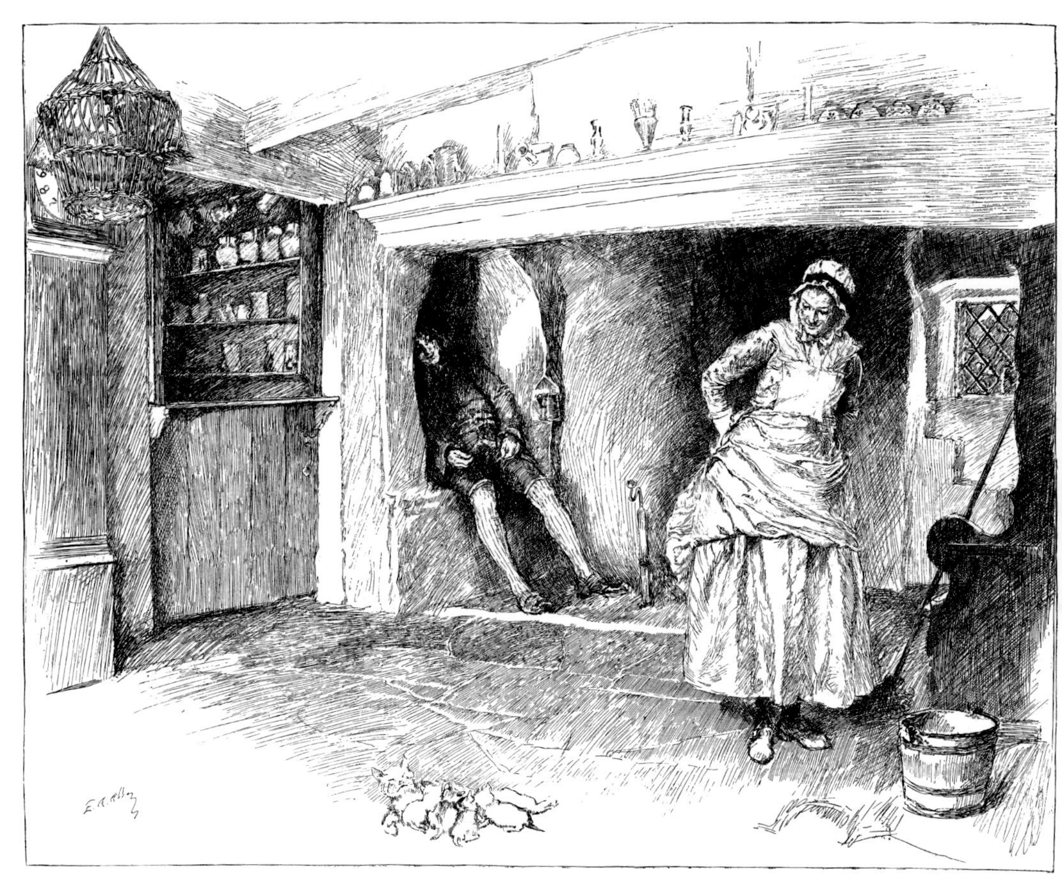

"The parlor splendors of that festive place."

The Deserted Village
Harper & Brothers, October 1902
Originally published in *Harper's New Monthly Magazine*, May 1902

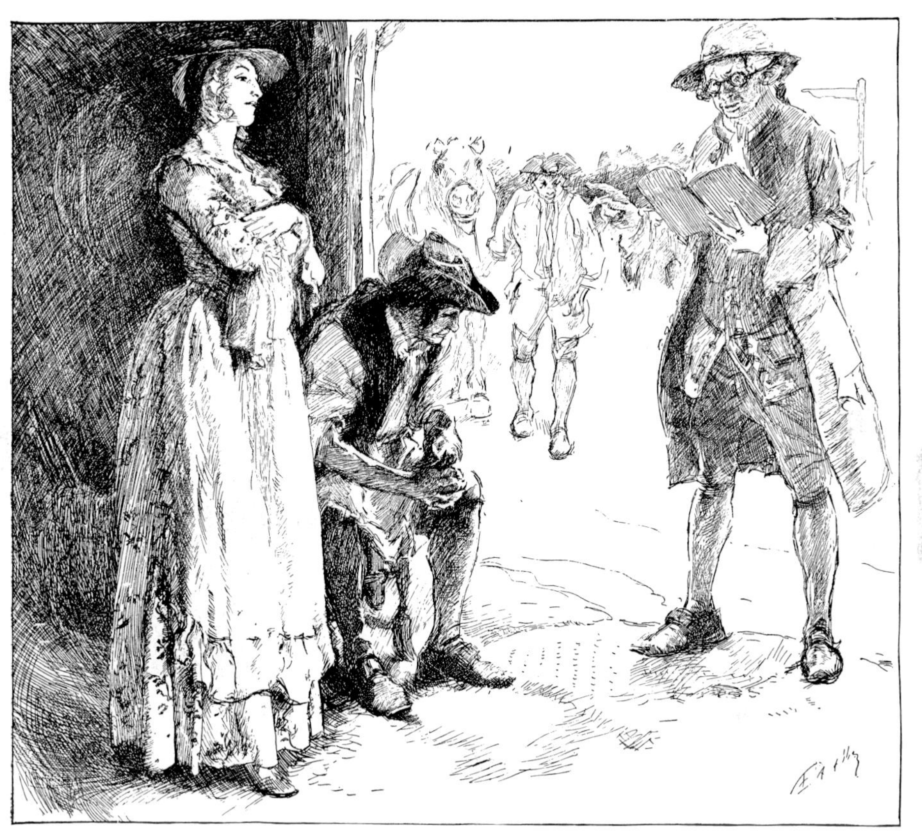

"Relax his ponderous strength, and lean to hear."

The Deserted Village
Harper & Brothers, October 1902
Originally published in *Harper's New Monthly Magazine*, May 1902

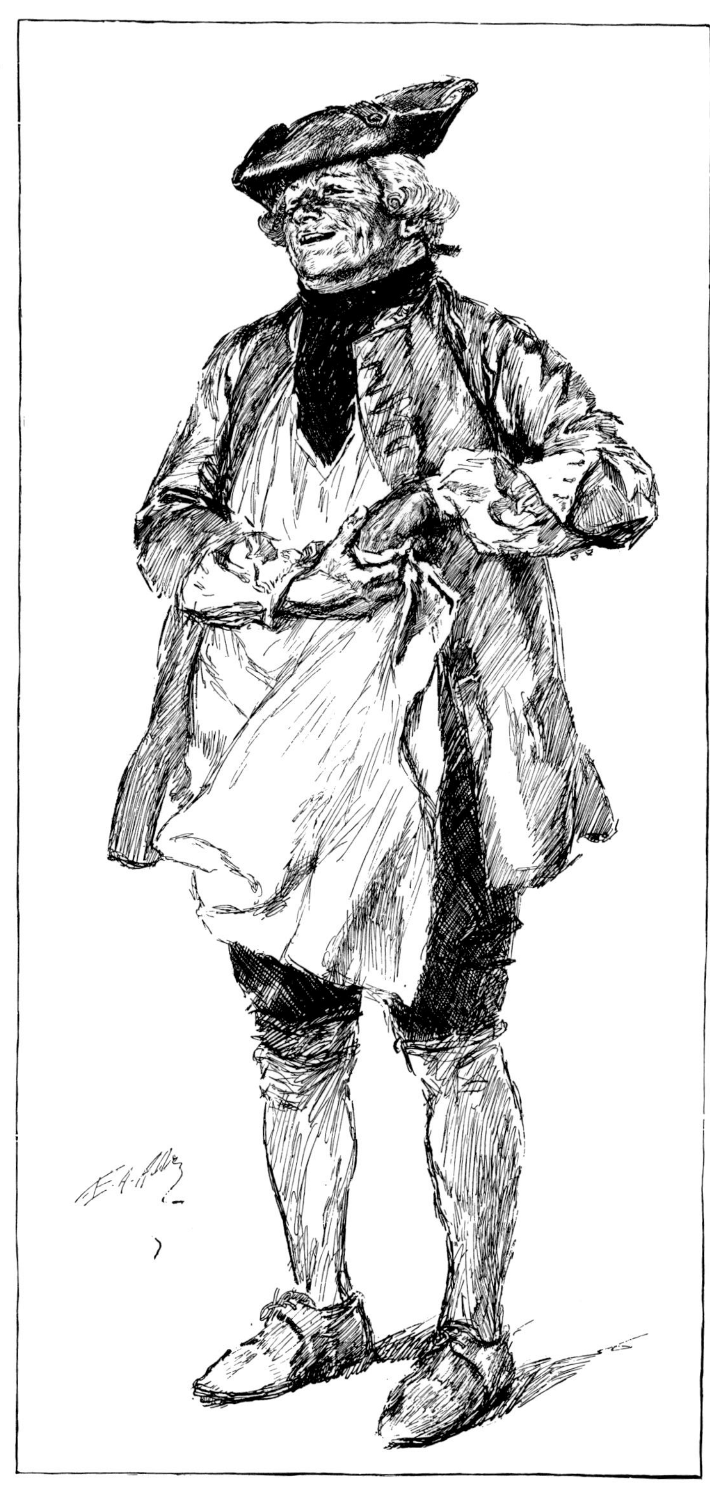

"The host himself no longer shall be found."

The Deserted Village
Harper & Brothers, October 1902

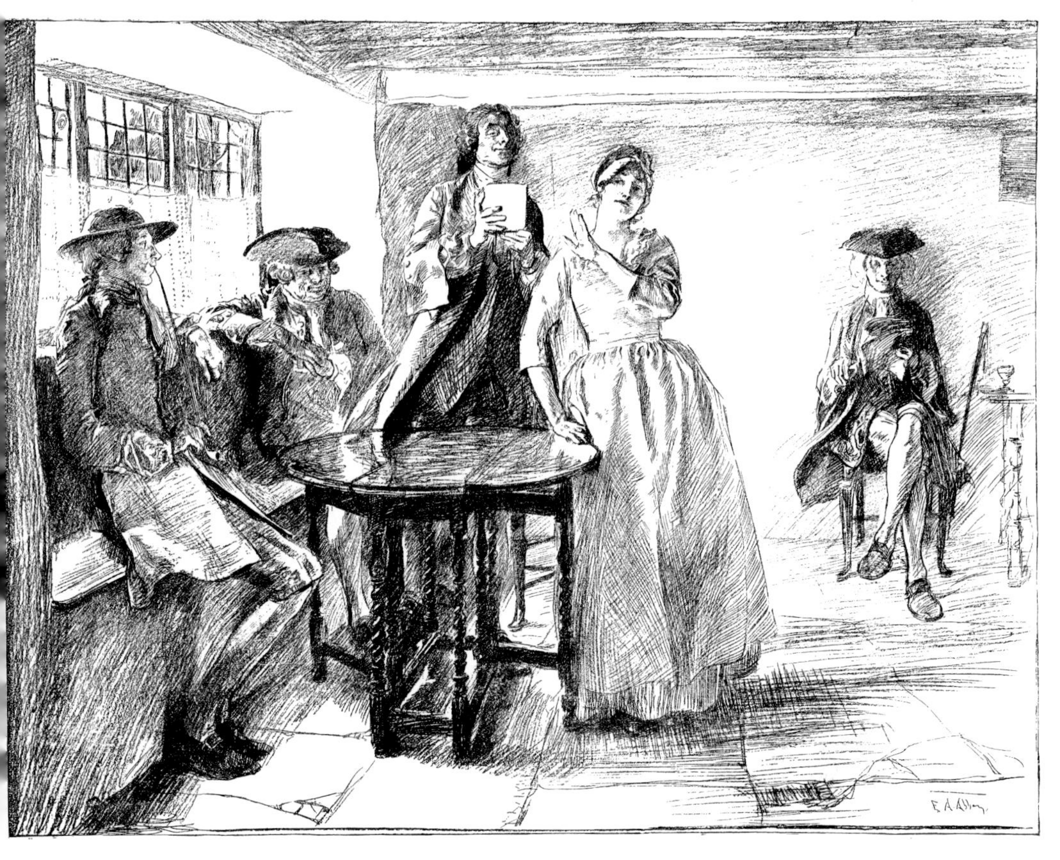

"Nor the coy maid, half willing to be prest."

The Deserted Village
Harper & Brothers, October 1902
Originally published in *Harper's New Monthly Magazine*, May 1902

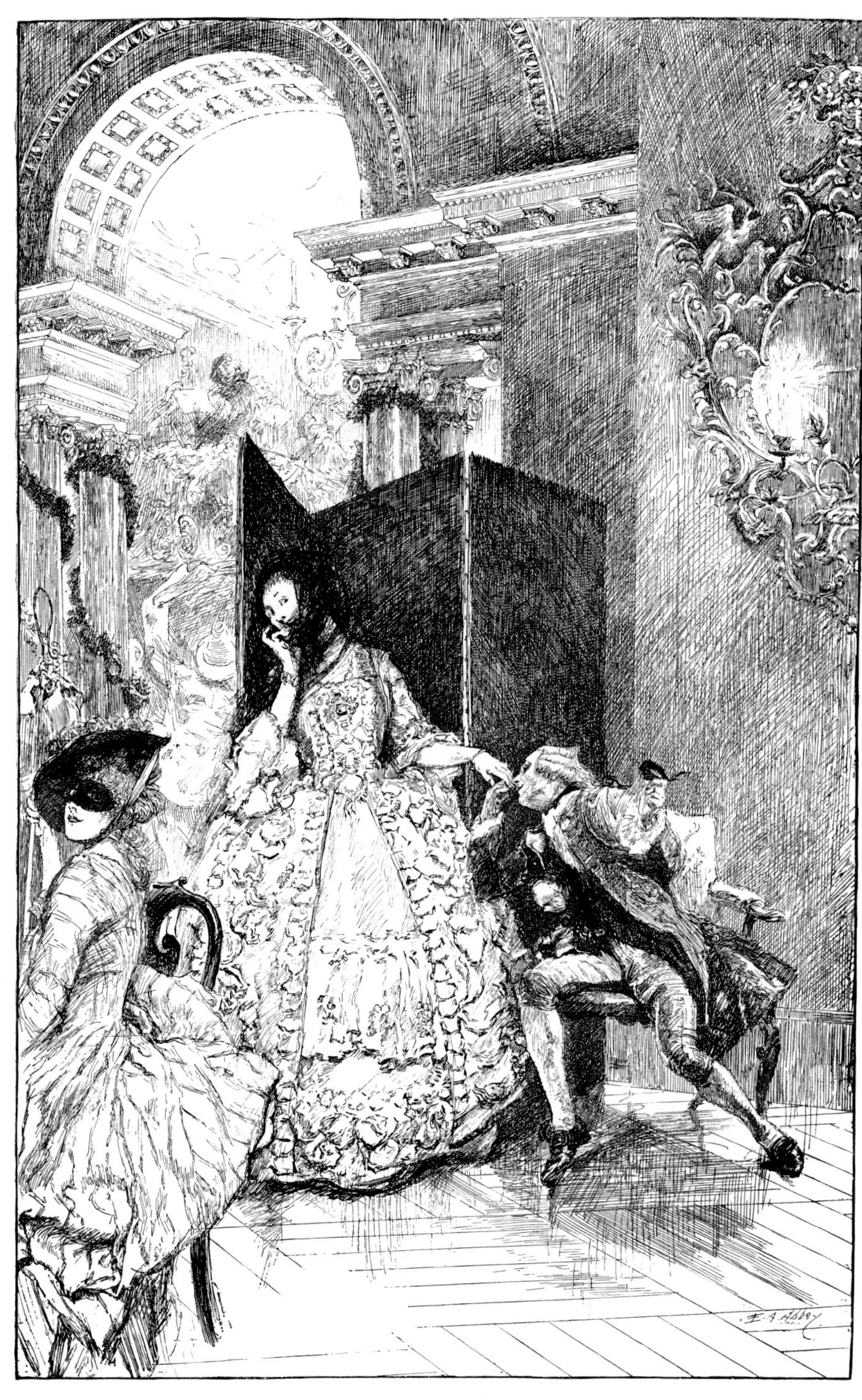

"But the long pomp, the midnight masquerade,
With all the freaks of wanton wealth arrayed."

The Deserted Village
Harper & Brothers, October 1902
Originally published in *Harper's New Monthly Magazine*, June 1902

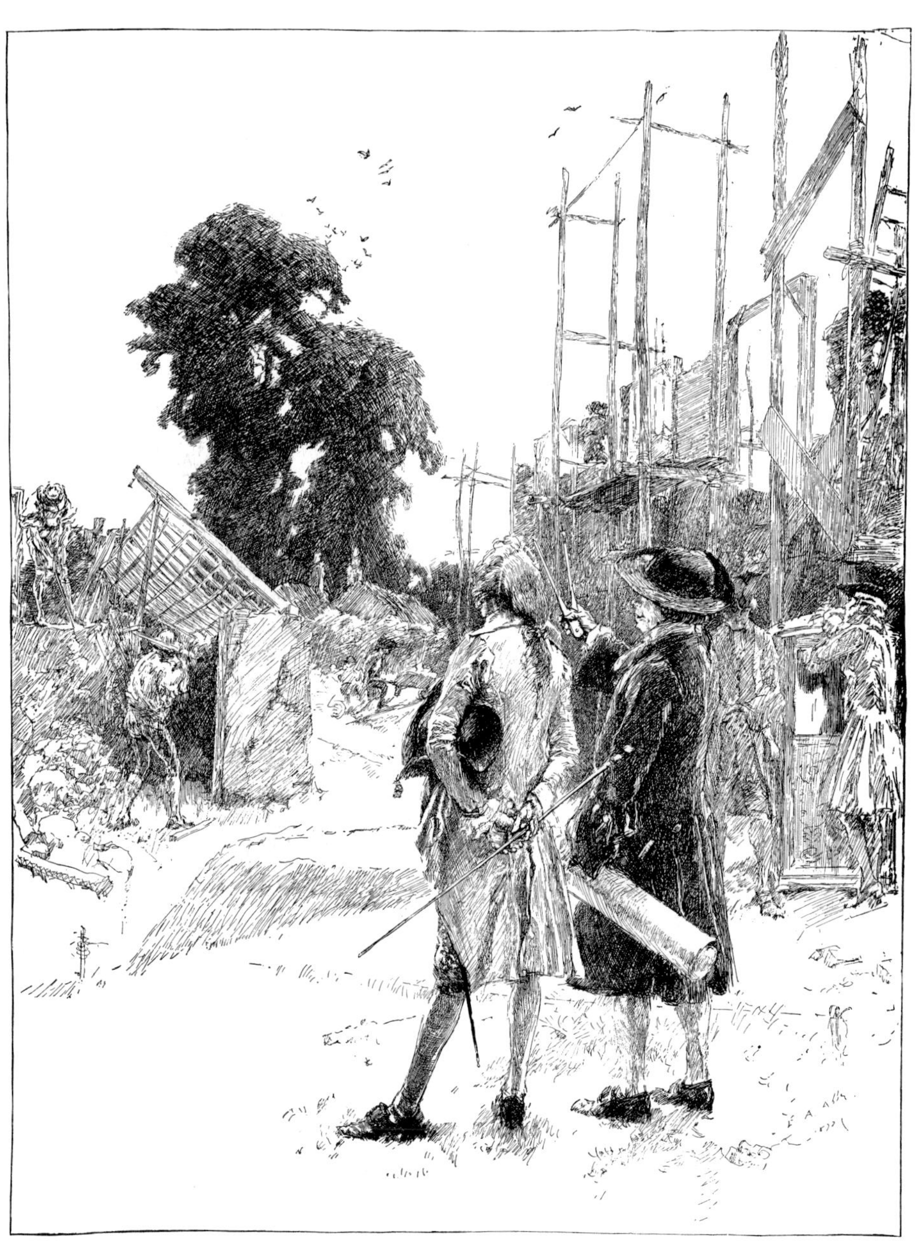

The Deserted Village
Harper & Brothers, October 1902
Originally published in *Harper's New Monthly Magazine*, June 1902

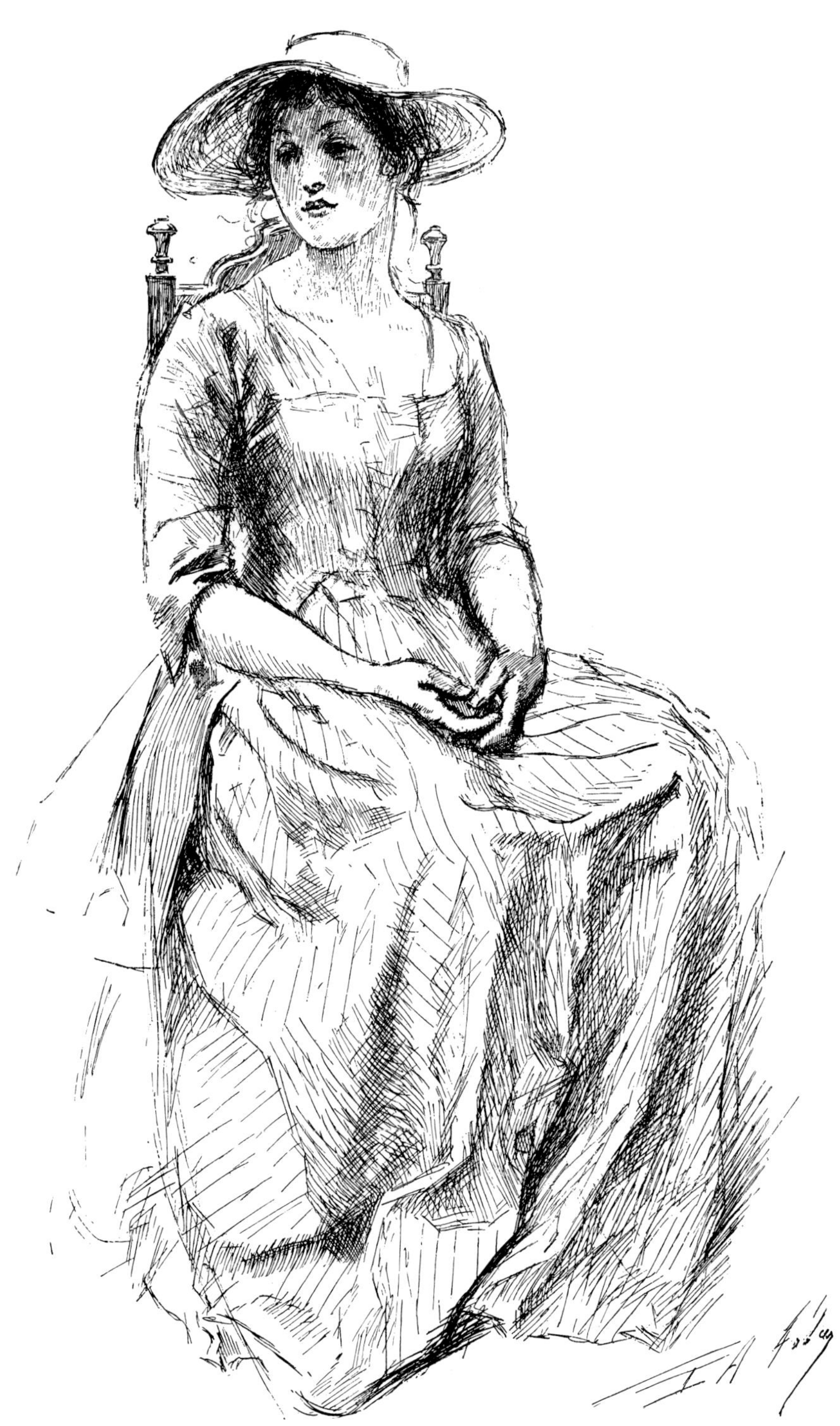

The Deserted Village
Harper & Brothers, October 1902

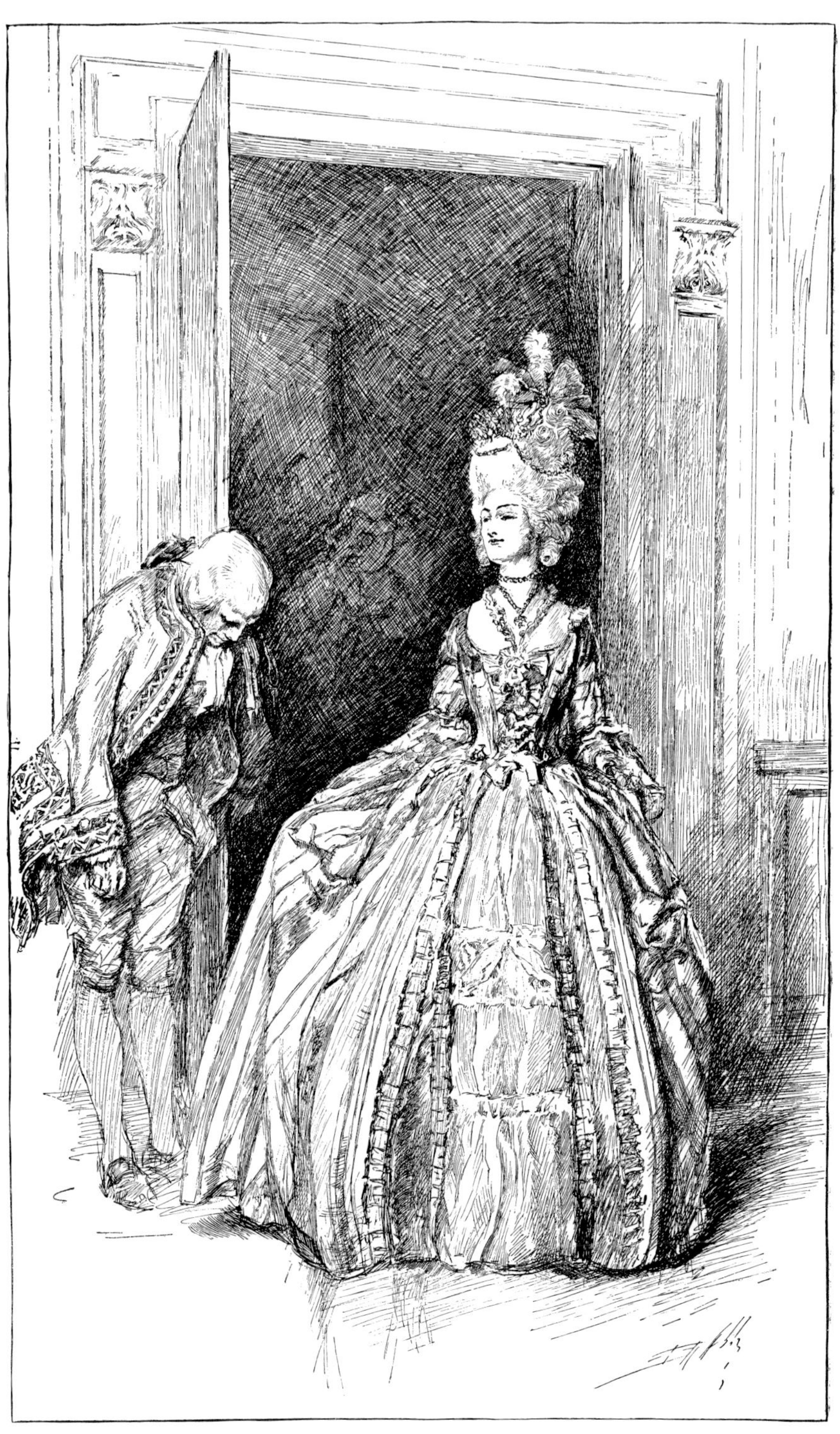

"She then shines forth, solicitous to bless,
In all the glaring impotence of dress."

The Deserted Village
Harper & Brothers, October 1902
Originally published in *Harper's New Monthly Magazine*, June 1902

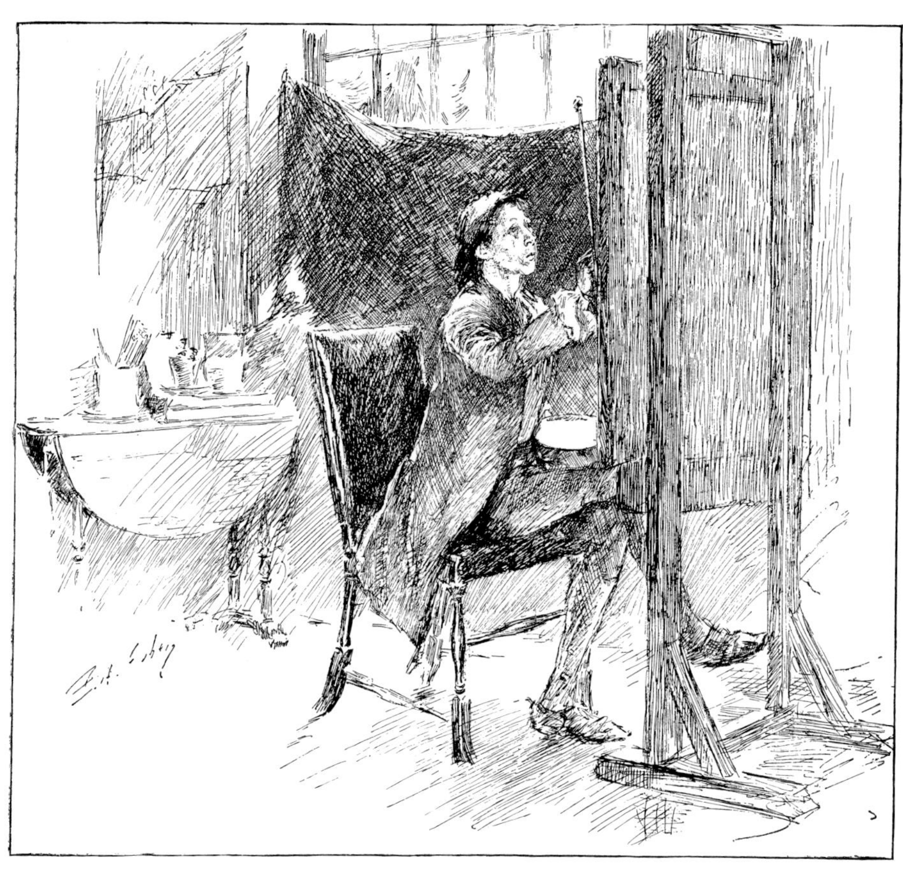

"There the pale artist plies the sickly trade."

The Deserted Village
Harper & Brothers, October 1902
Originally published in *Harper's New Monthly Magazine*, July 1902

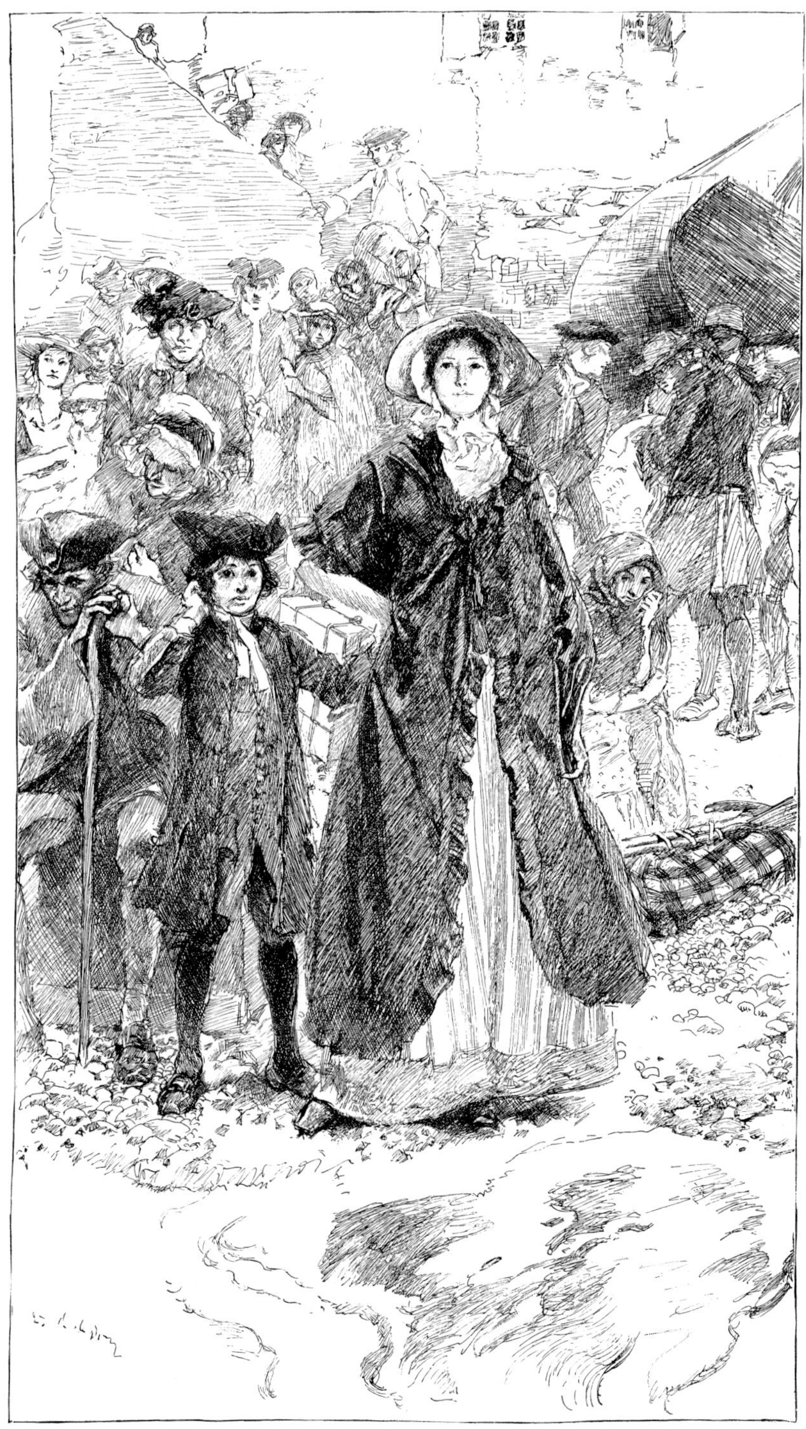

"Downward they move — A melancholy band —"

The Deserted Village
Harper & Brothers, October 1902
Originally published in *Harper's New Monthly Magazine*, August 1902

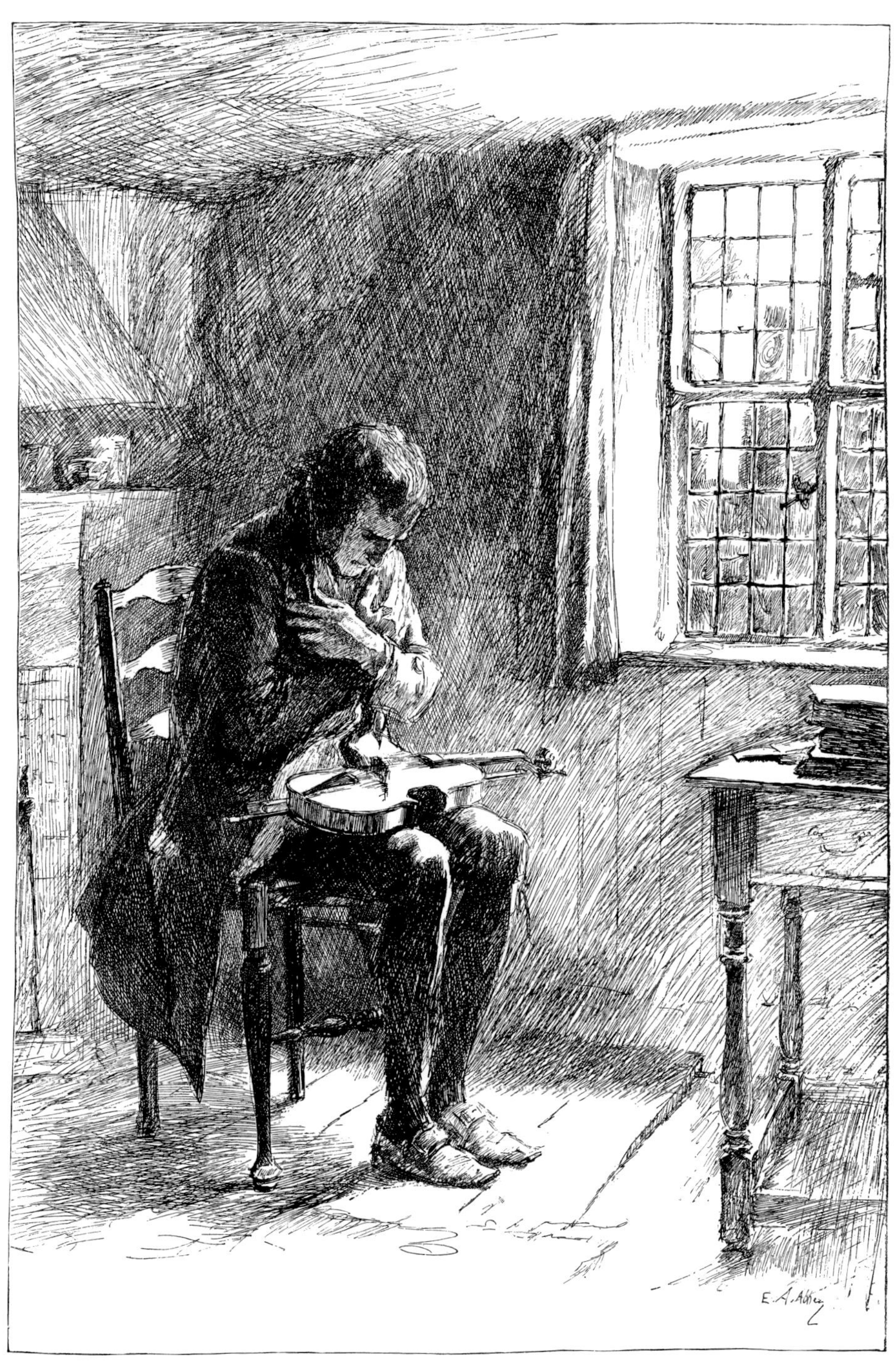

"Thou found'st me poor at first, and keep'st me so."

The Deserted Village
Harper & Brothers, October 1902
Originally published in *Harper's New Monthly Magazine*, August 1902

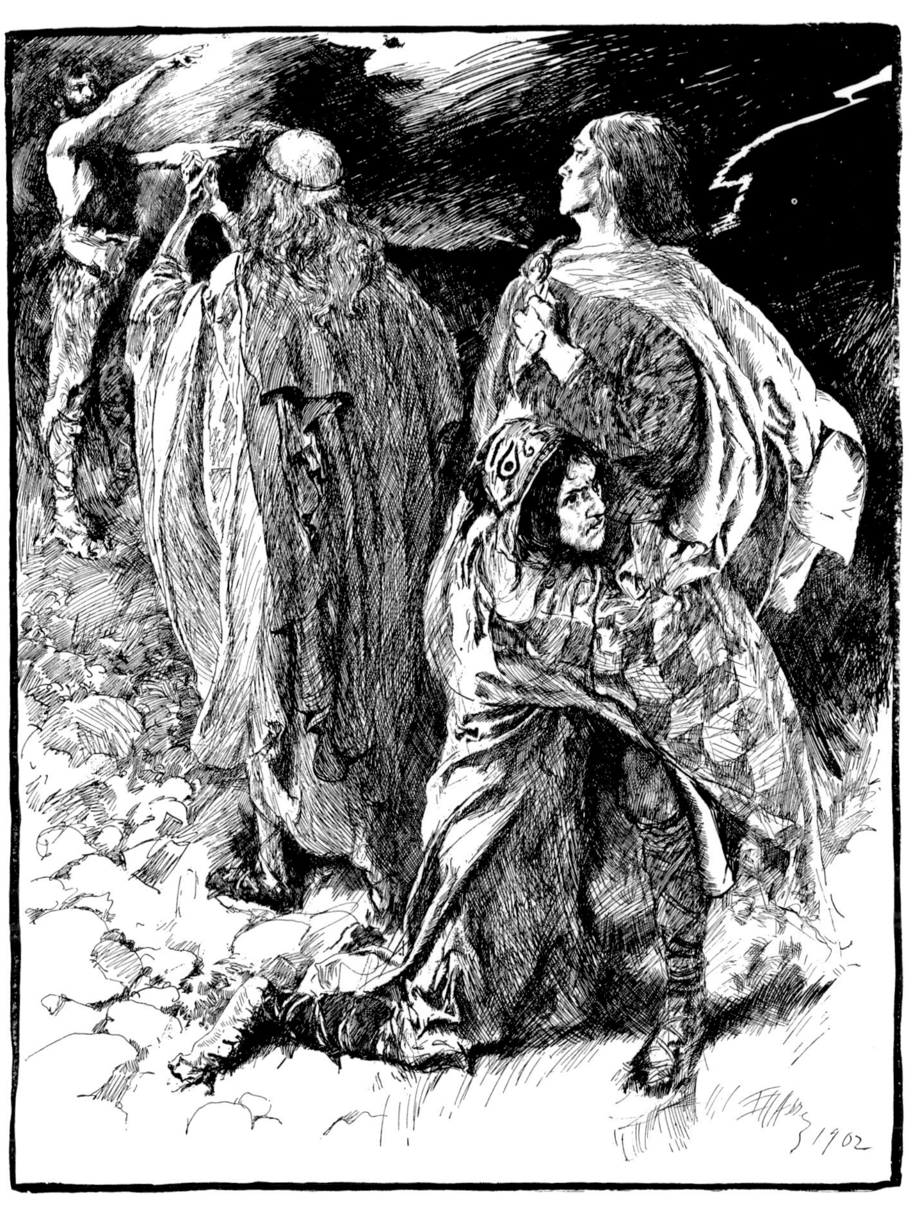

Harper's Monthly Magazine, December 1902
"King Lear"
Act III., Scene IV. — Lear, Kent, Fool and Edgar

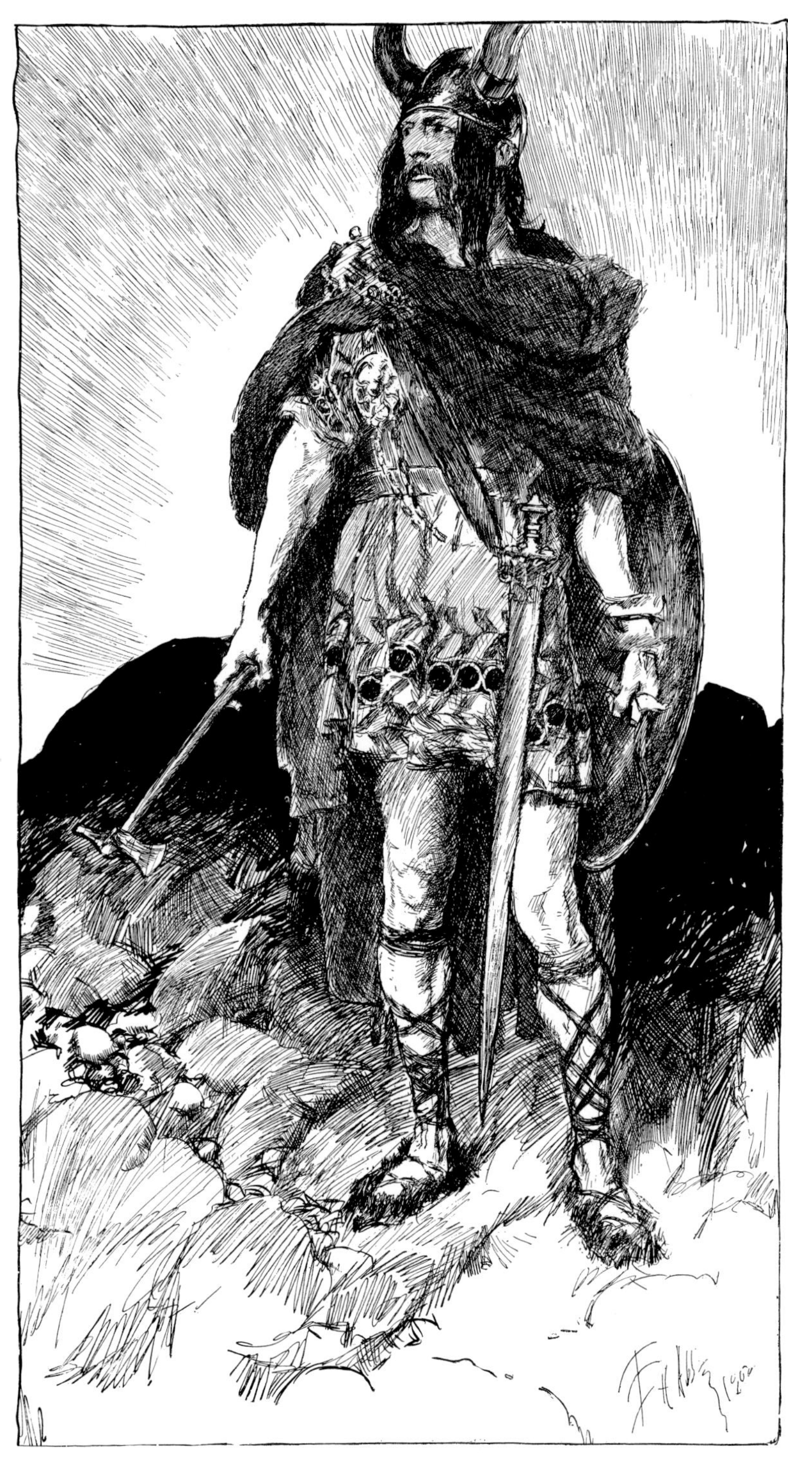

Harper's Monthly Magazine, December 1902
"King Lear"
Act V., Scene III. — Edgar, Armed

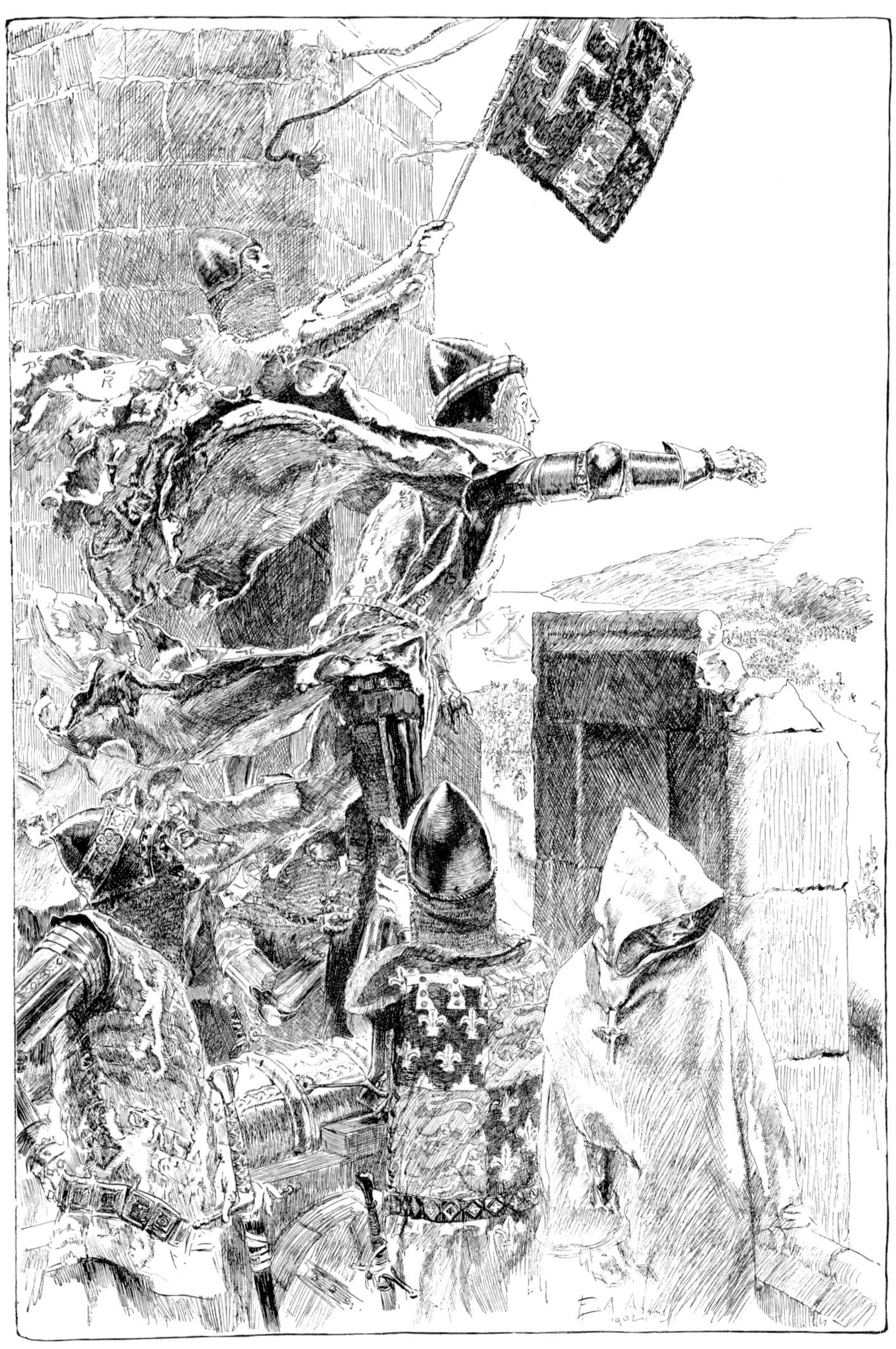

Harper's Monthly Magazine, March 1903
"Richard II."
Act III., Scene III. — The King on the wall of Flint Castle.

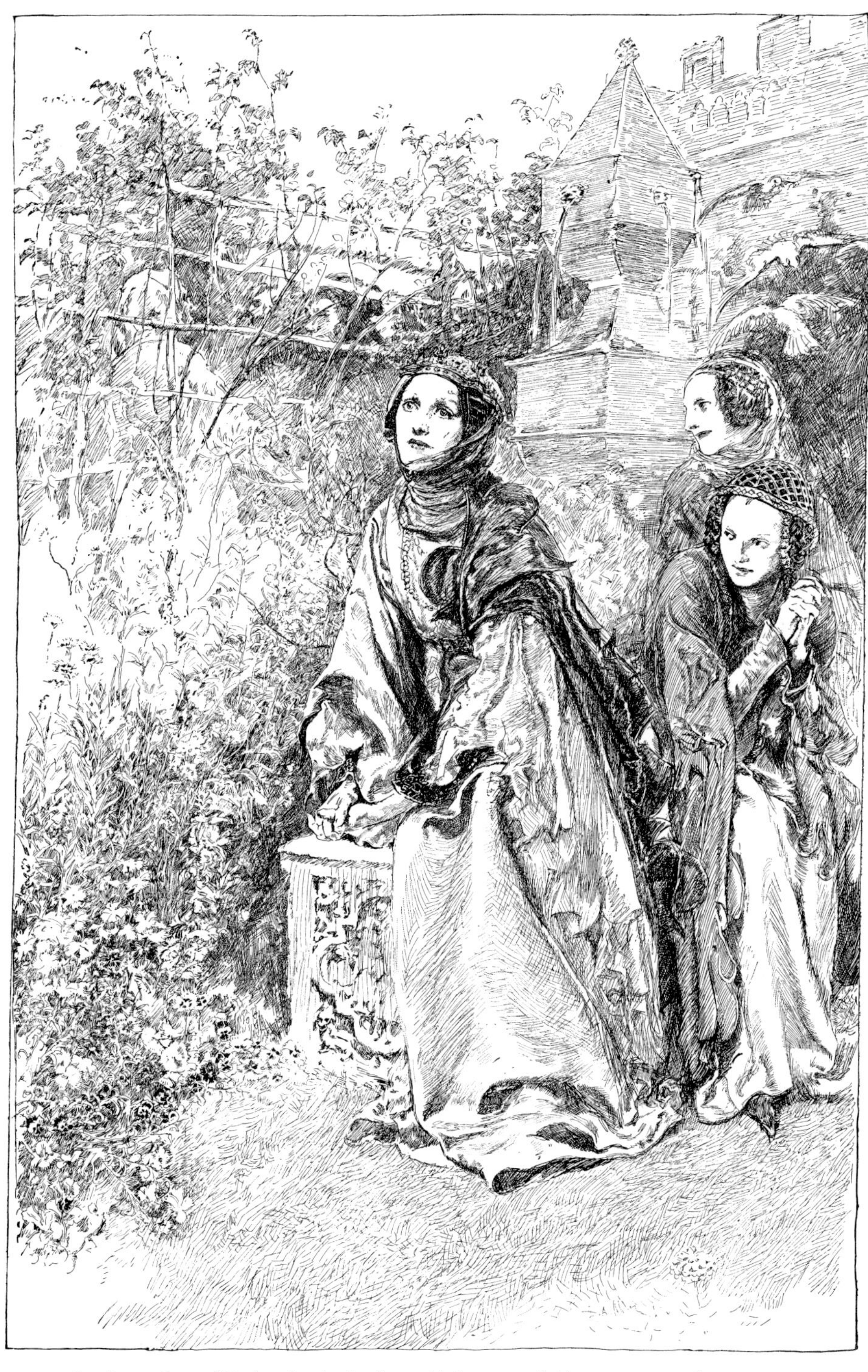

Gardener. "…and Bolingbroke hath seiz'd the wasteful king. — O! what pity is it.
Hat he had not so trimm'd and dress'd his land, as we this garden."

Harper's Monthly Magazine, March 1903
"Richard II."
Act III., Scene IV. — Langley. The Duke of York's garden.

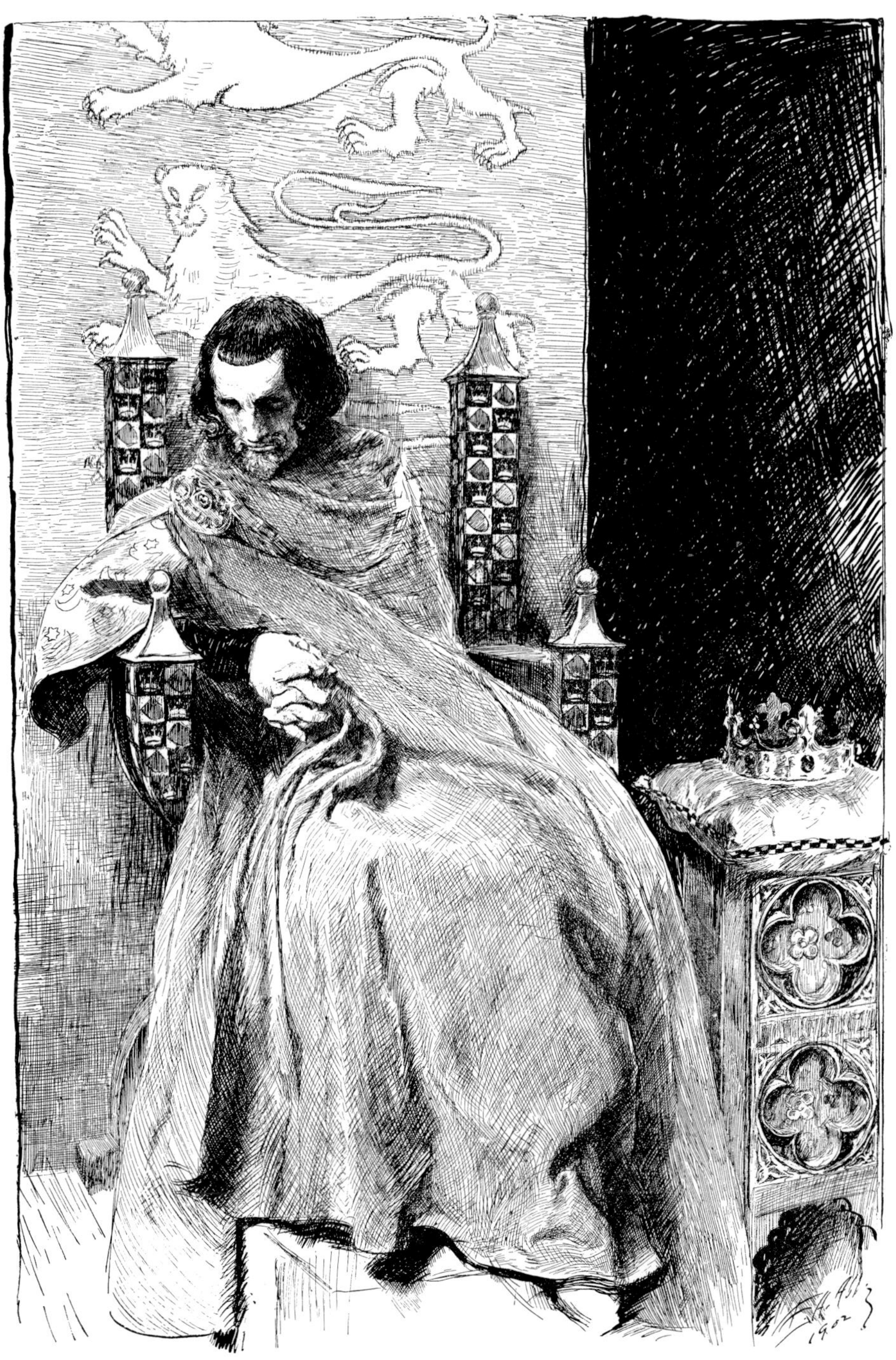

Harper's Monthly Magazine, May 1903
"King John"

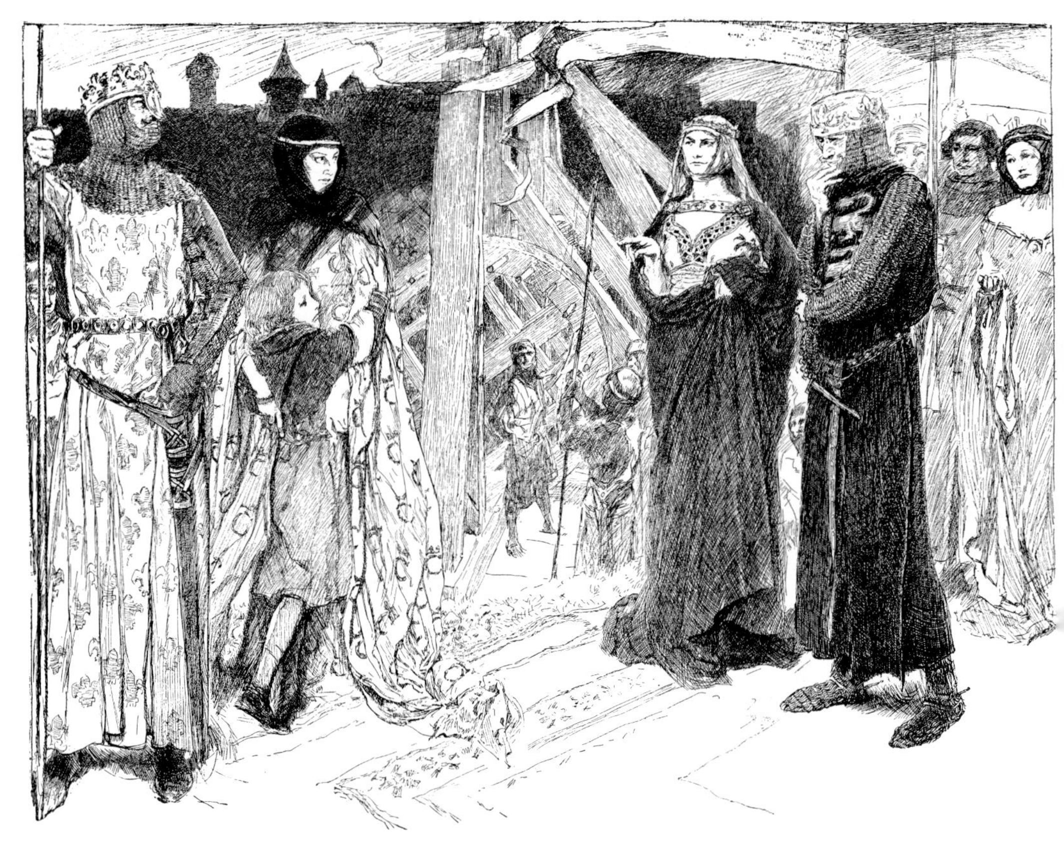

Elinor. "Come to thy grandam child."

Harper's Monthly Magazine, May 1903
"King John"
Act II., Scene I. — Before the walls of Angier.

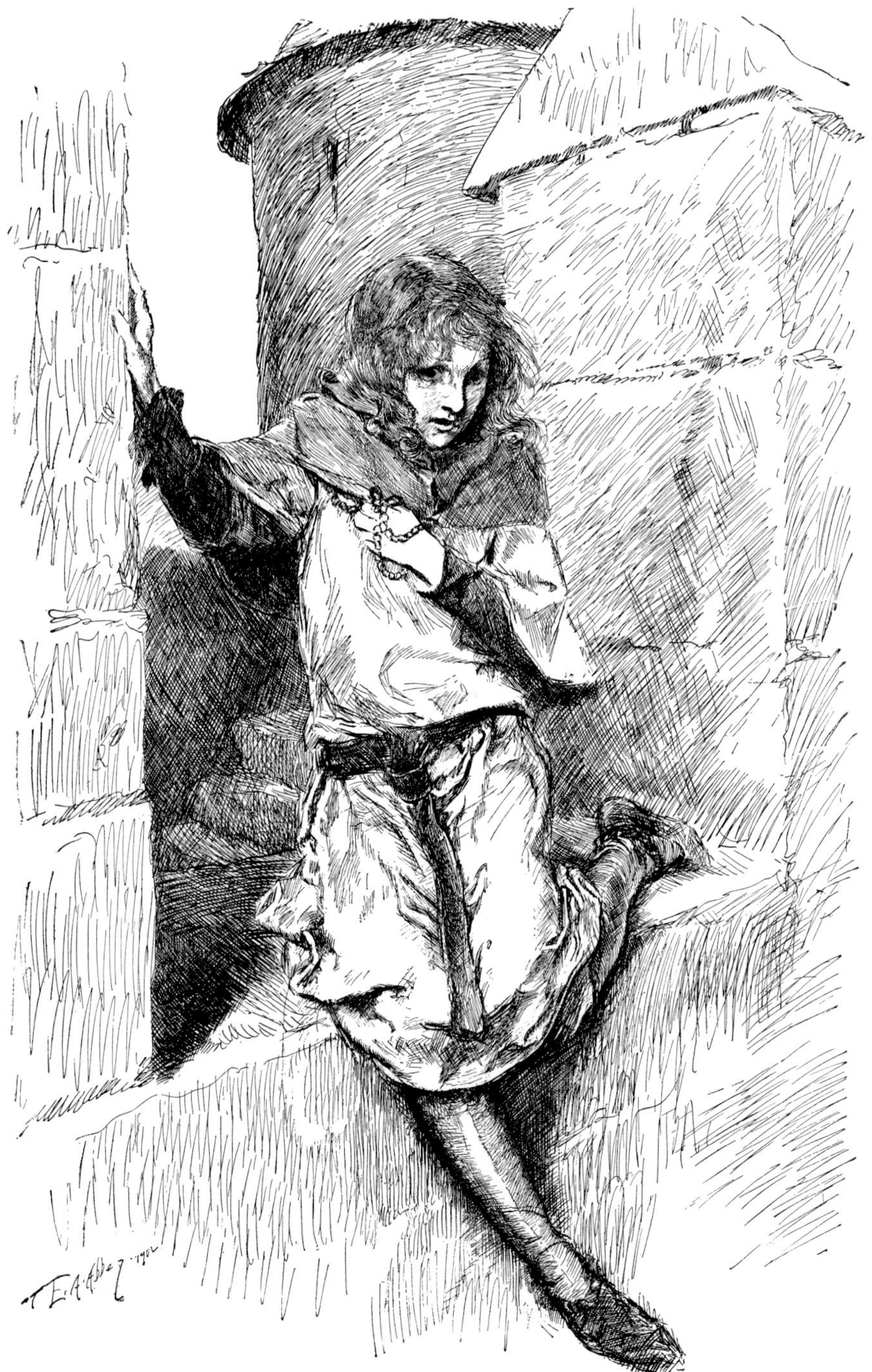

Arthur. "The wall is high; and yet will I leap down."

Harper's Monthly Magazine, May 1903
"King John"
Act IV., Scene III. — The Castle Walls.

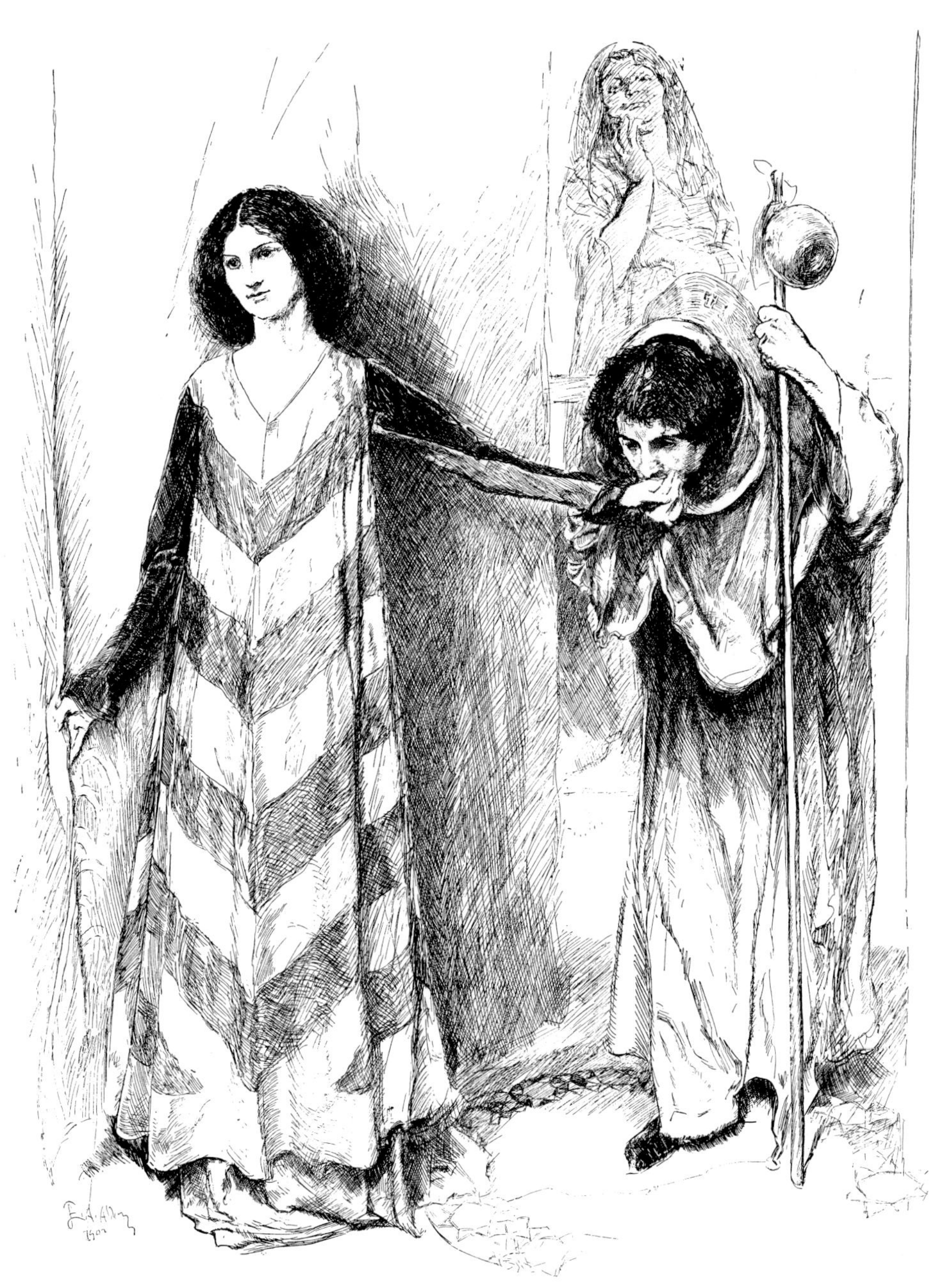

Romeo. "Have not saints lips, and holy palmers too?"

Harper's Monthly Magazine, July 1903
"Romeo and Juliet"
Act I., Scene V. — A hall in Capulet's House.

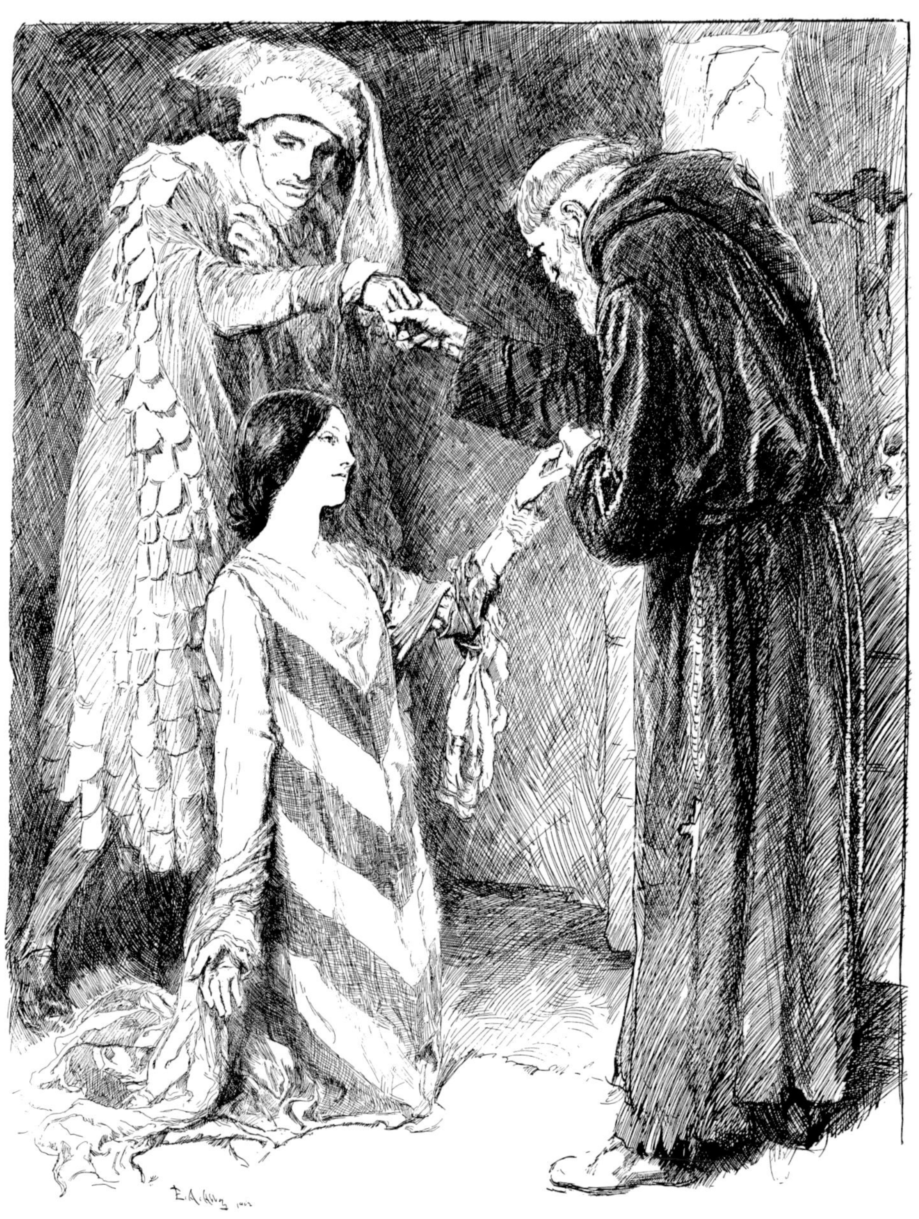

Friar. "Romeo shall thank thee, daughter, for us both."

Harper's Monthly Magazine, July 1903
"Romeo and Juliet"
Act II., Scene VI. — Friar Laurence's Cell.

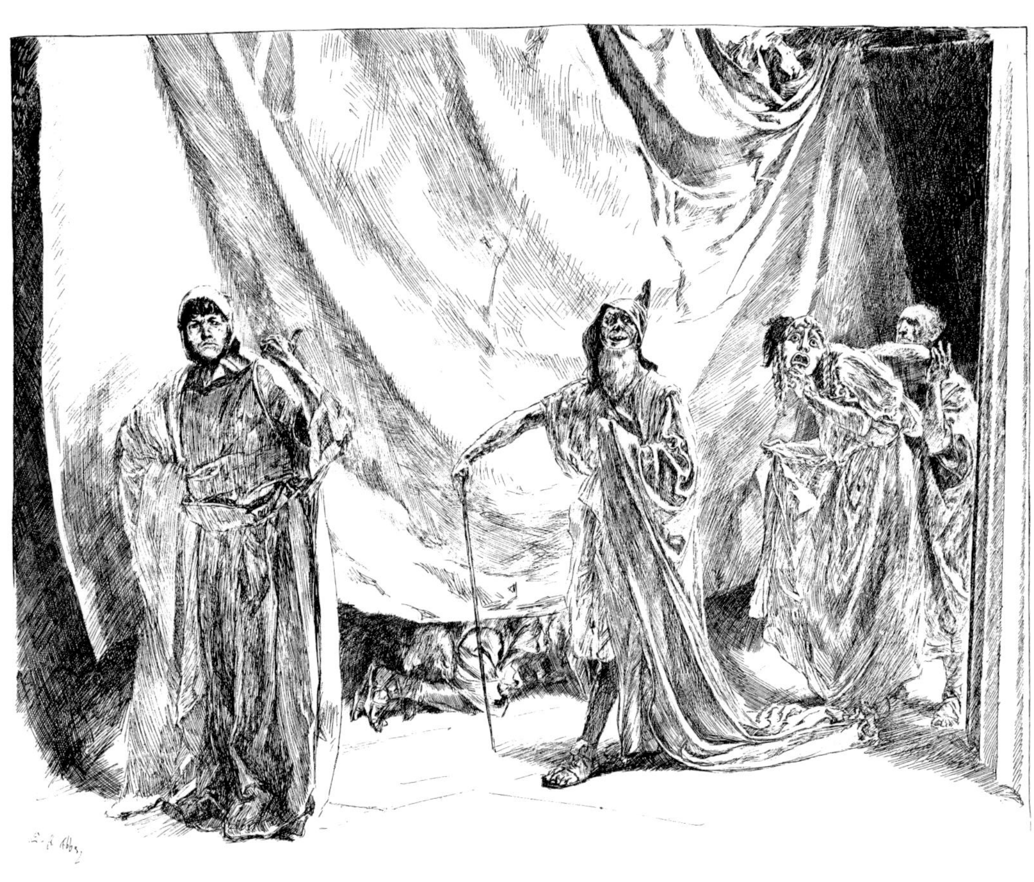

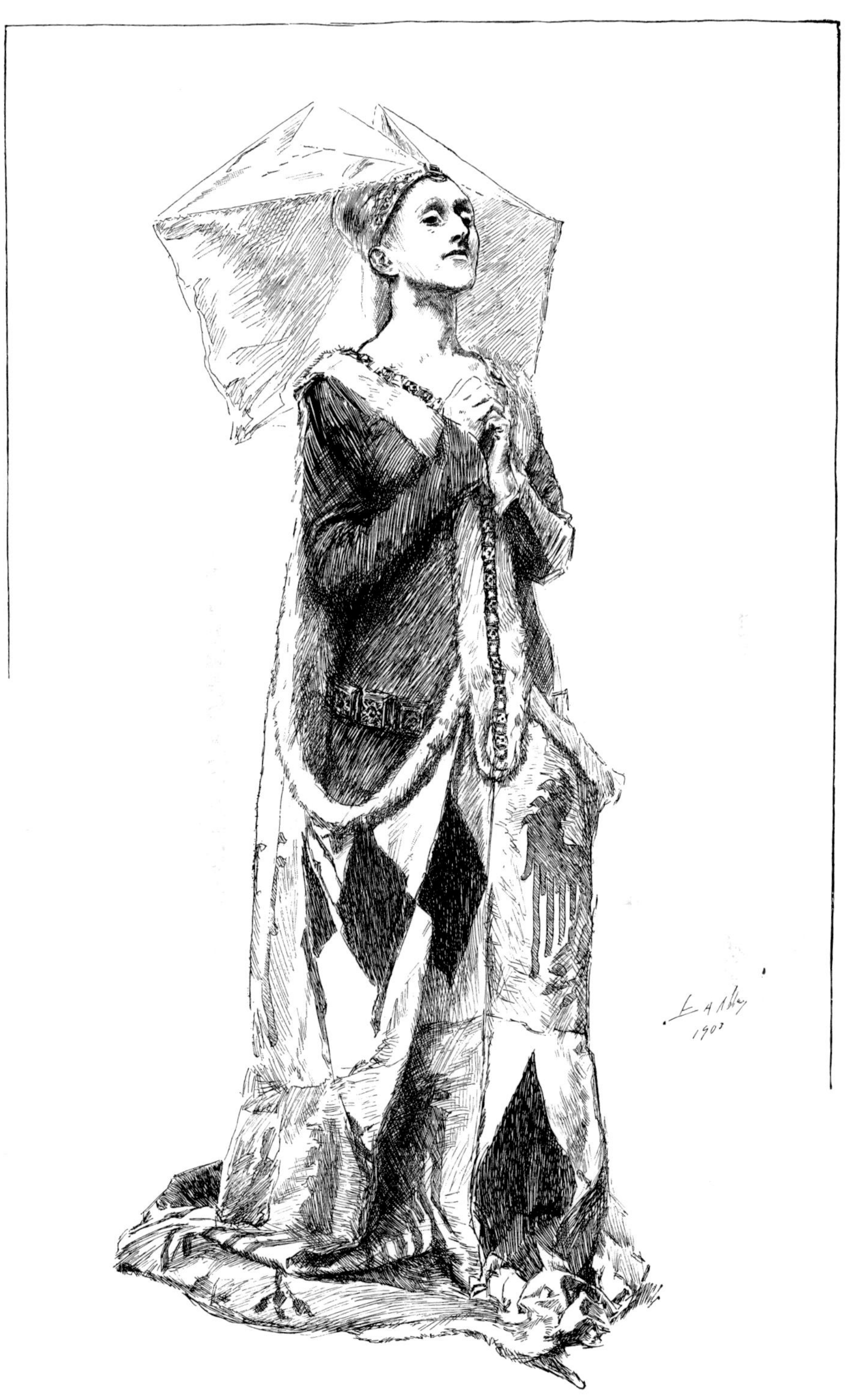

The Lady Anne Nevill.

Harper's Monthly Magazine, January 1904
"The Tragedy of King Richard III."

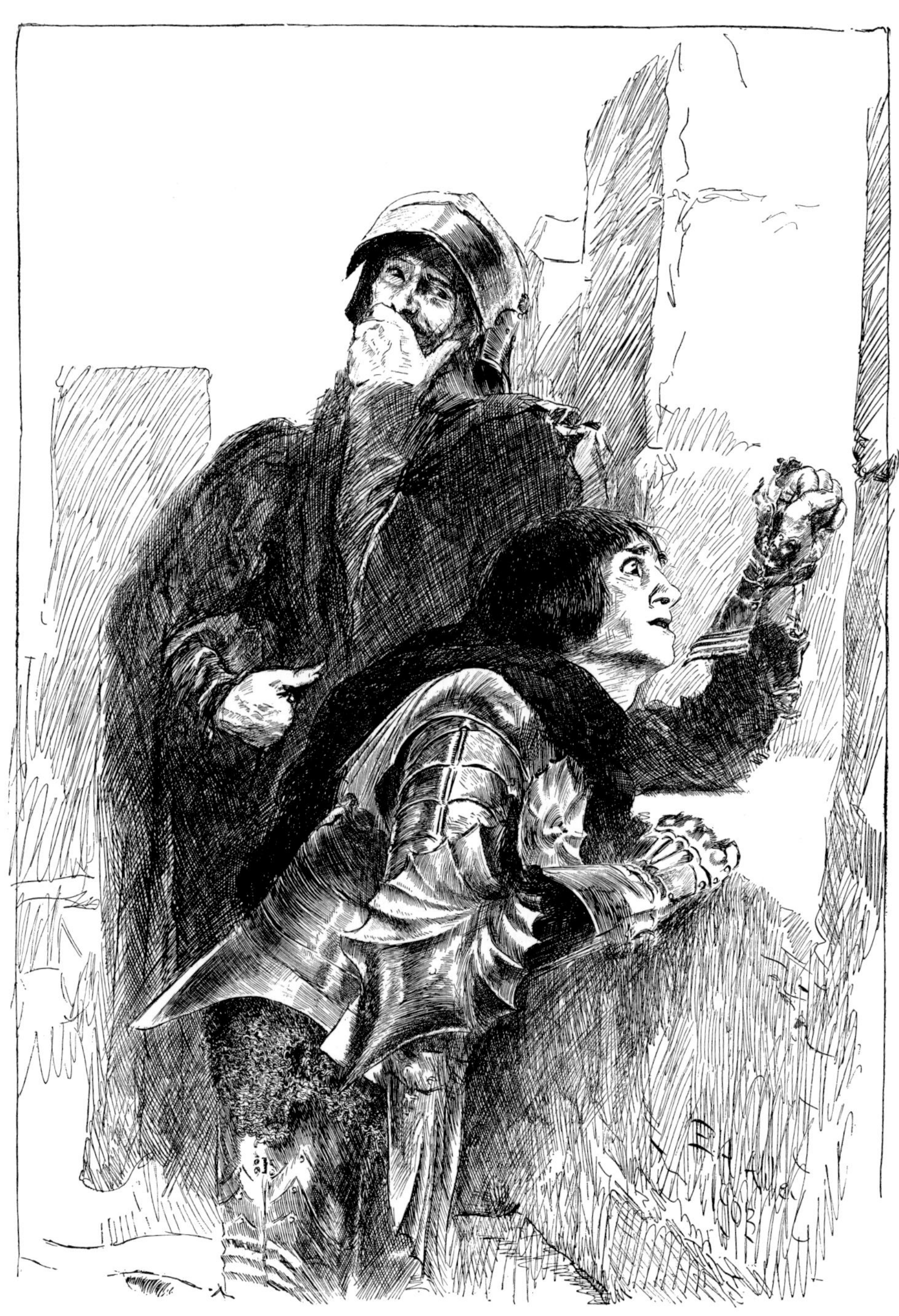

Gloster. "So dear I loved the man that I must weep.
I took him for the plainest harmless creature..."

Harper's Monthly Magazine, January 1904
"The Tragedy of King Richard III."
Act III., Scene V. — The Tower Wall.

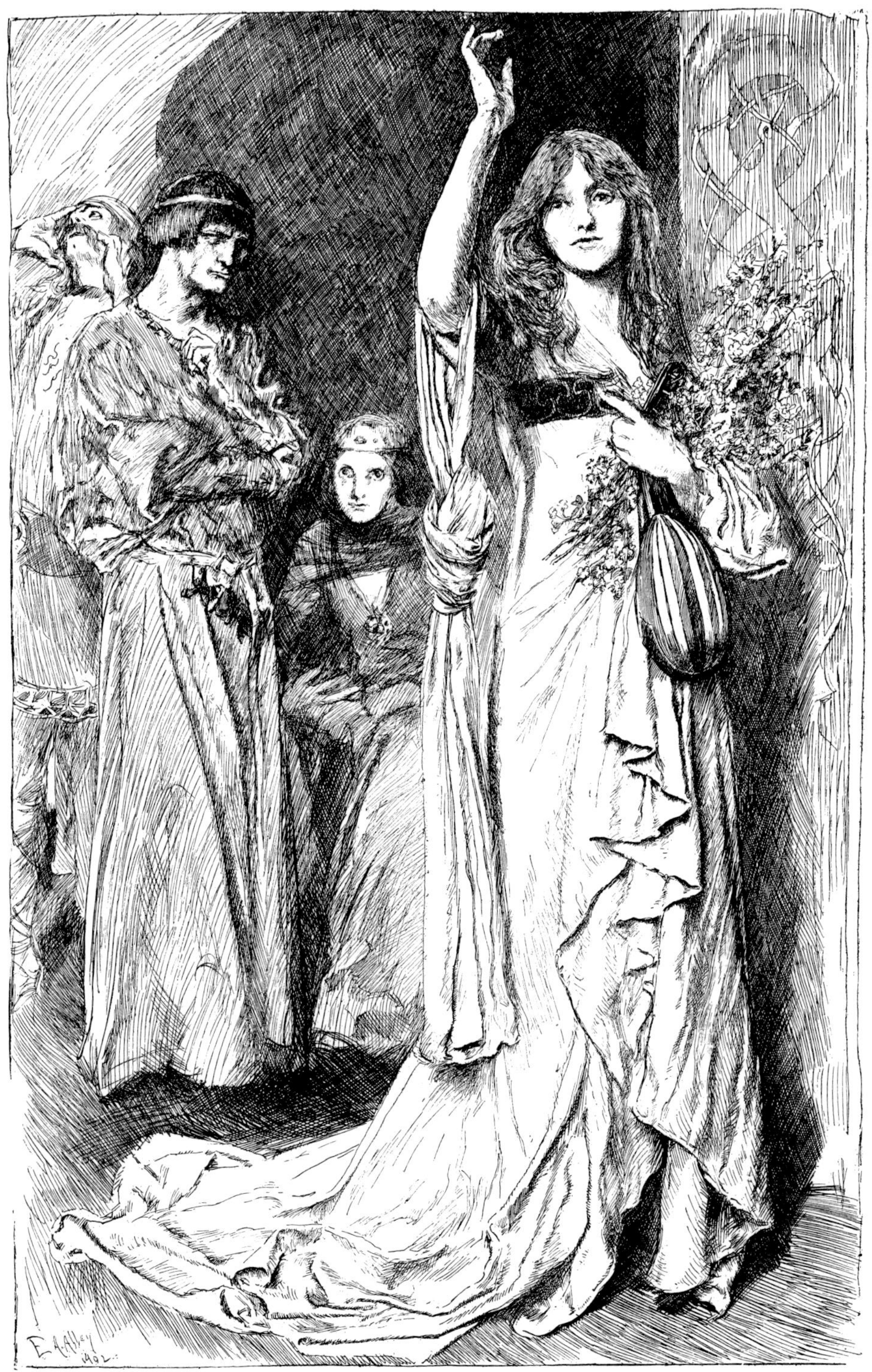

Ophelia. "And of all Christian souls! I pray God. God be wi' you!"

Harper's Monthly Magazine, May 1904
"Hamlet"
Act IV., Scene V. — Elsinore. — A room in the castle.

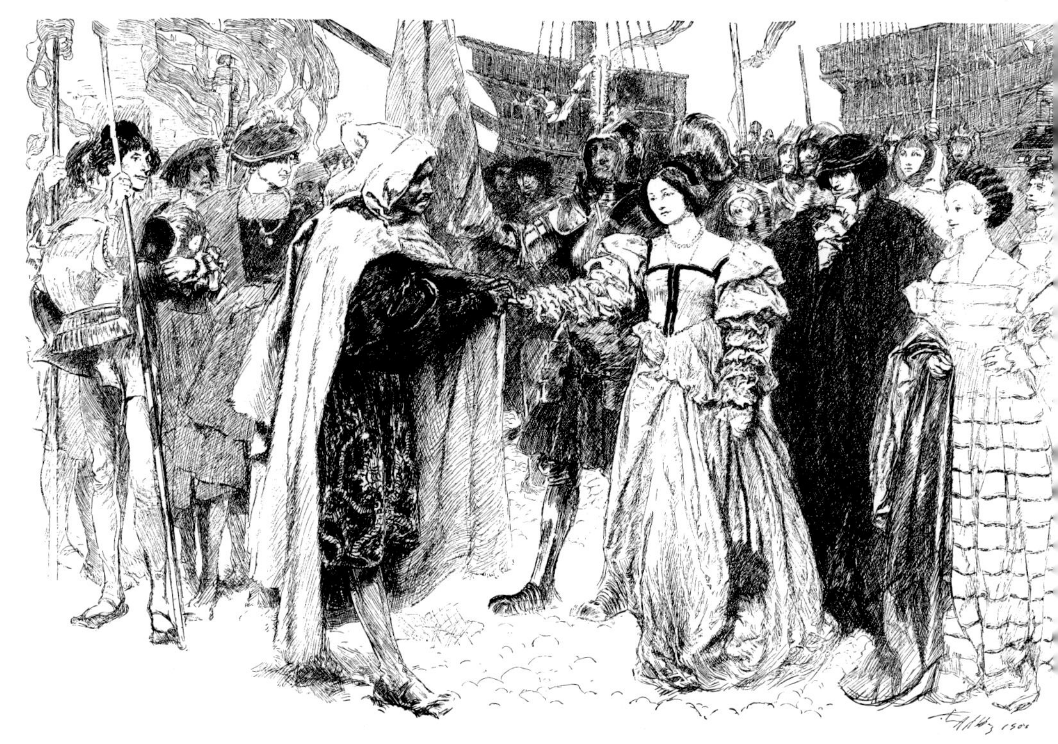

Othello. "O my fair warrior."

Harper's Monthly Magazine, October 1904
"Othello"
Act II., Scene I. — A Seaport Town in Cyprus.

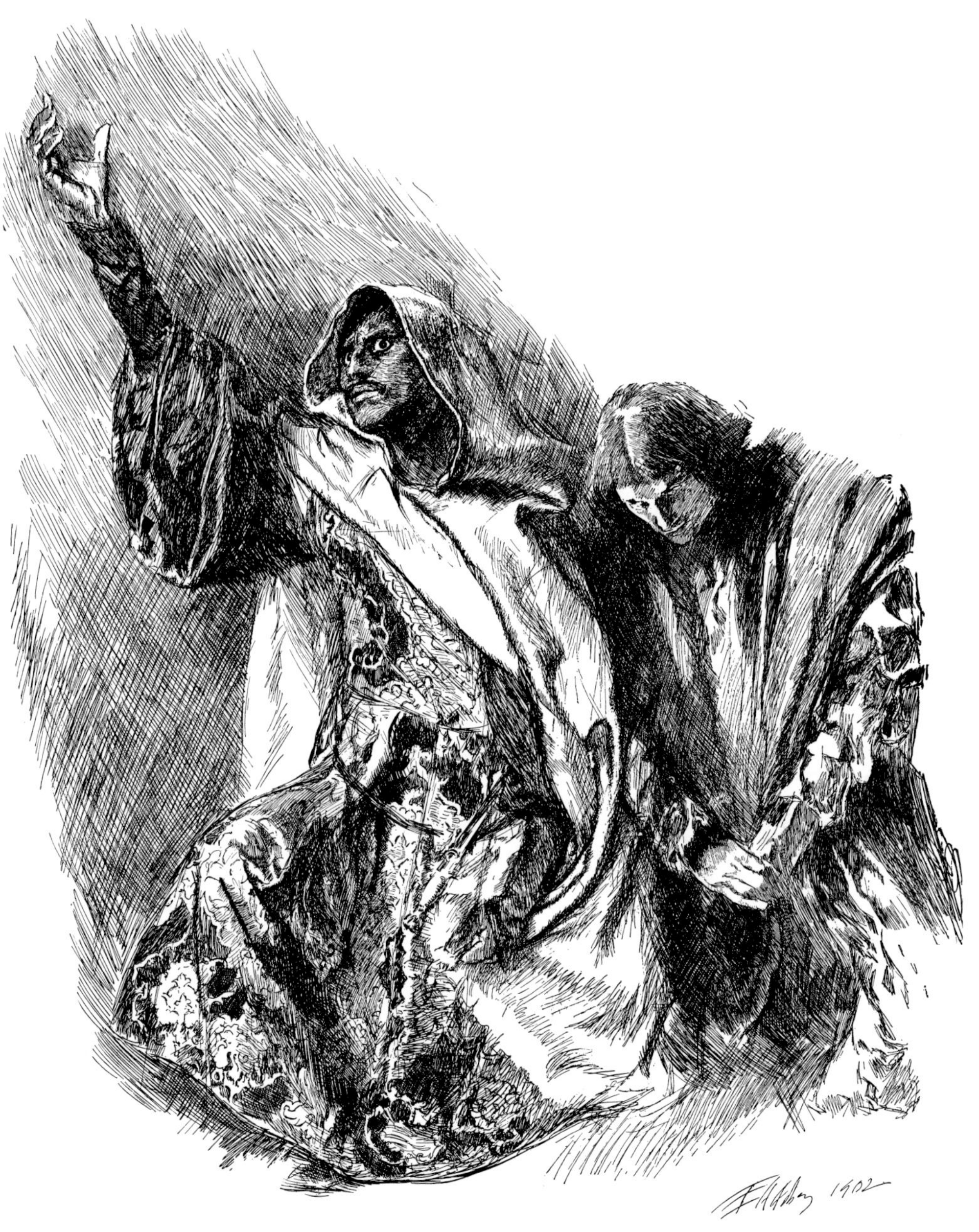

Othello. "Now, by yond marble heaven,
In the due reverence of a sacred vow, I hear engage my words."

Harper's Monthly Magazine, October 1904
"Othello"
Act III., Scene III. — Before the castle.

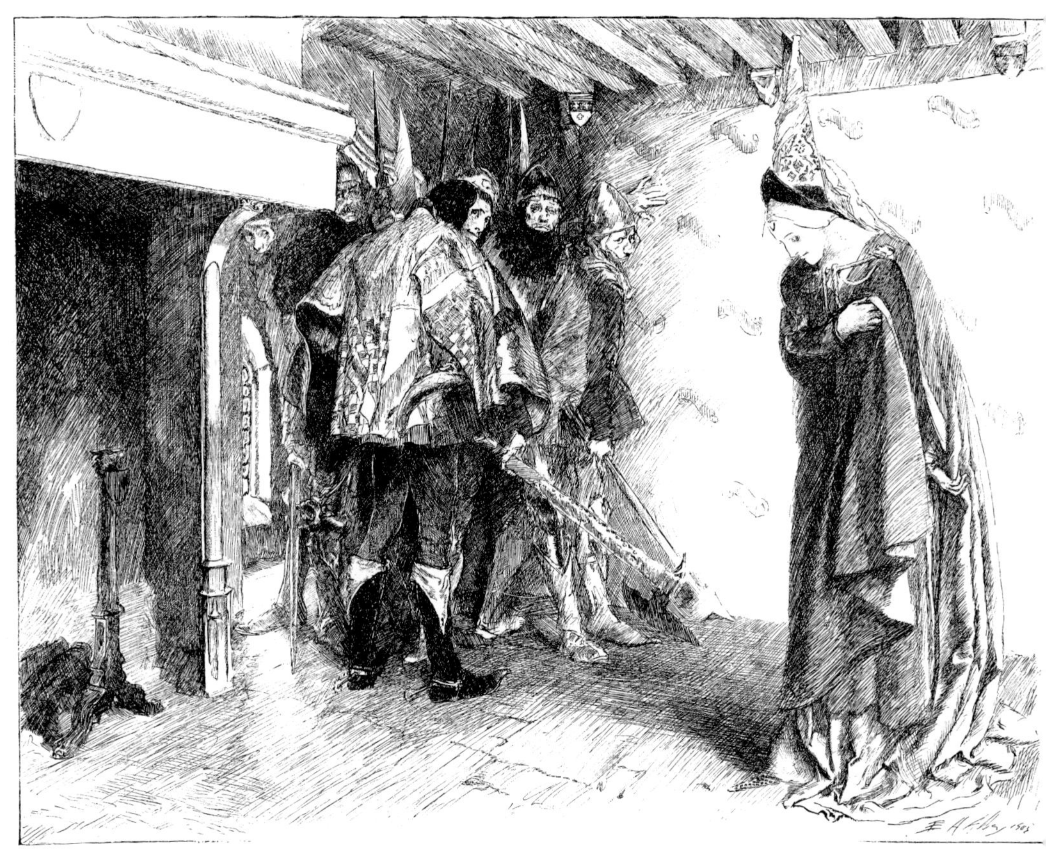

Talbot. "How say you madam?
Are you persuaded that Talbot is but shadow of himself?"

Harper's Monthly Magazine, November 1905
Shakespeare's "King Henry VI."
Part 1: Act II., Scene III. — Auvergne. The Countess's castle.

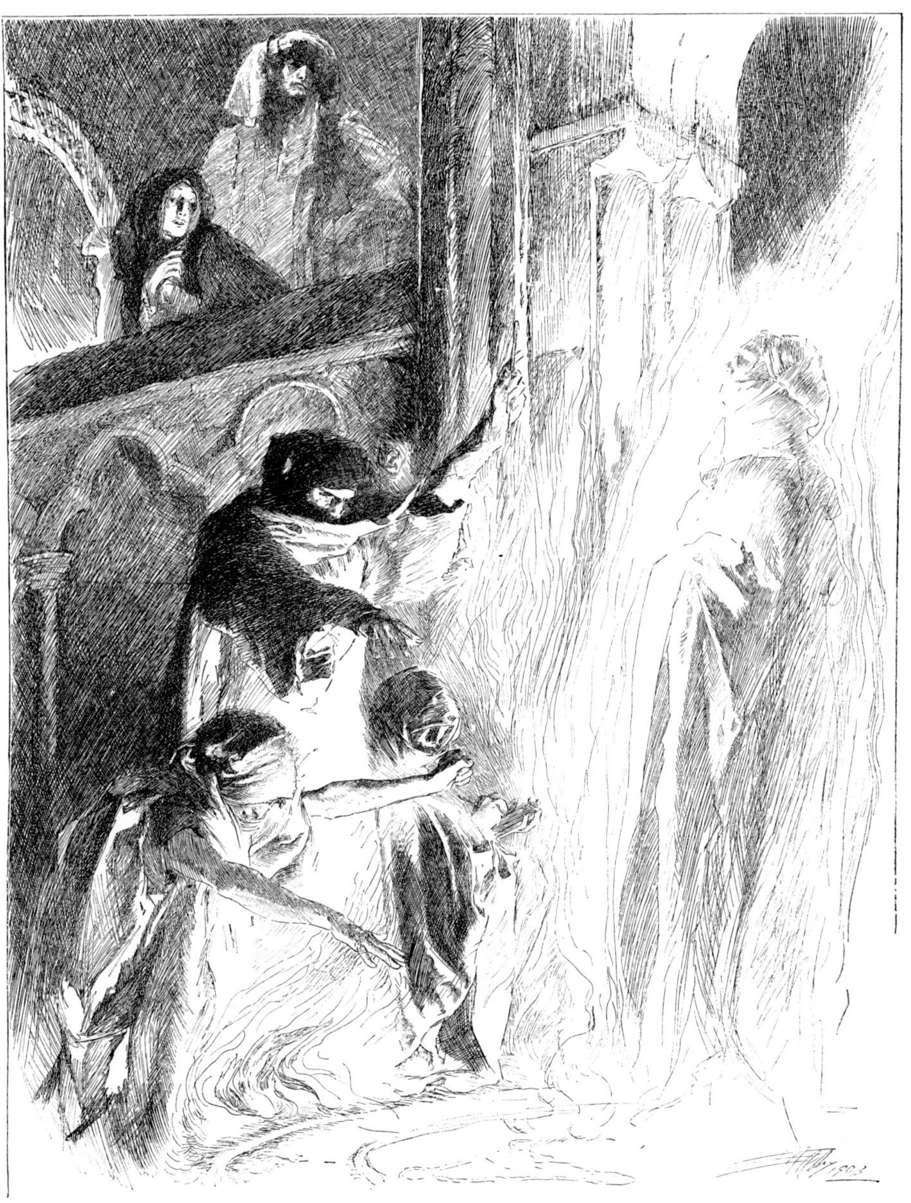

Spirit. "Adsum."

Harper's Monthly Magazine, November 1905
Shakespeare's "King Henry VI."
Part II: Act I., Scene IV. — Gloucester's garden.

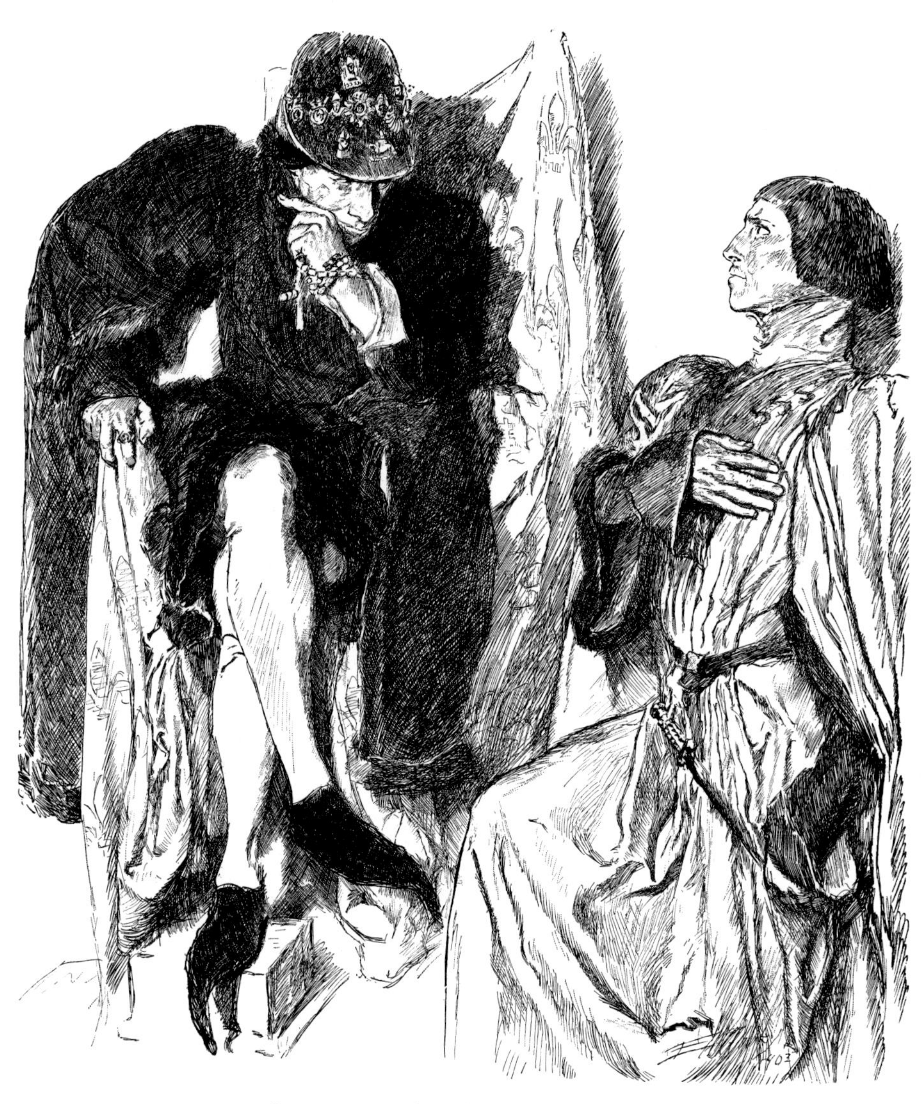

King Lewis. "Now, Warwick, tell me, even upon thy conscience,
Is Edward your true king?"

Harper's Monthly Magazine, November 1905
Shakespeare's "King Henry VI."
Part III: Act III., Scene III. — France. King Lweis XI's palace.

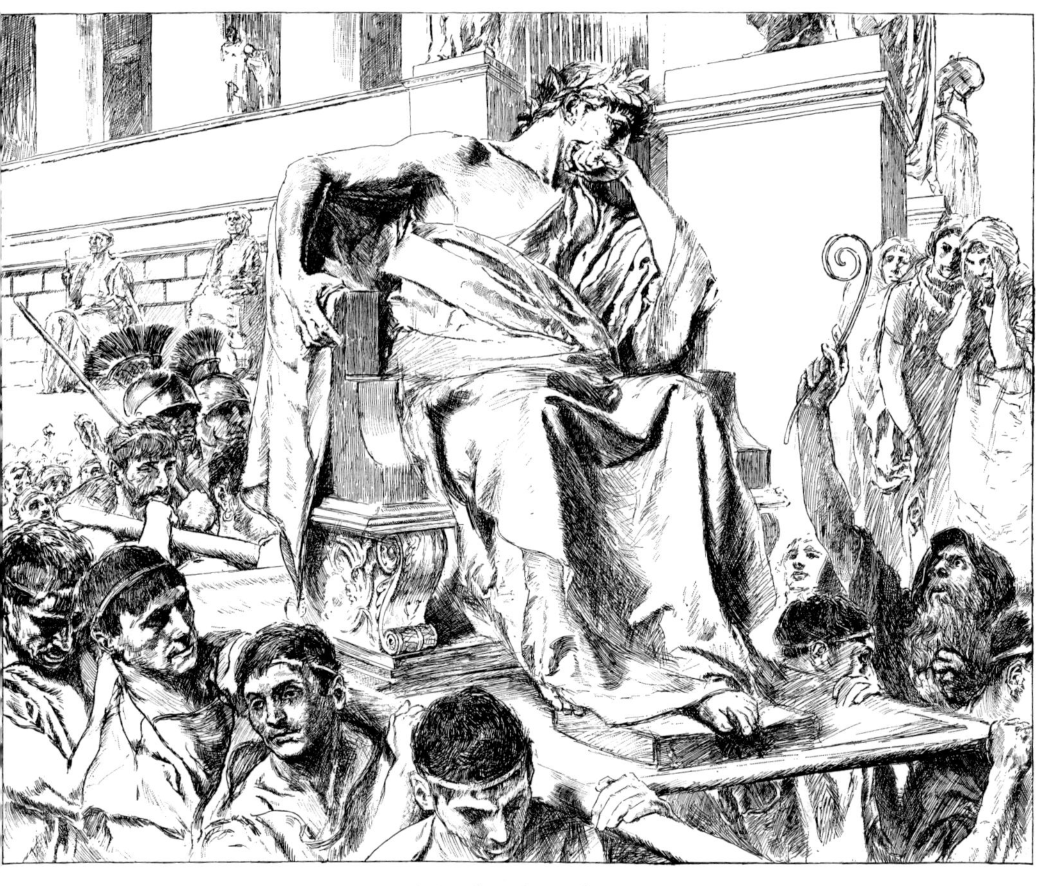

Ceasar. "The ides of March are come."
Soothsayer. "Aye, Ceasar; but not gone."

Harper's Monthly Magazine, February 1906
"Julius Cæsar."
Act III., Scene I. — Rome. Before the Capitol; the Senate sitting above.

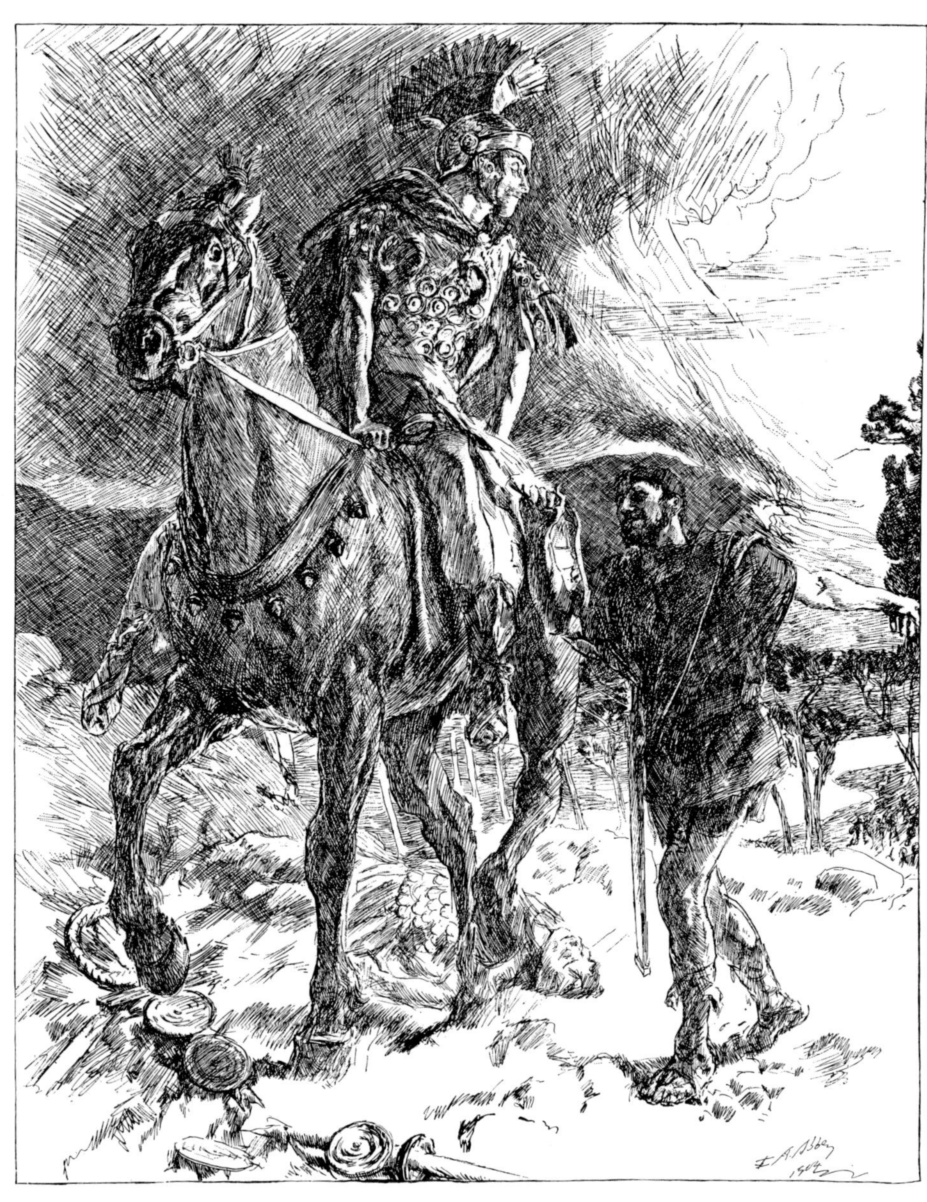

Cassius: "O, look, Titinius, look, the villains fly!"

Harper's Monthly Magazine, February 1906
"Julius Cæsar."
Act V., Scene III. — Another part of the field.

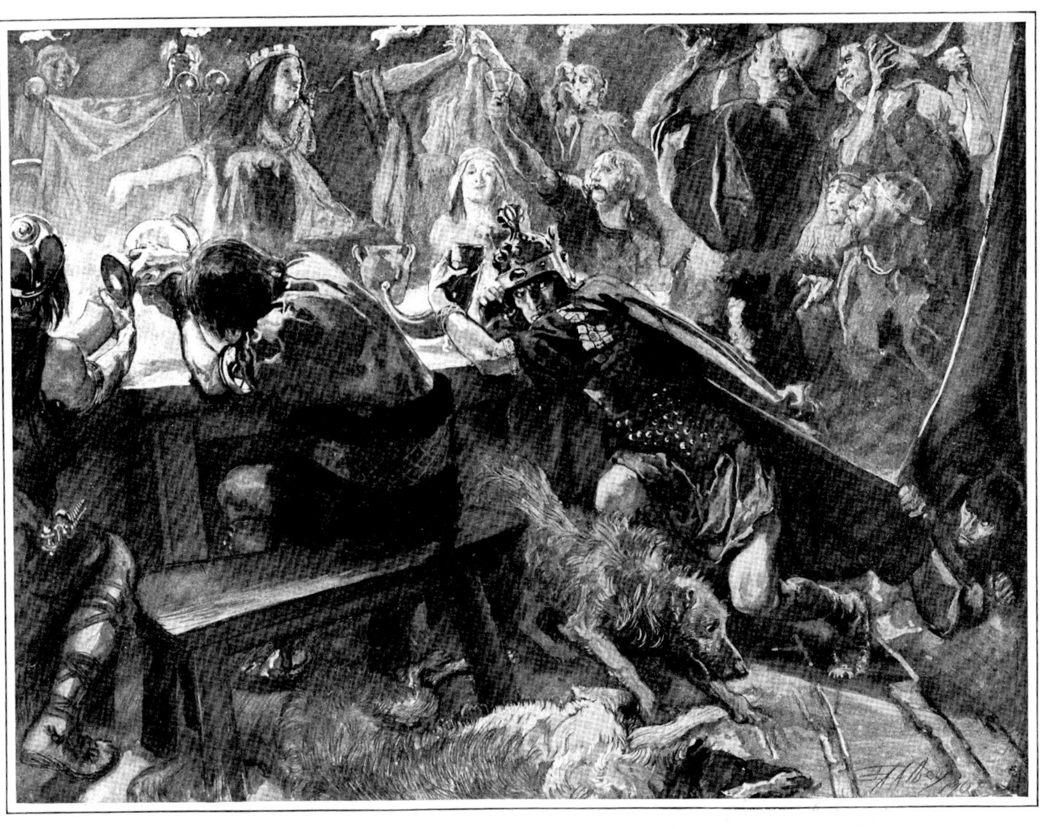

Macbeth. "There's blood upon thy face."

Harper's Monthly Magazine, November 1906
"Macbeth"
Act III., Scene IV. — The same. Hall in the palace.

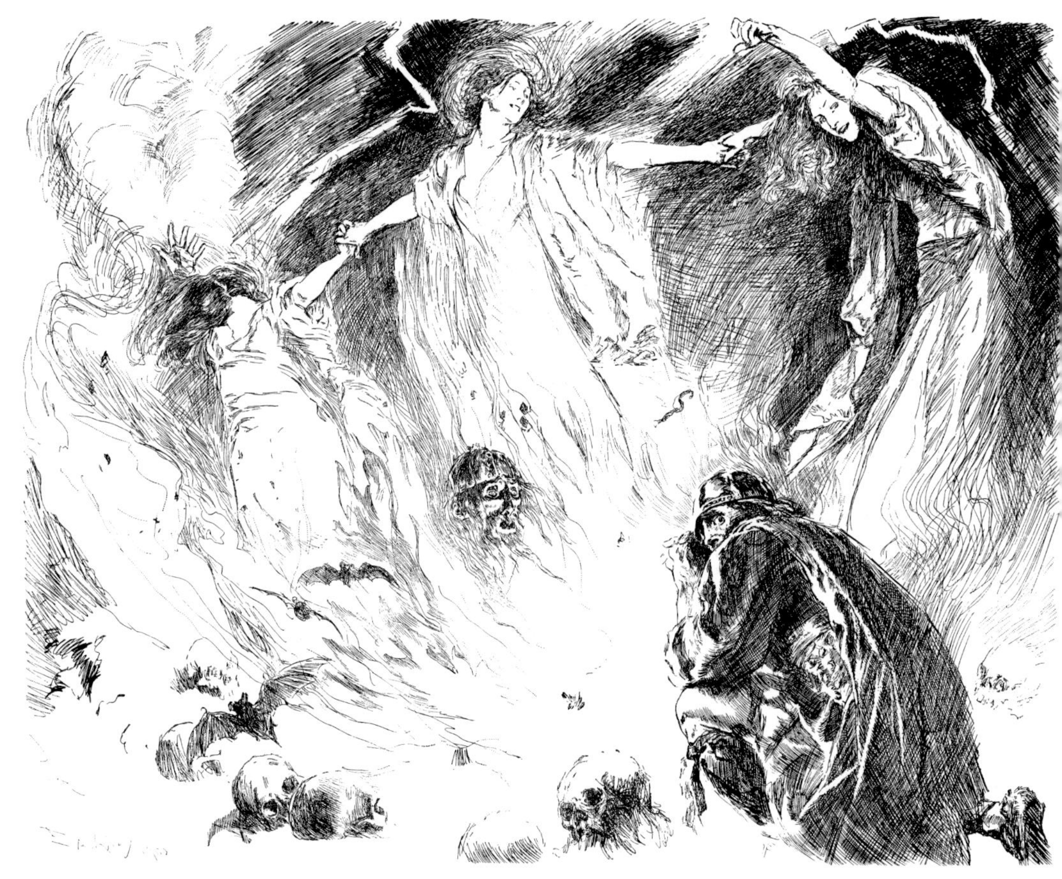

First Apparition. "Macbeth! Macbeth! Macbeth! Beware MacDuff."

Harper's Monthly Magazine, November 1906
"Macbeth"
Act IV., Scene I. — A cavern. In the middle, a boiling cauldron.

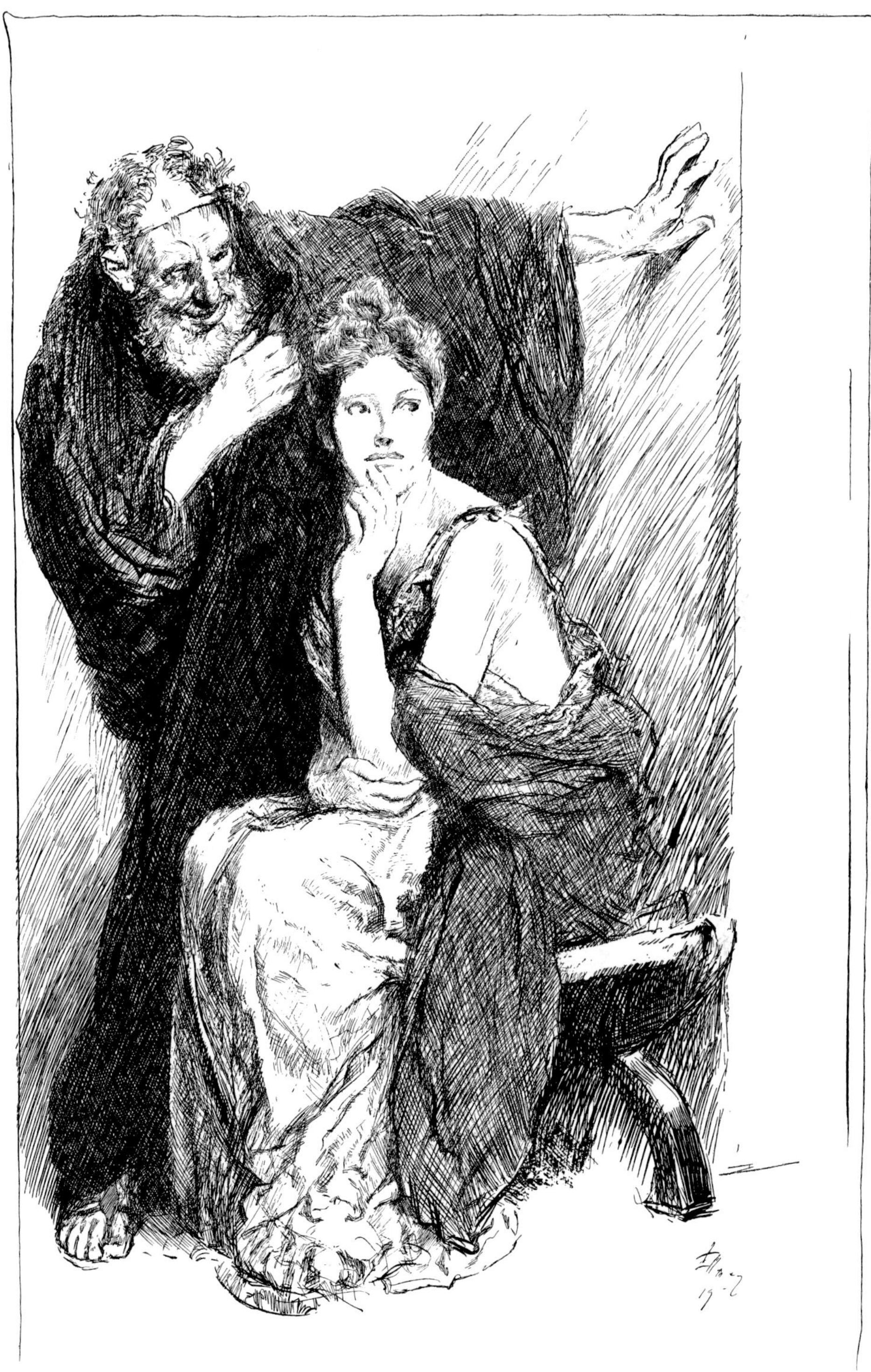

Cressida and her uncle.

Harper's Monthly Magazine, October 1907
"Troilus and Cressida"

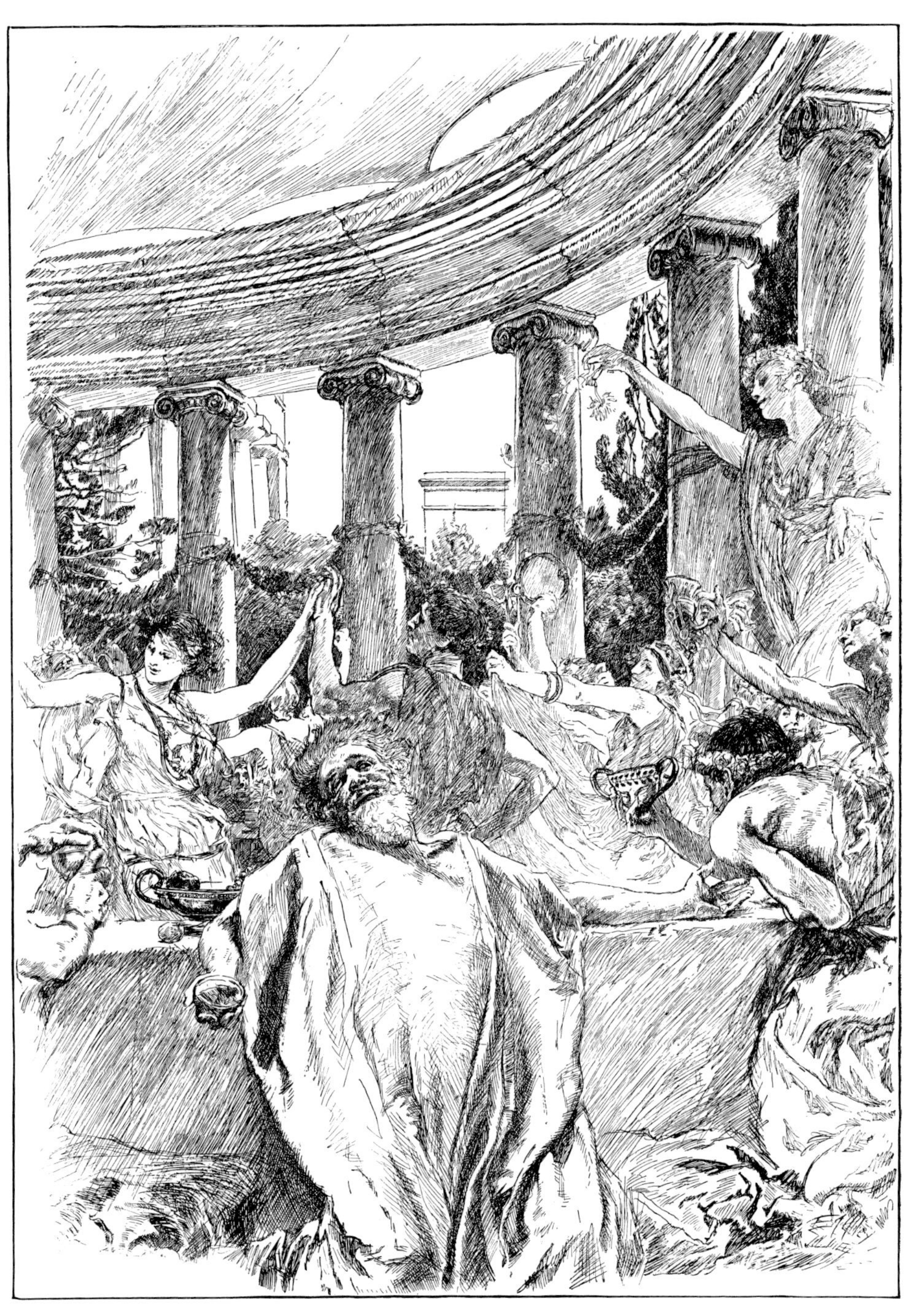

Apemantus. "Hey-day, what a sweep of vanity comes this way. They dance!"

Harper's Monthly Magazine, May 1908
"Timon of Athens."
Act I., Scene II. — A banqueting-room in Timon's house.

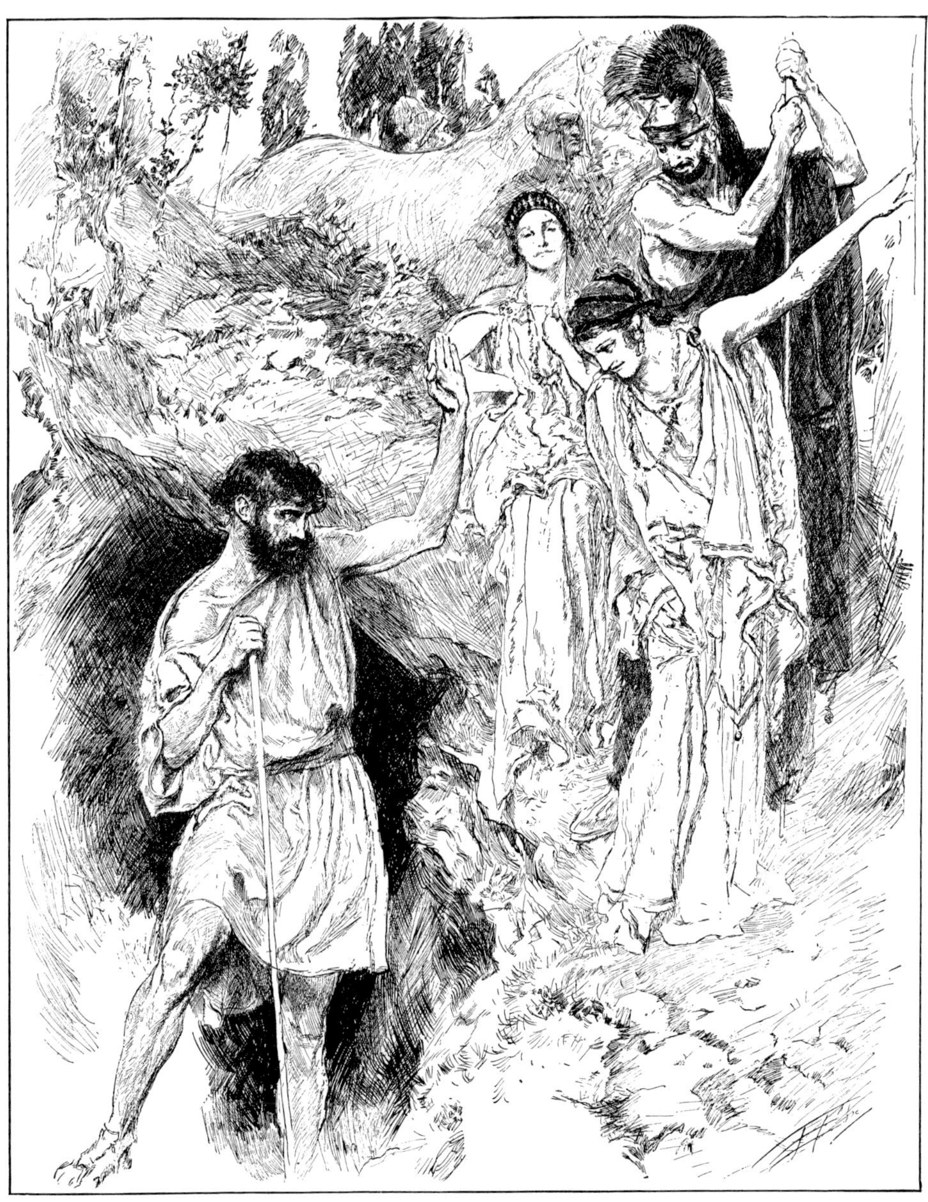

Timon. "I prithee, beat thy drum and get thee gone."

Harper's Monthly Magazine, May 1908
"Timon of Athens."
Act VI., Scene III. — Woods and cave, near the seashore.

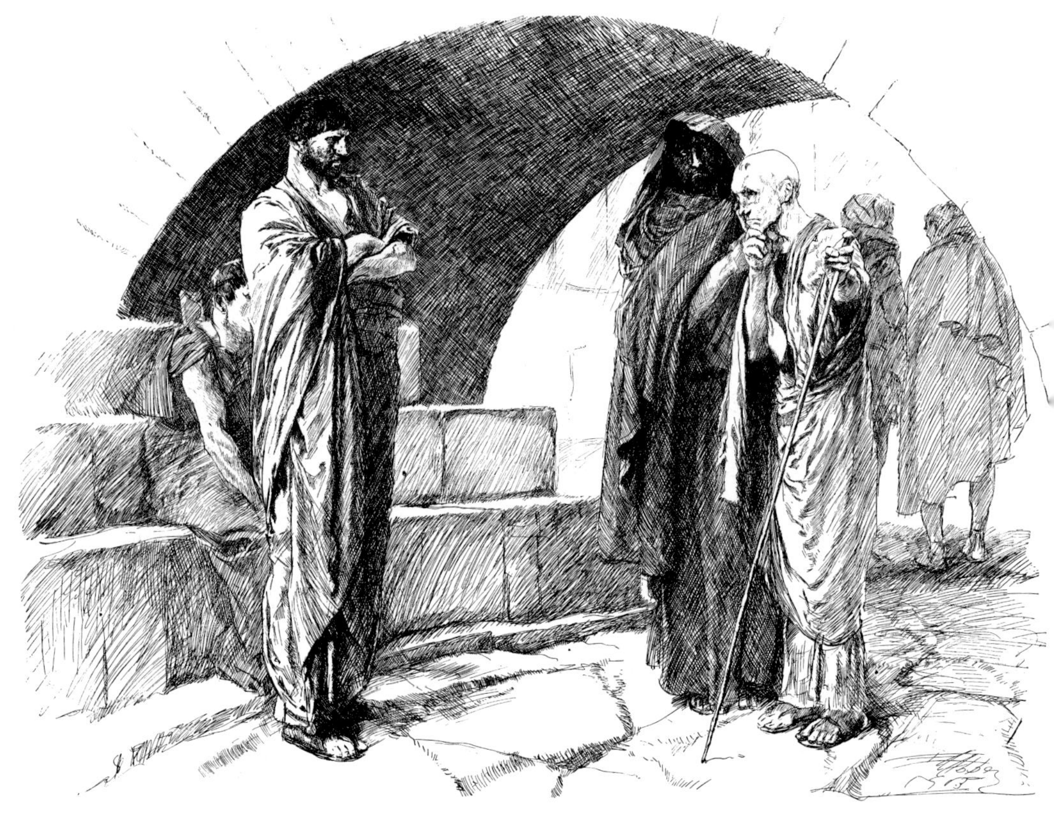

Coriolanus. "So, here comes a brace.—You know the cause, sirs, of my standing here."

Harper's Monthly Magazine, November 1908
"Coriolanus."
Act II., Scene III. — The same. The Forum.

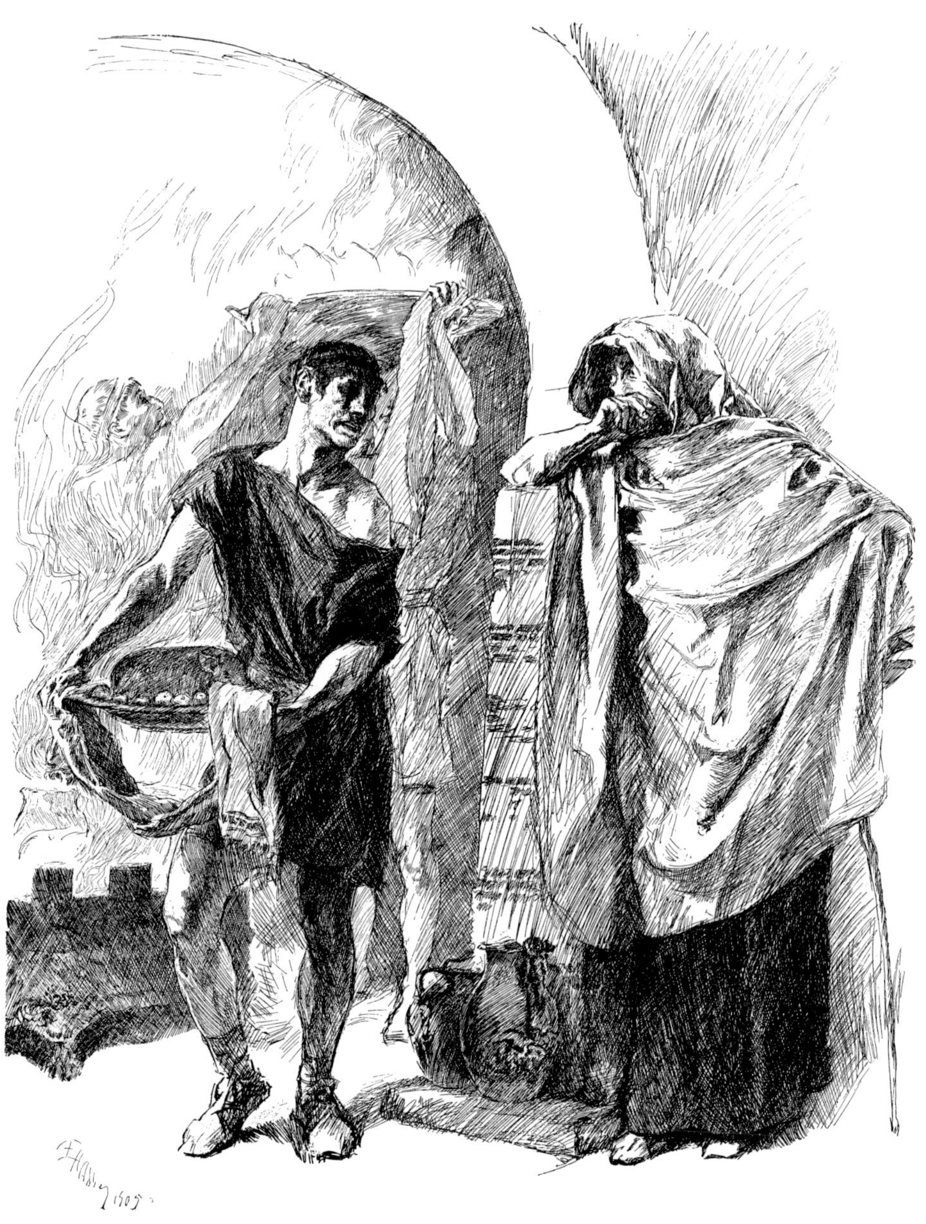

Servant. "What would you have, friend? Whence are you? Here's no place for you."

Harper's Monthly Magazine, November 1908
"Coriolanus."
Act IV., Scene V. — The same. A hall in Aufidius's house.

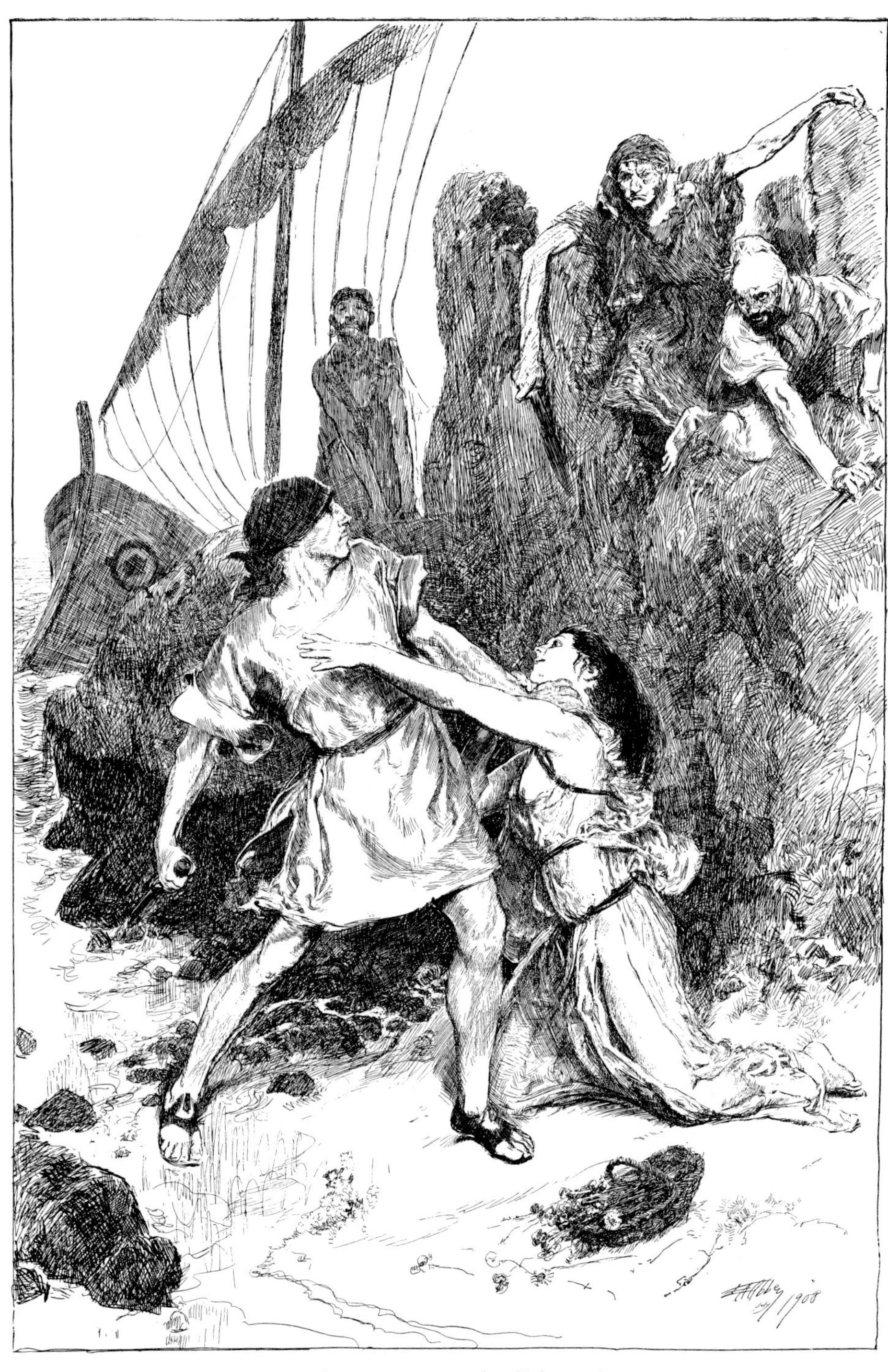

Leonine. "I am sworn. And will dispatch.
[Whilst Marina is struggling, enter the pirates]
Pirate. "Hold, villain!"

Harper's Monthly Magazine, February 1909
"Pericles"
Act IV, Scene I. — Tarsus. An open place near the sea-shore.

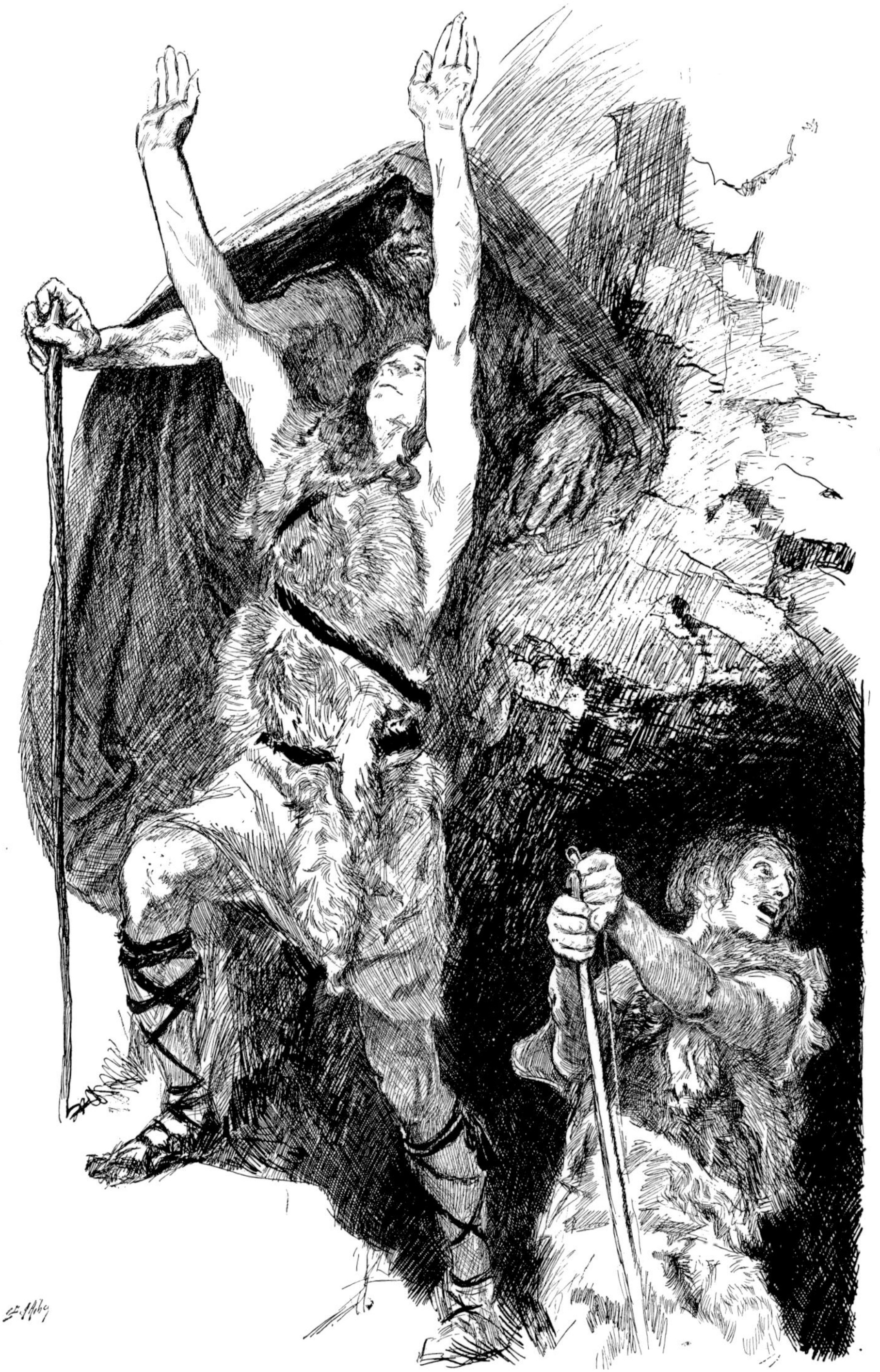

Belarius. "Hail, thou fair heaven!
We house I' the rock, yet use thee not so hardly As prouder livers do."
Guiderius. "Hail, heaven!" Arviragus. "Hail, heaven!"

Harper's Monthly Magazine, April 1909
"Cymbeline"
Act III., Scene III. — Wales: a mountainous country with a cave.

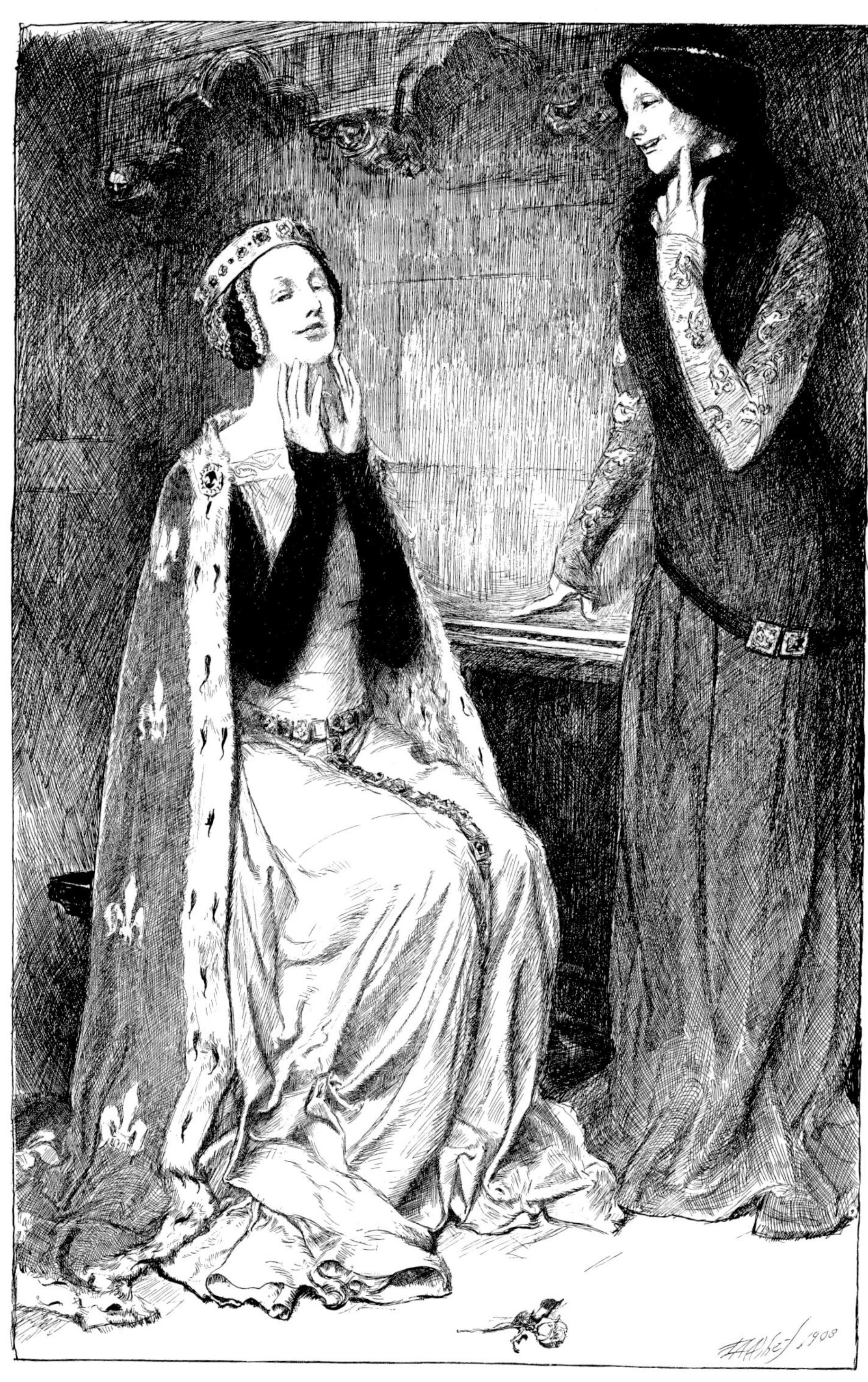

Katherine and Alice—The Lesson in English.

Harper's Monthly Magazine, May 1909
Shakespeare's "Henry V"
Act III., Scene IV. — The French King's palace.

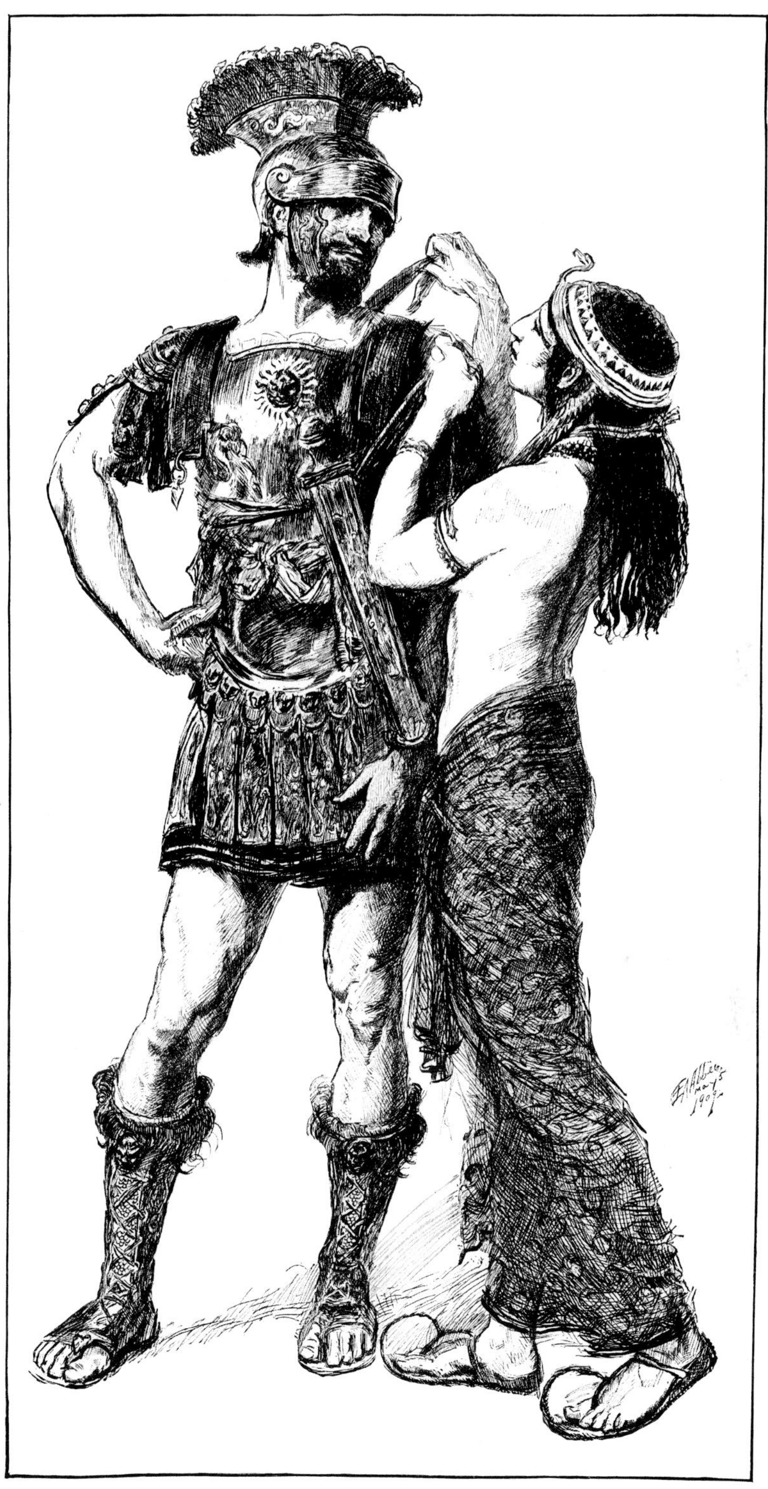

Cleopatra: "Sooth, la, I'll help; thus it must be."

Harper's Monthly Magazine, September 1909
"Antony and Cleopatra"
Act IV., Scene IV. — The same. A room in the palace.

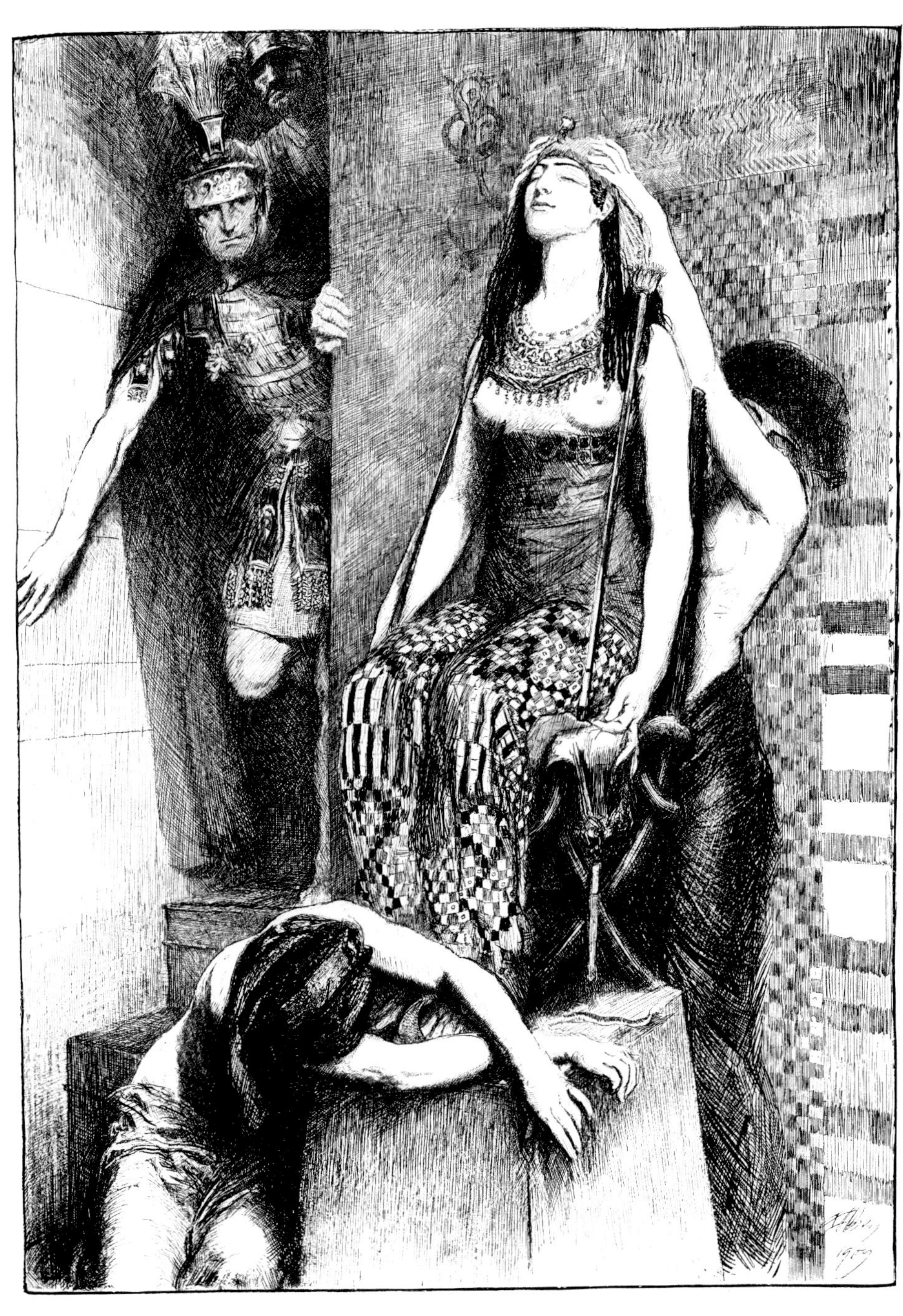

Harper's Monthly Magazine, 1909
"Charmian"
Act V., Scene II. — Your crown's awry; Ill mend it, and then play—

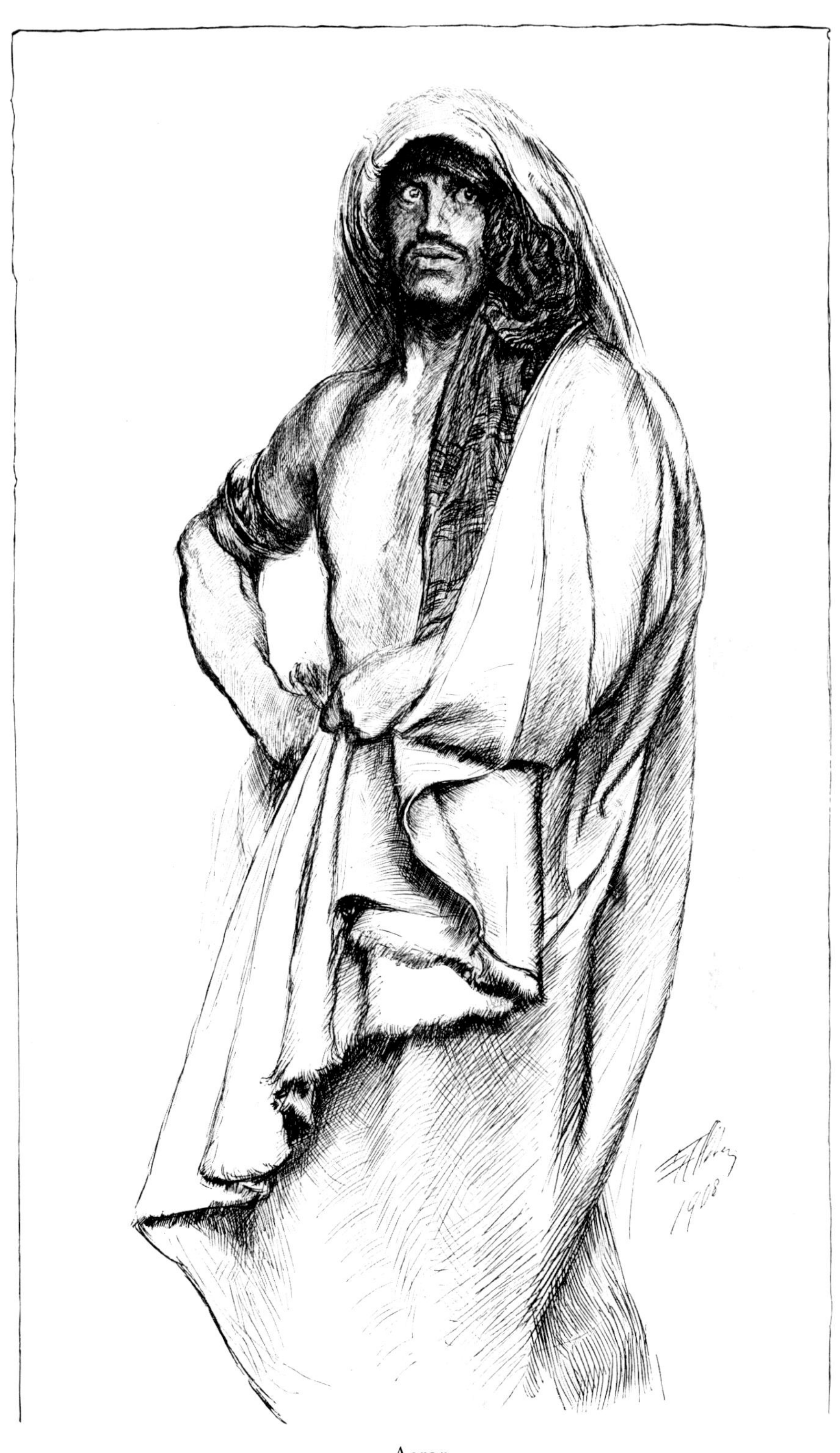

Aaron.

Harper's Monthly Magazine, October 1909
"Titus Andronicus."

AFTERWORD

by
John Fleskes

The Drawings of Edwin Austin Abbey focuses on the artist's published pen-and-ink works for Harper & Brothers. The material has been reproduced from books and magazines released during his lifetime (1852-1911). This volume serves to present Abbey's illustrations in an easy-to-reference collection. With a few exceptions, the art appears in chronological order. Pieces drawn for magazines in a given year are followed by imagery found within a book released during that same time. The source information is included for all art where the details were found. If captions and titles were elusive, we have placed those works based on the date found alongside Abbey's signature. Dual notations are shared in the cases where a piece appeared in both a magazine and a book.

   Work on this retrospective began in 2008, when rare original magazines and tear sheets where provided to us by the artists William Stout and Jim Silke. Next, the esteemed collectors Bud Plant and Jim Vadeboncoeur Jr. offered more material to expand upon our initial findings. The book came to approximately 200 pages at that time but was set aside before being revisited again in early 2020. The encouragement to begin anew came from Alice A. Carter—award-winning illustrator, art professor and author—who offered to write the extensive and enriched essay on the life of Abbey that opens this book. Furthermore, from her and Courtney Granner's personal collection came a series of rare Abbey books from which we could scan an extra 150 images. After combining these images with the material previously obtained, the book swelled to

400 pages. It should be noted, however, that this collection is not meant to be complete: Some drawings from Harper & Brothers publications are absent, along with those from *Scribner's* and various British publications. This is simply due to the source material not being available to us during the production of this book.

The impetus to publish a collection of Abbey's artwork stemmed from a desire to share his remarkable drawings with a larger audience. His position as an important figure in the history of the Golden Age of Illustration has always intrigued me. This explosive period began in the early 1880s and ran until the early 1930s. It was sparked by new printing methods that permitted greater fidelity in reproducing fine lines. This led to an increased demand by the public for publishers to include illustrations to accompany stories, articles and poetry.

Abbey was at the perfect place and time to experience this transitional phase. Initially, in the early 1870s, his drawings were interpreted by master engravers who created the woodblock plates that were used for publication. As highly skilled as these engravers were, the process was expensive and time-consuming and could not accurately depict the details in the original art. A decade into his profession, Abbey's drawings began to be shown more faithfully through the new photo-mechanical processes then in development.

Inspired by the rapid demand for illustration and the technological improvements of printing, Abbey's obsessive desire for greater accuracy in the details of his drawings only grew. (He could take weeks gathering authentic costumes, props and furniture for each historical drawing.) His commitment to the form helped to bring Abbey additional recognition, along with a favorable perspective of pen-and-ink art among the general audience. He also had the good fortune to garner approval within the major art circles of the day while gaining the approval of the most difficult of critics. Even now, well over a century after he completed his last work, Abbey's complete devotion to the art of drawing and his unwavering dedication toward research to ensure historical accuracy play a direct role in the approach that artists use today. Along with noted artists such as Gustave Doré, Howard Pyle and Daniel Vierge, Abbey set forth an invisible influence that permeates the industry to this day. With this, Abbey has our thanks.

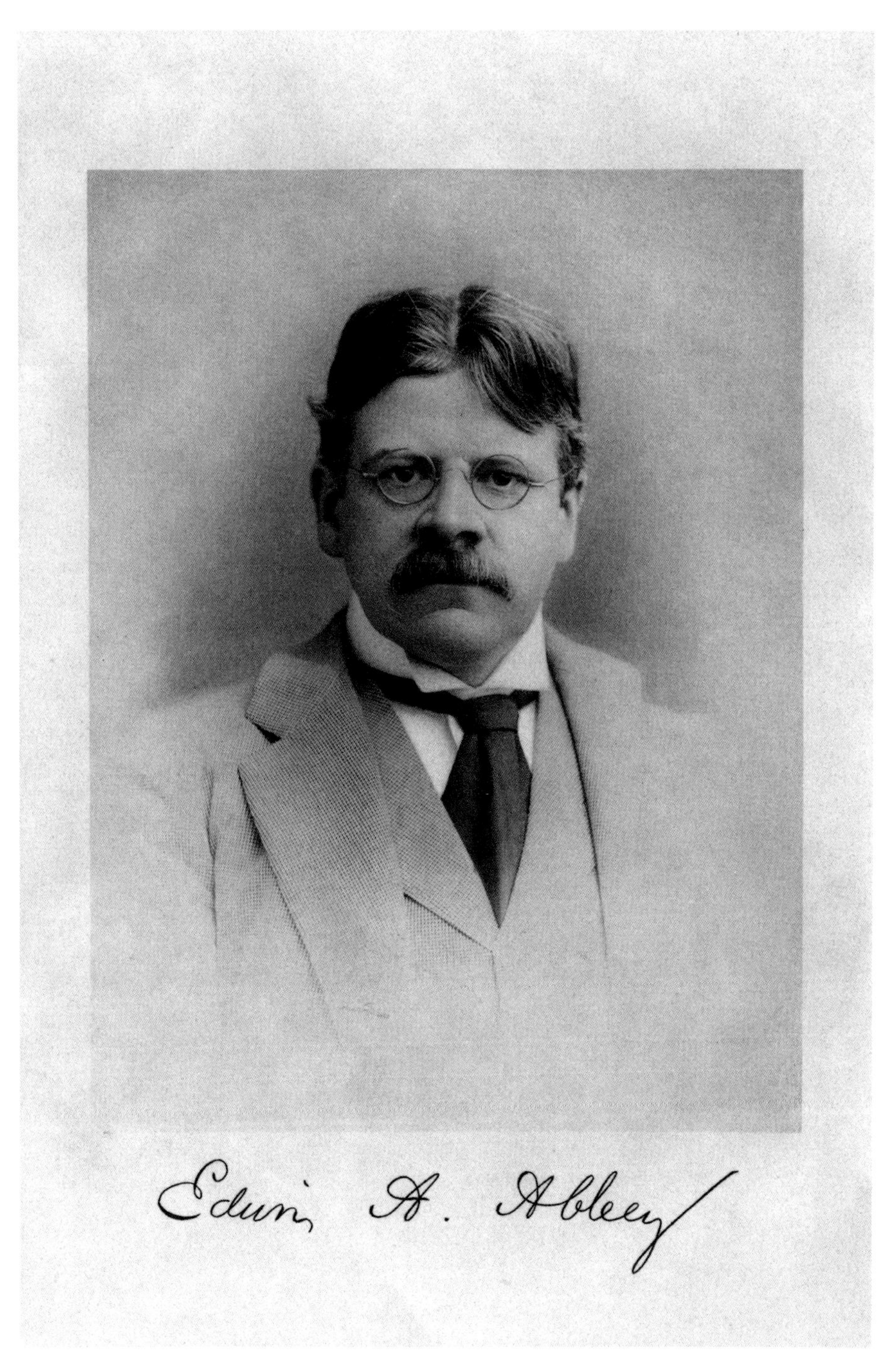

The Deserted Village
Harper & Brothers, October 1902

FOOTNOTES

[1] vangoghletters.org/vg/letters/let333/letter.html, Br. 1990: 335 | CL: 277, From: Vincent van Gogh to: Theo van Gogh, Sunday, 1 April 1883.

[2] E.V. Lucas, *Edwin Austin Abbey Royal Academician: The Record of His Life and Work* (New York: Charles Scribner's Sons and London: Methuen and Company Ltd., 1921), 4-5.

[3] E.V. Lucas, 5.

[4] E.V. Lucas, 197.

[5] Joseph Pennell, *The Adventures of an Illustrator* (Boston: Little, Brown, and Company, 1925), 68. Joseph Pennell was insulted when he showed a drawing to Charles Parsons and was asked, "Well, have you got anything else to live on? If you haven't you better saw wood."

[6] E.V. Lucas, 184.

[7] When Abbey was hired in 1871, the staff artists at *Harper's* were Charles Stanley Reinhart, the Civil War "special artists" Stanley Fox and Theodore Russell Davis, and the marine specialist Granville Perkins.

[8] Frank Luther Mott, *A History of American Magazines, 1741-1930, Vol. 2.* (Cambridge, Mass.: Belknap Press of Harvard University Press, 1953), 473. https://hdl-handle-net.libaccess.sjlibrary.org/2027/heb.00678. EPUB.

[9] Frank Luther Mott, 470.

[10] "Our Illustrations of the War," *Harper's Weekly*, volume 5, April 27, 1861. 258. https://research.wou.edu/c.php?g=551307&p=3785487

[11] W.A. Rogers, *A World Worthwhile: A Record of Auld Acquaintance* (New York and London: Harper & Brothers Publishers, 1922), 14-15. In this memoir, the cartoonist William Allen Rogers documented the working process of the Harper's art staff in the 1870s. "A double-page block for *Harper's Weekly* was usually made up of thirty-six pieces of boxwood about one inch in thickness, cut across the grain and highly

polished. The back of each piece of wood was hollowed out to admit steel bolts which ran through the adjoining section, and when tightened held the whole together in a single smooth block. A very thin film of Chinese white was rubbed into the surface of the block to kill the warm color of the boxwood and afford a surface for pencil lines. The first step in making the illustration was to draw a rough sketch on paper the exact size of the composite wood block. From this a tracing was made, which was rubbed down reversed on the block."

[12] W.A. Rogers, "Abbey at Franklin Square," *The Colophon: A Book Collector's Quarterly*, Part Six, 1931. (Pages not numbered.)

[13] E.V. Lucas, 23.

[14] W.A. Rogers, "Abbey at Franklin Square."

[15] *Scribner's Monthly: An Illustrated Magazine* launched in November 1870.

[16] Mott, 397.

[17] E.V. Lucas, 26.

[18] W.A. Rogers, "Abbey at Franklin Square."

[19] E.V. Lucas, 28.

[20] W.A. Rogers, "Abbey at Franklin Square."

[21] E.V. Lucas, 22.

[22] E.V. Lucas, 33.

[23] Many of the Tile Club members would later become famous. Among their ranks were the painter Winslow Homer, sculptor Augustus Saint-Gaudens and architect Stanford White.

[24] E.V. Lucas, 38.

[25] Joseph Pennell, *The Adventures of an Illustrator: Mostly in Following His Authors in America & Europe* (Boston: Little, Brown and Company, 1925), 34.

[26] E.V. Lucas, 47.

[27] E.V. Lucas, 55. At a luncheon given in his honor in 1908, Abbey said, "I came [to England] as soon as I could—because a collection of English works of art was shown at Philadelphia which profoundly impressed me."

[28] W.A. Rogers, "Abbey at Franklin Square."

[29] W.A. Rogers, "Abbey at Franklin Square."

[30] Harper's regularly sent writers and artists out on specific assignments for its travel features. However, this looser arrangement was more unusual.

Abbey had already illustrated three of Herrick's poems, and feedback from readers justified more of the same.

31 Rebecca N. Mitchell, "Robert Herrick, Victorian Poet: Christina Rossetti, George Meredith and the Victorian Recovery of Hesperides." *Modern Philology*, 113, no. 1 (2015): 88-115.

32 E.V. Lucas, 58.

33 J. Henry Harper, *The House of Harper: A Century of Publishing in Franklin Square* (New York: Harper & Brothers Publishers, 1912), 462.

34 E.V. Lucas, 63.

35 E.V. Lucas, 63.

36 Washington Irving, *The Sketch Book of Geoffrey Crayon, Gent.*, (New York: E.P. Dutton & Co., 1906), 251.

37 "Topics of the Time: American Magazines in England," *Scribner's Monthly*, XXII, 145 (May 1881).

38 E.V. Lucas, 70. Writing for the article "Some Glimpses of Artistic London," *Harper's Weekly*, November 1883, Joseph Hatton described George Boughton's home in detail and dubbed the imposing edifice "a red-brick oasis in a cultural desert." 838.

39 E.V. Lucas, 72.

40 E.V. Lucas, 73.

41 E.V. Lucas, 80.

42 E.V. Lucas, 82.

43 E.V. Lucas, 102.

44 E.V. Lucas, 103.

45 E.V. Lucas, 439-440.

46 S.G.W. Benjamin, "Present Tendencies of American Art," *Harper's Monthly*, March 1879, V.58, 496.

47 E.V. Lucas, 125. In 1883 Abbey sent Reinhart a letter of encouragement. "Barnard [the British illustrator Frederick Barnard] thinks your work is the best that is published in American magazines, and Fildes spoke of it the other evening in the warmest terms."

48 The lines are from William Blake's poem "And Did Those Feet in Ancient Time," written as a preface to his epic poem. *Milton: A Poem in Two Books*, 1804.

49 E.V. Lucas, 117.

50 Van Gogh mentioned Abbey in eleven letters written to his brother

Theo van Gogh and to Anthon van Rappard between October 22, 1882, and July 3, 1883. Van Rappard was a Dutch painter and a student of Abbey's friend and mentor Lawrence Alma-Tadema.

[51] E.V. Lucas, 97.

[52] "Robert Herrick: Selections from the Poetry of Robert Herrick With Drawings by Edwin A. Abbey," New York. Harper & Brothers. *The New York Times*, December 1, 1882, 3.

[53] E.V. Lucas, 138.

[54] E.V. Lucas, 102.

[55] W.A. Rogers, "Abbey at Franklin Square."

[56] Joseph Pennell, *Pen Drawing and Pen Draughtsmen: Their Work and Their Methods: A Study of the Art Today With Technical Suggestions*, 3rd ed. (London: MacMillan,1889), 225.

[57] *The New York Times*, "New Books," Monday, November 29, 1886, 2.

[58] Marion Mako, "Painting with Nature in Broadway, Worcestershire." *Garden History* 34, no. 1 (2006): 47-63.

[59] E.V. Lucas, 150.

[60] Sargent's large canvas was his famous work "Carnation, Lily, Lily, Rose." The painting was inspired when Abbey and Sargent were boating on the Thames and spotted Chinese lanterns hanging from trees on the riverbank. The title comes from the lyrics of "The Wreath," a tune the Broadway group enjoyed singing around the piano: "A wreath around her head she wore / Carnation, lily, lily and rose / And in her hand a crook she bore / And sweets her breath, her breath, compose." https://anothrosko.bandcamp.com/track/the-wreath

[61] *The New York Times*, "New Books," Monday, November 29, 1886, 2.

[62] E.V. Lucas, 154.

[63] Lawrence W. Levine, "William Shakespeare in America," *Highbrow/Lowbrow: The Emergence of Cultural Hierarchy in America* (Boston: Harvard University Press, 1988), 11-83.

[64] Henry C. Pitz, *Howard Pyle: Writer, Illustrator, Founder of the Brandywine School* (New York: Clarkson N. Potter, Inc.), 1975. 26.

[65] Henry C. Pitz, 26.

[66] E.V. Lucas, 157.

[67] E.V. Lucas, 169.

[68] Lucy Oakley, *Unfaded Pageant: Edwin Austin Abbey's Shakespearean*

Subjects from the Yale University Art Gallery and Other Collections (New York: Miriam and Ira D. Wallach Art Gallery, 1994), 31.

[69] E.V. Lucas, 125.

[70] E.V. Lucas, 185.

[71] *The Critic: A Weekly Review of Literature and the Arts.* December 15, 1888, 299.

[72] E.V. Lucas, 186

[73] E.V. Lucas, 189.

[74] E.V. Lucas, 178.

[75] E.V. Lucas, 185.

[76] "Literature 'The Quiet Life.'" *The Critic*, November 2, 1889, 211-212.

[77] M.H. Speilmann, "Edwin Austin Abbey, R.A. Part One," *The Magazine of Art*, volume 23, 1899, 117-118.

[78] E.V. Lucas, 208.

[79] E.V. Lucas, 215.

[80] E.V. Lucas, 228

[81] M.H. Speilmann, "Edwin Austin Abbey, R.A. Part Two" *The Magazine of Art*, volume 23, 1899, 195-196.

[82] E.V. Lucas, 326.

[83] E.V. Lucas, 267.

[84] "Edwin A. Abbey's 'Shakespeare,'" *The New York Times*, November 23, 1895.

[85] M.H. Spielmann, volume 23, 118.

[86] E.V. Lucas, 375.

[87] E.V. Lucas, 400-401. Abbey goes on to say, "I've met nearly all the great artists of my time and many of the lesser ones—but the big ones are always strong men. Women who stick at it always become wrecks—I have never known it otherwise." The Pennsylvania illustrator and painter Violet Oakley (1874-1961) took over the Harrisburg commission when Abbey died. Ironically, Oakley attributed Abbey's death to the difficulty of the assignment. "It was perhaps the most colossal commission that had been given to one man," she wrote. "And it was just too heavy for him."

[88] E.V. Lucas, 372.

[89] E.V. Lucas, 446.

[90] E.V. Lucas, 486.

[91] E.V. Lucas, 491.

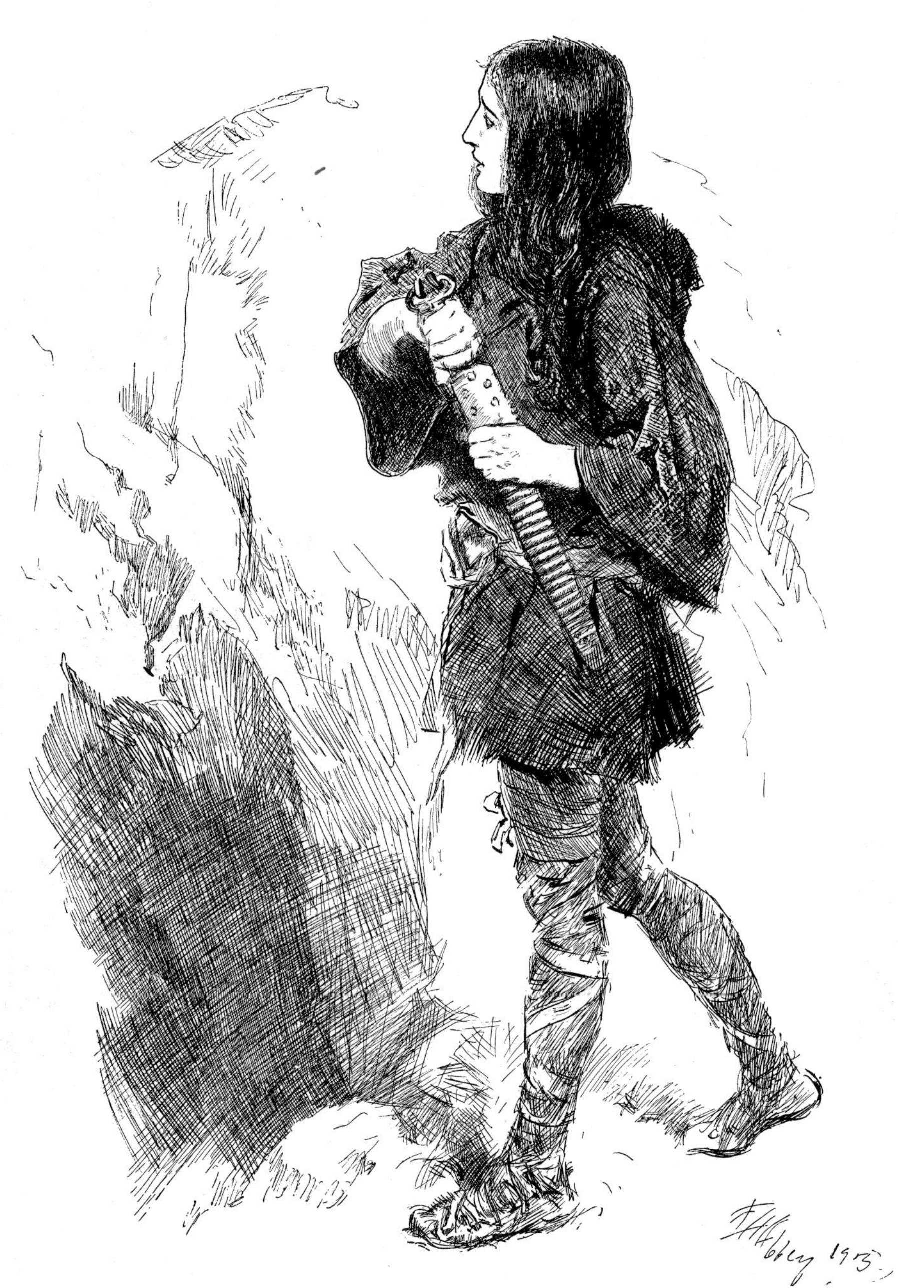